# THE
# PARTITION OF TURKEY

# THE
# PARTITION OF TURKEY

A DIPLOMATIC HISTORY

1913·1923

BY

HARRY N. HOWARD

HOWARD FERTIG

New York · 1966

PRINTED IN THE UNITED STATES OF AMERICA

BY NOBLE OFFSET PRINTERS

## TO MY BELOVED ELIZABETH

*"Doomed to know not Winter, only Spring, a being*
*Trod the flowery April blithely for a while"*—*R. L. S.*

# PREFACE

THE breakup of the Ottoman Empire was one of the most significant and fundamental results of the world war. In many respects, and without underestimating the other fundamental causes of the war, the great conflagration of 1914-1918 may be considered as a struggle of the Great Powers of Europe over the Turkish question in all its aspects. The Austro-Russian rivalry in the Balkans, the German-Russian contest for supremacy at Constantinople and in the Straits, the British desire for protection of Near Eastern routes to India, and the French ambitions in Syria, raised problems (to mention but a few!) which were to be settled not by diplomacy, but by the arbitration of war. The Lausanne conference, of 1922-1923, reached the latest definitive solution of the Turkish problem. This essay proposes to treat of the period most significant for the partition of Turkey, 1913 to 1923, though it has been deemed advisable to include materials which both antedate the period and which bring the work substantially to the present.

The writer became interested in the subject of the dissolution of the Ottoman Empire at the hands of the European Powers while he was making a study of the Mosul question, a few years ago. He has had access to the available published documentary sources, and it was his privilege to do archival study and research in the archives and libraries of Central and Balkan Europe in 1928, under the guidance and direction of his friend and teacher, Professor Robert J. Kerner, of the Department of History, of the University of California, at Berkeley.

The writer wishes to acknowledge his profoundest gratitude and indebtedness to Professor Kerner for his unfailing kindness, his friendly criticism, and his inspiring encouragement. Acknowledgement is due him not only for his assistance and direction during the early phases of the work, but also for his advice in all the stages of its preparation.

Further acknowledgement is due to Dean Howard Robinson, of Miami University, and to Mr. Joseph A. Brandt, of the University Press, University of Oklahoma, for general criticism of the manuscript. Professor Dawson Phelps, of the Mississippi Women's College, was kind enough to lend the necessary volumes of *Aussenpolitik*, containing

the Austrian documents. The writer wishes to thank Colonel E. M. House and Professor Charles Seymour, of Yale University, for their letters concerning the American attitude with reference to the question of Constantinople and the Straits. The writer is grateful to Count Sforza for his kindness in reading the work while in proof, and for his helpful suggestions. Finally he expresses his appreciation to his wife, Elizabeth Polk Howard, for her criticisms, her assistance in reading the proof, and for the compilation of the maps.

HARRY N. HOWARD.

Miami University,
Oxford, Ohio.
*July 18, 1931.*

# TABLE OF CONTENTS

## MAPS

# THE PARTITION OF TURKEY

# CHAPTER I

# A PREFACE TO THE PARTITION OF THE
# TURKISH EMPIRE, 1908-1913

## Introduction

THE world war witnessed the passing of four empires from the stage of international politics—Russia, Germany, Austria-Hungary and the Ottoman Empire. On the decline since the treaty of Karlowitz of 1699, the Turkish Empire had been preserved through the existing balance among the European Powers. Since 1844 the Porte had been recognized as "the sick man of Europe." From 1856 to the outbreak of the world war, one may reasonably state that most of the major crises in European politics were due to a possible, a probable, or an actually threatening partition of the dominions of the sultan. The great war was but the culmination, so far as Turkey was concerned, of this long process of dissolution. The end was the present definitive dissolution of the empire as represented by the treaty of Lausanne, signed on July 24, 1923. This essay represents a study and analysis of the problem, in the main, from the treaty of Bucharest, of 1913, to that of Lausanne.[1]

The first definite, important step leading to the partition of Turkey in recent years was the Austro-Hungarian annexation of Bosnia and Herzegovina, which was formally proclaimed on October 6, 1908. Prince Ferdinand of Bulgaria had proclaimed the independence of his principality on the previous day. Into the tangled diplomacy of this event we shall not enter. Europe was left in the face of an Austrian *fait accompli*. Turkey had been dismembered of two provinces, though it is true that they had been under Austrian administration since 1878.

If Bulgaria had obtained her independence through the annexation episode, a more unhappy fate was reserved for Serbia. Bosnia and Herzegovina, peopled with south Slavs, were akin to the Serbs in race and sentiment. A move toward the south was viewed with alarm by the statesmen of Belgrade. The utter alienation of any possible friendship for the Dual Monarchy was a result of Count Aehrenthal's forward action into the Balkans. Turkey, in the throes of the Young Turk movement, was obliged to accept the situation with such grace as the circumstances demanded, and received payment for the economic interests involved.[2]

Of the great Powers of Europe, Russia was the most vitally interested in the annexation episode. Indeed, M. Isvolsky, the Russian foreign minister, had met Baron Aehrenthal at Buchlau, in September 1908, to discuss the situation in the Balkans, in view of Austria's announced intention to proceed with railway construction in that region. Russia, defeated in the Far East in the war with Japan, faced with a revolution at home, now turned to the Near East for a solution of her historic question in the Straits. Accordingly, at Buchlau, came these interesting discussions. In return for passage of the Straits for Russian warships, it seems, Austria-Hungary was to be allowed annexation of Bosnia and Herzegovina. The latter apparently was dependent on Russia's securing the consent of the European cabinets to the proposal with regard to the Straits. Aehrenthal carried out the annexation, but Isvolsky failed to receive from the cabinets of Europe the much coveted solution of the problem of the Straits. Unable to act with Austria backed by Germany "in shining armor," Russia had to accept the situation.[3]

The next great step in the partition of Turkey came during the Italo-Turkish war of 1911-1912. As early as October 1909, Italy and Russia had reached a *rapprochement* on the conditions that Italy might annex Tripoli, while Russia might in the future gain passage of the Straits for her warships.[4] On slight pretext, Italy declared war on Turkey on September 29, 1911. The conclusion of hostilities found Italy in possession of Tripolitania in northern Africa, and in "temporary occupation" of the Dodecanese islands off the coast of Asiatic Turkey. The treaty of Lausanne, of October 18, 1912, gave Italy possession of both Tripolitania and Cyrenaica. The islands of the Dodecanese were to be evacuated and restored to Turkey when the conditions of the peace had been fulfilled.[5] Needless to say, Italy's "temporary" occupation has continued throughout the world war to the present day. Step by step the Ottoman Empire was going to pieces.

But the Italo-Turkish war had more far-reaching consequences. During the struggle, Italian warships had bombarded the forts of the Dardanelles, which led to the closing of the Straits. This action meant the loss of millions of rubles to Russian merchants whose products were tied up in the Black sea ports of southern Russia. This was to lead Russian statesmen to an attempt to solve an increasingly vexing problem in the near future. The war also had far reaching and most vital consequences among the states of the Balkan peninsula. Serbia, Bulgaria, Montenegro and Greece, each had minorities under the

Turkish yoke in Macedonia. Freed from Turkey during the course of the nineteenth century, these small Balkan states laid aside their own bitter hatreds for each other, saw an opportunity—Turkey being at war with Italy—to free Macedonia and the Aegean islands from the Ottoman Empire, and once for all to settle the age-old eastern question. In the early part of 1912 the Balkan alliances at last were formed, and in the autumn of that year the first of the Balkan wars broke out. To this episode we must now turn.

2.

### The Balkan League and the Balkan Wars

In December 1911, M. Charykov, the Russian ambassador to the Porte, made his famous proposal for a Turco-Slavonic league, in which Russia was to obtain passage of the Straits for her warships, in return for a guarantee of the territorial integrity of Turkey. Though there was opposition even among Russian circles,[6] from the Russian viewpoint, the proposal, whether likely to succeed or not, was perfectly natural, since the fundamental aim of Russian policy was a solution of the question of the Straits, not necessarily a matter of the partition of Turkish territories.[7] Indeed, since so many failures to settle the problem in consultation with the cabinets of Europe, and especially since the débacle of 1908-1909, many Russian diplomats had come to the conclusion that only direct negotiations with Turkey could solve the problem. The démarche of Charykov failed because Great Britain and Germany (though not openly) opposed this revival of the principles long ago enunciated in the treaty of Unkiar Eskelessi in 1833.[8] The Sublime Porte refused to make the necessary concession,[9] Charykov was thereupon disavowed on the return of Sazonov to his post at St. Petersburg, and the incident, apparently was closed.

It has been stated above that the Italo-Turkish war had grave influences in the Balkans. It became the signal for a Balkan revolt and for the formation of the Balkan league against Turkey. The negotiations for an alliance between Serbia and Bulgaria, which began in October 1911, resulted in a formal treaty on March 13, 1912. Both M. Hartwig, the Russian minister at Belgrade, and M. Nekliudov, the imperial minister in Sofia, played important rôles in engineering the alliance. Russia desired the Balkan league in order to prevent Austrian expansion in the Balkans and to postpone a settlement of the Turkish

problem, which might prove to the disadvantage of Russia. In view of the circumstances in the case, however, it is not at all unlikely that the alliance would have been concluded without outside direction.[10]

The treaty between Serbia and Bulgaria was signed formally on March 13, 1912. Its significant provisions were: (1) The two parties guaranteed their political independence and territorial integrity against an attack of any other state; (2) the parties agreed to oppose with all their forces any attempt on the part of any great Power to annex, occupy or attempt to take possession even temporarily, of any part of the Balkans then under Turkish suzerainty, if one of them considered such action contrary to its interests; (3) peace was to be made in common; and (4) a secret military convention was to be drawn up, and was to be an integral part of the treaty. The treaty was to remain secret and would enter into force at once.[11]

Annexed to the treaty of alliance was a secret agreement by which Bulgaria and Serbia were to divide the Turkish territory of Macedonia between them. By this agreement Serbia recognized the Bulgarian claim to the entire territory to the east of the Rhodope and the Struma, while the latter granted the Serbian claim to the country northwest of the Shar mountains. The region between the Shar, Rhodope, the Aegean and Okhrida (the "contested zone"), should an autonomous province prove impractical, was to be divided by a line running southwest from Mount Galem to Lake Okhrida. Serbia advanced no claims beyond this line, and Bulgaria accepted it, if the tsar of Russia, who was named arbiter, so decreed. The division assigned Struga, Skoplje (Uskub), and Kumanovo to Serbia; and Okhrida, Monastir and Ishtip to Bulgaria. Skoplje had been for a time the ancient capital of the old Serbian kingdom, while Okhrida had been the Bulgarian capital, as well as the seat of the Bulgarian patriarchate.[12]

This was the "convention de guerre" of which M. Poincaré complained when he visited St. Petersburg in the summer of 1912.[13] Sazonov wrote to Count Benckendorff on March 30, 1912, that a treaty of mutual defence between Serbia and Bulgaria had been concluded "with our cognizance". Bax-Ironside, the British minister at Sofia, knew of the treaty, and requested Isvolsky to inform Poincaré of its contents. Sazonov, however, believed that through his influence he would be able to control the actions of the Balkan allies.[14]

A secret military convention was added to the alliance on May 12, 1912. This agreement obligated Bulgaria to furnish 200,000 soldiers, and Serbia 150,000, in the event of hostilities. In case Rumania attacked

Bulgaria, Serbia was obliged to send 100,000 men to the middle Danube, or Dobruja theatre. If attacked by Turkey, Serbia was to send 100,000 men to the Vardar sector. If, on the other hand, Austria-Hungary attacked Serbia, Bulgaria was to place 200,000 men at Serbia's disposal. Other military agreements followed in June, August and September, 1912.[15]

Bulgaria and Greece reached an accord, without boundary delimitation, on May 29, 1912, in which they agreed on united action in case of war with Turkey. In a separate declaration, however, it was stated that in case of a Turkish war on Greece, due to the admission of Cretan deputies in the Greek parliament, Bulgaria should observe a benevolent neutrality toward her ally.[16] When Montenegro joined this grouping of the Balkan states, the alliances were complete, and the states were prepared to move against the Porte.

Nekliudov, the Russian representative in Sofia, was informed of the Greco-Bulgarian treaty on June 20, 1912, but did not believe that any serious complications would ensue because of the ancient hatred of the Greeks and Bulgarians against each other.[17] Events were not long in precipitating a war between Turkey and the Balkan allies. M. Hartwig, at Belgrade, reported to St. Petersburg on May 11, 1912, that an Albanian insurrection was in the making. Montenegro was aiding the movement, which was causing intense excitement in Turkey.[18] Neither Russia nor Austria desired a war in the Balkans which would upset the *status quo*. Sazonov counseled against any rash moves on the part of Bulgaria, which desired to use the alliance against the Turks. On September 30, Bulgaria, Serbia and Greece issued orders for mobilization against Turkey, after presenting demands to the Porte with reference to Macedonia. Sazonov and Berchtold issued a joint note to the Balkan allies on October 10, 1912, in which they warned them against upsetting the peace in the Balkans, assumed responsibility for all reforms in Turkey not infringing the sultan's sovereignty, and added that they would "tolerate at the end of the conflict no modifications of the present territorial *status quo* in European Turkey."[19]

But the concert of Europe was too late, for already on October 8, Montenegro had declared war, and within the next two weeks, Bulgaria, Greece and Serbia were in action. Turkey, meanwhile, had made her peace with Italy, and was to throw her forces into the Balkan struggle. From the very outset, to the wonder of all Europe and the world at large, the allies were victorious. The allied campaigns showed a decided political trend, each national army advancing into

23

the territory to which its people laid claims. Bulgarian soldiers advanced into Thrace, passed round Adrianople, and in October 1912 were facing the Chatalja lines, the outer defences of Constantinople. Serbian forces occupied the sanjak of Novibazar, uniting with Montenegro. They captured Skoplje (Uskub) and Monastir. In Albania, San Giovanni di Medua and Durazzo, on the Adriatic, fell to the victorious Serbian armies. The Greeks took Salonica, heading off the Bulgarians, while the Greek fleet took all the Aegean islands of Turkey except the Dodecanese, which had been under Italian occupation since the Italo-Turkish war. On December 3, 1912, Bulgaria and Serbia signed an armistice with Turkey, in which Greece took no part. Following the armistice the belligerents sent representatives to London, where under the presidency of Sir Edward Grey, an attempt was made to settle their differences. The meetings lasted from December 16, 1912 to January 6, 1913, when the conference suspended without making substantial gains.[20]

Meanwhile the Bulgarian approach to Constantinople had alarmed Sazonov. On October 31, the Russian foreign minister telegraphed Benckendorff that a dangerous situation would be created by a siege along the Chatalja line. He feared trouble in Constantinople and advised Sofia to be prudent and "halt in time." The Bulgarians were not to be allowed to advance farther and even more to threaten the Turkish capital. Sazonov continued:

*"The whole territory belonging to Constantinople must remain under the actual sovereignty of the Sultan. No compromises whatever are possible in this matter. We hope that Bulgaria will not place herself and Russia in the difficult position of our having to accentuate this still more emphatically at Sofia."*[21]

Intervention, Sazonov thought, could be successful only if immediate. Constantinople should be protected, though the remaining territory might be partitioned among the allies. An autonomous Albania under the suzerainty of the sultan could be provided, but Serbia must be assured her access to the Adriatic, and a rectification must be made on the Bulgar-Rumanian frontier.[22]

Grey, however, found it impossible to halt the Bulgarians before Constantinople. The Turks had collapsed and the Bulgarians already were pushing on to Constantinople, though Sofia announced its intention to withdraw after dictating the peace. The British foreign secretary had advised Madjarov, the Bulgarian minister at London, of the danger of alienating Russia in regard to Constantinople.[23]

24

Sazonov felt that the allies could be restrained concerning Constantinople by announcing that European Turkey up to the Adrianople line would be divided between them. He asked Isvolsky to inform Poincaré that the occupation of Constantinople by the allies "would cause the simultaneous appearance of our entire Black sea fleet in the Turkish capital." France should influence Berlin and Vienna in that respect.[24] Two days later he wired Isvolsky that he opposed temporary occupation of Constantinople, and that in such case the fleet would be sent and "would remain there precisely as long as the allies."[25] Grey was not surprised at the position of the St. Petersburg cabinet, but he thought that Constantinople might be made a "neutralized and free city," though that did not seem practical.[26]

This brought on a discussion of the possible future status of Constantinople. Poincaré asked Isvolsky on November 26, 1912, if Sazonov had changed his view on "neutralization of the Straits," as reported by Georges Louis.[27] Sazonov replied on November 28 that *the vital interests of Russia in the Straits cannot be protected by any legal guarantees or stipulations, as these could always be circumvented; we always must rather consider the question: by what actual force is it 'de facto' possible to protect a given status of the Straits from infringements?"*

It was to be presumed that Constantinople and a protecting territory would remain Turkish.[28] Both France and Great Britain promised Russia their support should, the question of the Straits be raised.

After the failure of the London conference in January 1913, the war was resumed. The Bulgarian army, with the aid of Serbian forces, took Adrianople, the Greeks occupied Janina, while the soldiers of Montenegro advanced into Scutari. Meanwhile the conference at London seemed unable to reach a solution of the difficulties. The Greeks already had alienated the Bulgars in the occupation of Salonica. The Serbs, shut out from the lower Vardar valley by both Greece and Bulgaria, sought an outlet to the Adriatic through Albania. But this attempt on the part of Serbia met the firm opposition of both Austria-Hungary and Italy, neither of which desired to see a new disturbing factor in a sea which both were considering "*mare nostrum.*" However, the intervention of the cabinets of Europe finally resulted in the making of the treaty of London, of May 30, 1913.[29]

The treaty of London was never ratified, but its terms are of considerable importance. Turkey ceded Crete and the European territory west of the so-called Enos-Midia line to the Balkan allies. The question of the Aegean islands, with the exception of Crete, was

reserved to the concert of Europe. Montenegro was obliged to surrender Scutari, and Albania was to form an independent state. Serbia
lost her Adriatic outlet, on account of the Austrian and Italian insistence on the "principle of nationalities", in the creation of an
independent Albania, and this fact led to the Serbian demand for
territorial adjustments in Macedonia. The Belgrade government
advanced the contention that the territorial features of the Serbo-
Bulgarian treaty of 1912 be revised and that it keep the territory
occupied, that it have a coterminous frontier with Greece, and an
Aegean outlet through Salonica. The government of Sofia remained
adamant and refused to admit the Serbian contention, a position in
which the Bulgarians were supported by Austria-Hungary. Greece was
making large claims on Macedonia, and both Greece and Serbia began
to fear Bulgarian aspirations in the Balkans. This was the situation
which led to the formation of the Greco-Serbian alliance, the breakup
of the Balkan league, and the outbreak of the second Balkan war—a
fratricidal conflict between the Balkan states.[30]

When the Turkish question proper was discussed among the
European representatives at Paris in the spring of 1913, Sazonov took
the position that such financial restrictions as would preclude a proper
defence of Constantinople should not be placed on the Porte. Content
with the *status quo* in the Ottoman Empire, with a weak government
in sovereignty over Constantinople and the Straits, Sazonov did not
favor inviting attack from other quarters, from Bulgaria, in particular,
as "the latter knows very well, that the Straits belong to Russia's
incontestable sphere of interest and that in this respect any weakness
or hesitation on our side is utterly inadmissible."[31]

Giers, the Russian ambassador in Constantinople, seemed convinced that the Ottoman Empire was on the decline, though Turkish
politicians could still count on the support of several Powers. He felt
that the introduction of an international element in the hitherto direct
Russo-Turkish relations would but "hinder and delay our historical
task to take possession of the Straits." Since Turkey was not a great
market, and since Russia had few investments in the country, Russia
was not interested in her regeneration. Giers desired only, therefore,
sufficient order in Turkey to guarantee the safety of the population.
"This would enable us to postpone the liquidation of Turkey until
the moment when our participation in this process of liquidation
would afford us the greatest possible advantages." Better relations

could be counted on, though in order to weaken Turkish resistance, Russia should eleminate the points of friction in her Turkish relations.[32]

Never ratified, the ink on the treaty of London was hardly dry before the Balkan allies were at war with each other over the division of the Macedonian spoils. Fearful of Bulgarian aggression and ambition, Greece and Serbia made an alliance on June 1, 1913, providing for common action against Bulgaria in the case of open conflict. The two parties agreed that since the partition of Turkish territories in Europe had been confided to the Balkan states, they would make no separate agreement with reference thereto with Bulgaria. They considered it their vital interest that no other state interpose between their respective possessions on the west of the Vardar river, providing for a common Greco-Serb frontier. If there should be disagreement with Sofia over the delimitation of the frontiers, the two Powers engaged to ask for the mediation or arbitration of the Triple Entente or of other European Powers. Should Bulgaria refuse, and war thereupon ensue, the two states were to aid each other with all their forces. Serbia was promised special privileges in the port of Salonica on the Aegean, and the railroad lines running from Skoplje and Monastir were to offer the Serbs special facilities.[33]

Again war seriously threatened to disturb the Balkans. Russia had been the arbiter in a possible Serbo-Bulgarian dispute over territorial questions in Macedonia, but Sazonov seemed unable to make any headway for a pacific solution of the issue. A peaceable solution of the Macedonian question was difficult under any and all circumstances, so conflicting were the claims and counter claims of Serbia, Bulgaria and Greece. At this particular time such a solution was well nigh impossible on account of the position of Bulgaria, whose intransigeance was supported by Austria-Hungary. The Dual Monarchy had been instrumental in preventing the Serbs from achieving an outlet on the Adriatic, through the creation of an independent Albania. And from the very opening days of the conference at London in December 1912, the Austrian statesmen used every opportunity to separate Bulgaria from her allies and to destroy the Balkan league.[34] Doubtless the Ballplatz was aware that if the Turkish question were settled in the manner apparently desired by the Balkan allies, the Austro-Hungarian question might be placed next on the *tapis*. Certainly the Serbian danger, created partly as a result of unsolved nationalistic problems in the Dual Monarchy, seemed more and more threatening in Vienna official circles.

As early as December 19, 1912, Count Berchtold wired Sofia that Geshov was aware of Austria's essentially friendly attitude toward Bulgaria's aspirations. "We wish a large and strong Bulgaria," he wrote. Under the condition that Bulgaria preserve a friendly attitude, Austria might be willing to support Bulgarian aspirations in the Balkans.[35] The Bulgarians reciprocated this desire for more friendly and direct relations with Vienna. On February 21, 1913, Count Tarnowsky had a long conversation with M. Danev about the Serbo-Bulgarian alliance, and drew from him the admission that the alliance was to last only for the duration of the war with Turkey. Somewhat later the finance minister told Tarnowsky:

*"Our alliance with Serbia has left a bad impression in Vienna. You can be certain that it is only against Turkey that we have concluded this accord. As soon as peace is made, we shall have no engagement with Serbia, nor toward Greece, as we have no engagement toward Russia. We—a Russophil government—we are all convinced of the necessity and possibility of our direct friendship with Austria-Hungary and of our 'rapprochement' to the Triplice. We foresee rivalries of the great Bulgaria with Russia, but we do not see any possible differences between our interests and yours, these interests being parallel."[36]*

At the same time, the Sofia government desired the support of Austria against the growing danger of Rumania. On March 10, Count Tarnowsky received assurances from Geshov that Bulgaria desired a more definite friendship with Austria-Hungary, "even as you wish ours". He gave assurances that he saw "no reason which could separate us, if only Bulgaria comes out of all these crises as she ought to."[37]

Despite the position of the Geshov-Danev government, which the Austrians, for good reasons of high politics, were pulling away from the Balkan alliances, Count Tarnowsky did not trust the government, and began to talk privately with the members of the opposition, Radoslavov and Ghenadiev, who continually warned him that the members of the government could not be trusted. But even these men recognized that Austria must support Bulgaria in the ever-present difficulties with Rumania.[38]

By May it was apparent that Serbo-Bulgarian relations were becoming more and more strained and that the breaking point was near at hand. On May 29 Geshov spoke very freely of the possibility of a war with Serbia. He told Tarnowsky that war was a distinct possibility, and asked: "What do you think of this war?" When Tarnowsky tried to avoid the question, the Bulgarian minister again said: "I must ask

you how your government envisages the question of war between us and Serbia." Tarnowsky again evaded a direct answer, and Geshov continued:

*"You understand that my hands are tied, but at present if war breaks out between us and Serbia, there is no longer any engagement, no more alliance, and the moment has come to ask you what Austria-Hungary counts on doing. Is war between Serbia and Bulgaria convenient for you; would you allow free course to events; or are you going to stop them by your attitude; do you want a Bulgaria strong and large, or not?"*

Tarnowsky could not answer all these questions, though he did tell the Bulgarian that Austria did desire "a strong and large Bulgaria under the condition that this Bulgaria should undertake a purely Bulgarian policy and enter no hostile combination against us." Geshov then asked the Austrian minister to ask Count Berchtold for instructions in reference to the expected Serbo-Bulgarian war, and he concluded: "Between us, I must tell you that the Serbs are entirely ready and we not yet."[39]

Berchtold gave his answer to the Bulgarian query the next day. Austria had no intention of "falling on Bulgaria" in the event of a war with Serbia. The future of Austria's attitude depended entirely on Bulgaria's relation to the Monarchy.

*"As we have declared repeatedly, and as your highness warned yesterday, we are ready to support the growth of Bulgaria, however only under the natural condition that they in Sofia follow a purely Bulgarian policy and enter no political combination which is directed against us."[40]*

The foundation had been laid for further conversations between the statesmen of the two countries. If Bulgaria could give the necessary assurances, there would be no question as to the policy of the Ballplatz. Relations between Serbia and Bulgaria, and between Rumania and Bulgaria, became increasingly strained.[41]

On June 18 Danev again approached Tarnowsky with reference to Austria's attitude in the event of a new Balkan war. The conversation was reported to Vienna, and Berchtold again stated his position on the matter.[42] The Bulgarians now gave the necessary assurances that they would not adopt a hostile attitude toward the Dual Monarchy, and on June 24, Berchtold expressed his satisfaction with the statement that "Bulgaria today is no longer on any side obligated to undertake active operations against Austria-Hungary." Berchtold was then evidently able to state his position more definitely.

"*In view of the openly hostile position of Serbia with relation to us, a further material and moral strengthening of Serbia at the cost of Bulgaria would be opposed throughout to our interests. Bulgaria can therefore in this case count not only on our sympathy, but also, if the circumstances then lead us to fear an undesired dénouement, can count on our active support, the latter however only under the condition that Bulgaria meets the wishes of Rumania in a measure, and gives such compensation for Rumanian neutrality, that it is possible for us to enter Bucharest with a certain right and with success for an understanding on this basis.*"[43]

The Austrian attitude was at least favorable to, if not actually instigating, a Bulgarian attack on Serbia, which would, of course, *ipso facto* mean the break up of the Balkan league. Just five days after Berchtold had stated definitely his position, on the night of June 29, 1913, the Bulgarian forces attacked the Greeks and Serbs all along the entire Macedonian front. A blunder, for which the Bulgarian government had to take full responsibility, had been made.[44]

Bulgaria was not to deal with Serbia and Greece alone, as has been intimated. Rumania was to enter the lists against her, and Turkey took advantage of the war between the Balkan allies in order to rectify conditions along the Enos-Midia frontier. On July 21, 1913, Enver Bey marched into Adrianople with his troops. Despite the protests of the Powers, the Turk was there to stay.[45]

Of much interest in the second Balkan war is the attitude of Rumania. The cabinet of Bucharest had remained aloof from the war of the Balkan allies against Turkey. On the eve of the war, October 3, 1912, Maiorescu, the Rumanian premier, announced that Rumania would "for the moment, preserve neutrality."[46] Rumanian statesmen, however, had long coveted the territory of Silistria-Balchik, in the Dobruja. With Bessarabia, this territory would give complete control of the Danube outlet into the Black sea to Rumania. From the beginning of the conflict, the policy of Bucharest was one of watchful waiting. While the Balkan allies were engaged in striking at the European possessions of Turkey, Rumania took every occasion to press her demands on Bulgaria. The government at Sofia, however, was willing to make only a slight rectification of the Dobruja frontier.[47]

Rumanian claims were not satisfied, and the question of Silistria-Balchik finally was referred to the European Powers for settlement.[48] The conference of ambassadors, meeting at St. Petersburg, to which the question was referred, arrived at a decision on May 9, 1913. The

judgment of the Powers gave Silistria to Rumania, and Bulgaria engaged to erect no fortress along the existing frontier, from the Danube to the Black sea.[49] In accordance with the provisions of the agreement, a mixed commission of Rumanians and Bulgarians met to delimit the new frontier. As neither side would compromise, the commission suspended meetings on June 30, 1913—the day following the treacherous attack of the Bulgarians on their erstwhile allies.[50]

Meanwhile the Rumanian government was following events in the Balkans very closely. On May 2, 1913, the Serbian government approached Rumania with a view to an alliance. This was followed on May 28 and June 22 by a similar move on the part of Greece. Maiorescu, however, answered evasively, but noted to King Carol that "we cannot intervene except when war breaks out between Greeks, Serbs and Bulgarians. At that moment our hands must be free, so that we shall be able to impose peace."[51] War did break out on June 29. On July 3 King Carol announced the mobilization of his army, and on July 10, Bulgaria and Rumania were at war.[52] The Rumanian armies marched into the disputed territory of Silistria-Balchik, while the Bulgarians, of necessity, retreated before them, almost without firing a shot.[53] Six days later, in his circular to the legations abroad, Maiorescu stated that Rumania had gone to war in order "to add now to her territory an assured frontier below the Danube."[54]

The war was to be of short duration. On July 19 Sofia offered to cede to Rumania the desired territory northeast of the line from Tutrakan to Balchik, in return for the withdrawal of Rumanian troops, her benevolent neutrality, and Rumanian support of Bulgaria in her contests with Greece and Serbia over the settlement of territorial issues.[55] Bulgaria did not intend to use the *entente* for a continuation of hostilities with Greece and Serbia.[56] On July 21, Ferdinand of Bulgaria appealed to King Carol for peace, while his urgent request in a similar end, to Vienna, met a rather frigid response.[57] The war came to a speedy end, and Bulgaria, crushed, was forced to accept the peace of Bucharest, signed on August 10, 1931.[58]

3.

## The Treaty of Bucharest

The conference of Bucharest, which was called to end the fratricidal war in the Balkans, met for the opening session on July 30, 1913.

The Balkan premiers, MM. Maiorescu, Pashich, and Venizelos were there, while Bulgaria was represented by M. Tonchev and M. Radev. On August 2, the Russian foreign minister agreed that "*it is in the general interest to create in the Balkans a situation as stable as possible which would carry in itself the guarantee of a long period of peace.*"

Like Austria-Hungary, Russia could not remain indifferent to too great a humiliation of Bulgaria. A moderating influence should be exercised both at Belgrade and at Athens in the interest of peace. Cavalla appeared to be most important for Bulgaria, and though Greece was unwilling to cede this port on the Aegean, she might be forced to do so if the unanimous pressure of the Powers could be brought to bear at Athens. An early conclusion of peace would react favorably on the problem of Adrianople.[59]

After two weeks of wrangling, the new allies imposed their will on Bulgaria. According to the decisions of the peace of Bucharest, Macedonia was divided on the general lines of the rule of *uti possedetis*. Montenegro and Serbia became coterminus through the division of the sanjak of Novibazar. Serbia obtained all of the old Serbia, including Monastir and the Vardar valley to Gevgeli. This gave her a common frontier with Greece and an economic outlet to the Aegean *via* Salonica, where Greece allowed the Serbs special commercial privileges. The rest of southern and western Macedonia, with Salonica and Cavalla, went to Greece. On the other hand, Bulgaria was limited to the territory north of the Belashitsa mountains and east of the river Mesta, cutting her off from a direct outlet to the sea. Rumania won the Silistria-Balchik portion of the Dobruja, including Dobrich. Greece, in addition, held Crete and the Aegean islands, which she had won from Turkey in the first Balkan war.

The most pressing question at the conference of Bucharest was that of Cavalla. Bulgaria demanded it for her outlet to the Aegean, but it was in Greek hands. The Powers of Europe were not in agreement on the question. Both France and Germany desired to leave the port in the hands of Greece.[60] Austria and Russia both insisted on giving Cavalla to Bulgaria, each in order to win that country over to its own Balkan policy. Indeed, both Austria and Russia reserved to submit this point of the treaty of Bucharest to the revision of the European cabinets.[61] On the eve of the signature of the treaty, M. Tonchev, the Bulgarian delegate, announced that though Bulgaria had to accept the treaty, the government of Sofia hoped to find "among the Great Powers a

support capable of bettering her position conforming to the sacrifices made by her and to the necessities of her economic and national development."[62]

Germany, however, appeared very much against a revision of the treaty and there was little likelihood of a fundamental change in its provisions.[63] On August 14 the Rumanian minister at St. Petersburg, M. Nano, reported that Sazonov would no longer insist on the question of Cavalla, and had abandoned the idea of revision of the treaty.[64]

Since Turkey was not a party to the peace of Bucharest, Bulgaria was forced to enter into separate negotiations for peace with that country. A treaty of peace finally was concluded on September 29, 1913, by which Turkey retained the Adrianople and Kirk Kilissé districts north of the Enos-Midia line, while the lower Maritsa formed the boundary near the Aegean coast. Turkey retained control of the railroad between Adrianople and Dedeagatch, on the Aegean. Bulgaria thus lost control of the only railway which would have given her access to the sea.[65]

By the treaties ending the Balkan wars, Serbia was increased in size by four-fifths the extent of her former territory. Montenegro received a like increase. Even Bulgaria obtained a one-fifth increase in size—though not in the territory she so much coveted. Greece was doubled in area. All the Balkan states received considerable increases in population, while Turkey lost two-thirds of her European population.[66]

Having examined the situation leading up to the Balkan wars, and having pointed out the significant territorial dispositions arising from those wars, we must now turn for a brief moment to another aspect of the Balkan situation in 1913—that of the relation of the Great Powers to the developments in the Balkan peninsula immediately following the peace of Bucharest. As already indicated, the two major Powers most vitally concerned were, naturally, Russia and Austria-Hungary. The Balkan league, though formed as a result of the conditions in Turkey and the Balkans, following the Italo-Turkish war, had been influenced, encouraged, and in many respects, engineered to a conclusion by St. Petersburg. Its breakup, through the action of Bulgaria (urged on by Austria-Hungary) and the mutual suspicion and distrust of the allies, meant a setback for, and a new orientation of Russian policy, with especial reference to Rumania. The dissolution

*treaty of Bucharest remained. Turkey, of course, was also sore and despoiled. Thus when the great war came, a year later, there were two Powers, Bulgaria and Turkey, hungering for a revanche and ready to take whichever side would give them a prospect of obtaining it. This naturally was the side of Austria and Germany. For Serbia was at war with Austria, while Greece and Rumania were sympathetic to Serbia or to the Western Powers."*[72]

The Balkan wars served as a prelude to all the carnage and destruction of the world war, and during the world war the Turkish Empire was to be destroyed.

HUNGARY

TRANSYLVANIA

BANAT

DANUBE

Belgrade

RUSSIA

BESS-
ARABIA

PRUTH RIVER

DNIESTER

BOSNIA

DALMATIA

RUMANIA

Bucharest

DANUBE RIVER

DOBRUJA

SERBIA

Nōvibizar    Misn

BULGARIA

Sofia

BLACK
SEA

MONTE-
NEGRO

Cetinje

ADRIATIC
SEA

Skutari

Skoblia

Ishtip

MARITZA

Adrianople    Midia

BOSPHORUS

Okhrida

Chatalja

Constantinople

Durazzo

ALBANIA

Monastir

Cavala

DEDEAGATCH

Enos

SEA OF
MARMORA

ITALY

Salonica

SAMO-
THRACE

Gallipoli

Brusa

IMBROS

CORFU

LEMNOS

MITYLENE

TURKEY

GREECE

ÆGEAN
SEA

Smyrna

Athens

Aidin

Corinth

MEDITERRANEAN
SEA

RHODES

CRETE

# CHAPTER II

# THE NEAR EAST ON THE
# EVE OF WAR

## The Liman von Sanders Mission

NOT only had the Balkan wars resulted in a complete upset in the peninsula, but they had destroyed the Balkan league, and had rendered imminent a breakup of the Ottoman Empire. In consequence of this condition of affairs, as we shall see, Russia and Germany were to meet face to face in a struggle at Constantinople over the question of the Straits, while Austria and Russia contested in the Balkans. Defeated during the war, Turkey seemed on the verge of collapse, and became the strategic point of diplomatic conflict between imperial Germany and tsarist Russia. In the Balkans, Bulgaria was isolated by the *entente* between Greece, Rumania and Serbia, who were pledged to the *status quo* under the treaty of Bucharest. Austrian policy looked toward reconstruction of a Balkan league with Bulgaria as the pivot of the alliance to be used in isolating and crushing the menace from the greater Serbia idea. In this alliance Bulgaria, Greece, Turkey and even Rumania, were to have their parts. Russia looked toward holding Greece, Serbia and Rumania together, and keeping Bulgaria in line with Russian Balkan aims. It is little wonder that in such conditions war was to break out in the summer of 1914, in the Balkans.

The failures of Turkey were attributed to her isolation in European politics, her internal disorganization and corruption. The Porte was in sad need of financial, civil, military and naval reforms. Drastic measures would be necessary if the empire were to recover from the disasters of 1912-1913.[1]

Moreover, the Berlin government was vitally concerned in the situation in Turkey. Almost since the advent of William II to the throne of the German Empire, the cabinet of Berlin had gazed toward the east to Constantinople and beyond, inspired by commercial and imperialistic ambitions. In 1903, the Bagdad railway convention had been signed, which when completed, would give German nationals a preponderant economic hold on the Ottoman Empire. Since the early 1880's the Turkish army had been under the tutelage of General von der Goltz Pasha. It was this German trained army which had been

39

crushed in the Balkan war. German prestige and interest were, there-fore, involved to a major degree in the rehabilitation of Turkey.

We shall not trace in any detail the need of reforms in Turkey. Financial assistance was needed and a British expert was placed in charge of the customs service. Civil reforms in the Armenian vilayets and elsewhere were required. The gendarmerie was placed under the efficient direction of the French general, Baumann. The navy, in dire need of rehabilitation, already had been placed in charge of the British seaman, Admiral Limpus. It remained to place the army under the training of a German officer.

The beginnings of the Liman von Sanders military mission date from the first months of 1913, while the first Balkan war was still in progress.[2] By the time the mission had matured on the completion of the contract with the Porte, it consisted of some forty-two capable officers of the German army. It is not necessary to insist that control of the army would mean virtual control of Constantinople and the Porte,[3] and would give Berlin a predominant position in a possible—and all too probable—partition of the Ottoman Empire. It is this latter phase of the question, in particular, which the writer proposes to develop.

Baron von Wangenheim, the German ambassador to the Sublime Porte, was convinced that Turkey, unaided, could not maintain her dominions intact. A partition of her territories was threatened by the various reform schemes of the Powers, which Germany should ward off, since her spheres of interest were not so easily delimited. Since the government of Berlin was in no position to profit from the occasion, Germany's policy should be to preserve the integrity of the empire as long as possible. Wangenheim's ideal of control over Turkey was modelled on the English treatment of Egypt.[4]

The project for the new mission was brought first to Russian attention when both George V and Nicholas II attended the marriage on May 24, 1913 of Princess Victoria Louise, daughter of William II. Reference was made to the plan of a military mission, and the tsar gave his consent.[5] On June 30, General Liman von Sanders was named as head of the mission to Turkey, though he was not to take his posi-tion in Constantinople until the Balkan peace had been determined. His powers were extensive. They included reorganization of the army, inspections of the armed forces, control of appointments in the Turkish military service, direction of military schools, and membership in the supreme war council of Turkey. The contract was to last for five years.[6]

The arrangements were carried on in strictest secrecy. When Sazonov passed through Berlin in October 1913, the mission was not mentioned in his conversations at the Wilhelmstrasse.[7] In November, however, news of the mission and its powers did reach St. Petersburg, and the incident developed into one of the most serious international disputes in the months preceding the outbreak of the war. Sazonov took a firm stand on the question when the obvious danger to Russian interests in Turkey became apparent. The conciliatory Kokovtsev, minister of finances and president of the council of state, who was in Berlin from November 17 to November 20, 1913, was asked to use the occasion to present the Russian case to Berlin. In these conversations, Bethmann explained that the mission was intended as no offense to Russia, and only to protect German economic interests in Turkey. Kokovtsev explained as frankly that, while Russia could understand the German position in sending a mission to Turkey, Russia's point of view "must change completely on the subject of the command by Germany of an army corps at Constantinople . . . . We take our stand on the principle that Constantinople must remain a Turkish capital, in whose integrity all the Great Powers are equally interested." His final suggestion was either for a modification of the general's powers, or for a change of residence from Constantinople to Adrianople.[8]

On Kokovtsev's return from Berlin, Sazonov pressed for a solution of the question. He telegraphed London and Paris on November 25, concerning German insistence on a military command in Constantinople. Already Berlin had the Hamburg-Bagdad scheme developed, and now the army was to be under German control. He urged a joint step of the Entente in Constantinople, pointing out that concessions to Germany "raised the question of equivalent compensations."[9] Pichon was in accord, but if the general were removed from Constantinople, he preferred to see him in Adrianople rather than in Smyrna.[10] Grey was ready to protest against the German action at Constantinople, but with an *identical*, not a *joint* note of the Powers. Sir Louis Mallet, the English ambassador in Turkey, was to point out the serious consequences of Turkey's action: "*The diplomats accredited to Constantinople would be under the dependence of Germany; the key of the Straits would be in the hands of Germany; a German general could, by his military measures, hold in check the sovereignty of the Sultan. Moreover, the balance of powers, by which even the existence of Turkey*

*is guaranteed, would be broken. To compensate the preponderance attributed to Germany, other Powers would claim from Turkey, like advantages."*[11]

Four days later Sazonov dispatched to London a copy of the instructions he would suggest for an identic note.[12] The note was based on Grey's previous idea, but Grey had now changed his mind; he thought Sazonov premature, and felt that they must now revert to the first idea of an official inquiry with the Porte. In the interim, Grey had learned that Liman's powers did not extend to the Straits. Besides, comparisons of an embarrassing nature were being made between the German general and the English Admiral Limpus, who was in the Turkish naval service.[13] Grey would not go further than to state to Turkey that France, England and Russia had heard that wide powers had been given a German general in Constantinople, creating for him an extraordinary position there. "We assume that Turkey would do nothing, by which the independence of the Turkish government, or the safety of the Straits and Constantinople, would be brought into question." Other Powers were interested, and would be glad to find out the particulars of the agreement with General Liman von Sanders.[14]

The change in Grey's attitude was a grave setback for Sazonov. He considered such a communication as "rather harmful than useful."[15] It was suggested to London that a removal of Admiral Limpus from Constantinople to Ismid might facilitate a removal of General von Sanders to Adrianople.[16] This, however, turned out to be impractical. Sazonov was much concerned over the lack of support he had from England, and complained to the British ambassador in St. Petersburg of the "organic fault" of the Triple Entente which was always "at a disadvantage in face of the firm block of the Triple Alliance."[17]

On December 13, the *démarche* was made, in which the three Powers requested the information as to the contract with General Liman. The grand vizier declared that the Straits, fortifications or the preservation of order in the capital were not in the province of the German mission.[18] But the concerted move of the Entente failed of any serious results.[19]

What would the government at St. Petersburg do? Such was now the question which was being asked both in Paris and London, as well as in the governing circles in Russia. While assured of French support, Isvolsky telegraphed on December 18 that the Quai d'Orsay feared particularly that if Russia adopted the standpoint of compensations

"this might easily lead to the liquidation of Asiatic Turkey." It was therefore necessary that he know definitely and explicitly Sazonov's plans. Sir Edward Grey expressed the fear that unless a change were made, Russia might make demands for a command in Armenia, which might signify the beginning of a partition of Asiatic Turkey.[20]

Meanwhile, no modification in the position of the military mission had taken place. On December 14, Liman von Sanders arrived in Constantinople.[21] A way out now appeared which would yield the form and keep the substance of German influence and control over Turkey. General Liman would be promoted in the German army and become a marshal and inspector-general of Turkish troops, but without actual command of troops in Constantinople.[21] This would amount, in reality, to an advance in his substantial powers.[22]

Almost giving up hope of a settlement, Sazonov moved for a *démarche* of the Entente in Berlin, but failed in his endeavors. On December 29, however, Sir Eyre Crowe (Grey was out of London) asked Benckendorff what Russia proposed to do if not successful in her demands. Specifically he wanted to know Russia's minimum demands: (1) modification of the contract, or compensations; (2) what coercive measures Russia proposed if Turkey did not accept; (3) and what extreme measures Russia was prepared to adopt.[23] The next day, Isvolsky reported similar questions from Paris. Doumergue wanted to know what Russia proposed, "in case their common action at Berlin and at Constantinople, should not have found the peaceful solution which they seek."[24]

Sazonov, himself, had drawn up on December 6, 1913, a memorandum on the situation in the Balkans and in the Ottoman Empire following the Balkan wars.[25] The Russian foreign minister sums up the situation in his statement of the case. The Balkan wars had shaken up the peninsula and threatened the integrity of the Ottoman Empire. While the final *débâcle* of Turkey had been announced for two centuries, it seemed the empire could not endure without the use of heroic measures. Internal dissensions, the attitude of the Balkan states, and the mutual rivalries of the Great Powers might precipitate matters.

*"In view of these considerations, all the Great Powers, without exception, are discounting from the present the possibility of a final dissolution of the Ottoman Empire and are putting the question of the previous guarantee of their rights and interests in the different provinces of Asia Minor. It is this which explains the increased activity of Germany, of Italy, and even of Austria, which, until now, has had no interest in Asia*

43

Minor—an activity tending to create and to consolidate the bases of their political pretentions in the future partition of the Ottoman Empire . . . .

"Doubts as to the stability and longevity of Turkey raise for us the historic question of the Straits and an evaluation of all the importance which they have for us from the political and economic point of view. There can be different opinions on the necessity or the absence of necessity for Russia to aspire to the possession of the Straits . . . . The question continues to remain open and the only conclusion that one can draw now is that it would be difficult for a responsible statesman in Russia who does not admit that, in case of a change in the status quo, Russia cannot admit a solution of the question contrary to her interests; in other words, that she cannot, in certain circumstances, remain a passive spectator of events. The taking possession of the Straits by another State than Turkey—is it admissible from the point of view of the interests of Russia?

"To answer this question it is necessary first to appreciate the present situation: the possession of the Straits by Turkey. The question of the safeguard of the Straits, a question so difficult and so complicated, actually is settled in a manner fairly satisfactory from the point of view of our direct interests. Turkey is a state not too strong, but not too weak; incapable of being a menace for us, and at the same time obliged to take Russia into consideration, who is more powerful than she . . . .

"Is the transfer of the Straits into the entire possession of another state admissible for us? To put this question is to answer it in the negative. The Straits in the possession of a powerful state would signify the entire subjection of the economic development of all southern Russia to that state . . . .

"In fact, whoever has possession of the Straits will hold not only the keys of the Black sea and of the Mediterranean. He will have also the key of the penetration in Asia Minor and that of hegemony in the Balkans, in consequence of which the state which replaces Turkey on the shores of the Straits will aspire probably to follow the way traced in their times by the Turks . . . ."[26]

In order to consider measures which might be necessary to take in the near future, Sazonov urged on the tsar, the early convocation of a special conference. The tsar approved these ideas of his foreign minister.[27]

Thereupon, a special conference was convened for January 13, 1914, to consider the possibilities of war and the question of the Straits. Count Kokovtsev presided at the meeting, and the foreign

minister, Sazonov, as well as the chiefs of the general and naval staffs were present. The immediate cause of the summoning of this important meeting was the presence of the German military mission in Constan-tinople.[28] The foreign office laid down the following principles for guidance and discussion in the conference: (1) Russia could not consent to the presence of a German general in command of troops in Con-stantinople, though Adrianople might be accepted; (2) the negotia-tions at Berlin and Constantinople should continue; (3) decisions must be taken to provide for backing up the demands by measures of com-pulsion; (4) compulsory measures might take the form of the occupa-tion of a point in Asia Minor, such as Trebizond or Bayezid, with notification of intent to remain until the demands were satisfied; (5) the measures should be communicated to France and England to learn their views; (6) the necessity for cautious and unanimous action of the Entente should be pressed in London and Paris. England and France agreeing, the following measures were proposed: (a) a rigid financial boycott of Turkey; (b) withdrawal of their representatives from Constantinople if this measure failed; (c) and resort to coercive measures after a fixed date. Should threats in the Caucasus be necessary, they should be secret and followed by prompt action. The results of the conference were to be transmitted to the tsar.

Kokovtsev favored conciliation and the use of financial pressure, and was opposed to the occupation of any territory in Asia Minor. After thoroughly discussing the issues presented, the conference decided to continue the negotiations in Berlin. The presence of Liman von Sanders in Constantinople was inadmissible, but an inspectorate over the Turkish army, apparently, had to be accepted. Recourse to measures of compulsion was to be taken only after the failure of negotiations, and then only in agreement with France and England. Should France and England fail to assist, "it does not appear possible to adopt means of pressure which might lead to a war with Germany."[29]

However, the acute phase of the episode was over when Liman was promoted to the position of lieutenant-general in the German army, and thereby became a Turkish marshal and inspector-general of the Ottoman army. This was notified to St. Petersburg on January 15, 1914.[30] Berlin had yielded formally to Russia, but the military mission remained in power. This was apparent from the letter of Sverbeiev, Russian ambassador in Berlin, on January 16, 1914. While he wrote that Berlin had done "everything in its power to fulfil our justifiable wishes," he had to note "the fact that General Liman's

relinquishment of the command of the first army corps is only a formal concession. The general retains his decisive influence upon the military questions of Turkey."[31]

The incident was neither closed nor settled.[32] On February 21, 1914, another special conference was called to consider plans for the occupation of Constantinople and the Straits, should there be danger of another Power seizing these vantage points.[33] At the outset, Sazonov explained that since events might take place through which the Straits might pass from the hands of Turkey to the detriment of Russia's vital interests, the government must develop a program "which should aim at the assurance of a solution in our favor of the historic question of the Straits." It was not to be assumed that operations against the Straits could take place without a general European war. In this case, Serbia would be fighting Austria-Hungary, while Bulgaria and Greece would doubtless range themselves on opposite sides. Rumania's position was, at this moment, rather doubtful.[34]

After an exhaustive discussion of all the military, naval and diplomatic measures to be adopted, the conference decided as follows: (1) The landing companies should be strengthened, and artillery sections were to be brought up to standard; (2) the ministries of finance, trade and industry and of the navy were to do all in their power to increase transport facilities in the Black sea; (3) the efficiency of the fleet must be increased, and the fleet strengthened in as short a time as possible by a second squadron of the latest types of battle cruisers; (4) immediate construction of the Caucasus railways for military purposes. The conference made it clear that Russia could not go to war and was determined not to do so. Russian plans against a third Power were possible only after 1917. Until then Russian policy in Turkey and the Straits was to preserve the *status quo*.

The mission had much wider ramifications in the field of diplomacy. It led directly to the move of St. Petersburg to transform the Entente into a triple alliance between Russia, France, and Great Britain.[35] Neither France nor England looked with approval on this step, however.[36] Failing that, Sazonov tried for a naval understanding with England, which was on the point of success when the coming of the war engrossed the attention of all Europe.[37]

The sending of the military mission of Liman von Sanders had brought to the fore the fundamental clash of interests between Germany and Russia in Turkey and the Straits. Already a German financial group was in control of the Bagdad railroad, the mainland route from

Europe into Asia, around which centered German interests in the Ottoman Empire. Military control was now to be superimposed on German economic influence in Turkey. It seemed to both St. Petersburg and others that the contest between the Teuton and the Slav for control in the Near East and in Turkey at last had come. Germany had thrown down the gage, and it was to be accepted.[38]

In its origins the military mission was much more than a technical group of military experts. Germany was confronted with losing out in the Near East, or gaining a very useful ally in a "coming world war." Politically, as we have seen, the sending of the mission aroused the hostility of Russia, forced her into an attempt to tighten the bonds of the Entente, led to the Turco-German alliance of August 2, 1914, and finally, brought Turkey into the world war.[39] Aside from the purely military aspects of the mission in Turkey, Liman von Sanders and his officers were intended to serve two general purposes. In the first place, the military mission would put Germany in a position of commanding importance to hold the Turkish Empire together, and thus dominate it both politically and economically. In the second place, when the dissolution of the Ottoman Empire finally came, with military control, the Berlin government would be able to obtain a full share of the country, along with the rest of the Powers, who were also anxious for a part.

2.

*Economic Preliminaries to the Partition of the Ottoman Empire*

One can understand neither the policy of Germany nor that of any other Great Power in Turkey without some knowledge of economic developments in the Ottoman Empire in the years preceding its downfall.

The forces of economic imperialism which tightened their hold on Turkey began their significant development during the Crimean war, when France and England taught the Sublime Porte to borrow. By 1875, the year in which the Porte became bankrupt, the public debt had reached a total of more than $1,000,000,000.[40] By the decree of Muharrem, December 20, 1881, the administration of the Ottoman public debt was created, and the debt reduced to $510,994,000. The council of the public debt, which was created by the decree, consisted of eight members[41] chosen to represent the various European

47

bondholders of Turkish securities. The council was given authority over duties on spirits, silk, stamps, salt, fish, etc., and served as an efficient collecting agency when foreigners began to invest in and construct railways in Turkey. In the end, the public debt controlled almost one-fourth of the total revenues of Turkey.

Financial and economic interests in Turkey had their fundamental political implications—particularly in their influence on the later plans and designs for the partition of the empire. Among these economic interests, railway construction played its peculiar part in the various projects for the partition of Asiatic Turkey. Before 1888, exclusive of Egypt, Turkish railways (in Europe) consisted of the Constantinople-Adrianople-Philippolis line and the Salonica-Mitrovitza line (1872). In Asia Minor there were the Smyrna-Aidin (1866), Smyrna-Cassaba (1866), the Constantinople-Ismid (1872), and the Mersina-Adana line (1886). Prior to 1888, the Germans had no railway interests in Asiatic Turkey. In 1899, however, an agreement between the Deutsche Bank and the Anatolian Railway Company, on the one part, and the Imperial Ottoman Bank and the Smyrna-Cassaba Railway (French) on the other, was reached. The part which the Administration of the Ottoman Public Debt played in railway construction may be seen in the fact that it finally became the intermediary between the government and the concessionaire in the major roads, including the German Bagdad project.[42]

It was in 1903 that the *Deutsche Bank* obtained its agreement embodying the Berlin-Bagdad railway scheme.[43] This was a concession for ninety-nine years, providing for the building of a railway line from Konia to Bagdad, via Adana, Aleppo and Mosul. The entire scheme, with branch lines in Syria and Mesopotamia, reaching to the Persian gulf, provided for a total of almost 2,400 miles of railroads.[44] By 1911 the Germans had more than £T 30,0 00,000 invested in Turkish railways.

The Bagdad project was of tremendous importance to Turkey. It would unify the country, build it up economically and politically, and in case of danger from without, enable the government the better to cope with a foe from beyond the frontiers. But the Bagdad railway scheme threatened French interests in Syria, the British in Egypt and Mesopotamia — particularly at Basra, commanding the Persian gulf — and the Russians in the Straits, and on the Caucasian and Persian frontiers. Incidentally, it gave Germany a vast stake in the Ottoman Empire—a stake either in its preservation, or in its partition. The

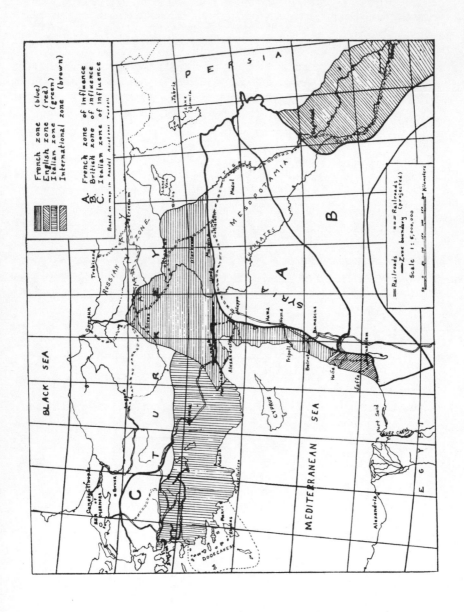

French zone (blue)
English zone (red)
Italian zone (green)
International zone (brown)

A. French zone of influence
B. British zone of influence
C. Italian zone of influence

Based on map in Naval Aviation Report.

═══ Railroads
═══ Railroads (projected)
—— Zone boundary

Scale 1: 6,000,000
50  0  50  100  150  200  250  Kilometers

PERSIA

Tabriz

Van

Erzerum

Trebizond

RUSSIAN ZONE

Samsun

FRENCH ZONE

TURKEY

BLACK SEA

Mosul

MESOPOTAMIA

EUPHRATES

Aleppo

Hama

Homs

SYRIA

A

B

Damascus

Tripoli

Beirut

Haifa

Jaffa

Alexandretta

CYPRUS

MEDITERRANEAN SEA

Port Said

SUEZ CANAL

Alexandria

EGYPT

C

DODECANESE

conflict with the interests of other Powers in the Near East, necessitated an agreement with each of them before the project could be completed.

France ranked second to Germany in the realm of railway construction in Turkey, with an investment of £T 18,842,560 (1911), with more than seven hundred miles in operation before the war. Aside from the Constantinople-Salonica line, the railways under French control were in Syria and Palestine—Smyrna-Cassaba, Damascus-Hama, and Jaffa-Jerusalem. Syria had become not only a great center of French cultural influence of long standing, but had developed into a very definite center of French investments in railways. The British, before the war, controlled only the Smyrna-Aidin railway of some 320 miles, with an investment of something over £T 4,500,000.[45] Nor were the British unmindful of their position of inferiority in the development of Turkish railways.

Neither Italy nor Russia controlled any Turkish railways. Indeed, one Russian writer states:

*"Russia, as is well known, played a very significant rôle in the general economic life of the Ottoman Empire. Neither in the imperial debt, nor in the Ottoman bank did Russian capital participate. Not a single kilometer of Turkish railways was controlled by Russia. Tsarist Russia struggled only to barricade Eastern Anatolia from European concessionaires."[46]*

Russia's great economic interests in Turkey centered in the necessity for an outlet through the Straits. Almost fifty per cent of her export trade went through this region, while from eighty-five to ninety per cent of her agricultural export reached the outside world only through these Turkish waters.

But if one examines the financial and trade statistics of Turkey before the war there is a slightly different story. By 1914 French capitalists had invested in Turkish securities a total of more than 3,350,000,000 francs, of which almost 2,500,000,000 were in the public debt. Germany came second with over 1,400,000,000 francs, of which more than 860,500,000 were in the public debt. Great Britain lagged with a total of only 807,958,496, the public debt investment being just above 500,000,000 francs. The French then controlled 60.08 per cent of the total debt of Turkey, while Germany had 24.52 per cent and England only 14.46 per cent.[47]

Trade statistics indicate still another angle of economic imperialism. In this realm Great Britain held an undisputed lead, though Germany

49

(and Italy) were making significant gains. Turkish exports to Germany jumped from 30,000,000 M (1900) to 70,100,000 M (1911). German imports to Turkey during the same period increased from 34,400,000 M to 112,800,000 M, an absolute gain of nearly 80,000,000 M. During this epoch Turkish exports to England dropped from 118,760,000 M to 100,660,000, while imports increased from 102,920,000 M to 177,160,000, exports representing a decrease from 35 per cent to 22 1·2 per cent of the total imports of Turkey. France had lost out in the trade with Turkey, dropping from second place in 1900, to a position inferior to Germany, Austria, and Italy in 1914.[48]

Thus by the eve of the world war, Germany and the Central Powers—and particularly Germany— held the dominating position in Turkish railways, ranked next to France in Turkish finance, and were making significant gains in Turkish trade. The mission of Liman von Sanders and the alliance of August 2, 1914, were but the political culmination of the already existing economic alliance. Well did Sir N. O'Connor (British ambassador in Turkey) insist in 1903, that "the Germans cannot put so large a capital into this country without being prepared to support the stability of an Empire in which they have staked so much. From the date of the signature (of the Bagdad Agreement) the German Government is directly interested in the highest degree in the maintenance of the Ottoman Empire."[49] Had the British ambassador added the counter-part of this policy—namely, that Germany would be interested in securing her share of Turkish territory around the *réseau* of the Bagdad project—he would have told the complete story. And, if the German spheres followed the line of the Bagdad route, that of France centered in her railroad territories. Likewise the British spheres centered around the Smyrna-Aidin railway and the neighborhood of Southern Mesopotamia. As will be pointed out later, by the spring of 1914, the western European Powers —Germany, France, England, and even Italy and Austria—were dividing Turkey into spheres of influence around their economic interests, preparatory to a possible partition of the Ottoman Empire.

3.

*The Political Preliminaries to the Partition of Turkey*

In November 1910, Russia and Germany came to an agreement with reference to the development of the Bagdad railway in Asiatic

Turkey. By this accord Germany recognized Russia's sphere in northern Persia, and undertook to construct no railroads therein. In return for this concession, Russia agreed no longer to oppose the Bagdad railway. Russia was to obtain from Persia a concession for the railway from Teheran to Khanikin, to be connected with the Bagdad line. Germans were to build this line, however, if Russian capitalists failed in the undertaking. Germany agreed not to encourage railway construction along the Caucasus frontier, which would be a strategic threat to Russia, as long as the Russian railways in that region were not completed.[50] The agreement finally was signed on August 19, 1911, following the Agadir crisis.[51]

The Potsdam accord was not in any real sense a project for the partition of Turkey. Nor did it foresee, necessarily, a division of Turkey into spheres of influence. The essential moves in that direction came in the years 1913-1914. After the Balkan wars, as Sazonov had pointed out in his memorandum of December 6, 1913, the Great Powers, without exception, were discounting in advance their claims on Asiatic Turkey.[52]

By an agreement between the Turkish and British governments in March 1913, the Porte recognized the special position of England in the region of the Persian gulf (southern Mesopotamia) and agreed to a policy of non-interference in Koweit, over which Britain's control had been established by the agreement of January 23, 1899, with the sheik. Basra was to be the terminus of the Bagdad route, unless and until Great Britain consented to its extension to the Persian gulf. Two British nationals were to sit on the board of directors of the Bagdad railway, and Lord Inchcape, of the British Indian Steam Navigation Company, was granted exclusive rights of navigation over the Tigris river from Kurna to Mosul, on the Euphrates from Kurna to Meskené, and on the Shatt-el-Arab. In return for these concessions, Great Britain would not oppose a four per cent increase in the Turkish customs duties.[53]

The Anglo-Turkish accord was, of course, a recognition on the part of Turkey, of an important English sphere of interest in the Ottoman Empire, as indicated in the agreement—in southern Mesopotamia and in Koweit. The Germans were fully informed as to the negotiations; indeed it was the German danger which had forced the British into the agreement of 1913, which was the prologue to the Anglo-German accord over the Bagdad railway, of June 1914. Both

51

Pallavicini and Giers, the Austrian and Russian ambassadors in Constantinople, were considerably alarmed by the English step. Turkey, already weak in Europe, now faced a serious threat against her territorial integrity in Asia. Knowing something of the German designs in Anatolia, Pallavicini feared that the Anglo-Turkish agreement signified an understanding between England and Germany having as its purpose the creation of "a kind of Anglo-German protectorate over Turkey."[54]

It remained for the Great Powers themselves to agree mutually on their spheres of influence, to outline their own *desiderata* in the future partition of Asiatic Turkey. The discussions between Germany, Italy and Austria, on the one hand, and between Germany, France and England, on the other, during 1913-1914, indicate clearly the policy which was to be followed. The members of the Triplice had talked over the problem of the partition of Turkey ever since the spring of 1913. Germany and France, and Germany and England arrived at their celebrated agreements on the Bagdad project in February and June 1914.

That Germany, Austria and Italy—the Central Powers—were developing definite plans for a partition of Asiatic Turkey in 1913-1914, during the year preceding the outbreak of the world war, no longer is subject to serious question. The "Drang nach Osten" already had taken very definite form for Germany, and German statesmen were considering Asia Minor (Anatolia) as a *"noli me tangere,"* on which the other European Powers should not encroach.[55] Italy, too, was much concerned about the future of Turkey, her interests centering particularly in the disposition of Albania in the Balkan peninsula, the Dodecanese islands, and in the prospects for Italian ambitions on the coast of Asiatic Turkey. Even the Austro-Hungarian Empire, faced with the greatest problem of nationalities on the continent of Europe, was ambitious to receive further territories at the expense of the Turkish Empire.[56]

On May 18, 1913, von Tschirschky, the German ambassador in Vienna, telegraphed Jagow that Berchtold had declared Austria's desire for the preservation of Turkey, but if the empire were to be partitioned, the Ballplatz would desire its share of the territory of Asiatic Turkey. Jagow had informed Berchtold of the German claims to the gulf of Alexandretta and the Mersina-Adana, and Anatolian districts, connecting these claims even with Armenia. Austria would desire the gulf of Adalia—the old provinces of Pamphylia and Cilicia. He

hoped that Austrian ambitions would not collide with German interests. Austria, also, would like the port of Haifa and its hinterland,
south of the French sphere in Syria. Italy, Berchtold felt, was a question. Doubtless Rome would want something in western Asia Minor,
despite recent accretions in northern Africa and in the Dodecanese
islands. Russia, too, would want territory on the Asiatic coast of the
Black Sea—which would open her way to the Bosphorus and the
Dardanelles.[57]

Nor was Italy slumbering. Grown more ambitious since the Italo-
Turkish war, Rome now stretched forth a hand toward the Adalia
vilayet on the coast of Asia Minor, where Italian economic interests
were developing rapidly. When Jagow heard of the negotiations of
the Nogara concern for concessions in Adalia, he complained to his
ambassador at Rome, Baron Flotow, that "economic interests in the
Orient have political consequences," and that Germany desired to
hold the Ottoman Empire together.[58] What both Austria-Hungary
and Germany feared was that Italy would obtain more than her share
of the bargain. The negotiations between Vienna, Rome and Berlin
continued, and on July 6, 1913, the discussions had gone far enough
for von Jagow to send to the German ambassador in Vienna a note in
which he outlined the sphere which Germany expected to obtain in
Asiatic Turkey. A map containing the necessary details, accompanied
the note.[59] The zones in Asia Minor which are mentioned in the note
were essentially the districts through which the proposed Bagdad
railway ran. They included mineral deposits, irrigation projects, and
ports. On July 15, 1913, Jagow informed Rome of this "zone de travail,"
always insisting, of course, that this was not a "sphere of influence."
In a very confidential note he outlined the German sphere in Asiatic
Turkey:

"The constructions of the Anatolian and Bagdad railroads and the
different works attached thereto (mines, irrigation projects, port constructions, etc.), pursued for some years by German capital, represent an
ensemble of concessions and interests which extend over a certain part
of Asiatic Turkey and form there a German zone de travail. This
zone de travail extends as far as the southern part of Asia Minor
where there are (précisément) several most important enterprises. Toward
the east this zone extends almost to Acre or even to Ladikia, while to the
west it extends as far as Alaja. From there its limit runs toward the
northwest and follows the line of the Taurus including the lake of Kirili
(lacus Carolis) which must supply water for the irrigation of the plain

53

*of Konia. Further, to the east and north, the boundary cannot be traced with precision, French and Russian interests not yet determined being involved.*"[60]

Just a few days prior to the sending of this telegram, San Giuliano, the Italian foreign minister, and the king and queen of Italy, had attended the Kaiser's annual yachting festival at Kiel, where Italy's ambitions both in the Balkans and in Asiatic Turkey were discussed.[61] Meanwhile, Austria and Italy were carrying on their own conversa' tions in regard to their respective shares of the Ottoman Empire. This is revealed not only from the German, but from the Austrian sources. A very important interview took place in Berlin in September 1913, between Count Forgach, of the Austrian foreign office, and Jagow, in which the two openly discussed a possible partition of Turkey.[62] Jagow informed Forgach that he did not share Wangenheim's faith in the strength of the Ottoman Empire. Within fifteen years, Turkey would go to pieces and a partition of Asia Minor would follow. Jagow had just had conversations with French and German banks over the Bagdad railroad questions. With England, also, there were important *pourparlers* on that issue, though a general understanding had not been reached. In case of a partition of the sultan's Asiatic heritage, Austria would want a sphere of interest on the southern angle of Asia Minor just opposite the island of Rhodes, as Berchtold had indicated in May. The Italian concessions in Adalia, both Forgach and Jagow agreed, would bring Italy easily into opposition with Eng' land. In conversations which Zimmermann, of the Wilhelmstrasse, had with von Szilassy, on October 30-31, the former used maps again to indicate the German desires in Asiatic Turkey. Jagow was repre' sented as very pessimistic about the future of Turkey, and counted on its division among the Powers of Europe.

The Austrian ambassador in Constantinople, Margrave Pallavicini, submitted the German tendencies to a severe analysis in a long report on December 29, 1913. For over a year, he points out, the Germans have spoken of spheres of interest in Turkey, and now believe that they can no longer remain mere "zones of work," but with the natural course of events must lead to a "partition of all Turkey." At Kiel Jagow drew the line between the Italian and German spheres of influence, laying the ground for a future political division of the empire. In view of the fact that the Bagdad railway tapped most of Asiatic Turkey, Pallavicini thought Germany would oppose partition of the country—instead it became the center of her schemes. The

German aim was "the creation of a German protectorate, under control of the army, after the English model, as it were, in Egypt." Whether Germany could carry through the program was another question. The Austrian suggested that Russia be bought off with Armenia, France with Syria, and England with Mesopotamia. Asia Minor could then be placed under a protectorate of the Triple Alliance! "Economically then, Thrace, with Constantinople in Europe, and all Asia Minor would be a single field of exploitation for Germany, Italy and for us."[63]

In a note of January 28, 1914, the ambassador of Italy at Berlin, Bollati, wrote Jagow that Rome accepted the German *zones de travail* in Asiatic Turkey. In return Italy desired a sphere of interest west of Germany's zone, on the gulf of Cos and Mendelia, to a line meeting the zones of the other Powers. The Italian government hoped these ideas would receive the same benevolence on the part of Berlin.[64] Three days later the Austrian ambassador, Szögyény, protested to the kaiser against the "unfriendly position" which Germany was taking toward Austria-Hungary "in the question of Asia Minor."[65]

Pallavicini greatly feared the results of the policy which Germany was following in the negotiations with Italy. In a long report to Berchtold, of March 23, 1914, he expressed the notion that the emphasis which Germany was giving to the "sphere of interest policy" would lessen distinctly the Turkish enthusiasm for Germany. Added now to the German policy was the Italian procedure in obtaining a sphere in southern Anatolia. Since Germany, Austria, Italy, France and England were engaged in discounting their shares of Asiatic Turkey, Pallavicini feared that one day the Turks might perceive that Russia was the single state not interested in a partition of the empire— and they might turn to Russia for protection and alliance.[66]

On April 18, 1914, Count Berchtold had an interview with the Italian foreign minister, San Giuliano, in which the two discussed their respective interests in Asia Minor. San Giuliano explained the Italian interests in Adalia—the Nogara concessions. Already there were negotiations between the British and the Italians over the Smyrna-Cassaba railroad. In return for recognition, Italy would view benevolently Austrian designs in Alaja westward along the coast of Asia Minor opposite the island of Rhodes.[67] But the Italo-Austrian negotiations remained fruitless. On May 19, 1913, the Nogara group signed an agreement with the English Smyrna-Aidin railway concern, by which the Italian company was to build lines to the south, and

the English to the north of the Smyrna-Aidin road, in the direction of the Bagdad railway. The agreement envisaged particularly the Adalia region and the region of Makri, for the development of ports and railways.[68] Lest there be doubt as to the Italian ambitions, Giolitti, Italian premier of the day, states:

*"The value of this concession (Adalia) for us was more remote than immediate and the reasons for seeking it political rather than economic for in the event of the break-up of the already sorely smitten Turkish Empire, it was as well to establish rights which would afterwards enable us to maintain the balance of power in the eastern Mediterranean. . . . So, after we had ascertained in Berlin what were the limits of the sphere of influence which Germany intended to reserve for herself in Asia Minor, we started negotiations in Vienna for defining the two spheres of influence, the Austrian and Italian. Owing, however, to later events, these negotiations were destined to remain fruitless."[69]*

Italy was holding the Dodecanese, and now was reaching out from those stepping stones into Asia Minor. Having obtained these, San Giuliano announced in the Italian Chamber of Deputies on May 26, 1914, that Italian economic and political interests of the first order were involved in Turkey, and that Rome stood for the preservation of the Mediterranean balance and "the maintenance of the territorial integrity of Turkey and her economic independence."[70]

Jagow little concealed his own attitude toward a possible partition of Turkey, and openly promoted the division of the empire into zones of influence. *Pourparlers* with France and England over the Bagdad railway, accordingly, were put under way after the close of the London conference, in the spring of 1913. The policy of the *Drang nach Osten* now took on a "concrete and definite form."[71] This was the beginning of "a partition of Turkey into economic spheres of interest,"[72] between Germany on the one hand, and France and England on the other.

After some months of diplomatic maneuvering, which had begun in the spring of 1913, the three Powers finally reached a settlement over the Bagdad railway on the eve of the outbreak of the world war in 1914. During the negotiations the German government was very careful not to indicate a trend toward a possible political partition of the Ottoman Empire. Purely the economic phases of the agreements were emphasized at London. Prince Lichnowsky wrote to Jagow on June 2, 1913:

*". . . I too am of opinion that it would be extremely unwise for us to enter into conversations with either Cambon or Pichon concerning*

*the partition of Asia Minor into spheres of interest; on no account must*
*we lead them to suppose that we would entertain the idea of dividing up*
*Turkey's possessions at some later date. That the French have designs*
*on Syria is just as well known as that these designs are being opposed*
*by England . . . . The disintegration of the latter (Turkey) would not*
*accord with British wishes if only for the reason that Great Britain would*
*not care to see us established as a Mediterranean Power and that it would*
*be difficult for Great Britain, from geographical considerations alone,*
*to pick out a suitable piece for herself. Now that we have repeatedly*
*emphasized the fact that we regard it as absolutely essential to maintain*
*the integrity of the Turkish possessions in Asia Minor, it would make a*
*most unfavorable impression if it got about that we had, behind England's*
*back, entered into negotiations with France for the partition of Asia*
*Minor . . . ."*[73]

However, during the course of the negotiations at London, Herr
von Gwinner, of the *Deutsche Bank,* seems to have hinted at the real
significance of the agreements to be made. He made several statements
"which have given the impression that we are already thinking of
broaching the subject of a partition of Asia Minor." Lichnowsky
therefore asked that hereafter Gwinner be instructed "that our attitude
has in no wise changed and that it is . . . dangerous to foster views
to the contrary."[74]

The French agreement with Germany was reached on February 15,
1914.[75] Affirming, as was usual in all such negotiations, the customary
desire that nothing be done which would work injury to the Ottoman Empire, the two Powers proceeded to delineate their economic
spheres in Asiatic Turkey. As was indicated in the negotiations between Germany, Austria and Italy, the Bagdad railroad project was
the nucleus of German claims, around which the German sphere was
drawn. French interests centered about Cilicia and Syria, where there
were not only educational and religious establishments, but considerable financial and railroad interests.[76] The terms of the agreement gave
France a sphere of influence in northern Anatolia for railway construction. The Black sea *réseau* was to be connected with the Anatolian
and Bagdad chain at Boli, Sivas, and Arghana Maden. Port and terminal
facilities at Heraclea were to be constructed in common, and the two
groups were to act together on construction of the railway, binding
the network to the interior of the country. The French sphere in
Syria was recognized. The French were to build from Tripoli (Syria)

through Homs to the Euphrates at Deir es Zor, where the Damascus-Hama railroad met the Bagdad line. The Germans were to build the line binding Alexandretta to Aleppo, and the latter via Meskené to a point on the Bagdad line in Mesopotamia. France recognized the German sphere of interest (*zone de travail*) around the Bagdad-Anatolian railway network. Separating the two zones was a neutral or "protected" zone running sixty kilometers south of the Alexandretta-Aleppo-Meskené line and prolongations; sixty kilometers north of the Tripoli-Homs-Deir es Zor line; and sixty kilometers on each side of the axis of the line from Homs to Aleppo. The zones were reserved exclusively to the exploitation of the respective national groups. Diplomatic measures to bring about the necessary increase in Turkish customs were agreed upon, and each group was to receive a subsidy from the Porte. The Deutsche Bank was to purchase from the Imperial Ottoman Bank its shares in the Bagdad railway, amounting to 69,400,000 francs. Suitable traffic arrangements were provided in annexes to the agreement.

At the same time, as we have seen, Great Britain and Germany were negotiating over their spheres in the Turkish Empire. Since the days of Lord Salisbury, English policy had changed from one of backing up the Ottoman Empire in any and all circumstances, to one which looked to a possible partition, in which British interests would be protected fully.[77] From the beginning, Downing Street looked askance at German economic and diplomatic predominance in Constantinople. The Bagdad railroad appeared to be a threat to the English both in Egypt, along the Suez route, and in southern Mesopotamia at Basra, striking at the very vitals of the British Empire.[78] When shortly after the London conference in 1913, the Wilhelmstrasse suggested an agreement over the Bagdad railway, the Foreign Office was not reluctant to negotiate. After conversations lasting a year, the two governments arrived at an understanding concerning their respective interests in Asiatic Turkey in June 1914.[79]

By the terms of the agreement London was no longer to oppose the Bagdad project, and Berlin was to obtain seats for two British nationals on the directory of the company. The British were to support a four per cent (eleven to fifteen per cent) ad valorem increase in Turkish customs. The terminus of the road was to be at Basra, and Great Britain was to control the gulf region in southern Mesopotamia. In return for British recognition of German irrigation projects in Cilicia, Britain received similar rights in southern Mesopotamia. The Anglo-Turkish agreement of 1913 was confirmed. The two Powers were to

influence the Porte to put the Shatt-el-Arab in navigable condition, which was to be open to all nations. Disputes over the convention were to be referred to the Hague court, if arbitration failed.

What Russia was expected to obtain from this partition of Turkey into economic spheres of interest is not very clear, though there was considerable loose talk about her rights to eastern Anatolia and Armenia. In view of the rapid changes that were taking place in the line-up in the Ottoman Empire, Russia did demand a delegate on the *Dette publique*, since that body had become a quasi-political organization, but Germany made consent conditional on the appointment of an additional German delegate to offset the Russian.[80] Sazonov suggested as early as July 1913, that an agreement might be made with the Porte to cede Russia the exclusive right for railroad construction in the frontier zones, and to guarantee Russian economic interests as defined by Russia. St. Petersburg would then renounce the convention of 1900 and agree to an increase in the Tuskish customs. Both Sazonov and Isvolsky were much concerned about the activities of French capitalists in northern Anatolian railways. On November 7, 1913, Sazonov wired Isvolsky in Paris: "Can we not be interested in the possible political consequences of an economic *entente* on the ground of the reciprocal recognition of spheres of influence of Germany and France in Asia Minor?"[81]

Russia had no tangible investments in Asiatic Turkey, and could not even expect to gain from the rights which France obtained in February 1914 for railway construction along the Asiatic shore of the Black sea. Her efforts, as already pointed out, were confined to barricading eastern Anatolia from foreign concessionaires. That Russia was against carving up the Ottoman Empire into spheres of influence as an economic preliminary to a later political partition of Asiatic Turkey is evident. Such a step would not be a suitable solution of the question of the Straits in a sense favorable to Russia. Shortly after the conclusion of the Franco-German agreement, in March 1914, Giers, the Russian ambassador in Constantinople, told Baron Wangenheim that the St. Petersburg cabinet had made a "complete alteration" of its policy toward Turkey. Russia could not consent to a danger to Constantinople at the hand of a third Power, and it would not suit Russia "to have Germany as a neighbor in Asia."[82]

On the eve of the war, then, plans were fully laid for a partition of the Turkish Empire, should the final and expected dissolution come. Wangenheim had complained in May 1913 that Germany was not ready for a partition of Turkey because her plans were not carefully

delineated. During the course of the year, from May 1913 to June 1914, Berlin had drawn up these plans very carefully, with her own allies, Austria-Hungary and Italy, and with France and Great Britain. In the end, as Prince Lichnowsky has stated concerning the agreements reached in 1914:

"*The real object of this treaty was to divide up Asia Minor into spheres of influence, although this term was anxiously avoided in view of the rights of the Sultan. Sir Edward Grey, too, repeatedly stated that there were in existence no agreements with France and Russia which in any way aimed at the partition of Asia Minor . . . . By this treaty the whole of Mesopotamia as far as Basra was included within our sphere of influence (without prejudice to already existing British navigation rights on the Tigris and the rights of the Willcox irrigation works), as well as the whole district of the Bagdad and Anatolian railway . . . . The coast of the Persian Gulf and the Smyrna-Aidin railway were recognized as the British economic sphere, Syria as the French and Armenia as the Russian.*"[83]

In the month of December 1913, as has been shown, the mission of Liman von Sanders came to reorganize the military establishment of Turkey. With the Bagdad road determined, and the spheres of interest later outlined, the Berlin government had completed its policy in Turkey. The military mission increased its hold on the Ottoman Empire. Perhaps the schemes of Germany stretched even as far as Afghanistan and Persia and into India.[84] At its best, German policy at this time, was one of insurance against every possibility. If Turkey went to pieces, Germany would obtain a major share of the Ottoman estate. If the Turkish Empire remained intact, through control of the army and domination of the Bagdad route, Turkey would be under the military and economic dominance of Germany.

4.

*The Crisis in Near Eastern Politics*

Having considered the Near Eastern problem from the angle of Asiatic Turkey and the plans for the partition of the Ottoman Empire, let us now turn once more to the Balkan tangle, from the late months of 1913, to the eve of the world war, and follow the threads of policy of the European cabinets in that troubled region.

After the treaty of Bucharest was signed, the Ballplatz was disposed to crush Serbia and the greater Serbian agitation, which the Dual Monarchy considered the most dangerous obstacle to her existence as a Great Power. So great was the danger of a break in Austro-Serbian relations that M. Pashich, the Serbian prime minister, came to Vienna, and on October 4, 1913, made definite overtures for more friendly relations to Count Berchtold.[85] Two weeks later, the Austrian government, seemingly determined to settle with Belgrade, sent an ultimatum to the Serbs demanding withdrawal of Serbian troops from beyond the Albanian frontier within eight days. The Serbs yielded to the Austrian threat of war.[86]

With the idea of ultimately crushing Serbia as a political factor in the Balkans, Vienna began to re-orient her Balkan policy with a view to reconstruction of the Balkan alliances, making Bulgaria the pivot of the scheme, and adding both Greece and Turkey, then holding Rumania faithful to the alliance, through fear of isolation in a sea of Slavdom. It has been indicated above that both Austria-Hungary and Bulgaria had moved in that direction as early as the winter of 1913— Austria-Hungary because of her fear of Serbia, and Bulgaria because of her desire for revenge. Conversations between Vienna and Berlin over this fundamental change in Balkan policy in June and July 1913, were leading to nothing because the Wilhelmstrasse desired yet to hold on to Bucharest as the chief make-weight in a Balkan alliance.[87] In a secret dispatch to Szögyény in Berlin, Berchtold noted that Serbia was becoming Austria's chief enemy in the Balkans since the wars of 1912-1913. It was therefore necessary to swing Bulgaria definitely to the Triple Alliance. Ghenadiev had already asked for an understanding, and Berchtold favored the idea, but felt he must have the support of both Germany and Italy. He thought that Greece might be induced to join the combination, and that Rumania could be held loyal to her old moorings. Count Stephen Tisza, the Hungarian premier, writing from Dresden, on August 25, supported Berchtold's ideas. Tisza considered the German policy in the Balkans not only a mistake, but as definitely compromising the future security of the German Empire. A connection between Bulgaria and Rumania must be supported in Bucharest "with all strength," and Bulgaria must be allied to the Triplice. "It is our life interest to prevent a standing grouping of Rumania with Serbia and Greece against Bulgaria, and the success of this action with reference thereto hangs chiefly on the German position in Bucharest."[88] But on September 13,

1913, Jagow wrote Wangenheim in Constantinople that though Sofia had offered an alliance to Vienna, in which Turkey also would be a member, he did not favor the project because a Greco-Turkish understanding should precede it. Besides King Carol of Rumania disapproved the idea, and von Jagow feared a war of *révanche*.[89]

Meanwhile Pallavicini telegraphed on September 8, that Turkish statesmen were ready for an understanding with Bulgaria. He felt that there were three Balkan factors which could be used to Austria's advantage—Albania, Bulgaria and Turkey. Tarnowsky, the Austrian minister at Sofia, complained on September 16, that Bulgaria's offer of an alliance thus far had received only sympathy from Vienna, and the rejoinder that "first Bulgaria should make an alliance with Rumania." He feared that Bulgaria might answer such a statement with immediate overtures both to Russia and Rumania. But again, there was no hope of German support. Baron Flotow wrote on September 23, that "as to the possibility of the conclusion of an alliance between Turkey and Bulgaria, Herr von Jagow does not believe." Jagow more readily believed in an alliance between Turkey and Greece, and in the eventual possibility of an alliance between Greece and Germany, though that, too, could wait.[90]

Berchtold explained his policy in Berlin, in October 1913. He told the kaiser that his efforts were directed "towards playing off the Balkan states against one another . . . . At present the conflict between Serbia and Bulgaria which remained from the second Balkan war was for this (purpose) of decisive importance, and means must above all be found to prevent these two Balkan States coming to terms, which could only happen at our expense." Bulgaria already had made moves in the direction of Vienna, but Berchtold "could only enter into such an orientation if our relation with Rumania was not thereby injured (tangirt) . . . . German policy would perhaps be of assistance to us in this." The kaiser felt that Belgrade could be either bought off or forced to fall in with Austro-Hungarian policy, and promised to support his ally.[91] It was not, however, until the summer of 1914 that Berlin finally gave full support to the Bulgarian alliance.

Bulgaria was now making very definite moves toward a close connection with the Dual Monarchy. Tarnowsky had a long conversation with Tsar Ferdinand on October 5, 1913, in which there was talk of an alliance between Bulgaria and Turkey, together with an agreement with Rumania—all gravitating toward the *Dreibund*. In early November, Ferdinand came to Vienna, not only for his physical and

political health, but also in order to clarify his relations with Austria. On November 6, he had a long interview with Berchtold at the Ballplatz. The subject of an alliance with Austria was discussed. The tsar of the Bulgars denounced the "cruel butchery" of the Bucharest treaty, stated he was on better relations with Rumania, and even offered to make good Roman Catholics of the Bulgarians![92] Berchtold favored the project, but postponed action. On November 11, 1913, he wired his representatives abroad that Bulgaria had offered a formal alliance. While not rejecting it, he pointed out that relations with Rumania must not be injured by such a move.[93] A week later Ghenadiev was in Vienna urging Austrian support and influence in Sofia. On November 23, Radoslavov, later premier, in an address at Plevna, declared that "the policy of Bulgaria must no longer be Russophil but independent."[94]

While no formal alliance was made at the time, the two countries were drawn toward each other by common political interests in the Balkans. Apparently no formal accord appeared necessary in Vienna. On the other hand Bulgaria was forced to play a double game, for she needed French money, and for that reason could hardly afford to alienate either France or Russia. One other policy was open to her: to combine with Serbia and Rumania to achieve their dreams against Austria-Hungary, in return for concessions in the Dobruja and Macedonia.[95] From this time on, Bulgarian policy vacillated between Austria and Russia, with Austria distinctly in the ascendency, until Bulgaria's entrance into the world war in the fall of 1915.

Many politicians in Sofia had turned rabidly Russophobe since the Balkan *débacle*. So practical a people, however, as the Bulgarians were not to be swayed by passing considerations of sentiment. On November 6, 1913, the same day on which Tsar Ferdinand was urging an alliance in Vienna, Ghenadiev, his finance minister, was in Paris denying such a move, and trying to obtain a loan on the Paris *bourse*. He told Pichon and Isvolsky that Sofia had neither conversations nor agreements either with Austria or with Turkey. Difficulties with Russia were not insurmountable, Bulgaria had no political aims in the Straits, and would like a political agreement with St. Petersburg. Isvolsky did not believe all that fell from Ghenadiev's lips, but urged a policy of forbearance on Sofia, believing the government could be controlled through a loan, of which that government was greatly in need.[96] Sazonov, however, had learned of the Vienna overtures of Bulgarian diplomacy and frowned on any financial support to the Radoslavov-Ghenadiev government.[97]

As we have already seen, the Balkan wars had altered completely the position of Rumania to the Triplice. The main obstacle to intimate relations between Rumania and Austria-Hungary was the Transylvanian question, which no responsible Austrian statesman had made any serious attempt to solve. There was now little likelihood that Rumania ever would take the part of Austria-Hungary in a conflict. Berchtold could not sanction a Bulgarian alliance, however, because it carried the possibility of still more injuring his relations with Rumania; and the Germans would not use their influence to improve Bulgaro-Rumanian relations. Wangenheim, German ambassador in Turkey, urged the possibility of a Turco-Rumano-Greek alliance—a policy supported in Berlin. In Wangenheim's opinion it would be impossible for a long time to improve relations between Rumania and Bulgaria.[98] Nevertheless, Bratianu, one of the most powerful of Rumanian statesmen, told both the German and the Austro-Hungarian ministers that the alliance "was a thing of impossibility," the chief obstacle being the Transylvanian question.[99]

But the Austrians continued their discussions in Sofia. Tarnowsky had an interview with Ghenadiev on December 11, 1913. The latter told him that the Bulgarians were aware that the way to Vienna lay through Bucharest. Since Bratianu was a Bulgarophobe a connection with Rumania seemed hardly possible. Again on December 29, both Radoslavov and Ghenadiev talked with Tarnowsky about the alliance, and about the much needed loan. No formal connection was possible at the time, though it was felt that a well-placed loan would do much good in Sofia.[100]

Meanwhile, Bulgaria and Turkey were in negotiations as to a possible understanding. Pallavicini, late in December reported a conversation with M. Toshev, his Bulgarian colleague in Constantinople, in which the latter urged a defensive Bulgar-Turkish alliance under the aegis of Austria-Hungary and Germany. It was to be based on Rumanian neutrality, and was to be used against both Greece and Serbia.[101] But again the negotiations for an alliance went on the rocks. The Bulgarians were afraid to make the alliance without external aid and influence. Sofia feared that the Turks might use such an agreement to win back western Thrace and the Aegean islands from Greece, leaving Bulgaria to face both Serbia and Rumania alone. Consequently, "it is impossible for the Bulgarian government to enter an alliance with

Turkey, without before receiving assurances from the *Dreibund*." Ghenadiev even expected Germany to use her influence with Greece for the cession of Cavalla to Bulgaria.[102]

Greece and Turkey, in the interim, had never settled the question of the Aegean islands. It will be remembered that Greece had won territory in northern Epirus (southern Albania) and the Aegean islands during the Balkan wars. Italy was in occupation of the Dodecanese islands. Turkey did not accept the solution of the question of the islands in behalf of Greece, because on the one hand Greek possession threat-ened the approach to the Dardanelles, and on the other menaced the security of Asiatic Turkey. War threatened from time to time.[103] The question had been reserved to the Powers of Europe for settlement. At Bucharest in August 1913 Greece had retained Crete and the islands occupied during the war. The Greco-Turkish treaty of November 1913 did not settle the issue. Germany and Austria, France and England, approved a settlement in favor of Greece. Neither Italy nor Russia, however, favored a settlement which would give to the Greeks command of the approach to the Straits of the Dardanelles.[104]

For some months there had been a German move (at times seconded by Vienna), not only to make peace between Greece and Turkey, but also to bring them both under the definite political influence of the Triple Alliance. As early as September 1913, Wangenheim, who was privately critical of the Grecophil tendencies of the Berlin cabinet, wrote that a new Balkan alliance along these lines would mean that Cavalla must go to Bulgaria, Salonica to Serbia, and the Aegean islands to Turkey. Only in case the islands were neutralized could Turkey give them to Greece, her chief enemy. The grand vizier would make such an alliance either with Greece or with Bulgaria, but the question of the islands was the chief stumbling block with Greece.[105] Vienna was awake to the possibilities, for Szilassy, Austrian minister at Athens, was pressing continually the importance of Greece in the Austro-German system since the Balkan Wars. Throughout January 1914, he wrote memoranda on the significance of Hellenism, and on January 9, he advanced the idea of a new Balkan confederation com-posed of Greece, Bulgaria, Turkey and Rumania against Serbia. Rumania might be doubtful on account of her Transylvanian dreams, but Greece might be won over with the Aegean islands with the exception of Tenedos and Imbros. Szilassy, however, was fearful of a Greek campaign in Asia Minor against Turkey. Germany, he felt, should be brought to this point of view.[106]

On January 30, Venizelos had a long interview with Berchtold in Vienna, in which the two discussed the possibilities of a mutual defensive alliance. Austria signified her willingness to consent to Greek possession of Chios and Mitylene.[107] Both Germany and Austria were now pushing an alliance between Turkey and Greece, though this did not appeal either to Pallavicini or Wangenheim. On April 17, 1914, Venizelos outlined a project for such an alliance to Bethmann-Hollweg, then at Corfu with William II.[108] The project called for a defensive alliance guaranteeing Turkey's European possessions, with respect for the *status quo ante bellum* in the Aegean islands, and nominal Turkish suzerainty over Chios and Mitylene. In a note of von Mutius, from Constantinople, however, the grand vizier is represented as desiring an alliance for five years and a military convention guaranteeing European Turkey. This would involve Greek recognition of Turkish sovereignty over the Aegean islands, with the exception of Crete, and maintenance of the existing régime in the islands.[109]

The propositions were far apart and it seemed little likely that an alliance would result. In fact, on May 7, 1914, Wangenheim wired Berlin, urging a Rumano-Bulgar-Turkish connection, and advising against a Greco-Turkish combination. "With our turning about to Greece the Rumano-Bulgar-Turkish alliance under German protectorate would be an impossibility." Greek dreams of Constantinople made relations with Turkey difficult.[110] However, when Wangenheim returned from Corfu, where he had gone to pay respects to his imperial master, he was ready to support a connection between Greece and Turkey.[111] Later in May the grand vizier asked Wangenheim to notify Venizelos that Turkey demanded Chios and Mitylene. Turkey asserted her position in the other Aegean islands attributed to Greece by the European Powers, and demanded the right to garrison not only Mitylene and Chios, but the island of Lemnos. Venizelos rejected this basis of an agreement, and asked Berlin to inform the Turks of his refusal.[112] The issue was never settled, for by this time events were taking place on the larger stage of world politics. In June the Austrian archduke was murdered. The world war was beginning.

All this time the negotiations with Bulgaria were being carried on. Not only were Vienna and Berlin endeavoring to hold Bulgaria with financial assistance, but to ally Bulgaria and Turkey under Austro-German auspices. Difficulties with the Pomaks in western Thrace had delayed the negotiations, according to a telegram of Count Tarnowsky, in Sofia. This was confirmed by Pallavicini. The Austrian ambassador

in Constantinople feared that if Bulgaria were unable to make an alliance under Austria and Germany, she might turn again to Russia, and Tarnowsky reported on February 18, that Bulgaria would make no alliance with Turkey, if a connection with the *Dreibund* seemed impossible. Without full German support no action could be taken. While the Turks felt that Bulgaria and Turkey were bound by common interests, the time appeared unfavorable for a treaty, and an alliance with or guarantee from Rumania would be necessry as a preliminary.[113]

The new tendencies in Austro-Hungarian Balkan policy were summed up in Count Stephen Tisza's memorandum on the foreign situation, of March 15, 1914.[114] The Balkan wars, he wrote, had created "a situation on our eastern and southern borders that requires on our part cool and calm consideration, but also consistent and tenacious action. The peace of Bucharest has brought about an entirely unsatisfactory condition, without the rectification of which no real, lasting peace is possible." Austria-Hungary must, therefore, in the future follow "a comprehensive, forward-looking *politique de longue main*" leading to a grouping of the Balkan Powers favorable to the Dual Monarchy—a policy which Germany must be led to follow. "Germany must perceive that the Balkans are of decisive importance, not only for us, but also for the German Empire." In the Balkans, it was the position of Russia, assisted by the "mad ambition" of Rumania and Serbia, and the "endangered position" of Bulgaria, which constituted the great problem for Austria-Hungary. ·

". . . *A combination that would reconcile Bulgaria with the rest of the Christian states under Russian patronage, and as the result of a successful war of conquest directed against our Monarchy, would assure Macedonia to Bulgaria, would complete the forging of the iron ring about us, for which Russia is so tenaciously and so consciously working, and make actual the military preponderance of the Entente on the Continent . . . .*

"*It is a matter of immediate necessity, to bring our plans with regard to Rumania, Bulgaria, Turkey, and Greece into accord with those of Germany. Only our firm coöperation with Germany can again secure our relations to Rumania. For that country, the conquest of Transylvania always remains the greatest lure, a great Rumania extending to the Theiss the most beautiful dream of Rumanian chauvinists. It requires self-control, and strong, sober discernment as well, to renounce this*

*fanciful picture and in alliance with us to secure present possessions and true independence, and avert the danger of a Russian protectorate."*

Unless Bulgaria's situation were ameliorated, menaced as she was not only by Serbia and Rumania, but also by Turkey, she might be thrown into the waiting arms of Russia. "For Bulgaria, expansion into Macedonia is a vital matter. If she cannot secure this in alliance with us, she will unconditonally throw herself into the arms of Russia and support the policy of conquest against us." For the Triple Alliance to cast off Bulgaria would be a "disastrous mistake."

The center of gravity of European politics lay in the Balkans and German and Austrian plans in that quarter must be harmonised. Only German coöperation could hold Rumania in the alliance and force modifications of the treaty of Bucharest in favor of Bulgaria—the only way of keeping that country in the Austrian orbit. Moreover the Turks must not be allowed to attack Bulgaria. To prevent this, intimate rela-tions between Athens and Sofia must be encouraged, and relations between Bucharest and Sofia smoothed over. Both Greece and Turkey should be brought into peaceful relations. The aims of Austro-German Balkan policy, then, must be to establish a grouping of the Balkan states favorable to the Triple Alliance, separate Greece and Rumania from Serbia, and reconcile them with Bulgaria, "on the basis of a natural expansion of Bulgaria at Serbia's expense." Withheld from any adven-ture, Turkey's Asiatic possessions were to be kept intact, and the Ottoman Empire drawn into the anti-Slav camp. Such was to be the new program for Austria-Hungary as outlined by the Hungarian premier.

When Pashich and Venizelos were in St. Petersburg, in February 1914, the lines of Russian policy in the Balkans and in Turkey were drawn more definitely. The tsar told Pashich that if peace were to be preserved Greece must avoid conflict with Turkey over the question of the Aegean islands, whose fate must be left to the European Powers. No loans should be granted either to Bulgaria or Turkey, under existing circumstances. Austrian and Italian occupation of Albania must be prevented by international occupation. Rumania should be brought into the Russian orbit and stand on the basis of the *status quo* of the treaty of Bucharest. The tsar condemned Ferdinand's Austrophil policy in Bulgaria, and believed he would have difficulty in holding his throne. Pashich envisaged possible concessions in Macedonia to Bulgaria "if she

were willing to help in the solution of the Serbo-Croatian question." On leaving, the tsar assured Pashich that "We will do everything for Serbia."[115]

Russian relations with Rumania had improved noticeably since the Balkan wars. Poklevsky-Koziel had reported as much since the opening of 1914. Rumania already had taken a stand to prevent a possible Greco-Turkish war, and her interest in keeping the Straits open to commerce was similar to that of imperial Russia. The attachment of Rumania to the treaty of Bucharest brought a firm understanding with both Serbia and Greece, the other holders of the spoils of war.[116] The community of interests with Rumania in the question of the Straits was emphasized at the Constanza meeting of June 1914, when the royal family of Rumania and the imperial family of Russia exchanged friendly greetings. Already in April, the tsar had told Paléologue, the French ambassador in Russia, that if Greece and Turkey went to war, with the closure of the Straits resulting, he would be ready to resort to force to reopen them.[117] There was to be no repetition of incidents such as those attendant on the Italo-Turkish war. The result of the Constanza meeting was an agreement that if another closure of the Straits were threatened in a further Greco-Turkish struggle, both Russia and Rumania would declare in common that "they could not remain indifferent in this situation of fact."[118] Sazonov concluded from further conversations in Bucharest, that a future war would find Rumania on the side which seemed most likely to succeed, but rather favorably inclined toward France, England and Russia.[119] Nor did the Austrians have serious illusions as to the future.

But Russian *rapprochement* with Rumania was not necessarily to be at the expense of Bulgaria. Indeed, St. Petersburg desired to swing Rumania from her leanings toward the Triplice into the orbit of the Entente, and at the same time to hold Bulgaria to her old anchorage. This line of policy, would, of course, serve to re-constitute the Balkan league with Rumania, Greece and Serbia, on the basis established at Bucharest, in August 1913. But it held out the promise of compensation to Bulgaria.

St. Petersburg, on the other hand, did not trust the government of the day in Sofia. The Radoslavov cabinet was distinctly Austrophil, and Sazonov would consent to no loan from Paris until an "independent"—pro-Russian—policy were assured. Only in that case could he work for a reconciliation between Bulgaria and Serbia, and bring Bulgaria back into the fold.[120] Radoslavov failed to obtain a loan

in France because he would not give a promise that the Bulgarian government would not follow a policy hostile to the Triple Entente. Failing in Paris, Sofia turned to Berlin for the financial support which was a matter of life and death to the cabinet, and submitted to the onerous terms of the German bankers.[121] Russian policy attempted to prevent this loan, which would signify the complete subjection of Bulgaria to Austro-German designs. Every means was exhausted, until in May 1914, when Savinsky, the new Russian minister at Sofia, the French minister, and representatives of financial interests, arrived at a plan of action.[122] Solution was difficult at best, however, and by July 3, the Radoslavov cabinet had concluded the German loan and carried it through the *Sobranje*. Though no political clauses appeared in the loan agreement, they apparently were understood between the parties to the transaction. The government at Sofia seemed to have been placed definitely in the orbit of the Central Powers.[123]

While Savinsky fully realized the great importance of separating Rumania from her connections with the Triplice, he was insistent that Bulgaria's political orientation was not a matter of indifference to St. Petersburg. Traditional ties were still binding. A new conflagration, he felt, would put Austria and Russia in opposite camps. In such an eventuality, Bulgaria's geographical and political position would play a significant rôle. Moreover, Savinsky sensed the direction of events when he wrote Sazonov on May 16, 1914:

*"A systematic conquest of the Near East in general, and of Bulgaria in particular, forms part of Germany's quite definite plan. They already have installed Sanders-Pasha on the Bosphorus and now they are impudently stretching out their hands towards Constantinople, and this from both sides, in Thrace as in Asia Minor . . . . They do all they can to induce Bulgaria to arrive at an understanding with Turkey.*

*"Bulgaria is thus being pushed towards the brink of a precipice. It is incumbent upon us, for the sake of our traditional policy, as well as in regard of our most vital interests, not to allow the Austro-German plan to be realized."*[124]

Meanwhile, Turkish policy toward the Entente in general and Russia in particular took an interesting turn in the spring of 1914. It will be remembered that at the secret conference of February 1914, Russia, in view of the German plans in Turkey, had determined on the measures to solve the question of the Straits, should events precipitate trouble in that region. This did not signify either a plot to seize the Straits, or even warlike activities for a solution of the question in

1914. Indeed the entire history of Russo-Turkish relations, centering as it does around the question of the Straits, is illuminating in this respect, and needs some reinterpretation. A recent Turkish writer, Ali Fuad, who points out that Russia is either "the greatest friend or enemy of Turkey," lays down a general rule in Russo-Turkish relations, when he writes:

*"Russia, following circumstances, will have recourse to these two methods, she will become in turn friend and enemy of the Porte, but her policy will be directed always and invariably toward the same end: to dominate Turkey. She will find herself always also in the presence of the interests of the western Powers whose principal rôle will consist in suspecting Russia in both cases and in taking precautions, in order to counteract her designs."*[125]

Such is the general principle. It is now clear that Russia might have solved the question of the Straits and her relations with Turkey in the spring of 1914, through a friendly *entente* with the Porte, had that possibility remained open. Mukhtar Pasha, the Turkish ambassador in Berlin, writes: "Everything proves that at this epoch the Russians had decided to proceed finally to the realization of what they called their historic mission, *free to Turkey to choose in this occurrence the rôle of ally or of adversary.*"[126] In February 1914 an agreement had been reached on the Armenian reforms, and Russo-Turkish relations had improved considerably.[127]

For some months it was apparent that there had been a "change" in Russia's policy toward Turkey. In Pallavicini's report of March 23, 1914, which we have already cited, he points out the dangers of the German policy which was leading toward a partition of the Ottoman Empire, notes the "complete alteration" in Russian policy, and expresses his fear that the Turks might turn to the Muscovite for an alliance, as the single Power opposed to a carving up of Asiatic Turkey.[128] On April 4, the Austrian ambassador further reports that there is no doubt that Russian policy has taken "another direction" from that hitherto followed. This change is ascribed to the sending of the German military mission to Turkey and to the division of Turkey into spheres of influence, discounting in advance the downfall of the Turkish Empire. Moreover, many Turks themselves were changing their course. The known attitude of the Powers, the Italian acquisition of the Dodecanese and Italian efforts in southern Anatolia, had their effect on Constantinople. Pallavicini learned that the Turks were becoming more and more fearful as to the future, and thought they

71

might turn to Russia. Halil Bey told him that Russia was pursuing a very active policy, and stated that a treaty between Russia and Turkey was "thinkable," on the basis of free passage of the Bosphorus for Russia, and a political guarantee for Turkey. The conclusion of such an agreement would place the Triplice in a "very unfavorable" position. The remedy was a Turco-Bulgarian alliance under the protection of Germany and the Dual Monarchy.[129] One thing was certain, in view of the circumstances: it would be impossible for Turkey to remain isolated, and the next few months would determine in what direction she was to turn for aid and comfort.[130]

But that which gave formal significance to a possible new orientation in Russo-Turkish relations and aroused the fears of both Pallavicini and Wangenheim, was the journey of the Turkish mission early in May 1914, to Livadia to pay a visit of respect and courtesy to the tsar of all the Russias. Talaat Bey, minister of the interior and chief of the mission, offered Russia an alliance on the very day of his departure for home. Sazonov was surprised and did not believe the offer to be overweighted with sincerity, but he did not turn down the proposal and left the matter open to further consideration.[131] The Turkish newspapers seemed very favorably impressed with the Livadia interview, and spoke openly of a prospective alliance with Russia. Pallavicini revived the shades of the Charykov proposal, of 1911, in which in return for a favorable solution of the question of the Straits, Russia would guarantee the territorial integrity of the Ottoman Empire.[132] In his address to the Duma, on May 24, 1914, Sazonov said:

*"The liquidation of the Balkan crisis has exercised a favorable influence on the connections between Russia and the Ottoman Empire, whose European possessions were a source of weakness. In the solution of the problem of her internal organization, Turkey will find Russia disposed to offer her assistance.*

*"The freedom of maritime commerce in the Straits conforms to Ottoman interests and answers to the vital needs of Russia, and can be realized only on the condition of the pacific development of Turkey.*

*"The evolution of the recent Armenian question witnesses the peaceful intentions of the present government of Turkey . . . . The conversations with the members of the extraordinary Ottoman embassy which came to Livadia gave us the impression of the serious desire of Turkey to establish with Russia relations answering to the interests of the two countries and conforming to the new political conditions."[133]*

Whether or not the new orientation of Turkish policy would have a chance of development, there can be no question that the Livadia interview disquieted the Austrians. Pallavicini was more and more convinced that it was the policy of Germany which had led the Turks to this pass, even though the German foreign ministry refused to get excited. And yet, the Austrian ambassador did not lay all the blame on the Germans. He felt that a large share of it must be placed on Italian shoulders. The Italians had begun in the Libyan campaign, and now they were making a detour through the Dodecanese into Asia Minor. Already the Turks had been aroused, and through the opposition of the other Great Powers which possessed interests in Asiatic Turkey, the Italian dreams would meet ship-wreck. Pallavicini felt that the Livadia interviews and those at Constanza signified a change in Turkish policy which could only be met with a Turco-Bulgarian connection under the Central Powers. Otherwise Russia might obtain a solution of her historic question in the Straits, and the Muscovite and the Turk might march hand in hand.[134]

Mukhtar Pasha, the Turkish ambassador in Berlin, favored the Russian *rapprochement* as a means of attaining Turkey's security, though he was perfectly aware of Russian aspirations in the Straits. Even as to Russian aims in Armenia, Mukhtar wrote on July 16, 1913, "Their principal objective remains always Constantinople." In this same dispatch, the Turkish statesman noted the impossibility of out-building Russia in the Black sea in the next four or five years, and that defence of Constantinople could be realized only by "a previous *entente* with one or several Mediterranean Powers." He concluded: "It is now necessary to be able to defend against Russia the seat of the califate and even the heart of the empire, *or even to adopt toward that Power a policy of conciliation and entente permitting her no longer to attack us.*"[135]

The Turkish move toward Russia was not isolated. In June 1914, it was followed up in England. Since February 1914, relations between Turkey and France had improved to such an extent that on April 25, the first series of a 500,000,000 franc loan was awarded the Ottoman Bank and floated on the Paris Bourse with the tacit consent of the Deutsche Bank. France had received concessions for more than 2,000 miles of railway in Asiatic Turkey following the agreement of February 1914, with Germany.[136] In June, Djemal Pasha, minister of marine, attended the review of the French fleet. In conversations at the Quai d'Orsay, he proposed an alliance with England, France and Russia,

holding out high hopes of closing the iron ring around the Central Powers. At the same time, the former grand vizier, Hakki Pasha, tried to reach an understanding on Armenian reforms, providing for English administrators in Armenia. This, naturally, met the objections of Russia.[137] In particular, however, any move toward Russia on the part of Turkey was blocked by the control which the Liman von Sanders mission and Baron Wangenheim, the German ambassador at Constantinople, now had over the Porte. This fundamental German control, in the end, precluded any possibility of a Russo-Turkish intimacy. Again let us quote Mukhtar Pasha:

*"As for the policy to be applied toward Turkey, it is not to be said that it must necessarily be of a hostile character. That would be to mistake the nature and the means which diplomacy uses to believe that the designs of Russia to extend her domination over the Straits must exclude every possibility of approaching the question pacifically. An intimate rapprochement with Turkey in the aim of creating a situation analogous to that established in 1832 (sic) by the treaty of Unkiar Eskellessi, could have satisfied Russia, as the facts related above demonstrate. The success of such a policy was moreover more advantageous than an expedition against Constantinople, which had to depend on problematical conditions and eventualities. It presented also risks and sacrifices which they were interested in avoiding. Thus, in case the Sublime Porte had been at the point of following a settled policy, intimate connections between it and St. Petersburg could have been established . . . . As every hope of direct understanding with the Turks disappeared before the Germanophil tendencies of the leaders, and particularly of the Young-Turkish military chiefs, the Russians persevered in their aim of taking possession of Constantinople, and searched for an understanding with England."[138]*

And Sazonov writes:

*"The Young Turk cabinet, frightened at the boldness of its own proposal, had evidently decided to abandon the plan contemplated by Talaat. It may also be that the German embassy, having learnt of his attempt to find a counterpoise to German influence in an alliance with Russia, had promptly put an end to all such aspirations. There is no doubt, however—and this has been confirmed from other sources—that the Young Turks hesitated before linking their fate with that of Germany; but the German ambassador, Baron von Wangenheim, and the military mission of General Liman von Sanders, finally succeeded in convincing them of her invincible might. Enver Pasha, the Minister of War, who*

74

had enjoyed the special favor of the Kaiser during his long stay in Berlin, and the numerous pro-Germans to be found in Turkish military circles, believed still more blindly in her power."[139]

It is sufficient to note, finally, that within the next month the lines of a Turco-German alliance were being drawn. The ruling powers in Young Turkey were being drawn definitely into the German circle.

When the Archduke Franz Ferdinand, heir apparent to the throne of the Dual Monarchy, was assassinated on a street of Sarajevo, on June 28, 1914, the lines of Austro-Hungarian policy in the Balkans and in Turkey were already definite. Tisza's famous memorandum of March 15, 1914, which had indicated the policy to be followed, became the basis of a memorandum drawn up in the Ballplatz in May 1914.[140]

At the very outset the Austrian memorandum noted that the Balkan situation "looked at from the point of view of Austria-Hungary as well as of the Triple Alliance, . . . cannot be described as at all favorable." Rumania no longer could be counted on definitely, Serbia had been enlarged in territory, and Greece, though not hostile, was allied to Serbia. The document outlined a project to reconstruct a Balkan alliance, with Bulgaria as the pivot, and with Greece and Rumania in line. The object of this new Balkan alliance was to isolate and finally to crush, Serbia. While Bulgaria had awakened "from the hypnotic spell cast by Russia," unless that country were won over to the Central Powers, she might become reconciled to Russia, and in the next upheaval receive Macedonia, while Serbia was aggrandized at Austrian expense. The great marplot in the Balkans was, of course, Franco-Russian influence.

"As Bulgaria sought and found a rapprochement to Turkey after the conclusion of peace, and as, on the other hand, the Porte discovered an inclination to form an alliance with Bulgaria and to enter into closer relations with the Triple Alliance, Franco-Russian influence has for some time been busily at work along the Bosphorus to counteract this Turkish policy, to draw Turkey over to the Dual Alliance and in this way to force Bulgaria to a change of face, either by means of complete isolation or by the coöperative influence of Turkey. Reports from Constantinople, to a certain extent corroborated by Talaat Bey's visit to Livadia, would indicate that these efforts, at least so far as Turkey is concerned, have not been entirely fruitless. By hinting at the alleged plans of other Powers for the partitioning of Turkey's possessions in Asia Minor, and effectually assisted by France's shrewd utilization of Turkey's financial necessities, Russia has so far succeeded in overcoming Turkey's historic distrust of

75

*her that Turkish statesmen are earnestly considering a* rapprochement *toward the other group of Powers instead of an association with the Triple Alliance."*

In the face of the upset in the Balkans, the Dual Monarchy was forced to take a very definite attitude. There was no time to lose. But what was to be done by the statesmen of the Dual Monarchy?

*"Our political object should be to show Rumania by our actions that we are able to find other pillars of support for Austria-Hungary. Any action to be undertaken for this purpose goes hand in hand with the real and timely necessity for devising new methods for counteracting the efforts of the Dual Alliance to erect a new Balkan alliance. Under the circumstances existing in the Balkans today, the only way to accomplish either the one thing or the other is for the Monarchy to accept the offer made a year ago by Bulgaria and repeated several times since, and to enter upon relations with that nation which would practically amount to an alliance. At the same time it should be the policy of the Monarchy to bring about an alliance between Bulgaria and Turkey, a plan to which both nations were up to a short time ago so favorably disposed that a compact was already drawn up, although it was subsequently left unsigned. Here, too, a continuation of the attitude of patient expectation to which the Monarchy was led by a far greater consideration for the alliance than was shown in Bucharest, would prove a great disadvantage impossible to overcome. Further holding off, and particularly the neglect of any counteraction in Sofia would simply be playing into the hands of the systematic and intensive efforts of France and of Russia. Rumania's attitude actually saddles the Monarchy with the necessity of conceding to Bulgaria that support for which she has for so long been suing, in order to frustrate the otherwise scarcely inevitable success of Russia's policy of circumscription. But this must be done as long as the road to Sofia and also Constantinople lies open."*

On July 5, 1914, Count Hoyos delivered Francis Joseph's letter with this memorandum to Berlin. The German government was, therefore, conversant with the fundamentals of Austrian policy from that date, and promised its full support.[141] Berchtold seemed determined on a policy of war against Serbia, while Count Tisza favored accomplishing the same fundamental result of crushing Serbia through the new alliance project in the Balkans.[142] At the meeting of the council of ministers on July 7, Berchtold presented his case, and was opposed by Tisza on the ground that previous diplomatic action must be taken. A diplomatic victory might be suitable, since "by the accession of

Bulgaria and Turkey to the Triple Alliance we may out balance Rumania and Serbia and perhaps induce Rumania to return to the Triple Alliance."[143] Tisza was a Magyar and wanted no more south Slavs in the empire, even in the event of war. This would avoid complications with Italy and gain the sympathies of England. "It is my belief that after a successful war it would be best to reduce the size of Serbia, by returning its newly acquired territory to Bulgaria, Greece and Albania, and to ask only certain important strategic corrections of the frontier lines."[144]

What took place in the next few weeks is familiar, if complicated, history, and need not be repeated. The Wiesner report was at hand on July 13. The next day, Count Stephen Tisza changed for a policy of war.[145] The ultimatum to Serbia was now being prepared. an ultimatum of such a character that its acceptance would be a virtual impossibility. On July 19, 1914, another conference was held in which the inevitable war was discussed. Berchtold accepted Tisza's demand that no Serbian territory be annexed providing that it did not apply to certain strategic points. That country had to be reduced "so that she would no longer be dangerous, by ceding as large parts of Serbian territory as possible to Bulgaria, Greece, Albania, and possibly to Rumania also."[146] The ultimatun was presented at Belgrade on July 23, and on July 25, was largely accepted. The same day Russia ordered partial mobilization. On July 28, Austria declared war on Serbia, and on July 31, the Russian general mobilization was decreed. Since July 24, Germany had made belated and futile efforts to preserve the peace. But the war machines were already in motion.

The story of the Austro-Hungarian and German maneuvers for a Bulgarian and Turkish alliance from the middle of July 1914, to the entrance of Turkey (October-November 1914) and Bulgaria (October 1915) in the world war, is reserved for later consideration. It will be sufficient here to relate that both countries followed the policy actively from the middle of July, and on August 2, 1914, German efforts in Turkey were crowned with success.

5.

*The Situation at the Outbreak of the War*

In the year preceding the outbreak of the world war the Near East scene monopolized European attention. The principal rivals in

the Balkan peninsula were Austria-Hungary and Russia, each of which was attempting to form a Balkan alliance against the other. At Constantinople both Russia and Germany were contesting for supremacy, engaged as they were in a conflict over the control of the Straits.[147] Both in the Balkan peninsula and in the Ottoman Empire proper, the interest of Russia centered primarily in a desire to secure a favorable solution of the question of the Straits.

The Balkan wars had split the Balkan peninsula into two warring camps. Serbia, Rumania and Greece, guarantors of the treaty of Bucharest, remained for the most part, under the aegis of the Entente. Russia, in particular, was the champion of this intimacy, both as a check on Austrian pressure in the Balkans, and as furthering her own ambitions in the region of Constantinople. In line with the same general policy of Russia, however, was the attempt to bring both Bulgaria and Turkey within the circle of Russian influence.

Opposed to the Russian designs in the Balkans, Austria-Hungary was pursuing the aim, since the summer of 1913, of dominating, isolating or crushing Serbia as a political factor in the Balkans. To the Dual Monarchy the dream of a greater Serbia on its southern frontier was the greatest danger. This policy was to be carried out through the organization of a Balkan alliance with Bulgaria at the pivot, but also including Greece and Rumania, in order to complete the encirclement of Serbia. Bulgaria began to pursue an Austrophil policy since the treaty of Bucharest, offering Vienna a formal alliance, and at the same time playing a game noted for its cleverness and duplicity. No alliance was concluded between the two countries, but the common interests of both bound them together. In the spring of 1914, Austria-Hungary, now supported actively by Germany, began serious negotiations with Sofia which led in July 1914, to a Bulgarian loan in Berlin, practically binding Bulgaria to the Triplice.

In Turkey two policies were followed. Berlin sent down the mission of Liman von Sanders to Constantinople, in December 1913, with the object of controlling the Porte and holding the Ottoman Empire intact as long as possible. This would mean military control of Turkey, which, coupled with the German control of the Bagdad railway, would give Germany virtual supremacy in the affairs of the empire. Turkey would become a vassal of Germany. The counterpart of this policy lies in the conclusion of the Bagdad railway agreements with France and England in 1914, and the conversations with Vienna and Rome, dividing Turkey into spheres of interest, and discounting in advance

the shares in a later political partition of the Ottoman Empire. At the same time, as we have seen, both Vienna and Berlin were working toward a Balkan alliance, which would include Turkey, Greece, Bulgaria and Rumania. Were such an alliance achieved, granting the elimination of Serbia as a Balkan factor, Germany's policy of *double insurance* in the Ottoman Empire would bar the Muscovite from Tsargrad, and bring the Bagdad route completely under the control of the Triplice.

The policy of the Triple Entente in the Balkans and in Turkey remains somewhat confused and lacked all semblance of unity. England and France were ready, and did negotiate agreements with Germany to divide Turkey into spheres of interest in which Germany would obtain the *réseau* of the Bagdad railway, England southern Mesopotamia, and France Syria. Russia stood for a policy of *status quo* in Turkey because she did not want Germany as her neighbor in the region of the Straits. In case no Great Power interfered in Turkey, Russia was content to let things remain as they were. The military mission of Liman von Sanders, however, struck at Russia in the most vital spot in the Near East—Constantinople and the Straits. This led the government at St. Petersburg to call the secret conferences of January and February 1914, to survey the possibilities of a solution of Russia's historic mission. Even at this date, Russia might have solved the question in a pacific manner, on the basis of Unkiar Eskelessi, had Turkey been either disposed or able to follow such a policy. Russia was determined on a solution, but would not be ready to undertake active measures until after 1917. As pointed out above, Russian policy in the Balkans looked toward the reconstruction of the Balkan alliance under her own patronage. This called for a *rapprochement* with Rumania, though not necessarily at the expense of Bulgaria. Distrust of the Sofia cabinet, however, led to financial and political pressure on Bulgaria, which resulted ultimately (together with the circumstances of Bulgaria's defeat in the second Balkan war) in that country's swinging toward Austria-Hungary and Germany.

The outbreak of the world war, then, found Serbia in active conflict with Austria. Greece and Rumania remained neutral but more or less favorably disposed toward the Entente. Bulgaria was on the point of allying with the Central Powers, while Turkey was led to her doom through the German alliance of August 2, 1914.

# CHAPTER III

# TURKEY IN THE WORLD WAR

## The Turco-German Alliance

THE German military mission had a much more fundamental influence in Turkey than the mere reorganization of the Turkish army and the creation of an effective instrument of war. Liman von Sanders and his mission became the chief make-weight in the alliance between Germany and the Porte which was concluded on August 2, 1914, and was one of the principal factors bringing Turkey into the war in October. Negotiations for a connection between Turkey and Germany had been going on for some time before the actual outbreak of hostilities in the fateful summer of 1914.[1]

Since the spring of 1914 the Austrian government had been attempting to arrange a Turco-Bulgarian alliance under the aegis of the Triplice—such an arrangement being but a development from the year 1913. Francis Joseph, in his letter of July 2 to William II, suggested an attempt "to reconcile Greece to Bulgaria and to Turkey; thus there would develop under the patronage of the Triple Alliance a new Balkan alliance whose aim would be to put an end to the advance of the Panslavic flood and to assure peace to our countries." In mid-July Count Berchtold inquired of his ambassador at the Porte, the Margrave Pallavicini, whether Turkey could be won over to the Central Powers. The reply was that Turkey had shown a turn toward Russia, and was distrustful of Italy, on account of her Asiatic aspirations. The important thing was to keep Turkey from joining the enemy group. German influence would be necessary to make an arrangement with Turkey. But the German foreign office was not yet certain of the utility of a Turkish alliance. Jagow wrote: "*Turkey could absolutely adopt no other attitude than that of balancing here and there between the Powers, or else joining herself to the strongest and most successful group. If Rumania stood firmly by the Triple Alliance, and if perhaps, Bulgaria should also seek to connect herself with us, it would unquestionably exercise some influence on the attitude of Turkey.*"[2]

In the center of a Balkan alliance attached to the Central Powers, Turkey might be useful—otherwise that country would be quite

useless as an ally. The Porte was weak and would be merely a passive factor in a possible war. Wangenheim insisted, however, that "it should be the policy of the Triple Alliance . . . *to arrange its relations so that in case Turkey should become a factor of power when years have gone by, the threads should not be severed.*" For the time being, Turkey should be advised to remain neutral—even as a neutral she would detain Russian troops on the Armenian frontier.[3] Meanwhile the German ambassador played none too skillfully with the alliance negotiations. On July 22 he wired Berlin that Enver Pasha wanted an alliance, but could not move until preparations were complete. Some connection was necessary. Turkey could not stand alone between the two great groups of European Powers. A majority of the cabinet favored the Triple Alliance, while the minority urged a connection with the Entente. This minority was a liberal moderate group to whom the free traditions of both England and France still had a fundamental appeal. Enver stated that "the present Turkish government earnestly desired to connect itself with the Triple Alliance, and would with heavy hearts decide on a pact with the Triple Entente, only if they should be turned away by us." The cabinet, however, understood the weakness of Turkey. The Porte might turn to a secondary alliance, either with Greece, under the Entente, or with Bulgaria, under the Triplice. The German ambassador remained unconvinced of the value of Turkey as an ally in her weakened condition.[4] When the kaiser read this dispatch, he noted on the margin: "*Theoretically correct, but at the present moment wrong. The thing to do now is to get hold of every gun in readiness in the Balkans to shoot against the Slavs for Austria, and so a Turkish-Bulgarian alliance may well be accepted! That is opportunist politics, and must be pursued in this case.*"[5] Instructions were sent accordingly to Wangenheim "to work in Constantinople along this line."[6] The next day, July 23, the grand vizier told Wangenheim that Turkey required an alliance only against Russia, not against France and England. While this eased the situation, the German ambassador again wavered. This was the crucial communication to Berlin, for in the marginal note the kaiser stated: "*She makes a direct offer of herself!!! A refusal or a snub would amount to her going over to Russia-Gallia, and our influence would be gone once for all! Wangenheim must express himself to the Turks in relation to a connection with the Triple Alliance with unmistakably plain compliance and receive their desires and report them! Under no circumstances at all can we afford to turn them away.*"[7]

Wangenheim no longer delayed. He telegraphed on July 27 that the alliance could be realized by dropping scruples, and corrected his estimate of Turkey's value as an ally "if the Turkish army were actually commanded by German officers. Its military worth would thereby be increased threefold." Liman had told him that he was making himself strong as leader of the fifth army corps. "German command of the army would have the inestimable advantage that Turkey, *in the event of war, would have to fulfil the obligations she undertook*."[8] It is perhaps not without interest to note that German command of the Turkish navy— if not command of the army—did assure Turkey's fulfilment of those obligations, and her entrance into the war.

A few days later, the grand vizier requested Wangenheim to submit the project for "a secret offensive and defensive alliance with Turkey against Russia" to Berlin. This would facilitate Turkey's entrance into the Triple Alliance. The terms were favorable in the extreme to Germany. (1) "Casus to occur whenever Russia should attack either Turkey or Germany or else Austria, or if either Germany or the Triple Alliance should make an attack on Russia." (2) The question of debts, capitulations, etc., was not to be raised. (3) The German military mission was to remain in Turkey. (4) "Turkey . . . would bind herself to find some method by which the supreme command of the Turkish army and the actual field command of one-fourth of the army should be given over to the military mission upon the outbreak of war."[9]

All of this was to be kept secret, even from the Turkish ministers. Even Pallavicini (who already knew of it) was to be kept in the dark. On July 28 a draft treaty in line with the kaiser's instructions was prepared,[10] calling for "strict" neutrality in the Austro-Serb conflict, but if Russia intervened and Germany were forced in, the *casus foederis* would arise for Turkey. The military mission remained in Turkey, with supreme command of troops. Germany guaranteed Turkey against Russia. The treaty was to be in force for the duration of the Austro-Serb conflict, and for troubles arising therefrom. "In case no war should take place between Germany and Russia as a result of this conflict, the treaty automatically becomes inoperative." But the Turks found the German limitation of the treaty "wholly unacceptable." The grand vizier told Wangenheim: "*It could not be demanded of Turkey that she bind herself to Germany at present, to find that she was left to look out for herself later, if Russia should wish to avenge herself on Turkey for her friendly attitude to the Triple Alliance.*

85

We would have to protect Turkey from all the possible consequences of her association with Germany . . . . He has been considering a term of seven years, but in no case would he be willing to let the compact run for a shorter time than General Liman's contract, which ran out at the end of 1918. It would only be logical if he were to insist that Germany, which desired by means of the Liman Mission to advance military reforms, should undertake to guarantee that Liman's activities should not be interrupted by a Russian attack."[11] War seemed imminent, and the Berlin cabinet decided on an immediate signature of the Turkish alliance. On July 31, the kaiser informed the Austrian military attaché in strictest confidence that he was about to conclude an alliance with Turkey "which would oblige the Turks actually to advance against Russia with five army corps under the chief command of Liman von Sanders and the leadership of the military mission, already increased to sixty officers."[12]

On August 2 there remained only the formality of signing the document. The treaty was arranged as ordered by the kaiser. The principal articles of importance stipulated:

"1. The two contracting parties agree to observe strict neutrality in regard to the present conflict between Austria-Hungary and Serbia.

"2. In case Russia should intervene with active military measures, and should thus bring about a casus foederis for Germany with relation to Austria-Hungary, this casus foederis would also come into existence for Turkey.

"3. In case of war, Germany will leave her military mission at the disposal of Turkey.

"The latter, for her part, assures the said military mission an effective influence on the general conduct of the army, in accordance with the understanding arrived at directly between His Excellency the Minister of War and His Excellency the Chief of the Military Mission.

"4. In case Turkish territories are threatened by Russia, Germany agrees to defend them if need be by force of arms.

"5. This agreement which has been concluded for the purpose of protecting both Empires from the international complications which may result from the present conflict, goes into force as soon as it is signed by the above mentioned plenipotentiaries, and shall remain valid, together with any similar mutual agreements, until December 31, 1918."

The agreement was subject to renewal, was to be ratified by the kaiser, and was to remain strictly secret.[13]

86

So the fateful alliance was made. Turkey was bound to Germany from August 2, 1914. The Liman von Sanders mission was the heart and center of the alliance which was to bring the Ottoman Empire into the great conflict. It was secret—only five persons in Turkey knew anything about the treaty. Only Enver and Talaat knew exactly what the treaty meant, and apparently, Enver alone was happy in the prospect of entering the war on the side of Germany and dealing a death blow to the mortal enemy, Russia. Austria knew of the alliance, but Italy was not informed, for obvious reasons. During the negotiations Turkey had asked for German aid for abolition of the capitulations, assistance in drawing both Rumania and Bulgaria into the orbit, a war indemnity, and retrocession of the Aegean islands to Turkey. In addition there were to be frontier rectifications to assure direct contact between the Moslem populations of Turkey and Russia in the east.[14]

The Turkish alliance was but a part of the scheme to draw both Rumania and Bulgaria into the Austro-German fold, as we have seen. Austria had been fostering the Bulgarian connection in particular, and desired to bring about an alliance between Turkey and Bulgaria as a preliminary. Berlin was not unwilling to bring Bulgaria in, providing an express guarantee of Rumanian integrity could be obtained. On July 6, however, Bethmann agreed to push the alliance project, and on July 12, Berchtold announced to Mérey in Rome that active negotiations would begin within the week. The kaiser did not conceal his distrust of Tsar Ferdinand of Bulgaria, but was willing to negotiate. On the other hand, Radoslavov approached Count Tarnowsky, on July 14, with a view to proposing a renewal of the offer of an alliance to the Triple Alliance. The Austrian minister had just returned from Vienna with a draft for an alliance and was ready to examine a Bulgarian project.[15] Tsar Ferdinand, however, took his time in examining the Austrian draft—doubtless he did not desire to precipitate Bulgaria into an altogether uncertain conflict.[16]

Meanwhile Pallavicini was active in promoting a Turco-Bulgarian alliance from Constantinople.[17] M. Toshev, the Bulgarian minister to the Porte, had several conversations with the margrave, and on July 21, he reported a conversation with Saïd Halim, Enver and Talaat. They had outlined the terms of an alliance whereby the parties were to undertake common action with Austria-Hungary in case of interference of another party in the Austro-Serb dispute. Bulgaria was to receive Macedonia, and Turkey was to obtain a guarantee of her territorial

integrity. The attitude of Rumania, it was felt, depended on the firmness of Vienna.[18] But, the Ballplatz, to reverse the picture, could come to no agreement with Bulgaria in a definitive sense, until the attitude of Rumania was beyond doubt.[19]

On July 25, the Sofia cabinet announced its intention to follow its own policy "by seeking to become attached to the Triple Alliance." The German minister, Michahelles, advised the government to make a "concrete proposition."[20] Already the German government was beginning to take a more than normal interest in the developments in the Bulgarian capital. Tsar Ferdinand was ready for discussions with Berlin and the negotiations took more definite shape. Michahelles reported on July 28, that the approaches of Savinsky had been rejected summarily by Sofia with the retort that "Bulgaria would not lift a finger for the benefit of Serbia."[21] On August 1, Berlin instructed the German minister to support Austria in bringing Bulgaria into the alliance, and at the same time assurances were given Rumania that there were no designs against her. It was important that Bulgaria give Rumania assurance that in case of war Bulgaria would act in accordance with the interests of the Central Powers, and on August 1, Tarnowsky was to obtain the promise from Bulgaria that Rumania need not fear as long as she stood with the Triplice.[22]

Germany declared war on Russia on August 1, 1914. On August 2, as we have seen, the Turco-German alliance was signed. On the same day, Radoslavov made a definite proposition to the Central Powers:

"1. *The Triple Alliance guarantees to Bulgaria her present territorial status against any attack of every kind, no matter from what source.*

"2. *The Triple Alliance promises Bulgaria its support in her efforts toward the future acquisition of her territory in which she possesses historic and ethnographic rights and which is under the domination of a country not belonging to the Triple Alliance.*"[23]

If Rumania entered the alliance, she had nothing to fear, but if she sided with Russia, Bulgaria was to have a free hand in the Dobruja. At the same time Berlin instructed Michahelles to agree to the proposal. Since the Turkish agreement had been signed, Turkey was protected. The alliance was to last for six years, with separate engagements with Austria and Germany. Early conclusion of the agreement was urged on Vienna.[24] Both Wangenheim and the German minister at Bucharest were informed the following day. The latter was to notify King Carol, and to ask "whether Rumania will now join us."[25]

At the same time the German government wanted to know "from a military point of view (what) Bulgaria promises to undertake."[26]

Tarnowsky was empowered to accept the project if his German colleague should receive instruction.[27] Meanwhile Germany was urging the Turco-Bulgarian negotiations to a speedy conclusion. Russia was trying to win over Bulgaria by far-reaching promises.[28] Tarnowsky, however, received no direct instructions, but the German minister approached Radoslavov on Bulgaria's "active obligations," proposing that Bulgaria obligate herself to march in full force at German demand "against any one of her national neighbors who may be on the side of the enemies of Germany."[29] This enemy was Serbia in particular, as Bulgarian action against that country would enable Austria to concentrate her forces against Russia. Finally on August 4, full powers to sign the compact were sent to Michahelles, but Tarnowsky, it seems (August 5), was not empowered to sign. Vienna was urgently requested to take action, and the German minister was instructed to: "Agree to formula. Also agree to Bulgaria's taking the field against Serbia."[30]

At this date no alliance with Bulgaria was signed. The wily Ferdinand was playing a very practical game. Neutrality had been announced, Bulgaria was biding her time, and the Radoslavov cabinet was waiting to see who would make the best offers and seemed most likely to wear the laurels of the victor in the world conflict.[31]

In the interim, Vienna and Berlin were meeting with little success in Bucharest. If the key to the Balkan situation lay in Rumania, as many felt, it was not to be placed in other hands. On the assassination of the Austrian archduke, King Carol expressed his sympathy to the aged Francis Joseph, but this was no commitment to the cause of the Central Powers. While there were indications that Rumania might follow the Central Powers, fundamental obstacles stood in the way. One of these was the presence of more than three million Rumanians on the soil of the Dual Monarchy. Another was Rumania's insistence on the preservation of the territorial dispositions of the treaty of Bucharest. On this proposition Greece stood with Rumania. When Count Czernin first spoke with King Carol about the alliance, the latter considered it very unsafe.[32] The kaiser urged his brother Hohenzollern to remain true to the alliance with the Central Powers. There were threats of publication of the compact. The German minister was even instructed to offer Bessarabia in the event of a favorable attitude

on the part of Rumania.[33] But Berlin was advised that popular sentiment was distinctly hostile to Austrian policy against Serbia.[34] Waldburg further advised the Wilhelmstrasse:

*"Bratianu desires that the Roumanians in Transylvania should be given certain assurances on the part of Hungary to the effect that after the war they would be granted greater rights. With regard to Bessarabia, Bratianu stated that it would only be of value to Roumania in the event that Russia had to surrender further territories also to Austria and to Germany, and should become so weakened that that province would actually remain a possession of Roumania permanently."*[35] As matter of fact, Bratianu had heard of the tempting offers which Russia was making to Bulgaria, and feared an attack on Rumania if she sided with the Central Powers.[36] Finally at a crown council on August 3, the government decided to remain neutral.[37] But it was a neutrality ever tempered by watchful waiting.

Along with Rumania and Bulgaria, Greece, too, remained aside from the struggle, and became one of the stakes in the war diplomacy in the Near East. Venizelos was on his way to Brussels to meet the Turkish grand vizier to settle the question of the Aegean islands when the war clouds began to threaten the coming storm. On July 25, he wrote from Munich that while reserving his attitude on the Serbo-Greek alliance,[38] Greece would never allow Bulgaria to attack Serbia and upset the treaty of Bucharest.[39] This was an answer to the appeal of Pashich for the aid of his ally.[40]

The kaiser, alarmed at rumors that the Greeks might attempt a sudden attack against the Dardanelles, made a strong appeal to his brother-in-law, King Constantine, on July 25. He advised the king that Turkey was desirous of making an agreement with Germany and also with Austria. Not only must Greece not attack Turkey; to the contrary, she must place herself on the side of the Central Powers. In his reply of July 27, Constantine denied considering "an attack on the Dardanelles or anywhere else. Both myself and my Government are very far from considering any adventurous policy." On the other hand, he could not perceive "how Turkey can help Austria without associating herself with Bulgaria." But an action which would result in territorial acquisitions in the Balkans for Bulgaria would upset the treaty of Bucharest, and could not, therefore, be sanctioned by Greece.[41] Another telegram from the kaiser (July 31) did not sway Constantine who was still fearful of Bulgaria. Much angered at the failure of Con-

stantine to do his bidding, William II ordered that Athens be informed that "I have made an alliance with Bulgaria and Turkey for the war against Russia and will treat Greece as an enemy in case she does not join us at once . . . ."[42] On August 4, Theotoky, the Greek minister in Berlin, wired Constantine: "*The Emperor informs Your Majesty that an alliance has been today concluded between Germany and Turkey; that Bulgaria and Rumania are equally ranging themselves on the side of Germany; that the German ships which are in the Mediterranean will be joined with the Turkish fleet in order to act together . . . .*" All the Balkans, according to Berlin, were arming against Slavdom, while Bulgaria and Turkey were pledged to fight against every state not following the same policy. On August 7, Constantine replied, stating that "I shall never forget that it is to him (the kaiser) that we owe Cavalla," but equally insisting that Greece could not go to war.[43]

To conclude the efforts in August 1914 to bring Bulgaria and Rumania into the war on the side of the Austro-Germans, Talaat Pasha and Halil Pasha went to Sofia and Bucharest during the middle of the month. Ostensibly purposing to settle the Greco-Turkish issue over the Aegean islands, the Turks worked for an alliance between Turkey, Rumania, Bulgaria and Greece, under German domination. The Bucharest cabinet would enter into no engagement, however, and it appears that the Radoslavov government would obligate itself only to preserve neutrality and guarantee Turkey against an attack from Bulgaria, in case Turkey allied with the Central Powers.[44]

2.

## The Incident of the "Goeben" and "Breslau"

The significance of the entry of Turkey into the world war on the side of Germany and Austria can hardly be overestimated. Since the Turks commanded the land and sea routes to three continents, whoever could win them over would hold the dominating position in the Near East. For Russia, as we have seen, Turkey was of vital importance as holding the Straits, the key to the economic and strategic security of all the Russias. For England, a favorable position in Turkey meant holding the route to India against friend or foe, protecting the Suez canal, and domination of the Straits. For Germany a position of dominance at Constantinople signified splitting her opponents in two parts, the one isolated from the other, and led clearly to the successful realization of the *Drang nach Osten*.[45]

How the Berlin government took advantage of its position of influence with the Porte through the Liman von Sanders mission and how the treaty of August 2, 1914, was made, have been related. Three days after the conclusion of the secret Turco-German alliance, Enver Bey, the negotiator of that treaty, offered a compact to St. Petersburg. Sazonov did not reject the offer, and at the suggestion of Giers, Russian ambassador at Constantinople, sent it to Paris and London, where it made no impression. Turkey, meanwhile, had declared her neutrality in the war, though she was in reality but playing a waiting game, while making demands on the Entente for the preservation of her neutral attitude. From the available documents it is evident that the tsar's government did more than either of its allies to keep Turkey out of war, if indeed, she would not come into the struggle on the side of the Entente.

But on August 10, 1914, two German cruisers, the *Goeben* and *Breslau*, passed through the Dardanelles to Constantinople. It was this factor which really sealed the fate of Turkey and finally brought that country into the world war. The Germans had commanded the Ottoman army under General Liman since December 1913. Since August 2, 1914, they had had an alliance with Turkey. By August 11, they had virtual control of the Turkish navy. It was this command which gave them the opportunity of forcing the Porte into open hostilities by the attack of the combined Turco-German fleet, under Admiral Souchon's leadership, on the Russian Black sea fleet and ports on October 29, 1914. Even after· this date, as will be shown, St. Petersburg was willing to keep the peace with Turkey if the naval and military officers of Germany were dismissed.

There is no gainsaying the influence which Turkey's action had upon the war. It split the Allied forces; cut off Russian wheat from the west and western munitions from Russia; precipitated the Russian débâcle and revolution, and probably prolonged the war by two years. Finally it led to the breakup of the Ottoman Empire.

On the outbreak of war in Europe there arose immediately the important question as to the attitude of Turkey toward the war, with its corollary, the attitude of each belligerent group toward the Porte.[46] On August 2, the Berlin government had made its treaty with the Young Turks—a fact apparently unknown to the Entente.[47] In broad outlines it may be said that British policy toward Turkey was: (1) To keep Turkey out of the war as long as possible, or at least until Egypt had been secured and the Indian troops moved safely through the Suez canal;

(2) to make it clear that any war was a result of an unprovoked Turkish aggression.[48] Greece was to be the pivot in a new Balkan alliance, for use against Turkey and the Straits. Neither France nor Britain, in particular, desired war with Turkey, for fear of their Moslem subjects in Africa and Asia, but they were unwilling to make the necessary sacrifices to conciliate Turkish opinion.[49] Already Berlin had begun the policy of arousing the Moslem world against the Allies—a policy which was to prove a dismal failure.[50]

At the outset Turkey declared a formal neutrality in the conflict, but adopted a policy of watchful waiting, to be guided by events. It was clear that any opportunity to regain lost ground would be seized eagerly. Mobilization was under way on August 3, but the grand vizier assured the Russian ambassador, M. Giers, that Turkey would observe neutrality, and that the mobilization was merely "precautionary."[51] On August 4, Grey advised Beaumont, the British chargé at Constantinople, to warn Turkey that neutrality would best serve her interests. As advice from "Turkey's oldest friend," he warned that her entrance on the German side would entail "the gravest consequences."[52]

Meanwhile the Porte was organizing all its forces in order to guarantee the territory of the empire. The grand vizier assured Beaumont that "the retention of the German military mission meant nothing and had no political significance. He regarded them as Turkish employees who were doing good work, and, as they had offered to remain, it would have been ungracious to refuse."[53] Indeed, the mission was doing "good work"—in Berlin it was considered as being on active service in time of war.

On August 3 an incident occurred which had consequences out of all proportion to its apparent importance. The Turks had building in England the two ships, *Sultan Osman* and the *Reschadieh*, for the Turkish navy.[54] Paid for by popular subscription, the ships would have given Turkey naval supremacy in the Aegean over Greece, and threatened Russia in the Black sea. Admiral Limpus, the British officer in command of the Turkish fleet, reported to the Porte that the Greeks were doing all in their power to prevent their arrival in Constantinople. And then, on the very eve of the entrance of Britain into the world conflict, the British admiralty sequestered the ships. While the government at London acted well within its rights according to international law, the fact remains that this one incident did more to arouse Turkish resentment against Great Britain than any other single event

93

at the time.[55] George V sent a personal message of regret to the sultan, but the incident was never closed.[56] Though Turkey was technically bound by her treaty of alliance with Germany, signed one day previous to the British action, the seizure of her two ships gave an excuse for the entrance of the *Goeben* and *Breslau* into the Straits, their "purchase" by the Porte, and the consequent precipitation of Turkey into the world conflict on the side of the Central Powers.[57]

The alliance with Turkey once formally signed, the Germans redoubled their efforts to bring Turkey into the war. The *Goeben* and *Breslau* played important rôles in the process. These two cruisers of the German fleet had taken part in the international demonstration before Scutari, Albania, in July 1914.[58] When the war broke out they were still in those waters. On July 27 the British Admiral Milne was ordered to aid French transports in crossing from northern Africa to France, and to watch for the German ships. The French Admiral Boué de Lapeyrère had like instructions.[59] If possible the German vessels were to be brought to action by both fleets and disposed of in the Mediterranean.[60]

But despite the secret treaty of alliance between Germany and Turkey, there were formal difficulties about passing the cruisers through the Dardanelles. Admiral Souchon, the German officer in command, was not, therefore, to proceed at once to the Dardanelles. Directed to go to Pola, the Vienna government protested its inability to aid him. The admiral was then given liberty of action to proceed to the Straits as he saw fit.[61] Admiral von Tirpitz, who was director of naval operations in Berlin, had plans for the entrance of the two ships into the Straits. On August 3, von Tirpitz asked that Wangenheim be informed that on the official announcement of the Turkish alliance, the two ships had been ordered to Constantinople. It was suggested that Souchon be placed "at the disposal of government to command Turkish fleet," and the ambassador was to "request whether we can assist Turkish fleet by offer of German personnel."[62] Here was a plan by which the German government would dominate completely the situation at Constantinople with both the army and navy in German hands. England's entry into the war now thought certain, Admiral Limpus was to be kept from making "improper use of the Turkish fleet." The Mohammedan watchword was to be sounded in the English colonies, and the Caucasus was to be revolutionized.[63]

By August 10 the German cruisers had slipped through the French and British fleets, passed the Straits, and were headed for Constantinople.[64] It was one of the master strokes of the war for the Germans, and, at the very best, one of the great blunders for the Allies.[65]

The passage of the Dardanelles became the signal for protests against the Porte's unneutral act.[66] Djemal Pasha describes the passage as unneutral and a "*casus belli*," for the Allies.[67] But the Entente was not anxious to precipitate trouble with Turkey. The Entente simply was not united on the Turkish issue, and made no *concerted* effort to smooth over a bad situation and keep Turkey favorable to the Allies. Sir Edward Grey wrote to Sir Francis Bertie in Paris on August 15, 1914, that they did not wish to foster any quarrel with Turkey. "It would be very embarrassing to us, both in India and in Egypt if Turkey came out against us." The independence and integrity of Turkey would be respected if she remained neutral, but if she sided with the Central Powers, "we could not answer for what might be taken from her in Asia Minor."[68] He had already so instructed Sir Louis Mallet, British ambassador in Turkey, adding that Turkey must repatriate the German officers on the *Goeben* and *Breslau*, afford peaceful facilities, and observe neutrality. The question of capitulations could be considered when proper reforms had been made.[69]

In order to pass over this very awkward situation, the Turks struck on the ingenious idea of a fake disarmament of the vessels and then resorted to the ruse of a fictitious sale which tricked neither themselves nor others.[70] Sazonov protested the illegal purchase, under the London convention of 1909, and both Germans and Turks admitted the sale to be pure subterfuge.[71] Admiral Limpus and the British naval mission were recalled from service with the fleet to the ministry of marine in Constantinople, and Souchon, of the German navy, succeeded to the command of the Turkish fleet.[72] Almost all the commands in the navy were given to German officers. The German cruisers were renamed the *Midilli* and the *Jawus*. The two ships sequestered by Great Britain had been replaced and they were to render distinguished service in the Black sea.[73]

The *Goeben* and *Breslau* incident is significant in that it indicates definitely that Turkey was to go into war on the side of the Central Powers. Up to this time the Germans were fearful lest their friends in Constantinople would reconsider the alliance of August 2. With the passage of the Dardanelles, however, there was no longer any question as to the issue. Grey wrote, "This means that Turkey has joined

Germany and may attack Egypt." The Turkish army was being mobilized, troops were reported moving toward Egypt, and transports in the Red sea were embarking for the Suez canal.[74] Mallet believed that Turkey would remain neutral but for the unsolved question of the islands with Greece. He informed the grand vizier that "His Majesty's government regarded Turkish fleet as annex of German fleet and that if it went into the Aegean we should sink it." The grand vizier assured Mallet that the fleet "had no intention of leaving the Dardanelles."[75] Fearing a naval *coup* on the part of Admiral Souchon, the British government thought the presence of a fleet before the Dardanelles a wise measure.[76]

Ambassador Morgenthau well summarized the significance of the *Goeben* and *Breslau* in the following statement:

*"The Goeben and Breslau . . . gave the Ottoman and German naval forces control of the Black Sea. Moreover, these two ships could easily dominate Constantinople and thus they furnished the means by which . . . the German navy . . . could terrorize the Turks. The passage of the Straits by these ships made it inevitable that Turkey should join Germany at the moment that Germany desired her assistance . . . and it likewise sealed the doom of the Turkish Empire . . . . With them the Turkish navy became stronger than the Russian Black Sea fleet and thus made it certain that Russia could make no attack on Constantinople."[77]*

3.

*Russo-Turkish Alliance Negotiations, August 1914*

Perhaps nothing throws so much light on the fundamental nature of Russian policy toward Turkey as the alliance negotiations between the two countries in August 1914. It will be recalled that Enver Pasha, who had made the German alliance, initiated the negotiations with St. Petersburg.[78]

On August 5, 1914, Giers reported that General Leontiev, his military attaché, had talked with Enver, who had explained that mobilization was not directed against Russia, and that if Russia so desired, and could quiet Turkish fears on the Caucasus, Turkish troops would be withdrawn. He then declared that Turkey was not bound to anyone and would act "conforming to her interests. If Russia desired to fix her attention on the Turkish army and use it for her cause, he did not think this combination impossible." Such an army

Russia could use to neutralize the armies of any of the Balkan states, or in coöperation with a Balkan combination against Austria. In return Turkey expected frontier rectifications in western Thrace and the solution of the Aegean islands question. Greece could obtain compensation in Epirus, Bulgaria in Macedonia, and Serbia in Bosnia and Herzegovina.[79]

When Leontiev expressed his surprise that the German officers had remained in Turkey, Enver replied that he did not doubt that Berlin was serving strictly German purposes, "with a view to bringing Turkey into its sphere of influence, but that purpose will not be accomplished, for the reason that Turkey will follow a course dictated solely by her own interests."[80]

Now arose the inevitable question of Bulgaria. General Leontiev suspected a convention between Turkey and Bulgaria. On August 5 Toshev, minister of Bulgaria in Constantinople paid a visit to Giers. At the suggestion that the time had now come for the return of Bulgaria to the Balkan league under Russian influence, he replied that Bulgarian sentiment was still against Serbia. Though neutral, Bulgaria would like a guarantee against Turkey. Sofia would find the desired guarantee in a "mutual obligation of Greece, Turkey, Bulgaria and Rumania not to take part in this war," as well as the germ of a Balkan *bloc* against Austria.[81] Toshev's ideas of compensation were so similar to those of Enver, that Giers suspected previous conversations between the two. Giers felt that such a proposal should not be rejected. "The formation of a Balkan *bloc*, with Turkey included, can only be useful to us at the moment when circumstances will permit us to be the masters of the Straits." Giers, therefore, would continue the negotiations, as Sazonov was urging, to gain time, but avoiding definite declarations.[82]

Enver made a concrete proposition on August 9.[83] He offered to withdraw the troops from the Caucasus frontier, and to concentrate them in the west as an earnest of his sincerity. The troops would be placed in Thrace for use either with or against Bulgaria. When the Entente was established the German military mission would be dismissed. Turkey would expect in return western Thrace and the Aegean islands and the signature of a defensive alliance with Russia for five or ten years. Sazonov moved very cautiously. Withdrawal of Turkish troops from the Caucasus meant concentration elsewhere; to demand it would signify weakness.[84] Giers thought the proposition should be accepted immediately. Time was pressing. Should "we obtain victory,

97

we shall always know how to recompense Bulgaria and Greece." A refusal meant German victory in Turkey. Even though Enver were to be doubted, Russia might thereby clear up a difficult situation in Turkey, when a refusal "certainly would throw Turkey into the arms of our enemies."[85]

Sazonov continued to temporize. He told his ambassador to let the Turks understand that Russia, with her Allies could threaten the existence of Asia Minor, if Turkey joined the Austro-Germans.[86] On the same day, August 10, Ponceau, in the Quai d'Orsay, advised Isvolsky of Turkish fears about Russian designs on the Straits. Ponceau told Isvolsky "that it might be advantageous for us to draw Turkey to the number of our enemies in order to make an end of her."[87] The next day Doumergue confirmed Ponceau, adding that "there is nothing to prevent us in the liquidation of the war, in settling the question of the Straits conforming to our views."[88]

Giers insisted on the urgency of the Turkish alliance. It meant exclusive influence in Turkey and the Balkans. It would eliminate the ever hostile German element in Turkey, while a rejection would throw Turkey into German hands. The historic moment had come.[89] This was, in other words, an opportunity to return to the basis of Unkiar-Eskelessi of 1833, to dominate and control Turkey through an alliance. Rumor of the German compact with Turkey spread. Only an immediate decision could save the day, deliver a mortal blow to Berlin, gain an advantage of 200,000 men, and put Austria in a serious strategic position.[90]

On August 10 the *Goeben* and *Breslau* had passed the Straits. This had altered completely the situation in Constantinople. Giers felt that an immediate decision was now necessary. Tomorrow would be too late. Turkey allied, a connection with Bulgaria was possible; rejection meant the opposition of both Powers.[91]

The Russians thought the Turco-Bulgarian alliance near conclusion. The project of Giers was to draw Bulgaria into a new Balkan alliance, with Greece and Serbia actively aiding. A union with Turkey was not inconsistent with this idea. Though rumor confirmed the German alliance, Giers was convinced "that it is so important for us to detach Turkey from Germany, that we must strive as long as there remains the least hope of success."[92]

Sazonov was acquainted fully with the Turkish overtures since the beginning of the conversations with Leontiev. On August 15, he sent the Turkish project to Isvolsky and Benckendorff in Paris and

London. Russia was ready to offer Turkey the following for Turkish neutrality: (1) Turkey was to commence demobilization of her army as an earnest of sincerity; (2) as an equivalent, the Entente would guaran-tee Turkish integrity; (3) Turkey was to have possession of all German concessions in Asia Minor, possession to be guaranteed in the peace treaty.[93]

We are now at the stage where France and England were apprised of the Russo-Turkish negotiations. What would be the attitude of the western Allies? Giers reported on August 15, that the grand vizier was favorably impressed with the idea of a territorial guarantee and the possession of the German concessions. The question was merely one of form. Already negotiations with the Greeks over the Aegean islands were under way in Bucharest.[94] The next day in conversation with Sir George Buchanan, British ambassador at St. Petersburg, Sazonov was told that the Porte was afraid of Russia and wanted a guarantee from France and England. Sazonov therefore thought necessary a guarantee à *trois*, as well as the promise of German economic concessions in Asia Minor, as he had outlined in his note of the previous day. Moreover he was willing to return Lemnos to the Porte, guaran-teeing the security of the Straits. Greece could be sure of Chios and Mitylene, Epirus would be given Greece in compensation for Lemnos.[95] Sazonov desired such a guarantee on the part of England and France, as he could scarcely hope to advance in his Turkish negotiations without their complete support.

Now alarmed, Giers telegraphed that the grand vizier was losing power, Enver might at any moment become the absolute dictator of Turkey, and that perhaps the German-Turkish alliance had been signed. The only possibility of saving the situation lay in accepting the alliance with Turkey.[96] This was August 16, 1914. Sazonov, on receipt of this warning from Constantinople, sent Enver's proposition to London and Paris:

"1. *The Turks recall their troops from the Caucasian frontier.*

"2. *They offer us in Turkey an army which could fight any Balkan country, Bulgaria included, if she marches against us.*

"3. *The German instructors to be dismissed from Turkey.*

"*For all that Turkey will receive:* (1) *In Thrace territory to the line of the 22° meridian;* (2) *the isles of the Aegean.*

"*At the same time a defensive alliance is considered for ten years between Turkey and Russia.*"[97]

If Sazonov wanted the opinion of London and Paris on the Turkish overtures, he was not to be kept waiting long. On August 17, Isvolsky reported that he had seen Delcassé, minister of foreign affairs of the republic. M. Delcassé "did not believe the *pourparlers* with Turkey could lead to anything and he thought it more conforming with our purposes to guarantee, without delay, the restoration of the Balkan *bloc* in directing it against Turkey." Moreover Delcassé was convinced that Bulgaria should have Thrace to the Enos-Midia line, while Greece could be promised Epirus, with the exception of Valona, which was to go to Italy. This, he thought, was the best way to reconstitute the Balkan league. It would leave Rumania free to strike against Austria, and would strengthen the Allied position against Germany. Occupied with these adversaries, no serious attack could come from Turkey.[98]

Nor did Sir Edward Grey mince words. The same day Benckendorff telegraphed to St. Petersburg that Grey had instructed Mallet to support his French and Russian colleagues in a guarantee of Turkish integrity and the return of the German concessions in Asia Minor, in case the Porte remained neutral. Grey was, however, entirely opposed to an offer of territorial increase to Turkey, and was particularly against the offer of Lemnos, which was virtually at the mouth of the Dardanelles. That would arouse Venizelos, in whom, in case of war with Turkey, Grey thought he had an immediate and certain ally. Grey, then, would go no further than an offer of territorial integrity and the German concessions, because of his fear of the consequences on both Greece and Bulgaria.[99] One should add, that Great Britain did not like to see Turkey, under a Russian alliance, with the control of the islands protecting the entrance of the Dardanelles. With the islands in Greek hands, England possessed a vantage point from which to attack the Straits.

Again, on August 17, Leontiev reported that war with Russia was taken for granted in Turkish military circles.[100] However, the following day, Giers, together with his colleagues offered the grand vizier the territorial integrity of Turkey, in return for the neutrality of the Porte. The declaration made a good impression, apparently, but Giers thought a promise of an increase of territory would have removed the crisis altogether.[101]

The French and British rejection of the Turkish offer sounded the death knell of any possible Turco-Russian or Turco-Entente *rapprochement*. Nevertheless, the Russian embassy kept up its efforts. Leontiev believed the alliance with its possible Balkan connections too valuable

to give up.[102] On August 19, Giers reports a conversation with Djavid Bey, minister of finance and partisan of the Entente. In his opinion the Allies would have to offer a written proposition to Turkey, with a treaty of guarantee for fifteen or twenty years. Likewise the régime of the capitulations would have to go. In return the German military mission would be dismissed. Djavid did not raise the Aegean islands question, save to indicate that negotiations with Greece were then under way in Bucharest.[103]

Giers thought the stipulation for the abolition of the capitulations acceptable. But a written guarantee for Turkey for a period longer than five or ten years was undesirable.[104] Djavid, likewise, had seen the French and British ambassadors. He repeated his proposition to them, not concealing his fear of Russia. He desired, not a common guarantee, but one from each of the Powers of the Entente—partly, doubtless, in order to divide the Allies. He had fixed no duration of the treaty. Giers had thought a fifteen year guarantee too long, and if a five year treaty were insufficient, he would stipulate no specified period. The question of capitulations was causing difficulties for both Mallet and Bompard, though Giers believed a settlement possible if the security and integrity of persons and domicile were assured.[105]

On August 20 Sazonov telegraphed to Isvolsky, asking that a common declaration of the three Powers be made in Constantinople in reference to the economic concessions in Asia Minor. The solidarity of the Entente in Turkey had a peculiar importance for Russia, which had not been supported in previous *démarches*.[106] The next day Sazonov had the reply of both France and England, which had not yet known of the entire proposition advanced by Djavid. If Paris and London could agree, Sazonov was convinced that he could propose a satisfactory capitulations régime to the Porte, preserving the essential rights of foreigners in the Ottoman Empire, and guaranteeing the fundamental rights of Turkey.[107]

At this point, having concluded the discussion of the alliance negotiations proper, it may be well to indicate in summary, the policy of the Entente, and the reasons for the failure of the negotiations between Russia and Turkey. The importance of the episode is of the first magnitude, for had Turkey come into the war on the side of the Allies —perhaps even if she had remained neutral—the war might have ended two years before 1918, the Balkans might not have been lost, Greece

might have been won, the Straits might have remained open, Russia might have been provisioned by the Allies and the revolution of 1917 thereby postponed if not forestalled.

The reasons for the failure of the negotiations seem apparent. In the first place the Germans had an alliance with Turkey since August 2, 1914. After the passage of the *Goeben* and *Breslau* through the Straits, with command of both army and navy, Berlin completely dominated the situation at Constantinople. Secondly, Enver Pasha and the grand vizier may not have been sincere in their proposals to Russia, since both had taken leading parts with von Wangenheim and Liman von Sanders in working out the Turco-German alliance. However, fundamental interests rather than matters of sincerity dictate the policies of nations, and had the leaders of Turkish policy received the necessary encouragement from the Allies acting in concert, they might have favored the Entente. In the third place, the French and British governments completely rejected any idea of a possible alliance with the Porte on August 17, by refusing to accede to the Turkish demand on the question of the Aegean islands. Finally Turkey had a fundamental fear of Russia, developed through many historical clashes —a fear not unlike that which countries of Latin-America feal toward the great colossus in North America. While Giers and Leontiev were positively convinced of the desirability of the alliance, Sazonov, though never rejecting the idea, was never able to convince France or England. Both France and England seem to have been too certain of an easy victory over Turkey to consider it worthwhile to make serious advances toward conciliation.[108]

In the end it was the alliance of August 2, 1914, and the control which Germany had over the army, navy and government of Turkey, which was to lead to all the consequences of the war with Turkey and to the later partition of the Ottoman Empire.

4.

*The Question of Guarantee and the Capitulations. Turkish Neutrality*

The question of the capitulations, which had been raised clearly in connection with the move of Turkey for an understanding with Russia and the Entente, was one of the most important problems in Turkey's relations to the European Powers. The capitulatory régime which dated far back in Turkish history, by 1914 bound the economic

development of the Ottoman Empire to the will of outside financial and political interests. The outbreak of the war gave the Turks an opportunity to press for the abolition of this hated system. The matter was opened in all its implications on August 20, when Djemal Pasha, minister of marine, broached the subject with Mallet, the British ambassador. Djemal proposed immediate abolition of the capitulations; return of the Turkish battleships which Great Britain had seized on August 3; renunciation of any interference in the internal affairs of Turkey; a guarantee of western Thrace if Bulgaria sided with Germany; restoration of the Aegean islands; and, finally an engagement to oblige the Central Powers to accept any agreement reached on the capitulations.[109] Sir Louis rejected the proposals in general and in severalty. He pointed out the difficulty of abolition of the capitulations, told Djemal the return of the warships was "impossible," considered renunciation of interference in Turkey "absurd," and the return of the Greek islands "impossible."[110]

On the other hand Sazonov and Giers were willing to make concessions to the Porte, as has been indicated, during the alliance negotiations. Turkey would be allowed to abolish the capitulations provided only that foreign interests and nationals were protected. In return the German officers of the military mission and of the fleet were to be dismissed and the *Goeben* and *Breslau* dismantled.[111]

Giers reported to Sazonov on August 27, that German victories in the west had aroused the hopes of the Turks. He felt that the Entente must lose no time in making a proposition to the Porte. Bompard, his French colleague, had no instructions on a written guarantee. The declaration must guarantee Turkey definitely as long as she remained neutral. Events were moving rapidly, and Giers wanted to do everything "to bring the Turks on our side."[112] This project, however, did not appeal to Delcassé, who had figured out already the compensations for Greece and Bulgaria at the expense of Turkey, should these states proceed against the Porte. His policy was to give western Thrace to Bulgaria, and Epirus, with the exception of Valona (which was to go to Italy), to Greece.[113] Naturally such a choice bit of information reached Turkish ears, and Giers rightly feared it would play into the hands of the Germans.[114]

The Porte was now ready to take the initiative. On September 8, Giers heard that the capitulations would be abolished very soon,[115] and the next morning the grand vizier admitted as much to Mallet. The latter, surprised, protested that the capitulations were not uni-

lateral in nature, and could be abolished only by agreement with the contracting parties. He did not expect to "allow British subjects to be judged by court-martial, especially so long as the army was in the hands of Germans." Mallet informed Grey the same day that the announcement of the abolition of capitulations from October 1, 1914, had been dispatched.[116]

No less surprised apparently were the Austrian, German and Italian ambassadors. Indeed Pallavicini, as dean of the diplomatic corps, was ready to present an indentic note of all the Powers in protest to the Porte.[117] Wangenheim disclaimed all responsibility for the move.[118] Sir Louis Mallet notified Grey that on September 10, identic protests would be sent. And on that date the protests were filed with the Sublime Porte.[119]

Sazonov telegraphed Giers on September 10, that he was willing to consider the abolition of the capitulations providing Turkey guaranteed the rights of foreigners, remained neutral and dismissed all German officers in her service.[120] Grey, however, was more adamant in his position. On September 16, he informed Mallet of his readiness to "consider reasonable concessions about capitulations," if the Porte remained neutral. He added a note of warning: "Perhaps we might also say that if they break the peace we cannot be responsible for the consequences; that we hope they will keep the peace, but whether they do or not in their own affair."[121]

Meanwhile on September 15, Giers reported a conversation with both Talaat and Halil. They told him they desired to enter an agreement on the capitulations, separating the economic from the juridical side of the question, economic freedom being the more important for Turkey. Their desire was, therefore, immediate suspension of the economic regulations. Giers felt "that we should now meet them on this ground, as our refusal might play into the hands of the Germans."[122] Two days later Djavid Bey, minister of finance, expressed the idea that Turkish demobilization could be brought about by the suppression of both economic and judicial capitulations. Giers asked instructions, and Sazonov wired on September 19, that he was ready to agree to suppression of the capitulations, with sufficient guarantees for foreigners, "if the Ottoman government will make a proposal covering the unconditional neutrality of Turkey; such a guarantee might be furnished by demobilization and the removal of all German military officers."[123]

An iradé increasing the customs duty was announced on September 22, and three days later other changes were made. Giers reported a more conciliatory attitude on the part of the government on September 25, and the disposition to grant concessions in judicial and penal capitulations, in return for fiscal equality of all nationals, and for an engagement to enter into negotiations for commercial treaties to replace the old capitulations. It was the intention to continue negotiations as long as hope of the maintenance of the judicial capitulations remained.[124]

News of the proposed abolition of foreign post offices, announced for October 1, brought renewed protests from the Powers.[125] On September 26, Sazonov warned the Porte of the consequences of its action: "The sympathy of Russia is at once a guaranty of tranquillity for Turkey and a most valuable promise of assistance, which it is not to the interest of Turkey to ignore."[126] Grey followed on October 1, warning Turkey not to alienate the sympathy of England "which constitutes a guarantee of present tranquillity, and a pledge of future support."[127]

But on October 1 the foreign post offices were closed. Again protests followed—without avail.[128] On the same day Halil Bey, president of the chamber of deputies, interviewed Giers relative to the régime of the capitulations. On agreement to allow Turkey economic freedom, the cabinet might instruct the authorities to suspend temporarily the suppression of the judicial capitulations, and a commission could be appointed to draw up a satisfactory system. His French and British colleagues assenting, Giers informed Halil that any accord depended on the preservation of the juridical régime, until a new order, satisfactory to the Powers, had been instituted. Giers saw little hope of progress.[129] Two days later the Russian embassy heard that the Lebanon statute would be abolished, and the Entente ambassadors protested it on October 5.[130] Objection was fruitless, however, for the Porte followed suppression of the Lebanon statute with molestation of Allied subjects, and the placing of all foreign schools under Turkish control.[131] The Turks were to be done with the old system of things.

Here ends, apparently, the episode of the capitulations in the period immediately preceding the war with Turkey. The European situation had given the Porte an opportunity to gain concessions on the matter, and finally to abolish the régime altogether.[132] From the available evidence on the question, it is quite evident that St. Petersburg was willing to concede more to the Porte than either Paris or London. The Allies of Russia did not want to pay too high a price for

Turkish neutrality. Yet as a result of Turkey's entrance into the war the Allies paid in the lives of thousands of young men who laid down their lives on the Gallipoli peninsula. On the other hand if Germany and Austria at first entered a protest against Turkey's uni-lateral action, they later withdrew from any further action in matter.[133] Turkey had played a waiting game throughout the episode, putting little or no faith in the promises of England, France or Russia. So important was the question of the capitulations, that it may be true, as Halidé Edib says: *"There is not the slightest doubt that, had the Allies consented to modify the supreme symbol of Turkish humiliation, the capitu-lations, twenty Enver Pashas would not have sufficed to drag Turkey into the general lunacy of the war."*[134]

5.

## Turkey Enters the World War

So diametrically opposed were the aims of the Allies in Turkey that they did not act in concert either in the promise of favors to the Porte or in their threats against the Ottoman government. Aside from the moves of the tsarist government, which were blocked by England and France in August 1914, no serious attempt was made to bring about a favorable attitude on the part of Turkey toward the Allies. The result was that the Turks were left to face the ever-increasing pressure of the Germans alone. The first steps taken by the Germans (together with those Turks who desired to enter the war on the side of the Central Powers) were the alliance, mobilization of the Turkish army and the passage of the *Goeben* and *Breslau* through the Straits. The next steps, to be taken in order, were the closure of the Straits in the latter part of September, and the attack of the Turco-German fleet on the Russian Black sea fleet at the close of October 1914. If at the beginning of the conflict immediate participation of Turkey was not desired, the Marne defeat forced the issue on Germany. Turkey, it is apparent, wished to postpone action, remain outwardly neutral, await a favorable turn in the negotiations with Rumania, Bulgaria and Greece, and complete her preparations before entering hostilities.[135]

Throughout August and September 1914, German soldiers, sailors, officers and technicians, as well as supplies, ammunition and artillery, poured into Constantinople *via* Rumania and Bulgaria.[136] Giers com-plained on September 3, that the vicinity of Constantinople was over-run with Germans. A mine laying flotilla was at work under the

direction of the *Goeben* and *Breslau*. The batteries on both shores of the Straits were under German command. Events might take place at any moment which would hurl Turkey into the war.[137] Mallet complained to the grand vizier that Turkey was not observing her neutrality and that "Constantinople and her neighborhood now form an armed German camp . . . that between 4,000 and 5,000 soldiers and sailors had arrived to date." The promise that the Turkish fleet should not enter the Black sea had not been observed.[138]

All this while the Porte innocently protested its neutrality, and Saïd Halim promised that the German officers of the *Goeben* and *Breslau* would be dismissed as soon as Turkish sailors could manage the ships.[139] There were warnings even from Turks that neutrality was the best, indeed the only policy to be observed. Rifat Pasha, the Turkish ambassador in Paris, telegraphed on September 4: "Germany is isolated and doomed to defeat. Hostility to the Entente may endanger our very existence. The only sane policy for Turkey consists in obtaining advantages from the Entente by pursuing strict and sincere neutrality."[140] Sir Louis Mallet was instructed on September 23, to warn the Porte on the consequences of its policy, pointing out its inconsistency with its declared neutrality. German officers and men were participating in the fleet and building up the defences of the Dardanelles. The officers and men of the *Goeben* and *Breslau* not only had not been dismissed, they were taking almost complete charge of the navy, and more were entering Turkey. Grey finally warned, "it will become clear that Constantinople is no longer under Turkish but German control, and that *open hostility will be forced on Turkey by Germany.*"[141] Turkey was already a German protectorate to be pushed into the world conflict whenever it best suited German interests to do so.

Late in August came reports that an attempt might be made to close the Dardanelles. German officers and sailors were arriving continually through Sofia and were soon placed along the shores of the Straits. Mallet was assured, however, that no attempt would be made to leave the Dardanelles.[142]

At this time an incident occurred which was destined to have very far-reaching consequences. On September 26, a Turkish destroyer was stopped outside the Dardanelles and turned back by a destroyer of the British fleet. The commandant of the Dardanelles, Colonel Weber, a German officer, thereupon closed the Straits. The British, French and Russian ambassadors entered immediate protest with the grand vizier. The latter, clearly disturbed, laid the blame for the action on the

British fleet. The ambassadors urged immediate opening of the Straits. This the grand vizier seemed to favor, stating that he did not desire war.[143] Prince Saïd Halim in fact, promised to reopen the Straits, if the British would withdraw the fleet from the entrance of the Dardanelles.[144]

But Grey refused to consider a withdrawal of the fleet. The Straits had been closed unnecessarily he thought. Though Britain had no hostile aims against Turkey, an effective watch over the Straits had to be maintained as long as the German officers remained. The request of the grand vizier could not, therefore, be entertained.[145] The foreign office thought Berlin had planned the closing of the Straits for some time and laid all the blame on the Germans.[146] Grey notified Mallet that the British fleet would be withdrawn when the German officers and crew left. They "would then have no fear of hostile action on the part of the Turks."[147]

The closure of the Straits, coming as it did a full month before Turkey entered the war, was not only a blow which cut a line of communication between the western Allies and Russia, but it indicated the supreme control which Germany had over the Turkish government, and must be taken as a presage of events which were to take place during the month following. The day after the closure of the Straits by the Germans, Rifat Pasha sent another warning to his government: ". . . *German interferences must promptly be brought to an end . . . . The Entente is ready to condemn us to death if we act as enemies. Germany has no interest in saving us. She considers us as a mere tool. In case of defeat she will use us as a means of satisfying the appetite of the victors, in case of victory she will turn us into a protectorate. The Entente is in a position to injure us even in the event of Entente defeat. We are on the direct road to dismemberment. We should recall the fact that an extremist foreign policy has always been the cause of our misfortunes. It even made possible the miracle of a Balkan alliance against us."*[143]

Berlin was now determined clearly to draw Turkey into the war. As early as August 20, Wangenheim was using pressure to induce the Porte to enter the struggle. Djavid Bey, the grand vizier and Djemal Pasha were opposed.[149] When Liman von Sanders and the officers of the German military mission asked permission of the kaiser early in September to return for active service in the field, he was told:

"*H. M. the Emperor and King charges me to remind your Excellency that your Excellency should consider your employment in the present capacity as any other employment in war. It is the positive order of His*

*Majesty that your Excellency subordinate any views diverging from the policies of the imperial ambassador as approved by His Majesty, etc."*[150] Turkey was yet neutral, but the German government considered its military mission as being already on active war service. On September 5, Wangenheim informed Enver Pasha that the time had arrived for action —possibly in Egypt or by a descent on Odessa.[151] Admiral Limpus, of the British naval mission in Turkey ,was recalled by his government on September 13, in view of his impossible situation.[152] German pressure was now becoming more and more evident as the controlling factor in Constantinople. The Turkish press was subsidized.[153] About September 20, Wangenheim intended to send the *Goeben* and *Breslau* into the Black sea under the flag of Germany, and was opposed by the Turkish cabinet and General von Sanders, since the ships had appeared three days before under the Turkish flag. Wangenheim told the grand vizier, however, that "the German vessels were only to a certain extent under Turkish control, and that they were destined to serve, not only Turkish, but principally German interests." He promised that "German officers would not challenge the Russian fleet."[154]

On September 22, Pallavicini urged the Porte to break with Russia. Five days later Vienna urged her ambassador to use every means at his disposal to call forth an action of the Turkish fleet against Russia.[155] The move was again repeated on October 2, when Pallavicini urged action on the hesitating grand vizier, as a means of exerting pressure on both Bulgaria and Rumania. The latter, however, feared a possible defeat in the Black sea, which would imperil Constantinople.[156] Giers reported the following day that Turkey was overflowing with German officers, men, weapons and ammunition. They had fortified the Straits and were creating difficulties on all frontiers. A struggle was on in the cabinet, between Enver and those who desired peace, "but the most probable outcome is that the Germans themselves will create an in-cident to precipitate Turkey into war."[157] Pallavicini renewed his efforts on October 5, insisting to the grand vizier that both the Austrian and German governments felt "that the Turkish fleet should now be attacking the Black sea coast."[158] The time for action had arrived.

By this time the Entente had lost the situation in Constantinople entirely. The Turks continued to temporize. Fear of Bulgaria and the need for money appear to have been the principal difficulties in the way of immediate action. On October 11 a meeting took place at the German embassy in which Enver and Talaat took part. Turkey obligated her-self to open hostilities on receipt of financial aid from Germany. The

first instalment had been received, and a second instalment was due October 21. Giers understood if then the grand vizier refused to go to war, Enver and Talaat would remove him from office.[159]

Already the press of Constantinople had been bribed, the effects of which were evident.[160] Funds were now being turned to use for active war preparations. On October 22, Mallet understood that the Turks had received £1,000,000 and when they had received £4,000,000 they would enter the war.[161]

Still the Porte delayed. Pallavicini complained "the grand vizier hesitates always."[162] On October 22, he had urged war again on Halil and the minister of the interior. Both thought it wiser to wait until the situation in Egypt and the Caucasus had cleared. Not certain of Italy, they desired to wait until spring before taking the field. Halil went to Berlin on October 27, to seek a postponement. Enver, Talaat and Djemal, however, were now in active preparation for an Egyptian campaign. Enver was indeed ready for the great adventure—an adventure in which he himself was to play the rôle of a Turkish Napoleon and liberator. Already, on October 22, he had the necessary orders and instructions for both military and political action drawn up. The Turkish fleet under the command of Admiral Souchon was to attack the Russian fleet without a declaration of war, and only after a Russian declaration of hostilities was the sultan to summon his people to battle. The Balkan states were to be aligned with Turkey under the aegis of Germany and Austria. On the same day he issued the necessary orders to Admiral Souchon:

"*The Turkish fleet will gain the naval supremacy in the Black Sea.*

"*Seek the Russian fleet and strike it without a declaration of war, wherever you find it.*"[163]

Mallet reported on October 27, that Enver had advised Pallavicini "that he was determined to have war, whatever his colleagues might desire. Turkish fleet would be sent into Black sea and he could easily arrange with Admiral Souchon to provoke hostilities . . . . Fleet has in point of fact, today gone into Black sea, so it is impossible to foretell what is in store."[164]

What was in store was very soon revealed. After many insistent demands Admiral Souchon had obtained the consent of the government to engage in maneuvers in the Black sea. The consent came through the vice-commander of the Bosphorus forts on October 27. The next day the German admiral created a *fait accompli* by attacking the Russian fleet and bombarding ports on the Russian Black sea

littoral, Theodosia, Novorossysk and Odessa. The *Goeben* had sunk a mine layer, while the *Breslau* destroyed fifty petroleum depots and fourteen military transports. News of all this reached Constantinople on October 29.[165] Apparently the members of the Turkish government knew nothing of the projected attack. The Germans had taken the Turkish fleet into the Black sea and had deliberately engaged the Russians, attacked unfortified towns, and without a declaration of war, had forced the hand of Turkey.

Immediately Giers advised St. Petersburg of the attack. With his French and British colleagues he offered the suggestion that the Porte could either break off relations with the Allies, or immediately remove all military and naval officers of Germany from Turkey. Sazonov, however, promptly ordered Giers to turn over the embassy to the Italian ambassador, and leave Constantinople.[166] On October 30, the grand vizier expressed his "poignant regret," adding the attack was entirely against the orders of the Porte. He intended to address the Russian government directly, but authority was already passing from his hands.[167]

The Russian ambassador left Constantinople on October 31. His English and French colleagues followed him.[168] The Turks now tried negotiations directly with Petrograd. On November 1, Fahr-Eddin, chargé at Petrograd, expressed his regrets to Sazonov and moved for an investigation. Sazonov informed him that it was too late to investigate, but "if the Sublime Porte decided upon the immediate dismissal of all the German military and naval officers and men, it might not be impossible to reach some basis of satisfaction to be given by Turkey for the illegal act of aggression against our coasts and for the damage thereby inflicted."[169] Some members of the Turkish government, it seems, were already prepared to take such action in order to preserve peace. At a meeting held in the home of Halil Bey a majority of the ministers were opposed to the war, and proposed giving complete satisfaction to Russia and the Entente by dismissing all the German officers and men in the Turkish service. Talaat, minister of the interior, though acknowledging this as the only way of preserving neutrality and peace, insisted on the impossibility of such action "as the city of Constantinople and the government of Turkey were under the threat of German guns."[170]

Even at the last moment the evidence indicates the willingness of Russia to have peace with Turkey, providing the latter would remove the German officers from the Ottoman service. Indeed Liman von Sanders himself writes:

"*In those days it was stated in Constantinople that even after the action with the Turco-German ships in the Black sea, Russia was willing to recognize Turkish neutrality, provided the German military mission and men of the Goeben and Breslau were at once returned to Germany; and that the Turkish government declined . . . .*"[171]

Through the action of the *Goeben* and *Breslau* in the Black sea the Berlin government had attained its purpose of precipitating Turkey into the war. It had assured that Turkey would "fulfil the obligations she undertook," as Wangenheim had desired during the feverish days of July, when he was negotiating the Turkish alliance. Final action came through the combined command and direction of the Turkish army and navy.[172]

The Black sea venture brings into quick relief the true significance of the *Goeben* and *Breslau*, for these two vessels led the attack of October 28, 1914, which, in turn, brought Turkey into the war. Professor Stahl, former under chief of the naval general staff in Russia, says:

"*This incursion entrained the closure of the Dardanelles during all the duration of the war and the rupture of our maritime communications with the Allies, which compromised our provisioning in arms and ammunitions . . . . It modified to our disadvantage the correlation of the forces in the Black sea, checked our plans, aggravated the conditions of war in the Black sea where it destroyed our supremacy . . . . Under the influence of the Entente, the commandant of the fleet of the Black sea received the order to wait before acting until the first shots had been fired by the enemy; thence an unforeseen attack of the Germano-Turkish fleet against Sebastopol, Odessa and other ports of the Black sea . . . . After the arrival of the Goeben our littoral was exposed to the attacks and bombardments of the enemy cruisers; devastations resulted from this. The insecurity of maritime communications, due to the same cause, entrained the capture and destruction of our transports . . . . The fleet of the Black sea no longer had its freedom of action, hence the impossibility of blocking and bottling the Bosphorus, the difficulties and lack of success of the blockade of Anatolia, the impossibility of barring the way of*

*enemy transports . . . . The incursion of the Goeben had as a result the prolongation of the war and the fatal consequences which that prolonga-tion involved.*"[173]

The closing of the Straits in September 1914 was full of dire consequences for Russia, for it cut off that country permanently from her western allies, and probably prolonged the world war by several years. It was this event, which, coupled with the corrupt and in-efficient bureaucracy of Petrograd, led to the downfall of the tsarist régime and ushered in the rule of the Bolsheviks in 1917. By entrance into the great conflict, with all the dangers which such action signified for Russia, the Porte forced the Russian government to seek the "radical" solution of the question of Constantinople and the Straits in 1915.[174]

On October 31, 1914, the tsar of all the Russias issued a proclama-tion of war against the Ottoman Empire. It contained these significant words:

*"Under German command the Turkish fleet has had the treacherous effrontery to attack our Black sea coasts. We share with all the peoples of Russia the unshakable conviction that the rash intervention of Turkey will only hasten that country's downfall and open the Russian path towards the solution of the historic problem which our ancestors have bequeathed to us on the shores of the Black sea."*[175] The solution of the question of the Straits—the question of a secure outlet to the free sea—became thenceforth the major issue of the world war for Russia.

Russia declared war on Turkey on November 4, and Great Britain and France followed by declaring war the next day. From November 1914 to the end of October 1918, the Ottoman Empire was in open conflict with the Allies, having been brought into war by German military and naval command of the Turkish forces.[176] On November 14, the sultan proclaimed a "jihad" or holy war against the "infidels." But, as we shall see, the holy war ended in dismal failure, when even the Arabs took action against their Ottoman rulers.[177] As if to add assurance to the treaty of August 1914, a further Turco-German alliance was signed on January 11, 1915, but it could save neither the Germans nor the Turks.[178] In the words of Mr. Asquith's Guidhall speech of November 9, 1914, "The Turkish Empire has committed suicide, and dug with its own hands its grave."[179]

Turkey's entrance into the world struggle was the direct result of the sending of the Liman von Sanders mission to Turkey in 1913, the signing of the alliance of August 2, 1914, and the passage of the *Goeben* and *Breslau* through the Straits in August 1914. From that moment, the Entente had lost control in Constantinople, and Turkey's entrance into the war was largely but a question of time. Germany had made a military protectorate out of Turkey and was intent on using that country as a pawn in the world war to be used when the requirements of war necessitated Turkish action. The moderates in Turkey did not want war. The militarists hesitated only because of the unpreparedness of Turkey and because of the attitude of the Balkan states, particularly Bulgaria. With the failure of the Marne drive on the western front, however, the Germans determined to bring Turkey into the war. The opportunity came when Admiral Souchon made his famous attack on the Russian fleet and ports along the Black sea on October 28, 1914. Perhaps no better judgment has been passed on the situation than that of the Angora tribunal of independence, of August 22, 1926: ". . . *The whole Turkish nation was dragged into the war as a result of a* fait accompli, *the work of a German admiral who received his orders from the kaiser. In other words, a great and historic empire had become a toy of this German admiral whose very name was unknown to the Turkish people. Turkish ministers who submitted to such steps look more like obedient, submissive servants of the kaiser than ministers responsible for the welfare of Turkey.*"[180]

The failure of the Allies to act in concert in their attempts to conciliate Turkey proved disastrous to them. Great Britain and France turned down any consideration of the Turco-Russian project of alliance which was drawn up in August 1914. The evidence indicates a greater willingness on the part of the tsarist government to make concessions to the Porte in the discussions concerning both Turkish neutrality and the abolition of the capitulations than either of the other two allies. The truth is that Russia did not want war with Turkey and sought to achieve a solution of her historic problem of an outlet to the free sea through diplomatic channels. This attitude is evident even after the encounter in the Black sea of October 29, 1914. Any effort on the part of the Entente, however, probably was in vain from the beginning, in view of German control over the Turkish government.

The significance of Turkey's entrance into the great war would be difficult to overestimate. Immediately the Ottoman Empire—whether

in the region of the Straits, in Palestine and Syria, or in Mesopotamia—became one of the major scenes of the war. Great Britain alone employed more than one million men against the Turks. Probably the war was prolonged by two years on account of the decision of the Germans to force Turkey into the war. In the end Turkey's entrance into the struggle involved not only the doom of the Ottoman Empire, but through the closure of the Dardanelles and the Bosphorus, and the consequent isolation of Russia, it brought on the downfall of the empire of the tsars.

# CHAPTER IV

# CONSTANTINOPLE AND THE STRAITS

## The Supreme Issue for Russia

THE entrance of Turkey into the world war made the question of Constantinople and the Straits the supreme issue for Russia. Twice during a decade the Dardanelles had been closed, and now, in the hands of an enemy, the control of this vital passage became Russia's dominating problem in the war. The steady and clear development of Russian policy with reference to the problem of Constantinople and the Straits can now be traced with precision.[1] At the beginning of the struggle, Russian official and public opinion was uncertain about the ultimate disposition of both Constantinople and the Straits. The Anglo-French operations against the Dardanelles early in February 1915, however, not only crystallized sentiment and opinion, but forced the St. Petersburg government to demand the "radical" solution of the question in favor of Russia. This led to the secret agreements of March and April 1915, by which both France and England were forced reluctantly to cede Constantinople and the Straits to the Muscovite. The age-old struggle for the possession of *Tsargrad*, in fulfilment of Russia's "historic mission" appeared to have reached a successful conclusion.[2]

The predominating influence of the *Goeben* and *Breslau* over the fate of Turkey has been described already. Now in German hands, the Straits were closed on September 27, 1914, by a German officer, Colonel Weber. This was more than a month before Admiral Souchon took his Turco-German fleet into the Black sea, attacked the Russian fleet and defenseless ports on that sea, and thereby brought Turkey into the war. Little wonder is it that Tsar Nicholas declared in his proclamation of November 1914 that Turkey's action would but hasten the fulfilment of "Russia's historic mission on the shores of the Black sea."

While the war opened to Russia the opportunity for a favorable solution of the Straits question, St. Petersburg had no definite plans as to the ultimate disposition of the Straits and Constantinople. Indeed Paléologue reported on September 26, 1914, that Sazonov had told

him the Turks must remain in Constantinople, though he had not decided the final fate of the city. Freedom of the Straits must once for all be assured. Passage was to be guaranteed by: (1) non-fortification of the Dardanelles; (2) a commission assisted by naval force to police the Dardanelles and the sea of Marmora; and (3) a Russian coaling station to be established at the entrance of the Bosphorus.[3] On October 13 Isvolsky reported that the Quai d'Orsay would support the Russian claims, and "Russia will claim, of course, the freedom of the Straits and sufficient guarantees . . . . Russia will have the complete support of France, who can act in a favorable sense in this question . . . at London."[4]

Just after Turkey had entered the war, Sazonov declared to Paléologue that Russia would have to make Turkey pay dearly for her action. Guarantees on the Bosphorus were necessary, but "as regards Constantinople," he did not "want the Turks to be cleared out." Gladly would he "leave them the old Byzantine city with a good sized kitchen-garden all round. But no more!"[5]

On November 3 the British fleet bombarded the forts of the Dardanelles and troops were rushed to the defence of Egypt. The attack was little more than a demonstration of force against the Turks. Four days later, on November 7, Delcassé informed Isvolsky that it would be well to develop a common plan of action of the Entente in regard to Turkey in view of the complexity of the interests involved.[6] On November 9, Grey, who at once recognized the significance of Russia's position with reference to the Straits, declared to Benckendorff, Russian ambassador at the court of St. James, that if Germany were defeated, the question of the Straits could only be settled in conformity with Russia's interests.[7] Within a few days of Grey's pronouncement, George V himself told Benckendorff that "as for Constantinople it is clear that it must be yours."[8] Finally, on November 14, Buchanan, the British ambassador at St. Petersburg, presented a memorandum to Sazonov, which stated that "the government of His Britannic Majesty . . . have been led to recognize the question of the Straits and Constantinople must be solved in the manner Russia desires," but in agreement with France and England.[9] Sazonov was dissatisfied with this declaration, but received no further comfort from his Allies at the time. Four days later the Russian minister gave his consent to the British annexation of Egypt, which had been placed under British protection as early as August 6, 1914.[10]

In a conversation with Paléologue on November 21, 1914, the tsar clarified the position of his government on the Turkish question. He stated: "The Turks must be expelled from Europe . . . Constantinople must in the future be neutral, with an international régime." Western Thrace to the Enos-Midia line was to go to Bulgaria. Exclusive of Constantinople, the rest of the territory from that line to the shores of the Straits was to be Russian.[11] At this point Paléologue delineated the French spheres of interest in Palestine and Syria and the emperor agreed that France should have this part of the Turkish heritage.[12] Delcassé, informed that England had obtained Russia's consent to the annexation of Egypt, offered no objection, as he would now obtain British consent to French incorporation of both Tunis and Morocco.[13] Meanwhile Paléologue was certain that the question of the Straits would "raise complications between Russia and England."[14]

Complications of a very serious nature did, indeed, arise in the very near future, at the inception of the Dardanelles campaign—a campaign which appeared to Russian statesmen to have not only the object of winning the war, but seizure of Constantinople and the Straits before the Muscovite could get there. It was this campaign which led, more than anything else, to the Russian demand for the cession of *Tsargrad* and the the Straits by treaty to Russia.

2.

### The Constantinople Treaty

The problem of the Dardanelles presented one of the major strategic issues of the war, rivaling in importance the western front in France, or the eastern front in Russia. Until the forts of the Dardanelles were crushed and the Straits opened, Russia could not be provisioned, nor could Russian grain find a market in the west. Communications between Russia and her western Allies were severed and the Germans were astride the main lateral line of contact at Constantinople.[15] An attack on the Dardanelles, if successful, offered fair prospect of bringing the war to an early and favorable conclusion. At a stroke all danger to Egypt could be removed, the Balkans secured, the unwavering support of the Arabs assured, and an end could be put to the hesitation of Italy.[16] These were stakes of the greatest importance. At the very beginning of the war, in August 1914, Winston Churchill, first lord of the admiralty, favored seizing the Straits with the assistance of

Greek forces.[17] Admiral Lord Fisher had pointed out that a purely naval attack on the forts of the Dardanelles could have no hope of success.[18] A force of at least 100,000 men would be necessary for the task of pushing through to Constantinople. Lord Fisher states "What the Admiralty wanted was a force, not merely to enable them to make good the passage of the Straits . . . but one large enough to seize their ultimate objective which was Constantinople." The sailors, who viewed the problem from the standpoint of naval strategy, had to give in reluctantly to the political desire of "getting possession of the Straits," even though the venture was something of an "experiment" which could be abandoned at will if it were too difficult an undertaking.[19]

A plan for an attack on the Dardanelles had been presented by the admiralty before the cabinet as early as November 25, 1914, but nothing seems to have developed from it at the time.[20] Early in January 1915, however, General Sir John Hanbury Williams, attached to the Russian armies, reported a conversation with Grand Duke Nicholas, the Russian generalissimo, on the necessity of relieving the Russian forces on the Caucasus front.[21] Sir George Buchanan telegraphed this information to London on January 2, 1915, stating that the grand duke had *"asked if it would be possible for Lord Kitchener to arrange for a demonstration of some kind against the Turks elsewhere, either naval or military, and . . . cause . . . the Turks to withdraw some of the forces now acting against Russians in the Caucasus, and thus relieve the position of the Russians."*[22] The next day Kitchener wrote Churchill that he did not see "that we can do anything that will very seriously help the Russians in the Caucasus."[23] But on January 3 a reply was sent to Buchanan, who was to assure the grand duke that a demonstration would be made against the Turks, though it was feared that little relief could be brought to the hard-pressed Russians.[24] However, in a private letter to Churchill, Kitchener wrote that "the only place that a demonstration might have some effect in stopping reinforcements going east would be the Dardanelles."[25] The Russian request for a diversion against Turkey was to be turned into a great campaign for control of the Straits.

The actual decision to attack the Dardanelles with a naval force was reached by the war council on January 13, 1915. The admiralty was to "prepare for a naval expedition in February to bombard and take the Gallipoli Peninsula with Constantinople as its objective."[26] Fisher informed the Grand Duke Nicholas of the project to attack the

Dardanelles on January 19, and hoped for the coöperation of the Russian fleet—the fleet which had been bottled up in the Black sea by the *Goeben* and *Breslau* in the fall of 1914.[27] Sazonov communicated the British plan to military headquarters on January 21, 1915, expressing the idea that if Russia could not take appropriate part in the campaign it should be postponed. Sazonov asked first for a purely Russian expedition against the Straits, then appropriate Russian representation, or postponement of the expedition. Neither the Grand Duke Nicholas nor General Danilov shared the views of the foreign minister, because of the general importance of the campaign to the war.[28] Though a "diversion" against Turkey did not signify a major operation against the Dardanelles, Churchill claims to have secured Russia's favorable attitude toward the project, and the promise of active support by France in the attack, which was launched in February 1915.[29]

At this juncture came the offer of Venizelos for Greek participation in the coming campaign against Turkey. The dream of a new Hellenic empire with its heart and soul centering about St. Sophia and Constantinople had been revived.[30] The attack of the British fleet began with the bombardment on February 19, 1915. Venizelos saw his opportunity and quickly grasped it. At the crown councils of March 3 and 5, called for consideration of the war problem, he urged participation in the operations against the Dardanelles. The general staff was opposed to the policy of Venizelos in offering an army corps and the Greek fleet to the Entente. Failing to secure the assent either of the council or of King Constantine, Venizelos resigned office as premier on March 6.[31] On the eve of his resignation, however, the Greek premier communicated his program for action to the Allies. The offer stated, "without having any political views on Constantinople and the Straits, we have such interests of a moral and commercial order there that we could not be disinterested in their fate."[32] Great Britain replied that she would accept the assistance of Greece if both Constantine and Venizelos were in full accord on the proposition.[33] Paris was willing that Greece participate providing Greek efforts were not limited to the Dardanelles alone, and that Greek troops go to the aid of Serbia and take part in the general war.[34]

Sazonov was neither evasive nor reluctant in his attitude. As early as February 27, 1915, Demidov had informed him from Athens that the Dardanelles campaign was arousing intense interest and that some leaders saw in it an opportunity for Greece "to accomplish—in accord

with the Triple Entente—the great historic task."[35] Diplomatic dispatches indicating that Greece would be interested in participating in the campaign with a view to internationalizing Constantinople and the Straits after the manner of Crete, fell into Sazonov's hands. He advised Demidov that "the imperial government could not admit that the future of Constantinople and the Straits be settled other than in absolute conformity with the capital aspirations of the Russian people." For a war against Turkey, Greece might be compensated in Asia Minor, but not in the region which Russia had to control "to assure our outlet toward a free sea."[36] He had already instructed his minister at Athens that Russia "cannot under such conditions admit the participation of Greek troops in the entrance into Constantinople of the Allied armies."[37] Both the British and French governments had been advised of this attitude.[38] On March 4 Grey indicated the possibilities of Greek assistance to Count Benckendorff. When the latter interposed objections, Grey stated that the admiralty had attached great importance to the matter of Greek assistance. Greece could be offered compensations in Smyrna. Moreover success in the Dardanelles would have an important influence on the Balkans and Italy. Benckendorff stated that Sazonov would be very firm in his opposition, especially since Russian participation seemed remote.[39] Churchill was determined to win over the Greeks for his Dardanelles project. He wrote on March 6, 1915: "If Russia prevents Greece helping, I will do my utmost to oppose her having Constantinople. She is a broken power but for our aid, and has no resource open but to turn traitor—and that she cannot do."[40] On March 7 Sazonov informed Athens that Greek collaboration was not desired "for the taking of this city."[41]

Sazonov's fears in regard to Greek entrance into the Dardanelles campaign apparently were not groundless. For on March 5, 1915, Sir John Stavridi, a Greek millionaire in London, wrote Venizelos that Lloyd George had urged Greece to side with Britain in the war, "for he foresees for us, for a Greece considerably grown yet under the aegis of England, a brilliant and more important future in the Orient." Lloyd George told Stavridi that England was working for the restoration of the Balkan alliance, the mission of Noel Buxton being sent to the Balkans in order to accomplish that purpose. In return for the cession of Cavalla to Bulgaria, Greece was to receive the Smyrna district in Asia. As to Constantinople:

"*As you know already, the desire of France and of England is that Russia not become all powerful in the East. And if it is France and England who take Constantinople, their idea is to render it an international city. Certainly for us that would be a thousand times better than to see it definitely in the hands of Russia.*"[42] The British project was to put the Greeks in Constantinople in order to keep the Russians out, and evidently the Russians were not unaware of this feature of the program.

Meanwhile the campaign against the Dardanelles had served to crystallize Russian sentiment in regard to Constantinople and the Straits. Neither the tsar nor Sazonov had been definite in November 1914 as to a solution of the question, save that any solution must be in accordance with Russia's interests. Evidently this was not sufficient for Baron Taube and other members of the council of state, who drew up a memorandum for the tsar, late in November 1914, urging more precision in the statement of the Russian *desiderata*. It would be unfortunate, they wrote, that after so many sacrifices, the Russian people should be recompensed only by the reconstitution of Poland, while France solved the question of Alsace-Lorraine through outright annexation, and England took over Egypt. Russia should obtain Galicia and gain control over Constantinople and the Straits.[43] Doubtless this internal pressure from the council of state had something to do with the more precise definition of Sazonov's demands in the spring of 1915.

When the Duma met on February 9, 1915, it was enthusiastic about the prospects of reaching a fundamental solution of the problem of Russia's outlet to a free sea. Goremykin spoke of Russia's "future on the shores of the sea which washes the walls of Constantinople." Miliukov, leader of the Cadets, stated that "we can now be certain that Constantinople and the Straits will become ours at the opportune moment through diplomatic and military measures." Sazonov, however, was more reserved in his declaration. He said: "The day is at hand when we will see the solution of the economic and political problems now raised by the necessity of securing Russian access to the open sea."[44]

When Sir Edward Grey began to entertain the idea of a separate peace with Turkey through negotiations with a liberal group in that country, Sazonov ordered Isvolsky and Benckendorff to have nothing to do with the project, as the demands of public opinion in Russia had advanced considerably with reference to the question of the Straits.[45] Doubtless the St. Petersburg government felt that these

overtures were but another attempt to prevent a solution favorable to Russia. Isvolsky reported on February 23 that the press of Paris was taking a great interest in the Dardanelles and suggesting "various combinations of an international character." Though not suspecting the French government, he urged the formulation of a clear policy, and asked for definite instructions for his conversations with Delcassé.[46] The tsar's marginal annotation of February 25, 1915, instructed Sazonov that "it was necessary to inform our ambassadors of the future situation of the Straits," and forced him to define his position. Two days later the Russian ambassador at Paris heard rumors of sending the Armenian financier, Gulbenkian, a former counsellor of the Young Turk government, to Constantinople to provoke a *coup d'état* on behalf of the Entente.[47]

By February 28 Sazonov had formulated a program of action in accord with Paléologue and Buchanan, in case the Porte demanded peace, under the hard pressure of the Allied fleets at the Dardanelles. Armistice conditions were worked out providing for the surrender of the German ships in the Turkish naval service and the relinquishment of all German officers, soldiers and sailors. All batteries on the Bosphorus and the Dardanelles were to be dismantled and the mines in the water were to be removed. The Allied fleet was to remain at Constantinople and Allied troops were to occupy the forts around Constantinople.[48]

Sir Edward Grey announced in the House of Commons on February 25, 1915, that Russia's access to the open sea was favored in Great Britain, but "the precise form in which it will be realized will no doubt be settled in the terms of peace."[49] Grey's statement satisfied neither Sazonov nor Russian official or public opinion. The meeting of the Duma had been held on February 9. Sazonov had not yet committed himself to the radical solution of the problem of the Straits. By March 1 he was forced to that issue.[50] On that day Sazonov told Paléologue that the entire country was demanding the radical solution of the problem— a solution which would guarantee to Russia a fundamental control over Constantinople. Hitherto Grey had spoken in general terms about settling the question "in conformity with Russia's desires." Now the time for plain speech had come. "The Russian people are now entitled to know that they can count on their Allies in the realization of their national task. England and France should say openly that they agree to the annexation of Constantinople by Russia when the day for peace arrives."[51]

Sazonov, in other words, was no longer satisfied with the uncertain and indefinite promises of Great Britain and France. Nor was he content to see Russia pushed out of Constantinople either by the Allied forces operating in the Dardanelles, or by the Allies acting in conjunction with the Greek army and navy. Nor was a separate peace with Turkey to forestall the accomplishment of the historic task. Buchanan telegraphed Grey on March 1 that the Russian public was entirely dissatisfied with his position. Sazonov wanted a statement that "His Majesty's Government favored a settlement of question of Constantinople and Straits that would accord with views of Russian government and aspirations of Russian people."[52] Great Britain long had opposed Russia in the region of the Straits, but now had changed "entirely" and was taking the lead "in sympathy" with Russia.[53] As the price for consent to Russian aspirations in the Straits, Britain asked for Russian assent to annexation of the neutral zone in Persia (as in 1907) and all the central part of Iran, including the Ispahan region. Sazonov agreed to this proposition.[54]

On March 1 Isvolsky reported to Sazonov that Delcassé still urged direct participation of the Russian army and navy in the Dardanelles operations. He stated that an arrival at Constantinople, with the Turkish government gone, would put the question of a collective occupation of the city before the Entente. This, in turn would signify the end of European Turkey.[55] Delcassé was much disturbed at Sazonov's statement to Buchanan. When Isvolsky told him that Russia was determined to assure her free access to the open sea, the French foreign minister replied that he was consenting "to an international administration of Constantinople and the neutralization of the Straits." France, however, would do everything to aid Russia in the fulfilment of her historic dream. This was to be subject to two stipulated conditions. The Straits were to be under an international régime similar to that of the Danube, and fortifications were to be forbidden.[56] The French press continued to discuss an internationalization of the Straits, and Isvolsky feared that Constantinople might be taken without Russia, which would be "extremely disfavorable." He felt that circumstances demanded direct explanations among Grey, Delcassé and Sazonov, "on the future, not only of Constantinople and the Straits but also of Asiatic Turkey."[57]

In a memorandum which M. Sazonov presented to Paléologue and Buchanan on March 4, 1915,[58] the Russian government laid down claims which admitted of no misunderstanding. In this famous note,

Petrograd claimed the left bank of the Bosphorus, the sea of Marmora, and the Dardanelles, as well as Thrace to the Enos-Midia line. On the Asiatic shore the demands included the Sakaria river to a point on the gulf of Ismid. The islands of the sea of Marmora, and likewise, Imbros and Tenedos, commanding the approach to the Dardanelles, were to be under the control of Russia. Any other solution, according to the memorandum, would be "insufficient and unstable." In return for favorable consideration, Russia promised to receive "with sympathy" the English and French desires in Turkey and elsewhere.

Sazonov's memorandum, with its specific demands and definite claims, made a strong impression on Delcassé. The French foreign minister, however, felt that the question was so important that it should be submitted to the direct examination of the three prime ministers. Sazonov rejected this suggestion so as to take no chances in a matter so vital to Russia's strategic and economic interests.[59] On March 8, in a memorandum of the French embassy, Sazonov was informed that Russia could "count absolutely on the benevolence of the government of the republic," when the question of Constantinople and the Straits was to be decided. This question, as well as the entire problem of the Near East would be decided "definitely in the treaty of peace," in accordance with the declaration of September 5, 1914.[60] The next day Delcassé told Isvolsky that he considered the question of Constantinople one of the most difficult of all the issues raised by the war. France, of course, would not contest the Russian claim, but desired guarantees of non-fortification and freedom of commerce. But the question "must be part of the general settlement of the war and not the object of a special accord."[61] On March 10 Delcassé appeared to Isvolsky to have given assent to Russian possession of Constantinople and the Straits with the stipulations indicated, and seemed ready to support the proposition in London.[62] In reality Russia was to have more difficulty in gaining French consent to her program than with the government at London. France had no intention of giving in until the ineluctable circumstances of war required it.

At the same time Isvolsky reported that the occupation of Constantinople must be prepared not only from the military and administrative viewpoint, but from the financial and economic as well. Russia should take the initiative in drawing up plans for occupation. The ambassador had learned that the English and French directors of the *Banque ottomane* were planning to return with the landing of troops, and would be followed by the delegates on the council of the Ottoman

public debt. Hence, it was necessary that Russia play an appropriate rôle in the period of transition under Allied occupation.[63]

Meanwhile, on March 6, 1915, Sir George Buchanan presented a memorandum on the question of Greek assistance in the Dardanelles operations.[64] Grey confirmed what Sazonov had said in the Duma about Russian aspirations in the Straits. He considered Greek help in the Dardanelles very important, however, and thought a refusal dangerous. England had never cared to promise Greece "any part of the Straits," but was willing to offer Smyrna and its environs to Greece as compensation. As for the Dardanelles, England was only trying to attain a common end, "with all the disinterestedness possible concerning the aspirations of Russia in this region, and with full conscience that the direct results will be neither advantageous nor disadvantageous for England, but only for Russia."

On March 12 the British government had formulated a definite answer to the Russian demand for the cession of Constantinople and the Straits.[65] The memorandum insisted that the Russian demands had gone much beyond what London had been led to expect and that British assent involved a complete reversal of a century-old policy with reference to the Straits. Such assent would be given on certain conditions, which, however, would not affect Russian control over the region. These conditions involved making Constantinople a free port for goods in transit to and from non-Russian territory, and granting commercial freedom for ships passing through the Straits. Both conditions had been granted already. Since Russia alone would now gain the direct benefit from the operations against the Dardanelles, the British government requested that no obstacles be placed in the way of any power which offered to coöperate with the Allies on reasonable terms. Greece was the only power likely to desire participation in the Dardanelles expedition. The British government also hoped that Petrograd would try to calm Bulgaria and Rumania "as to Russia's possession of the Straits and Constantinople being to their disadvantage," and to do everything possible to bring these two states into the war. In addition, the rights of England and France were to be guaranteed, the holy Moslem places protected, Arabia was to remain under independent Moslem rule, and the neutral zone in Persia was to revert to the British sphere of interest. In return for these concessions to London, Sazonov asked for "full liberty of action" in the Russian sphere in Persia.[66]

But these concessions to Russia were subject to even more serious conditions. A brief memorandum of March 12, 1915, from the British embassy, states:

*"If the war ends in a triumphant conclusion and if the aspirations of Great Britain and France in the Ottoman Empire as well as in other regions are realized, as exposed in the Russian communication . . . the government of His Majesty will give its consent to what is exposed in the memorandum of the imperial government on the subject of Constantinople and the Straits."*[67]

Sazonov now returned to his negotiations with the Quai d'Orsay to secure French consent to Russia's aspirations in the region of the Straits. On March 18 he telegraphed to Isvolsky that while he had entire confidence in Delcassé personally, the imperial government desired that *"the consent of France to the complete satisfaction of our desires be expressed to it in the most formal manner and under a form similar to that of the British government."*[68] Paris finally acceded to the Russian demands on April 10, but only after St. Petersburg had given complete satisfaction to the French designs on Asiatic Turkey.

Paléologue notified the imperial government on March 14 that France desired to annex Syria, including the region of the gulf of Alexandretta, and Cilicia to the Taurus mountains.[69] The next day Paléologue explained that Syria also comprised Palestine.[70] Sazonov, however, felt that if Russia satisfied these demands of Paris, the problem of the holy places being involved, it would be necessary to study the question further.[71] To this Delcassé agreed, though he insisted on Syria, Cilicia and parts of Palestine, with special examination of the problem of the holy places.[72] On March 16, the tsar, in conversation with Paléologue, gave his consent to French annexation of Syria, Cilicia and Palestine, though France had not yet given formal consent to Russian acquisition of the Straits.[73] Isvolsky reported on March 26 that French financial circles, former Ambassador Bompard, and the ministry of foreign affairs, were drawing plans to begin activity in Turkey as soon as Allied troops had taken Constantinople. It was, therefore, necessary for Russia to designate persons for a mixed occupation of Constantinople.[74] Two days later Isvolsky advised Sazonov that certain influential circles in Paris still favored an international organization for Constantinople and neutralization of the Straits. Though the government was preventing a press polemic, through censorship, a favorable attitude could be expected neither from Bompard nor from Poincaré. The French and British operations in the

Dardanelles had suffered heavy losses, and the fact that Russia was taking no part in that expedition was proving "extremely disadvantageous." Isvolsky was convinced that "all these efforts can lead to happy results only in case we take the principal military and naval rôle in the taking of Constantinople." At any rate it was extremely important that measures be taken providing for appropriate Russian representation in any mixed occupation of Constantinople.[75] On April 1 Isvolsky inquired of Sazonov whether Paléologue had made the promised written communication with reference to Constantinople, and when, four days later he reminded Delcassé of the matter, the latter explained his failure as due to his "absence of memory."[76] The French embassy gave a belated consent to Russian acquisition of the Straits and Constantinople only on April 10.[77] The final seal was placed on the Constantinople-Straits accord during the negotiations for the entrance of Italy into the war, when both London and Paris explained that by Italy's adherence to the declaration of September 5, 1914, nothing would be changed, the question of Constantinople and the Straits being considered as definitely settled.[78]

In March and April 1915, then, Russia had won the concession of *Tsargrad* and the waters of the Straits from her reluctant Allies. Great Britain had been the traditional enemy of Russia in the Near East, always barring the way to Constantinople, and the passage from the Black sea to the Mediterranean. Throughout the nineteenth century the English policy held as an article of faith. The twentieth century witnessed a change. In 1903, the committee of imperial defence went on record "that the exclusion of Russia from the Straits was not for Great Britain a primary naval or military interest." And the director of naval intelligence reported:

*"It may be stated generally that a Russian occupation of the Dardanelles, or an arrangement for enabling Russia to freely use the waterway between the Black sea and the Mediterranean, such as her dominating influence can extract from Turkey at her pleasure, would not make any marked difference in our strategic dispositions as compared with present conditions."*[79] Doubtless this decision of the committee of imperial defence was influenced by the increasing part which Germany was playing in the Near East and the desire for a balancing factor in Russia. Though conceded in principle at this early date, it was hoped that the concession need not be made, and then only for other compensations.

However that may be, it was only the pressure of the trying days of the war which brought England to the point of ceding Constantinople and the Straits to Russia.

The French attitude on the Straits negotiations with Russia during the spring of 1915 is the most conclusive proof not only of the lack of unity of Franco-Russian policy in the east, but of any pre-war collusion based on the alliance for the settlement of the question of the Straits and that of Alsace-Lorraine. Some publicists have argued the existence of an agreement on these two problems inherent in the Franco-Russian alliance on the basis of the diary of Georges Louis, former French ambassador in Russia. In no case is documentary evidence adduced. The policy of the Quai d'Orsay during the negotiations of 1915 is conclusive proof to the contrary.[80]

Viscount Grey has confessed that "the British operations against the Dardanelles came near to impairing our relations with Russia . . . . It was agreed . . . that the promise of Constantinople must be made: but neither we nor the French liked the thing."[81] Lord Bertie, British ambassador at Paris, who hated the Russians only less than he did the common enemy, urged "the advisability of England and France (in this matter England comes before France) getting to Constantinople before Russia, so that the Muscovite may not have it all his own way in deciding the future of that city and the Straits, Dardanelles and Bosphorus."[82]

Nor was this the end of the story. In February Grey had undertaken certain negotiations with liberal and moderate Turks for the conclusion of a possible separate peace. Sazonov had rejected these moves of the English foreign minister. During April and May 1915, Djavid Bey, former Turkish minister of finance, went to Geneva, Switzerland, with the obvious purpose of entering into negotiations with the Entente.[83] He engaged certain French statesmen in conversation, though Delcassé denied any reality in these overtures.[84] On May 28 Delcassé informed Isvolsky, however, that the Turks had tried to enter into *pourparlers*. Though the French foreign minister apparently remained firm in his intention to throw the Turks out of Europe, he asked Isvolsky to obtain the attitude of St. Petersburg.[85] Sazonov replied two days later that he saw no obstacle in a prudent examination of the Turkish proposal, providing "the irrevocable decision of the Allies to give Constantinople and the Straits to Russia" be revealed to them.[86] This, of course, made a separate peace virtually impossible, for the Turks could hardly be expected to surrender their capital to

Russia. However, it indicates Russia's intention to allow nothing to interfere with the fulfilment of the historic mission in Turkey.

While Russia was demanding Constantinople, as we have seen, the possibility of her being able to dispose of military and naval forces to coöperate with the Allies in taking the city and the Straits steadily diminished. Many felt that the acquisition of Constantinople would remain a mere dream despite the promises of the Allies. General Janushkevich, chief of the general staff, on the other hand, thought that in view of Russia's great services on her own main front, the war would end with the favorable solution of the question of Constantinople.[87]

Meanwhile there were overtures from another quarter. In a private letter to the tsar, dated March 10, 1915, the Princess Maria Vasilchikova, who had been detained at Kleinwartenstein, Austria, advanced the idea of a separate peace with the Central Powers. She had talks with certain Austro-German diplomats on the subject. When the princess asked: "What of the Dardanelles?" they replied, "The Russian tsar has but to ask it—and the Straits will be free." On March 30 the princess wrote the emperor that these same men had told her "that England intends to keep Constantinople for herself and to create in the Dardanelles another Gibraltar." Later, on May 27, 1915, she saw Jagow, the German foreign secretary, and heard still more about English designs on the Straits, but the German promises were extremely vague.[88] Nekliudov, Russian minister at Stockholm, reported on July 20, 1915, that Germany was willing to offer Russia Constantinople and the Straits if she would make a separate peace, since it was impossible to take the region by force of arms.[89] But to all these overtures both the tsar and his government turned a deaf ear.

The Dardanelles campaign, which had begun in February 1915, was making no progress. This brilliant scheme of Winston Churchill, which would have isolated the Central Powers, gained control of Constantinople and the Straits, opened the route to Russia, crippled Turkey, and brought Italy, Greece, Rumania and Bulgaria into the war on the side of the Allies, had failed virtually by the summer of 1915. Begun as a naval operation, by March it was apparent that landing operations on an extended scale were necessary if Constantinople were to be taken. The offer of the Greeks had been turned down by Russia in early March. Russia was pressing her own claim to Constantinople, while the British were intending to use the Greeks, not only to take Constantinople, but as a pivot of a new Balkan alliance

against Turkey, and so forestall the Russian claim. A late March attack on the forts of the Dardanelles had done much damage but suffered heavy losses. The navy had failed to achieve Constantinople in four weeks, as Churchill had promised so confidently in January. After March 18 Limon von Sanders learned of the plan for a land attack, and of the assemblage of 90,000 troops for that purpose. The first landing took place on April 25. The months of May, June and July 1915 were marked by waiting and delay. This proved costly to the Entente in the Balkans, and failed in the break-through to Constantinople. In August, the attacks were renewed, but by this time the Turks were able to concentrate heavily in the Galipoli peninsula, with about 500,000 troops available to meet the Allies. Turkey was now on the defensive in Mesopotamia, but Russia no longer threatened. Bulgaria was on the verge of joining the Central Powers. By August 8 the Anzac attack at Suvla was checked, due to the work of Liman von Sanders and the initiative of Mustapha Kemal.

By this time the Salonica expedition was in the offing, with the object of relieving Serbia and pressing through the Balkans. On October 15 Sir Ian Hamilton was replaced by General Munro as commander of the forces operating in the Dardanelles. The campaign had failed, and on December 8, orders were received to evacuate the peninsula. Perhaps the most brilliant part of the campaign, the evacuation was carried out in December 1915 and January 1916.

The reasons for the Allied débacle in the region of the Straits are both diplomatic and military: diplomatic in the sense of lack of unity among the western Allies and Russia, and in the refusal to allow the Greeks to enter the struggle; and military in another sense. The British employed over 400,000 men in the campaign, while the Turks used 800,000—Turkish bayonets in the last analysis had barred the way. The failure of the expedition lost Bulgaria to the Allies, lowered Entente prestige in the east, probably prolonged the war by two years, and was one of the main contributory causes in precipitating the Russian catastrophe of 1917. Even this, however, did not end the illusion of Russia as to the possibility of obtaining the Straits and Constantinople.[90]

At the end of August 1915, the Grand Duke Nicholas became commander of the Caucasus region, with General Alexeiev as chief of staff. This change, in conjunction with the Allied failure at the Dardanelles, had serious consequences. General Alexeiev believed the liquidation of the ill-fated Dardanelles campaign a necessary prelimi-

nary toward a separate peace with the Turks, and was extremely skeptical of seizing Constantinople. The success of the Russian forces operating against Turkey and the capture of Erzerum in the winter of 1916, brought Alexeiev back to his peace project. Prince Kudashev, writing to Sazonov on February 18, 1916, explained Alexeiev's ideas. Hopes founded on Turkey, in particular, acquisition of the Straits by Russia "scarcely have a chance in the future." The main task ahead was the defeat of Germany, which alone would entail tremendous sacrifices. Peace with Turkey could be obtained without sacrifice of real interests, and giving up only for a time the seizure of the Straits. A separate peace, moreover, would facilitate the successful conclusion of the war for the Allies. The move failed, however, due to Sazonov's insistence on the Constantinople issue. No peace was to be allowed to interfere with that problem. At last the tsar himself vetoed any idea of a separate peace with Turkey, when in a marginal annotation on a dispatch (September 2, 1916), he stated: "It is necessary to make an end of Turkey. In any case her place is not in Europe. Therefore we must have no relations with the (Turkish) opposition."[91] Further expeditions against the Straits were planned, despite the almost obvious impossibility of carrying out any of them.

While Alexiev and Kudashev were formulating their ideas of a separate peace with Turkey, in view of the evident impossibility of obtaining immediate control over Constantinople and the Straits, certain moves in the direction of peace were taking place in western Europe. Colonel E. M. House was in London talking over the prospects of peace with the members of the British government. As to the Near East and the Ottoman Empire, House noted in his diary for February 14, 1916:

"*We all cheerfully divided up Turkey, both in Asia and Europe. The discussion hung for a long while around the fate of Constantinople. George and Balfour were not enthusiastic over giving it into the hands of Russia, Grey and Asquith thinking if this were not done material for another war would always be at hand. I suggested the neutralization of Constantinople . . . .*"[92]

In a memorandum of Sir Edward Grey, dated February 22, 1916, the British foreign minister quotes House on the now familiar proposition indicating that President Wilson was ready, if France and England thought the moment favorable, to propose a conference to put an end to the war. If the Allies accepted the idea and the Germans rejected it, in all likelihood the United States would enter the struggle against

Germany. Grey quoted House to the effect, that among other things, "the acquisition by Russia of an outlet to the sea", should be a part of the basis for peace. Apparently Colonel House did not go beyond the idea of neutralization and internationalization of the Straits in his project, for there is no evidence that he favored outright Russian acquisition of Constantinople and the waters of the Straits.[93] In fact, Colonel House himself writes:

"*I feel very sure . . . that my suggestion to the British in 1916 went no further than that Russia should be permitted at all times to have an outlet to the seas through the Dardanelles. I am certain that I did not believe at any time that she should have further territory either in Europe or Asia.*"[94] That the British were still reluctant to allow the Muscovite control at Constantinople, even after they had been forced to concede in the spring of 1915, does not seem open to serious question or doubt.

Having obtained the consent of France and England to Russia's possession of Constantinople and the Straits, the tsarist government desired to publish the agreement. Already the question had become an internal as well as an external issue, and it was felt that publication of the document would assure the home front in Russia and quiet the fears of disaffected elements. No longer was the accord to remain a secret, preserved in the diplomatic chancellories of Europe. Negotiations were carried on throughout the year 1916 between the three governments (and Italy). Britain was concerned with the effect of publication on India; France hesitated and suggested a new manifesto on Poland. Russian military circles feared the results on the Rumanian military situation if the secret were disclosed. Finally the western Allies were informed that Russia would be content with a brief declaration. On December 2, 1916, M. Trepov, the prime minister, stated in the Duma:

"*An agreement which we concluded in 1915, with Great Britain and France, and to which Italy has adhered, established in the most definite fashion the right of Russia to the Straits and Constantinople . . . . I repeat that absolute agreement on this point is firmly established among the Allies.*"[95]

3.

### The Result of the Russian Demand

Throughout the war imperial Russia held on to the dream of Constantinople and the Straits. Once Turkey came into the conflict

# Negru, Matthew
# Wed May 08 2013

EMAIL

p22318999

The partition of Turkey; a diplomatic history, 1913-1923, by Harry N. Howard.
36294159893004

**Newton Main**

the problem of a free access to the open sea became the principal object of the war for Russia. The Russian demands, however, were never clearly defined until expressly formulated in March 1915, when, after the beginning of the Dardanelles campaign and the attempt to bring Greece into the war against Turkey, Sazonov made his famous demand for Constantinople and the Straits. Neither England nor France desired to concede in regard to the question, but both were forced to do so on account of the grim circumstances of the world war. Russia was not to be denied in those supreme moments of her sacrifice. In January and February 1914, at the secret conferences held to consider the problem of the Straits following Germany's dispatch of the Liman von Sanders mission to Turkey, the Russian government decided that those waters could be acquired only in a general European war. Unable to take action until 1917 because of naval inferiority, unable to move with sufficient troops because of the war on the eastern front, it was the irony of fate that in the expected European war Russia could not send either military or naval forces to operate against the Straits.

By her demand for Constantinople and the Straits, Russia opened up the entire question of the future of Turkey—a fact which was to lead to the secret treaties and understandings of 1915-1917, which partitioned the sultan's heritage among the members of the Entente. It is perhaps more than a mere strange coincidence that the agreement of March 1915 and those which were to be executed in the following year were "substantially the same" as the propositions for a "peaceful partition (of the Ottoman Empire) made by the tsar to Aberdeen's Government in 1853"—a policy now to be carried out "after seventy years of agony."[96] The negotiations for and the fate of these Allied agreements in regard to the partition of the Turkish Empire, will be considered in a later chapter.[97]

# CHAPTER V

# ITALY, THE BALKANS AND THE TURKISH QUESTION, 1914-1916

## National Prizes in the Turkish Question

WITH the outbreak of the world war, both sides in the conflict became anxious to add new recruits to their armies from the ranks of the neutral states. In Mediterranean and eastern Europe, Italy and Rumania had long standing treaties of alliance with the Central Powers. Hence a declaration of neutrality signified a breaking of ancient ties and a probable later connection with the Entente. Greece seemed favorable to the Entente in the beginning, and under Venizelos, was anxious to participate in the operations against the Dardanelles. Bulgaria, since the Balkan wars of 1912-1913, was following a pro-Austro-German policy, and until her entry into the struggle, mystified the diplomats of the Entente.

Each of these Powers had an interest in the Turkish question. Italy had a threefold interest. She was determined to assure herself a secure hold on the Dalmatian littoral at the expense of Austria, failure to obtain which was to lead to the rupture between the two countries. The grant of this territory by the Entente, on the other hand, led to difficulties with the Serbs, who were supported by Russia. Again, Italy was interested in the settlement of the question of the Straits. Fear that France, Britain and Russia would determine the question without her had much to do with the final decision in the spring of 1915. It was this question, too, which brought on the difficulties with Russia during the Italian negotiations. The St. Petersburg government, having won a reluctant concession of Constantinople and the Straits from her Allies, was not going to allow a new partner to upset the bargain. A final interest of Italy lay in her possession, since 1912, of the Dodecanese, and her aspirations in the Adalia vilayet on the coast of Asiatic Turkey. The treaty of London, of April 1915, paid Italy dearly for her "sacred egoism" in entering the war, though paper promises and actual territorial acquisitions varied widely in scope.

Greece, almost doubled in population since the Balkan wars, and greatly increased in size, inherited further trouble with the Turk. On the eve of the war, the question of the Aegean islands had not

been settled. Though the Athens government did not fulfil the obligations of its alliance with Serbia, it became intensely interested in the Anglo-French operations against the Dardanelles. Other problems in which Greece was concerned were those of the internationalization of the Straits, western Thrace, northern Epirus, the Dodecanese, and of the acquisition of the Smyrna region in Asia Minor. Had the policy of Venizelos prevailed, it is not unlikely that Greece would have realized some of these aspirations. As it was, Russia opposed Greek entrance in the Dardanelles campaign with Constantinople as the objective, Venizelos and King Constantine disagreed, and only the defection of the former in 1916 brought a semblance of participation in the war on the side of the Entente.

Bulgaria, the connecting link between Turkey and the Central Powers, was the key to the Balkan situation from the beginning of the war to her final decision for the Triplice in the fall of 1915. Guided by Tsar Ferdinand and Radoslavov, in the Austrian orbit, the Sofia cabinet seems to have been bound to Vienna since August 1914. Despoiled by the victors in the war of 1913, Bulgaria now demanded revision of the treaty of Bucharest. She claimed satisfaction of four *irredenta*: (1) Serbian Macedonia, (2) Greek Macedonia, (3) Thrace, (4) and the Dobruja. When one notes the struggle for Balkan leadership between England and Russia, and adds the evident Bulgarian fear of Russian domination in the Straits, the chain of circumstances bringing Bulgaria in the war is well nigh complete.

Rumania's connection with the Turkish question is important, though not so direct as that of Italy, Greece and Bulgaria. Her national aspirations could be satisfied only at Austro-Hungarian expense, some 3,000,000 Rumanians living in the Dual Monarchy. By the possession of Bessarabia, then in Russian hands, she could liberate other Rumanians, bar Russia's Balkan approach to the Straits, and threaten the Russian port of Odessa. While the Bucharest government had grave misgivings as to Russian control of the Straits—Rumania's only outlet to the open sea—the feeling prevailed that a change in the sovereignty of the Straits would result from the war, and that Rumania could not prevent it. Conviction that the Entente would win was a decisive factor in her resolution to enter the war.

Allied diplomacy in the Balkans during the war hardly can be viewed as an edifying spectacle. Russia had tried to keep Turkey neutral, or to bring her into the war on the side of the Entente, as an ally of Russia. This proposition had met with rebuff in the middle of

August 1914. Both Downing Street and the Quai d'Orsay were determined on the formation of a Balkan alliance of Greece, Bulgaria, Rumania and Serbia, for use against Turkey and the Central Powers. England, in particular, was using Greece as the pivot of a new Balkan alliance. Russia blocked Greek participation, when the Athens cabinet offered to assist, because of her fear of British domination in the region of the Straits, with Britain using Greece as a puppet. Nor was there unity in the Bulgarian negotiations. Having failed to win Greece, Britain then tried to win supremacy in Bulgaria over Russia. The result was a checkmate and failure in the negotiations for a Balkan alliance. Though substantial offers were made to Bulgaria, her conviction that German arms were invincible brought that country into war against the Entente. The case of Rumania is that of a government, abiding its time, playing for good bargains and securing them, and then striking after it is too late. Here again the Allies were divided. France and England favored Rumanian participation in the war, while Russia preferred to have the Bucharest government remain neutral, as the best guarantee against Austro-German penetration in the Balkans and Turkey. Russia did not value highly Rumanian arms, not did she wish to create a larger Rumania on the road to the Straits. However, Russia acted in concert with her Allies to bring Rumania into the war, in 1915 and 1916.

Such, in brief, is the tangled story of the Italian and Balkan negotiations preceding the entrance of these countries into the war. We must now trace them in some detail.

2.

### Italy's Entrance into the World War

When Italy declared her neutrality on August 3, 1914,[1] both the Triplice and the Entente vied with each other in their offers to bring about favorable action on the part of Rome. It is not necessary to enter into all the details of the negotiations. Italian *irredenta*, long in the hands of the Dual Monarchy, could be satisfied only at the expense of Austria. These included the Trentino, the Dalmatian coast and other parts of Austria. The Austrian frontier, moreover, was strategically unfavorable to Italy. Aside from these serious grievances, the Austrian

invasion in the Balkans was upsetting the balance, without compensation to Italy. As early as July 25, 1914, the Quirinal had asked for an exchange of views on the matter.[2]

After the death of San Giuliano in October 1914, the office of foreign affairs fell to the lot of Sidney Sonnino, son of a Scotch mother and an Italian Jew, who knew how to bargain. Still haggling about the Austrian advance in the Balkans, the Italians increased their claims.[3] The German share in any compensations which Italy might obtain from the Central Powers was nothing, since Germany had no lands which Italy could claim. Her contribution was to send Prince Bülow to Rome in December 1914. He learned that while the majority of people favored neutrality, this was only on the presumption of obtaining "the fulfilment of certain national aspirations."[4] On January 11, 1915, Bülow was informed that harmony between Italy and Austria was impossible until the irrendentist formula of "Trentino and Trieste" was removed.[5]

Berchtold gave way to Burian at the Ballplatz in January 1915. The latter continued the ill-starred negotiations with Rome, but with as little success.[6] On March 27, 1915, Burian informed Avarna that in return for a friendly neutrality and Austrian liberty of action in the Balkans, Italy would receive territory in southern Tyrol, including Trentino.[7] Italy replied that the offer was insufficient, and demanded immediate cession.[8] On April 8 Sonnino presented claims for Gradisca and Gorizia in the Isonzo valley, the establishment of Trieste as an autonomous city, cession of the archipelago of Curzola, Austrian disinterestedness in Albania, renunciation of Austrian rights under Article VII of the Triple Alliance, and recognition of the Italian occupation of the Dodecanese.[9] Burian rejected this project.[10]

Italy was now preparing to enter the war against Germany and Austria.[11] They knew at the Quirinal that the most important concessions were at Austrian expense, and that Vienna naturally had great difficulty in surrendering her own territory.

It was not difficult, of course, for the Entente—in particular, France and England—to give in to the Italian demands for territory under the Habsburg dominion. The day following her declaration of neutrality, Rome sounded the Entente as to a possible entry into the war against the Central Powers. Sazonov was willing to grant Trieste to Italy, and had no objection to her annexation of Trentino, if his allies were in accord.[12] The Italian ambassador at St. Petersburg, Carlotti, however, informed Sazonov that aside from the Trentino, Italy

desired the possession of Valona, and predominance in the Adriatic. In return, Rome would consent to Greek and Serb acquisitions on the Adriatic.[13] France, apparently, was willing to grant these claims.[14] On August 7 England consented, and added the necessity of promising Trieste. Grey thought the *pourparlers* could be conducted by Sazonov.[15] Sazonov felt that in return for such great concessions, Italy should be urged to enter the war immediately.[16] He outlined a project on August 10, whereby Italy would receive the Trentino, Trieste and Valona, in return for such action, and desired a prompt reply.[17]

Sir Edward Grey now took the initiative in the negotiations, a step which the Quirinal preferred.[18] At the same time, the Italian demands worried Sazonov and caused him to urge the strictest secrecy in the negotiations, lest the Serbs be aroused.[19]

During the next week or so the negotiations continued, but little was accomplished. It was clear that Italy would not enter the war against the Allies. When she would fight was another question. Krupensky telegraphed Sazonov on August 22, that Italy desired the assurance that in case of war, Russia would draw off most of the Austrian army.[20]

Meanwhile, Rome continued to delay, and was in the midst of conversations with Austria.[21] On September 19 the question of a possible occupation of Valona arose, and Sazonov warned that if it were done with Austrian consent, the whole situation would be altered.[22] On October 4 the British ambassador presented the Italian claim to occupy Valona, but Sazonov saw no reason to give his consent.[23] No change occurred during the month of December, though Salandra had made a speech in the Italian Chamber, which was anti-Austrian in tone.[24] On December 10, 1914, the Italian ambassador at St. Petersburg outlined the important interests of Italy in Albania, when he heard of a project to divide it between Greece and Serbia. Sazonov informed him that an occupation of Valona by Italy would be contrary to the decisions of London, in 1913. On December 25, however, Italian troops occupied the city. This disquieted both the Serb and Greek governments, and led Sazonov to protest to the Italian ambassador.[25]

By this time it appeared that Italy was deciding to move toward active participation with the Entente, though the Austrian negotiations had not failed definitely.[26] The French and British began to insist on Italy's entry at the price of considerable territorial acquisitions. Sazonov was not at all enthusiastic, and advised a revision of the offers made in the fall of 1914. On March 8 he proposed that Italy's gains be

scaled down to the new circumstances, that Italy take the initiative in the negotiations, and operate against both Austria and Turkey, since she desired compensations in Turkey.[27]

Again Italy's "sacred egoism" asserted itself. Delcassé agreed that Italy should take the initiative, and must fight both Austria and Turkey. Isvolsky wrote on March 10, that "the Italian government does not intend absolutely to participate in the operations against the Straits and Constantinople." But Delcassé feared to revise the promises made to Rome.[28] On the same day Benckendorff reported that Grey was much impressed with the Italian overtures. Grey thought that England would not oppose the Italian retention of the Dodecanese.[29] St. Petersburg was ready to agree to the major part of the Italian demands by March 15. It raised no objection to Italy's right to annex Trentino, South Tyrol, Trieste, Istria, the islands of the Quarnero and Valona. In case of the partition of Turkey, Italian claims in Adalia and the Dodecanese were recognized. An autonomous Albania was to be constituted. Sazonov reserved the right to make changes more favorable to the Serbs.[30] He informed Carlotti on March 24 that the Dalmatian claims were entirely unacceptable because they infringed on Serbian rights for an outlet to the Adriatic.[31] The next day Sazonov telegraphed Benckendorff that the Entente should not go beyond certain limits in the negotiations with Rome, nor sacrifice Serbian and Montenegrin interests to Italy. Already very important concessions had been made. Italy only could obtain her desires in Austria at a minimum effort with the aid of the Entente.[32] In a memorandum which Buchanan gave Sazonov on March 26, 1915, the British government, having learned that Rumania was about to decide for the Allies, again urged action in reference to Rome.[33] Sazonov was unconvinced, and thought that Grey should be more firm in his attitude. A few days later Buchanan advised Sazonov that Italy was ready to make slight concessions to Serbia on the Dalmatian littoral, though the Italian demands would make the Adriatic an Italian lake.[34]

Grey was insistent on the necessity of Italian aid, and though Sazonov partook neither of the fears of Grey nor of Delcassé, he gave in. He would not accept the responsibility for a break with Italy.[35] While he had no objection to Italian demands on Asia Minor, Sazonov protested against Grey's generosity in regions where England and France were not primarily concerned.[36] On April 4 he informed the Grand Duke Nicholas that he was ceding to Italy, though he had fears of the Serbian reaction. Sazonov could not hold longer against Franco-

British pressure.[37] But new concessions were necessary. On April 15 Petrograd signified its willingness to further changes, including a virtual Italian protectorate over Albania, on condition that Greece receive northern Epirus, Montenegro retain northern Albania with Scutari, St. Jean de Medua and Alessio, and that Serbia and Greece be assured a common frontier.[38]

The concessions made, Russia felt that Italy should come immediately into the war. The Italians desired a month's delay. Sazonov was not inclined to sign the treaty under that condition, as he felt that Italian aid would have only a moral, not military importance.[39]

On April 18 Benckendorff sent Sazonov the draft declaration by which Italy was to adhere to the declaration of September 5, 1914, with an obligation not to make a separate peace. Added in pencil was the following statement:

*"It is decided that all the conventions relative to the future peace, adopted by the Allied Powers before Italy rallied to these Powers, remain in force and will not be submitted to any later (ultérieur) examination."*[40]

This was an assurance to Russia that Italy's action would not upset the cession of Constantinople, which had been secured in March. On April 15 Poincaré addressed the tsar urging Russia's assistance in securing the aid of Italy.[41] The following day Buchanan told Sazonov that "after the complaisance we have shown Russia in the question of Constantinople," it seemed that Russia should not insist on a time limit for Italy's entry into the war. Were Italy lost, Rumania and Bulgaria and Greece would join the Entente.[42] Buchanan presented on April 21 Grey's draft of agreement for Italy's adhesion to make peace and war in common with her Allies. While Sazonov complained that the treaty with Italy had been written without his collaboration, he would sign the accord.[43] He wanted Italy to recognize the agreement on Constantinople and the Straits. But Grey thought this unwise, since the Allies already had conceded the claims of Russia. Once Rome had adhered to the declaration of September 5, 1914, she could be informed of the situation, and "must consider the question of Constantinople and the Straits as a settled affair."[44]

In another letter, Poincaré informed the tsar that Italy's decision would not affect the accords previously reached.[45] With this assurance, Russia was willing to sign the treaty of April 26, 1915, guaranteeing Italy's entrance into the war in the following month.[46] Italy had won

her concessions in Austria, the Balkans, and in Asia Minor.[47] On May 4 the cabinet of Rome denounced the Triple Alliance at Vienna, and on May 22 declared war against Austria.[48]

3.

## Greece and the World War

In Greece the course of events during the world war centers about the personalities of Venizelos and King Constantine. At the outbreak Venizelos was at Munich on his way to Brussels to settle the issue of the Aegean islands with the grand vizier of Turkey. In answer to the plea of Pashich on July 25, 1914, Venizelos replied that he would propose war against Bulgaria if the latter intervened against Serbia.[49] As already indicated, on August 4, 1914, the kaiser informed Constantine of his alliance with Turkey, that Bulgaria and Rumania were joining the Triplice, and that the *Goeben* and *Breslau* were sailing to Constantinople. Personally sympathetic, Constantine insisted on the impossibility of offering Greek aid to Germany.[50]

Venizelos believed in the victory of the Entente, and from the outset he urged Greek participation on that side. On August 18, 1914, he offered Greek help to the Allies, to be used, apparently, against Turkey. Churchill urged Greek participation from the beginning, but Grey, though favoring the idea, feared to hasten the matter, on account of Russia. Turkey had not yet entered the war and the Allies were lukewarm in their reception of the Greek offer.[51] The British did suggest an understanding between the British and Greek staffs for action against Turkey. Constantine and Admiral Kerr, head of the British naval mission to Greece, worked out a project for such action, with Greek participation only in case Turkey attacked first. Whereupon Venizelos offered his resignation. While Greece could not move without securing the Bulgarian frontier, Venizelos felt that if that were assured, war against the Porte could be undertaken.[52] Though Venizelos remained in office, he was now clearly in disagreement with the King. Insinuations as to the pro-German policy of Constantine now became general.

Events were moving rapidly elsewhere in the Balkans. Bulgaria, officially neutral, ever menaced Serbia, and became increasingly hostile in attitude. Rumania was neutral, but negotiating with both sides. In mid-August, the Bucharest cabinet had invited Greece and Turkey

148

to settle the islands question, but with the purpose of forming a neutral Balkan *bloc* to oppose Russia in the Straits.[53] By this time, too, the Entente was beginning to formulate ideas concerning a renewed Balkan alliance. Bulgaria was the pivot of the Russian scheme. When Britain failed in Greece, she tried to oust Russia from supremacy in Sofia, with consequent confusion, and the reluctant loss of Bulgaria to the Allies.[54]

On November 22, 1914, the Allies offered Greece the southern portion of Albania except Valona, in return for her immediate aid to Serbia. Venizelos refused because of Rumania's failure to guarantee Bulgaria's conduct.[55] No important development took place until January 23, 1915, when the British minister at Athens informed Venizelos that in return for Greek assistance to Serbia, the Entente would offer important territorial gains to Greece in Asia Minor. In turn Bulgaria could be given concessions in Macedonia.[56] While the offers were purposely vague, the next day Venizelos presented the first of his memoranda to Constantine urging Greek participation in the war. In return for an empire in Asia Minor, Greece would give up Cavalla to Bulgaria and withdraw objections to Serbian concessions to Bulgaria. In addition Greece would ask, if Bulgaria extended beyond the Vardar, that Serbia cede to Greece the Doïran-Gevgeli district. In this way the Balkan league could be reconstructed for service with the Entente.[57]

Constantine was unconvinced, however, and on January 30 Venizelos presented a second memorandum which was even more optimistic than his first. Rumania had refused joint action in aid of Serbia as long as Bulgaria was not in line. Venizelos now turned specifically to Sofia. The Cavalla, Drama, Seres district, territory of two thousand kilometers, would be ceded to Bulgaria. Its Hellenic population was 30,000. Venizelos had his eyes on 125,000 square kilometers in Asia Minor with a Greek population of 800,000.[58] The general staff, Venizelos had to confess, was not allured by these dreams. Neither was Constantine, though a greater Hellas beckoned in the words of his prime minister.

In the interim Turkey had entered the world war. On November 3 the forts of the Dardanelles were bombarded. The British decision to attack the forts had been reached on November 25. Only in January 1915, however, was the move set on foot, when the Russian appeal for a diversion against Turkey reached London. With the failure of the first naval attack on February 19 the necessity of new troops for land operations became apparent. Venizelos offered three divisions of troops to the Allies on March 1, 1915. He did this without

royal consent, and Colonel Metaxas of the general staff resigned in protest. At the crown councils of March 3-5, 1915, Venizelos presented his case, to which Constantine was opposed.[59] As we have seen, Venizelos, then on the very eve of his resignation, made an official offer to the Entente. England and France desired Greek assistance, but Russia rejected the offer under the conditions in which it was made. Russia did not favor the establishment of Greece in Constantinople under the aegis of Great Britain.[60]

With the resignation of Venizelos, M. Gounaris became premier. Though there were to be general elections in June 1915, Gounaris remained in office from March until August, when Venizelos again returned to power. Gounaris announced a policy of benevolent neutrality toward the Entente. On April 12 the Entente again made an offer of Asiatic territory for Greek collaboration—namely, territory in the Aidin vilayet on the coast of Asia Minor.[61] Asked to define the territory more specifically, Elliot, the British minister, told Gounaris that the note meant "Smyrna and a substantial portion of its hinterland." Neither Deville nor Demidov had instructions from their governments.[62] In its reply of April 14 the Gounaris cabinet stated its willingness to coöperate immediately if the Entente would guarantee Greek territorial integrity, including northern Epirus and the islands, during the war and for a definite period after the war.[63] Gounaris announced on May 1, that his government would remain neutral since this assurance was not given.[64] On May 9 Constantine declared that the refusal of the Allies to give the necessary guarantee was the reason for Greek failure to enter the war. When Poincaré heard this he stated that such a guarantee would exclude Bulgaria from joining the Entente, since she would see Cavalla lost forever.[65] Meanwhile, Prince George, brother of the king, was in Paris negotiating and urging Constantine to action. "In entering into the alliance we gain everything, in remaining aside we lose all. Be generous, think that it is a question of Saint Sophia and have confidence in the God of Greece."[66] He urged action despite the fact that the Allies would not alienate Bulgaria by guaranteeing Cavalla to Greece—though they disclaimed any intention of forcing Greece to surrender it.[67] Under these conditions nothing more could be done with the Gounaris cabinet.

The elections of June 13, 1915, returned Venizelos to power, and he became prime minister of Greece at the end of August,[68] when Bulgaria was on the verge of a decision for the Central Powers. Again

the question of Cavalla was on the table, and again the Entente protested that it would offer Cavalla to Bulgaria only with Greek consent.[69]

When Bulgaria mobilized in September, Greece counter-mobilized.
The Serbian treaty once more came into controversy, and this issue,
among others, gave rise to the Allied expedition at Salonica. On September 23 Venizelos, after Constantine's refusal to entertain the idea,
asked the Allied Powers if they were prepared to send 150,000 men
to fulfil the Serb obligations against the Bulgars, under the treaty of
May 1913.[70] The answer was in the affirmative, and the first forces
landed at Salonica under formal protest on October 3, 1915.[71] On the
next day Venizelos delivered a vigorous address urging immediate
entry into the war. Constantine exacted his resignation as prime minister on October 5.[72] Zaïmis now became premier and remained in power
until November with the provisional support of Venizelos. He announced a policy of neutrality consonant with the interests of his
country.[73] Bulgaria declared war on Serbia on October 12, but Greece announced that the *casus foederis* did not arise.[74] England offered Greece the
island of Cyprus on October 16, if she would come to the aid of Serbia.[75]
On November 4 Zaïmis was forced to resign by the Venizelists.[76]

The Skouloudis ministry followed, lasting until December. By this
time there was little question of active participation in the war. The
government announced its policy of benevolent neutrality on November 8. Meanwhile, the chamber had been dissolved, but Skouloudis
remained in power. The Entente used this fact as an excuse to interfere
in the internal affairs of the country.[77] Troops were kept at Salonica
under Sarrail, Corfu was occupied for the Serbian army in exile, and
Castellorizo, off Asia Minor, was taken over.[78] Greece was in the hands
of the Allies. On December 28, 1915, Constantine told Sir Francis
Elliot that "Greece is thinking above everything of her territorial
integrity: she does not wish to see the Russians at Constantinople.
Germany has guaranteed our territorial integrity so long as we remain
neutral."[79]

In April 1916 the Allies pressed for the passage of Serbian troops
from Corfu to Salonica, to which Greece finally gave her consent.[80]

A Bulgarian force took Fort Rupel, commanding the Struma entrance of southern Macedonia, on May 26. The surrender was arranged
by the Greek and the Bulgarian governments. Zaïmis again took over
the government when Skouloudis was forced to resign in consequence
of this affair on June 23, 1916. The Bulgarians even entered the long

coveted seaport of Cavalla, as well as the Seres and Drama districts in September 1915. The Greek garrison of 8,000 men surrendered without firing.

This was the last straw for Venizelos. Making a final appeal to the king,[81] he set out for Crete and on September 27, established his own revolutionary provisional government. On November 24 the Venizelist government declared war on the Central Powers and Bulgaria.[82]

The Allies were now prepared for sterner measures in Greece. The Lambros ministry had been formed in October 1916. The Entente demanded the surrender of Greek artillery, demobilization of certain forces, expulsion of undesirables, control of police and railroads, and the occupation of certain points in Athens. Fighting took place when French and British marines landed and marched on Athens. Demands were made for Constantine's resignation. Both Italy and Russia opposed this action.[83] In June 1917, M. Jonnart was sent out as high commissioner and on June 11 he demanded the abdication of the king, which was announced the next day. Venizelos was then asked to assume the reins of government, and on June 30, 1917, the Greek government broke off relations with the Central Powers and was in the war.[84] It was this action which became the basis for future Greek claims on the Turkish Empire after the world war had ended.

4.

### Bulgaria and the Balkan League

Bulgaria was the pivot of the Balkan situation during the war. Geographically this small nation formed the connecting link between the Central Powers and Turkey. Hence her importance to the Triplice in opening up a sure and certain route for the transport of men and munitions to Turkey, and the crushing of Serbia, which barred the way.[85] Though many indications pointed toward a possible Austro-German *entente*, the Radoslavov cabinet declared its neutrality on the outbreak of the war, and began a *realpolitik* in negotiating with both sides.[86] The re-formation of a Balkan union around Bulgaria, a policy which Russia early adopted, demanded the satisfaction of Bulgaria's national aspirations in the Cavalla, Seres, Drama district in Greek Macedonia, Serbian Macedonia, Thrace and the Dobruja. Of these the Macedonian question was of outstanding importance. Satisfaction of any of these claims would come only at the sacrifice of an ally or

possible ally of the Entente—Serbia, Greece and Rumania. Failure to settle these issues, fear of Russian domination in the Straits, Anglo-Russian rivalry for supremacy in the negotiations with the Sofia cabinet, and belief in ultimate victory of German arms finally brought about Bulgarian action against the Allies.

Both England and Russia engaged in a struggle for supremacy in Bulgaria after the British failure in the Greek negotiations, when Britain tried to dominate the situation in Sofia. As early as August 5 Sazonov telegraphed his chargé at Belgrade that he felt Bulgarian aid only could be assured by the immediate cession of Ishtip and Kotchana with Macedonia to the Vardar. In case of victory Bulgaria could obtain the "contested" zone outlined in the treaty of 1912. For her neutrality Sazonov was willing to offer this territory to Bulgaria at the end of a victorious conflict. Should Pashich agree, guarantees could be given to Russia, which would in turn transmit them to Sofia.[87] The Serbian cabinet, however, refused to make the desired concession, seeing in Greece and Rumania a guarantee against a Bulgarian attack.[88]

In a long conversation with Radoslavov, Savinsky promised the minister-president "fine compensations" if Bulgaria remained neutral. But more definite statements were necessary, for he learned that Germany and Austria had given a written promise of Pirot and Nish, and Macedonia with the Vardar, and Salonica, in case of German victory.[89] Sazonov asked Savinsky, on August 9 to notify Radoslavov that he expected an answer, and three days later Sofia announced its decision "to keep the strictest neutrality and provide for the defence of her territory."[90]

Both France and England were now developing the idea of reforming the Balkan league. Talaat and Halil Pasha were in Sofia during the middle of August, but Savinsky was informed on August 18 that no agreement had been signed.[91] Anglo-Russian rivalry for leadership was becoming apparent.[92] Sazonov instructed Savinsky to advise the Sofia cabinet that they could resume normal relations with Russia, and on August 25 he suggested that Greece might cede the purely Slav districts in Macedonia south of Serbia.[93] Delcassé proposed that Bulgaria be offered Thrace to the Enos-Midia line, in case Bulgaria opposed resistance to a hostile Turkey.[94]

It was in August that Mr. Noel Buxton began his journey to the Balkans in the hope of creating a Balkan federation. He had submitted a memorandum to Grey for securing Bulgarian armed neutrality, thus freeing the other Balkan states from danger. England was to take the

lead in these efforts.[95] Mr. Winston Churchill was particularly enthusiastic over the Buxton mission and the propsect for English leadership in this quarter of the war.[96] Unless Bulgaria were secured, as has been indicated, the British pivot in Greece could not stand. Sazonov, evidently, had known this in August, and had urged *primarily* the Bulgarian alliance.

Both government and press in Bulgaria became increasingly hostile to the Entente during September. The government again proclaimed its neutrality on October 1, and refused Russia the right of free transit of arms or equipment through Bulgaria to Serbia.[97] This would have been an unneutral act, but that fact did not prevent arms, munitions and men from going through from Germany to Turkey.[98]

Sir H. Bax-Ironside, the British minister at Sofia, informed his colleagues on October 4 that England viewed Bulgarian desires with sympathy and was ready to offer financial support to her if she proved friendly.[99] On the same day Radoslavov told Savinsky that Bulgaria would never fight Russia, but at the end of the war might occupy Macedonia. Savinsky informed him that if Bulgaria remained neutral, Russia would give satisfaction to her aspirations.[100]

Russia received no satisfactory answer to her overtures, and in November 1914, the Allied ministers made further advances toward Bulgaria, as well as attempts to induce Serbia to make concessions in Macedonia.[101] On November 2 Savinsky again saw Radoslavov but made little progress. He felt that the three Powers acting in concert might be able to accomplish something. Now that Turkey was definitely in the war Sazonov was willing to offer Bulgaria Thrace to the Enos-Midia line for war against Turkey, and Macedonia (as of the 1912 treaty) for aid against Austria. Savinsky was to speak informally of it, at the same time offering to protect Bulgaria's coast and to assure Rumania's attitude.[102] Sazonov repeated his offer on November 5, but the Radoslavov government again refused. Bax-Ironside would win Bulgarian assistance through a guarantee of immediate occupation of the region east of the Vardar.[103] Savinsky was persuaded that a declaration squarely promising Bulgaria Macedonia, the lure of which was so great that no Bulgarian government could resist the offer, would be successful. The three states could give the necessary guarantee. Pashich could not but understand, for Bulgarian action would entail that of Rumania and Greece.[104] On November 9, Sazonov transmitted to Sofia the identical text of a note on which he, Paléologue and Buchanan had agreed. It guaranteed to Bulgaria, for war against Turkey, the

Enos-Midia line in Thrace and the Vardar line in Macedonia.[105] Savinsky did not feel that this offer would make the Bulgars over-enthusiastic. At the same time he reported that the British minister had been making advances toward Radoslavov with view to seizing the initiative in the Balkans—a direct threat at Russia's own position there. This was the beginning of a rift between England and Russia for supremacy in the Balkans.[106] On November 15 Bax-Ironside had made a démarche with Radoslavov and Dobrovitch, Ferdinand's secretary, offering Bulgaria Thrace (Enos-Midia) and Macedonia (Vardar), as well as financial assistance. His answer, received two days later, declared the intention of Sofia to remain neutral, though no attack would be made on Rumania if she moved with the Entente.[107]

Concessions to Bulgaria depended mainly on Serbian good will, and already obstacles were met from that quarter.[108] On November 17 Savinsky transmitted the following recommendations which the three ministers were sending their governments: (1) The three Powers must not make a new proposition, but develop those already made; (2) Bulgaria must receive after the war a guarantee of acquisitions in Macedonia on the 1912 basis; (3) as proof, the Powers must grant freedom to occupy the territory to the Vardar at once; (4) a promise without immediate occupation will lead only to vague results; (5) the pourparlers must be secret from Serbia, which will be placed before a fait accompli. This was the only means of holding Serbia to the desired concessions.[109] Instead, on November 24, the three ministers presented Radoslavov with a note declaring that if Bulgaria engaged to keep a strict neutrality toward Rumania, Greece and Serbia to the end of the war, the Allies would promise "great territorial compensations," which would be increased if she came into the war against Austria and Turkey. As Savinsky had feared, such a vague declaration met with the response that Bulgaria would remain neutral.[110]

The conduct of Bulgaria continued to inspire distrust. As early as December 4 France had protested against her unneutral conduct in allowing the port of Dedeagatch to be used as a base of supplies for Turkey. Radoslavov denied the allegation.[111]

Sazonov proposed to France and England on December 1 that they declare in common: (1) At Athens, that if Greece came to the aid of Serbia, she would be guaranteed against Bulgaria; (2) they would notify Bulgaria of such intention, and promise her concessions in Macedonia after the war, as well as the Enos-Midia line in Thrace; (3) They would ask the Rumanians to join the démarche of the three,

guaranteeing Greece against an attack.[112] The move was without effect, neither Greece nor Rumania would yield, and when the Allies presented their declaration on December 9, 1914, the response was again that Bulgaria intended to preserve a strict neutrality.[113]

All the Allied efforts in Bulgaria had met with a definite failure.[114] Perhaps the American minister in the Balkans, Mr. Vopicka, had sized up the situation when he wrote on September 30, 1914, that "Bulgaria is trying to get through her diplomacy what she lost on the battlefield last year . . . . Bulgaria is trying to get Macedonia from Serbia, Cavalla from Greece, and Silistria from Rumania without war." None of these countries was willing to cede, and it looked as though nothing was to be done at Sofia.[115]

The Austro-German diplomats in Bulgaria were far from idle during this time. On December 2, 1914, Count Tarnowsky reported to Berchtold that Radoslavov was not satisfied with the promise of Serbian territories, and asked for a written guarantee. But Austria was not disposed to give definite promises as long as Bulgarian troops remained inactive. She would guarantee Serbian lands occupied by these soldiers. Advised that the Entente had given a written promise of Macedonia and Thrace, Tarnowsky replied that the Triplice would offer more. They asked only that Bulgaria take it. Radoslavov apparently considered the Entente proposition the more favorable. Pressed for entrance into the war, however, he demurred that the country was not ready, and demanded a written promise from both Germany and Austria.[116] Sofia was taking no chances either with the Entente or with the Central Powers.

It became increasingly evident that sentiment was swinging clearly toward the Central Powers when Dr. Momchilov, vice-president of the *Sobranje*, declared in the Vienna *Reichspost* of December 25, 1914, that "all Bulgaria knows that Russia, intending by her policy to have the Dardanelles, becomes an enemy for Bulgaria . . . ."[117] He assured Vienna publicly of Bulgaria's attitude. When Russia first mobilized, Sofia took it as an indication of Russia's determination to settle the question of the Straits. Sazonov desired to use the port of Burgas as a base of operations against the Bosphorus and Turkey, but was refused. The Bulgarian government, never enamoured with Russian domination at Constantinople, favored an international solution, and Radoslavov actively urged a Balkan league of Bulgaria, Greece and Rumania against the Russian danger.[118]

Bulgaria was not, however, ready to enter the war. Her attitude depended on the outcome of the Austrian offensive against Serbia.[119] In his speech to the *Sobranje* on January 4, 1915, Radoslavov reiterated his neutrality, and denied any understanding with Austria. The trend of the government was well portrayed when the second instalment of the 500,000,000 franc loan, concluded in Berlin in July 1914, was paid. Increasingly it was felt that the Radoslavov cabinet was binding itself to the Central Powers.[120]

Obtaining the necessary concessions for Bulgaria was difficult under any circumstances. But in the latter part of December 1914 it was particularly so, for by this time the Serbs had driven the Austrians entirely out of the country, and had retaken Belgrade. The Serbs were intransigeant in the matter of Macedonia, and Delcassé was suggesting that the Entente take the situation in hand and impose a settlement on the Balkan states. Rumania might be induced to set an example by ceding the Dobruja.[121]

In January 1915, Noel Buxton, who had returned from his Balkan journey, laid down principles for winning Bulgaria and re-forming the Balkan league. His proposal included: (1) An arrangement dictated by the Allies, in which England was to take a part equally prominent with Russia and France; (2) definite proposals to Bulgaria, which should be communicated to the opposition parties; (3) in the event of victory, a definite promise of Bosnia, Herzegovina, and an outlet to the sea through Dalmatia to Serbia, which was then to cede Macedonia (on the 1912 basis) to Bulgaria; (4) Bulgarian security against Turkey, and the cession of Cavalla by Greece, conditioned on the promise of Smyrna to Greece.[122]

Isvolsky reported his conversations with Buxton on January 10, 1915. When Delcassé spoke with him on the Smyrna concession, however, the French foreign minister observed that Smyrna, where France had large financial interests, was bound up with the whole question of Asiatic Turkey, and any action must take that fact into consideration.[123]

Rumors of a new offensive against Serbia induced Delcassé to make another proposal for a Balkan démarche.[124] His program, telegraphed to Sazonov on January 28, 1915, called for good relations between Bulgaria and Serbia, with concessions conditioned on a Serbian outlet to the Adriatic. Greece was to unite with Serbia in return for Asiatic territory, and Bulgaria was to receive the Enos-Media line in Thrace and Macedonia after the war. Both Monastir and Uskub (Skoplje) remained Serb. Financial aid was to be given Bulgaria, which was not only

to refrain from attacking Serbia, Rumania or Greece, but to move against Turkey. Rumania was to be brought into the camp of the Entente and to make concessions in the Dobruja to Bulgaria.

When these propositions were presented to Pashich, he complained that Serbia could not cede more than the Vardar line in Macedonia, that Greece and Rumania should make concessions, that Russia should not have held out such large hopes to Bulgaria, and he threatened to resign if more were demanded of his country.[125] Sazonov was willing to concede when Serbia entered her Adriatic heritage, but Savinsky felt that the propositions would not lure Radoslavov, who had been promised as much for neutrality.[126] In the meantime, Delcassé was certain that large concessions to Serbia on the Adriatic would irritate Italy.[127] The final result was that the proposed declaration never materialized.

Early in February the French government sent the Duke of Guise to Sofia to influence Ferdinand, the grandson of Louis Philippe, but he was unable to accomplish anything with his wily kinsman.[128]

The first week in February 1915, witnessed a meeting at Paris, at which Lloyd George proposed sending a mixed army to Serbia for the purpose of influencing Greece, Rumania and Bulgaria. Millerand, French war minister, opposed the plan, and Russia received it with caution. The Grand Duke Nicholas consented at first only to the sending of a single Cossack regiment, but later expanded this to a brigade of infantry.[129]

While the months of March and April were occupied with the negotiations which resulted in Italy's entrance into the war, the Balkan negotiations continued. Operations against the Dardanelles were beginning, the success of which would alter radically the entire situation in the Balkans. Success would entrain the entrance of Bulgaria, Greece and Rumania; failure would lose the Balkans.[130]

On February 15 Grey proposed that the Powers declare to Sofia their general sympathy for Bulgaria, and to ask her conditions for action. Delcassé felt that Radoslavov and his government were already too much bound to the Triplice to be subject to pressure, but thought a decisive influence would be exercised "by the issue of the Allied operations against the Straits and Constantinople."[131] Radoslavov informed Savinsky on February 26 that Bulgaria particularly wanted Cavalla from Greece, and would renounce Salonica forever, in return. The Russian minister was convinced that Sofia could be purchased at that price, if Greece were out of the question.[132] This was confirmed

on March 1, 1915, in a telegram which Radoslavov sent to his minister in London, instructing him to "continue to emphasize the Bulgarian decision of a strict neutrality but useful to the Triple [Entente? Alliance?] and for that, demand the Dobruja, Macedonia with Cavalla."[133]

Serbia remained adamant on the Macedonian question. Bulgarian *comitadjis* continued their activity throughout March, and on March 22 Pashich begged the Powers to enter into no *pourparlers* with Sofia to the detriment of Serbia.[134] Only three days later, however, Paléologue, in a conversation with Madjarov, the Bulgarian minister in Russia, again offered Macedonia and Thrace, with financial aid, and guarantees against Rumania and Greece, if Bulgaria came to the Entente's aid.[135] Meanwhile, Sazonov was not impressed with the Greek offer of aid to Serbia, and instead proposed that the Powers protest against the activities of the Bulgarian *comitadji*, armed and organized by the Austrians, who aimed to destroy the Serbian-Nish-Salonica railways. Delcassé declared for a categorical statement at Sofia that an attack on Serbia would mean war with the Entente, and suggested a Russian landing at Varna. Savinsky believed that such a landing would rally the people of Bulgaria to Russia.[136]

Negotiations with Rumania were now in full sway, and the demands of the Bucharest cabinet were causing trouble in both Russia and Serbia.[137] The latter part of April brought news to St. Petersburg of a possible Turco-Bulgarian neutrality compact, by which Turkey was to cede the Enos-Midia line in Thrace—a bargain which Germany and Austria were encouraging.[138]

In May efforts to bring Bulgaria into the war were redoubled. Italy was moving into action against the Central Powers. Perhaps Rumania would follow the example of her Latin sister. On May 4 Sazonov agreed with Grey's proposition to renew active negotiations at Sofia, and both were to undertake conversations. From May 19 to 24, 1915, Sazonov advised Savinsky of his willingness to cede Bulgaria immediate possession of the Enos-Midia line in Thrace for an attack on Turkey, and after the war, when Serbia had her Adriatic outlet, Macedonia (on the 1912 basis). In addition the Powers would influence Greece to surrender Cavalla, comprising the Seres-Drama district, if Grey and Delcassé were willing. Rumania would be asked to give up a part of the Dobruja.[139] This meant giving most of what Bulgaria demanded. Stantsiov, Bulgarian minister at Paris, already had demanded of Delcassé both the "contested" and "uncontested" zones in Macedonia, Cavalla and part of the Dobruja.[140] Doubtless this overture was

produced by Italy's adhesion to the Allied cause, and the favorable position of the Allies in the Gallipoli peninsula. At any rate, the Sofia cabinet was making a bid for large stakes. Sazonov suggested to Nish that Serbia should be willing to cede the Egri Palanka-Sopot-Okhrida line in Macedonia after the war, but it availed little.[141] Grey telegraphed Rodd in Rome on May 26 that with Italy's adherence the time to bring Bulgaria into action had arrived. He, too, suggested that Serbia concede Macedonia, including Monastir, when Serbia obtained Bosnia, Herzegovina and a part of the Dalmatian coast. Bulgaria would then receive Thrace and the Allies could influence Greece to give up Cavalla in return for Smyrna.[142]

Italy was asked to join the démarche, and on May 29, 1915, the Entente definitely offered Bulgaria the territories outlined both in Thrace and Macedonia, and guaranteed to use all their efforts to obtain Cavalla from Greece and the Dobruja from Rumania.[143] This was the supreme moment in the negotiations with Bulgaria. Austria, however, submitted a more luring offer on June 5 when, in return for her *neutrality*, Bulgaria was promised at the end of the war, all of Serbian Macedonia, and the territories given to Greece and Rumania in 1913, if these Powers declared war on the Triple Alliance.[144]

The Bulgarian reply to the Allied note did not come until June 14, and when it did arrive, it merely asked for further explanations.[145] Meanwhile the Sofia cabinet was in negotiations with Turkey for the retrocession of the right bank of the Maritza in return for a favorable attitude toward Turkey and the Central Powers. Austria and Germany increased their pressure on Radoslavov, who, much disappointed at not receiving an immediate cession of Serbian Macedonia from the Entente, was more than ever inclined to Austria and Germany.[146] When Sir Valentine Chirol arrived in Sofia on an official mission in July, the situation seemed hopeless.[147]

Having failed to secure Bulgaria in May the Allies had recourse to other means. The British government proposed to use the projected Salonica expedition to occupy the "uncontested" zone in Macedonia and thus to guarantee it to Bulgaria. As Grey wrote to O'Beirne, who had succeeded Bax-Ironside at Sofia, "The Allies can, and if necessary will, refuse to recognize any extension of Serbia until she has conceded the uncontested zone . . .; they will arrange with Serbia for Allied forces to occupy to the Vardar as a guarantee to Bulgaria."[148] Without a sufficient guarantee of Macedonia, Bulgaria would not move. The Serbian government would not yield, despite the pressure of the

Allies, and protested against the Italian gains on the Adriatic. Many preferred to fight Bulgaria rather than surrender Macedonia.[149] When the four Allied ministers presented an identical note on August 4 demanding the Macedonian concession, in return for Serbia's aggrandizement, Pashich protested that it was almost impossible to give in. Serbia required a guarantee of her own future on the Adriatic, which in turn aroused the objections of France and Italy. The government at Nish did not want to yield in Macedonia if Italy were to control the Dalmatian littoral, while Greece raised objections on the Cavalla cessions.[150]

On August 3 the Entente ministers presented a note to Bulgaria guaranteeing Macedonia and immediate possession of Thrace to Enos-Midia, signifying their refusal to allow Greek or Serbian gains until they had conceded to Bulgaria.[151] Both Greece and Serbia protested and the note was without effect.

Bulgaria was now preparing to enter the war on the side of the Central Powers. O'Beirne reported to Grey on August 20 that Sofia was nearing a decision and only a faint chance of one favorable to the Allies remained.[152] German successes in the east—particularly the Russian break at Gorlice on May 2, which resulted in the retreat from Galicia—and the Allied failure at the Dardanelles had their inevitable influence. In July, under pressure from German great headquarters, Austro-German efforts to bring Bulgaria into the struggle were renewed vigorously. Indeed, General von Falkenhayn, chief of staff of the imperial armies, seems preëminently to have appreciated the importance of the Balkans, and Bulgaria in particular. Nor was von Hindenburg unaware of the vital significance of Bulgaria as the connecting link between Turkey and the Central Powers. Toward the latter part of August, Lieutenant-Colonel Gantshev was sent to German headquarters to negotiate terms.[153] The presence of the Duke of Mecklenburg-Schwerin at Sofia was but a presage of the course of events.[154]

Apparently the Allied pressure on Serbia had brought that country to desperation in the summer of 1915. Count Tarnowsky had reported from Sofia as early as May 22, 1915, that there were certain signs of a possible overture from Serbia to the Central Powers for a separate peace. In August it appeared that M. Marghiloman, the Rumanian statesman, was attempting to mediate along this line. Toward the end of September von Jagow was hoping that a Serbian surrender might obviate the necessity of a great Balkan campaign. But the desire of Austria-Hungary and Bulgaria to destroy Serbia as a political factor in

the Balkans finally triumphed over the more conservative and practical aims of Berlin.[155] Whatever the plight of Serbia, on August 20 and 21, Pashich appeared before the *Skupshtina* and declared the position of the Allied governments on the issue of Macedonia, the central point of conflict between Serbia and Bulgaria. The Entente informed Radoslavov on August 21 that Bulgaria would be guaranteed Macedonia if she attacked Turkey immediately.[156] On August 28 Pashich himself made an overture toward Bulgaria with an offer of the Vardar line in Macedonia; but this did not suit the more exacting Bulgarian premier. Only in September did Nish yield and agree to the cession of Macedonia (on the 1912 basis), with the exception of Skoplje and Prilep. In return the Serbs expected Croatia, Slovenia and a part of the Adriatic littoral, as well as a common Greco-Serb frontier. The Powers now could occupy the territory as a guarantee.[157]

But it was too late. Negotiations between Turkey and Bulgaria, which had been engineered for some time from the German embassy in Constantinople, resulted in the Turco-Bulgarian treaty of September 3, 1915.[158] By the terms of this agreement, in return for Bulgarian "neutrality," Turkey ceded Thrace, including the district of Mustapha Pasha to the Aegean sea at Enos, the right bank of the Maritza, and the district north of Adrianople and Dedeagatch. The Serbs and Russians rightly understood the significance of this overture. Bulgaria was going to war against the Allies.[159]

Events moved rapidly. On September 6 Bulgaria signed a treaty of alliance with Germany and Austria. The treaty provided for mutual aid against attack from a bordering state, and was to remain in force unless renewed, until December 31, 1920. A military convention signed the same day gave supreme command of the Austro-German-Bulgarian forces to Mackensen, whose object was "to bring about and assure as soon as possible *liaison* by land between Hungary and Bulgaria," and consequently communication between the Central Powers and Turkey. Within thirty days from the signature of the convention, the Austro-German forces were to advance on Serbia from the north, and five days later the Bulgars were to march. A secret convention delimited the territorial compensations Bulgaria was to receive. These involved both the "contested" and "uncontested" zones in Macedonia. In case Rumania joined the Entente, Bulgaria would obtain the Dobruja territory lost in 1913. If Greece proved hostile, Bulgaria would acquire Cavalla. Finally Austria and Germany engaged to lend Bulgaria 200,000,000 francs to be paid in four instalments.[160]

The Allied ministers added to their previous offers on September 13 by promising Bulgaria after the war, not only the "contested" but the "uncontested" zone, for a declaration against Turkey.[161] But on September 21 the Bulgarian army mobilized. While Radoslavov announced to the world the purely precautionary and non-aggressive character of the mobilization, he telegraphed Vienna to pay the first instalment of the loan, in fulfilment of the terms of the alliance.[162] In accordance with the Turkish agreement, immediately on the issuance of these orders, Turkey ceded the right bank of the Maritza, as well as the territory north of Adrianople, between the Tunja, the Maritza and the frontier. Turkey was taking no chances with Sofia.[163]

The Allies had received no reply on their offer of September 13 and Sazonov warned Savinsky on September 21 that if a satisfactory answer were not forthcoming, the Allied ministers would leave the Bulgarian capital. He did not want to precipitate matters however.[164] Instead, every effort was made to conciliate Bulgaria. When Pashich was finding extreme difficulty in ceding the "uncontested" zone in Macedonia, Sazonov was suggesting placing it at the disposal of the tsar. On September 28 Grey announced to the House of Commons that British policy in the Balkans was based on agreement between the Balkan states, on the principle of nationalities, and had no hostile intention against Bulgaria unless she proved aggressive.[165]

Sazonov again warned Radoslavov against any hostile action on October 2. Two days later France, England and Russia presented a twenty-four hour ultimatum to the Sofia government. Radoslavov replied the same day in a note characterized by its insolence and duplicity, which was quite unsatisfactory to the Entente. Whereupon, on October 7, 1915, the Allied ministers left the Bulgarian capital and broke off diplomatic relations.[166]

William II had saluted the Bulgarian alliance "with joy," for Bulgaria had now joined Germany, and a direct connection with Turkey could be opened up by land through the Balkans, once Serbia had been crushed. On September 29 orders for a Bulgarian attack on Serbia had been sent from Vienna, carried by Captain Prince Windischgraetz through Bucharest to Sofia. The forces of the Central Powers crossed the Danube into Serbia on October 7. Three days later the general secretary of the Sofia foreign office advised Tarnowsky that an incident would have to be created in order to make the war properly defensive and save Constantine's position in Greece. This incident took place as arranged and the Bulgarian forces crossed the

Serb frontier, beginning the march into Macedonia on October 11.[167] All the Allied attempts to relieve Serbia were dismal failures, and by February 1916 that country was entirely in the hands of the Central Powers. Eventually the remnants of the Serb army found refuge in the island of Corfu, where they were rebuilt into an efficient fighting force to be used in reconquering Serbia in the closing months of the war. An allied Mitteleuropa, under the domination of Berlin now stretched from the Persian gulf to the North sea, untroubled by the small Slav state which had barred the way.

What was to be done with Serbia? General Falkenhayn proposed in November 1915 that the war with Serbia be brought to a speedy close, and that terms be offered on the basis of complete surrender, and union of "what is left of Serbia with Montenegro and Albania, under the Montenegrin dynasty."[168] Count Metternich, who had succeeded the late Baron Wangenheim as German ambassador at Constantinople, expressed himself as in favor of a separate peace with Serbia, and was distinctly opposed to the entire disappearance of Serbia from the Balkan map. Likewise he looked on the independent existence of Albania as a farce. Radoslavov, somewhat naturally, appears to have been in favor of the complete destruction of the Serbian kingdom. The Margrave Pallavicini was in agreement with his German colleague, on the ground that with the disappearance of Serbia, a big Bulgaria would become the dominant Slav state in the new Balkans, and would be quite as dangerous as Serbia had been. "It seems to me not out of the question that this Great Bulgaria also might come into the wake of Russia and pursue under her aegis a far-sighted policy at the expense of the Monarchy." The aim of the Monarchy then should be to create a new equilibrium in the Balkans, preserve a Serb state "small but still capable of life," support Greek aspirations in southern Albania, stir up the Bulgarians—and above all prevent any sort of Balkan unity.[169]

Most cynical of all was the attitude of Count Stephen Tisza, the stern Calvinist premier of Hungary. In two memoranda addressed to the Emperor Francis Joseph and to Baron Burian in December 1915, Tisza proposes not annexation of Serbia to the Dual Monarchy, but cutting the country to pieces, and its division among its neighbors. Tisza realized the danger of annexing any part of Serbia to Austria-Hungary and the addition of new Slav elements to the empire's racial melting pot. He therefore proposed that Bulgaria annex Macedonia and the Serb territory east of the Morava river. Albania was to take

land both from Serbia and Montenegro; and Serbia was to be excluded from the Adriatic. Hungary was to annex the territory around Belgrade, and the district along the south bank of the Save and Danube. In order to prevent the danger imminent in such an annexation of Slav territory, German and Magyar colonization was to be introduced. As if to add the final blow, this small, mangled state was to be "bound by economic and military ties to the Monarchy," and the Karageorge dynasty was to disappear.[170] Such were the Austrian plans for "reconstruction" in the Balkans.

Meanwhile all opposition, as has been pointed out, to the policy of Tsar Ferdinand and the Radoslavov clique in Bulgaria was without avail. A final appeal of the opposition on September 17, 1915, did not influence Ferdinand. Bulgaria was determined to achieve her aims under the supposedly invincible arms of Austria and Germany. Radoslavov, in announcing the war declaration to the *Sobranje*, proclaimed the danger of Russian possession of the Straits, the insufficiency of Allied offers, and his unflinching faith in German victory.[171] The Bulgarian premier was anxious to crush Serbia and secure possession of Macedonia. The decision which Radoslavov and Ferdinand had made was to cost Bulgaria dearly, but the Rubicon had been crossed, and there could be no turning back until the very end of the great conflict.

The diplomacy of the Central Powers, directed by the high command, was a complete success in Bulgaria. The Allies, though divided in their Balkan policy, had made substantial offers to Bulgaria, but they were either of such a general nature, or (when specific) came so late as to be ineffective. Yet it is conceivable that Bulgarian interests might have dictated an action in favor of the Entente, as many of the opposition leaders at Sofia wanted, and as the results of the world war amply demonstrate. Why, then, did Bulgaria finally turn to Germany and Austria? The answer seems to be apparent. The Bulgarian government desired to secure immediate occupation of Macedonia; the personal policy of Ferdinand and that of the Radoslavov cabinet clearly followed an Austro-German orientation since 1913; the failure of the Allies at the Dardanelles, and the seeming invincibility of German arms naturally influenced the government; Bulgaria feared Russian domination at the Straits; and, lack of unity in Allied Balkan policy gave the Central Powers a better chance to dominate at Sofia.[172]

## Rumania and the War

If Italy followed a policy of "sacred egoism," Rumania pursued that of "national instinct." Each country had been the ally of the Triplice since the 1880's; each had declared its neutrality at the outbreak of the war; each had national aspirations which could be fulfilled at the expense of the Dual Monarchy. Both states from the beginning followed a program of bargaining, offering their services at a high price—so high, indeed, that it was only through the pressure of France and England that Russia agreed to their entrance into the war.[173] Bratianu, prime minister in the Bucharest cabinet, had a clearly defined policy from the inception of the conflict. That policy was to declare Rumanian neutrality and wait until the certainty of Entente victory. Rumania must be the enemy of Austria-Hungary, but since the war would be a long one, he would not enter the struggle, until the last stages, when Rumania could achieve her aims at Austrian expense with minimum effort. In it all Bratianu miscalculated only on the time of Rumanian entry. The result was a terrible defeat for Rumanian arms, though the country achieved all her national aspirations through the victory of the Entente.

At the outbreak of the war Rumania declared her neutrality despite the Germanic tendencies of the Hohenzollern monarch, the insistence of the conservatives, and the terms of the alliance of thirty years' standing with the Central Powers. The crown council of August 3, 1914, had decided that issue.[174]

Rumania's interest in her 3,000,000 *confrères* in Austria-Hunagry, virtually precluded her attachment to the Austro-German forces. Neutrality signified a policy of watchful waiting, with ultimate war against the Dual Monarchy seemingly in view.[175] So far as the question of Turkey is concerned, Rumania was involved in the attempts to form a Balkan league, and in the solution of the Straits question, in accordance with her interests. Relations with Bulgaria centered about the Dobruja, which Rumania had seized in 1913.

As early as July 30, 1914, Sazonov wired Poklevsky, the Russian minister at Bucharest, that he could offer Transylvania to Bratianu for entrance into the war. This was in line with French ideas.[176] At the same time Austria was offering special arrangements for the Rumanians of Austria-Hungary to win the favor of Bucharest.[177] On August 9

Sazonov proposed to London and Paris that they attempt to win Rumania on the promise of the coveted Transylvania. Blondel, the French minister, thought at this time, however, that Rumanian neutrality was more valuable to the Entente.[178]

Bratianu signified his willingness to act with Russia early in September providing Rumania's territorial integrity were secured and territorial increases at the hands of her enemies guaranteed. Poklevsky recognized the value of definite connections with Rumania, since it was hardly possible to prevent her growth in the event of Allied victory.[179] The Russian victory in Galicia produced an enormous influence in Bucharest, and it looked as though Rumania would march with the Entente, if Italy moved in that direction.[180] Doubtless it was this fact which led Austria to propose in mid-September to grant a special status to Rumanians in Transylvania, frontier rectifications in Bukovina, and to offer Rumania all Bessarabia and Odessa. The Ukraine, as a vassal of Austria, would form a protecting buffer against the Russian bear.[181]

Already on September 16 Sazonov had instructed Poklevsky to offer immediate possession of southern Bukovina and Transylvania, then in Russian possession, if Rumania would enter the war. On hearing of the Austrian proposal he urged his minister to propose "not only autonomy, but the annexation of Transylvania."[182] When Poklevsky made this declaration Bratianu demurred, asking for written promises from the Entente. In reply, Sazonov wanted Bratianu to understand that he was asking Rumania to occupy territory without effort, but that the most to be offered for neutrality would be Transylvania, after the war.[183] Bratianu then asked if this were a proposition for neutrality. This led Sazonov to work out a formula with Diamandy, Rumanian minister at St. Petersburg, whereby, in return for recognition of Rumania's right to annex "provinces of Rumanian population" in the Dual Monarchy including part of Bukovina, Rumania was to observe a benevolent neutrality toward Russia.[184] Bratianu proposed two additional points—that Russia guarantee Rumania's present territory and the river Pruth for a boundary in Bukovina. The accord was to remain secret, and was formulated on October 1. Two days later Sazonov notified the embassy at Bucharest.[185]

Sazonov instructed Poklevsky to explain that he would not use armed force to protect Rumanian territory, and that "benevolent" neutrality meant prohibition of transit for enemy munitions across Rumania, and the privilege of such transit from Russia through Rumania

to Serbia. Bratianu, however, hoped that in case of Rumania's entrance into the war, Russia would aid with troops. On the other hand, he did not see how he could prevent munitions crossing to Turkey and Bulgaria over Rumanian soil. This would arouse Austrian and German hostility and prevent Rumanian war supplies from coming from Germany—supplies which were necessary for a possible campaign against the Central Powers.[186]

The Turkish declaration of war influenced Bratianu, who now felt that if Bulgaria marched against Serbia, Rumania could not occupy the desired Austrian territory. Fear of Bulgaria carried great weight at Bucharest. Bratianu refused any concessions to Sofia in the Dobruja, though some opposition leaders envisaged such in the interest of happier relations.[187] By this time public opinion was frankly on the side of the Entente, and even the members of the conservative opposition were in favor of war with the Central Powers. As Count Czernin wrote to Berchtold after the death of the king, there were only two parties left in Rumania—those who believed in immediate war, and those ("our friends") who believed in delay, since Austria was not yet beaten.[188] Both Filipescu and Ionescu were advising war, but Bratianu hesitated on the pretext of unpreparedness. Great Britain and France were ready to extend financial assistance. Sazonov, on November 14, insisted that Rumania must enter the war and take Transylvania before the Serbs were crushed. Four days later he suggested informing Bucharest of Radoslavov's formal statement of November 17, promising neutrality, but Rumania was not ready for action. Bratianu told the Belgian minister that he would not cede the Dobruja to Bulgaria, unless he obtained Bessarabia from Russia—with the evident intention of securing Rumania's Danubian outlet to the Black sea. This did not prevent him from expressing his regret at Serbian and Greek obstinacy in failing to cede parts of Macedonia to Bulgaria.[189]

As we have seen—it was in December 1914—in view of the impending Austrian drive against Serbia, the Entente began to redouble efforts to re-constitute the Balkan *bloc*, and to bring Rumania, Bulgaria and Greece into their ranks. This demanded wide-reaching concessions to Bulgaria in Macedonia and the Dobruja. France was urging immediate action by Rumania, only to receive the answer that Bucharest was unprepared for a decision. On December 2 Sazonov advised Diamandy of the Austrian danger to Serbia, and expressed his lack of faith in the reasons of Bratianu.[190] While Bratianu realized the supreme importance

of the Balkan *bloc*, he rejected the idea of a sacrifice to Bulgaria. Sazonov thought that a concession in the Dobruja would facilitate action in Serbia, while Bucharest could obtain compensation in Transylvania. But Bratianu objected that concessions in Macedonia alone would satisfy Sofia—and he was partially correct—the Dobruja being only of secondary importance. Nor would he consent to a concession without an assurance that the Entente already had persuaded Bulgaria to intervene on their side. For these reasons Poklevsky thought it best not to open the subject officially.[191] Both the French and British ministers were instructed to concert with Poklevsky, and Sazonov felt that concessions from both Serbia and Rumania were necessary. Trubetzkoy, Russian minister at Nish, telegraphed Sazonov on December 14 that Rumanian action would have influence in Serbia. He would like a conditional promise from Bratianu to attack, if Bulgaria moved against the Serbs. Two days later Sazonov wired Bucharest that efforts must be directed toward forming the Balkan *bloc*. Macedonian concessions especially were necessary, but Rumanian action in the Dobruja would set an example for both Serbia and Greece. He suggested an accord between Bratianu and Pashich for a simultaneous transfer of territories to Bulgaria. Greece would be asked to join only a *fait accompli*.[192] Delcassé, however, did not approve the idea, as he felt that neither Bucharest nor Nish would concede, save by the imposed authority of the Allies.[193]

Throughout this period neither Count Czernin nor Busche, the Austrian and German ministers, spared efforts to hold Rumania to the Central Powers. Czernin knew that an agreement with Bratianu was impossible, but were he overthrown and Marghiloman or Maiorescu installed, territorial concessions in Transylvania and Bukovina might be effective. Certainly the promise of special political status to Rumanian minorities in the Monarchy, which alone Tisza was willing to grant, was not efficacious. More and more, opinion was becoming pro-Entente.[194]

Sazonov complained to Diamandy on January 10, 1915, concerning the attitude of his country. On the one hand the government prepared for war, and on the other it was attempting to form a neutral league to prevent Balkan domination by the Slavs, and Russian supremacy in the Straits. He wanted a frank exchange in view of Rumania's supposed "benevolent neutrality" toward Russia. When Poklevsky broached the matter with Bratianu, he was told that Rumania had attempted to form no such league, but was preparing to join in the fray

169

when Italy answered the summons of the Entente. Russia knew of Rumania's policy in regard to Bulgaria, and Bratianu hoped for a Bulgaro-Serb accord. On January 22, 1915, Sazonov learned that Rumania was then in negotiations for the formation of a Greco-Serb-Bulgarian alliance against Russia and Serbia "in view of preventing the Slav danger in case Russia occupies Constantinople and the Straits." Greece was fearful lest her interests, in view of a partition of Turkey, would be endangered unless she adhered to this accord.[195] Sonnino informed Carlotti on February 19 that Rumania would never accept a plan placing the Straits in the hands of any single Power—Russia. While the negotiations for the cession of Constantinople to Russia were being initiated, Grey advised Bucharest that the freedom of commerce in the Straits would be guaranteed.[196]

The Bulgarian minister at St. Petersburg, Madjarov, wrote Radoslavov on March 3, 1915, affirming that Rumania was favorable to the Entente. Having concluded a loan in London, on the condition that it was not to be used against Allied interests, Rumania would march when Russia had a sufficient number of troops in Bukovina, when Italy entered the war, or when Bulgaria joined. In exchange for Transylvania, Bucharest would cede the Dobruja to Bulgaria.[197]

When the negotiations with Italy approached a successful end, Rumania showed renewed signs of activity. Her demands were very heavy. On April 21, 1915, Poklevsky wired Sazonov that Rumania desired not only Transylvania, the Pruth line in Bukovina, and the Banat, but the active military coöperation of Russia.[198] Russia felt the demands were exaggerated, and Neratov relegraphed Isvolsky on April 30 to advise Delcassé that "if, renouncing the ethnographic principle, Rumania insists on annexing almost all Bukovina to the detriment of Russian interests and all the Banat at the expense of the Serbs," an accord would meet almost insuperable difficulties. He hoped these demands would not be encouraged by the Allies.[199] The next day Bratianu explained to Poklevsky that he was preparing to enter the war with the briefest delay, since Italy was on the verge of action. The territorial acquisitions expected were large: Bukovina to the Pruth, Transylvania, the Banat to the Tisza, and a large part of Hungary. Poklevsky protested against such exactions, but advised a conciliatory answer. Meanwhile Delcassé had assured Isvolsky that he would counsel Bucharest to be moderate.[200]

Sazonov was ready on May 2 to negotiate with Rumania to bring her into the Entente. But when the full extent of the Rumanian demands

became evident, he told Diamandy that "such demands were not acceptable." He could not sacrifice both Russian and Serb interests.[201] This was on May 3. On the same day the Grand Duke Nicholas telegraphed St. Petersburg that Rumania was of little importance, in view of Italy's imminent action, and her demands "absolutely in-acceptable."[202] Whereupon Bratianu told Blondel that unless Rumania were given the desired concessions she would not march with the Allies.[203] Sazonov would not concede. Under pressure from Paris, however, on May 19 he signified his willingness to accept a compromise outlined by Paléologue, whereby Rumania would receive the Sereth line in Bukovina and the northeast part of the Torontal district in the Banat.[204]

While the developments in Italy pushed Rumania to make further requisitions of the Entente, that fact did not preclude simultaneous negotiations with Austria and Germany. As the Italian zero hour dawned, Rumania's demands on Austria increased. Bukovina and the Banat were at stake in the Austro-Rumanian negotiations for Rumanian neutrality. Convinced as he was that Rumania was lost, Tisza would listen to no suggestions from Czernin or others concerning the cession of any Hungarian territory.[205] On the other hand, Tisza was quite willing to cut off the territory of other countries. In December 1915 he wrote: "*Cut off from the body of the Serbian state all that has been promised to Serbia and Montenegro which naturally belong to it, cut Montenegro off from the Adriatic, and we need only to annex the north-west corner of Serbia to separate Serbia and Montenegro from the outer world and to make them wholly dependent on the Monarchy.*"[206] No more conciliatory, Burian informed Czernin on May 23 that a victorious Russia would never allow a strengthened and enlarged Rumania to bar her way to the Straits.[207]

Berlin was naturally more willing to sacrifice Austro-Hungarian territory to Rumania and urged conciliation. Neither Erzberger, of the German Reichstag, nor Bethmann-Hollweg, however, were able to move Tisza, when they urged a territorial cession in June 1915.[208] Both Bethmann and Jagow were in Vienna on June 25, 1915, attempting to use pressure on Burian to cede territory in return for the right of passage of munitions across Rumania to Bulgaria and Turkey. Tisza had undergone a slight conversion, but when the offer was made in Bucharest, it met a refusal.[209]

The long drawn out bargaining with the Allies continued. On June 18 Bratianu signified his willingness to enter the war, two months

after the signature of a political accord with the Entente, with a military agreement fixing the exact conditions.[210] The Russian general staff was now in favor of pacifying Rumania, in view of the military situation. Favorable action, the military felt, would close the Rumanian frontier to military provisions for Turkey. Rumania could be given some supplies of war. In the Banat, Serbia could be protected by a zone around Belgrade.[211] But Bratianu stood his ground. This exasperated Delcassé, since practically all the concessions had been made. The French minister was of the opinion that satisfactions to Rumania would call for Serbian aggrandizement not only in Bosnia, Herzegovina, and a part of the Dalmatian coast, but also in Croatia. This might win both Rumania and Bulgaria, and lead to the formation of the Balkan union.[212]

The Russian defeat at Gorlice, the retreat from Galicia and the indifferent success of the French offensive in the west brought renewed demands for Rumanian participation, but these failures distinctly cooled the ardor of Bratianu and his followers. Isvolsky wired Sazonov that a failure in the Rumanian negotiations would be laid at his door.[213] Sazonov's answer of June 30 was that Russia was ready to satisfy all Rumania's requirements in Bukovina, under the condition that she enter the war within five weeks. Bratianu, however, insisted on the entire Banat.[214] He seemed willing to surrender Semlin and a protected zone about Belgrade, and on July 10 Sazonov urged pressure on Rumania in the loan negotiations at London. [215] At the same time Sazonov, in agreement with France and England, was giving in to all Rumania's claims for territory in Transylvania, Bukovina and the Banat. In return, Rumania was to promise to go to war within five weeks after the signature of a political convention, to prohibit passage of war materials to Turkey, give up the Dobruja and Balchik to Bulgaria, and to cede to Serbia in the Banat.[216] Russia had given in only at the insistence of France and England. In both military and diplomatic policy, it seemed that the desires of Petrograd must be subordinated to London and Paris.[217]

Final efforts to hold Bulgaria in leash were now being made. On August 14 Bratianu told Poklevsky of a conversation with the Serbian minister, in which the latter expressed the willingness of his government to surrender the Vardar line in Macedonia. The prospect of the London loan to Rumania in September again aroused Sazonov's hopes of bringing pressure on Bucharest.[218]

Bulgaria's entrance into the war brought renewed abuse from the western Allies on Russia's Balkan policy. Great importance was attached to the Balkans. The German operations in the peninsula would now not only drive a wedge between the Allies, but would open completely the road to Asia Minor. Isvolsky telegraphed on October 12, 1915:

*"They remarked that after the war it is Russia which will obtain the most advantages to the detriment of Turkey, and that if she does not participate in the common [effort?] France and England will be obliged to re-examine (remettre à l'étude) their decision on the subject of Constantinople and the Straits."*[219]

The Rumanian loan negotiations at London brought tempting offers from the Central Powers. It was learned that Germany had offered a large loan, and the cession of Bessarabia and Bukovina after the war, in return for Rumanian action against the Entente.[220]

But Bratianu remained true to his course. At the beginning of November he informed the English minister that he would not allow a Russian army to cross Rumania to aid Serbia. His military terms for Rumanian assistance to the Entente included an Anglo-French army of 500,000 men in the Balkans, a Russian army of 200,000 in Bessarabia, an attack of these armies on Bulgaria, a Russian offensive against the Austro-Germans from the Baltic to Bukovina, and the assurance of war munitions and supplies from France and England. Until all these conditions were realities Rumania would retain a free hand. For the time being, therefore, Rumanian aid seemed out of the question, despite the demands of Filipescu and Ionescu for immediate action.[221] General Alexeiev, it is interesting to note, had outlined a plan for a gigantic drive through the Balkans, which would finally entrain both Greece and Rumania.[222]

Rumania's attitude thus far was the result of many factors. Among these, as indicated, the question of the Straits played its inevitable rôle. Rumors that the Straits had been promised Russia in the spring of 1915 had spread naturally, and knowledge of Russian aims in the war caused fear in many Bucharest political circles. Paléologue had proclaimed in March that Russia's ambitions might prevent both Italy and Rumania from joining the Entente.[223] In a remarkable address before the Rumanian chamber of deputies on December 16-17, 1915,[224] M. Také Ionescu, conservative Ententophil, urged action with the Allies as the only way of realizing her national dreams at Austro-Hungarian expense. As to the Straits, he said: "Does it depend on us who will take

the Straits? . . . . It may be that the Russians will take the Straits. It may be that the Allies will take the Straits. One thing, however, is certain—that the Turks will not stay in the Straits." Rumania could not be the deciding factor in any case. In the end, apparently, this attitude prevailed.[225]

Nevertheless, Rumania was not ready to unfurl her battle flags and send her legions into the great conflict. During the latter part of January 1916, Bratianu's policy was placing his country in a dangerous position. The Central Powers were adopting a threatening attitude, with a possible ultimatum in view. Russian troops would be necessary to protect Rumania from a Bulgarian attack in the Dobruja, the real object of which was to enable Rumania to concentrate her forces for the seizure of Transylvania. On January 26 Sazonov actually proposed an offensive of the Salonica expedition against Bulgaria, if the latter threatened Rumania.[226] The Russian general staff drew up a project for helping Rumania, but as Diamandy received no instructions, nothing came of it.[227] Poincaré made an appeal to the tsar on March 1 for pressure on Rumania. Nicholas replied that Russia was doing everything in her power to hasten the action of the Bucharest cabinet.[228]

Relations with the Central Powers were eased when a commercial treaty was signed with Germany on April 7, 1916. Nor was this treaty without political significance. The closing of the Dardanelles and the attitude of Bulgaria forced most of Rumania's agricultural products towards Vienna and Berlin. The treaty produced a most unfavorable impression on Russia.[229]

By this time the Russo-Rumanian negotiations met the active opposition of the Russian general staff. In a memorandum of April 1916, Basili, of the diplomatic chancery of general headquarters, stated that under the conditions demanded, not only would the unity of the tsar's armies be destroyed, but Rumanian occupation of Transylvania would be a strategic blunder and lead to her own isolation.[230] Moreover the Russians believed that tempting German propositions might be made to Bratianu.[231]

Brusilov's brilliant June offensive, which was sweeping everything before it, again aroused excitement in Bucharest, and the negotiations for entry into the struggle received fresh impetus. It was the supreme moment for Rumanian action, as Sazonov rightly informed Paléologue. On June 25 France virtually demanded that Russia no longer put any obstacles in the way of a favorable advance of Rumania. But Bratianu himself was not ready for a decision and the moment passed.[232] In the

entire course of Bratianu's cool calculating policy, this was the grave error, since it later entailed Rumania's humiliating defeat at the hands of von Mackensen, when his forces marched into Bucharest in December 1916.

On June 29 Blondel was instructed to offer the necessary supplies to Rumania, and Bratianu informed him that Rumanian neutrality could not last much longer. A few days later, on July 4, Poklevsky wired Sazonov that the Bucharest cabinet was ready to sign a military convention and political agreement guaranteeing territorial acquisitions.[233] Sazonov received these suggestions with good grace, and was prepared to make a military convention providing for the near entry of Rumania into the war.[234] France now put pressure on Bratianu. Briand advised Blondel to tell Bratianu that "if the intervention of Rumania is to do any good, it must be immediate." All the conditions for action had been fulfilled.[235] By July 27 the military accord, fixing Rumanian action for August 14 and providing for an offensive of the Salonica expedition was ready. General Alexeiev, however, found it inacceptable.[236] The Quai d'Orsay now put pressure on St. Petersburg. The pro-German Sturmer, who had replaced Sazonov at the foreign ministry, insisted that Rumania sign the military convention not later than August 14 and that operations begin not later than August 22, if possible. Russia had given up her demand for guarantees in the Banat, but if Rumania refused, she would lose all the advantages offered to Bucharest.[237]

On August 18 the political and military conventions were signed. Rumania was guaranteed the Banat, Transylvania and the plain of the Tisza, and the Bukovina to the Pruth.[238] Russia was obligated to divert a part of her forces to protect Rumania in the Dobruja, and the Allies were to begin their Salonica offensive.[239] But on August 26 both King Ferdinand and Bratianu assured Czernin of Rumania's desire to remain neutral. The next day a crown council decided for war and the declaration of hostilities was presented in Vienna.[240] Operations began on August 28, 1916.

Austrian failures against Italy, Allied successes in both west and east, and the prospect of ultimate victory had finally brought Rumania into the war. But if the Allies felt that a small but powerful friend had come to their aid, they were soon to be disillusioned. The Rumanian forces enjoyed a short victorious march into Transylvania, which was poorly defended—a grave tactical blunder for which the Central Powers were not unprepared. Within three months, thanks to the Austro-German offensive under Falkenhayn and Mackensen, and the

Bulgarian drive from the south into the Dobruja, the Rumanian forces were crushed. The capital was moved to Jassy, and on December 5 the Germans entered Bucharest. Bratianu won his ultimate victory only with the triumph of the Allied armies, after having suffered a terrible defeat and the humiliating peace of Bucharest.[241]

6.

*Failure of Allied Diplomacy in the Balkans*

Allied Balkan policy proved to be a fiasco. The Allies lost Turkey through the control which Germany had over the Porte since 1913, and because of the failure of England and France to accede to the Russian project of an alliance in August 1914. Russia would not permit Greece to enter the war as the pawn of England at the Dardanelles, and forestall her own claims to *Tsargrad* and an outlet to the free sea. The English failure to win Greece as the pivot of a Balkan alliance led to her efforts to replace Russian supremacy in Bulgaria. Russia had made Bulgaria the pivot of her Balkan policy from the beginning of the war. This Anglo-Russian contest in Sofia, coupled with the control which Germany had developed (and despite the fact of substantial promises made to Bulgaria by the Entente), led to the defeat of Allied diplomacy there. Russia made every effort to bring Rumania into the war, though preferring neutrality in principle, and under pressure from England and France surrendered to practically all Rumanian territorial desires. Rumania entered late and proved more of a liability as an Allied belligerent, than she would have been as a neutral. Both Italy and Rumania made such military demands on Russia as to divide her forces and thus materially contributed to the weakening of the main Russian front against Germany. This was exactly what competent military and diplomatic circles of Russia had feared. The results of such a diversion of Russian forces are too well known to need chronicling here.

Concessions of territory in each case were complicated and difficult. Bulgaria demanded Macedonia as the keystone of her territorial acquisitions in order to satisfy not only the dream of an outlet to the Aegean, but to "free" certain Bulgarian nationals in that country. Greece would not give up her share of Macedonia without guarantees in Asiatic Turkey. Serbia refused to yield her part of Macedonia without assurances on the Adriatic littoral. Both met the opposition of Italy, supported by France and England. Rumania would not concede

the Dobruja unless Greece and Serbia would submit in Macedonia, and a guarantee of Bulgaria's action with the Entente were obtained. It was thus that the Macedonian question became entangled with the most serious and complex of all Near Eastern issues and led to an insoluble impasse from which there appeared to be no escape. Added to these difficulties was the fact that Greece, Rumania and Bulgaria were all interested in blocking Russian designs in the Straits, and at intervals attempted to form their own *bloc* to achieve that purpose.

Allied diplomacy therefore met with inevitable failure in the Balkans. Probably doomed from the beginning, it was impossible to re-form the Balkan league for a concerted attack on Turkey. Each Balkan state pursued its own course in the war. Each Great Power among the Allies followed its own policy in the Balkans. Rumania was crushed soon after her entrance into the war, and while Serbia was overrun, Bulgaria was the first of the Central Powers to surrender to the Allies. The war had begun in the Balkans, and in that quarter of the world it was to end. How the conclusion of hostilities in the Balkans led to the general *dénouement* in November 1918, and how this situation was used by the British in an attempt to gain control not only over Constantinople and the Straits, but of a substantial part of Turkey, will be related in the chapter which follows.

# CHAPTER VI

## THE SECRET TREATIES AND THE PARTITION OF TURKEY, 1915-1918

## The Inter-Allied Agreements, 1915-1917.

TURKEY'S entrance into the world war foreshadowed her own doom; in the words of Mr. Asquith, the Porte had "committed suicide". The question of Constantinople and the Straits—their cession to Russia in March-April 1915—has been considered. From the Russian viewpoint this problem dominated the whole question of the partition of Turkey. Indeed, the Russian demand with reference to Constantinople and the Straits furnished the western Allies with a pretext and a basis for the partition of the rest of the Ottoman Empire. The action of the Entente in carving up the Sultan's estate in Asiatic Turkey had been preceded by economic preliminaries over a period of years—economic preliminaries which had grave political consequences for the empire. As we have seen, with the exception of Russia, the Powers of Europe had by the spring of 1914 succeeded in delimiting their respective spheres around their economic and strategic interests. Russia had remained aside from the movement; she did not dominate a single kilometer of railroads, and her commerce with Turkey was limited. Yet fifty per cent of her export trade went through the waters of the Straits. Russia's real interests, apart from the Straits, namely the economic and strategic key to the Russian Black sea coasts, were centered in Turkish Armenia. Only a portion of Armenia, it will be recalled, had fallen to Russia in 1878, thanks to the imperial diplomacy of Benjamin Disraeli. The Armenian plateau served both as a Russian Asiatic approach toward the region of the Straits and as a strategic threat against the British position in India.

Italy was almost in a similar situation until early 1914, though her trade with Turkey was growing by leaps and bounds, and though she held the Dodecanese and had aspirations in the Adalia vilayet on the coast of Asia Minor. While more recent, Italy's claims were none the less real, as her "sacred egoism" in entering the great war amply demonstrated. Rome was not only to receive large territories at Austrian expense, but demanded fulfilment of her Asiatic dreams.[1] Syria, where France especially had at stake such great financial, political and cultural interests, might serve as a strategic offset against the British

preserve in Egypt and the Suez neighborhood. France had claimed special privileges and rights in Syria since the days of Suleyman the Magnificent, and now sought to consolidate her position in this vital region in the Near East. Great Britain, ever constant guardian of all routes to her rich empire in India, had long since watched over the Straits, bolstered up the Turkish Empire against Russia, and now was concerned greatly in obtaining Mesopotamia. The Mosul vilayet in the "land of the two rivers" was believed to contain great quantities of oil, while the Diala district might furnish the much needed cotton for English cotton mills. With Arabia, Mesopotamia would become another link along the route to India, whether by land, through the Suez canal, or the Red sea and Persian gulf.[2] Moreover, within this territory an Arab state or confederation was to be erected under British control—a project which would serve the purpose and take the place of the old empire which was to be no more.

Five secret agreements forecast the end of the Ottoman Empire. The first of these, as we have seen, was that between England and France (to which Italy was later added), on the one hand, and Russia on the other, by which Russia was to rule at Constantinople and hold undisputed sway over the Straits. The second was the treaty of London, April 26, 1915, which satisfied Italian demands. France and England had hinted at their own share of Turkey during the negotiations with Russia over Constantinople. These negotiations led to the Anglo-Franco-Russian agreement of March-April 1916, by which these Powers marked out their particular spheres in Asia Minor. In May 1916 France and England, in turn, delineated more definitely their part of the Turkish heritage. The process was completed by the treaty of St. Jean de Maurienne of April 19-21, 1917, in which Italy was given further assurances of territory in Asia Minor.[3]

The negotiations which Great Britain conducted simultaneously with two contesting Arab leaders—the Emir Hussein of the Hejaz and Ibn Saud of the Nejd—were to cause grave controversies and give rise to conflict both between England and France and between England and the Arab rivals. The Bolshevik denunciation of the secret treaties in November 1917 and the position which President Wilson took in his famous address on the Fourteen Points in January 1918, brought on a revision of the agreements before the Paris peace conference. All this is part and parcel of the story which follows.

The Turkish war forced Russia to a final settlement of the Straits question. The negotiations leading to this agreement have been

described in a previous chapter.[4] Russia finally had wrung from France and England the long-dreamed-of control at Tsargrad and the Straits. This agreement gave Russia Constantinople and supremacy over the entire region of the Straits on both the European and Asiatic shores, with the islands of the Marmora, and Tenedos and Imbros, at the entrance of the Dardanelles. These rights of Russia, however, were not to prejudice those of France and England.

England had made her own territorial exactions in return for her consent to Russian demands in the region of the Straits. Russia had to recognize the British position in Egypt. The neutral zone in Persia, delimited and defined in the accord between the two countries in 1907, was now to be an English sphere of influence. Petrograd reserved only the territory in the northern zone, and asked for frontier rectifications on the Afghan border. An independent Arab state or confederation was to be created and placed under Moslem authority, while Palestine, in view of its peculiar religious and strategic position, was to be placed under an international régime.

Italy commanded a high tribute for her services to the Entente when she entered the war in May 1915. The treaty of London gave the Quirinal not only large territorial concessions at Austrian expense, but also rights in Adalia on the Asia Minor littoral. All the twelve islands of the Dodecanese, which Italy had held since the war of 1912, now went to her in full possession. Her territory in Asia Minor, centering in the Adalia vilayet and its hinterland, was to be proportional to that of the other Powers. This zone was to be established in conformity with the "vital interests" of France and England. But if France and England and Russia should in the course of the war, occupy certain districts of Asiatic Turkey, the territory adjoining Adalia was to be left to Italy, who reserved the right of occupation. Finally, Italy associated herself with the Allied declarations concerning Arabia.[5] Italy was beginning to take her place among the foremost Powers in the Near East.

The Constantinople agreement among France, England and Russia, foresaw further Allied engagements with reference to the partition of Asiatic Turkey. France had raised the issue very early and definitely in March 1915. But on March 20, Sir George Buchanan, the British ambassador in Petrograd, informed Sazonov that the British government thought it essential that an independent Moslem power be created in some other center, on the disappearance of the Turks from Constantinople. This would be the heart of the political

life of Islam. The holy places would be the nucleus of this projected state. The new Moslem empire probably would include Arabia. But the London government thought it premature to deliberate on the question of an "eventual partition between the Powers of Mesopotamia, Syria, Palestine and the adjoining regions, as long as the question of a Moslem Empire is not settled."[6] The British were anxious that nothing be done in the way of prejudicing their control over either Arabia or Mesopotamia, and were already showing an interest in a new Arab empire, which as Turkey had done before, would bar the way of any foreign Power to India.

By early 1916 negotiations for a partition of Turkey were far advanced. England had already gained Russian assent to her position in Egypt and Mesopotamia, while the French position in Syria was recognized. These diplomatic maneuvers led to the Anglo-Franco-Russian agreement in March-April 1916, and to the Sykes-Picot accord of May 1916. As will be pointed out later, simultaneous negotiations were carried on with the Arabs of the Hejaz under the Emir Hussein through the London foreign office, while the government of India bargained with Ibn Saud of the Nejd.

Early in the summer of 1915 the British had begun their conversations with Hussein. In December of that year Georges Picot and Sir Mark Sykes were appointed to prepare an agreement relative to the French and English shares of the Ottoman Empire. The Anglo-French negotiations necessitated Russian cooperation, and this fact brought Sykes and Picot to Petrograd in March 1916 to reach an accord with Russia on the partition of Turkey.[7] The result was the now famous engagement among the three Powers outlining their portions of the empire. The essential project was contained in the memorandum of March 9, 1916, which included the substance of the agreement already reached between France and England.[8] The two western Powers were ready to take under their protection the independent Arab kingdom, which was divided into two zones of influence, while Palestine was reserved for an international administration. France was to receive the coastal strip of Syria, the Adana vilayet, Cilicia and territory in southern Kurdistan, including Kharput.[9] Great Britain obtained Mesopotamia with Bagdad and Basra. Moreover, England stipulated that the two ports of Haïfa and Acre in Syria should belong to her. Alexandretta was to be a free port. Previous concessions in the territories were to be recognized in principle, and proportional parts of the Ottoman public debt were to be assumed.[10] Russia was to

receive Armenia and a part of Kurdistan, including the vilayets of Erzerum, Trebizond, Van and Bitlis. The limit of Russian acquisitions on the Black sea was to be determined later at a point west of Trebizond. It is interesting to note that Sykes contested the Russian position in Armenia for the reason that it was too dangerous a neighbor to Mosul.[11]

A few weeks later the Sykes-Picot agreement, which was embodied in the Grey-Cambon exchange of May 9-16, 1916, was concluded. This document defined in particular, the French and British shares of Asiatic Turkey, by which France was to receive an administrative zone (blue) which included Cilicia, a part of central Anatolia, the Lebanon, and the Syrian coastal strip. Great Britain acquired an administrative zone (red) comprising Mesopotamia with Bagdad and Basra, with the ports of Haïfa and Acre, on the Syrian coast. In addition two zones of influence were created. In the French zone (A) was embraced the land southeast of the French administrative zone, and north of the British (B) zone, comprising Damascus, Aleppo, Homs and Hama, and Mosul. The British zone of influence enclosed territory between Palestine and Mesopotamia, and stretched beyond Tekrit. Within these two zones of influence the two Powers provided for the establishment of an Arab state or confederation under the suzerainty of an Arab chieftain. As indicated in the Russian agreement, Palestine (the brown zone) was to be under an international régime. Within their respective spheres of influence the French and English reserved the right of priority on loans and enterprises and the right to supply advisors and foreign officials to the Arabs. Alexandretta was to be a free port as stipulated in the earlier accord with Russia. They agreed that the Bagdad railway was not to be prolonged beyond Mosul in the French zone, nor beyond Samara in the British, until a railroad joining Bagdad and Aleppo through the Euphrates valley was completed, and then only by coöperation. Finally neither of the two states was to enter into negotiations with a third Power for the cession of its rights, other than to an Arab state or confederation, save with the consent of both signatories. Great Britain entered an engagement not to cede Cyprus without French consent. Other articles dealt with the various interests of the two Powers in their respective zones.[12]

France and England had, then, in May 1916, outlined their allotments in Asiatic Turkey. The French had long desired Syria—and in French official and public circles Palestine was but a part of Syria.[13] France had obtained also a part of Anatolia, as well as the Mosul

vilayet. It was Sir Mark Sykes' idea to place the French in Mosul in order to create a buffer between Russia and England in Asia Minor. And, as we shall see, when Russia ceased to be a factor to the north of Mesopotamia (Iraq), the coveted territory went back to Great Britain. Great Britain had sought and obtained further protection of the route to India.[14]

Much later a final Allied arrangement concerning Asiatic Turkey was concluded at St. Jean de Maurienne, on April 19-21, 1917. Since 1914 Italy had certain interests in Adalia. During the war Balfour had had long conversations with Imperiali, the Italian representative in London, with a view to settling the pressing Italian claims. Italy demanded the inclusion of Mersina and Adana in the Italian sphere, but the French refused this concession. On the other hand, the British rejected the cession of Smyrna to Rome, because that vilayet was being offered to the Greeks. The Italians rejected an offer of territory on the gulf of Scala Nuova, including Konia. The government at Rome refused to take part in the Salonica expedition, where its troops would have been of use, but demanded representation in all expeditions in Asia Minor. Finally, however, notable satisfactions to Italian desires were made in the agreement of St. Jean de Maurienne, after the United States had entered the war. By the terms of this treaty, Italy recognized the engagements in the Sykes-Picot accord, and obtained further concessions for herself in Asia Minor, in Adalia and the Smyrna region. Free port privileges were given to France and England, their colonies and protectorates. As in the Franco-British accord, the three Powers engaged to respect their reciprocal interests, while Italy recognized the agreements previously concluded. In conclusion, the document provided for an arrangement that in case all the desires and plans of the Powers could not be carried out, "the maintenance of the Mediterranean equilibrium shall be fairly taken into consideration . . . in any change or arrangement affecting the provinces of the Ottoman Empire as a consequence of the war." However, the accord was to be subject to the approval of the Russian government and its express consent was to be obtained.[15] Since the Petrograd government failed to give its consent to the treaty, both France and England were able to contest its validity at the peace conference, and Italy received nothing from the bargain.[16]

Such, in brief, was the Allied scheme for the partition of Turkey following a victorious war. Russia was to have control over Constantinople and the Straits, Armenia and a part of Kurdistan. France was

to obtain Syria and central Anatolia, with a zone of influence including the Mosul vilayet. England was to obtain Mesopotamia, including Bagdad and Basra in the south. Italy was to retain the Dodecanese, occupied since 1912, and to have Adalia with its hinterland, and the Smyrna region, on the mainland. Indeed the activities of the Allied Powers in Asiatic Turkey during the world war cannot be appreciated without a fundamental understanding of these secret treaties and the circumstances which produced them.

Let us now retrace our steps, in order to follow the course of the war in Asiatic Turkey. This will reveal the way in which the Entente, and Great Britain in particular, won the Arabs by promising them autonomy and freedom,—a condition that made possible a victory for Allied arms in that quarter of the world.

2.

### The Arabs and the War in Asiatic Turkey.

Three great British armies carried on the war against the Turks. One landed at Basra, advanced through the Tigris and Euphrates valleys, and attempted throughout the war to control Mesopotamia and bar that route to India. A second came up from Egypt into Palestine and advanced to the conquest of Syria—to protect the Suez canal. In the end more than 200,000 British and Arab forces operated in the Syrian region, while the French had but 6,000 men employed in the territory which they so much coveted. The third expedition coöperated with the royal navy and tried to force the Dardanelles with Constantinople and the control of the Straits as the fundamental objective.

In October 1914, British and Indian troops were ordered to demonstrate on the Persian gulf, and, if possible, to occupy Abbadan island and Basra, with the purpose of protecting the oil works and pipelines. These forces pushed north under the command of General Townshend with the object of controlling Mesopotamia. They were checked, however, by superior Turkish forces under the command of von der Goltz Pasha. By November 1915, Townshend had reached Ctesiphon, but he was compelled to surrender to the Turks at Kut-el-Amara in May 1916, just at the time when the members of the Entente were agreeing on the partition of Turkey.[17] In rather striking contrast to the British débacle, Russian troops, in February 1916, had gained Erzerum, advancing thence to Trebizond and south to Bitlis and Van.

187

Armenia was conquered. The Russian advance had much to do with arousing the Armenians against the Turks, which, in part, led to the wholesale massacres of these people by the Turks during the world war.[18]

Djemal Pasha had developed plans, earlier in the war, for a Syrian campaign in order to threaten and take both the Suez canal and Egypt. By February 1915, these had matured and the attack which had been planned so carefully proved a dismal failure.[19] This threat, however, finally led the British to undertake their own offensive in Palestine and Syria, and induced them to arouse the Arabs to action against the Osmanli.

Two weeks before the war with Turkey began, Great Britain inquired of the Emir Hussein of the Hejaz what his attitude would be in case of war with Turkey, and he gave an evasive answer. When the sultan declared a holy war and attempted to fire the Moslem world against the Entente, England began in earnest to counteract that influence by inciting the Arabs to fight their old enemies. Long dissatisfied with Ottoman rule, and more recently perturbed by the senseless tactics of Djemal Pasha's policy in Syria and the Lebanon, the Arabs were not unready to negotiate.[20] They believed in the freedom which would come from the common Allied victory.

The Arab negotiations follow two conflicting trends. The India office bargained with Ibn Saud, sultan of the Nejd, and center of the puritanic Wahabite sect. As early as October 1914, Captain Shakespeare of the royal navy, who was well acquainted with Arabia, was sent out to get in touch with Ibn Saud. Relations with the Emir Hussein were established through the London foreign office, with Sir Henry MacMahon, British high commissioner in Egypt, conducting the negotiations from that nearby vantage point.

From the beginning, Hussein gave a willing reception to the British overtures. In a letter which he wrote on July 15, 1915, the sherif made known the conditions of his adhesion to the British cause against Turkey. England must recognize "the independence" of the Arab countries limited on the north by Mersina and Adana, to the 37th parallel, including Biridjek, Urfa, Mardin, Jezireh and Amadia, to the Persian frontier. On the east the Arab territory was limited by the Persian frontier, on the south by the Persian gulf and Indian ocean, with the exception of Aden, and on the west by the Red sea and the Mediterranean to Mersina. Likewise, material and moral support must be furnished, in return for which England would receive

priority in economic concessions. Sir Henry answered on August 30, 1915, that discussion of frontiers was premature. The sherif, however, insisted on an immediate discussion in a letter of September 9, which MacMahon forwarded to London on October 18. In this he included a statement of Hussein's representative in Cairo, declaring that the Arabs would oppose by armed force the French occupation of the Aleppo, Hama, Homs, Damascus districts; but with this exception, they were willing to accept modifications of the northwestern frontiers proposed by the sherif.[21]

MacMahon replied to Hussein's *démarche* on the order of London on October 24, 1915. He now denied the purely Arab character of the Mersina-Alexandretta districts, as well as that of the parts of Syria to the west of Damascus, Hama, Homs and Aleppo. With that modification, and without prejudice to existing treaties with Arab chieftains, the boundaries were accepted, "and in regard to those portions of the territories therein in which Great Britain is free to act without detriment to her ally, France," MacMahon was empowered to make a definite proposal to Hussein. The proposal was: (1) subject to the modifications indicated, Great Britain undertook to recognize Arab "independence" in the limits and boundaries proposed by the sherif of Mecca; (2) Great Britain was to guarantee the holy places against aggression and to recognize their individuality; (3) England would offer her advice, and would assist the Arabs in establishing suitable forms of government; (4) the Arabs, on the other hand, were to seek the advice and guidance of Great Britain only, and all foreign advisors were to be British; (5) the Arabs recognized the special interests and position of Great Britain in the vilayets of Bagdad and Basra.[22]

Hussein accepted the exclusion of Mersina and Adana, but maintained his pretentions to Aleppo and Beirut in his reply to the British offer on November 5, 1915. He also sustained his claim to the Basra and Bagdad vilayets, but offered the British the right of temporary occupation in return for pecuniary considerations, and consented to recognize the special agreements with the local chieftains. On December 14 MacMahon took note of Hussein's declaration, but stated that in view of French interests in Syria (Aleppo and Beirut) a final letter would be necessary.[23]

On November 23, 1915, Sir Arthur Nicolson, permanent undersecretary of state at the foreign office, informed M. Picot of the Arab negotiations and of the demand of Hussein. At a second meeting on December 21, Picot advised Nicolson that the French government

accepted Arab administration of Damascus, Homs, Hama and Aleppo—but only under French influence.[24] Little else, either of British ambition in the Arab world or of the aspirations of the Arabs themselves, seems to have been revealed to the French.

The grand sherif notified the British government on January 1, 1916, that in order not to disturb the Franco-British understanding, he would waive his claims to the Lebanon during the war. He assured MacMahon, however, that he "could be certain that at the first occasion, once the war is ended, we shall reclaim what we leave to France." At the end of the month, January 30, MacMahon informed Hussein that he had received orders to accede to all his demands, acknowledged his desire not to disturb the alliance, and assured him of the lasting nature of Anglo-French friendship.[25]

What were the engagements now assumed by the British in reference to the Emir Hussein? It seems clear that Great Britain was undertaking, conditional on an Arab revolt, to recognize Arab independence, south of the 37th parallel, except in Bagdad and Basra, and exclusive of districts where French interests predominated.[26] It also appears that Great Britain, without the knowledge of her allies, was attempting to construct an Arab state or confederation under positive British control. Finally, it is evident that Hussein had more far reaching ambitions which he did not renounce in his agreement with the British—such as claims against the British in southern Mesopotamia and against the French in Syria which he proposed to settle at the end of a victorious war.

Meanwhile, the government of India had been negotiating with Ibn Saud, through Captain Shakespeare. While Ibn Saud was not unwilling to make an agreement with Britain, he wanted specific, definite understandings. Having learned of the threatening attitude of the sherif of Mecca after the first Turkish defeats, the sultan of the Nejd wrote to Sir Percy Cox, expressing his fear lest Hussein attempt to establish his authority over the Nejd, and protesting against any pretensions he might have in that direction. Sir Percy calmed him, saying that the Hejaz operations were to be restricted, and could not create any danger for the Nejd, whose integrity Great Britain guaranteed. On December 25, 1915, Ibn Saud and the British government mutually engaged to maintain their friendship, and to liquidate their special interests. This agreement was ratified on July 18, 1916, by the viceroy of India at Simla and the secretary of state for India at the foreign office in London. Great Britain recognized that the Nejd,

Qatif, Jubail, ports and territories along the Persian gulf belonged to Ibn Saud, "independent sovereign of these countries and absolute chief of the tribes residing there," and guaranteed their protection. Ibn Saud, in turn, engaged to make no treaties with any other state, nor to allow foreign interference or concessions without British consent, whose advice he was to follow. The routes to the holy places were to be kept open. In conclusion, Ibn Saud was to abstain from any interference in Koweit, Bahrein, Qatar and Oman, all of which were either under British protectorate or bound to Great Britain by treaty.[27]

From the opening of 1916, Ibn Saud became the chief supporter of Great Britain in eastern and southern Arabia in the same manner that Hussein had become in western Arabia. Both were heavily subsidized by the British treasury for their efforts in the Allied cause.[28]

It is of no little interest to note that England appears to have made diametrically conflicting engagements with these Arab chieftains. The British definitely had promised an Arab state under Hussein including the territory south of the 37th parallel, with the exception of Bagdad and Basra and those districts where French interests predominated. The India office had promised a part of these territories in central and eastern Arabia to Ibn Saud as sovereign and independent lord. Neither chieftain knew of the engagements to the other—a fact which was to lead to very serious complications following the war. If the Arabs were kept in ignorance, the French were not informed of the engagements, as M. Pichon told the peace conference in March 1919.[29]

But Hussein desired much more than he ever actually was to receive. Satisfaction of all his ambitions for an Arab state would compromise not only the British claims, but directly would contravene French interests in Syria, as well as those of his rival Ibn Saud. Nor did the grand sherif agree to the British reservations on Syria, Palestine or Mesopotamia. He merely waived his rights for the moment in the interest of Allied harmony and victory in the war. The British were forced to tread easily, therefore, so conflicting were the aims, lest the Arabs be alienated and go over to the side of Turkey.[30]

The fundamental desire of Great Britain seems evident from the negotiations and the campaigns. The three principal campaigns against Turkey struck at the very vitals of the Ottoman Empire—the Dardanelles, Syria and Palestine, and Mesopotamia. Every one covered a route to India, land or sea. The negotiations with both Hussein and Ibn Saud carefully reserved to England the control of all concessions, advisors and supervision of foreign relations. Britain was constructing

another buffer along the route to the heart of her empire. The Turks were gone—now an Arab state under British influence would arise to take their place. Both France and Italy saw, in this development, a threat to their own position in the Near East. Particularly was this true of the French position in Syria. As for Russia, that government, recognizing the Sykes-Picot accord, promised France and England to support an Arab state when the Arabs themselves should establish one. This was in May 1916. The year following, Russia, in the agony of the November 1917 revolution, ceased to be a party to the treaty, published its terms to the world, and denounced its share of the bargain.[31]

Some doubt prevailed whether Hussein and the Arabs of the Hejaz actually would raise the standard of revolt, for in December 1915-January 1916, the evacuation of the Gallipoli peninsula made abundantly clear the Allied failure at the Dardanelles. This had a profound effect in the east. On June 10, 1916, however, a rebellion occurred at Mecca, and on June 27 the sherif issued his proclamation of revolution against Turkey. Not long after, Arab forces occupied Jeddah, laid siege to Medina, and finally cut the Hejaz railway. On October 5, 1916, Hussein formed an Arab cabinet, called an assembly and proclaimed himself king of Arabia. In November a second proclamation called on all Arabs to fight against the Turk. On November 4 the emir was crowned king, and in December he actually received British recognition as king of the Hejaz.[32]

The ground for the Arab revolt had been well prepared. The British forces under General Maude were now pushing the Turks along the upper Tigris. In February 1917, Kut was retaken, and the following month witnessed the fall of Bagdad.[33] In April, the English were in Samara, just eighty-one miles north of Bagdad. General Allenby succeeded to the command following the death of Maude in June 1917, and conducted the campaign in Palestine. By November and December 1917, the Palestine sector was invested with British troops and Jerusalem was retaken. By the end of the year Turkish authority had been swept from the northwestern part of Arabia and Hussein himself held sway over the region. No small part of this triumph was due to the Emir Feisal, who had taken up arms, thanks to the brilliant work of Colonel Lawrence, and had operated throughout the war in coöperation with British forces. The advance went steadily on through 1918. Only two days prior to the armistice, the last of the Turkish troops were defeated at Shergat, leaving open the road to Mosul,

though British soldiers did not reach that point until after the armistice with Turkey. Before the end of the war the British had thrown almost 1,000,000 men into the eastern campaigns against the Ottoman Empire.[34]

3.

## The Dénouement

We must now turn our attention once more to the moves and counter-moves which were being made on the diplomatic chess board. Following her declaration of war on Turkey (August 21, 1915), Italy inquired about the Straits agreement. However, Sazonov was able to postpone consideration until the Quirinal had taken similar action against Germany one year later. The agreements partitioning Asia Minor had been drawn up in the spring of 1916 and it was now the policy of tsarist Russia to prevent Italy from securing Smyrna as her share of Turkey—a point too close to the zone of the Straits. On December 2, 1916, however, Italy gave her final consent to Russia's acquisition of Constantinople and the Straits, on condition that Italian claims in the Orient and elsewhere be supported by Russia. At the same time the cabinets of Petrograd and Rome exchanged notes on the maintenance of the Racconigi accord of October 1909.[35]

The question of the Straits again came to the fore when Sazonov instructed Isvolsky on the eve of the inter-allied conference to be held in March 1916 that the secret treaties "must remain inviolable and must not again be put in question"—engagements including that with France and England over Constantinople and the Straits, Syria and Asia Minor, and the treaty of London with Italy. Russia was ready to grant France and England freedom in fixing the western frontiers with Germany in return for a similar liberty of action for Russia in the east with both Austria and Germany. The Polish question was to be excluded from the discussions.[36] When, during the latter days of the tsarist régime, M. Doumergue, while attending the inter-allied conference at Petrograd, attempted to get Russia's assent to redrawing the French frontiers in return for previous French consent to the Straits agreement, Pokrovsky, last of the tsar's foreign ministers, refused. France wanted a political separation between Germany and the trans-Rhine provinces established, possession of Alsace-Lorraine,

and a special position in the Saar valley. Pokrovsky finally assented on the identical conditions which Sazonov had proposed in March 1916. An agreement was worked out by March 11, 1917.

In a memorandum of March 6, 1917, Pokrovsky wrote to the emperor that it was indispensable to acquire the Straits before the conclusion of peace, otherwise "it is scarcely probable for us ever to acquire Constantinople and the Straits and the accord thereon will become a simple scrap of paper."[37] This document was transmitted to Basili, at general headquarters, where General Alexeiev outlined the difficulties of an expedition against the Straits and insisted on its utter impossibility.[38]

But in March 1917 the tsarist régime came to an end and was replaced by a *bourgeois* Provisional Government with Prince Lvov as premier and Professor Paul Miliukov as foreign minister. Miliukov attached so much importance to an expedition against Constantinople that further plans for a possible campaign were drawn up. On April 24 Basili wrote to Neratov that, in view of internal circumstances and technical reasons, "we must envisage seriously the possibility . . . of being obliged to renounce from now to the end of the war our acquiring the Straits." An expedition appeared out of the question, and "*it is certain that if we come to the conclusion that it is impossible for us to dominate in the Straits, then the continuation of the struggle with Turkey, which does not threaten us, would have from the point of view of our interests but a single aim: to force her to turn from our enemies and to recognize our control over the Straits.*" This, Basili felt, was much better for Russia than neutralization of the Straits, for it would give her security of passage, without the interference of the Powers. If Russia could not acquire the Straits and place a *fait accompli* before the conference of peace, then she might act by a convention with Turkey.[39] This was but a reversion, as will be seen, to the basis of Unkiar Eskelessi (1833), to which the Russians had returned as late as 1911 and even 1914.

Internal developments of such a nature as to prevent any possibility of action against the Straits were now taking place in Russia. The attitude of the Provisional Government toward the secret treaties was defined clearly when on March 18, 1917, Miliukov sent a declaration to the Russian representatives abroad that Russia "will remain mindful of the international engagements entered into by the fallen régime."[40] Miliukov's statement only served to widen the breach between the government and the extreme socialists of the Petrograd

Soviet, which was already becoming a powerful influence in governmental circles. The Soviet was to be done with the whole fabric of the secret treaties, and on March 27 it called on "the peoples of the world" to take the questions of peace and war into their own hands. Later Kerensky, who had become minister of justice, made a declaration on the internationalization of Constantinople which brought from Miliukov a communication to the London embassy that it was necessary to persuade British opinion that Russia had no intention of renouncing her claims.[41] Meanwhile, on March 23, Italy, France and England had signified their consent to ratification of all the accords concluded between them.[42]

Doubtless the extreme attitude and popular agitation of the Petrograd Soviet had much to do with the statement which Prince Lvov issued to the Russian people on April 10, when he declared: ". . . *The Provisional Government considers it to be its right and duty to declare at this time that the purpose of free Russia is not domination over other nations, or seizure of their national possessions, or forcible occupation of foreign territories, but the establishment of stable peace on the basis of the self-determination of peoples . . . ."*[42]a

So heartened was the All-Russian Conference of the Soviet of Workers' and Soldiers' Deputies, that on April 25 it resolved to "support with energy all the efforts of the Provisional Government along this line." But now the Allies were no longer content with the Russian position. On May 1 Miliukov explained that his government, though safeguarding its own rights, would "in every way, observe the obligations assumed toward our Allies." He was "in full accord" with the Allies and felt "absolutely certain that the problems which have been raised by this war will be solved in a spirit that will afford a firm basis for lasting peace . . . ." Now the Pretrograd Soviet answered with a storm of protest which finally led to fighting in the streets of Petrograd and to demands for the resignation of the foreign minister. In the end the government was forced to announce on May 5 that the note of May 1 had in mind "only the attainment of those objects named in the declaration of April 10 . . . ."[42]b

While accepting the interpretation of the Provisional Government, the Soviet lost confidence in its leaders, appealed to the people to rally to the revolution, and called upon the socialists of all countries for "peace without annexations and indemnities on the basis of the self-determination of peoples." On the same day, May 15, 1917, Miliukov,

who was now completely at variance with both the Kerensky government and the ideals of the Soviet, resigned. There is something pathetic in the note which he sounded on May 22, 1917 at the congress of the Cadet party, when he declared: "*I admit quite frankly, and stand firmly by it, that the main thread of my policy was to get the Straits for Russia. I fought, unfortunately in vain, against those who favored the new formula (no annexation, and no indemnity, and the right of self-determination), and that Russia should free the Allies from their obligations to help her secure sovereign rights over the Straits. I would say, and say it proudly, and regard it as a distinct service to the country, that until the last moment that I was in office, I did nothing which gave the Allies the right to say that Russia has renounced the Straits.*"[43]

Miliukov had fallen because of his stand on the question of Constantinople and the Straits. When he was forced to resign the portfolio of foreign minister, the government, though remaining "steadfastly loyal to the cause of the Allies," declared for a "peace without annexations, without indemnities, and on the basis of the self-determination of peoples."[43]a Under the hammering blows of the Petrograd Soviet, the Provisional Government had abandoned finally the secret treaties by which Russia had hoped to fulfil her historic mission.

While President Wilson doubtless knew the fundamental nature of the secret treaties between the Allies, the extent of his knowledge remains problematical. When the late Lord Balfour came to Washington with the British mission in April 1917, there were discussions as to future territorial dispositions following the war. Balfour and Colonel E. M. House agreed that attempts at a separate peace might be made with both Austria and Bulgaria. It was agreed that Serbia should receive Bosnia and Herzegovina, and return a part of Macedonia to Bulgaria. Rumania should have, perhaps, Bessarabia and the Banat. Austria, they thought, should be composed of Bohemia, Hungary and Austria proper.

"*Constantinople was our next point. We agreed that it should be internationalized. Crossing the Bosphorus we came to Anatolia. It is here that the secret treaties between the Allies come in prominently. They have agreed to give Russia a sphere of influence in Armenia and the northern part. The British take in Mesopotamia (and the region) which is contiguous to Egypt. France and Italy each have their spheres embracing the balance of Anatolia up to the Straits.*"[44] House told Balfour at this time that "it is all bad." Balfour was very hazy in his explanation of just what the treaties included.[45] On April 30, 1917,

House, Wilson and Balfour were in conference at the White House. Here again the question of Constantinople and the Straits arose, and the question of their internationalization was discussed. House sensed the heart of the problem when, though agreeing in principle, he pointed out the difficulties which would arise in connection with a consequent attempt to internationalize the straits between Sweden, Norway and continental Europe, as well as the Suez and Panama canals. But neither Wilson nor Balfour thought "that the two questions had much in common."[46]

When Sir Herbert Samuel presented a memorandum on "The Future of Palestine," to Prime Minister Asquith in January 1915, the great Liberal leader was not attracted by the prospect "of this proposed addition to our responsibilities" and was surprised at finding "this almost lyrical outburst" proceeding from the mind of the brilliant Jew. The only other partisan of the proposal seemed to be Lloyd George, who, Asquith says, "does not care a damn for the Jews or their past or their future, but thinks it will be an outrage to let the Holy Places pass into the possession or under the protectorate of 'agnostic, atheistic France'." It will be remembered that the secret agreements of 1916 left Palestine under an international régime. Steps were now to be taken to bring that coveted strategic territory along the Suez definitely into British hands. Much water, not altogether untroubled, had run under the bridge since 1916.

November 2, 1917, brought forth the famous Balfour declaration concerning the British position in Palestine. It stated that: "*His Majesty's government view with favor the establishment in Palestine of a national home for the Jewish people and will use its best endeavors to facilitate the achievement of this object, it being clearly understood that nothing shall be done which may prejudice the civil and religious rights of existing non-Jewish communities in Palestine or the rights and political status enjoyed by Jews in any other country.*"[47]

This was a vague enough commitment, assuring the Jews a "national home" and offering protection to non-Jewish elements, including, of course, the Arabs, who had lived in the country for some 1300 years. It foreshadowed trouble for the future between Arabs and Jews, by the very generalities of the formula. The Balfour declaration was a master stroke of diplomacy, for doubtless it would serve to rally international Jewry from both camps to the cause of the Allies, with all the financial and moral support of which the Jews were capable. But what

did the Balfour declaration mean? It was susceptible of any interpretation which would best meet the interests of His Majesty's government
at the time. If it were to British interest to evacuate Palestine, such
action would not violate the strict letter of this "promise" to the Jews.
Palestine was to be a "national home," not a national state for the Jews.
If British interests in the near and middle east and India dictated a long
tenure in Palestine, the declaration would become a sacred pledge of
national honor to remain in that much troubled country. It is no mere
coïncidence that in the year 1918 Palestine finally passed into British
hands.

The attitude of the Bolsheviks toward the secret treaties and the
partition of Turkey had been clearly defined by the spring of 1917,
when they forced Miliukov out of the foreign ministry. When they
gained control under the slogan of "All power to the soviets" in
November 1917, they carried their resolutions into effect. As early
as October 20, 1917 the instructions of the central executive committee
to Skobelev, Russian representative to the Allied war conference at
Paris, had stipulated among others, the following aims of the war:

*"Turkish Armenia to receive full autonomy and later, when it has
a local government and international guarantees, the right of self-determination."*

*"Serbia and Montenegro to be restored and to have material aid from
the international assistance fund. Serbia should have access to the Adriatic. Bosnia and Herzegovina to be autonomous."*

*"Disputed areas in the Balkans to have temporary autonomy to be
followed by plebescites."*

*"Rumania to have back her old frontiers, with the obligation to give
Dobrudja temporary autonomy at once and the right of self-determination later. Rumania to bind herself to put into force immediately the
clauses in the Berlin treaty about the Jews and to give them equal rights
with citizens of Rumania."*

*"To reëstablish Greece and Persia."*

*"To neutralize all straits which give access to inland seas;
also the Suez and Panama canals . . . ."*[48]

In the famous "Decree of Peace" of November 8, 1917, the All-
Russian Convention of Soviets of Workers', Soldiers' and Peasants'
Deputies, unanimously proposed an immediate peace, on the familiar
basis of no annexations and no indemnities. It abolished "secret
diplomacy," and was to begin publishing the secret treaties. The statement declared: *"The government abrogates absolutely and immediately*

*all the provisions of these secret treaties in as much as they were intended
in the majority of cases for the purpose of securing profits and privileges
for Russian landowners and capitalists and retaining or increasing the
annexations by the Great Russians."*[49]

On November 22, 1917, the Soviet government informed the
Allied ambassadors of its stand and proposed it as a basis for an
armistice and peace. A few days later, November 28, 1917, an appeal
to the people of the belligerent countries stated that "we have published the secret agreements of the Tsar and the bourgeoisie with the
Allies *and have declared them not binding for the Russian people.*"
Immediate peace was urged, and it was announced that Soviet Russia
would begin negotiations with the Central Powers on December 1—
alone, if the Allies would not join.[49]*a*

Doubtless, the "Mohammedan workers in Russia and the East"
were more vitally concerned in the Soviet position on the secret treaties,
and to these peoples an appeal was made on December 7, 1917.

*"We declare that the secret treaties of the deposed Tsar as to the
annexation of Constantinople, confirmed by the late Kerensky government—are now null and void. The Russian republic, and its government,
the Council of the People's Commissars, are opposed to the annexation of
foreign lands: Constantinople must remain in the hands of the Moham-
medans.*

*"We declare that the treaty for the division of Persia is null and
void . . . .*

*"We declare that the division of Turkey and the subduction from it of
Armenia, is null and void. Immediately after the cessation of military
activities, the Armenians will be guaranteed the right of free self-determination of their political fate."*[49]*b* Not free Russia, but "the robbers of
European imperialism," were the enemies to be feared. The publication of the secret treaties by the Bolsheviks created a sensation. Naturally the Turks were quick to inform the Arabs of these revelations, as indications of Allied duplicity in dealing with them. But while
Hussein and the Arabs were shocked to know of the Franco-British
understandings, they remained loyal to the Entente.[50]

Meanwhile, on December 19, 1917, an appeal "to the toiling,
oppressed and exhausted peoples of Europe" denounced the secret
engagements, and urged all peoples to join in the peace negotiations
at Brest-Litovsk, which were to open three days later. At the first
plenary session of the Brest-Litovsk conference, Leon Trotzky, who
led the Soviet delegation, insisted on no annexations and no indemnities,

but made little impression on the delegates of the Central Powers. On December 29, the conference was interrupted until January 8, 1918, in order, as Trotzky announced, "to give the last opportunity to the Allied countries" to take part in the peace negotiations. No reply being received, on February 10, 1918, the Soviet delegation declared: "*If the war was ever a war of defence it has long ceased to be so for either side. If Great Britain has taken possession of the African colonies, Bagdad, and Jerusalem, it is no longer a defensive war; if Germany is occupying Serbia, Belgium, Poland, Lithuania and Rumania, this is also no defensive war. It is a struggle for the partition of the world . . . .*"[50]a Confronted by the failure of the Allies to join the peace conference, and by the imperialistic designs of Germany and Austria on her territory, Russia refused to sign a treaty. Trotzky announced that "we are withdrawing from the war, but we are forced to refuse to sign a peace treaty." Under pressure from Lenin, however, the treaty was signed on March 3, 1918, when German forces began the march on Petrograd.

Russia had collapsed. The treaty of Brest-Litovsk proved to be one of the severest contracts ever imposed on one Power by another in modern history. Courland, Lithuania and Poland on the west were cut off from Russia. The fate of these territories was to be determined by Germany and Austria in agreement with their respective peoples. The Ukraine was to be torn away from Russia. Moreover, the treaty of Brest-Litovsk called for the immediate evacuation of the eastern provinces of Anatolia, Ardahan, Kars and Batum. In April 1918, the Turks had retaken Trebizond, Erzerum, Mush and Van. An Armenian republic was constituted in Erivan, and that unfortunate little state started again on its unhappy career.

On March 19, 1918, Count Hertling, the German chancellor, explained to the Reichstag that Lithuania and Courland had been "united" to Germany, while Livonia and Esthonia would be in "friendly" relations. The independence of the Ukraine was acknowledged on February 8, while that of Finland received recognition on March 7.[51] This was followed on May 7 when the Rumanians were forced to sign the humiliating peace of Bucharest. By this treaty Rumania lost the passes leading from Transylvania into Wallachia, while the Bulgarians took the part of the Dobruja lost in 1913. In return Rumania was offered Bessarabia.[52]

The treaty of Brest-Litovsk, then, pushed Russia from the Baltic, cut away the Ukraine, and left Russia with a foothold on neither the

European nor Asiatic shore of the Black sea. By offering Bessarabia to Rumania, the Germans would not only estrange Rumania and Soviet Russia, but take away Russia's Balkan land approach to the region of the Straits. Russia was put back into the position of a land-locked, isolated state—a situation similar to that which the country had occupied before the days of Peter the Great.

The action of Soviet Russia at Brest-Litovsk gave Lloyd George occasion to declare before the House of Commons, on December 20, 1917, that, "of course, the fact that Russia has entered into separate negotiations absolutely disposes of any question there may be about Constantinople."[53] Nor was the English prime minister slow to take advantage of his opportunities in such a situation.

On December 28, 1917, the British labor conference passed some important resolutions on the aims of the war, its hand being forced, doubtless, by the earlier pronouncements of the Bolsheviks. With reference to Turkey, the conference went on record against "*handing back to the universally execrated rule of the Turkish government any subject people which has once been freed from it. Thus whatever may be proposed with regard to Armenia, Mesopotamia and Arabia they cannot be restored to the tyranny of the sultan and his pashas.*" On the other hand the Laborites were opposed to any imperialistic schemes, and suggested that these territories be placed under "supernational authority, or league of nations." As for Constantinople, that city "should be made a free port, permanently neutralized, and placed (together with both shores of the Dardanelles and possibly some or all of Asia Minor) under the same impartial administration."[54]

A few days later, on January 5, 1918, Lloyd George declared before the same gathering that Britain was not fighting "to deprive Turkey of its capital, or of the rich and renowned lands of Asia Minor and Thrace, which are predominantly Turkish in race."[55] But he continued: "*While we do not challenge the maintenance of the Turkish Empire in the homelands of the Turkish race with its capital at Constantinople—the passage between the Mediterranean and the Black sea being internationalized and neutralized—Arabia, Armenia, Syria and Palestine are in our judgment entitled to a recognition of their separate national conditions.*" The form of that recognition was not determined, though the prime minister was definite in his assertion "that it would be impossible to restore to their former sovereignty the territories to which I have already referred." As to the arrangements with the Allies, the Russian collapse had altered the conditions, and the British government

was "perfectly ready to discuss them with our Allies." This state-ment is of extreme importance, for it indicates the trend of events. Lloyd George was generous about the Turkish "homelands." He was glad to give assurances about Constantinople and the Straits, now that Russia was no longer involved. But nowhere did he indicate a willing-ness to restore any of the territories to which England aspired. An internationalization and neutralization of the Straits would give control over these waters to the British navy, and enable England to dominate that trade route and highway to the Russian Black sea shore. Inciden-tally, the speech reassured the home front as to liberal war aims, and stimulated enlistments in India, where some 70,000,000 Moslems were vitally concerned with the destiny of the Caliphate, which had been in the hands of the Turkish sultans since the days of Sultan Selim I.[56]

The Lloyd George pronunciamento foreshadowed the Wilson Fourteen Points of January 8, 1918, the formulation of which had been long in the making. The diary of Colonel House indicates that, as early as August 1917, the general terms of the secret treaties were common property, and Wilson's opposition to them definite. "They know in Turkey . . . of the secret treaties which the Allies have made among themselves in which they have cheerfully partitioned Turkey." On October 13, 1917, House refers to a conference with Wilson, in which Wilson thought he should advocate the effacement of Turkey from the map, the parts of which should become autonomous along racial lines, and not divided among the belligerents. On December 1, 1917, Wilson cabled House in Paris to protest against the secret treaties. In his address, however, he laid down only the general principle as stated in point XII which deals with the disposition of Asiatic Turkey. This part of the famous Fourteen Points address declares:

*"The Turkish portions of the present Ottoman Empire should be assured a secure sovereignty, but the other nationalities which are now under Turkish rule should be assured an undoubted security of life and an absolutely unmolested opportunity of autonomous development and the Dardanelles should be permanently opened as a free passage to the ships and commerce of all nations under international guarantees."*[57]

The declarations of Allied policy called for counter statements from the Central Powers. Count Hertling, replying to Wilson and Lloyd George, on January 24, 1928, announced that "the integrity of Turkey and the safeguarding of her capital which is connected closely

with the question of the Straits, are important and vital interests of the German Empire also. Our ally can always count upon our energetic support in this matter."[58]

Halil Bey, the Turkish foreign minister, on February 7, 1918, gave his general adherence to the principle that national groups not independent before the war should receive institutions in accordance with "the constitution of each individual country." As for the Straits, they "will remain open in future to international traffic as in the past, and and on the same conditions."[59] Such conditions as these were hardly of a nature to satisfy the demands of the Allies who were determined to have freedom of passage of the Straits under "international" guarantee.

These diplomatic maneuvers were carried on throughout the spring of 1918, with the fate of peoples, and those of Turkey in particular, hanging in the balance. On February 25 Hertling, answering Wilson's address of February 11, declared: *"The Entente is fighting for the acquisition of portions of Austro-Hungarian territory by Italy . . . . The Entente is fighting for the severance of Palestine, Syria and Arabia from the Turkish Empire. England has particularly cast an eye on portions of Turkish territory. She has suddenly discovered an affection for the Arabians, and she hopes by utilizing the Arabians to annex fresh territories to the British Empire, perhaps by the creation of a protectorate dependent on British domination."*[60] Count Hertling was quite correct in his estimate of the situation, though he neglected to mention Germany's own reason for her interest in that region of the world, namely ultimate domination over the whole of the Ottoman Empire through the Bagdad railway as well as other economic concessions, and through military control.[61]

The closing months of the world war brought renewed activity on both the fighting and diplomatic fronts in the Near East. Unprepared to carry on the war in unison, the conclusion of hostilities, as we are now about to see, was to find each of the Allied Powers pursuing its own particular aims at the expense of a fundamental solution of the great problems involved. By August 1918, the British government appeared to favor a new Balkan balance, urging both Rumania and Serbia to cede territory in the Dobruja and Macedonia in the interest of a Balkan equilibrium. Should Turkey cease to be a European Power, her successor in eastern Thrace could be only Bulgaria, which might

be assured a free hand as regards Turkish Thrace up to the line of Enos-Midia or even of Midia-Rodosto. A Balkan customs union was considered.[62] Moreover the foreign office had now come to the conclusion that Bessarabia was historically Rumanian and that the hope of progress lay in union with Rumania.[63] Doubtless the British were not blind to the fact that Bessarabia in Rumanian hands would block Russia's approach to the Straits and enable Rumania to threaten Odessa.

The American attitude toward the coming problems of peace now became much more definite. On September 21, 1918, Mr. Lansing prepared a memorandum for the guidance of the American peace commissioners.[64] The principles laid down for Turkey and the Balkans are very significant. (1) Germany was to be blocked from the routes to the Near East. (2) Rumania was to be given sovereignty over Bessarabia, Transylvania and the upper portion of the Dobruja, leaving the central mouth of the Danube as the Bulgarian boundary. (3) Croatia, Slavonia, Dalmatia, Bosnia and Herzegovina were to be united with Serbia and Montenegro and to form a single or federated state. (4) The boundaries of Bulgaria, Serbia and Greece were to follow generally those existing after the first Balkan war; Bulgaria was to surrender to Greece more of the Aegean coast, and was to obtain Turkish territory to the district surrounding Constantinople. (5) Greece was to obtain more of the Aegean coast, and the Dodecanese, with possible territory in Asia Minor. (6) The Ottoman Empire was to be reduced to Anatolia, with no possessions in Europe, though this "requires consideration."

Lansing conceived of Constantinople under an international protectorate or a government acting as mandatory. The commission or mandatory was to have "the regulation of the Dardanelles and Bosphorus as international waterways." Both Armenia and Syria were to be protectorates of such Powers "as seems expedient from a domestic as well as an international point of view." Both were to have self government as soon as possible, and the open door principle was to be observed. Palestine was to be put under an autonomous or international protectorate or under a Power designated as mandatory. Arabia would receive consideration as to full or partial sovereignty of the state or states to be established. Great Britain was to be full sovereign over Egypt or to exercise a complete protectorate.

In the official American commentary on the Wilson Fourteen Points, which appeared in October 1918, Serbia appears as Jugoslavia with access to the Adriatic, while Rumania is accorded Dobruja,

Bessarabia and probably Transylvania. Bulgaria, on the other hand, is offered a part of Dobruja (as before 1913), as well as Thrace to the Enos-Midia line, or possibly to Midia-Rodosto as Lansing had outlined. Macedonia was to be allotted only after an impartial investigation, the basis of the investigation being the southern line of the "contested" zone in the Serbo-Bulgarian treaty of 1912. Albania was to be put under a protectorate, possibly of Italy, with the northern boundary substantially as of the London conference of 1913.

Constantinople and the Straits were to be internationalized, either collectively or under a mandate of a league of nations. The Turks were to be restricted to Anatolia, while the coast lands, "where Greeks predominate," should be placed under international control, with Greece as the most likely mandatory. Armenia should be given a Mediterranean port, under a protecting Power. Though the French might claim this protectorate, it was felt that the Armenians would prefer Great Britain. Syria had been allotted to France already in the secret agreements of 1916. The best mandatory for Palestine, Mesopotamia and Arabia appeared to be Great Britain, whose forces had thoroughly conquered all these territories by this time. Guarantees for the mandatories in Asia Minor were to be written in the peace treaty, containing protection for minorities, the open door and the internationalization of the railroad trunk lines.[65]

While the American government in principle, was opposed to the secret treaties partitioning Turkey among the members of the Entente, and was insisting on the idea of mandates, a careful perusal of its documents indicates territorial dispositions in Asiatic Turkey in striking accord with the secret treaties. This applied neither to Italy nor to Russia, however. But the French position in Syria is clearly recognized, and the British position in Mesopotamia, Palestine and Arabia is accepted. Even in the American program the possibility of the disappearance of the Ottoman Empire from the map is announced openly. Finally the American government favored the internationalization of Constantinople as sound, time-honored American doctrine—though it was not to be applied to the Panama canal.

While the doctrines and principles sounded in the Wilson address of January 8, 1918 and further statements of policy struck a responsive chord in Soviet Russia, M. Chicherin, who was now people's commissar for foreign affairs, found occasion to point out some omissions in the American program. In a note of October 24, 1918, Chicherin "complimented" the American president on his stand and inferred that Wilson

meant "*that the masses of the people must everywhere first become the masters of their own fate in order to unite afterwards in a league of free nations. But strangely enough, we do not find among your demands the liberation of Ireland, Egypt, or India, nor even the liberation of the Philippines, and we would be very sorry to learn that these people should be denied the opportunity to participate together with us, through their freely elected representatives, in the organization of the League of Nations.*"[65]a

Meanwhile, the end of the war was approaching. British arms were victorious throughout Mesopotamia, Arabia, Palestine and Syria. On October 1, 1918, Feisal entered Damascus at the head of his own Arab forces. Having conquered Mesopotamia, Palestine and Syria—the British moved on. Not until after the armistice did they reach the vilayet of Mosul in northern Mesopotamia. But when the Russians collapsed on the Caucasus frontier, the English were forced to take over another land passage to India. The British objective was far reaching. The plan was to cover the Mesopotamian conquests, to put hands on the oil of Baku and to create a zone of security as large as possible around the Indian Empire. The scheme called for the taking of Enzeli, on the Caspian sea, *via* Persia, then Baku. A naval, military and political base was to be established at Baku, and the oil would be controlled. From this vantage point, the British would coöperate with the Christians of Urmia, the Transcaucasians and anti-Bolshevist elements of the Trans-Caspian, arouse an anti-Turkish Moslem federation in the Caucasus and Turkestan, and exercise an international mandate over western and central Asia. The first British mission, under Dunsterville, reached Baku in the summer of 1918, but was forced out in September. A second mission under Malleson regained Baku in November 1918, and obtained control of the railroad to Batum. This point was evacuated August 24, 1919. The Transcaucasus region furnished a point from which to attack, not only Turkey, but the Bolsheviks in Soviet Russia.[66]

It was a favorable moment for Britain. Germany was out of it, Russia was now in the throes of one of the most gigantic political and social revolutions in history, while France was absorbed in shaping her own Rhine frontier in the west. Turkey was awaiting the death sentence of her national existence. The time was ripe for England to realize her world policy—could she now hope to establish an effective domination on the land and sea routes to the crown jewel of the British Empire, India?

Having borne the brunt of the battle against Turkey, Great Britain was determined to have her own way in the armistice and peace with Turkey.[67] Measures were taken quickly, once the opportunity developed, to obtain control in the Near East and to oblige Turkey to treat with the British alone. The Bulgarian army, operating against Franchet d'Espérey's army of the Orient, broke into retreat, and on September 29, 1918, an armistice was signed. On October 2 the *Sobranie* accepted the terms and the next day Tsar Ferdinand abdicated in favor of his son Boris III. The army was to be demobilized.

The defection of Bulgaria was the beginning of the end for the Central Powers. Not only did it cut the vital communications between Turkey and the Central States, but it left open the southern flank to the menace of Allied arms. Turkey was ready to capitulate on October 5. The same day, Maréchal d'Espérey formulated his fundamental plan of action in the Balkans. It stipulated:

"*1. The Bulgarian army being* hors de cause, *our principal objective is to liberate all Serbia and to menace Austria-Hungary.*

"*2. To hold the important strategic points of Bulgaria in order to keep in touch with Rumania and to cut the communications between the Central (Powers) and Turkey.*

"*3. To put into operation in the briefest delay the means necessary to act against Turkey for opening the Dardanelles by a sharp attack on the isthmus of Bulair in a way to permit the entrance of the Allied fleets in Marmora.*

"*4. To operate against the Austrian forces of Albania which gravely threaten our advance, to free Albania and Montenegro.*"[67a]

To carry out his plan of action, the French general intended to use a total of seventeen divisions along the Serbian front. A French division was to form the advance guard moving toward Rumania. An English brigade was to move on Varna, Burgas and Dobritch, while mixed garrisons were to occupy the capital and other important points in Bulgaria. Finally, a southern section of the army, composed of five divisions, with Adrianople and the Aegean sea as the objective, was to be placed under the command of a French general.

D'Espérey advised his government, "I shall act without waiting." This telegram caught the members of the Entente unaware—without military unity, the Allies had fundamentally opposed national ambitions in the Balkans. On October 7, 1918, Clemenceau notified d'Espérey of the aims of the supreme war council of the Allies. Not only did the Allies intend to free Serbia and to regain contact with Rumania

for offensive action against the principal enemies, but "to isolate Turkey in order to force her to an armistice and to open to us free communication in the Black sea."[67b] Such was the scheme for the early conclusion of the great conflict when the final act of the war drama was already being staged.

Whatever may have been the aims of France toward penetrating the heart of the Central Powers, Great Britain desired to concentrate her attention on the Near East and Turkey in particular. The Turkish capital could be attacked only from Thrace, and General Milne, in command of the British right wing of d'Espérey's army was to be detailed for this important task. Lloyd George now obtained from Clemenceau the right of the British to exercise a superior authority over the entire region of Constantinople. On October 7, 1918, the French prime minister sent the following self-explanatory order to General d'Espérey: "1. *The eastern section of the Allied army which will march on Constantinople will be placed under the direct command of an English general, himself placed under the direct orders of the C. A.A. 2. This eastern section, charged with the march on Constantinople, will be composed principally of English troops, but will include also some French, Italian, Serb and Greek troops. 3. Reciprocally, English troops will take part in the operations toward the north.*" This order gave the British unquestioned supremacy both on land and sea in the region of the Straits, and enabled them, almost without consulting either France or Italy, to impose the armistice on the beaten Turks.

Admiral Calthorpe, commander of the British Mediterranean fleet at Malta, hastened to Mudros on October 11 to lay the ground for an armistice with Turkey. Immediate negotiations were delayed until the English had an assured position in Syria and Iraq (Aleppo and Mosul), and had established their influence at Constantinople. General Townshend, who had been a prisoner of war in Turkey since his surrender at Kut-el-Amara, served as an intermediary and advised the Turks to ask for the protection of England. This suggestion was accepted, and Izzet Pasha sent Townshend to Mudros on October 20 to propose the suspension of hostilities. The proposal included opening of the Dardanelles to the British fleet, autonomy of Iraq and Syria under the Sultan, a similar position for the Caucasus, evacuation of Iraq and Syria by the Allies, fixation of the European frontier of Turkey in the 1913 boundaries, and the liberation of British prisoners.[68]

On October 22 Calthorpe invited the Turks to send envoys to Mudros, and the next day he received orders from London containing the bases on which the armistice was to be signed. These were: The opening of the Dardanelles to Constantinople, and the opening of the Bosphorus into the Black sea; occupation by the Allies of the forts of these Straits.[69] Possibility of occupying Constantinople by Allied troops appears to have alarmed the Turks, but the difficulty was avoided by allowing the Allied naval squadrons to arrive before the troops, who were only to guard the city.[70] Finally, on October 30 the armistice was signed in the name of the Allies, though the Italians and French knew its exact contents apparently only after its signature.[71]

The terms of the Mudros armistice opened up the Dardanelles, guaranteed access to the Black sea and provided for Allied occupation of the forts along the Dardanelles and Bosphorus. The Turkish forces were to be demobilized immediately, except where necessary to preserve order. Their disposition was to be "determined by the Allies, after consultation with the Turkish government." All war vessels in Turkish waters were to be interned in such ports as directed, while free use of all ports for Allied vessels was granted. Article VII gave the Allies "the right to occupy any strategic points in the event of any situation arising which threatens the security of the Allies." The Turks were ordered to withdraw all troops in northwestern Persia and Transcaucasia. The Allies were placed in control of all railroads. They were to occupy Batum, and Turkey was to raise no objection to the occupation of Baku. (The British were already there.) Article XVI provided for the surrender of all garrisons in Hejaz, Assir-Yemen, Syria and Mesopotamia to the nearest Allied garrisons, and all Turkish troops were to be withdrawn from Cilicia, except those necessary to preserve order.

All Turkish officers in Tripolitania and Cyrenaica were to surrender to the Italians. Other articles of importance required the immediate departure of all Germans and Austrians. Compliance with orders regarding the disposal of equipment, arms and ammunition was mandatory. An Allied representative was to be attached to the Turkish ministry of supplies to safeguard Allied interests. Article XXIII stipulated that "in case of disorder in the six Armenian vilayets, the Allies reserve for themselves the right to occupy any part of them." Finally, Turkey was to cease all relations with the Central Powers. Hostilities were to cease at noon, October 31, 1918.[72]

Turkey had surrendered. The Entente—particularly Great Britain —was in control. The Straits were entirely in the hands of England. This was in accordance with the fundamental desires of London, which wanted to control the entire region of the Straits and Constantinople in order to use it as a base of operations possibly against the Germans in Russia, or as a vantage point for an economic blockade against Bolshevism.[73]

The British seemed determined to get control of the Near East not only against their enemies the Turks, but also against their allies the French. They had already gained supremacy over the French in the region of Constantinople and had forced Clemenceau to recognize that fact. They had also won a fundamental supremacy in Mesopotamia, Palestine and Syria. Only a few French troops coöperated in these campaigns—not more than 6,000 in Syria. Feisal was now in Damascus. But English troops had not yet occupied Mosul. Britain hastened the march of her armies of Iraq on Mosul, and the naval and military forces of Calthorpe and Milne on Constantinople. Having secured the right to enter any territories of Turkey in order to guarantee security and preserve order, British troops pushed on to the Mosul vilayet. The advance was ordered on November 1 1918, the day after the armistice with Turkey went into effect.[74] All garrisons in Iraq were ordered to surrender. At the approach of the British, troubles occurred in Mosul. The Turks accused the British of inciting the disorders to secure a pretext for occupation. On November 15, 1918, the soldiers of Britain entered the vilayet. By the end of November the Turkish commander was led to complain that Great Britain was penetrating to the interior of Diarbekir and would end by "making us retreat as far as Sivas."[75] Evidently England was determined that the Turks should evacuate the entire region.

Meanwhile, grave difficulties confronted the French in Syria— apparently, the Arabs were not enamoured with the *mission civilizatrice* of France. On November 9, 1918, just two days before the war with the Central Powers ended, France and England issued their joint declaration on Arab policy. They avowed purely altruistic motives. Their aim was "*the complete and final emancipation of all these peoples so long oppressed by the Turks, and to establish national governments and administrations which shall derive their authority from the initiative and free will of the peoples themselves. To realize this, France and Great Britain are in agreement to encourage and assist the establishment of native governments in Syria and Mesopotamia, now*

*liberated by the Allies, as also in those territories for whose liberation they are striving, and to recognize those governments immediately after they are effectively established."* Nor were the two Powers desirous of imposing foreign institutions on the Arabs. "Such is the part which the two Allied governments have set themselves to play in the liberate territories."[76]

Undoubtedly the Arabs expected too much from this declaration of their "liberators." At any rate, they hoped to determine their own future, without consulting the French in Syria, where a large Arab population did not desire French rule. Feisal, who had been in Paris in 1916, to reach an accord with the Quai d'Orsay, came again in 1919 to the peace conference to plead the cause of Arab independence, and to unite the pople of Syria with those of Mesopotamia without French interference. The fact that Colonel Lawrence, who had done so much to bring the Arabs into the war, accompanied the Arab leader, indicates British support in this project.[77] But the story of the peace conference is reserved for later consideration.

In December 1918, shortly before the peace conference of Paris was to convene, Great Britain added further assurances to her position in the east by forcing the French to surrender Mosul and to change Palestine from an international zone to a British sphere of interest. This alteration occurred in December, when Clemenceau visited Lloyd George in London. What brought about the change of attitude on the part of Clemenceau and the desire of Lloyd George for the retrocession of Mosul and Palestine to England? There were several factors. The fact that Britain had played such a preponderant part in the eastern theater of the war was used to considerable advantage by Lloyd George.[78] The French had experienced considerable difficulties in Syria, and in order to reach ultimate agreement, Clemenceau had gone to London. When he requested his Welsh friend to confirm the French position in Syria and Cilicia, Lloyd George "made demands for certain places which he thought should be included in the British zone of influence, namely, Mosul." In addition, he asked for Palestine. On his return to Paris, Clemenceau urged a favorable consideration, which resulted in the memorandum of February 15, 1919, by which France gave formal consent to these changes.[79] Russia no longer on the north, Britain retained the territory of Mosul in her own hands. In Palestine Great Britain adopted the policy that a British Palestine, a "national home" for the Jews, was much safer as a guard

for the Suez canal than one under *international* control. It was sound policy for Great Britain to internationalize the Straits. It was unsound policy to internationalize Palestine.

Doubtless there were other reasons for the exchange. Victor Bérard, speaking before the French Senate on July 28, 1920, declared that Clemenceau had surrendered Mosul and Palestine to Lloyd George in return for "Metz and Strasburg without plebiscite, the Saar basin, Rhine occupation, complete security and coal without a money advance."[80] André Tardieu, however, puts the trade on three conditions: (1) France was to obtain by the exchange her part of the Mosul oil; (2) Great Britain was to support France unconditionally at the peace conference on the basis of the secret treaties; (3) the mandates established, the French mandate for the zones created by the Sykes-Picot accord (including Syria, with Damascus and Aleppo, Alexandretta and Beirut), would be supported.[81]

Great Britain now had made several fundamental alterations in her position in Asiatic Turkey, following the Russian débacle and the Turkish defeat. That France considered her position "legally" secure on the basis of the secret agreements—and despite the fact that the entire edifice of these treaties seemed to be tottering—is clear from Pichon's statement before the French Chamber on December 29, 1918. The French foreign minister declared: "We have in their (Turkish) empire incontestable rights to safeguard; we have them in Syria, the Lebanon, in Cilicia and Palestine." These rights were based on historic title, on agreements, on contracts and on the aspirations of the peoples. Though Pichon recognized the complete freedom of the peace conference in dealing with the secret treaties, he felt that "these agreements established with England continue to bind England and us . . . and that the rights which have been granted to us . . . are rights acquired from the present."[82] While Feisal appeared to be in popular control of Syria, French policy was to use him, as it were, in securing peaceful acquiescence of French designs in Syria. This, evidently, was the position of the French republic as the peace conference began to discuss the question of Turkey and the Near East in the winter of 1919.

4.

*The Situation in the East*

Such was the situation in the east at the close of the world war. Turkey was completely at the mercy of the Powers of Europe—ready

for the operating table. During the course of the war the Entente had made agreements for the partition of the Ottoman Empire among England, France, Russia and Italy. Great Britain had entered into separate negotiations with the Arabs during 1915-1916, with a view not only to securing their aid during the war, but with the definite purpose of establishing British supremacy throughout Mesopotamia, Arabia, Palestine, and perhaps, Syria. An Arab state or confederation might take the place of Turkey as a bulwark along the route to India. The conflicting promises made to Hussein of the Hejaz and to Ibn Saud of the Nejd, together with the conflict in the promises made to the French and the Arabs in Syria was to lead to serious complications and difficulties in the post-war years. The predominant part played by Great Britain in the theater of Asiatic Turkey gave her the lead in the negotiations for an armistice and peace. When the Bolsheviks published and denounced the secret treaties in November and December 1917, the whole question of Asiatic Turkey came before the world —a world somewhat shocked and disillusioned by this revelation of realistic Allied aims in Asiatic Turkey. President Wilson was fundamentally opposed to the secret treaties, of which he knew the essential outlines. Wilson's opposition led to the establishment of the liberal principle of the mandate system. But in the end, the significant territorial dispositions of the secret treaties remained intact. Shortly before the peace conference, however, Great Britain was able to secure both Palestine and Mosul, was dominant in the Transcaucasian region and in virtual control of Constantinople and the Straits. The Ottoman Empire had ceased to exist. At the peace conference it was to be carved up among the members of the Entente.

# CHAPTER VII

# THE TURKISH QUESTION AT THE
# PEACE CONFERENCE

## The Turkish Question

NO MORE important question confronted the peace conference at Paris than that of Turkey. In its ensemble, the Turkish problem involved issues of world-wide importance and significance. Once more the statesmen of the world were trying to reach a solution of an age-old Eastern Question. And once more the Eastern Question was to prove not only a stumbling block on the road to world peace, but also was to give rise to serious disputes and grave rivalries among the Great Powers of Europe.

The disposition of Turkish territories among the members of the Entente involved many difficult and complicated issues. The question of Constantinople and the Straits alone, as one writer, Mr. Leonard Woolf, puts it, would indicate the probabilities of future war or peace. He states: "*Constantinople and the narrow Straits upon which it stands have occasioned the world more trouble, have cost humanity more in blood and suffering during the last five hundred years, than any other single spot upon the earth. Certainly during the last hundred years it has been the chief European center of international unrest. From it and about it, have radiated continually international rivalries and hatreds and suspicions. It was the direct origin and cause of a large number of the wars fought in the nineteenth century. It is not improbable that when Europe in her last ditch has fought the last battle of the great war, we shall find that what we have again been fighting about is really Constantinople.*"[1]

This judgment, passed in 1917, practically has been confirmed by the documentary materials published since the world war. At any rate, the problem of the Near East and Turkey must be assigned, if not the chief, at least a major share, in the causes which finally led to the great conflict. Would the peace conference, which was called to settle the issues arising from "the war to end wars," give a solution to the time-honored question of the Orient? Would the rivalries of the Powers recede before the necessity of a fundamental world solution of the problem in the interests of world peace? Both in Europe and in Asia territories were to be cut away from the Turkish Empire. In

Europe, the Thracian question involved Greece, Turkey and Bulgaria, as well as the ambitions of the Great Powers. In Asia arose the questions of the future Turkish state and the problems of a separate Armenia, Kurdistan, Arabia, Mesopotamia, Syria, Palestine and Hejaz. Were these Asiatic territories to become independent or to be placed under the mandates of the European nations? The fate of the Straits and Constantinople had to be determined.

Since the Russian revolution, the subsequent denunciation and publication of the secret treaties, and the advent of the United States into the war and the troubled sea of European politics, the Allied and Associated Powers had been forced to make liberal promises with reference to Asiatic Turkey. The peace conference was faced with the secret treaties dividing Turkey between France, England, Russia (now out of it), and Italy on the one hand, and the British obligations to the Arabs on the other. A conflict between the Powers at the conference ensued. Moreover the Arabs clashed with the French in Syria and called into question the entire edifice of the secret agree-ments. Both Greece and Italy claimed a wide share of Turkey on the western shores of Asia Minor. President Wilson did not consider himself bound by these agreements, but was unable to obviate the difficulties which they brought about. His plan was to erect a league of nations, with a mandatory system to solve the problems of retarded peoples. This, in the end, under one form or another, was the solution adopted. So difficult and complicated, however, was the Turkish question, so vital were the conflicting interests of the Powers involved, that it was not until August 10, 1920, that peace was at last dictated to the Turks at Sèvres. But the treaty of Sèvres proved abortive, aroused the Turks to heroic resistance, and led only to further conflict and disturbance in the east. Only the treaty of Lausanne in July 1923 finally brought forth a settlement of the Eastern Question.

2.

*Turkey before the Paris Conference*

When the Paris conference met in January 1919, it appeared that all the Powers (Russia being absent) were agreed that Turkey was to be broken into its component elements. The Straits were to be inter-nationalized. Armenia, Syria, Palestine, Arabia and Mesopotamia were to be separated from the former Ottoman Empire. However, the fact

that the Powers of the Entente had spheres of influence in the various parts of Turkey led to a clash of interests and widely different views as to the ultimate disposition of the territory.[2] In particular, France and England engaged in a bitter struggle not only over their respective shares of Asiatic Turkey, but over the control of Constantinople and the Straits.

Shortly after the opening ceremonies of the conference, the Turkish question in all its angles presented itself. Already it had been the subject of memoranda, informal conference and debate.[3] As early as December 16, 1918, Jan Christian Smuts, of South Africa, had written a memorandum embodying certain principles which he desired to see written into the treaty of peace. Europe was being "liquidated," he said, and he wished to have the "peoples and territories formerly belonging to Russia, Austria and Turkey" placed under the mandate of the league of nations. He did not want annexation of any of these territories by any of the victorious Powers. The rule of "self-government, or the consent of the governed to their form of government" was to be "fairly and reasonably applied." He felt that such a principle might be applied to such territories as upper and lower Mesopotamia, Lebanon and Syria, though not to Armenia or Palestine.[4] Strangely enough, General Smuts did not wish to place the African territories conquered by British arms under the mandate system. It remained for President Wilson to do that, particularly in his first Paris draft for a league of nations, dated January 10, 1919. In this important document, the American president had stated: "*In respect of the peoples and territories which formerly belonged to Austria Hungary, and to Turkey, and in respect of the colonies formerly under the dominion of the German Empire, the league of nations shall be regarded as the residuary trustee with sovereign right of ultimate disposal or of continued administration in accordance with certain fundamental principles . . .; and this reversion and control shall exclude all rights or privileges of annexation on the part of any Power.*"[5] The Wilson program called for the exclusion of any right of annexation by any European Power, the rule of self-determination, and stipulated that "all policies of administration or economic development be based primarily upon the well-considered interests of the people themselves."

This was the status of the problem of Turkey when it came before the representatives of the Powers on January 20, 1919. Lloyd George, speaking for Great Britain, pointed out that the "doctrine of a mandatory for all conquests in the late Turkish Empire and in the German

colonies" had now been accepted. But he insisted on the recognition of three classes of mandates: (1) mandates applicable to countries civilized, but not yet organized, such as Arabia, where "a century might elapse before the people could be properly organized;" (2) mandates applicable to tropical countries; (3) mandates were to be applied only to conquered parts either of the Turkish Empire or of the German Empire. This would exclude Smyrna, Adalia and Northern Anatolia from the system.

President Wilson, apparently did not fall in with the line of thought of his British colleague. He did not feel that one should begin a discussion as to a possible partition of Turkey at this time. It had been suggested that America take a mandate in Turkey. He felt that the American people would be very reluctant not only to undertake such a task, but would be disinclined to send troops into Turkey. "But even if it was suggested that American troops should occupy Constantinople, or Mesopotamia, it was evident that they could not do so as they were not at war with Turkey." It would be very unwise, President Wilson thought, "to accept any form of mandate until they knew how it was intended to work . . . ." Wilson's statement filled Lloyd George "with despair." The British statesman was concerned only with immediate peace and was anxious to get British armies back home and demobilized. He had no ulterior motive or design in Asiatic Turkey. Signor Orlando, the representative of the government at Rome, declared that "Italy had only one simple and perfectly just desire, namely, that a proper proportion between the Allies should be maintained in respect of the occupation of those territories." All he asked was that "Italy obtain its share of mandates or territories to be militarily occupied."[6] This was to be Orlando's position whether a temporary mandatory were appointed or the territorial *status quo* maintained. Italy was demanding her place in the Turkish partition.

On January 30, 1919, further discussion took place in the supreme council. Already it had been decided that such territories as Armenia, Syria, Palestine, Arabia and Mesopotamia were to be separated from the Turkish Empire—their ultimate disposition was yet to be determined. Mr. Lloyd George now moved to include another territory in the lands to be taken from the Turks: ". . . *He did not realize that it was separate. He thought Mesopotamia and Armenia would cover it but he was now informed that it did not. He referred to Kurdistan, which was between Mesopotamia and Armenia . . . .*" In reality Mr. Lloyd George was interested in securing a buffer between Mosul and

Turkey proper. Wilson again stated his objection to placing American troops in Turkish territory, to which Lloyd George countered with the story of British military burdens. Great Britain had no intention of accepting a mandate for either Syria or Armenia. *"He thought the same thing applied to Kurdistan and the Caucasus, where there were rich oil-wells. He did not think that Great Britain had the slightest intention of being the mandatory even in the case of the oil-wells of Baku, but somebody had to be there to protect the Armenians and to keep the tribes and sects in Lebanon from cutting each other's throats and attacking the French or Turks, or whoever else might be there . . . ."* President Wilson "could think of nothing the people of the United States would be less inclined to accept than military responsibility in Asia," but would endeavor to gain such acceptance if it were desired sincerely. He suggested that the military authorities study and report on the question of military occupation. Clemenceau felt that withdrawal of troops would be very difficult as long as Russia was an uncertain factor. Finally, on motion of Lloyd George, the Powers decided to ask the military representatives of the Allied Powers to report "as to the most equitable and economical distribution among these Powers of the burden of supplying military forces for the purpose of maintaining order in the Turkish Empire and Transcaucasia pending the decisions of the peace conference concerning the government of Turkish territory."[7] The meeting concluded its labors by adopting the following significant resolution: . . . *"The Allied and Associated Powers are agreed that Armenia, Syria, Mesopotamia and Kurdistan, Palestine and Arabia must be completely severed from the Turkish Empire. This is without prejudice to the settlement of other parts of the Turkish Empire."*[8]

Mandates, in accordance with the program of Wilson and Smuts, were to be set up in behalf of the territories thus detached from Turkey. Certain communities had reached the stage where independence could be recognized provisionally, subject to mandates until able to stand alone. This was particularly true, it was thought, of the parts of Turkey such as the territories named. The wishes of the communities were to be "a principal consideration in the selection of the mandatory Power." On January 30, 1919, the European Powers had decreed the end of the Turkish Empire. It remained for those Powers to fight over the spoils of the dismembered Empire. How the European statesmen considered the mandate principles—from the idealistic and material standpoints—the coming months were to indicate.

On February 3, 1919, M. Venizelos, the Cretan who had long fought the battle for the union of all Greeks under the flag of Hellas, appeared before the conference to present the claims of his government. He began by asking for northern Epirus, the Aegean islands (including the Dodecanese, Imbros and Tenedos), Thrace and Western Asia Minor. Northern Epirus he claimed on the basis of Greek population, where there were 120,000 Greeks to only 80,000 Albanians. According to Venizelos the population of the Dodecanese consisted of 110,000 Greeks contrasted with 12,000 of all other nationalities. "Greece claimed not only the islands of the Dodecanese, but all the Aegean islands, including those which for strategic reasons owing to their situation at the entrance of the Straits had not been attributed to Greece by the conference of London after the Balkan war." The Greek premier made no demand for Cyprus because he felt that since England had offered the island during the war she would now be "sufficiently magnanimous to surrender Cyprus to Greece."[9]

Thrace was to be Greek. Bulgaria was to cede western Thrace, depriving herself of an outlet to the Aegean, and to receive access to the Mediterranean through the Straits, which were to be internationalized. Moreover Greece would allow Bulgaria a commercial outlet at Cavalla or Salonica. Venizelos made no request for Constantinople, however, though "in reality Constantinople was a Greek town." It should be internationalized and placed under the league of nations— including the vilayet of Constantinople, the sanjaks of Ismid, Gallipoli, Biga and a part of Brusa. The sultan should be made to leave and go to Konia or Brusa, and a small Turkish state should be confined to Asia.[10]

The next day the shrewd Greek premier continued his address. He now claimed western Asia Minor west of a line drawn between Kastzoirzo and the sea of Marmora, excluding the Straits area, basing his pretensions on Wilson's twelfth point, namely, the geographical and historical unity of the country and the Greek majority in the population of the country. Nor were the islands along the shore to be excluded. With the exception of Constantinople, according to Greek figures, 1,132,000 Greeks dwelt in Asia Minor, mostly merchant classes living along the Mediterranean littoral.

Armenia, Venizelos thought, should include the six Armenian vilayets, with Russian Armenia and Trebizond and Ardana, as well as Cilicia. As to the military problems involved in the Greek ambitions,

he assured the conference that they were not great and "would present no difficulties." The Greek disaster of 1922 demonstrated the contrary of that position.

At the conclusion of his statement Lloyd George moved that the Greek claims be examined by an expert committee composed of two representatives of the United States, the British Empire, France and Italy.[11]

Not until March 6, and then only after several meetings, was the committee on Greek territorial claims ready with its recommendations. The United States, France and Great Britain accepted Greek demands in the southwestern part of northern Epirus, but drew the frontier between the Voyansa and Zrevos rivers, while Italy opposed them. Great Britain and France alone, however, supported the Greek aspira- tions. Italy, for obvious reasons, and the United States, voted for the existing boundary. All four delegations accepted the claims of Greece in eastern and western Thrace, with modifications, though the Italians made reservations. The reservations for western Thrace asked that Dedeagatch be left to Bulgaria, leaving the whole of eastern Thrace in the hands of the separate state of Constantinople, whose boundaries were not yet determined.[12] In western Asia Minor, Italy would make no recommendations at all because the settlement could not be separated from the general solution of Anatolia as a whole, and because the regions to which Greece aspired had been to a large extent the subject of cer- tain well known international arrangements. In other words, Greek interests clashed with those of Italy, for the Italians felt their interests had been secure under the secret treaties of 1915 and 1917 which promised Rome territorial acquisitions in the Smyrna and Adalia regions.[13]

Sir Eyre Crowe, the British representative on the committee, informed his Italian colleague on March 1, 1919, that the 1915 agree- ment referred only to Adalia, while the 1917 accord was invalid for want of Russian approval. France took a similar stand, though she would not oppose Italy on the question of the islands. Mr. Wester- mann, the American delegate, stated that the United States was not bound by the secret treaties, but he also was opposed to the Greek position. Both the British and American delegates, however, accepted the French proposition of March 1. This project stipulated: (1) if the peace conference decided to grant the Greek demands in western Asia Minor, the boundary should include Aivali, on the north coast, Soma, Kirk, Agatch, Alashehr, and Scala Nuova on the south coast;

(2) if the Greek claims were not accepted, in case Anatolia were put under a Great Power, this part of Asia Minor should not be placed under the same Power.

Neither Great Britain nor France would make recommendations concerning the Dodecanese, but Westermann supported the Greeks. However, neither Imbros nor Tenedos, at the entrance of the Straits, were to be fortified. Castellorizo, in view of its proximity to the mainland, was to remain under the state ruling over the Asiatic littoral. But were that sovereignty Turkish, Castellorizo was to be Greek.

The report of the committee on Greek claims came before the central committee on territorial questions on March 7, 1919, but no unanimous agreement was reached. The French and British representatives urged acceptance of the report, but were faced with the opposition of the United States and Italy.[14] Later during the month of March the American delegation appears to have undergone a change of attitude, perhaps on account of the fact that other members believed more strongly in Greek ambitions in Asia Minor, and the general political situation. Westermann gained the impression that either House or Wilson, or House alone, had accepted the Smyrna proposal.[15] Venizelos continued to press his claims for the Asiatic coast of Turkey,[16] the ultimate result of which was to be the Greek military débacle of September 1922.

Others were demanding a share of the Turkish estate. The Emir Feisal was received in Paris in January 1919, and decorated with the *croix de guerre*, though the government of France made it clear that he was received, not as representing the head of a state, but as a distinguished guest.[17] On February 6, Feisal appeared before the conference to present his case for the Arabs. In a memorandum which he presented on January 31, 1919, Feisal had asked for the independence of all Arabs in Asia from the Alexandretta line south. This would include Syria, Iraq, Jezireh, Hejaz, Nejd and the Yemen. Since the Hejaz was already independent and Aden under British protection, these were later excluded from the demand.[18]

Feisal's claims were based on the fact that the Arabs were a civilized people, had a common language, natural frontiers, and the almost one hundred per cent Arab population of the country. Socially and economically, he asserted, the country was a unit. The Arabs had fought on the side of the Entente and independence had been promised them by the British. Moreover the principles of Wilson were involved. The Arabs in Syria, Damascus, Beirut, Aleppo, Tripoli, Latakia and

other districts had declared for independence and had hoisted the Arab flag before the arrival of Allied forces. This flag had been lowered provisionally until the conference had settled the question. Recognized as belligerents during the war, Feisal now demanded independence for the Arabs. He asked fulfilment of the promises of November 1918.[19]

Syria claimed her independence and place in the proposed Arab confederation. Some people in the Lebanon asked for French protection, but desired economic union with Syria. Palestine should be left for the mutual consideration of the interested parties, and constituted an exception in the Arab ambitions for independence—at least temporarily. Feisal suggested an international inquiry into this problem. On Lloyd George's question as to Arab military operations, Feisal replied that the Hejaz had furnished some 100,000 men to the Allied cause, and outside the Hejaz, had operated in Syria. In reply to President Wilson, he stated that he was there to ask for the independence of his people and for their right to choose their own mandatory. The Arabs had fought for the principle of their own unity and freedom and now sought to realize it. Feisal did not include the Kurdish peoples as Arabs.[20]

A week later the problem of Syria proper was considered when Dr. Bliss appeared before the council. His plea was for a commission of investigation in Syria and the Lebanon.[21] At the same time representatives from Syria and the Lebanon were introduced, mostly at the instigation of the French. M. Chekri Gamen insisted on the distinct character of Syria—to annex it to Arabia would be a political mistake. He desired a Syria completely separated from Arabia, but including Palestine, where the Jews could be autonomous. The government should be a constitutional monarchy, under the guardianship of France. Two days later further pleas for a French mandate were heard on behalf of Syria and the Lebanon.[22] But when Mr. Lansing raised the issue of sending a commission of investigation to Syria on February 18 the question was postponed.[23] Investigating commissions might arouse the people and scatter the seeds of discontent.

On February 26, 1919, the Armenian delegation presented its demands to the conference. Both M. Aharoman, president of the republic, and Boghos Nubar Pasha made statements. The substance of the Armenian claims may be found in the addresses and a memorandum presented the same day. Armenian aspirations called for an Armenian state including: (1) Cilicia, with the sanjaks of Marash (including Khozan, Djebel-Bereket, Adana, with Alexandretta); (2) the six vilayets of Erzerum, Bitlis, Van, Diarbekir, Kharput, Sivas,

and a part of Trebizond, giving access to the Black sea; (3) the territory of the Armenian republic of the Caucasus, comprising Erivan, the southern part of Tiflis, the southwest part of Elizabetpol and Kars, except the northern part of Ardahan. This territory was to be liber- ated from Turkey, and put under the joint protection of the Powers, with a mandate for twenty years.[24] As will be pointed out later, few of these claims were to be granted, and the Armenian question proved well-nigh insoluble at Paris.

The Zionist cause was heard on February 27, 1919. The problem of Palestine was a complicated one at best and an equitable solution was difficult to find. Despite the pretentions of the Jews to the country, David Hunter Miller, legal advisor to the American delegation, had pointed out to President Wilson in January "that the rule of self- determination would prevent the establishment of a Jewish state in Palestine," even as it would preclude "the establishment of any auton- omous Armenia," since both peoples were in a decided minority. Nevertheless Mr. Sokolow, who made the first statement for the Zionists, asked for the recognition of the historic right of the Jews to a national home in Palestine.[25] Both Great Britain and France had recognized Palestine as such a national home, and President Wilson had signified his approval. On January 3, just before the conference opened, the Emir Feisal and Mr. Weizmann, president of the Zionist organization, had signed an agreement pledging their friendship, and promising after the peace conference to delimit the boundaries. Pales- tine was to be a national home for the Jews, but Arab rights were to be protected. There was to be religious freedom, and the Mohammedan holy places were to be placed under Moslem control. Moreover agree- ment was stipulated on matters before the conference, while disputes were to be referred to Great Britain. These last two points, and the fact that the treaty was signed in London, indicate British supervision of the arrangement as well as Britain's determination to control affairs in the region of the Suez canal.[26] The Zionists preferred a mandate under the league of nations, and the mandatory was to promote Jewish immigration and preserve local self-government. But a Jewish home in a country overwhelmingly Arab in population and tradition could not but give rise to serious complications.

Like the other enemy states, Turkey was not allowed a voice at Paris, though General Sherif Pasha, delegate of the congress of Liberal Turks of Geneva presented several memoranda for the consideration of the conference. The Liberal Turks disclaimed any responsibility for

the entrance of Turkey into the war, but placed the blame for the action on the ruling clique of the day. A "memorandum on the claims of the Kurds" proposed an independent Kurdistan, formed fo the vilayets of Diarbekir, Kharput, Bitlis, Mosul and the sanjak of Urfa. Since the Arabs and Armenians were to be given their independence, it could not be denied to the Kurds. But, in essence, the Liberal Turkish elements stood for the integrity of Turkey. Constantinople, they felt, must remain Turkish and Moslem—"Constantinople being a Turkish city *par excellence*, without which the very existence of Turkey cannot be conceived . . . ." Turkey without the historic capital, would be a country without a heart, like a body "deprived of its source of life". To internationalize such a Turkish city would be a grave mistake. "To internationalize this city which, by its geographical position, shines on two continents, is to create a central *foyer* appropriate to certain subversive ideas which tend to prevail against the very principle of nationalities."[27] But any such pleas were in vain, for the Allies had their own aims with reference to Turkey, and those who had definite aspirations in Turkey were to use the principle of nationality only in so far as that principle furthered their ambitions.

The claims and counter-claims of the peoples in the Near East, the clash of interests of the Great Powers over the disposition of the territory in Asiatic Turkey, and the opposition of the United States to the secret treaties, brought that problem before the council of four on March 20, 1919.[28] That France and Great Britain were in conflict with each other during the course of the war, not only over military and naval operations in the Near East, but also over the territorial problems in that region, has been demonstrated amply. The territorial questions over which the two countries were now to quarrel so bitterly involved their rivalry in Asiatic Turkey and resulted in a serious conflict of interests in the matter of Constantinople and the Straits. This conflict, which developed during the early stages of the war (even before Russia was eliminated) continued throughout the struggle, disturbed and threatened the deliberations at the peace conference, prevented a solution at Paris and culminated in the Greco-Turkish war of 1919-1922.

M. Pichon, the French minister for foreign affairs, brought the secret treaties before the conference in a discussion of the Arab question on March 20. The Sykes-Picot agreement, he said, had for its purpose the detachment of the Arabs from the Turks, and the

settlement of the claims of Great Britain and France in Asia. Great Britain had no political aims in Syria—only economic interests which France desired to protect. France had sent only a small number of troops to Syria because of the demands on her own western front. Great Britain, however, had been concerned far more in the Turkish campaign. The disproportion of troops involved had resulted in many incidents, and M. Clemenceau had thought it best to bring the matter before the London government.

M. Pichon read the joint declaration concerning Arab policy which the two governments had issued on November 8, 1918. The British government did not evince great interest, the difficulties continued, and Clemenceau journeyed to London in December 1918 in order to patch up the differences. Asked to confirm the French position in Syria and Cilicia, Lloyd George demanded that Mosul and Palestine be placed definitely within the British zone of influence. On his return Clemenceau urged that this suggestion be examined in "the most favorable spirit," and the result was the French memorandum of February 15, 1919, giving in to the British position.[29]

The French were frank in declaring they did not want the responsibility of administering Palestine, though they preferred to see it "under an international administration". But France wanted the entire Syrian region treated as one under the mandatory of France. When Lloyd George desired to lighten the British burden, on January 30, 1919, by a redistribution of troops in Asia Minor, the French were ready to occupy Syria and Cilicia. Great Britain already had occupied Mesopotamia, including Mosul, and Italy was to march into the Caucasus and Konia.[30]

But the British wished to limit the French zone in Syria on the east and south involving the Jebel Druse, which France refused. As M. Pichon stated, "it was enough for the Chamber to know that the government were in negotiation with Great Britain for the handing over of Mosul." This had resulted in a proposal in the budget committee for a diminution of credits for Syria, and "in consequence, the minimum that France could accept was what had been put forward in the French government's note to Mr. Lloyd George, the object of which had been to give satisfaction at his desire for the inclusion of Mosul in the British zone."[31]

In answer to Pichon, Lloyd George explained that Britain had no question with France regarding Syria. That difficulty had been cleared up in London with M. Clemenceau, "at which time he had said he

wanted Mosul with the adjacent regions in Palestine." He wished "to acknowledge the cordial spirit in which M. Pichon had met our desires."[32] However the whole Syrian campaign had fallen to Great Britain, French troops being negligible. When Britain was carrying on the *brunt* of the battle *in the west*, from 900,000 to 1,000,000 British and Indian troops were fighting in Turkey and the Caucasus—almost the entire war in the east. Despite this fact, "M. Pichon seemed to think that we were departing from the 1916 agreement in other respects, as well as in respect to Mosul and Palestine."[33]

Lloyd George contested the French position in regard to the Arabs, insisting that the zone of French administration did not include Damascus, Homs, Hama or Aleppo. In the French zone of influence (A), France was pledged to support an independent Arab state or confederation under the suzerainty of an Arab chieftain. In this zone France would have priority of economic rights and privileges, as well as the right to supply advisors at the request of the people. This was, however, a question between France and Hussein, not the concern of Great Britain.[34]

M. Pichon replied that the adoption of the mandatory principle had altered the situation fundamentally—and France asked for the recognition of her mandate in Syria. On Lloyd George's further insistence that French occupation of Damascus would violate the treaty with Hussein and the Arabs, the French minister denied that France had made any such treaty with the Arabs.[35] Moreover France had been kept in the dark about the treaty. The British prime minister contended that the Sykes-Picot accord was based on a British engagement with Hussein, and that by signing that agreement, France was bound likewise to the treaty with Hussein. Even by the Sykes-Picot accord Damascus, Homs, Hama and Aleppo were not included in the "zone of direct administration, but in the independent Arab state." Pichon did not contest the point, though France had not recognized the Hejaz in 1916. He believed that France could reach an agreement with Feisal, if Great Britain would use her good offices to such a purpose. Such was the French position in securing a mandate for Syria and establishing French influence in that region.[36]

Although President Wilson was not indifferent to the Franco-British understandings and was interested in the commitments to Hussein, he felt that the disappearance of Russia had altered the basis of the secret treaties concerning Asiatic Turkey. His main desire was to know whether France was acceptable as a mandatory in Syria

and Great Britain in Mesopotamia, since the mandate principle had been adopted on January 30, 1919. Moreover other questions were involved, for if Cilicia were placed under Syria, Armenia would be cut off from the sea. The United States wanted no territory in Turkey, though some had suggested a mandate. On Wilson's suggestion, General Allenby, the conqueror of Palestine, explained that French occupation in Syria would result in serious trouble among the Moslems and Arabs, who might make war against the French under the leadership of the Emir Feisal. Already there had been difficulties in Damascus, Beirut and Aleppo.[37]

President Wilson urged the sending of an international commission to investigate the situation in Syria. Clemenceau accepted "in principle," but insisted on "guarantees," and that the commission should investigate Palestine, Mesopotamia and Syria, as well as other parts of Turkey. Nor was Lloyd George enthusiastic. Mr. Wilson was to draft the terms of reference of the commission.[38] In the end, however, the French objected, refused to send members, and England in turn backed down. Mr. Wilson then appointed President Henry C. King of Oberlin college and Charles R. Crane as a commission of investigation in Asia Minor.[39] Yet not until May 1919 was the commission under way, arriving at Jaffa in June.[40]

Meanwhile Feisal returned to Syria in March, later to be chosen king, and an Arab national congress meeting at Damascus demanded the withdrawal of Allied troops.[41] French efforts at conciliation evidently had failed. On March 25, 1919, an informal meeting of the British and French experts took place. Colonel Lawrence, Miss Gertrude Bell and Sir Valentine Chirol represented the British, while French interests were represented by Robert de Caix, Philippe Millet, Henri Brenier, Gauvain and d'Espeyran. All were opposed to sending a commission to Syria, as it would unsettle the country. The project to send the commission had resulted in the French failure to conciliate Feisal according to Lawrence. It was agreed that if a responsible French representative approached Feisal with a proposal there might be a chance of success. This proposal included: (1) a French mandate for Syria; (2) permission to the Syrians to elect their own prince in a national assembly convened at Damascus; (3) the position of France to be similar to that of Britain in Egypt. The Lebanon and possibly the territory of the Jebel Druse could be autonomous under Feisal.

Colonel Lawrence added that the movement for Arab unity had no serious political value for the present or the near future, and that there was no connection between the Emir Feisal and his father, the king of the Hejaz. He was against the Sykes-Picot boundaries, insisting that a proper division would extend the zone of economic dependence on Damascus and the Syrian boundaries far southeast of the Jordan. The French experts seemed to approve this project.[42] Though there may have been no real chance of Arab unity on account of differences among the Arabs themselves and the geographical nature of the country, the position of Colonel Lawrence is not without interest in view of his own earlier activities among these peoples.

3.

### The Constantinopolitan State

The fate of Constantinople and the Straits had come up for consideration early in the conference. The general agreement, vague and ill-defined though it was, favored an international settlement under a mandate of the league of nations. As early as December 2, 1918, this solution was suggested to Mr. David Hunter Miller by Lord Eustace Percy, of the British foreign office. The United States, Lord Eustace thought, might accept such a trust . . . "He went so far as to suggest that if the formulation of general principles were attempted the Panama canal would come in the same class as the Straits to which I replied pleasantly as expressing my personal views that such a grouping seemed hardly among the possibilities. I regard Percy's conversation as an effort to convey to me without stating them as such some of the British ideas which have been formulated, and that his Panama canal suggestion was an attempt to show difficulties in the way of idealistic principles of United States . . . ."[43] Mr. Miller should have countered by placing the Suez canal "in the same class as the Straits" as well. Again, on January 11, Miller reports a meeting with Lord Robert Cecil, Colonel Lawrence, Lionel Curtis and others, at which there was unanimous sentiment among the British present "that the United States should take Constantinople, and agreement . . . that it should take Armenia . . . ." Colonel Lawrence, who was openly anti-French in attitude, expressed the hope "that the United States would administer Syria."[44] The idea that the American government take over Constantinople seemed to be general. The British did not want the French there, the

231

French did not want the British in occupation, and neither desired an Italian mandate at that vital point in the region of the Straits. Hence the desire for an American mandate. As Armenia had few resources to be exploited, it too, might well go to the United States. As the American legal advisor pointed out, American interests in Turkey were largely sentimental, and largely limited to Armenia, though even then the United States was interested in the "open door" in the exploitation of the oil of Mosul. Miller commented as early as January 10, 1919 . . . . "*Doubtless the United States will get such of those (mandates) as Great Britain thinks too difficult for herself, and those will lie in the hands of the United States as a bulwark of the British Empire; such as Armenia. The rest will go to Great Britain, to France, and Japan, who, with theoretical responsibilities to the league of nations, have among them an absolute veto on every act of the executive council.*"[45]

Throughout March and April the experts worked on the project of the Constantinopolitan state. Until its structure and boundaries were determined, there was difficulty in formulating the outlines of the rest of Thrace, Turkish Anatolia and the Smyrna region of Asia Minor.[46] Its area, according to an American memorandum of uncertain date, ought to include the entire littoral of the Straits including that of the sea of Marmora. An area was to be reserved for Turkey in Anatolia about the size of the state of New Mexico, with a population of some 5,700,000 overwhelmingly Turkish.[47]

It was about this time that Italy became particularly nervous, both on the Fiume question and that of Asia Minor. Lloyd George and Clemenceau suggested on April 21, 1919, that Rome might compromise on the Adriatic, if given an Asiatic mandate. Clemenceau thought this mandate might cover a part of Anatolia, touching the territory mandated to Greece, and the Constantinople and Armenian mandates.[48] Mr. Wilson did not favor the idea, while Lloyd George suggested an Italian sphere such as Britain had in various parts of the world. The Italian delegation left the conference on April 24 because of Wilson's opposition on the Adriatic question, and did not return to Paris until May 5, 1919. On April 30 it was announced that an Italian warship had gone to Smyrna, and it was suggested that all the Powers send warships to that center of trouble. On May 5, Lloyd George announced Italian occupation of the harbor of Marmaris as a coaling station. A battalion was at Konia by agreement, and troops had been landed at Adalia, and possibly at Alaja.[49]

232

At the same time Lloyd George suggested the impossibility of an immediate settlement of the mandate problem in Turkey. There should be a redistribution of troops. The United States would send troops to Armenia and Constantinople, Britain would come out of the Caucasus, France could garrison Syria, and the Greeks occupy Smyrna. The Italians were not mentioned in this scheme and Lloyd George's announced intention to withdraw British troops from the Caucasus was "in order to have them ready to counteract any move by the Italians."[50] On May 6 Mr. Wilson stated definitely that the United States could not send troops to Turkey since it had not been at war with that country. Italy might be compelled to get out of Anatolia, however, because of her dependence on the United States for credits. An Italian mandate for Asia Minor would be a cause for grave friction.[51] At the same time Wilson thought that the only advantage in allowing Italy to keep Fiume was that it would break the treaty of London, giving the Dodecanese to Italy.[52]

The council of four again pondered over the Italian situation, when Lloyd George raised the mandate question. Rather naïvely (at least) he suggested that an Italian mandate in Anatolia might solve the immigration question in America. Mr. Wilson advanced a proposition favoring the uniting of the Smyrna district and the Dodecanese to Greece. Mr. Nicholson, a British expert, indicated a line on the map excluding the Bagdad railway from the Italian zone.[53] Again Lloyd George brought forward his plan for an American mandate over Armenia and Constantinople, a French mandate over northern Anatolia, with Italy in southern Anatolia, including the port of Makri (and possibly Mersina), and the German shares in the Heraclea and other coal mines. But the Italians demanded Scala Nuova in addition. The American, true to his earlier pronouncements, would not promise American acceptance of a mandate for any part of Turkey.[54]

The next day, May 14, Lloyd George presented his plan for the reorganization of the Turkish Empire, which had been worked out by Nicolson.[55] This proposition involved: (1) an American mandate for Constantinople and Armenia; (2) full Greek sovereignty over Smyrna and Aivali, the Dodecanese and Castellorizo; (3) spheres of influence in the rest of Asia Minor, with a Greek mandate for the territory adjacent to Smyrna. Italy was to have the mandate for the southern seaboard, from west of Makri to the point where Armenia strikes the Mediterranean. France was to receive the mandate for the rest of the "future Turkish state."

President Wilson's idea was to set up a Turkish state in northern Anatolia, under a "loose" French mandate, as it would be better not to have the French and Italian mixing in southern Anatolia—both with advisors at the Turkish capital. Lloyd George urged this as "the great argument against dividing Anatolia." According to Wilson, southern Anatolia should be a self-governing unit with Konia as the capital, and an elected governor-general. As an alternative, Lloyd George proposed that the sultan remain in Constantinople, as sovereign over all Turkey, leaving France, Italy and Greece to overlook parts of Anatolia, while the United States supervised the activities of the sultan at Constantinople.[56]

Another very important decision was reached on this date. On April 12 Venizelos reported serious troubles in Smyrna and Aidin and urged strong, immediate measures. The Greeks had made preparations for a landing at Smyrna.[57] May 14 witnessed a landing of Greek forces under cover of British and French vessels and the U. S. S. Arizona and five American destroyers. This was the definite beginning of the terrible Greco-Turkish drama of 1919-1922 which ended so disastrously for the dreams of a greater Hellas in Asia Minor as well as for Venizelos.[58]

News reached the council of three on May 17 that Italy had followed the example of the Greeks and had landed five hundred men at Scala Nuova. A formal protest was lodged with the government at Rome. Lloyd George circulated a memorandum prepared by Arthur James Balfour to the members protesting against the division of Anatolia. Mr. Balfour did not believe that the old Turkish Empire had been so bad as to warrant such treatment and was particularly afraid that the partition contemplated would "deeply shock large sections of Mohammedan opinion." The English statesman felt that "we must admit that no such scheme would ever have been thought of, if it had not been necessary to find some method of satisfying Italian ambitions." Under his plan Turkey would remain an undivided state without a mandatory, with much diminished territories, but with substantially the same status as that of the old empire. The sultan was to "reign at Brussa or Konia as his predecessors had formerly reigned at Constantinople." But now something had to be found for the Italians in Asia Minor. It would be better, Balfour thought, if the Italians played no part at all, but they "must somehow be mollified, and the only question is how to mollify them at the smallest cost to mankind." His whole object was "to give the Italians something which they really like," and they

234

showed a great liking for concessions, particularly in southern Anatolia in Adalia. But if Balfour's program was intended to take care of the Italian situation, it is to be noted that this most English of statesmen did not neglect to preserve all that Britain desired. Constantinople would not be the Turkish capital, Turkey would not control the Straits, and Great Britain would retain all that she had gained in Mesopotamia and Palestine.[59]

The Moslems of India did lodge a protest against the Italian and Greek action in landing on the coast of Asiatic Turkey. This led Lloyd George on May 19 to ask the withdrawal of the Italian mandate altogether, and get Italy out of Asia Minor entirely.[60] Wilson, also impressed by the Moslem sentiment, suggested leaving the sultan in Anatolia, and perhaps in Constantinople under French advice. But Lloyd George replied that if France were to be the *single* advisor of Turkey, "he would have to ask for a re-examination of the whole question of mandates in the Turkish Empire."[61] He wanted a solution of the problem, but not one which would place France in such control over Constantinople and the Straits.

Later in the day the Italian intervention in Asia Minor came into the discussion. The Italians had claimed that "anarchy" had forced their action, which was in the sphere allotted to Italy in 1915. Consequently, Italian intervention was similar to the Greek landing at Smyrna and that of the French at Heraclea, and was not intended to compromise the final settlement. Lloyd George answered that the Greek landing had the approval of the supreme council and that the two cases were not comparable. If Italy did not remove her troops he would disinterest himself entirely in Italian claims in Asia Minor.[62]

On May 21 the fertile mind of Lloyd George brought forth another mandate scheme for the Turkish Empire. Under this new plan the United States was to have the mandate over Constantinople, the Straits, Armenia and Cilicia. Anatolia was to remain undivided, save for the region to be united to Greece. Either the United States would assume a "light" mandate for Anatolia or there would be no mandate at all for that territory. France was to have a provisional mandate for Syria, until the report of the commission which was sent there, and, in like manner, Great Britain assumed the provisional mandate for Mesopotamia. Until Russia's reorganization, America was to have the mandate for the Caucasus. Italy was entirely excluded from any Turkish mandate by this project.[63]

The reasons for this newest British proposal were asserted to be the Moslem (Indian) objection to the destruction of Turkish sovereignty—and there is no doubt but that Indian influences had great weight with British ideas on the partition of Turkey. They lay also in the British desire to preserve the freedom of the Straits through an American mandate, without the interference of either France or Italy. Britain had done nine-tenths of the fighting against Turkey, and now the British cabinet had decided that it was "bad policy" to partition Anatolia. But even an independent Turkey would require "some" foreign control, and such control should be exercised by America, because the Turks would distrust a European mandate, for fear that Turkey might become a "mere colony." Moreover, "it was impossible . . . to make Italy sole mandatory in Anatolia and if France alone exercised this power Italy would be jealous."[64] How Great Britain felt about the prospect either of Italian or French control is not difficult to conjecture—hence the desire to have the United States assume the obligation.

Evidently President Wilson penetrated the heart of his British colleague's project when he again announced his serious doubt as to American acceptance of responsibility for Anatolia. This seems even more clear when Wilson added that even "if the United States were the mandatory of the Straits they would not in the least object if the sultan were advised in stipulated matters by other Powers on the subject of the government of Anatolia." At this, Lloyd George replied that if the United States could not accept a mandate for Anatolia, "it would be better for the sultan to clear out of Constantinople."[65] The entire British scheme of things would be wrecked. M. Clemenceau objected strongly to the new British project and urged that France "surely ought not to be expelled from Asia Minor on two such grounds as the Mussulman question and the Italian question."[66]

Damad Ferid Pasha, head of the Turkish delegation, was allowed to read a statement before the supreme council on June 17, 1919. He did not condone the crimes of Turkey during the war, but insisted on a peace with Turkey in accordance with the Wilson principles, based on the *status quo ante bellum*. In Thrace he asked for a line northwest of Constantinople, a frontier for the defence of both Constantinople and Adrianople. In Asia Minor, Turkey claimed the territory bounded on the north by the Black sea, on the east by the Tigris river and the Turco-Persian frontiers as before the war. This would include the vilayets of Mosul and Diarbekir, as well as a part

of Aleppo to the Mediterranean. Likewise the islands near the coast should remain Turkish in order to protect the mainland. Turkey would discuss the Armenian frontiers. As to the Arabs, Turkey would grant autonomy to Syria, Palestine, Hejaz, Assyr, Yemen and Iraq—under Ottoman sovereignty. Turkey would negotiate with England concerning the status of Egypt and Cyprus. The Ottoman people would never accept "the dismemberment of the empire or its division under separate mandates."[67]

These were impossible demands, for the Powers already had promised "freedom" to the subject peoples and were even more determined to keep what they had gained for themselves in Asia Minor, Syria, Palestine, Arabia and Mesopotamia. In a bitterly denunciatory letter of June 25 Clemenceau libeled the entire nation of Turkey.

". . . There is no case to be found either in Europe or Asia or Africa, in which the establishment of Turkish rule in any country has not been followed by a diminution of material prosperity, and a fall in the level of culture; nor is there any case to be found in which the withdrawal of Turkish rule has not been followed by a growth in material prosperity and a rise in the level of culture. Neither among the Christians of Europe nor among the Moslems of Syria, Arabia and Africa, has the Turk done other than destroy wherever he has conquered; never has he shown himself able to develop in peace what he has won by war. Not in this direction do his talents run."[68] As long as such an attitude prevailed, there could be little question of an equitable solution of the Turkish problem.

In view of Wilson's pending departure, Lloyd George again raised the Turkish issue on June 25, 1919. He outlined the future frontiers, but left the final disposition of the territories until the American attitude on the acceptance of a mandate were known definitely. To this Wilson agreed, while Clemenceau pointed out that the question of Constantinople was involved. Mr. Wilson asserted that the amputations would involve Mesopotamia, Syria and Armenia. Allied troops would remain to preserve order. Lloyd George was worried about the Armenians and Clemenceau had the Italians in mind. Italy's actions were entirely unauthorized by the conference.[69]

Wilson's proposal was to "cut off all that Turkey was to give up; and to oblige Turkey to accept any conditions with regard to oversight or direction which the Allied and Associated governments might agree to." He thought a mandate over Turkey would be a mistake, but "some Power ought to have a firm hand." Constantinople and the Straits were to be left as "a neutral strip;" already they were in the hands

of the Allies. "He would make the sultan and his government move out of Constantinople and he would say what was ceded to the Allied and Associated Powers." This, however, was not final. Lloyd George pointed out that it "involved the question of whether the Turk was to go out of Constantinople." Wilson considered that question as settled—in his opinion "they ought to be cleared out."[70]

The question of the Turkish mandates again occupied the attention of the council of four the next day. Mr. Wilson agreed to present the plan for an American mandate for Constantinople and the Straits to the American Senate. The difficulties in respect to the Asiatic settle-ment arose, he said, from the Italian attitude. M. Clemenceau said that "he was inclined to refuse discussion of Asiatic questions with the Italians for the present." And Lloyd George was afraid that Italian intervention would "cause unrest among the Mohammedan population of the world"—India. Wilson was so exasperated that he thought the Italians "should be asked clearly to state whether they remained in the Entente or not." If so, Italy must take her part with the Allies "and do nothing independently." Lloyd George insisted that Italy had gone beyond even the grants of the St. Jean de Mau-rienne agreement.[71] On June 28 the United States, Great Britain and France warned Rome that her action, unless curbed, would "mean the loss of all claims to further assistance or aid from those who were once proud to be her associates."[72]

Meanwhile the King-Crane commission had gone to Asia Minor for the purpose of investigation. Lloyd George had stated on June 25 that he had received a telegram from Feisal, in Syria, complaining that the commission was not an Allied body. Feisal had interpreted a telegram from General Allenby to the effect that Britain would assume a Syrian mandate, but was advised that "in no circumstances would Great Britain take this mandate."[73] The King-Crane commission spent the late spring and summer months of 1919 in Asia Minor, and re-turned to Paris in September. Its findings were of such a character that even the American government saw fit to suppress them, to avoid "embarrassing" the peace conference in general—and France in particular. In general, the commission recommended: (1) an Armenian mandate, excluding Cilicia, which was to go with Anatolia; (2) an international Constantinopolitan state, under a mandatory, separate from Turkey; (3) a mandatory for a separate Turkish state; (4) no terri-tory to be set off for the Greeks, who could be given autonomy in Smyrna under the general mandate for Turkey; (5) a single general

mandate for all Asia Minor (not including Mesopotamia and Syria) with Armenia, the Constantinople state, and the Turkish state; (6) the United States to assume this general mandate.[74]

There was no official Russian delegation at Paris during the peace negotiations. This did not prevent such men as Prince Lvov, Sazonov, Chaikovsky, and Maklakov from presenting memoranda to the conference concerning Russian interests. Naturally these interests centered about Constantinople and the Straits. Bratianu's demand of February 1, 1919, for Bessarabia (among other large territories) was granted provisionally on February 18, 1919.[75] Rumania had occupied the territory "temporarily" ever since March 1918—a fact which led to the confiscation of the Rumanian gold reserve of $80,000,000 by the Bolsheviks and the deportation of M. Diamandi, the Rumanian minister in Russia, by way of reprisal. The action taken by the peace conference, in line with both British and American policy, would bar Russia's land approach to the Straits, and enable Rumania to threaten Russia's Black Sea coast. The Russian political conference (composed of the above named men) protested against the Rumanian occupation, but their protests were as ineffective as those of the Soviet Union.[76] Neither liberal nor Bolshevik Russia desired to see Russia blocked in that direction when a rejuvenated country resumed its march toward Constantinople.

Since Constantinople and the Straits were to be put under mandate, the Russian political conference naturally urged the only solution as a Russian mandate over the region, under the league of nations. Constantinople in other hands would be a constant menace to Russian interests. The sole régime consonant with Russian interests, they argued, must be on the following basis: (1) the real guarantee of freedom of passage of the Straits for commerce during war and peace; (2) freedom for warships of riverain Powers of the Black sea in war and peace; (3) closure of the Straits to the warships of non-riverain Black sea Powers in war and peace. A neutralization of the Straits, permitting free passage of outside (British) war vessels into the Black sea was against Russian interests, to which the *ancien régime* was preferable.[77] Naturally the conference neither could nor would do anything. As Lloyd George was later to explain, Russia was now relieved of a very burdensome problem.

The supreme council administered a stinging rebuke to Venizelos early in July for advancing too far in Asia Minor, whereupon the Greek premier ordered a further advance. The Italians were already

in serious difficulties with the peace conference. This fact, doubtless, together with the desire to settle their own mutual differences, led Venizelos and Tittoni, the Italian foreign minister, to make their agreement of July 29, 1919, to give each other reciprocal aid and comfort before the conference. Italy agreed to support Greek pretentions in both eastern and western Thrace, as well as in northern Epirus, in return for certain concessions. Greece engaged to support Italian sovereignty over Valona and confirmed the neutralization of Corfu. If her claims in Thrace and Epirus were satisfied, Greece was to renounce to Italy her ambitions in Asia Minor beyond the Meander. Certain commercial privileges in Smyrna were to be given to Italy. Italy ceded to Greece the sovereignty of the isles which she had occupied in the Aegean, though Italy was to retain Rhodes, with guarantees of religious and cultural rights. In case Italy or Greece did not obtain full satisfaction of all claims, however, complete liberty of action would be resumed.[78] On July 22, 1920, Italy denounced the treaty, and as a result, Venizelos threatened not to sign the treaty of Sèvres.

The provisions relative to Turkey in the treaty of Versailles, which Germany signed on June 28, are of considerable interest. By article 147 Berlin recognized the British protectorate over Egypt and renounced the régime of the capitulations.[79] By article 155 Germany recognized and accepted all arrangements which the Allied and Associated Powers "may make with Turkey and Bulgaria with reference to any rights, interests and privileges whatever which might be claimed by Germany or her nationals in Turkey and Bulgaria."[80] Austria and Hungary were forced to assume an identical obligation,[81] while from the former territories of the Dual Monarchy were created the new Jugoslavia, the greater Rumania and the new parts of Italy. German interests—including the Bagdad railway—were now to be liquidated in favor of the Allies.

Article XXII of the covenant of the League of Nations—identical with article XIX as presented by Mr. Wilson on February 14, 1919—embodied in the treaty of Versailles, provided for the establishment of the mandate system in the parts of Turkey which were to be separated from the former Ottoman Empire.[82] This all but completed the process of partition, though the Allied Powers had not yet allocated definitely the territories involved.

Not until November 27, 1919, was the treaty of Neuilly signed with Bulgaria.[83] Venizelos had won his battle with Bulgaria when the

treaty decreed Bulgarian loss of the Aegean shore to Greece, though of course, Sofia retained the Black sea coast line.[84] Strategic rectifications were to be made for Jugoslavia and Rumania on the basis of the situation existing on August 1, 1914.

During all this time Great Britain was pursuing a policy, the object of which seemed to be to gain complete control in the Near and Middle East. Some Englishmen even talked of gaining a British mandate for Constantinople, while others attempted to gain control by treaty with Turkey. The Greeks were to be used to defeat the almost exhausted Turks, and possibly against Russia, while Baron Wrangel and General Denikin and the "White" armies were supplied with the necessary munitions to be used against the Bolsheviki. Already Baku and Batum were in British hands. On August 9, 1919, a treaty with Persia was signed, which gave Britain practical control over the affairs of that country and made Persia a virtual protectorate.[85] Afghanistan completed the territories under British control stretching from the Mediterranean and Red sea to the very gates of India.

On September 13, 1919, Lloyd George threatened Clemenceau with an evacuation of British troops from Syria and Cilicia, including the Taurus tunnel. Such a withdrawal would leave Great Britain in occupation of Palestine from Dan to Beer-Sheba, and Mesopotamia, while France, with her meagre forces, would be left at the mercy of the Arabs who were already threatening her seriously in Syria. This policy of Lloyd George seems to be the counterpart of the British attempts, now well known, to gain control of the region of Constantinople, and of the project to construct an Arab confederation at the expense of the French in Syria. Clemenceau was prepared to discuss the boundaries between Palestine and Syria, and between Syria and Mosul. He began to fear the impossibility of the dissolution of the Ottoman Empire. While Syria and Mesopotamia were under mandate, Feisal might realize his plans against the French in Syria. The wisest course, Clemenceau felt, was to keep the sultan in Constantinople, with a French advisor. Lloyd George thought that no British government "could accept any such plan. The only solution for a government of Constantinople was an American mandate."[86] An accord in line with Lloyd George's suggestion was reached on September 15, 1919.[87]

Lloyd George's remark about Constantinople is interesting in the light of a supposed secret treaty between England and the Constantinople government of September 12, 1919, by which England was

to dominate Turkey completely. By this agreement England guaranteed the territorial integrity of Turkey, Constantinople was to remain
the seat of the caliphate, while the Straits were placed under English
control. The Turks were not to oppose an independent Kurdistan—
necessary as a buffer for the vilayet of Mosul. The spiritual authority
of the sultan was to be placed at the disposal of England in Syria,
Mesopotamia and other places, while England engaged to put down
any rebellion in Turkey, and to support the Turkish claims before the
conference. Finally Turkey renounced her rights over Cyprus and
Egypt.[88] From this time on, the British, for one reason or another,
were no longer enthusiastic over forcing the Turk out of Constantinople. A Turkish government at that historic and strategic point
could be controlled by the British fleet.

4.

### The Treaty of Sèvres and the Dissolution of Turkey

As already indicated in the above discussion, after months of
deliberation, the Allies were unable to dispose of the Turkish question
at Paris. It is true that there was general agreement that Constantinople
and the Straits were to be internationalized and that the Ottoman
Empire was to be partitioned according to the provisions of the secret
treaties. But the publication and denunciation of these documents by
the Bolsheviks and the attitude of President Wilson had brought them
into notoriety and had forced a revision of the original scheme, especially in the adoption of the mandate principle for Syria, Palestine
and Mesopotamia. But the fate of the rest of Turkey was not yet
determined definitely. The last of the American delegation left Paris
in December 1919 with no peace treaty yet signed with Turkey. Nor
was one possible on account of the rivalries of the Powers over the
spoils of the old empire, the Greco-Turkish war, and the rise of
Mustapha Kemal Pasha. Lloyd George claimed that there could be
no settlement with Turkey "till we know what the United States is
going to do," and in the United States, as we shall see, a distinctly
hostile sentiment against accepting any responsibilities in Turkey
precluded whatever chance there was for the moderating influence of
the United States on the peace with Turkey.

As early as April 1919, France and England had signed the Long-
Berenger oil agreement, which became the basis of the San Remo oil

agreement of April 24, 1920. By this arrangement England and France delimited their oil interests in Russia and Rumania, British and French colonies, and particularly in Mesopotamia. France was allowed a twenty-five per cent share in the exploitation of the oil.[89] This action on the part of the French and English governments—which seemed all too anxious to gather up the spoils of war—led to the most vigorous opposition on the part of the government of the United States, which, though it assumed no responsiblity for the Near East, desired to partake of all the benefits.[90]

At San Remo (April 24, 1920) the Allies finally concluded their labors by accepting the English terms of peace with Turkey, though the document was not signed until August. As Lloyd George explained the situation before the House of Commons, on April 29, 1920: "*We have to guard the Straits—that is in our charge—Palestine and Mesopotamia, including Mosul; the French have got to protect Cilicia; and the Italians undertake to protect the district of Adalia.*"[91] Such was the euphemistic language by which the British prime minister described the grasping activities of England and the Entente in Asiatic Turkey.

The entire program of San Remo stipulated: (1) maintenance of the sultan at Constantinople; (2) the right of the Allies to occupy European Turkey and the Straits zone; (3) the creation of an Armenian state not comprising Trebizond, or Erzingan, but having access to the sea; (4) abandonment by Turkey of Syria, Palestine, Mesopotamia, Arabia and the islands of the Aegean. The United States was asked either to assume the Armenian mandate, or at least to delimit the boundaries of the unhappy state. Mr. Wilson, indeed, did submit the question of the American mandate to the Senate on May 24, 1920, but it was rejected by that body on June 1, 1920.[92]

The Turkish question already had caused grave difficulties between Great Britain and the Moslems of India, who were sensitive on any point touching the caliphate. During the peace negotiations these difficulties recurred and complicated the problem of a settlement with Turkey. On March 19, 1920 a Moslem delegation representing their more than 70,000,000 co-religionists of India had lodged a vigorous protest with Lloyd George against the Turkish treaty. Opposed to the removal of the sultan from Constantinople, they objected to a parti- tion of Turkey in the interests of the very Powers who had asserted they were not fighting against the Turkish people or to deprive them of their "homelands." Moreover the Allies, as Lloyd George explained

243

to the Moslems, were but trying to free the subject nationalities from the oppression of the Turks. The Moslem delegation also presented a strong protest to the supreme council at San Remo.[93]

Nevertheless, after months of work on the project, a treaty based on the ideas developed at San Remo, was presented to the Turkish delegation headed by Damad Ferid Pasha on May 11, 1920. Its terms were severe and brought forth a bitter reply from the Turkish delegation on July 8, 1920. Fundamentally, as the Turkish memorandum recognized, it was "a question of dismemberment." But it is best to quote the words of the Turkish document itself: "*Not only do they detach from Ottoman territory in the name of the principle of nationalities, important provinces erected into free and independent states (Armenia and Hejaz) or independent states under the protection of a mandatory (Mesopotamia, Palestine and Syria); not only do they amputate Egypt, Suez and Cyprus in favor of Great Britain; not only do they demand that Turkey renounce all her rights and titles over Libya and the isles of the Aegean sea, they pretend, moreover, to despoil her, in the name of nationalities of eastern Thrace and the region of Smyrna . . . in favor of Greece . . . .*

"*Again, they prepare the detachment of Kurdistan, and in an indirect manner, the partition of the rest of the country into zones of influence.*

"*On the surface, more than two-thirds of the territory of the Ottoman Empire would be thenceforth separated from it . . . .*

"*To these amputations, the project of treaty adds the gravest injury to the sovereignty of the Ottoman state.*

"*At Constantinople itself, Turkey would not be at home. At the side of his imperial majesty the sultan and of the Turkish government—even above them—a 'comission of the Straits' would reign over the Bosphorus, the Sea of Marmora and the Dardanelles. Turkey would not even be represented in this commission, while Bulgaria would send a delegate to it.*"[94] Broken and subdued, with their government under the very guns of the Allies, the Turks did not care to sign their own death warrant. In all justice, they asked the Allies to carry out their own sentence. But the Constantinople government was compelled to sign the treaty of Sèvres on August 10, 1920.

By the terms of the treaty of Sèvres, the Turkish state was left in Constantinople, along the shores of the Marmora, and in the Gallipoli peninsula. In Asia Minor, Turkey was forced to renounce Syria, Mesopotamia and Palestine, which were placed under the mandates of France and Great Britain. The Hejaz was to be a free and independent

state.[95] Smyrna was to be administered by Greece for a period of five years, under Turkish "sovereignty," after which it was to belong to Greece if the local parliament or plebiscite so decreed. Greece gained Imbros and Tenedos, which controlled the entrance of the Straits[96] —a fact which doubtless accounts for the provision. This would place the islands at the disposal of the British navy. Armenia was to be a free and independent state, including the vilayets of Erzerum, Trebizond, Van and Bitlis, whose boundaries were to be decided by President Wilson. Turkey renounced to England all her rights in Egypt, the Sudan, and Cyprus. In addition she gave up, in favor of Italy, all claims to the Aegean islands.[97]

In the regulation of the Straits the treaty was drastic, under the guise of an internationalization of those waters. Although the "rights and title" of Turkey over Constantinople were not affected, yet if Turkey failed to observe the treaty, the provisions would be modified still more in favor of the Allies. Article 37 delcared:

*"The navigation of the Straits, including the Dardanelles, the Sea of Marmora and the Bosphorus, shall in future be open, both in peace and war, to every vessel of commerce or of war and to military and commercial aircraft, without distinction of flag.*

*"These waters shall not be subject to blockade, nor shall any belligerent right be exercised nor any act of hostility be committed within them, unless in pursuance of a decision of the council of the League of Nations."*

In order to insure the "freedom" of the Straits, Turkey had to delegate control over the Dardanelles, Marmora and Bosphorus to a commission of the Straits, which was given an extended authority. The commission was to be composed of representatives of the United States (when willing), the British Empire, France, Italy, Japan, Russia (when a member of the League of Nations), Greece, Rumania, Bulgaria and Turkey (when members of the League.) The Great Powers were each given two votes. The commission of the Straits was to exercise its authority "in complete independence" of the local authority. In case of interference with freedom of passage, an appeal to the Allied forces could be made. The commission was to exercise the duties of the previous health and sanitation bodies, and necessary police forces were to be placed under its direct orders.[98]

Articles 57-61 laid down the rules and regulations governing navigation of the Straits. These stipulated that:

(1) *Belligerent warships were not to revictual, except to complete passage of the Straits and reach the nearest port of call, and repairs only to make seaworthy were to be made;*

(2) *Passage of belligerent vessels was to be made with "the least possible delay;"*

(3) *The stay was not to last more than twenty-four hours, save in cases of distress, and opposing belligerent vessels were to depart at an interval of twenty-four hours;*

(4) *The League of Nations was to lay down any other war rules for the Straits.*

Prizes were to be subjected to similar regulations. "Except in case of accidental hindrance of the passage," no troops were to be embarked or disembarked, nor were munitions or other war materials to be landed in the regions under the commission's control. But article 60 stipulated that nothing in the above provisions "shall be deemed to limit the powers of a belligerent or belligerents acting in pursuance of a decision by the council of the League of Nations"—a council of which the Allied Powers were themselves the dominating members.

An annex attached made provision for the organization of the commission of the Straits. The chairmanship was to be on a two year rotatory basis among the United States, Great Britain, France, Italy, Japan and Russia. Decisions were to be taken by *majority*, and the chairman was to have a casting vote. Abstention from voting was regarded as a negative vote against any proposal. The commission was empowered "to prepare, issue, and enforce" as well as to amend and repeal the regulations for the Straits. Since there was little likelihood of the United States taking its position on the commission, and since Russia was diametrically opposed, this placed the Straits in the hands of the Allied Powers against Turkey.[99]

But if the Powers were to carve up the Turkish Empire and take away almost every vestige of Turkish sovereignty over the Straits, they were also to subject what remained to economic, judicial and financial bondage.

The preamble to the financial section of the treaty stated in mellifluous words that "the Allied Powers, desiring to afford some measure of relief and assistance to Turkey," were to organize a group of representatives of the British Empire, France and Italy to supervise the financial, economic and administrative policy of the country. By article 246 of the treaty it was decreed that the old council of the Ottoman public debt should now consist only of representatives of British, French

(including a representative of the Ottoman bank) and Italian representatives—the German and Austrian members were eliminated definitely. So severe were these regulations, so complete the authority of the council, that Dr. Blaisdell has remarked:

*"Not a single item of the economic order in Turkey as forecast by the Sèvres treaty would have remained within the sole jurisdiction of the Turkish government. Currency improvement, economic regeneration, tax reform, government financing both domestic and foreign, tariff policy, concessions, all resources of the country (even those not assigned to meet charges on the foreign debt); all fell within the domain mapped out for the international financial commission. By this ring of economic servitudes Turkey would have become effectively shackled to the Allied Powers . . . ."*[100]

In addition to the treaty of Sèvres a tripartite agreement was reached between Italy, France and England by which Italy was to receive her share of Turkish territory. Italy was granted rights in southern Anatolia and Adalia, France in Cilicia and the western part of Kurdistan bordering on Syria. This was done in order to "help Turkey to develop her resources, and to avoid international rivalries which have obstructed these objects in the past."[101] It was stipulated that equality in all international commissions in the reorganization of Turkey, as well as equality of economic treatment, should prevail. None of the three Powers was to infringe on such rights in the reserved spheres of the others. The Italians obtained the right to exploit the Heraclea coal mines.[102]

Italy and Greece reached an agreement concerning Asia Minor. Turkey already had renounced the Dodecanese to Italy in the Sèvres treaty. In the Greco-Italian agreement of the same date, however, Italy renounced the Aegean islands to Greece.[103] Rhodes was to remain under Italy, but Italy agreed to permit a plebiscite when England decided to give Cyprus to Greece. In return Greece confirmed Italian commercial privileges in Smyrna.[104] But this agreement was denounced by Count Sforza, on July 22, 1922, a few weeks after he had become Italian foreign minister.

A final treaty between the Allied and Associated Powers and Greece allocated the territory of Thrace to Greece. Bulgaria obtained only a right of free transit across this territory to the Aegean in the parts assigned to Greece, under special conventions between the two countries. Bulgaria, however, was to have a permanent lease of part

of Dedeagatch, under the guarantee of the League of Nations.[105] Perhaps it should be noted that with Thrace in Greek hands, Great Britain would have a European land approach to Constantinople. The cession of Thrace is paralleled, as we have seen, by the surrender of the islands of Imbros and Tenedos at the mouth of the Straits, which would in the future, as in the past, give Great Britain convenient naval bases for operations against the Dardanelles. With such an arrangement the British position in this region would be supreme.

Such then was the treaty of peace with Turkey. The Powers had set themselves to partitioning the empire and sharing the spoils among the victors and had placed the rest of "independent" Turkey under economic, judicial and financial bondage to the same Powers. But the treaty proved abortive and remained only the extreme expression of the intentions of the Allies with reference to the Turkish problem. The two great victors in the spoils of Sèvres were Great Britain and Greece. The losers were both Turkey and Russia. As a Russian diplomat was led to complain, the treaty of Sèvres, through the provisions concerning the Straits, exposed the entire southern coast of Russia (2,230 kilometers) to the attacks of any state which might be at war with her. Moreover the Russian port of Batum was "internationalized," Persia was given free access to the port. This gave the Allies the right of transit through Persia *via* of Transcaucasia and the Caspian sea, for possible action against the Soviet Union.[106] Within less than a year both Turkey and Russia presented a united diplomatic front against the danger common to both.

At Sèvres the Powers had agreed that the frontiers and mandate terms for Asia Minor should be laid in a mutual agreement for submission to the council of the League of Nations. Accordingly a second conference at San Remo met on December 23, 1920, where France and England agreed on "certain points connected with the mandates for Syria and the Lebanon, Palestine and Mesopotamia".[107] Boundaries were delimited at the expense of Syria, whereby Palestine secured the headwaters of the Jordan and Litani. Mosul was officially allocated to Great Britain, and the British again engaged not to cede Cyprus without the consent of France. The agreements with reference to railways and oil pipelines enabled Great Britain to get her oil to the sea through Syria, to connect up her railway system in Mesopotamia with that of the Hejaz, and have another link in the Cape to Cairo-India scheme of imperial communications.[108] Great Britain and France

had settled the question of the Near Eastern mandates to their own satisfaction, and in the face of vigorous American opposition, had confirmed their earlier oil agreement.

This was the culmination of the Sèvres policy in the Levant, marking the apogée of British policy in the Near East. Great Britain had obtained all her *desiderata* in the partition of the Ottoman Empire. Not only had Great Britain obtained Mesopotamia (with Mosul), Palestine and the formal recognition of her position in Cyprus and Egypt, but she had opened up the Straits in peace and war to ships of both commerce and war. Demilitarized (but not *neutralized*), the Straits were at the mercy of the British fleet, and Britain was able to subdue, not only Turkey, but to strike at Russia in the Black sea.

But the policy pursued at Sèvres and beyond proved disastrous in the end. The Turks were to rise against it, to expel the Greeks from Asia Minor, to threaten the British in the region of the Straits, and finally to reassert their right to an independent national existence.

# CHAPTER VIII

# THE GRECO-TURKISH STRUGGLE

## The Turkish Revolution

WHEN the Allies forced the Turkish delegates to sign the treaty of Sèvres on August 10, 1920, they grossly miscalculated the latent powers of resistance yet remaining among the Turks of the Anatolian plateau. If England thought the Turk would disarm peaceably and obediently accept the dictates of the supreme council, she was soon to be disillusioned sadly. As the Turks had warned at Sèvres, it was impossible "to destroy peacefully . . . twelve millions of people resolved to defend their independence."[1]

How the Greek forces landed at Smyrna in May 1919, under cover of British, French and even American men-of-war, has been related. It was this event which inspirited the Turks as a people, inflamed in them a national patriotism, which, under the guiding genius of Mustapha Kemal, was finally to drive the Greeks into the sea at Smyrna in 1922. Already deprived of their richest lands in Mesopotamia, with Arabia, Palestine, Syria, Armenia and Kurdistan detached, and with seaports gone, the nationalist Turks were not to permit Greece to take Smyrna and thus cut off another slice of Turkey in the program of Allied imperialism.[2] The Turkish people defied the Sèvres treaty, revolted from the Constantinople government, organized a republic at Angora, and declared Mustapha Kemal president.[3]

Mustapha Kemal Pasha had proved his metal during the Dardanelles campaign as a fearless, capable and intelligent soldier and man. At the conclusion of the war, he saw his country defeated and broken, and witnessed the vacillating policy of the government at Constantinople. The Ghazi himself told of his reactions at this time in his famous six-day speech before the Grand National Assembly in Angora in 1927:

"On May 19, 1919, I landed in Samsun. At that time the situation in Turkey was as follows: The group of Central Powers to which the Ottoman régime was allied had been defeated in the world war. The Ottoman army had completely disintegrated. A harsh armistice had been decided upon, and years of war had left the nation poverty-stricken and exhausted. Our country's leaders had been forced to flee for their

lives. Sultan Vahideddin, in whose degenerate person the throne and the caliphate were united, had agreed to humiliating peace terms merely to be able to save his own skin and preserve his throne. Damad Ferid Pasha's cabinet was powerless, worthless, and discredited. It bowed to the will of the sultan, and tolerated any situation that maintained the security of the sovereign. The Allied Powers did not consider it necessary to respect the terms of the Armistice. Foreign officers and officials, as well as their agents, extended their Powers unduly.

"Faced with this determination on the part of the foreign Powers to destroy and annihilate the Ottoman Empire, our country found itself in a state of dark uncertainty. We lived in a condition of perpetual apprehension. Those of us who endeavored to understand how frightful a catastrophe had befallen us did all we could to take measures that would rescue us from our plight. The army existed in name only . . . ." No one supected the treason of the sultan-caliph—no one would think of Turkey without a caliph. No one thought that Turkey could be revived without the assistance of one of the victorious Great Powers. Yet there was no great state, apparently, to which the Turks could turn.

The fact that Kemal, none too well liked at Constantinople, was sent out to Eastern Anatolia as inspector of the third army, gave him his opportunity. He examined the condition of the third corps at Sivas and the fifteenth corps at Erzerum, and was struck by the terrible condition of his countrymen. He became convinced that the old order of things, with the sultanate and caliphate "had become preposterous". But one course remained open—"the shaping of an entirely new Turkish State founded on national independence". He had to persuade the people to rebel against "the Ottoman sultan, against the caliph, and against everything Mohammedan. The whole Turkish nation and the whole Turkish army had to be won over to the idea of revolution." And a new social structure had to be built on the wreck of the old.[4]

On the night of June 21, 1919, while at Amasia, he ordered that a congress be assembled at Erzerum on July 10, adding that the nationalist congress at Sivas should send three representatives. The appeal urged that Constantinople was incapable of ruling over the country any longer—Anatolia was to rule. In response to these activities, the government at Constantinople, acting under the inspiration of the British high commissioner, issued an order for the return of Mustapha, and condemned his program in Anatolia. But the work

continued, and after a month of futile effort on the part of Constantinople to block the operations in Anatolia, the sultan dismissed Mustapha Kemal from his service on July 8, 1919.

The congress at Erzerum, over which the great Turkish leader presided, convened on July 23, 1919, and lasted for fourteen days. The congress demanded that the government refuse to submit to foreign domination and occupation; otherwise the nationalists would assume control. A national assembly was demanded, which was to take even the Constantinople government under its control.

The activities of the congress at Erzerum were broadcast throughout the country. Another congress, meeting at Sivas in September, was attended by delegates from all over the country. The Sivas congress adopted on September 9 a declaration which stated the political platform which the nationalists under the leadership of Kemal now had formulated. This declaration made a plea for the unity of Turkish territory, opposed the occupation of Allied troops, objected to an independent Armenian state, denounced the Greek activities in western Asia Minor, called for the defence of the sultanate and caliphate, and resolved to fight for Turkish integrity. This action of the Sivas congress was followed by renewed vigor on the part of the Constantinople government against the nationalists, and Mustapha Kemal was outlawed.[5]

But the nationalists kept on with their work, and were even in communication with Constantinople, demanding that the cabinet of Damad Ferid Pasha de dismissed, an election held, and a national assembly called. A most significant demand was that the government committee of the congress at Sivas become the constitutional government of Turkey. The result of all this agitation was the dismissal of Damad Ferid in late September and the summoning of Ali Risa Pasha, who was outwardly conciliatory toward the group at Sivas, to the position of grand vizier. Providing the new government defended the cause of the nation, did nothing important without convening the proposed national assembly, and appointed delegates to the peace conference who represented "the desires of the nation," the Sivas government promised its support. In October 1919, the Constantinople government was definitely defeated when the nationalist deputies gained a decided majority in the elections. With the downfall of Damad Ferid, the new grand vizier, Ali Risa Pasha entered into negotiations with Kemal and signed a protocol which for the first time recognized the representative character of the movement at Sivas. Nevertheless,

"the sultan's government and the nation faced each other as bitterly as two hostile Powers preparing for future strife."[6]

The Turkish nationalist deputies met at Angora, in the heart of Anatolia, formulated a definite national policy, and adopted the "national pact," the declaration of independence of the new Turkey. This remarkable document, consisting of six brief articles, proclaimed the unity of the peoples of Anatolia and Turkey—clearly of Ottoman majority—which formed a whole not admitting of division. The Arabs in enemy occupied territory, formerly an integral part of the old Ottoman Empire, and the people of western Thrace, were to choose their own fate in complete freedom. The pact guaranteed the rights of minorities, but Turkey was to "enjoy complete independence and liberty" in the government of the nation, in order to assure her development along modern lines. For that reason the nationalists were opposed to any restriction inimical to their political, judicial and financial development. As to the Straits and Constantinople, the national pact declared:

*"The security of the city of Constantinople, which is the seat of the caliphate of Islam, the capital of the sultanate, and the headquarters of the Ottoman government, and of the Sea of Marmora, must be protected from every danger. Provided this principle is maintained, whatever decision may be arrived at jointly by us and all other interested governments concerned, regarding the opening of the Bosphorus to the commerce and traffic of the world, is valid."[7]* Turkey demanded her security at Constantinople, and that being guaranteed, the Straits were to be open to commerce in agreement with the Powers. Even the Constantinople government adopted the national pact on January 28, 1920, since the Allies refused recognition to a parliament not meeting in the legal capital. Reasons of a highly political nature dictated this stand of the Allies.

On March 16, 1920, Allied (British) forces under General Milne marched into Constantinople, seized the public buildings, arrested and deported many nationalist leaders, and kept the degenerate sultan on his throne, despite his overwhelming repudiation by the Turks themselves. An Allied *communiqué* which was issued to explain this high-handed action of the military, stated:

*"1. The occupation is provisional.*

*"2. The Entente Powers have no intention of destroying the authority of the sultanate. They desire on the contrary to reinforce it in all places which shall remain in submission to the Ottoman administration.*

256

"3. *The Entente Powers continue in their intention not to deprive the Turks of Constantinople, but if—which God forbid—any general troubles or massacres occur, this decision will probably be modified . . . .*"[8] The Allied occupation of Constantinople, which took place almost five months before the treaty of Sèvres was forced upon the Turks, explains Lloyd George's change of policy in reference to keeping the Turk in Constantinople. It will be recalled that during the peace conference at Paris he first favored an American mandate for the region of Constantinople and the Straits, or failing that, throwing the sultan out of the Turkish capital. In September 1919, a possible secret agreement with Ferid Pasha, however, gave England control over the Constantinople government and dominance in the Straits. Peace was delayed. The Moslems had protested against the removal of the caliphate from Constantinople. Lloyd George was forced to explain his position in the House of Commons on February 26, 1920. Why were the Turks not forced out of Constantinople? The explanation: Britain wanted "freedom of the Straits," which would give her access to the new nations arising on the Black sea, and desired to "protect" the minorities in Turkey. Turkey had no navy, America had rejected a mandate, and Russia now was "out of the competition for a very unpleasant task". Hence, as the British prime minister stated, Great Britain was there to insure this freedom and to protect the Armenians. Were Mr. Lloyd George an Armenian, he "would rather know that the men who are responsible were within reach of Allied forces, and that I had the protection of the British fleet, and that if they ordered massacres and murders and outrages Constantinople could be laid in ashes." Mr. Lloyd George would "*feel more secure if he knew that the Sultan and his ministers were overlooked by a British garrison, and that out in the Bosphorus the British ships were within reach of them, than if he were at Konia, hundreds of miles across the Taurus mountains from the nearest Allied garrison and the sea with its great British ships and their guns out of sight and out of mind.*"[9]

The Greek aggression at Smyrna probably did more than any other factor to precipitate the nationalist movement in Turkey, but the British action at Constantinople added the finishing touches. The move of March 16, 1920, was the immediate cause of the removal of the entire nationalist government to Angora, where the British ships and the British guns were "out of sight and out of mind". In the

security of the Anatolian plateau the Turks were to work out their own destiny with their own blood and treasure, their own courage and intelligence.

The parliament at Constantinople met for the last time on April 11 and was dissolved. On April 23 the Grand National Assembly declared its adhesion to the national pact, denounced the Constantinople government from the date March 15-16, 1920, and elected Mustapha Kemal president of the republic.[10]

It is perhaps not without significance that this action of the nationalists coincides almost to a day with the conference at San Remo where the Allies were deliberating on the partition of the old empire among themselves. Soon after the opening session of the assembly, a law of fundamental organization, vesting sovereignty in the people, and placing the powers of government in a unicameral legislature (elected by manhood suffrage), was enacted. Ministers of the government were to be elected by and be responsible to this body, which exercised sovereign rights in both domestic and foreign policy. At the head of the government stood the president and vice-president, elected by the assembly.[11]

2.

### The Greco-Turkish War

Having landed at Smyrna, the Greeks were advancing from this foothold into the interior of Turkey because of "strategic necessity." When Mr. Lloyd George was so anxious to bring Greece into the world war against the Turks, he promised a brilliant future "under the aegis of England." From 1919 to 1922 his aim was to back up Venizelos in the Asiatic venture. Greece was to impose the terms of peace on Turkey. England, already overburdened, could not dispose of men, but could furnish supplies, if Greece would assume this task. As Venizelos wrote from London on March 19, 1920, ". . . We must not expect any aid in men on the part of England concerning those countries which interest us immediately . . . . England will dispose of the necessary army for Constantinople and the Straits."[12]

A little more than a month after the occupation of Constantinople, as we have seen already, the Allies accepted the English terms of peace at San Remo in April 1920. Great Britain obtained formal assent

to her position in Mesopotamia, Palestine and "guardianship" of the region of the Straits. France and Italy were allotted their respective shares of Turkish territory in Syria and Adalia.

In June 1920, the British prime minister gave further aid and comfort to the Greeks at the Hythe conference, when Venizelos offered Millerand and Lloyd George an army of 90,000 men with which to destroy the Turkish nationalists. The consent of Italy was necessary and for this reason the conference of Boulogne met during the latter part of June. Count Sforza, then Italian foreign minister, was entirely opposed to the Greek project for action against Turkey.[13] One month later at the Spa conference of July, Venizelos again urged his proposition, and was still opposed by Italy, but had the loyal backing of the London government.[14] In fact, Lloyd George, who was none too secretive about his attitude, explained his position to the House of Commons on July 21:

*"Mustapha Kemal was supposed to be marching with great forces to drive the Allies out of Asia Minor, and even Constantinople was supposed to be in peril . . . . After going into the matter [with Venizelos] very closely, the British government came to the conclusion that the best thing to do would be to use the force at the disposal of the Greek government for the purpose of clearing up the situation . . . . M. Venizelos expressed the opinion that he would be able to clear up the whole of the neighborhood between Smyrna and the Dardanelles in the course of fifteen days."*[15]

There was yet formal unity among the Allied Powers, though the rift both in east and west was becoming more and more apparent as the days passed. Already France and England were opposed over the French Rhine policy and the question of German reparations, and their programs in the Near East were beginning to diverge in a fundamental sense. But with this nominal backing in 1920 the Greeks were enabled to take the offensive which before the end of 1920 brought them into occupation of considerable portions of Asia Minor, including the ancient capital of Turkey, Brusa. The year 1921 witnessed even greater military successes on the part of the Greeks and brought them within some two hundred miles of the new Turkish capital at Angora, which the Greeks failed to take, and their military situation thereafter became steadily worse. In December 1920, Constantine had returned to his throne in Athens, and the Allies considered this "disloyal" conduct toward them.[16]

The Turks were now threatening the Greeks in Smyrna, menacing the French in Cilicia, and even were bringing anxiety to the British in the region of the Straits. Moreover there was continual jealousy on the part of the French against the British who were reigning supreme at Constantinople, and both Italy and France were engaging in secret negotiations with the Turks. Doubtless it was this situation which forced the summoning of the London conference in February 1921 to consider the ever pressing problem of the Levant.[17] Lloyd George took the helm at the meeting of February 21, 1921 and directed the discussion. The Greeks considered themselves perfectly capable of overwhelming the Turks, though General Gouraud, who had had enough experience with the Turks, warned them to the contrary.[18] Both the Constantinople and Angora governments were represented, but when Tewfik Pasha took his position at the conference, it was only to yield to Bekir Sami Bey, the foreign minister of the Angora government. Bekir Sami Bey suggested an inquest into the situation of the Near East. Such an impartial investigation as was urged by the nationalist leader would signify that the policy followed at Sèvres was a mistake, but it was accepted.[19] The Turks naturally were willing to consent to a commission of inquiry, but early in March the Greeks rejected it.[20] Despite this, however, Lloyd George privately encouraged the Greeks to continue their war against the Turks, if their technical advisors urged the necessity of security. Immediate renewal of hostilities in Asia Minor was the result.[21]

But it was not to be easy sailing for the Greek forces operating against the nationalist armies of Turkey. At first defeated, by the summer of 1921 Greek troops were in Afium-Karahissar and Kutaja. The front lasted for one year, when in August 1922, the Greek lines broke and ended in the disaster at Smyrna. The diplomatic episode back of this struggle is important.

If the Angora government was proving its prowess on the field of battle, its conduct in the field of diplomacy was superb. Early in 1921, Turkey settled her relationships with her neighbors, renewed friendships with France and Italy—thus separating these two Powers from England—and became the friend and ally of Soviet Russia.

By the tripartite agreement of August 10, 1920, France and Great Britain pledged to Italy the guarantee of certain economic rights in southern Anatolia. On March 13, 1921, Bekir Sami Bey signed an accord with Count Sforza, recognizing Italy's right of economic exploitation (Italo-Turkish collaboration) in Adalia, Afium-Karahissar,

Kutaja, Aidin, Konia and the coal mines of Heraclea. In return, Italy engaged to support all the demands of the Turkish delegation on the restoration of Thrace and Smyrna to Turkey.[22] This led to Italy's withdrawal of her forces from Adalia in June, and later in the year to an agreement with Kemal. As if to add assurance, the Italians made another agreement with the Constantinople government.[23]

The French were not long in following the Italian example. As early as 1920, Paris had observed the rise of the nationalists and had seen the necessity of coming to terms with the Turks in order to protect the French position in Syria. General Gouraud, who had been sent out to Syria, was willing to make concessions in the Syrian mandate and in Cilicia in February 1921. The war between France and Turkey came to an end in the next month.[24] But if the war seemed threatening to the French in 1920, in 1921 it was evidently ominous. Paris now figured definitely on making friends of the Turks, obtaining concessions, and protecting Syria. Hence, M. Franklin-Bouillon, who had gone to Angora on a "private" mission in 1920, returned the next year as an emissary of the Quai d'Orsay, and made the Angora accord of October 1921, bearing his name.[25]

The Angora agreement was important, not only in what it contained, but particularly because it signified a separate peace with Turkey, without consultation with Great Britain, and therefore marked a definite line of cleavage in the policies of the two countries in the Levant. By this agreement France ceded to Turkey some 10,000 square kilometers of territory, including the evacuation of Cilicia, and the retrocession of land running east and west from the gulf of Alexandretta to the Tigris, opposite Jeziret-ibn-Omar. The Bagdad railway, from the Jaihan river in eastern Cilicia to Rasul-Ain, in the northern part of Mesopotamia, went to Turkey.[26] Moreover France engaged to allow the Turks to send troops by rail from Meden-Ekbes to Choban Bey and Nisibin, in Turkish territory. Finally, the Angora government accepted the transfer of the Bagdad railway section between Bozanti and Nisibin, as well as the branches in Adana, to a French group, with all rights, privileges and advantages attached to concessions on exploitation and traffic.[27]

In a covering letter, Yussuf Kemal Bey, the Angora negotiator, informed Franklin-Bouillon that his government was disposed to grant concessions for iron, chrome and silver in the Kharshut valley for ninety-nine years, with fifty per cent Turkish participation. Turkey desired French specialists and would view with favor other requests

for concessions.[28] Proclamations in accordance with the agreement were promulgated by the French and Turkish authorities in the following December. [29] France had not only made peace with Turkey—she was making a strong bid for economic and political influence with the Kemalists. Turkey had gained a friend, and was now enabled to concentrate her strength against the Greeks along the Sakaria river.

The British foreign minister, the capable and brilliant Lord Curzon, took vigorous exception to the action of France in making the Angora accord with Turkey, which was aimed directly at Great Britain. Lord Curzon complained of France breaking "the close and unwavering coöperation" of the two governments in the east. Specifically he objected to a separate peace with Turkey, the violation of the Sèvres and dependent treaties, modification of the Syrian frontier, and encouragement of a Turkish threat against the British position in Iraq. He feared a possible secret agreement, and could not believe that Paris would make such an agreement "without prior reference to His Majesty's government."[30]

But the Quai d'Orsay was not moved. France and Britain, opposed in their Rhine policy, were at the sword's point in Asia Minor. At this time, it will be remembered, England was abandoning France to solve her own difficulties on the Rhine, and was attempting by every artifice, naval, military, or diplomatic, to gain supremacy not only over Mesopotamia, Arabia and Palestine, but in the region of Constantinople. In return the French, who had their own aims and ambitions in the Near East, and who were perfectly aware of the British aspirations, broke with England over Turkey, made a separate peace with Kemal, and gave a veiled support to the Turks in the struggle with Greece. In both east and west the Entente, which had stood the test of the world war, appeared to be at an end.

Turkey had renewed relations with France and Italy in March 1921. In the same month the Angora government became the friend and ally of Soviet Russia. Soviet Russia was returning to the policy of Unkiar Eskelessi, utilizing an Asiatic policy directed against the British Empire just as tsarist Russia had done in the pre-war days. England was interested in opening the Straits at Sèvres in order to menace Russia on the Black sea, and already had begun to build buffer states against the Soviet Union in Asia.[31] In answer to this policy, Russia was developing a security system for her protection both in Europe and in Asia. On May 7, 1920, a treaty with the republic of Georgia brought that country into the orbit of Russia. A treaty with

Persia, signed February 26, 1921, renounced all the rights of the late tsarist régime, but gave the Soviet Union the right to send troops to Persia to prevent an attack on Russia, should this danger occur. Under Russian influence, Persia refused to ratify the earlier agreement with England of August 1919.[32] Two days after the treaty with Persia an agreement was signed with Afghanistan, in which the two parties mutually pledged to do nothing, either militarily or politically, against each other. Afghanistan was to receive "financial and other material aid" from Soviet Russia.[33] Both Turkey and Russia had operated in Armenia in the fall of 1920. The Turks had occupied a great part of Armenia, leaving only the district of Erivan to the Armenian state, and Armenia became sovietized in order to escape further torture. By the end of February 1921, all three Transcaucasian republics, Armenia, Georgia and Azerbaijan were under Soviet influence, and conquered.[34] This was the reply of Bolshevik Russia to the British threat in Asia.

But it remained for Russia and Turkey to settle their accounts. On March 16, 1921, Yussuf Kemal Bey signed a treaty of friendship and virtual alliance with the government at Moscow, after *pourparlers* lasting more than a month. The treaty of Moscow, which fits into the general scheme of treaties of security by which Russia sought to protect herself, gave to Turkey both Kars and Ardahan, while Batum was placed under a Russo-Turkish *condominium*. Russia accepted the abolition of the capitulations, and both parties mutually pledged themselves not to recognize any treaty or pact imposed on either by force. Moscow recognized the government at Angora, with all the territories claimed in the national pact.[35] Article 5 stipulated:

"*With a view to guaranteeing the freedom of the Straits and their free passage for commercial purposes to all countries, both parties agree to entrust to a special conference, composed of delegates from all the riverain states, the drafting of the definitive and international status of the Black sea and of the Straits, on condition that its decisions shall not prejudice the absolute sovereignty and the safety of Turkey and of her capital, Constantinople.*"[36] Soviet Russia also began to furnish arms and money to Turkey, hoping not only to bolshevize the Turks, but to strengthen the Turkish position on the Straits, as a protection to Russia. Likewise, and for the same reason, the Soviet government was interested in strengthening Turkey against the imperialism of the western Powers.[37]. Turkey was to be incorporated into the Russian system of security. Turkey, on the other hand, accepted Russian aid

as a necessity, but did not wish to become communist. Emissaries from Russia who were intent on carrying the new gospel to the nationalists, mysteriously disappeared on their arrival in Turkey.[38]

Chicherin advised Kemal not to make any agreement with England, and Bekir Sami Bey's trip to Europe caused some alarm in Moscow, which was not allayed by the French accord of October 1921. However on October 13, 1921, Turkey concluded the treaty of Kars with Armenia, Georgia and Azerbaijan, delimiting their frontiers, recognizing the territories included in the Turkish national pact, and confirming the provisions of the earlier treaty of Moscow with Soviet Russia. Georgia now received Batum, which was made a free port for Turkey. The provisions relative to Constantinople and the Straits were identical with those of the treaty of Moscow.[39]

By 1921, then, Turkey had succeeded in completely altering her international position by means of a veritable diplomatic revolution in the east. In western Europe the Angora government had succeeded in winning both Italy and France from any solidarity they may have had with England. But the Turks had accomplished much more. They had settled accounts with their neighbors, had made a virtual alliance with Soviet Russia, which had vital interests at stake in the Straits. With these new factors involved, there can be little wonder at the Greek débacle in September 1922.

Meanwhile the Greeks resumed the offensive in June 1921. Lord Curzon was now prepared to offer the mediation of England, and to recognize the growing power of Angora. He put before the Paris conference of June 22, 1921, a proposal to make Smyrna an autonomous province under Turkey, but with a Christian governor.[40] Despite the warning that all responsibiluty would "fall exclusively on the Greeks themselves", Athens rejected the offer.[41] The war continued, and on August 10, 1921, the supreme council washed its hands of the problem and announced its "strict neutrality" in the struggle.[42] The fact that Turkey was in agreement with both France and Italy, however, had a sobering effect on Athens in the autumn of 1921. In October, Gounaris, the Greek prime minister, accompanied by Baltazzi and Rangabé, went to Paris and London, in the interest of the Greek cause in Asia Minor. Briand was none too comforting in his attitude toward the Greeks.[43] After some discussion, the Greek emissaries placed their unfortunate country in the hands of Lord Curzon, who outlined a project for peace in the Near East.[44] Yet Curzon's stand did not prevent Lloyd George from declaring his great "friendship" for

Greece, and promising "to use all his political action," in her favor during the negotiations, though in the war with Turkey, "it was impossible for him to give [Greece] a positive support".[45]

By the end of December 1921, Curzon had obtained cabinet approval for his proposals. A meeting with France and Italy, which was to have been held in January 1922, failed because of the fall of the Briand cabinet. Poincaré came to the office of premier. At the meeting of the supreme council at Cannes early in January, Curzon proposed an autonomous Smyrna under the protection of the League of Nations, and a small territorial rectification in Thrace. Both France and Italy appeared to be willing to accept the English proposals as a basis for peace, though Poincaré would do nothing to help Greece. The fall of the Italian cabinet in February added further difficulties.[46]

The fact that all was not well with the Greek forces in Asia Minor brought from Gounaris his letter of despair to Curzon on February 22, 1922. Lack of supplies, want of money and resources were exhausting the Greeks, while the Turks were receiving help not only from Russia, but from "certain of the Allied Powers." Greece needed immediate reinforcements, fresh war materials, and financial aid.[47] England could not furnish the necessary aid, and Curzon urged a diplomatic solution of the war in his reply of March 6.[48] Italy having formed a new ministry, Lord Curzon proposed an armistice in the Near East.

It is at this juncture that the Moslem question in India again arises in connection with the Turkish problem. The presence of the Greek prime minister in London caused the rumor among the Indian Moslems that England would support Greece in order to crush Mustapha Kemal, and gave rise to the caliphate agitation. The viceroy of India urged this factor on the government at London, and forwarded a final request to the secretary of state for India, Mr. Montagu, on March 7, 1922. In particular, Lord Reading urged on behalf of the Moslems, "subject to the safeguarding of the neutrality of the Straits and of the security of the non-Moslem population," the following: (1) evacuation of Constantinople; (2) suzerainty of the sultan in the holy places; (3) restoration of Ottoman Thrace (with Adrianople), and Smyrna. Montagu's premature publication of the communication of the viceroy, without the knowledge or sanction of the cabinet, shocked Curzon, and brought on the resignation of the former from the government. Lord Curzon wrote to Mr. Austen Chamberlain on March 9, 1922: "If the policy

of H. M. G. is the policy of the viceroy and Montagu, then let Montagu go to Paris in my place, and fight to obtain Adrianople and Thrace and the holy places for his beloved Turks."[49]

Toward the end of March, however, Curzon, Poincaré and Schanzer met at Paris and on March 27 issued their pronouncement to Greece and Turkey, containing propositions for peace between the two countries. The Allied ministers called for the reëstablishment of the Turks and Turkish dominion "in the areas which may fairly be regarded as their own, with the historic and renowned capital of Constantinople as the centre, and with such powers as may enable them to renew a vigorous and independent national existence." The Allies proposed an armistice, which the Greeks accepted, though they required four months for the withdrawal of Greek troops. If Turkey accepted, she would recover Anatolia, and Turkish sovereignty in Asia Minor would exist "unimpaired from the Mediterranean to the Straits and the Black sea, and from the borders of Transcaucasia, Persia and Mesopotamia to the shores of the Aegean." The Turks, however, were to be admitted to the Asiatic shore of the Dardanelles only under the provisions of the demilitarized zone, where an Allied force remained "in order to safeguard the free and unimpeded entrance of the Straits." Gallipoli, Chanak, Lemnos, Imbros, Tenedos, Samothrace and Mitylene (at the entrance of the Straits) and the islands of the Marmora, were to be demilitarized. Proposals concerning Thrace, Constantinople and the capitulations were outlined as a basis of the future peace.[50]

Whether or not the Turks would accept the armistice as the exhausted Greeks had done, was a different question. With a good, well equipped army, a friendly Russia, the Entente divided, and the Greeks confessing defeat, it seemed altogether unlikely. Both Constantinople and Angora received the note, urging the immediate necessity of a conference within three weeks to bring about peace.[51] The Sublime Porte answered on April 8 with a vague note which signified little either in content or political significance.[52] The Angora government replied on April 5, agreeing in principle to an armistice, but insisting on guarantees against a renewal of the Greek offensive. In a second note of April 23, Angora, answering an Allied note of April 16, reiterated its desire for peace, but with continued insistence on the necessary guarantees. The Turkish nationalists were taking no chances.[53]

But the war continued. A Greek note of July 29, 1922, informed the Allied Powers that occupation of Constantinople by Greek troops was the only means of imposing peace on Turkey. The Allies replied that the inter-Allied military command had received orders to "repulse by force any military movement directed against the occupied zone".[54] The Athens government followed its announcement by landing 25,000 soldiers at Rodosto. The Greek dream of entering Constantinople was hopeless, for the final drive of the already exhausted army in Asia Minor proved a disaster.

These circumstances prompted Lloyd George to make his famous address to the House of Commons on August 4, 1922, in which he clearly indicated the British position, when he declared:

*"I forget who it was who said that we were not fair as between the parties. I am not sure that we are. What has happened? Here is a war between Greece and Turkey. We are defending the capital of one of the parties against the other. We must not overlook that fact, and it is a very important fact. If we were not there, there is absolutely no doubt that the Greeks would occupy that capital in a very few hours, and that would produce a decision. There is only one way now in which the Greeks can have a decision, and that is by marching through almost impenetrable defiles for hundreds of miles into the country. I do not know of any army that would have gone as far as the Greeks have. It was a very daring and a very dangerous military enterprise . . . . There are even suggestions, not altogether, perhaps, without foundation, that the Kemalist forces are being reëquipped from Europe. The Greeks, under other conditions, would have been entitled to blockade the coast of Asia Minor . . . . Peace the Kemalists will not accept, because they say we will not give them satisfactory armistice terms:* but we are not allowing the Greeks to wage the war with their full strength. We cannot allow that sort of thing to go on indefinitely, *in the hope that the Kemalists entertain, that they will at last exhaust this little country, whose men have been under arms for ten or twelve years, with one war after another, and which has not indefinite resources. That is the position. We only want to see a just peace established . . . ."*[55]

Lloyd George well knew that the British were not so much defending the capital of the old Turkey at Constantinople as holding it for themselves. Nor could the British prime minister have been unaware of the fundamental intention of his own government in encouraging the futile Greek advance into Asia Minor—namely, the achievement of British aspirations against Turkey. In both Athens and Angora the

Lloyd George speech was taken as an invitation to the Greeks to renew the struggle. Parts of it became a Greek army order. On August 18, the Turkish army struck along the entire front of the Sakaria river. Before a month had passed, the Greeks had fled in panic across the Anatolian plateau. On September 9 the Turks occupied Smyrna, and by September 20 there were no more Greek soldiers to be found in Asia Minor.[56]

So flushed with victory were the embattled Kemalists that they were tempted to move north to try conclusions with the British in the region of the Straits, but the sound judgment of the Turkish leader prevented a useless conflict. On September 11 the Allied commissioners in Constantinople advised the Turks that they would not permit a violation of the zone of the Straits.[57] The next day Great Britain asked France and Italy to aid in the defence of the Straits by armed force, while British troops were already proceeding to the danger zone.[58]

### 3.

### The Turkish Victory

The defeat of the Greeks relieved Angora from looking to Moscow for military and diplomatic support for the time-being—and Russia and Turkey were almost bound to disagree over the question of the Straits, as well as over economic and political problems.[59] By the Moscow treaty of 1921, Russia and Turkey agreed to settle issues regarding the Straits in a conference of the riverain Black sea Powers.[60] When Turkey made the October 1921 accord with France, the Soviet government took fear, but was assured that Turkey would take no action opposing the Russian treaty.[61] As the Turks advanced toward the Straits in August 1922, Russia, for her own good reasons, held to the policy of supporting the sovereign rights of Turkey over Constantinople and the Straits, and stood for the protection of Russian interests in that region and in the Black sea.[62] On September 13, 1922, M. Karakhan sent a note to Lord Curzon bitterly denouncing the entire Allied policy in the Near East, in which he declared that the fate of the Straits was to be decided by a conference of the riverain Powers as provided in the treaty of Moscow, which alone Russia recognized.

". . . *Russia cannot consent to the Straits being opened to the battleships of any country, and, in particular, that Great Britain, with*

the consent of her Allies, should have control of the Straits without the consent, and against the wishes, of the Powers who have vital interests in the Black sea, and who should have the right of decision as to the fate of the Straits.

"Russia, Turkey, the Ukraine, and Georgia, to whom belongs practically the whole of the Black sea coast, cannot admit the right of any other government to interfere in the settlement of the question of the Straits, and will maintain the point of view above set out even if the contrary point of view is backed by military or naval superiority . . . ."[63]

At the same time the Moslem members of the Indian legislature protested to the viceroy and cabled London urging neutrality in the Greco-Turkish war. As a basis for peace, the Moslems suggested that Turkey retain Thrace with Adrianople, the abolition of international control over Constantinople and the Straits, with guarantees for freedom of passage, and the retention of the sultan and caliph in Constantinople.[64]

On September 15 Great Britain sent an appeal to the Dominions, and to Greece, Jugoslavia and Rumania to help defend the Straits against a possible Turkish aggression, and the next day an official communiqué explaining the predicament of the government was made public.

". . . The approach of the Kemalists forces to Constantinople, and the Dardanelles and the demands put forward by the Angora government . . . if assented to, involve nothing less than the loss of the whole results of the victory over Turkey in the late war. The channel of deep salt water that separates Europe from Asia and unites the Mediterranean and the Black sea affects world interests, European interests, and British interests of the first order."[65] And His Majesty's government was to ask the world to help defend that little, but important "channel of deep salt water." While M. Poincaré had already shown his interest in the Straits and had expressed his "solidarity" with Britain, the action of the London government (of which Paris knew nothing) profoundly surprised him. The French premier wired London on September 18 that "the French government has been profoundly surprised at the grave initiatives publicly announced by the British cabinet on the subject of the affairs in the Orient before any entente with its allies and particularly with France." France was "absolutely in accord" on the necessity of preserving the freedom of the Straits, but differed with London "on the proper means to realize it", and seriously feared the consequences of the British policy in the entire Moslem world.[66]

The next day Poincaré ordered that all French troops at Chanak and all other points along the Dardanelles be withdrawn, and the Italians quickly followed that example, leaving the British to face the Turks, should they make the attempt to cross the demilitarized zones. Among the British dominions, Australia and New Zealand alone favored action in the Dardanelles, and offered to send troops to the assistance of the mother country. Neither Jugoslavia nor Rumania was moved to fall in line with Great Britain.[67] On September 19, the government at Washington, though affirming its interest in the Straits, refused to take any other action.[68]

Lord Curzon left for Paris to confer with Poincaré and Count Sforza on September 19. The next day France, England and Italy agreed on the necessity of calling a conference for the settlement of the Eastern Question, to which France, Great Britain, Italy and Japan, Rumania, Jugoslavia and Turkey were to be invited to send representatives. Russia and her vassal states were not to be invited, doubtless in order to present the Soviet Union with a *fait accompli*, and to assure a solution of the problem of the Straits in accordance with the desires of the Allies.[69] On September 23 an invitation was sent to Turkey, advising the Turks of the summons of a conference on the affairs of the Near East, on the basis of the return of Turkish Thrace to the Maritza and Adrianople to Turkey. A conference was to meet at Mudania to arrange an armistice between Greece and the victorious Turks.[70]

On September 24 Mr. Lloyd George made a public statement explaining his policy in the Near East. The first and primary consideration directing British policy was "our anxiety as to the freedom of the seas between the Mediterranean and the Black sea." The closing of that narrow strip of water had been responsible for the collapse of Russia and the defeat of Rumania, as well as the prolongation of the world war by two years. The original program with reference to Turkey, the British prime minister was forced to admit, had broken down completely. The original idea had been that America should undertake the mandate for Armenia as well as the Constantinopolitan state; that France should take the mandate for Cilicia; that Italy accept the responsibility for Adalia, and that the Greeks occupy the vilayet of Smyrna. But America rejected the Armenian mandate, the French surrendered Cilicia to the Turks in 1921, the Italians withdrew from southern Anatolia, and the Greek hopes for a greater Hellas in Asia Minor were now dashed to the ground. Meanwhile the Turks were threatening to advance into Europe.

"We therefore, have regarded it as a matter of paramount importance to the interests of European peace that the war in Asia Minor should not spread in Europe. We have . . . taken steps to strengthen our position in the Dardanelles . . . , with a view of achieving two objects: First, that of securing the freedom of the Straits, and second, that of preventing the prairie fire, which devastated Asia, from crossing the narrow seas and lighting the dry timber in the Balkans.

"We do not wish to hold Gallipoli and Chanak in the interests of Great Britain alone. We do not consider that Great Britain alone should have the sole responsibility there. We believe those important shores should be held under the auspices of the League of Nations in the interest of all nations alike . . . .

"But the freedom of the Straits remains. That is of vital interest to us as a maritime and commercial power and to civilization throughout the world. That we can maintain, and the fight that we are putting up at the present moment is the fight to insure that, whatever happens at the peace conference, we shall not abandon the policy of securing the freedom of the Straits . . . . That is why we are taking the steps which we have already taken, and we shall do our best to secure an immediate conference between all the Powers concerned in order to establish permanent peace . . . . I want to make it clear that we do not want a second Gibraltar in the Dardanelles. We want the League of Nations to keep the Straits open for all nations."[71]

But there were Powers in eastern Europe which did not accept the British thesis concerning the guarantee of freedom of the Straits. On September 24 the Soviet government sent a note to the Entente, Bulgaria and even Egypt, urging a conference "of all interested Powers, in the first place—Black sea Powers," to deal with the Turkish problem. Azerbaijan, Armenia and Georgia joined Russia in a declaration of September 27 stating that they "would not recognize any decision which would be taken without the participation of the Transcaucasian republics and against their interests."[72] The next day the Soviet government advised Angora that Soviet Russia, the Ukraine and the Transcaucasian republics expected representation at the coming conference.

The Angora government accepted the conditions of the armistice on September 29, 1922, and promised not to attack the neutral zone about Chanak and the Straits, providing the Allies would cede Constantinople with eastern Thrace to the Maritza river, including

Adrianople.[73] About the same time Kemal telegraphed General Harrington, the British commandant at Chanak, to evacuate the Asiatic
side of the Straits, as the French and Italians had done, and insisted
that no Greek vessels pass the Dardanelles. Harrington warned the
Turks not to advance or threaten the British position, which was now
being reinforced.[74] The British general had the complete support of the
London government in this action.

The American government noted its satisfaction at the calling of
a conference to settle the Eastern Question, and trusted "that suitable
arrangements may be agreed upon in the interest of peace to preserve
the freedom of the Straits pending a conference to conclude a final
treaty of peace between Turkey, Greece and the Allies."[75] Moscow,
on the other hand, protested its exclusion from the conference, and
warned the Allied Powers that "Russia would recognize no decision
taken without her participation and against her interests." The Soviet
government favored Turkish sovereignty over Constantinople and the
Straits in order to protect its own interests. The western Powers, but
above all Great Britain, refused to restore sovereignty over the Straits
to Turkey "in the name of freedom of the Straits, but in reality in
order to maintain there their own domination." Efforts to settle the
crisis in the Near East without the participation of the interested
peoples "can give no positive result nor avoid the imminent risk of a
new war". In consequence Russia proposed especially a conference of
the Black sea Powers to determine the régime of the Straits.

*"The freedom of the Straits, in the name of which Europe is preparing
a new effusion of blood, signifies only freedom for the Powers to block the
Straits at a moment and under any pretext whatever, and to separate
thus the entire Black sea from the rest of the world.*

*"The Russian government is also a partisan of freedom of the Straits,
but a freedom which concerns only merchant ships, and which frees
entirely at the same time the Straits and the Black sea from the presence
of foreign naval forces."*[76] Another note from Moscow protested against
the blockade of the Straits and demanded the removal of all limitations
on commercial ships passing through the Dardanelles and the Bosphorus.[77]

As a result of these negotiations following the Turkish victory over
the Greeks, a conference to arrange an armistice between the two
belligerent Powers met at Mudania, where the instrument was drawn
up and signed on October 11, 1922.[78] The Kemalists had demanded
the immediate occupation of Constantinople and eastern Thrace, but

on account of the fact that the Allies now were united again formally, the Turks were unable to press that issue to a favorable conclusion. The armistice stipulated that the Greeks withdraw from Thrace behind the left bank of the' Maritza. Allied forces were to occupy the right bank, including Karagatch, and were to be withdrawn only when the Angora government could take over the territory. Neutral zones, which the Turks promised to respect, were to be drawn up, and Turkish troops were not to be moved into eastern Thrace until the ratification of the treaty of peace.

The Turks had won their war for independence against the Allies and had returned to Europe. Greek hopes in Asia Minor were crushed beyond recovery, though Constantine had abdicated the throne once more, and Venizelos had returned to power.[79] The Turks under Mustapha Kemal were now in possession of practically all the territory they had claimed under the national pact and it remained only to complete their task after the conference of Lausanne. The policy of Lloyd George in the region of the Straits was almost a complete fiasco. That policy was not only to secure the lion's share in the break-up of the old Turkey, but to dominate and control the Straits and Constantinople. France had obtained only Syria, while Italy was crowded out of Asia Minor. Both Italy and France appear to have understood the fundamental aims of British policy, and from 1921 to the disastrous end in 1922, they held aloof from the futile Greek venture on which Mr. Lloyd George had set his heart and mind. The end found the Greeks routed before the victorious armies of the Turkish nationalists, and England appealing for French and Italian aid in protecting British control of the Straits. They answered by withdrawing their troops from the Chanak region, not desiring to risk the possibilities of another conflict in that quarter of the world. Deserted at home and abroad, on October 19, 1922, Lloyd George was forced to resign the office of prime minister, when the conservatives withdrew from the government coalition—a withdrawal due primarily to the failure of the eastern policy of the government.[80]

Though the policy of Lloyd George had ended so disastrously in the defeat of the Greek armies in Asia Minor, Great Britain was yet to attempt to achieve her aims in the Straits and Turkey through the exclusion of Russia from the conference at Lausanne, which was to meet in November 1922. How the Lausanne conference dealt with the problem, how the Turks fought for the independence which they

had won on the battlefield, and the fundamental antagonism between Russian and British interests in the region of the Straits, will be related in the next chapter.

# CHAPTER IX

# THE TURKISH VICTORY AT LAUSANNE

## Introduction

THE conference of Lausanne, which met from November 1922 to July 1923, was one of the most important diplomatic gatherings after the world war. It marked the definite triumph of Turkish nationalism under Mustapha Kemal, the disastrous defeat of Greece and the end of Hellenic dreams in Asia Minor, and signified a victory of French over British policy in the region of the Near East. The conference was to consider the eastern problem in all its ramifications, bring about peace in the Levant, and make a new régime of the Straits. The long struggle of the Turks for national independence was one of the great epics of recent world history. That independence won on the battle-fields of Asia Minor was to be completed by no less notable victories in diplomacy at Lausanne.

Lord Curzon went to Lausanne with the avowed intention of making peace between Turkey and Greece, enabling Turkey to reconstruct herself, drawing Angora away from Russia, Persia and Afghanistan, and pointing the country toward western Europe.[1] The British program called for the exclusion of Russia from the conference proper and allowing the Soviet government and its allies to be heard only in the discussions of the régime of the Straits. On September 27, 1922, France, England and Italy invited Russia to Lausanne to participate in these restricted discussions regarding the Straits. On October 18, 1922, Chicherin advised the Soviet representatives in England and Italy that in seeking a lasting and enduring peace in the Near East ". . . *Soviet Russian Government sees itself forced earnestly to stand on her participation in the Conference on Near Eastern questions as a whole without any limitation. Relying at that time on her right to support the arrangements of the Russo-Turkish Moscow treaty that the final working out of the international statute must be given over to the Black sea riparian states, the Russian government, in view of the approaching call of the conference, will examine the whole complex of Near Eastern problems, informs them of its demand for participation on equal terms with other negotiating Powers.*" On November 2 Chicherin replied to the Allied proposition, stating that an attempt to decide the question

of the Straits apart from the remaining questions, basic to any solution of the problems of the Near East, would not give the results expected at the conference and would not lead to a permanent settlement of the question of the Straits satisfactory to all the interested Powers. Russia demanded the participation of the Ukraine and Georgia.[2] But the Allies were able to limit Russian participation on the excuse that Russia had taken part neither in the Sèvres treaty nor in the Greco-Turkish war.[3]

Invitations to the conference were issued on October 27, 1922, and the Angora government accepted on October 31. However the fact that Constantinople was also invited to send representatives to Lausanne led the Grand National Assembly on November 1 to end the dual government, by declaring the deposition of Mohammed VI, and voiding all acts of the Constantinople government since March 16, 1920. On November 5 the sultan's authority ended when Refet Pasha took over the government in the name of Angora. Abdul Mejid Effendi, second son of Abdul Aziz who was deposed in 1876, was elected to the caliphate on November 18.[4]

Anglo-French differences still seemed to forebode ill for the conference. Great Britain, in order to present a united front to the Turks, urged that an Allied program be formulated before the opening of the conference. On November 18, Italy, France and England reached an agreement on fundamental principles.[5] Though asked to send representatives to the conference on October 28, the American government contented itself with sending "unofficial observers". The United States had not been at war with Turkey, but was particularly interested in the preservation of the freedom of the Straits; maintenance of the régime of the capitulations; protection of educational, philanthropic and religious institutions; protection of minorities; and preservation of the "open door" for American enterprises in the Near East.[6]

No conference since the world war faced greater difficulties or had to solve more complicated problems than that at Lausanne. The Turkish victory over the Greeks had upset completely the whole situation in the Near East. The manifold questions before the meeting at Lausanne, which constituted a veritable Gordian knot, were: (1) territorial and political problems of vast importance dealing with Thrace, the Aegean islands, and the régime of the Straits; (2) the problem of minorities, which had been one of the main difficulties with the

old Ottoman government; (3) the problem of the régime of the capitulations, involving the judicial, financial and economic organization of Turkey.

If these issues were of great importance to the Allies, they were of *vital* significance to the Turks. The nationalists had won a great victory on the field of battle. They came to Lausanne to fight for Turkish territorial integrity, and to preserve its sovereignty from infringement, either through international control over the Straits or through the judicial or financial capitulations.[7]

President Haab of the Swiss federation welcomed the conference on November 20.[8] Ismet Pasha, the Turkish delegate, who was to distinguish himself as a diplomat no less than as a general, spoke of the new position of his country as a free and independent state. At the first plenary session on November 21 the conference organized, adopted rules of procedure, and prepared itself for the onerous tasks ahead.[9]

Following the adoption of the rules, Mr. Richard Washburn Child, the representative of the United States, indicated that the American delegation would take no part in the negotiations, sign no documents, or assume any engagement, but would be present at all discussions, and expected to be treated on a footing of perfect equality with all the other delegations.[10] The conference decided on November 22 to allow the Bulgarian delegation to present its case in regard to the Aegean and to be heard with regard to the problem of the Straits. Both Albania and Belgium were to be heard on the question of the Ottoman public debt.[11]

After many crises, the first conference ended in the rupture of February 4, 1923, when the Turkish delegation refused to sign the draft treaty presented by the Allied Powers on January 31. The *impasse* came over the problem of the capitulations, since the Turks refused to accept either that régime, or a substitute which provided international guarantees for a juridical régime of similar import under another name. Nor would the Turks assign the vilayet of Mosul to Great Britain. Ismet Pasha made this clear in his note of February 4, 1923, emphasizing Turkey's concessions on the Thracian question, the internationalization of the Straits, and Gallipoli. In order not to delay peace, however, he proposed to exclude the Mosul question from the conference and settle it between Great Britain and Turkey within the period of one year.[12] A final meeting on Sunday, February 4, failed to reach any solution. M. Bompard is said to have seen Ismet shortly

before departing for Paris, and wired Poincaré that Turkey had yielded on the capitulations. The conference was to be resumed on Ismet's return from Angora,[13] and the Mudania armistice was to remain in force during the interval. The Turks left Lausanne on February 7 for Angora.[14]

On March 6 the Grand National Assembly voted the treaty drafted at Lausanne unacceptable because of its conflict with the national pact, but decided to reopen the negotiations with the Allied Powers. The basis for the treaty was to be: (1) complete abolition of the judicial and financial capitulations; (2) postponement within a fixed time of the Mosul settlement and the economic clauses; (3) acceptance of the Karagatch clause, abandoning the Turkish claim to the 1913 frontier west of the Maritza delta; (4) insistence on the claim for Greek reparations for damages in Anatolia; (5) acceptance of all other points settled at Lausanne; (6) immediate evacuation of occupied territories by the Allies after peace.[15] These propositions, which accepted internationalization of the Straits, were sent to the Allies in Ismet Pasha's note of March 8, 1923.[16] Though surprised at renewed discussion of questions considered settled, the Allies notified the Angora government on April 1 of their willingness to discuss the points raised.[17] On April 7 the Turks were ready to send delegates to Lausanne for the discussions which were to reopen on April 23.[18]

Events of grave importance influencing the problems before the conference took place during the interim. Evidently in the aim of securing American aid and influence and splitting the Allies, the Grand National Assembly on April 10, ratified the Chester concession, whose interests conflicted with French rights on the Samsun railway concession of 1914. News of this action alarmed both the British and French, and led to a protest from Paris to both the Washington and Angora governments. Greece was mobilizing on the Thracian frontier, and the tense situation on the Syrian frontier caused the dispatch of General Weygand, one of France's greatest fighting generals, to the Near East.[19]

The main problems before the second gathering were those of the capitulations, the Ottoman public debt and the question of economic concessions.[20] The conference closed on July 24, 1923, with the signing of the final acts. The compromises which were made will be discussed in the pages that follow. The problems will be treated separately in the order of their consideration at Lausanne. These were: (1) *territorial questions*, including the Thracian frontier, the Aegean islands, the

régime of the Straits, the Mosul question, and the problem of minorities; (2) *the capitulations and the régime of foreigners;* (3) *economic and
financial problems*, including concessions, the Ottoman public debt,
and the protection of foreign economic interests.

2.

## Territorial Questions—The Thracian Frontier

The problem of the Thracian frontier, which came before the
conference on November 22, 1922, involved not only the fate of
western Thrace, but was of importance to Greece, Turkey and Bulgaria,
as well as to certain of the Allied Powers since it touched the question
of the Straits. This territory had been placed at the disposition of the
Allied Powers by the treaty of Neuilly with Bulgaria in 1919.[21] The
Allies ceded Thrace to Greece in the treaty of Sèvres, August 1920,
but gave Bulgaria the right of free transit to the Aegean and a lease
for a port in Dedeagatch under the guarantee of the League of Nations.[22]
The treaty of Sèvres also surrendered eastern Thrace to the Chatalja lines
to Greece, and forced Turkey to renounce her rights therein.[23] But the
treaty of Sèvres, thanks to the uprising of the Turks against the imperialism of the western Powers, proved abortive. The Mudania
armistice of 1922 stipulated that the Greeks withdraw behind the left
bank of the Maritza from the Aegean sea to the Bulgarian frontier.[24]

This was the situation in Thrace when the Lausanne conference
met. When Ismet Pasha was asked to state his position with reference
to the issue, he claimed the Thracian frontier of the treaty of Constantinople of 1913, and demanded a plebiscite for western Thrace.[25]
These demands met the firm opposition of M. Venizelos, who was
supported by both the Jugoslav and Rumanian representatives. Both
urged the creation of a demilitarized zone in Thrace from the Black to
the Aegean sea.[26] That afternoon M. Stambulisky presented Bulgaria's
plea for an economic outlet to the Aegean which had been promised
in the treaty of Sèvres, and which Bulgaria needed in order to gain
access to the Mediterranean free from dependence on the Straits. He
suggested a neutral zone in western Thrace under the guarantee of the
Allied Powers. Bulgarian access to the sea could not be secure across
territory which was either Greek or Turkish.[27]

Lord Curzon took up the issue and examined the juridical basis of
the Thracian question, but insisted on the Maritza river as the frontier

281

for Turkey. The Allied Powers had agreed on a demilitarized frontier from twenty to thirty kilometers wide on either side of the Maritza between eastern and western Thrace, into the neighborhood of Dedea-gatch and Enos. This would remove the threat from Adrianople. Lord Curzon suggested a form of international control, with a neutral strip, which would remove the military menace and give Bulgaria an outlet to the sea. A sub-commission would consider the problem. Curzon rejected the Turkish idea of a plebiscite for western Thrace as being out of the question.[28]

On November 23 then, the Turkish delegation was confronted by four propositions in western Thrace: (1) adoption of the Maritza frontier for eastern Thrace; (2) constitution of a neutral zone; (3) creation of an outlet on the Aegean for Bulgaria; and (4) international-ization of the railway to the Aegean sea.[29] Ismet insisted on the 1913 frontier and asked for an examination of the question of the neutral zone. Wishing to assure a Bulgarian outlet to the sea, the Turkish delegate had no objection to an international organization enabling Bulgaria, Turkey and Thrace to use the railway.[30]

The next afternoon General Weygand read the report of the sub-commission dealing with the problem, recommending a thirty kilometer demilitarized zone from the Black sea to the Maritza, and, following that river to the Aegean. A second part of the report dealing with Bulgarian access to the Aegean recommended an international commis-sion to supervise Dedeagatch, which was to be a free port.[31] A Bulgarian note attached declared that if Bulgaria did not receive Dedeagatch in full sovereignty, it should be placed under an autonomous régime.[32] The Turks would not consent to the demilitarized zone unless the Powers gave a guarantee for its inviolability, though they would not consent to any foreign supervision over the territory. Again Ismet insisted on the 1913 frontier and desired an express statement that Turkish sovereignty over the territory would not be impugned.[33]

Lord Curzon recognized the seriousness of the problem of neu-tralization which Ismet had opened—involving fundamentally the same problems of political security which have so often troubled the diplomats of western Europe, and particularly those of France. Natu-rally the Turks did not want to disarm their territories unless dis-armament were followed by neutralization and guarantee against attack. But Lord Curzon thought the problem of neutralization "raised a very large question" of "an ominous character", that would arise again in the problem of the Straits, "which could not be decided at

the conference table and would have to be considered by the various governments concerned."[34] M. Barrère, the representative of France, supported his British colleague in this question.[35]

Both the eastern and western Thracian questions were reopened by Ismet on November 25, only to meet Lord Curzon's definite rejection of a plebiscite for western Thrace. The Allied Powers offered only a small enclave between the 1915 boundary and the Maritza.[36]

The first commission completed its labors and reported with the other commissions on January 31, 1923. Turkey received full sovereignty over eastern Thrace, subject to the demilitarized zones protecting the Greek and Bulgarian frontiers. While the Allies ceded the Maritza bridge, they completely rejected a plebiscite for western Thrace, following the precedent set by the head of the British delegation. Including the garrison of Constantinople, Turkey was allowed to have a force of 20,000 men in eastern Thrace.[37] The frontiers of Thrace were laid down in the draft treaty.[38] The draft convention provided *demilitarization* of the frontiers, but did not stipulate *neutralization* or *guarantee* of the territory.[39] Complaints on these provisions by one of the bordering states could be filed with the council of the League of Nations.[40]

The Turkish note of February 4, 1923, accepted the Thracian frontier, and in return for the Allied concession in raising the military limitation in Thrace, the Turks were ready to give up their claim to the 1913 frontier, including Karagatch and the Kuleli-Burgas (Demotika) railway.[41]

At the second session, Turkey won Karagatch in return for conceding the claim for Greek reparations in Anatolia. Tension between the two countries had reached a high pitch when this settlement was reached on May 19, 1923.[42] Jugoslavia opposed this solution, but withdrew the objection, and Venizelos formally acceded on May 26.[43] On July 17 a protocol transferring Karagatch and the isles of Tenedos and Imbros to Turkey, was signed with the final acts of the conference on July 24, 1923.[44]

The conference apparently lost sight of Bulgaria's plight. Bulgaria rejected the proposal of November 24, 1922, to demilitarize western Thrace and internationalize the railway to the sea. Likewise the Sofia delegation refused the lease of a site on the Aegean between Demotika and Makri, which was recommended on January 26, 1923. Nor did Venizelos' offer of harbor rights at Salonica meet with favor in Sofia, for the reason of insufficient guarantees.[45]

## The Aegean Islands

The conference took up the problem of the Aegean islands—involving Lemnos, Samothrace, Imbros and Tenedos—on November 22, 1922. On account of their proximity to the Dardanelles, Ismet Pasha proposed that Imbros and Tenedos be returned to Turkey, as suggested in 1913, for he doubtless had not forgotten the lessons of the world war, when such islands were used by the British as naval bases for operations against the Straits. The head of the Turkish delegation proposed that all the other islands—especially Lemnos, Mitylene, Chios, Samothrace and Nikaria—given to Greece in 1913, be placed under a special régime.[46] Lord Curzon suggested that the fate of Imbros, Tenedos and Samothrace be examined in connection with the question of the Straits, since obviously they were part and parcel of that problem. He rejected the idea of an autonomous régime for the other islands and advised that they be placed under Greek sovereignty and neutralized.[47] The commission thereupon resolved to refer to a sub-commission the matter of the sovereignty over Tenedos and Imbros, together with the problem of the demilitarization of Samothrace and the other islands.[48] Ismet Pasha, however, did not regard the Thracian issue as settled and could not agree to calling Turkish sovereignty over Tenedos and Imbros into question.[49]

General Weygand reported for the sub-commission on November 29. The Turkish delegation had refused to take part in the deliberations of the sub-commission without the Russian delegation, since the islands were bound up with the question of the Straits, and the Russian delegation had been invited to the conference to discuss that problem. The conference adopted the recommendations of the sub-commission dealing with the demilitarization of Mitylene, Chios, Samos and Nikaria. The situation of Tenedos, Imbros and Samothrace was to be examined, as was proper, in connection with the complicated problem of the Straits.[50]

Articles 12 to 16 of the draft treaty submitted to the Turks on January 31, 1923, dealt with the islands.[51] The draft confirmed Greek sovereignty over the eastern Mediterranean islands, other than Imbros and Tenedos, and stipulated demilitarization in order to remove the obvious menace to Turkey. Tenedos and Imbros, which the treaty of Sèvres had given to Greece, were now to have a local autonomous

administration under Turkish sovereignty—a significant fact when one considers their strategic position at the entrance of the Dardanelles. Finally, Turkey renounced all right and title in the territories sur-rendered to Greece.

In the Turkish note of February 4, 1923, Ismet accepted the local administration in Tenedos and the Dodecanese proposal in favor of Italy.[52] A later Turkish counter-proposal added the Rabbit islands to Turkish sovereignty, but renounced the claim to Castellorizo.[53] Turkish protests led to a provision in the final draft recognizing special arrangements between Turkey and a limitrophe country.[54] Article 4 of the annex to the convention of the Straits stipulated the demilitariza-tion of Samothrace, Lemnos, Imbros, Tenedos and the Rabbit islands.[55]

4.

## The Question of the Straits

Perhaps the greatest international issue at Lausanne was that of the Straits, comprising the Dardanelles, the sea of Marmora, and the Bosphorus. During the war Constantinople and the Straits, un-der the hard pressure of the great conflict, were promised to tsarist Russia. With Russia in collapse, Great Britain had sought her own domination in this region—a policy which reached its zenith at Sèvres in 1920. By 1922 Turkey had revived and Russia had returned to the scene of action. The old secular struggle between Russia and England was now resumed with the Soviet government playing the rôle of the tsarist régime. Three theses concerning the Straits were presented at Lausanne: (1) the British proposition, intended to preserve the "freedom" of the Straits, under a pseudo-international scheme, which would give a position of dominance to the British fleet; (2) the Turkish project, preserving Turkish sovereignty, but giving a re-stricted freedom; and (3) the Russian plan, insisting on Turkish sover-eignty, but closing the Straits to warships, with the Black sea remain-ing virtually a Russian *mare clausum* navally. The two Powers which fundamentally fought the diplomatic battle over the question of the Straits at Lausanne were, of course, Russia and Great Britain.

The Russian delegation arrived at Lausanne on December 1, 1922, accompanied by the Soviet delegations from the Ukraine and Georgia. The discussion of the problem opened on December 4. When Ismet Pasha presented the Turkish viewpoint, he cited the national pact,

which declared for the security of Constantinople, but acknowledged that the Turks were ready "to subscribe to any decision which may be taken by common agreement between the Turkish government and . . . the Powers concerned . . . with a view to ensuring the opening of the Straits to world trade and to international communications."[56] Beyond that general statement Ismet refused to commit himself at the time.

M. Chicherin, the first delegate of Soviet Russia, insisted on permanent freedom for commerce in the Bosphorus, the Marmora and the Dardanelles. But, "the Dardanelles and the Bosphorus must be permanently closed both in peace and war to warships, armed vessels and military aircraft of all countries except Turkey."[57] Security for Turkey could be provided only by "the reestablishment and full maintenance of the rights of the Turkish people over Turkish territory and waters." Turkey should have full powers to defend the Straits against any attack with all the means at her command.[58]

The Russian scheme was more pro-Turk than the program of Ismet Pasha. It would make the Black sea a *mare clausum* and enable Russia to dominate those waters as well as the Straits ultimately. Moreover the fact that Russia had an alliance with Turkey revived British fears of Unkiar Eskelessi.[59]

M. Duca, of the Rumanian delegation, opposed closure of the Straits to ships of war, or placing them in the control of any single Power. The European Powers long since had internationalized the Danube, freedom of which could never be real "unless this international river were free up to its final outlet, the Straits." Rumania insisted on a "régime of complete liberty", and could "not agree to the key of the Straits being in the pocket of one Power alone, which could open or shut the gate at its will." An international régime should be established and the Black sea be neutralized. Having obtained Bessarabia in 1918, now in complete control of the Danube outlet to the Black sea, Rumania did not propose to see Russia dominant in the Straits, or even playing the supreme rôle unchallenged in the Black sea.[60] M. Duca was defending not only the position of his own government, but was representing the views of all the members of the Little Entente, of which Rumania was a member. Czechoslovakia, one of whose principal routes of import and export leads through Rumania to the Black sea, was directly interested in freedom of the Straits, as

likewise was Poland. The Bulgarian delegation took a similar position and asked for representation on any international administration which might be organized and given authority over the Straits.[61]

Lord Curzon was surprised at this "reversal" of the old policy of the Russia of the tsars. Closure of the Straits, he pointed out, would but create Russian predominance in the Black sea—of which the Soviet delegation was, no doubt, not unaware. If opening the Straits was to the advantage of the strongest naval Power (Great Britain), closure put the Black sea at the mercy of Russia.[62] In contrast, Curzon placed the Allied proposition for the regulation of passage in peace or war through the Straits, and the demilitarization of both Asiatic and European shores. The Allies sought "no special advantage" but desired to secure the Black sea states from danger, treat the Straits as an international waterway, and secure the existence of the Turkish capital on this route.[63]

The rules laid down allowed complete freedom for commerce in peace and war, Turkey being neutral; complete freedom for neutral commerce, Turkey being belligerent. Means taken by Turkey to prevent enemy passage were not to interfere with neutral vessels. Subject to limitation of number and stay, there was to be entire freedom in peace for vessels of war. The total force which any *one* Power could send through the Straits was not to be greater than that of the most powerful fleet in the Black sea. In the event of total demilitarization of the Black sea, the Powers *individually* reserved the right to send (and maintain) a force of three ships, *only one* of which was to exceed 10,000 tons. In time of war, Turkey being neutral, complete freedom as in peace was to prevail, but when belligerent, only neutral war vessels were to be allowed entry.[64]

To ensure the execution of these rules, the Allies proposed demilitarization of the European and Asiatic shores of the Bosphorus and Dardanelles, and the creation of an international commission which was to have charge of technical services, and to supervise and inspect the demilitarized zones. The commission would be composed of one member each from France, Great Britain, Japan, the United States, Russia, Turkey, Greece, Rumania and Bulgaria. The Turkish member was to be president. The Allies were prepared to discuss the question of guarantee and neutralization, about which the Turks were so meticulous. The Allies, of course, had reversed their former policy of

forbidding passage of the Straits to Russian warships, but were now able to dominate the Black sea through their own navies, and had no fear of a Russian threat in the Mediterranean.[65]

At this point, Mr. Child, the American "observer", presented the American position with reference to the Straits. The Washington government stood for complete freedom of commerce and trade the world over. The discussion involved "the freedom of all those nations which border on the Black sea, and of all those nations outside the Straits who desire to reach them on their friendly errands." The United States could not accept the position that the future of commerce in the Black sea was "the exclusive affair" of the riverain states. It was the concern of all nations. "The unlimited control of the Straits and the Black sea by any one nation is against the policy of the world." Mr. Child viewed disarmament of the Black sea as the guarantor of freedom there, while armament "to keep the Straits open is in fact a danger to the freedom of the Black sea." The American representative was urging a policy in reference to the Straits which was the exact contrary to that which his own government was pursuing in the region of the Panama canal. If, as Mr. Child stated, disarmament were the best assurance of freedom in the region of the Black sea, and if armament were the greatest danger to that freedom, then the same principle would apply to the strategic waters of the Caribbean sea.

Mr. Child could not agree with the Russian delegation in proposing the exclusion of warships from the Black sea. No nation had gone further than the United States in the direction of naval disarmament.

*"Ships of war are not necessarily agents of destruction; on the contrary, they may be agents of preservation and serve good and peaceful ends in the prevention of disorder and the maintenance of peace. We, I believe in common with every commercial nation, wish access to every free body of water in the world, and we will not be satisfied if our ships of war may not pursue their peaceful errands wherever our citizens and ships may go."*[66]

Ismet Pasha accepted the Allied proposals on December 8, with certain reservations. Turkey desired a guarantee securing the region of the Straits with Constantinople against a possible surprise attack from land or sea, and, in time of war (Turkey being a belligerent), indispensable technical control of the Straits. In addition Ismet urged Turkish sovereignty over Tenedos, Imbros and Samothrace, an autonomous régime in Lemnos, and a means of defence at Gallipoli.[67]

Chicherin was opposed completely to the Allied scheme for internationalization of the region of the Straits. Lord Curzon had insisted on international control over the Straits in order to guarantee "freedom" of passage at all times and in all circumstances. Chicherin adverted to both the Panama and Suez canals in order to demonstrate the contrary of the British position. Russia was asking for Turkey only what the United States and Great Britain already possessed at Panama and Suez, both of which had full right to fortify and protect their respective waterways, while the United States was even contemplating, for additional security, a second interoceanic canal in Nicaragua. The ideal solution, according to the Soviet foreign minister, would be naval disarmament on every sea; the only possible compromise was Turkish sovereignty over the Straits, and closure to warships. The régime for demilitarization, free passage of warships and an international commission, meant the end of Turkish independence and was unacceptable to Russia. Moreover the system was a means of attack on Russia. Individually fleets entering the Black sea could not exceed the largest Black sea fleet (Russian)—*combined they would be three times as great.* Even with limitation of armament in the Black sea, the Powers each could station three vessels there as a constant threat.[68]

Lord Curzon replied to the Turkish proposal on the afternoon of December 8. He was glad Ismet had recognized the principle of demilitarized zones, provided adequate guarantees were given. Curzon believed the guarantees given were sufficient, but thought the question of political guarantee worthy of examination. He did not feel that the Marmora could be excluded from the Straits, and insisted on the demilitarization of the Bosphorus, though modifications in behalf of Constantinople might be possible. He had no objection to the *transit* of troops in the demilitarized zones. The point on arsenals, naval stations and the extent of the demilitarized zones could be examined. Tenedos, Imbros, Samothrace and Lemnos should be demilitarized, but Samothrace must remain Greek.[69]

The Russian delegation now demanded that they be allowed to take part in the entire discussion of the question of the Straits and the Black sea. Lord Curzon gave assurances that he had no desire to exclude them.[70] This did not preclude the Allies from treating privately with the Turks, however, and led to the Russian protest of December 11, 1922. Chicherin submitted a plan to Ismet restricting the passage of

warships to one-third the Russian Black sea fleet, but Ismet demurred that concessions must be made toward the Allies. Turkey was being drawn away from her Russian moorings.[71]

The new Allied scheme for the régime of the Straits was presented to the Turks on December 18.[72] The new proposal reduced the demilitarized zones, permitted the transit of Turkish troops in the zones, and allowed the Turkish fleet to navigate and anchor in the Straits. To guarantee the security of the Straits, the Allies proposed an individual or collective appeal to the council of the League of Nations as to measures to be taken in event of a menace imperiling freedom of the Straits or of the demilitarized zones. The Powers agreed to contribute to such measures. Should unanimity in the council fail, the Powers individually agreed to take such measures as two-thirds of the council might approve.[73] But this was not the complete individual and collective guarantee which the Turks desired for their political security.

Both the Russian and Turkish delegations presented counter drafts at this meeting. Chicherin asserted that even the third Allied draft proved the intention against Russia, while giving Turkey only an illusory satisfaction through the League guarantee. The idea was to separate Turkey from Russia "and to expose Russia to the full weight of attack by the other Powers".[74] The Russian draft,[75] on the other hand, affirmed Turkish sovereignty over the Straits, while Samothrace and Lemnos were to be autonomous. Complete freedom of commercial vessels and aircraft was to be preserved. But, "in virtue of long-established principle, the Straits are recognized as closed to the war vessels . . . of all fleets, except that of Turkey."[76] In exceptional cases, Turkey could permit passage of light war vessels. In time of war Turkey was to enjoy the rights allowed belligerents by international law. To provide for commercial shipping, an international commission was proposed. The essential object of Moscow came to light in article 21 of the Russian draft:

"*The contracting Powers are agreed to elaborate and sign within three months from the adoption of the present regulation an international act recognizing the Black sea as a* mare clausum *of the littoral Powers, even in the event of changes being made in the régime of the Straits which may modify the above stipulations.*"

Such a program signified Russian dominance in the Black sea as well as ultimately in the Straits, and met not only the opposition of Bulgaria, Rumania and the Allies, but received a distinctly cool reception from Turkey.[77]

The Turkish counter project provided a restricted freedom of the Straits. It admitted the principle of freedom with reservations on the limitation and regulation of warships, and accepted demilitarization, with guarantees for Turkish security. Turkey did not want, however, an international commission over the Straits, and desired a collective and individual guarantee to respect the inviolability of the Straits.[78]

On December 19 the Allies categorically rejected the Russian proposal as out of the question, and proceeded to examine the Turkish memorandum. Lord Curzon was not prepared to concede any new ground to the Turks, and apparently the Allies had reached the limit of generosity.[79]

In the main the Turkish delegation agreed with the Allied project, but did not want the commission of the Straits to supervise demilitarization, and objected to Greek representation on that body. Nor did Ismet feel secure under a political guarantee of the League of Nations—he demanded an *individual and collective guarantee of the Powers*.[80] Chicherin characterized the Allied draft as a "flagrant violation of the security of Russia and her Allies, of the independence of Turkey, and of the interests of general peace".[81]

In the afternoon of the next day, however, the Allies stood their ground firmly, and the Turks capitulated. Ismet Pasha had consented to demilitarization of the Straits, freedom of passage, and the establishment of an international commission, *but did not receive the desired satisfaction of a political guarantee*.[82] The Allies were demilitarizing the Straits—not guaranteeing the region against seizure by another Power.

The draft treaty, as we have seen, was ready on January 31, 1923, and on February 1 Ismet Pasha finally accepted the new régime of the Straits, despite the opposition of Soviet Russia. Indeed rumors of a split between the Soviet government and Turkey led Raouf Bey, Turkish minister of foreign affairs, to declare on January 7, 1923, that the friendship and coöperation were unchanged and that "we are resolved to promote the welfare of our country by remaining faithful to this friendship which is beneficial to both sides."[83] M. Chicherin positively refused to sign the treaty because the new régime threatened

the security of Russia and her vassals, made a stable and peaceful situation in the Near East impossible, imposed new additional armaments on Russia, violated the treaty of Moscow between Russia and Turkey, violated the independence and sovereignty of Turkey, and threatened the security of Constantinople.

"*Taking account of the fact that the draft convention concerning the régime of the Straits presented by the inviting Powers threatens the security and vital interests of Russia, the Ukraine and Georgia;*

"*That it makes it impossible to establish a stable and peaceful situation in the Near East and on the Black sea;*

"*That it will result in imposing on Russia and the other countries an additional burden of naval armaments and places an obstacle in the way of establishing general peace . . . .*

"*The Russo-Ukrainian-Georgian delegation do not agree to the draft of the inviting Powers, make it clear that they are irreconcilably opposed to the whole policy of domination and violence expressed in this draft, and wish to emphasize the inability of the present conference to accomplish work of real peace.*

"*At the present time, there is no agreement with Russia, the Ukraine and Georgia. There have been no negotiations nor even attempts at negotiations with them. Under these conditions there cannot be any decision in the Straits question. There is none and there will not be any without Russia, the Ukraine and Georgia. If the convention is signed without Russia, the Ukraine and Georgia, the latter will retain an entirely free hand and complete liberty of action. If certain Powers sign this convention without Russia, the Ukraine and Georgia, the Straits question remains and will remain open.*"[84]

Despite the Russian refusal to sanction the Straits convention, the Turks had accepted it, and the document remained virtually as determined in the draft of January 31, 1923, with the exception that Turkey later obtained a garrison at Constantinople and on the Gallipoli peninsula. During the interval between the two conferences, the Grand National Assembly voted to renew negotiations on March 6, but insisted on the *complete abolition of the judicial capitulations.*[85] It was on this basis of a bargain for abolition of the capitulations, evidently, that final acceptance of the new régime of the Straits was given in the treaty of July 24, 1923. During the second part of the Lausanne conference a Soviet delegation headed by M. Vorovsky came to express its views with regard to the Straits, but on May 11 M. Vorovsky was murdered by a Swiss who had served in the Russian

army during the war. Finally, however, though deeply outraged by this incident, and opposed in principle to the convention of the Straits, M. Chicherin announced his intention of sending Nicolas Jordansky (from Rome) to sign it because the Turks had accepted it. The signature was placed on the convention on August 14, 1923 at Rome.[86] But the Soviet government did not cease to view the new régime of the Straits as other than a menace to Russian security.

The Straits convention of Lausanne consists of twenty articles, with an annex to article 2, which lays down the rules for passage of both commercial and war vessels and air craft through the Straits.[87] Article 1 stipulates:

*"The high contracting parties agree to recognize and declare the principle of freedom of transit and of navigation by sea and by air in the Strait of the Dardanelles, the Sea of Marmora and the Bosphorus, hereinafter comprised under the general term of the 'Straits'!"*

The first section of the annex deals with *merchant vessels, including hospital ships, yachts and fishing vessels and non-military aircraft.* In time of peace there is to be "complete freedom of navigation and passage by day and by night under any flag and with any kind of cargo". In time of war, Turkey being neutral, there is also "complete freedom", and the rights and duties of a neutral Turkey do not allow her to take any measures which may interfere either with navigation through the Straits or the air above. In time of war, when Turkey is a belligerent, there is to be freedom of navigation for neutral vessels and non-military aircraft, if they do not in any way assist the enemy. But while Turkey has "full power to take such measures as she may consider necessary to prevent enemy vessels from using the Straits", they are not to be of such a nature "as to prevent the free passage of neutral vessels".

The second section of the annex deals with *warships, including fleet auxiliaries, troopships, aircraft carriers and military aircraft.* In time of peace war vessels are given "complete freedom", but the maximum force which any *one* Power may send through the Straits is not to exceed that of the *most powerful* of the littoral states of the Black sea. However, the Powers "reserve to themselves the right to send into the Black sea, *at all times and under all circumstances*, a force of not more than three ships, of which no individual ship shall exceed 10,000 tons." This, assuredly, is an interesting feature of the program in the light of the demilitarization of the Straits and the possibilities for an attack on Russia. Turkey had no responsibility for the number of war

vessels passing the Straits, though the Straits commission was to keep a record of such passage and to keep account of the naval forces in the Black sea in order to carry out the above provisions.

In time of war, Turkey being neutral, there was to be complete freedom for war vessels, though this was not to be "applicable to any belligerent Power to the prejudice of its belligerent rights in the Black sea". Whatever rights or duties a neutral Turkey had, she was not "to take any measures liable to interfere with navigation through the Straits", whose waters as well as the air overhead "must remain entirely free in time of war, Turkey being neutral, just as in time of peace". But warships and aircraft of belligerents were to undertake no hostile acts within the Straits.

In time of war, Turkey being a belligerent, neutral war vessels were to enjoy "complete freedom". Nor were any measures which Turkey might take to prejudice the free passage of neutral vessels of war or aircraft. Submarines were to pass only on the surface, and strict rules were laid down for military aircraft. Warships in transit were not to remain longer than the time necessary to effect passage.

Special provisions relative to sanitary measures were provided in the convention. Warships having had cases of plague, cholera, or typhus (during the preceding seven days), or which had left an infected port in less than five days, had to go through quarantine. A similar rule applied to merchant vessels. War and commercial vessels calling at a port in the zone of the Straits were subject to the international sanitary regulations. Even these seemingly innocent sanitary regulations had their political inplications with reference to passage of the Straits and brought on a dispute between Angora and the Straits commission in 1924.

The demilitarized zones in the region of the Straits include the Gallipoli peninsula, both Asiatic and European shores of the Dardanelles, the Bosphorus and the sea of Marmora, running about seventy-five miles along the shores of the Dardanelles and sea of Marmora and from three to fifteen miles inland. Along the shores of the Bosphorus, the zones run the entire length at a depth of over nine miles inland. All the islands of the Marmora with the exception of Kizil Adalar are demilitarized. In the Aegean sea the Rabbit islands, Imbros and Tenedos, which belong to Turkey, and the Greek islands of Lemnos, Samothrace, Chios, Mitylene, Nikaria and Samos, are demilitarized. But, with the exception of Lemnos and Samothrace, Greece may keep a limited military force in the islands, and Turkey may transport troops

through both the demilitarized zones and islands, while both Powers in case of war and in pursuance of "belligerent rights", may modify the provisions for demilitarization in the Straits convention.[88]

No permanent fortifications, artillery organization, sub-marine engine of war, military air base, or naval base is to be allowed to exist in the demilitarized zones, subject to the exception that a garrison of 12,000 may be maintained at Constantinople and a naval base and arsenal may be constructed there.

The Straits convention, in order to secure execution of the stipulations concerning the freedom of the Straits, provides for the creation of an international *Commission of the Straits*, with headquarters at Constantinople. It is to be composed of one representative each from Turkey (whose representative is to be president), France, Great Britain, Italy, Japan, Bulgaria, Greece, Rumania, Russia and Jugoslavia. On accession to the convention, the United States is entitled to representation. The governments represented are to pay the salaries of their representatives. The commission is to carry out its functions under the auspices of the League of Nations, to which it furnishes an annual report. The fundamental duty of the commission is to see that the provisions relative to warships and military aircraft are carried out, and it is to "prescribe such regulations as may be necessary for the accomplishment of its task". But the convention is not to "infringe the right of Turkey to move her fleet freely in Turkish waters".

Turkey had desired an individual and collective sanction or guarantee for the zone of the Straits, a proposition which the Allies refused to accept. Instead, the Powers in order to assure that demilitarization of the region of the Straits would not endanger Turkey, and that no act of war should threaten the freedom of the Straits or the safety of the demilitarized zones, provided in article 18:

"*Should the freedom of navigation of the Straits or the security of the demilitarized zones be imperilled by a violation of the provisions relating to freedom of passage, or by a surprise attack or some act of war or threat of war, the high contracting parties, and in any case, France. Great Britain, Italy, and Japan,* acting in conjunction, *will meet such violation, attack or other act of war or threat of war*, by all the means that the Council of the League of Nations may decide for this purpose."

Such was the convention of the Straits formulated at Lausanne. Through it the Allies obtained freedom of passage of the Straits and demilitarized the zones of the Dardanelles, the Marmora and the Bosphorus. Demilitarization, however, was not followed by what the

Turks considered an effective neutralization or guarantee of security. The Allies rejected a collective and individual guarantee of the Straits which they stripped of armaments. Instead they merely pledged themselves to adopt such measures as the council of the League of Nations may approve by unanimity. Greater safety would result under article X of the covenant of the League, if and when Turkey becomes a member of that organization, though recent interpretations have eliminated much of the "security" from that much debated article. One may conclude then, that Turkey and the region of the Straits are safe only in time of peace. In time of war, even when neutral, Turkey is seriously handicapped, and when at war, the entire zone of the Straits is peculiarly subject—as always—to superior sea power. Such demilitarization too, as the Soviet government has insisted ever since, constitutes a direct menace to Russia on the Black sea. This fact has led to the continuance of close Russo-Turkish relations and the constant preparations which the Turks are known to be taking in order to defend the Straits against attack. Nor can it be said that the Lausanne solution of the question of the Straits is necessarily definitive.[89]

Freedom of the Straits is, indeed, desirable and in line with the best modern tendencies, but there is no more fundamental reason for internationalizing and demilitarizing these narrow waters between the Black sea and the Aegean than for internationalizing and demilitarizing the Suez and Panama canals. This has been essentially the Russian and Turkish position. Lord Percy suggested as much to David Hunter Miller at the peace conference in 1919. Colonel House similarly advised both President Wilson and Arthur James Balfour in the spring of 1917. If one waterway is to be placed under an international régime and disarmed, the others in all fairness and logic, though not in fact, fall in the same category. The difference in the situation lies purely in the fact that both England and the United States have the power to exclude outsiders from their reserved zones at Panama and Suez. In a word, there is no question of world politics peculiar to the region of the Straits. There is, however, a very fundamental question of international waterways—a question involving the Panama canal, the Suez canal, the Straits of Gibraltar and others—to which the same principles should be applied impartially.

Nor is it clear that the Straits properly can be neutralized or demilitarized in an attempt to solve that problem without general naval reduction or disarmament. Opening the Straits, as under the Lausanne régime, signifies ultimately, predominance of the greatest sea power—

Great Britain—in those waters and in the Black sea, as Chicherin pointed out. Closure as surely means Russian predominance in the Black sea, as Lord Curzon insisted. Neither proposition constitutes a solution under existing conditions in naval armament. To protect herself Russia must arm to the teeth in order to block any Power which might attack her Black sea coast. The problem of the Straits and the Black sea cannot be separated and solved without the action of the Great Powers in a general reduction of naval armaments. Without this, and without a fundamental solution of the entire problem of international waterways, there can be no essentially international settlement of the question of the Straits.

## 5.

### The Mosul Question

The problem of the Mosul vilayet had remained unsettled since 1918 and constituted one of the principal obstacles to the establishment of peace in the Near East. This important piece of land had been assigned to France by the secret treaties of 1916, but as we have seen, the British won back the territory from France in December 1918. The Turks did not accept the status of Mosul, continually opposed the British position, and the question presented one of the great problems at Lausanne—so great, in fact, that a settlement proved impossible, and had to be postponed for future solution between Turkey and Great Britain.

The importance of the Mosul vilayet both to England and Turkey has been indicated in a previous chapter. Economically, politically, and militarily, the vilayet was of extreme significance to both countries. In a strategic and political sense, the struggle for Mosul was a phase of the renewed secular contest between Russia and Great Britain and constituted "one of the central problems of this struggle for the route to India". Mosul is a crossway near the center of three important land routes to India: (1) the northern route—Moscow-Orenburg-Tashkent-Samarkand-Bokhara-Kabul-Peshavar; (2) the central route—Moscow-Rostov-Baku-Tauris-Teheran-Ispahan-Kerman-Quetta, or the variant via Caspian sea from Baku-Krasnovodsk-Merv-Herat-Kandahar-Quetta; (3) the southern route—London-Constantinople-Mosul-Bagdad-Kerman, or Bagdad-Ispahan to Quetta. In particular, the Mosul vilayet commands this southern route to India.

"Against a Russian attack, coming from the north or east, and against a Turkish attack, coming from the west, this crossway holds the defence of all the routes opening on the plain of Mesopotamia. From the point of view of offense, its position permits a flank attack on every important Russian advance attempted against Bagdad from the Persian plateau."[90] Mosul occupies a most important position in relation to Kurdistan, on account of the large number of Kurds in the territory, while geographically it dominates Kurdistan. Doubtless Mustapha Kemal understood the importance of the territory in making his demands for it. In Turkish hands, Mosul would constitute not only a constant menace against the English in Iraq (Bagdad) and the French in Syria, but would place the Turks in possession of all the routes of invasion descending on Aleppo, Bagdad and Damascus. The fact that Mosul dominates the headwaters of the Tigris, and that there are possibilities of large quantities of oil there increase its economic importance. In Turkish hands oil concessions could be used to excite the mutual jealousies of the Great Powers, as the Turks found out at Lausanne. French, English, and even American oil concerns engaged in a long struggle for priority rights in future exploitation. This contest or "oil war" in the Near East will be considered later.

Not desiring to discuss their claims before the entire Conference, Lord Curzon and Ismet Pasha made a vain attempt to settle the problem through a private exchange. The only result of this spirited correspondence was to reaffirm the positions of the two parties and to increase their determination to hold on to the coveted territory.[91] Failing to settle the matter privately, Lord Curzon brought the question before the territorial and military commission on January 23, 1923.[92] He called on Ismet Pasha to state the Turkish question, who summed up his case for the retention of the vilayet as follows:

"1. *The great majority of the population in this vilayet consists of Turks and Kurds.*

"2. *The inhabitants of the vilayet urgently demand that they may be restored to Turkey, for they know that in that event they will cease to be a colonized people and become citizens of an independent state.*

"3. *Geographically and politically this vilayet forms an integral part of Anatolia, and it can only maintain close relations with the ports of the Mediterranean, which are its real outlets, if it remains united to Anatolia.*

"4. *All the treaties, agreements and conventions which England may have concluded in regard to a country which is still legally part of the*

Ottoman Empire can have no legal value, the more so because the populations have not been given a chance of expressing their wishes freely and
safe from all pressure and foreign occupation.

"5. As Mosul is the point of intersection of all the roads connecting
the southern parts of Anatolia, its possession is indispensable to us for
the economic life and the security of that region.

".6. The Mosul vilayet was taken away from us, like many other
parts of our country, after the suspension of hostilities and contrary to
the conventions which had been concluded: it ought, therefore, to be
restored to us like the other districts which suffered the same fate."[93]

The Allies had no intention, of course, to restore any of the Asiatic
territories taken from Turkey as a result of the world war. In his reply,
Lord Curzon repeated the contentions he had made in the correspondence with Ismet. Great Britain had occupied Iraq, had placed a king
on the throne of the country, and Mosul, Bagdad and Basra were under
a common mandate of the League of Nations, for which Great Britain
was responsible. Great Britain thus, was bound by a threefold obligation—to the League of Nations, the king of Iraq and the people —and
therefore Great Britain could not surrender the territory to Turkey.[94]

Lord Curzon alluded to the subject of oil, which had been "widely
and constantly discussed in the press of the world". Oil had nothing
to do with his case, which he had presented "on its own merits quite
independently of any natural resources there may be in the country".[95]
But if oil had nothing to do with the argument, it had much to do with
the British position in Mosul. Lord Curzon observed that the Turks
had sent representatives to London to offer concessions in Mosul. He
became specific when he insisted on the validity of the Turkish Petroleum Company's concession of 1914. However, since oil "is a commodity
in which the world is interested" it would be a mistake to exercise a
monopoly. Even if oil were there, both Iraq and Anatolia would profit
by British exploitation. That was the substance of the oil affair. In the
British position it was "nil".[96]

Just how much the "world" was interested in the oil may be judged
from the fact that immediately following that session—in the evening—
the delegation of the United States presented a memorandum denying
specifically the rights of the Turkish Petroleum Company and insisting
on the principle of the open door for American oil companies. Standard
Oil and the famous Chester concession were particularly interested
in the oil of the vilayet. The oil war at Lausanne had opened, with the
United States and Great Britain the chief contestants.[97]

But there was no agreement. Lord Curzon, therefore, proposed that the problem be put before the council of the League of Nations for its impartial decision.[98] Ismet Pasha rejected arbitration of the dispute in general, and in particular took exception to arbitration by the League of Nations.[99] Lord Curzon countered by insisting on action by the League, asserting that Turkey would be on a footing of entire equality with Great Britain, since Turkey would be represented on the council for the purposes of the dispute. With the provision for unanimity in the covenant, no decision could be taken without Turkish consent.[100] If the Turkish delegation refused, Lord Curzon would appeal to the council, under article XI of the covenant, since the problem threatened to disturb the peace of the world.[101]

But Ismet rejected the English proposal, urged a plebiscite to determine the fate of the territory, and asked Curzon to recognize the restoration of Mosul to Turkey. Whereupon Curzon announced his decision to appeal to the council of the League.[102] Curzon took this action on January 25, 1923, and announced it on January 31 to the conference.[103] By February 4, however, the Turks had rejected the treaty, objecting particularly to the provisions with reference to the régime of the capitulations. At the same time Ismet suggested the exclusion of the Mosul issue from the conference and settlement "within the period of one year . . . by common agreement between Great Britain and Turkey."[104] The same day, at an informal meeting in Lord Curzon's room at the Beau Rivage hotel, Curzon indicated his assent to postponement of the settlement, to allow direct negotiations, providing that in case of failure, the question would then be referred to the League of Nations. Meanwhile the *status quo* "existing in the region" should be observed.[105] Ismet Pasha accepted the proposal on behalf of his delegation.[106]

Just as the first part of the conference of Lausanne was ending in failure and Ismet Pasha was leaving for Angora, M. Bompard, former ambassador of France at Constantinople and now representing his country at Lausanne, conferred with the chief of the Turkish delegation and informed him that the draft terms of the treaty were not final and left open the road to compromise.[107] Already M. Poincaré, though announcing the complete solidarity existing between England, Italy and France, told the French Chamber that France "will continue to play at Lausanne a rôle of prudence and conciliation".[108] The Allies, in literal turth, were no longer united even diplomatically against the Turks as the second part of the conference was to reveal so distinctly.

In the interim the Angora government ratified the Chester concession, giving Americans far reaching rights in the development of Anatolia, which conflicted with both French and British interests. While the main lines were determined, the Mosul question again came before the conference, when Sir Horace Rumbold, now chief British delegate, demanded that the British stipulation on the preservation of the *status quo* on the Turco-Iraq frontier be defined in the treaty. Ismet Pasha thought there was no change in the *status quo* while the question was in suspense.[109] Nothing in the way of a solution had been found by the end of May 1923.[110] But on June 4 the Mosul question was coupled with the Angora accord of October 1921, when General Pellé, delegate of France, insisted on the full force of that accord with all its annexes. Ismet demurred, hoping for an early solution of the Mosul issue, which was now bound up with the question of the Allied occupation of Turkish territory. When the Turks demanded the evacuation of Constantinople and Chanak on April 24, the Allies refused on the ground that the treaty became effective only on its full ratification.[111]

On June 26 England and Turkey reached an agreement on Mosul. The frontier was to be settled within nine months by direct negotiations, or failing that, the problem was to be referred to the council of the League of Nations, as Lord Curzon had urged during the earlier part of the conference. Meanwhile the two governments mutually engaged to respect the *status quo* pending the solution of the question by the council, "of which the final fate will depend on that decision."[112] On July 7 Sir Horace Rumbold announced that the evacuation of territory would take place within six weeks of notification to the Allies of ratification of the treaty, and the negotiations regarding Mosul would begin from the date of the evacuation operations.[113] But the question was not to be settled definitely until January 1926. In the end Great Britain won the legal right to retain the territory.[114]

6.

*The Question of Minorities*

A final problem of extreme gravity before the territorial and military commission at the Lausanne conference was that of the national and religious minorities, dealing with the fate, not only of the Greeks of Turkey, but also of the Armenians. Turkey was not the only

European (or Asiatic) country facing the difficult and complicated problem involved in the presence of religious and national minorities—especially the Orthodox Greeks and the Gregorian Armenians. But under a military empire like that of the sultans, situated as it was in a geographical *milieu* which formed a highway to three continents, and which became a subject of prey of certain nations interested in the Near East, the problem of minorities was bound to become accentuated. With the passing of the Ottoman Empire and the rise of a new nationalist Turkey, the character of the question of the minorities underwent a change. But while desiring to assure the minorities of the new Turkey a right to live in the republic, the Turkish delegation at Lausanne was no less determined to allow no infringement of Turkish sovereignty under the pretext of the Allies of protecting the national minorities. Turkey was resolved to permit no renewed partition of her patrimony by the Allies in the interest either of the Greeks or Armenians.

The question of the minorities first arose as early as December 1, 1922, when the late Dr. Fridtjof Nansen, sent to the Near East by the League of Nations, read a paper on the exchange of Greek and Turkish minorities, suggesting mutual exchange under the supervision of the League.[115] Ismet Pasha was surprised at the raising of an unexpected issue, which involved not only the exchange of prisoners, but that of the entire question of minorities.[116]

A sub-committee, formed to consider the problem, read its report on December 12. Lord Curzon emphasized the world interest in the problem, which involved the Turkish population of western Thrace, the Greek population of Constantinople, the Armenians, Nestorians, Assyrian Christians and the Jews. The plan of the sub-committee called for written guarantees for minorities in the treaty, similar to those made with the new central European states, and demanded a commission of the League of Nations in Constantinople to supervise the task.[117]

In reply Ismet Pasha delivered a long address denouncing the centuries of calumny heaped on Turkey and reviewing the history of the question from the Turkish standpoint. His theme was that the minorities in the Ottoman Empire had suffered only because foreign Powers had interfered with the internal affairs of the country and had aroused the subject peoples against the government. This, of course, left much to be desired either in the way of an analysis or a solution of the difficulties. In conclusion he rejected supervision of the problem by

the League of Nations, because the solution depended on the exclusion of all foreign interference. The question could be solved by the mutual exchange of Greeks and Turks, and the best guarantees in the future, he thought, lay in the laws and liberal policy of the new Turkey.[118]

Lord Curzon did not agree with the Turkish delegate, and Venizelos did not favor an exchange of Greek and Turkish minorities. Neither favored Ottoman legislation as a solution of the problem. Turkey could not claim a position superior to that of the new succession states in central Europe, all of which had been forced to sign treaties with guarantees for their national minorities.[119] Mr. Child, the American observer, urged that "strong measures should be secured for the safety of these peoples".[120] The French, Italian, Jugoslav, Greek and Armenian delegations supported the Curzon proposals.[121]

Ismet Pasha replied the next day, alleging Greek atrocities against the Turks in Anatolia, and insisting on an exchange of the Greeks, even in Constantinople, as "a painful necessity, but logical".[122] The Jews, never troublesome to their Turkish rulers, could remain in Turkey. He could not consent to a fresh attempt at a partition of Turkey for the Armenians, who already had a Soviet republic in Erivan. Nor could Turkey agree to the formation of an international commission which would intervene constantly in the internal affairs of the country. However, Turkey would accede to guarantees similar to those laid down for the new states in central Europe.[123] That was the limit to which the Turkish republic would commit itself.

Lord Curzon reminded the Turks that the eyes of the world were upon them, and urged the League of Nations as a proper instrument to solve the entire complex of problems.[124] Ismet answered his British opponent on December 14. As soon as peace was concluded, Turkey was ready to enter the League, as Lord Curzon had suggested. He refused to concede an Armenian home in Turkey, however, and rejected the international commission on minorities. Turkey would grant amnesty to offenders of the last few years, and would conclude the necessary treaties protecting the subject nationalities in the country.[125]

Lord Curzon was glad to hear Ismet's declaration in regard to the League of Nations, but questioned the efficacy of treaties guaranteeing minorities in Turkey, and proposed further study of the issue.[126] Venizelos did not desire compulsory exchange of Greek and Turkish peoples, but if necessary, reserved the right of limiting its application.[127]

The report of the sub-commission on minorities was presented on January 9, 1923.[128] In essence it was almost a complete Turkish victory, for it provided guarantees by treaty, but abandoned the plan for an international commission. This appeared to satisfy the Turkish delegation, but Lord Curzon regretted the Turkish refusal to allow a League commissioner to remain in Constantinople, and deplored the Turkish stand on the Armenian question. He denied the charge that the Allies had a political end in urging a national home for the Armenians and Assyro-Chaldeans—a denial which neither quieted Turkish fears nor moved them to concede to the wishes of the British foreign minister.[129]

The commission discussed the report on the exchange of populations on January 10. No agreement had been reached on the main issue. Turkey insisted on removing the Greek patriarchate from Constantinople as a condition of allowing the Greeks to remain there. Lord Curzon proposed to retain the patriarchate, but eliminate its political and administrative character and activities.[130] France, Rumania, Jugoslavia and Greece hoped for such a solution.[131] After a careful examination, Ismet withdrew his objection, on Lord Curzon's assurance that the patriarchate would be shorn of political influence.[132]

This led to the decision for mutual exchange of the Greek and Turkish population, except the Greeks of Constantinople and the Moslems of western Thrace.[133] The special draft convention between Greece and Turkey on the exchange of populations was signed on January 30 by the Turkish and Greek representatives.[134] Compulsory exchange was to take place after May 1, 1923.

The result was a Turkish victory in almost every respect. There was to be no supervision by the League of Nations, though the provisions of the treaty were placed under the guarantee of the League of Nations and were declared to be of international concern. Both the patriarch and the Greeks were to be permitted to remain in Constantinople. The question of the Armenian home, due to the firmness of the Turkish opposition, was dropped from further consideration.[135]

7.

*The Capitulations and the Régime of the Foreigners*

The Turks were determined to win not only their territorial integrity at Lausanne, but to secure sovereignty over their country through the abolition of the entire régime of the capitulations. Abolition of the capitulations had been declared as early as October 1, 1914,

and was recognized by Germany in January 1917. The Allies, however, had revived the régime under military control following the armistice and had eliminated the delegates of the Central Powers from the council of the Ottoman public debt. One of the primary objects of Turkey at the Lausanne conference was to rid the country of the hated foreign interference under the capitulations which threatened the national sovereignty. Moreover the Turkish national pact was "opposed to restrictions inimical to our development in political, judicial, financial and other matters".[136]

The question first came into consideration on December 2, 1922, before the commission on the régime of foreigners (second commission) under the presidency of Marquis Garroni. Garroni described the origin of the capitulations as the spontaneous act of the Ottoman govern-ment, dating from the days of Suleyman the Magnificent. However the régime was regarded as diminishing the sovereignty of a state, Turkey's demand for its abolition was intelligible, and the Allies were disposed to meet the demand "in principle". Turkey needed foreign aid and for this purpose guarantees would be needed. Such was the Allied position.[137]

Ismet was gratified at Allied acceptance of the abolition of the capitulations, but made it clear that his government would not agree to a suppression in form "but maintained in substance".[138] The Allied position was that suppression of the capitulations must be mutual, and while they accepted in principle, a satisfactory substitute must follow.[139] Baron Hayashi supported his colleagues, adding that Japan had taken twenty years in the same process of reconstruction. Mr. Child upheld the position of the Allied Powers—Americans too had interests at stake in the new Turkey.[140] In response Ismet read a long memorandum reviewing the history of the capitulations and concluding with the statement that Turkey could not assent to reëstablishment of the capitulatory régime or to any similar project, but was ready to make general arrangements for reciprocity based on the principles of inter-national law.[141]

The next meeting of the commission took place on December 28, 1922. Garroni indicated the willingness of the Allies to place foreign subjects on the same footing with Turkish citizens in regard to taxation and to make foreign citizens and companies subject to Turkish law. The Allies proposed to give Turkish courts full right to try foreigners under certain conditions. As to the composition of the courts there was disagreement. The Allies suggested a majority of foreign judges

305

in the Turkish courts, chosen by Turkey on the recommendation of the Permanent Court of International Justice. Until Turkey had created an acceptable judicial system, a transitory régime would be necessary.[142]

But such ideas were not at all pleasing to the Turkish delegation. Sir Horace Rumbold reported the failure of his commission on account of the "intransigeance" of the Turks. The Turks insisted on the sufficiency of their legislative guarantees, and rejected a transitory period under foreign supervision.[143] Ismet Pasha rejected foreign judges in Turkish courts as a violation of Turkish sovereignty even worse than the capitulations.[144] M. Barrère observed that France could not accept the blank rejection of these proposals, while Baron Hayashi again urged Turkey to go slowly in abolishing the capitulations as the Japanese had done in the late nineteenth century.[145] Mr. Child upheld the "sanctity of obligations" and "the fundamental equity" of foreigners who had invested in Turkey, in general support of the Allied position.[146] Lord Curzon, much disappointed, felt that no treaty could be made if Turkey were not willing to compromise.[147]

On January 6, 1923, Ismet delivered a carefully prepared speech on the capitulations. He again rejected a special régime for foreigners, but asserted his willingness to negotiate treaties regarding the conditions under which Allied nationals could settle in Turkey.[148] This was a re-assertion of the previous stand, which the Powers were careful to note.[149]

Garroni reviewed the work of his commission on January 27, 1923. The Allies were willing to abolish the capitulations and place foreigners in Turkey on the same fundamental basis as the Turks themselves, but the Turks rejected the plan for foreign judges to be chosen by Turkey. A new system provided for a judicial commission of five judges, two Turkish and three foreign jurists, recommended by the Permanent Court of International Justice, and all nominated by the Turkish government. Turkey then was to select legal advisors, on the nomination of the commission, who were to sit in the courts when foreigners were affected. The Allies asked for a declaration from Turkey to this effect. The system was to remain only for the period of transition until Turkey had built up an acceptable legal and judicial system.[150]

M. Serruys explained the work of his commission, which was to devise a fiscal régime for foreigners in Turkey, with guarantees in international law, and to provide for the revival of treaties to which

Turkey had been a party, and her adherence to other treaties. Turkey refused to exempt foreign property from capital levies for war purposes.[151]

The Allies submitted the draft convention on January 31—a convention which abolished the system of the capitulations in principle.[152] A further draft convention, however, with a declaration annexed, stipulated the conditions which the Allies deemed necessary during the period of transition. It provided legal counsellors who would not only advise, but in some cases actually sit in the Turkish courts, a condition which the Turks would not accept.[153] The concessions of February 3-4 dropped the judicial functions, leaving only the advisory powers.[154] Ismet Pasha rejected the new proposal, and on February 4 submitted a counter draft proposing to take into Turkish service European jurists for not less than five years, who were to be under the department of justice, and to take part in the reform of legislation. They would receive complaints from foreigners on the administration of justice, but were given no control over arrests.[155]

In his turn Lord Curzon refused to consider the Turkish counter-proposals, and Ismet Pasha would not give in. The conference broke up. When it reopened it was on the basis that the abolition of the capitulations be recognized. Indeed it was understood that the Turks were standing firm on the abolition of the capitulations in return for conceding on the internationalization of the region of the Straits. The second part of the Lausanne conference reached a deadlock on the judicial system on May 4, 1923, when Ismet again rejected foreign interference in judicial processes.[156] On May 19 the Allies accepted the Turkish standpoint on foreign educational, religious and charitable institutions, placing them solely under Turkish law. [157]

The final draft convention, signed on July 24, 1923, was a complete victory for the Turks. The declaration concerning the administration of justice proposed to take into the Turkish service for not less than five years, a number of European jurists as Turkish officials. They were to serve in the ministry of justice, take part in the legislative commissions, and receive complaints on the administration of justice—otherwise they were not to interfere in the administration of the law.[158] Turkey had succeeded in abolishing the centuries old capitulations, had eliminated foreign interference from the judicial system, and was to be sovereign in her own household. Having made fundamental concessions in the Straits, the Turkish nationalists stood firm and won freedom in judicial matters.

## Economic and Financial Questions

If Turkey came to Lausanne determined to win her territorial integrity and her judicial and political freedom, she was no less resolved to secure financial and economic liberation from a time-honored bondage to western Europe. These questions came under the province of the third commission, which held its first session on November 27, 1922, under the presidency of M. Barrère, the first delegate of France.[159] Ismet Pasha considered the main problems before the commission to be those of the Ottoman public debt and Greek reparations for damages in Anatolia resulting from the Greek occupation and retreat.[160]

The problem of the Ottoman public debt is a long and complicated one. As we have seen already, the Turks had been taught the borrowing process during the Crimean war, and, facing an outstanding debt of $1,000,000,000 in 1875, the country became bankrupt. On December 20, 1881, the council of the Ottoman public debt was created by the decree of Muharrem, the debt was reduced to $500,000,000, and certain important monopolies were assigned to the council for the service of the debt. During the world war the Allied nationals on the council of the Ottoman public debt ceased to serve—though the Turkish government permitted them to remain—and from 1914 to 1924 virtually no payments were made on the outstanding obligations of the public debt. Turkey paid dearly for her participation in the war, not only in the loss of over 400,000 men killed and a similar number of wounded, but incurred a war debt of more than $2,000,000,000, of which amount the Central Powers advanced almost $1,500,000,000 in the form of war loans.[161] The treaty of Sèvres brought a settlement neither to the problem of the public debt nor to any other major issue before it.

On the afternoon of November 28, 1922, Ismet Pasha presented the Turkish case concerning the Ottoman public debt and the question of Greek reparations. Since the Ottoman Empire had ceased to be, its debt should be distributed among the successor states, and Ismet proposed a sub-commission to deal with the question of the debt. He opposed paying the expenses of the post-war occupation of his country by the Allies, and insisted on reparations from Greece for her devastations in Anatolia since 1919. Venizelos, on the other hand, rejected payment of the Greek share of the Ottoman debt on technical grounds,

and stood firmly against the Turkish position with reference to reparations. Greece, Venizelos contended, had come into the war against
Turkey as the ally of the Serbs—a war in which Turkey had been the
aggressor. But even if Greece were the aggressor, she had occupied
Smyrna and other territory at the invitation of the Allies, and might
therefore demand larger damages from Turkey.[162] M. Ninchich, of Jugoslavia, indicated his country's willingness to accept its part of the debt
as a successor state.[163] Ismet, in turn, continued to insist on the recognition of Greek reparations for actions in Anatolia.[164] Barrère, however,
expected Turkey to assume the debt, leaving only the question of
distribution open, the share of each successor state being determined
on the basis of its contribution toward the general revenues of the
late empire. The Allies would consider the elimination of the expenses
of the military occupation since it had been of long duration.[165]

On January 13, 1923, the commission considered the report of the
financial sub-committee. There was a great difference in point of view.
The sub-committee took the distribution of the debt only up to the
outbreak of the world war.[166] Ismet Pasha contended that since the
empire had had a legal existence during the entire war, war loans and
debts should likewise be distributed among the succession states.[167]
Both Bompard and Curzon objected to the proposal of the Turkish
delegation, which would add an £T18,000,000 internal loan and
£T150,000,000 to £T170,000,000 paper currency issue to the debt.[168]
Venizelos proposed that railway charges be divided among all the
succession states or be excluded, and was ready to refer the question
to the Permanent Court of International Justice. The question of the
shares of the debt and payment of coupons was next considered.[169]

The chief difficulty of the day came when Ismet, after accepting
reciprocal responsibility (save as regards Greece) for reparations,
refused to pay damages growing out of the Allied occupation of Turkey.[170] It was in line with the best Turkish tradition at Lausanne to
refuse the institution of a sanitary commission composed of four doctors
(under a Turkish president), which was to exercise sanitary control
over the Straits for five years.[171] The Turks would permit no interference in the Straits under the guise of sanitary regulations.

The question of concessions caused considerable difficulties, as it
produced rivalry over the economic possibilities of Turkey among the
Powers, particularly among Great Britain, France, Italy and the
United States. The Allies desired to place the holders of concessions
before the war in full possession of their rights. The Turks opposed

such a principle on the ground that the new Turkey was determined to set her own house in order under the new conditions now prevailing in the country. They rejected outright any assurance to the *Régie* concession and the French loan of 1913, since it had not received parliamentary approval. New concessions were to conform to new economic conditions in Turkey. Nor did the Turks approve submission of such questions to arbitration by an international body, insisting, as they always did at Lausanne, on the sufficiency of Turkish law.[172] Moreover Ismet Pasha categorically rejected the Allied proposition that the council of the Ottoman public debt should control economic concessions in Turkey as well as the public debt itself—there was to be no reversion to any relic of the old capitulations under a different name.[173] This proposition, too, met the objection of Mr. Child, the American representative, on January 26, 1923, and the provision was therefore modified.[174]

M. Bompard presented the draft convention on January 31, 1923. He emphasized the distribution of the debt—Turkey being the only Power emerging from the war with a reduced debt. A commercial convention had been prepared giving tariff freedom to Turkey, liberating the country from that peculiar type of economic bondage.[175] Ismet would not sign the convention and on February 3-4, the Allies further reduced Turkish debts and payments, and urged that Greco-Turkish claims be settled by direct negotiations, or failing that, by arbitration. Finally they offered to eliminate the proposal that the proceeds of existing or future concessions should be applied to reparations, and to do away with the control over concessions which was to have been exercised by the council of the Ottoman public debt.[176]

In his memorandum of February 4 Ismet accepted the distribution of the public debt among the succession states in proportion to revenue, and the principle that railway debts be paid by the states on whose territory the railways were located. He also accepted division of the debt by the administration of the public debt, and agreed to pay overdue coupons. With reference to sanitary problems, Ismet granted everything except the international board, but was ready to employ European doctors in the Turkish sanitary administration as advisors for a period of five years. Turkey would accept the commercial convention proposed by the Powers on the condition of the abolition of the capitulations in the treaty.[177] At the meeting of February 4, 1923, the question of Greek reparations brought its serious difficulties, but

Lord Curzon finally proposed settlement of the problem between the parties, and Ismet accepted this means of finding a solution.[178]

Turkey would not accept the economic clauses of the treaty which would place her "in a position of economic servitude."[179] The Allies asked the Turkish delegation to reconsider the matter, but were met with a firm refusal.[180] Memories of the economic servitudes registered in the treaty of Sèvres were too fresh to admit of any compromise at Lausanne.

On March 6, 1923, the government at Angora decided to resume negotiations, but only on the basis of absolute abolition of the capitulations. Servitude—judicial, economic and financial—had to be eliminated if the new Turkey were to pursue her course unfettered. When the conference met again at Lausanne on April 22, it was with the assurance that peace would be made, but the Turks were to stand firmly on their position with reference to the capitulations.

On May 8, 1923, the conference accepted the report of the financial sub-commission, with the exception of the part on the Ottoman public debt.[181] The difference of opinion arose over the opposition to the Turkish insistence on payment to the bond-holders in paper francs.[182] On May 18 the Allies agreed to the Turkish position with reference to sanitary regulations in the region of the Straits, namely, that the necessary sanitary control be placed in the hands of a Turkish board, on which a number of European doctors were to serve for a period of five years. This would eliminate the factor of foreign control over the sanitary service in the Straits.[183] On May 26 the Greco-Turkish dispute concerning reparations, which had threatened the conference more than once, was solved by the Greek cession of Karagatch in return for Turkish renunciation of Greek reparations.[184] The Allies renounced all claims for damages against Turkey on May 28.[185]

It was rumored on May 15 that a British group which represented Mosul oil interests had bought control of the Anatolian railway—the Asiatic end of the Berlin-Bagdad line. It was to pay $25,000,000 to rebuild 900 miles and construct 1,2000 miles of railroad as provided in the original concession.[186] On June 16 it was reported that a monopolistic concession had been granted an Anglo-French concern for control of Turkish import and export trade.[187]

The problem of concessions assumed particular importance during the second part of the conference. Throughout June Mr. Grew, who had succeeded Mr. Child as the American observer, was active in opposing those clauses of the treaty which confirmed the validity of

the pre-war contracts, when all the formalities of the concession had not been fulfilled. This policy, as the Allies believed, indicated not only the American insistence on the traditional "open door," but active support of the Standard Oil Company and the Chester concession, both of which were interested in oil concessions in Mosul and Palestine.[188] The controversy over concessions in Turkey involved not only American companies, but the *Régie générale des chemins de fer,* the Turkish Petroleum Company, a British concern claiming oil rights in Mosul and Bagdad, the Armstrong-Vickers, limited, and others. But more will be said of this contest in the succeeding chapter. The controversy reached its climax on June 17.[189] Ismet Pasha conceded neither to the British nor to the French interests, insisted on determining the validity of all the claims by judicial process and concluded that Turkey "would regulate in entire independence the conditions of her economic existence".[190] Mr. Grew was gratified at the settlement of the problem of concessions, but trusted that it did not infringe on any American rights. As to the Turkish Petroleum Company, whose title the American government had contested since 1919, he indicated that the American attitude of the past years had not altered—whereupon Sir Horace Rumbold informed him that the British attitude toward the same company had not changed. In the end Turkey refused to confirm the Turkish Petroleum Company's concession in the treaty, despite Rumbold's warning that his government considered the 1914 contracts binding, and would hold Turkey responsible for "any failure in the obligations then contracted".[191]

The entire question of concessions was removed to a subsidiary annex of the treaty which provided that "concessionary contracts . . . duly entered into before the 29th day of October 1914 . . . are maintained."[192] Both Vickers-Armstrong and *Régie générale* were to receive new concessions, but the Turkish Petroleum—on account of the American position—was not even mentioned in the annex.[193] Negotiations for consideration in Mosul oil rights between the Standard Oil Company and Turkish Petroleum were already under way, however, and the Chester concession seemed suddenly to have lost its diplomatic support and to have faded from the scene.[194]

Meanwhile the conference reached an agreement on July 8 concerning the Ottoman public debt and other economic questions.[195] Turkey recognized the debt, which was to be distributed among the succession states, according to principles determined by the council of the Ottoman public debt.[196] The Lausanne conference finally settled

312

the public debt at £T141,666,299 ($623,331,715.60), Turkey being responsible for £T84,597,495 ($372,228,978), while the rest was divided among the succession states of the late empire.[197]

While Turkey had not won complete economic and financial freedom at Lausanne, the way had been paved for progress in that direction. In February 1928, a draft contract was signed which practically would replace the decree of Muharrem of 1881 and the old council of the Ottoman public debt. The council was now to hold its sessions at Paris, the Ottoman bank was to carry its accounts, the Turkish government was to have charge of the administration of its own revenues without outside interference, and the old capitulations were now eliminated. Turkey had regained her "sovereign financial rights".[198]

9.

*The American Treaty of Lausanne*

The American and Turkish delegations signed a treaty of friendship and commerce on August 6, 1923, providing for the renewal of normal relations between the two countries.[199] Following the same general lines as the previous treaty between Turkey and the Allied Powers, it completely abolished the capitulations and recognized Turkey's full equality with other nations.[200] Naturally the resumption of regular diplomatic relations by the other Powers necessitated American action, but the question of ratification became a political and religious issue in the American senate and the treaty failed of approval by that body on January 18, 1927.[201]

American relations with Turkey were put on a formal basis only by the *modus vivendi* reached between Admiral Bristol, the American high commissioner at Constantinople, and Tewfik Rushdi Bey, on February 17, 1927, at Angora. Regular diplomatic representation was resumed on October 12 of that year when Mr. Joseph C. Grew presented his credentials as the ambassador of the United States to the Angora government.[202]

10.

*Conclusion*

The treaty of Lausanne marks the end in the long process of the dissolution of the Ottoman Empire which had begun as early as the

313

treaty of Karlowitz in 1699. The conference of Lausanne confirmed the system of mandates by which France and England achieved their respective positions in Syria, Iraq and Palestine. It recognized the British protectorate in Egypt and the annexation of Cyprus, as well as the Italian position in the Dodecanese. The question of Mosul remained to be settled in 1926, when the British finally retained that important piece of territory. On the other hand, the Turk was back in Europe, having obtained Constantinople and eastern Thrace with Adrianople. If the treaty arising from the Lausanne conference had sounded the death knell of the old Ottoman Empire by cutting away vast territories, it had signaled the coming of the new Turkish republic, which was freed from ancient restrictions, and in the process of becoming a modern nation. On the other hand Armenia was forgotten and the Bulgarians were shut off from an outlet on the Aegean sea. Greece was forced to abandon her dreams of an Asiatic empire after her defeat by the Turks, and after Lausanne was engaged in consolidating her position at home and in the newly acquired western Thrace.[203] A new régime for the Straits had been instituted, placing those waters under an international control, but in reality opening the route to the Black sea to British sea power, and endangering both Turkey and Russia. This arrangement was to lead to the continuance of Turco-Russian friendship, to the development of a strong Russian fleet in the Black sea, and left the problem fundamentally unsolved.

The Ottoman Empire had ceased to be. But a new national state of Turkey had arisen in Anatolia under the guiding hand of Mustapha Kemal who directed its destinies along the path of modernization. The country was free from the entire system of the hated capitulations, liberated from antiquated financial and economic bondage, and ready to begin life anew in a revived and independent spirit. After ten years of struggle, the long Odyssey was ended—Turkey had won her war for independence.

# CHAPTER X

# THE LEAGUE OF NATIONS AND THE
# NEAR EASTERN MANDATES

PRIOR to the conference of Lausanne, England and France had consolidated their mandatory rule in Palestine, Mesopotamia and Syria. The conference at San Remo in April 1920 had witnessed the signing of an oil agreement between France and England for a division of the oil rights in Mesopotamia. At the same time, Great Britain received formal sanction of her rights in Mesopotamia, Palestine, and Mosul, and obtained control over the Straits. France had remained contented with her Syrian mandate, while Italy was satisfied with the prospects of obtaining Adalia. The treaty of Sèvres of August 1920, forced the Turks to accept an "international" régime of the Straits and to recognize a partition of their territories under the mandate system. At a second conference of San Remo in December 1920, France and England had settled "certain points" in regard to their mandated territories. The treaty of Lausanne added the finishing touches to the structure by internationalizing the region of the Straits and guaranteeing the positions of the Powers in their respective parts of the late Ottoman Empire.

I.

## The League of Nations and the Mandates

At the time of the signature of the armistice of Mudros on October 30, 1918, the British army was already administering Syria, Palestine, and Mesopotamia; and Cilicia was occupied toward the latter part of 1918. O. E. T. (enemy occupied territory) south, which included Palestine, alone was fully in British hands; O. E. T.'s west and north, comprising Beirut and the Syrian coast as well as Cilicia, were in the control of France; while the Emir Feisal had established an Arab government at Damascus in O. E. T. east, under the general direction of the British commander-in-chief. In each part of the enemy occupied territory, whether under French or Arab immediate control, British officers represented General Allenby. This situation, of course, was purely temporary, pending the signing of peace with the defeated Turks. But as the months wore on, the French began to insist on the fulfilment of the promises of 1916, the Arabs began to protest against the secret treaties which would deprive them of their independence and

unity, and the British were caught between the upper and nether millstones of obligations to both sides. Finally, as we have seen, on September 15, 1919, France and England came to an agreement whereby the Syrian littoral and Cilicia came under the control of France, but the French were not to occupy the cities of Damascus, Aleppo, Homs and Hama, which were under the rule of the Emir Feisal. Friction continued between the Arabs and the French despite the attempts of Feisal at moderation and his promises to the French high commissioner, General Gouraud, who had been sent out to the Levant in November 1919. A compromise between the Pan-Arabs and France which was reached by 1920, stipulating French rule along the Syrian coast and Cilicia, while Feisal ruled at Dasmascus under French influence, did not lead to harmony between the two parties. On March 10, 1920, an Arab congress meeting in historic Damascus elected the Emir Feisal king of Syria and proclaimed "the complete independence of Syria within its natural boundaries from Mount Sinai to the Taurus, and from the Syrian desert to the sea, without any protectorate, mandate, or any form of foreign interference."[1] Feisal refused to have anything to do with the San Remo conference which met in April 1920, well realizing as did other intelligent Arabs that it meant the end of the dream for independence. Yet it seems that the British, ever careful to encourage a possible Arab confederation at French expense, favored recognition of the emir's position at San Remo, but met the opposition of the Quai d'Orsay.[2] M. Briand made the charge before the French Chamber of Deputies on June 25, 1920, that England had installed Feisal in Syria— in order to disconcert the French.[3] Not long after, on July 19, 1920, Mr. Ormsby-Gore declared in the British House of Commons that boundaries meant nothing in the Arab world, and "the tribesmen of Mesopotamia and of Syria are linked inseparably, both in their political outlook and in their aspirations . . . . Our pledges are most specific to the Arabs; to the French they are less specific."[4]

Following the San Remo conference, Feisal definitely rejected the French mandate in May 1920. Determined to settle accounts, Paris authorized Gouraud to present an ultimatum to the emir, which he did on July 14. The ultimatum demanded absolute disposal of the railway from Aleppo to Rayak, abolition of conscription, acceptance of the French mandate and Syrian currency, and punishment of all offenders against the French occupation.[5] Feisal's delayed acceptance was followed by a stronger ultimatum, and after a short resistance the French entered Damascus on July 25, 1920. Feisal was forced to leave

the country and subsequently became king of the new state of Iraq, which the British were creating in Mesopotamia.[6] He took refuge in Palestine, while the French subdued the rest of Syria to their mandatory rule. A civil administration was set up, and on September 1, 1920, the independence of the Greater Lebanon was proclaimed, with Beirut as its capital. During September and October the states of Aleppo, Damascus and the territory of the Alaouites and the emirate of Hauran were created.[7]

Palestine remained under British military occupation from the end of the war until July 1, 1920, when a civil administration was instituted, with Sir Herbert Samuel, the brilliant English Jew, as British high commissioner. The announced policy of the British government was to grant equal treatment to all classes and races of people and to provide a national home for the Jews. An order in council provided the constitution of the country, but in 1922 a new constitution was promulgated. It provided for a high commissioner, commander-in-chief for the armed forces and an executive council, on which religious groups should be represented. If the French had their difficulties in Syria, the British encountered serious troubles with the Jews and Arabs. Lord Balfour's declaration of 1917 favored a Jewish national home in Palestine. The difficulties of carrying out such a program may be realized when one notes that out of a total population in Palestine of some 802,000 people, only 104,000 are Jews, while the Arabs account for 615,000 and the Christians 75,000.[8] The Arabs, who had lived in Palestine for more than 1300 years, could not understand the wisdom of establishing a Jewish national home in a country overwhelmingly Moslem, and were not unwary of the dangers which might arise out of a large Jewish immigration encouraged by the British. In 1920 and 1921 there were very serious riots against the Jews in various parts of the country—the worst of the outbreaks being at Jaffa—but these were suppressed by armed force. When an Arab delegation visited England in July 1921 to present its case in regard to Palestine, the colonial office at London assured the delegation that Arab rights would be protected, but the government stood firmly on the Balfour declaration with reference to the Jewish national home. The Arabs refused coöperation with the mandate authorities when it was proposed to create a legislative council, consisting of a high commissioner, ten officials and ten elected members representing Moslem, Christian and Jewish elements in the population. The advisory council remained, and a bureaucratic system of government carried on the administration

and legislation of the Palestine mandate.[9] England did not propose to jeopardize imperial interests along the route to India through the Suez canal.

Up to the time of Feisal's overthrow in July 1920, Transjordania had been administered from Damascus. But in November 1920, Abdulla, son of Hussein and brother of Feisal, was on his way to Syria to re-establish sherifian rule at Damascus. It was at this time that Great Britain asked Abdulla to forego the Damascus venture, and become ruler in Transjordania, under a mandate of Great Britain. Accordingly an arrangement was drawn up in March 1921, in July Great Britain made a grant of £180,000 to Abdulla's government, and since September 1922, Transjordania has been a distinct part of the mandate for Palestine.[10]

From 1918 to 1920, Mesopotamia was under British military occupation. A very serious nationalist uprising and insurrection broke out among the Arabs from July to December 1920, which threatened grave difficulties for the British in Iraq and even extended into the French mandate of Syria.[11] Sir Percy Cox, who had been appointed British high commissioner in Iraq, arrived in Bagdad on October 1, 1920, however, and immediately began the task of organizing a civil government and establishing a council of state under the Naqib of Bagdad as president. This was to endure until a national assembly could be formed to frame an organic law for the country. Foreign and military affairs were in the hands of the high commissioner, who also had a veto on any action of the council of state. British advisors were attached to each ministry.[12]

After some time spent in reorganizing the country, the question of a native ruler became very important. Several candidates appeared for the high office—Feisal, who had been forced out of Syria, Sayid Talib Pasha, the sheikh of Mohammerah, Ibn Saud of the Nejd, Agha Khan and a Turkish prince. Feisal and Sayid Talib were the outstanding candidates for the throne of Iraq. The latter, however, had made himself objectionable to the British authorities, who deported him to Ceylon. This action, which left the Emir Feisal the sole candidate for the throne of Iraq, together with the conference on Arab affairs at Cairo in March 1921, practically decided the fate of the kingship and of Iraq, and clearly indicated the will of the London government.[13]

Feisal left the Hejaz for Iraq in June 1921. On June 16 the Naqib of Bagdad proposed arrangements for his reception. On June 14,

Winston Churchill, then colonial secretary at London, announced that Great Britain favored and would support the emir as king of Iraq, if elected. This announcement reached Bagdad on June 16 and served to clear the air.[14] Less than a month later, on July 11, the council of state resolved that Feisal be declared the king of the country. Sir Percy Cox, however, insisted on a popular referendum to ascertain the "will" of the people. It is noteworthy that at the ensuing "election," Mosul, the troublesome Kurdish district on the Iraq-Turkish frontier in the north, entered vigorous objections, while Suleimania refused to take any part in the election at all. Previously Suleimania had rejected "almost unanimously, any form of inclusion under the Iraq government."[15] Kirkuk, likewise, rejected Feisal's candidacy. While the emir appears to have received an overwhelming majority of ninety-six per cent of the votes, the four per cent against him came almost solidly from this Kurdish district.[16]

Sir Percy Cox installed Feisal as king on August 23, 1921, without representation from either Suleimania or Kirkuk at the coronation ceremonies.[17] There was yet no constitution for the government of the country, and the British had no mandate from the League of Nations for the administration of the territory. Not until the treaty of October 10, 1922 was signed did the relations of the two countries become regular, and it was not until 1924 that Great Britain had what may be termed a mandate from the League of Nations.

Meanwhile the problem of the mandates for the Near East—Palestine, Syria and Mesopotamia—was coming before the League. The Mesopotamian mandate had been on the agenda of the council as early as December 1920, but its terms were not made public until February 1921.[18] The contest over the mandates in this section of the world, into which not only England, France and Italy, but even the United States of America entered, was a long and bitter one.

The American government had witnessed a very fundamental interest in mineral and oil exploitation in the Near East shortly after the world war came to a successful conclusion. Particularly was this true of the former Turkish territories of Palestine and Mesopotamia. On May 21, 1919, the American commission to negotiate peace received from the Department of State at Washington the following telegram:

"*American oil interests are seriously considering examination of Mesopotamia and Palestine with a view of acquiring oil territory. Will such activities meet approval American government and will conditions*

*of treaty be such as to permit American companies to enter that territory under terms of equality as compared with foreign companies in their relations to their respective governments . . . . People having this matter under consideration are not connected in any way with the Standard Oil group."*[19]

What were the American oil interests seriously considering the oil prospects in Mesopotamia and Palestine? Despite the implication of the above telegram, it is known that the Standard Oil Company was interested in both Palestine and Mesopotamia. Much more important for the time being was the Ottoman-American Development Company over whose destinies Admiral Colby M. Chester, formerly of the United States navy, presided. Admiral Chester had gone out to Turkey as early as 1899 on the time-honored task of protecting "American interests" in the domains of the sultan. Turkey was somewhat anxious that American capital be introduced into the country as a counter-weight against French, English and German concessions. Both England and Germany strenuously opposed any American interference in the game of concession hunting in the lands of the "sick man of Europe." Admiral Chester seems to have had the support of Washington and the backing of the powerful New York chamber of commerce in his efforts, and finally in 1908 Abdul Hamid granted him a concession, which the Young Turks later confirmed. The difficulties encountered in the Turco-Italian and Balkan wars, however, prevented development of the claims, and during the world war all action on the project was suspended. Following the war, with the coming of the oil struggle between the United States and Great Britain in the Near East and elsewhere, the American government indirectly protected the Chester concession, by opposing the validity of the Turkish Petroleum Company's grant in the same general territory of Mesopotamia. The Turkish Petroleum Company, which was the most serious rival of the Chester group, after a long struggle, had won a concession for the exclusive exploitation of the oil in Mesopotamia from Bagdad to Mosul in June 1914. The Turkish Petroleum Company then included the following participants: (1) the English group controlling seventy-five per cent of the stock, including Sir Ernest Cassel's National Bank of Turkey, the Royal-Dutch Shell Oil Company, and the Anglo-Persian Company, which was under the control of the British government; and (2) the German group with twenty-five per cent, under the Deutsche bank.[20] In November 1915, the Anglo-Persian Oil Company was informed that the agreement no longer possessed any legal validity.

The British organization, then, had no concession in the strict sense of that term, but only a promise of one, though Lord Curzon was not far from correct when he declared that the war alone had prevented the consummation of the Turkish Petroleum Company's concession in Mesopotamia.[21]

Now let us revert to the diplomatic struggle over oil in the mandated territories and point out its relation to the entire question of mandates in the territories of Palestine and Mesopotamia. Shortly after the conference at San Remo, on May 13, 1920,[22] Mr. John W. Davis, American ambassador in London, presented Lord Curzon a note, declaring that the United States had been informed of the assignment of the mandates for both Mesopotamia and Palestine. The Washington government felt that British occupation had already given advantages to oil companies in Great Britain in both these territories. To prevent the possibility of any discrimination, the United States government suggested that: (1) the mandatory adhere to the mandate principle agreed to at Paris; (2) that "equal treatment in law and in fact" be accorded to all nationals; (3) that no exclusive concessions or privileges be granted; and (4) that reasonable publicity be given the terms of the mandate.

Perhaps it was due to the San Remo convention that Lord Curzon did not answer the American note immediately, for no reply could be given apparently without a prior understanding with the Quai d'Orsay. In the interval, on July 28, 1920, the American government took note of the San Remo agreement on oil, and stated that such a convention would "result in a grave infringement of the mandate principle." Curzon replied on August 9 denying the American charges of discrimination, and equally ridiculing the idea that England was striving for an oil monopoly, since the British Empire controlled some four and one-half per cent of the world production, while the United States produced over eighty per cent of the world supply of oil at that time. The British foreign minister, however, did not state that if the United States unquestionably had control of the present production, Great Britain had control of the greater part of the oil reserves outside of the United States.[23] While appreciating the American position, Curzon asserted a principle diametrically opposed to that of the Washington government when he insisted that the question of mandates could be discussed only in the council of the League of Nations, of which the United States was not a member.[24]

When Mr. Colby returned to the controversy on November 20, 1920, he took particular exception to Curzon's statement that the terms of the mandates could be discussed only in the council of the League of Nations. The rights exercised by the Allied and Associated Powers in the mandated territories accrued directly as a result of the war against the Central Powers. As a participant in that struggle, the United States, though not at war with Turkey, made victory possible over Germany and her allies, and could not consider itself or any of the Associated Powers "debarred from the discussion of any of its consequences, or from participation in the rights and privileges secured under the mandates provided for in the Treaties of Peace." The terms of the mandates were to be submitted to the council, but "the United States is undoubtedly one of the Powers directly interested in the terms of the mandates, and I, therefore, request that the draft mandate forms be communicated to this government for its consideration before their submission to the Council of the League."

Such was the legal question back of the American position. The State Department seemed quite as much interested in petroleum, which was the material factor at the basis of the splendid principles it was enunciating. The danger of exhausting America's reserves of oil made it a fitting subject for negotiations. Mr. Colby continued:

*"The fact cannot be ignored that the reported resources of Mesopotamia have interested public opinion of the United States, Great Britain and other countries as a potential subject of economic strife . . . . To cite a single example: because of the shortage of petroleum, its constantly increasing commercial importance, and the continuing necessity of replenishing the world's supply by drawing upon the latent resources of undeveloped regions, it is of the highest importance to apply to the petroleum industry the most enlightened principles recognized by nations as appropriate for the peaceful ordering of their economic relations."*[25] Nor could the American government reconcile the San Remo oil agreement, giving Great Britain predominant control over the oil resources of Mesopotamia, with the principle of economic fair play and equality as embodied in the mandate principle. Lest there be any misunderstanding between the two governments, Mr. Colby particularly contested the validity of the concession of the Turkish Petroleum Company in Mesopotamia.[26]

Following the note of November, on December 23, 1920, Great Britain and France had defined their mandates, and upheld the San Remo oil agreement of April 1920, as well as outlining and delineating

the territories involved. The covenant of the League of Nations, it appears, contains no provision for the exchange of territories under mandate, such as is found in this agreement, which enabled Great Britain to extend her designs for the all-rail route to India, and within her own territorial limits to construct rail and pipelines connected with the Hejaz, Bagdad and Mosul lines.[27]

This was the status of the Anglo-American conflict when the issue of the "A" mandates was brought before the council of the League of Nations on February 21, 1921. In view of the American protest to the League and the unsettled conditions in the east, Mr. Balfour moved adjournment of the question until more peaceful times.[28] In his note of February 21 Mr. Colby took exception to the Mesopotamian mandate and the Japanese mandate over the island of Yap and called attention to his earlier request of November 20, 1920 (to Lord Curzon), that the draft mandates be submitted to the United States for approval before coming before the League. This was the only way in which the United States could express an opinion on the subject.[29] In its reply of March 1, 1921, the council took note of American interest and declared that the rights of the United States were "not likely to be questioned in any quarter." But the council reminded the government at Washington that it was primarily concerned not with the allocation of the mandates as such, but with the terms of the administration under the mandate. Since the United States insisted on the necessity of its express approval of these terms in order to insure their validity and guarantee American rights, the council invited that government to discuss the problem at the session of the council at which they were to be considered.[30] The state department neither answered the invitation nor again expressed its views on the subject to the council, though it later achieved practically all its purposes.[31] On June 15, 1920, Mr. Gastao da Cunha requested that the Allied Powers arrive at a complete agreement with the United States in order to avoid further delay on the question.[32] No objections were raised to Mr. H. A. L. Fisher's proposition that the mandate terms be forwarded to Washington for approval without the consent of the council, and this procedure was adopted.[33]

The final drafts for Mesopotamia and Palestine were published in August 1921, but were not then approved by the council.[34] Similarly September 1921 passed without action by the League with reference to the mandates. Failure to make any decision was due very largely

to three principal causes: (1) the United States was opposed to consideration of the mandates without its express, definite and previous approval
of the terms: (2) the Greco-Turkish war had left the entire Near East
in an extremely unsettled condition; and finally (3) events on the
northern frontier of Iraq—in the Mosul vilayet, over which Great
Britain and Turkey were struggling—precluded any precise definition
of the mandate.[35]

In the spring of 1922, the question of the "A" mandates again came
before the council of the League. Lord Balfour explained on May 17
that Washington had agreed in principle to the mandate terms, and
July 15 was set for the consideration of Palestine.[36] This brought the
problem before the council finally on July 19, 1922. When M. Viviani,
the representative of France, asked for discussion of the Syrian mandate
before that of Palestine, Balfour objected that the meeting had been
set aside especially for the consideration of Palestine. The Marquis
Imperiali, Italian representative on the council, would not consent
to consideration of the Syrian problem, because it was still subject to
negotiations between Rome and Paris. Viviani declared that the
mandates already had been delayed for two and one-half years, while
Balfour countered with the statement that the problem would have
been settled in February but for the position of the United States.
Imperiali, however, stood his ground and insisted "on the absolute
necessity" of agreement with Italy. Whereupon Viviani refused to
consider the Palestine mandate and Balfour moved adjournment pending
receipt of Imperiali's instructions from Rome.[37] On July 22 Italy was
ready to assent to the Syrian mandate of France, under reservations
pending an agreement between the two countries, and the council
approved. The Palestine and Syrian mandates were to go into force
simultaneously, as soon as France and Italy were in accord.[38] Final
approval on that basis was given by the council on July 24, 1922.[39]
On September 16 the council gave its approval to Balfour's memorandum
outlining a special régime for Transjordania, placing that district under
the British high commissioner in Palestine.[40]

It was not until September 29, 1923, that the Palestine and Syrian
mandates became effective legally. France and the United States reached
an agreement regarding Syria on April 4, 1924, protecting American
rights in Syria and preserving the "open door" theoretically.[41] The
Anglo-American treaty concerning Palestine was signed on December
3, 1924.[42] It is rather noteworthy that Great Britain succeeded in
obtaining "full powers of legislation and of administration save as they

326

may be limited by the terms of this mandate," in Palestine.[43] On the other hand, France, in striking contrast, received no such far-reaching powers of action or control in Syria.[44]

Great Britain carried on in Iraq without a mandate, her relation with the Bagdad government being regulated by the treaty of August 10, 1922.[45] By this alliance the British government engaged to give armed support and assistance to the state of Iraq. A British high commissioner and staff were to reside in Iraq and were to have a guiding hand in practically all governmental matters of importance. In all international affairs and in questions of finance the advice of the high commissioner was binding on the government. Great Britain was to use her good offices to obtain Iraq's membership in the League, in which case the treaty would terminate. Otherwise it was to last for twenty years. Disputes were to be submitted to the Permanent Court of International Justice. Other articles regulated internal affairs in the country.[46] A protocol added on April 30, 1923, stipulated the termination of the treaty on Iraq's entry into the League, which, in any case, was to terminate four years after the ratification of peace with Turkey.[47]

Meanwhile the trouble with Turkey on the nothern frontier of the Mosul vilayet continued, and when the treaty finally was ratified by the constituent assembly, it was with the express proviso that it "shall become null and void if the British government shall fail to safeguard the rights of Iraq in the Mosul vilayet in its entirety."[48]

It now remained to establish definite legal relations with the League of Nations. Conditions had vitally changed, for a king was on the throne of Iraq, and a treaty of alliance existed between Great Britain and the new state.[49] In June 1924 the question was before the council of the League, which was already apprised of the new situation.[50] On September 19, 1924, Lord Parmoor, representative of the British Labor government in Great Britain, reëmphasized that "the whole situation in Iraq has been profoundly modified since the original draft mandate was drawn up."[51] On September 27 the council adopted the draft instrument of the British government establishing the legal relationship of the new state and of Great Britain to the League. In this draft, Great Britain assumed responsibility for Iraq's fulfilment of the alliance, the terms of which were not to be modified without the consent of the council. Iraq's admission to the League would terminate the alliance, but if at the end of the period, Iraq were not in the League of Nations, the council was to decide on the measures to

be taken under article XXII of the covenant.[52] With the end of the world war, Great Britain had established Iraq as another bulwark on the road to India, but it was not until September 1924 that the relation between the two countries was placed on anything like a mandatory basis under the League of Nations.

2.

## Arab Relations After the World War

The inter-relations of the countries cut off from the late Ottoman Empire in the Near and Middle East have been far from happy since the world war. The Emir Feisal was driven from his Syrian throne by the French, only to be put on that of Iraq by the British government. The British placed Abdulla, Feisal's brother, on the throne of Trans-jordania and brought that territory (once under the Damascus government) definitely under the mandate of Palestine. A provisional frontier between Iraq and Syria was laid down in September 1919, but at the end of 1928 neither the Syro-Turkish nor the Syro-Iraq frontier had been determined.[53] The frontier between Palestine and Syria was laid down in the agreement of February 1922 (ratified on March 7, 1923), leaving the headwaters of the Jordan and the Litani in British hands.[54]

The chief troublemaker among the Arabs since the war was undoubtedly the picturesque and powerful Ibn Saud of the Nejd.[55] Ibn Saud played a negligible part in the world war, but played that part very carefully and with circumspection. As already indicated, the Emir Hussein, king of the Hejaz, had negotiated with the foreign office at London in 1915 and had laid claims to an Arab kingdom south of the thirty-seventh parallel, while the British government had recognized Ibn Saud as sovereign lord of most of southern and central Arabia in the treaty of July 18, 1916. Both Arab leaders were rather heavily "subsidized" by the British government during and after the war in order to keep them subservient to British aims.[56]

Following the war, however, Hussein conducted himself in such a manner that he was brought into enmity with the French in Syria, his pretentions to the caliphate alienated the Moslems in India, while his hostility to Ibn Saud led to conflict and defeat at the hands of this ancient enemy. Pursuing the same course which was adopted during the war, the British government in 1923 sought to make a treaty of alliance and protection with the king of the Hejaz and to build a policy

about him as well as about his son, the king of Iraq. The treaty, which was prepared under the Balwin ministry, was continued by the government of MacDonald, and stipulated an obligation on the part of Great Britain to recognize Arab independence in Mesopotamia, in Transjordania and in the vilayets situated in the Arabian peninsula, with the exception of Aden—and Great Britain was to support this independence of the Arab states. It was a reversion to the earlier ideas developed during the war. Palestine was to continue as a British mandate but Arab rights were to be guaranteed. On the other hand, Hussein obligated himself to recognize the special position of Great Britain in Mesopotamia, Palestine and Transjordania, in return for British protection to the Hejaz. The question of Palestine proved the stumbling block in the treaty, and Hussein refused to append his signature to the document.[57]

The refusal of the king of the Hejaz to sign the alliance with England led to the loss of his throne and to his defeat at the hands of Ibn Saud. When the Nejd chieftain opened his campaign against the Hejaz in the fall of 1924, Hussein called on the British government to protect him from the wrath to come, but the appeal fell on deaf ears, and the British Labor cabinet refused to interfere. Mr. MacDonald, anxious to wash his hands of the matter, simply declared that the British government was adhering "to their traditional policy of non-interference in religious matters, and are not prepared to be entangled in any struggles for the possession of the holy places of Islam which may be entered upon by the independent rulers of Arabia."[58] On October 3, 1924, Hussein abdicated the throne and Ibn Saud occupied Mecca. He became king of the Hejaz on January 8, 1925 and received recognition from France, Great Britain, Russia and the Netherlands.[59] The deposed Hussein declared that he had lost his throne because "I did not sign the treaty with Great Britain. I did my best to lead the English to annul the Balfour declaration. I should prefer to see Ibn Saud master of all Arabia than to see the Arabs under the yoke of a foreign Power."[60]

Having conquered the Hejaz, Ibn Saud continued to foster border raids across the Iraq frontier, which were only partially settled in the Bahra agreement of November 1925. Efforts of the British government to bring about a friendly agreement between the king of the Hejaz and Nejd and the king of Iraq finally proved successful with the signature

of an accord on February 24, 1930, in which the two sovereigns provided methods of settling their differences and promised to forget old family feuds.[61]

But the settlement of frontier difficulties did not mean peace in the former territories of the Ottoman Empire—whether in Egypt, Palestine, Syria or Iraq. It will be remembered that on February 28, 1922, the British government ended the protectorate of 1914 over Egypt and had given the country independence. But independence was given only with the understanding that the following matters be reserved absolutely to the government of Great Britain: (1) the security of the communications of the British Empire in Egypt—the Suez canal; (2) the defence of Egypt against all foreign aggression or interference, direct or indirect; (3) the protection of foreign interests in Egypt and the protection of minorities; and (4) control of the Sudan, including the headwaters of the Nile. In consequence, Great Britain notified all other Powers of the newly acquired "independence" of Egypt and advised them that it would "regard as an unfriendly act any attempt at interference in the affairs of Egypt by another Power" and would "consider any aggression against the territory of Egypt as an act to be repelled with all the means at their command."[62] It is perhaps needless to state that as yet no amicable settlement has been reached between Egypt and England, on account of the insistence of Britain on the control both of the Sudan, and the Suez canal, through armed forces. The latest failure occurred on May 8, 1930 with the conclusion of the Anglo-Egyptian conference at London.[63]

If Britain faced almost insuperable difficulties in Egypt, both France and Great Britain had their serious problems to settle in the newly mandated territories of Syria, Palestine and Iraq. On December 7, 1924, the French created a new state of Alexandria, setting off this district from Aleppo and Damascus. In the summer of 1925 a great rebellion against France broke out among the Jebel Druse, which was only quelled by 1927 after France had poured some 30,000 soldiers into the country. This did not prevent the Arabs from agitating for independence, and on June 9, 1928, a Syrian constituent assembly meeting at Damascus, declared the country an "independent sovereign state," which, however, the French high commissioner rejected. Conditions in Syria appeared to be improving in 1930, and on May 22 M. Henri Ponsot, the French high commissioner promulgated a statute in place of the 1928 constitution declaring Syria a republic with a parliament and a Moslem president.[64]

330

Great Britain reaped the whirlwind in Palestine as a result of misleading promises made during the war, when in August 1929, outbreaks between Jews and Arabs resulted in the death of more than two hundred and over three hundred wounded. The MacDonald government, after sending troops to quell the disorders, appointed a commission to investigate conditions in the mandate of Palestine. This commission made its report on March 31, 1930. Rightly the commission found the cause of the dispute in Arab hostility toward the Jews "consequent upon the disappointment of their political and national aspirations and fear for their economic future." The commission advised the British government: (1) to adopt a clear and definite policy in Palestine which would affirm the rights of non-Jewish elements (the overwhelming majority) in the country; and (2) to permit no more excessive Jewish immigration to Palestine as in 1925-26, and to consult the Arabs regarding Jewish immigration. It was asserted that "the absence of any measure of self-government is greatly aggravating the difficulties of local administration", but no constitutional reforms were recommended.[65] Transjordania, a creation of the "exigencies or accidents of international politics," has caused Britain almost as much difficulty as has Palestine. An agreement of February 20, 1928, failed to recognize the independence of the country, which was yet to be controlled by a British resident acting in behalf of the government of Palestine.[66]

Even in Iraq, which has been considered generally as the best example of the "A" mandates in former Turkish territory, the path of Great Britain has not been strewn with roses. A nationalistic sentiment has developed among certain classes who are anxious that the Iraqi manage their own affairs without foreign interference. A new treaty between Great Britain and Iraq, which was signed on January 13, 1926, extended the duration of the mandate for a period of twenty-five years, in order to take care of the requirements of the League of Nations when it awarded Mosul to Iraq.[67] This did not satisfy the demands of the government of Iraq and on December 14, 1927 another treaty was signed.[68] By this latest treaty Great Britain recognized Iraq "as an independent sovereign state" and the two parties pledged peace and friendship in their mutual relations. Article VIII stipulated:

*"Provided the present rate of progress in Iraq is maintained and all goes well in the interval, His Britannic Majesty will support the candidature of Iraq for admission to the League of Nations in 1932."*

The treaty was a disappointment to the Iraqi, who wanted immediate independence. When the Labor government came into power in England it faced a serious problem of discontent, and announced on September 19, 1929 that it would support Iraq's candidacy for admission to the League in 1932, would inform the League council of the decision not to proceed with the 1927 treaty, and that Great Britain would notify the League in January 1930 of the proposal to recommend Iraq membership in the League of Nations in the next two years. It looked as though Great Britian were preparing to create a second Egypt in Iraq, since "independence" was being offered along similar lines.[69]

Yet despite the difficulties there has been economic and political progress in Iraq. The Iraq branches of the Bagdad railway have been so highly developed that within one week's time one can travel from Bagdad to London. A railway now runs from Kalat, which is just south of Mosul, to Bagdad, while Bagdad and Basra were connected by rail as early as 1920. Great possibilities for economic development in Iraq lay in the exploitation of oil in the Mosul vilayet, since the award of the League of Nations in December 1925, while the prospects for irrigation and a return to the ancient prosperity have been enhanced considerably, since the headwaters of the Tigris river are in that vilayet and the great Diala project is just south of the boundary.[70] But more is to be said of the problem of Mosul in its proper connection with the Anglo-Turkish dispute following the conference of Lausanne.

# CHAPTER XI

# THE NEW TURKISH REPUBLIC

## The New Turkey after the Lausanne Conference

FOLLOWING the Lausanne conference the Turkish republic set out definitely on the path of westernization and modernization. When the Allied Powers invited both the Constantinople and Angora governments to Lausanne, the government at Angora abolished that at Constantinople, destroyed the sultanate and proceeded to alter the fundamental structure of the government of Turkey and to strike at the very basis of the old society.[1] On November 1, 1922 the political powers of the Ottoman caliphate were transferred to the Grand National Assembly at Angora. This was followed on March 3, 1924, by a series of three laws which assigned the functions of the former caliphate to a department of religious affairs in the office of the prime minister, abolishing the caliphate, and unifying the educational system of the republic. The new constitution of April 20, 1924, vested sovereignty in the nation as represented in the grand national assembly. By the decrees of September 2, 1925, the religious orders in Islam were suppressed leading to the further secularization of the republic. The spring of 1926 witnessed the adoption of the Swiss civil code, the Italian criminal code and the German commercial code of law, with changes only to meet the peculiar conditions of Turkey. These codes, of course, are entirely independent of the religious element, and replace the old law of the Koran which had been used in the Ottoman Empire. The last vestiges of Islam as a religion of state were eliminated on April 9, 1928, when the Grand National Assembly amended the constitution of 1924 by abrogating the article II which had declared "the state religion of Turkey is the religion of Islam." Henceforth Turkey was to be a completely secular republic without religious moorings or anchor. In November 1928 a law was passed establishing the new Latin alphabet for the Turkish language which was to go into effect in December of that year.[2] In March 1930 a law providing suffrage for woman was passed. During the same year the name of Constantinople was changed to Istanbul and that of Angora became Ankara. The

emancipation of women and the change in the dress of both men and women in Turkey were significant moves in the direction of westernization, even if only in the matter of psychology.

The Turkish reforms naturally had their influence both on the position of foreigners in Turkey and on that of the national and religious minorities. Foreigners have been placed largely on a footing of equality with the Turks and do not appear to have suffered thereby after the abolition of the capitulations. And at the end of 1928, "the minorities problem was nearer solution in Turkey, where it had once worked such havoc, than it was at that time in many East-European countries . . .; and it might be prophesied that the vestiges of discrimination would diminish in proportion as the national self-confidence of the Turkish community increased."[3]

While Turkey was making such progress in the field of cultural, religious and legal reform, somewhat of a set-back occurred in the realm of politics, when in 1925, the country took on more and more of the aspect of a dictatorship, under the iron hand of Mustapha Kemal Pasha. The government, doubtless, in order to prevent disaffection at home, and in order to hasten westernization, felt that a firm hand was necessary. A law for the maintenance of order was passed which only came to an end in 1929. A serious revolt did take place in 1925 among the Kurds, and there have been sporadic outbreaks since then. But in 1930 the situation had quieted sufficiently for an attempt to be made toward the establishment of a more liberal régime, through the organization of a party in opposition to the powerful People's party and the dictatorship. The failure of this opposition to develop raises many serious questions as to the future régime of Turkey. But the answer to that question lies, possibly, beyond the frontiers of the new republic. The sultanate will not be revived. But "whether military figures, with a party behind them, can maintain dictatorial power very much longer will depend on what is going on in the world in general and in Europe in particular."[3]a

### Turkish Foreign Relations

The foreign relations of the new Turkish republic since the conference of Lausanne have centered about several problems, chief of which have been the question of Mosul, the problem of the Straits, and the establishment of normal relations with the other nations of the world.

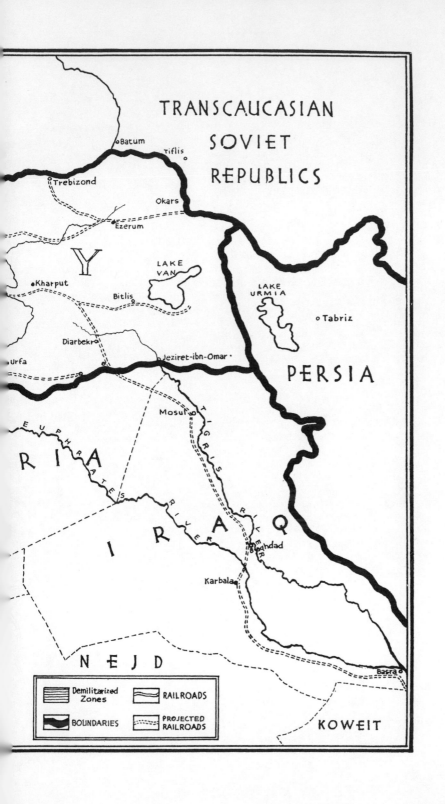

Having failed to settle the Mosul issue at Lausanne, British and Turkish delegates met in conference at Constantinople on May 19, 1924, to solve the problem by direct negotiation.[4] By this time the British had discovered the Assyro-Chaldeans (a Christian people), who lived in the vilayet of Hakkiari, just north of Mosul, and were laying claims to that territory in order to provide another buffer between Turkey and Iraq.[5] When the British delegate, Sir Percy Cox (former high commissioner in Iraq), insisted on the inseparability of Mosul from Iraq, Fethy Bey, the Turkish plenipotentiary, pointed out the inconsistency of this position with the Sykes-Picot accord of 1916, which had placed the Mosul vilayet in the French zone of influence. Sir Percy gave the fundamental history of the cession of Mosul when he replied with engaging frankness:

*"It is entirely true that during the first years of the war, Great Britain and France had envisaged the cession of the vilayets of Basra and Bagdad to Great Britain. It is important, however, to recall that this proposition was meditated between the two Allied Powers at a time when they expected that a third Allied Power, Russia, would be their neighbor on the north. From the most profound knowledge of the local condition (it is) clearly shown how impracticable this arrangement was, and it has consequently been abandoned . . . . In any case, there has never been any question of the surrender of the vilayet of Mosul to Turkey."*[6]

Under these conditions there could be no settlement of the problem. As a result the question came before the council of the League of Nations on September 30, 1924, at which time both Turkey and Great Britain were represented on a "footing of equality."[7] The British maintained not only the demand for Mosul, but requested the vilayet of Hakkiari as well.[8] The Turkish delegation held to the same position taken up at Lausanne. Neither Power would concede to the other. Whether either of the Powers would accept a ruling of the council in the matter was problematical. Lord Parmoor (of the Labor government) accepted the rôle of the council when M. Branting, the *rapporteur* put the question on September 25, 1924. Fethy Bey refused to accept a final arbitration of the League, but did accept the position of the council under article XV of the covenant.[9] Trouble on the Iraq-Turkish frontier continued, and on October 29 the council determined the so-called Brussels line as marking the *status quo* frontier pending the settlement of the dispute. The provisional line ran north of Mosul but did not include Hakkiari. Both parties engaged to respect it.[10] On October 31, 1924, the council appointed a commission to go to

Mosul to investigate conditions and to report.[11] The commission proceeded to the vilayet, made a thorough study of the problem and reported its findings to the council on September 3, 1925. The report favored uniting Mosul with Iraq under the condition that it remain under the mandate of Great Britain for twenty-five years and with the proviso that the rights of the Kurds be guaranteed.[12]

Both parties complained of frontier incidents and both pledged to observe the *status quo*.[13] The British government was prepared to assume the mandate over Iraq (including Mosul) for a period of twenty-five years.[14] Tewfik Rushdi Bey, the Turkish representative before the council, announced that his country could not accept the report, did not recognize the Iraq mandate, and wanted Mosul.[15] In view of Lord Curzon's promise at Lausanne that Turkey would take part in all of the voting with the members of the council, Turkey now refused to abide by the decision of the council, since, of course, as a participant in the dispute, it actually had no vote.[16] This situation brought the question of the council's rôle before the permanent court of international justice on October 22, 1925. The Turks were not represented when the British jurists presented their case though certain memoranda and documents were given to the court.[17] On November 21, 1925, the court handed down an opinion holding that the council had full powers to decide the question, but that the parties to the dispute could not vote in the decision.[18] The British government acknowledged the decision, while the Turks rejected it, on December 8, 1925.[19] The council adopted the advisory opinion of the court and the Turks refused even to attend any further meetings of that body.[20]

On December 16, 1925, the council awarded Mosul to Great Britain, laying down the Brussels line as the northern frontier of Iraq. Great Britain accepted the responsibility for the mandate over a period of twenty-five years.[21] The League had finished its task and Great Britain had won Mosul from Turkey. The British parliament accepted the decision on December 21, 1925.[22]

The day following the decision of the League, on December 17, 1925, Turkey and Russia signed a treaty mutually pledging to abstain from any aggression against each other and each bound itself not to "take part in any alliance or agreement of a political character with one or more outside powers directed against the other contracting party, as well as in any alliance or agreement with one or more outside powers directed against the military or naval security of the other contracting party."[23]

The decision of the League of Nations had thrown Turkey again into the waiting arms of Soviet Russia. Opinion in Turkey was aroused against the decision awarding Mosul to Britain. On December 18 Mustapha Kemal called an extraordinary cabinet and the government announced its preparedness to meet every situation "with reference to the Mosul territory."[24] But a military council wisely decided against war on December 25, 1925. War was not only a serious business, but might involve the introduction of Russian troops into Turkey—and they might be reluctant to withdraw. Nevertheless the Turks concluded that Great Britain was their determined enemy.[25]

Great Britain, as we have seen already, concluded a new treaty with Iraq on January 13, 1926, embodying the new obligations with reference to the vilayet of Mosul.[26] But before the British could settle with Turkey, France and the Angora government had settled their difficulties on May 30, 1926, by a treaty in which the two states promised to maintain friendly and neighborly relations.[27] Not until June 5, 1926, did Great Britain and Turkey reach a fundamental settlement. The treaty of that date recognized the mandate of Iraq and accepted the Mosul decision of the council with but slight change. Iraq was to pay Turkey a ten per cent royalty on oil rights in Mosul or to settle at the option of Turkey by payment of a sum of £500,000.[28] On June 17, 1926, it was announced that the Angora government had accepted such payment in lieu of the royalties.[29]

We must now turn our attention again to the international oil situation centering about the Mosul·vilayet since the Lausanne conference. As previously indicated, the Angora government ratified the Chester concession on April 10, 1922, doubtless in order to secure American diplomatic support. The concession of the Ottoman-American Development Company was one of the most stupendous projects ever planned in Turkey. This project involved the construction of three railroad systems totalling in all some 4,385 kilometers or about 2,800 miles. Preference was to be given to the road extending from Alexandretta bay to Kharput and Arghana, thence to Bitlis, through the vilayet of Mosul, to Kirkuk and Suleimania. One branch of this section led from Kharput to Sivas, while another was to lead from Kharput to Van. A second great section of the system was to be constructed from Angora to Sivas, from Sivas to Samsun, and from Chalty to the Black sea, while a parallel branch was to run from Trebizond to Erzerum. The third division was to connect Angora with Samsun *via* Yazgod

and the Angora-Sivas lines, with the terminal at Ulu Kishla, of the Bagdad railway *via* Caesarea. A section was to extend from Erzerum to Bayezid on the Persian frontier.

But more than railroads was involved. The Chester group obtained wide-reaching mineral rights in the territory traversed by the railways to a depth of twenty kilometers on each side of the road, including copper, gold, platinum, lead, zinc, iron, nickel and other minerals. Large concessions for oil exploitation involved the fields of Van, Erzerum and Bitlis, as well as those of Mosul.[30] Rather suddenly the Chester group disappeared from the scene at Lausanne, the Standard Oil Company took its place, and the United States and Great Britain prepared to settle their oil problems.[31]

More than a year prior to the final settlement with Turkey the Turkish Petroleum Company had obtained the concession for the oil rights in Mosul, and in Bagdad in March 1925. The British concern was given exclusive oil rights in the areas of Bagdad and Mosul for a period of seventy-five years, at the end of which term the property was to revert to the government of Iraq.[32] But by this time the Turkish Petroleum Company was not a purely British affair. The American group of companies, headed by the Standard Oil Company of New Jersey, now had a twenty-five per cent interest in the exploitation of Mosul oil. The long oil struggle in Mesopotamia was at an end and American nationals had won their rights under the principle of the "open door."[33]

The second great problem in relation to Turkey following the Lausanne conference was that of the Straits. The treaty of Lausanne had internationalized the Straits, placed those waters under an international commission, and had demilitarized the shores without giving a corresponding guarantee of the Powers—the result of which was not only a threat to Turkey, but a constant and serious menace to the security of Russia on the Black sea. As early as December 2, 1922, while the Lausanne conference was yet in its early stages, M. Litvinov, chairman of the Russian delegation at the Moscow arms conference, had declared that the Soviet government "*considers it its duty to watch over the protection of the shores of Russia with its own forces until it is able to conclude corresponding agreements with sea-powers whose military vessels could easily enter the seas washing the shores of Russia, an agreement which should guarantee Russia real safety and the inviolability of its unarmed shores, accessible to direct attack even from the more distant of the mighty sea powers . . . .*"[34] The Lausanne conference did not present Russia with an agreement which would guarantee either her

real safety or the inviolability of her unarmed shores, and though signed by the representative of the Soviet Union, the provisions dealing with the Straits were considered a menace to the security of the Black sea. Consequently when M. Chicherin was invited to send a delegation to the Rome naval conference which was called by the League of Nations in February 1924 to apply the principles of the Washington conference to non-signatories, the commissar for foreign affairs lent a willing ear. Chicherin's note of acceptance of the invitation, dated March 15, 1923, stated:

*"At the Lausanne conference it [the Soviet Union] defended the principle of closing the Straits for warships, the result of which would have been a diminution of the chances of armed conflicts at sea and the reduction of naval conflicts."*[35]

The Rome conference, like that at Lausanne, proved a disappointment in the way either of political guarantees or of naval reduction. Russia's 1921 naval tonnage was 490,000, recognition of which was now demanded as necessary for the security of her shores. Without the guarantee of the Washington treaties dealing with the Pacific, in abnormal relations with most states, these demands of the Soviet Union cannot be regarded as very excessive, if one fairly considers the naval requirements of such a Great Power. Yet the demand of the Russian delegation surprised the other Powers at Rome. In a note of February 21, 1924, the Russian naval delegation introduces the very sound principle that the safety of a state lies either in armaments or in conventions of disarmament and guarantee such as those provided at Washington in 1922, and states that "the Union will be satisfied with a total tonnage of 280,000 tons, but only provided that the following conditions are accepted:

"1. *That the council of the League of Nations is replaced in the draft (drawn up by members of the League) by another organization.*

"2. That the Bosphorus and the Dardanelles (Straits) are closed, in accordance with the proposal which we made at the Lausanne conference.

"3. *That vessels belonging to non-riparian states of the Baltic are forbidden access to the Baltic by the Sound and Belt.*

"4. *That the Straits of Korea are demilitarized (disarmed).*

"5. *That the vessels of war at present retained at Bizerta are restored to the Union.*"[36]

The Powers, of course, refused these conditions, with the consequence that Russia continued to build in the Black sea and elsewhere, possessing since 1924 the strongest fleet in that region—123,618 tons.

What could not be achieved at Rome in international agreement with the naval Powers, had to be attained through a bilateral treaty with Turkey. The failure of both Russia and Turkey to achieve their security at Lausanne led to the continuance of close relations between the two countries. This culminated in the treaty of Paris, December 17, 1925, when Turkey, one day after the decision awarding Mosul to Great Britain, fell into the arms of the Soviet Union. This convention enhanced the security of both Turkey and Russia, but only in the sense that both were faced with a common danger, and sought this means of protection as a way out. Russia was seeking compensation not only for Locarno, but for the menace in the region of the Straits, and against the British position in Mosul—and for this latter danger Turkey sought the pledge of Russia.[37]

Soviet or tsarist, communist or otherwise, Russia still faced the eternal problem of an outlet to the free sea. In a discourse delivered at Kamenev-Podolsk in 1924, Leon Trotsky is purported to have remarked:

"We must cry aloud that we need Constantinople and the Straits. A country such as ours cannot suffocate for the caprice or the interests of anyone. That is why Bessarabia is indispensable to us. It constitutes the first step on the road of Constantinople. Be persuaded of it, the Straits will belong to us sooner or later, even if England and France, forgetting the promises made during the war, wish to prevent us from obtaining them."[38]

As a part of the general problem of the Straits, the question of Bessarabia continued to disturb Russo-Rumanian relations, and was not solved even by the early ratification of the Paris anti-war pact (the so-called Kellog pact) which certain of the eastern European states put into operation on April 15, 1929. Russia and Rumania merely agreed to settle the affair in a peaceful manner. Turkey adhered to this convention on April 3, 1929.[39]

The Turks had their own peculiar problems with reference to the Straits aside from the matter of armament or their relations with the Soviet Union. The question of sanitary regulations within the zones of the Straits proved to be of political importance when the Turkish government raised the issue in November 1924 over the passage of

two British destroyers through the Straits in transit without signalling their sanitary condition. The government at Angora, on March 3, 1925, was informed by the commission of the Straits that under the terms of the Lausanne agreement "no obligation of this order was imposed on ships of war." In spite of this, the sanitary authorities still tried to intervene in the passage of war vessels. Ships coming from the Aegean were to be held at Chanak while those coming from the Black sea were to be held at Kavak for sanitary formalities. Such regulations applied to war and commercial vessels alike. The commission felt that a medical visit at these points was useless. The Turkish government, nevertheless, persisted in its attitude. When the international sanitary convention, signed at Paris, June 21, 1926, declared against any sanitary visit on ships *in transit* across territorial waters, the Turks made the following reservation:

*"The Turkish government reserves the right for the sanitary adminis-tration to place sanitary guard on board every ship of commerce passing the Straits without a doctor and coming from an infected port, in order to prevent the ship touching a Turkish port. It is understood, nevertheless, that the delays and expenses which might be involved in this regard will be a minimum."*

The commission still felt in 1927 that this regulation should be suppressed, but the government at Angora was determined to uphold its rights.[4ʲ]

Despite the security which Russia gained through the treaty of December 17, 1925, when Russia and Turkey were confronted with a common danger, after Lausanne, the face of Turkey was turned toward the west and away from Russia. This had been one of Lord Curzon's expressed and primary aims at the conference in 1922-1923. The period of Russia's ascendency in the Near and Middle East drew to a close after 1925, when not only Turkey, but Persia and Afghanistan pursued independent policies, without either Russian influence or dictation.[41]

On May 30 1928, Turkey and Italy signed a treaty of friendship, conciliation and neutrality, the first political pact which the Turks signed with a western European Great Power after the war. This treaty was an offset against that with Russia in December 1925. By this pact, the two Powers undertook not to enter into any combina-tions directed against the other and to remain neutral in case one of them became involved in a conflict. From the Italian viewpoint the treaty aided in consolidating the influence of Italy in the eastern Mediterranean, which had constantly increased since 1900. Nor was

343

this treaty without its economic background, for by 1927 Italian commerce in the Straits had gone beyond some 2,600,000 tons, out-stripping the British by more than 500,000 tons.[42] Mussolini followed his Turkish pact with a Greco-Italian pact of similar portent on September 23, 1928, but was unable to establish such an accord between Turkey and Greece, until on June 10, 1930, these two Powers, after so many years of struggle, finally signed a pact of friendship.[43]

That Turkey was turning away still more from her Russian moorings became more evident when on October 12, 1929, a strong British naval squadron headed by the *Queen Elizabeth* sailed through the Dardanelles and paid an official visit to Constantinople—the first friendly visit of British naval forces since pre-war days. The British Admiral Field and the British ambassador went to Angora on October 14, where they had a long interview with the Ghazi. It was felt that the visit emphasized a change in Anglo-Turkish relations similar to that in 1840 and 1881. Moreover the opposition of Turkey toward the introduction of Russian communism had brought on a distinct coolness in Russo-Turkish relations. On March 1, 1930, a treaty of commerce and navigation between Turkey and Great Britain was signed on the basis of the most-favored nation for a five-year term.[44]

Meanwhile renewed advances on the part of the U. S. S. R. toward Turkey took place on December 17, 1929—exactly four years after the treaty of 1925—when M. Karakhan, assistant commissar for foreign affairs, visited Angora (Ankara) and signed a pact amplifying the treaty of 1925. As if to offset such action, the Turkish government was reported ready to join the League of Nations, if given a semi-permanent seat on the council—a modification of an earlier demand for a permanent seat which the Turks had made in view of their position in the Moslem world. This representation could no longer be demanded on account of the secularization of the Turkish state. However the new request seemed to be having serious consideration in view of the possibilities of drawing Turkey completely out of the Russian orbit.[45]

2.

## Turkey Turns Westward

From the end of the world war to 1923, the Allies—Great Britain and France—set up a system of mandates in the territories formerly belonging to the Ottoman Empire, in Syria, Palestine and Mesopotamia.

This process of partition, begun in 1915, was developed during the Paris peace conference of 1919, was sanctioned by the conference of Lausanne and approved by the League of Nations in 1923. The final step in the partition of Turkey was taken when the council of the League of Nations awarded the vilayet of Mosul to the British mandate of Iraq in December 1925, which became an integral part of the British treaties with Iraq and Turkey in 1926.

For the League of Nations the system of mandates theoretically provided a trusteeship pending the development of retarded peoples until they should be able to take their proper places in the society of nations. In the former parts of Asiatic Turkey some of these peoples had reached already a reasonably high stage of development. Under a mandate, France was enabled to establish her control over Syria, despite evident unpopulatiry and a very serious rebellion among the Jebel Druse in 1925. Under the same mandate system Great Britain was able to build up a great bulwark of territories consolidating her strategic position along the route to India in both Iraq and Palestine. With Mosul ceded to Iraq, Great Britain not only obtained control over vast resources of oil, but gained an important strategic territory which would enable her to attack either Turkey or Russia, or protect Iraq from the advances of both Powers. By British control over the kingdom of the Hejaz and the Nejd and over other parts of southern Arabia, Great Britain continued to guard the approaches to India through the Red sea and the Persian gulf. Egypt added protection from the African side to this block of states on the other side of the Suez canal and the Red sea. In other words, the system of buffer states which England had built up extended from Egypt, across Palestine and Iraq to Afghanistan. Finally, through the internationalization of the entire region of the Straits, the British achieved their own solution of that world problem by placing both the Straits and the Black sea at the mercy of British seapower. For a long time Great Britain had upheld the Ottoman Empire as the best bulwark against any Power which might threaten India, the crown jewel of the British Empire. When a third Power, Germany, threatened to come into control over Turkey, the British abandoned the policy of the integrity of Turkey, took up that of the dismemberment of the old empire and after the war achieved the protection of India through the establishment of mandates among the Arabs. Italy received no mandate for any territory in Asia Minor as

she had desired, but did retain the islands of the Dodecanese in the Aegean sea, despite the pronounced disapproval of both the United States and Great Britain.[46]

Before the year 1913 the Turkish Empire was as large as European Russia and contained a population almost as great as that of the French republic. After the world war the Allies tore away from that empire a total territory in Asia alone of almost 600,000 square miles, with a population which may be estimated at 14,000,000. Of this territory detached from Turkey, Great Britain, either by mandate (Palestine and Iraq), protectorate, or sphere of influence, had a nominal control over all but 60,000 square miles (the French mandate of Syria), with an estimated population of 11,000,000.[47]

After the world war the new Turkish republic was a small compact and intensely nationalistic state composed of almost 14,000,000 people living in an area of some 282,627 square miles. European Turkey was limited to about 8,819 square miles and possessed a population of about 1,044,306 people, most of whom lived in the region of Constantinople. Asiatic Turkey contained a population of 12,615,969 living in an area of about 275,808 square miles centering in the Anatolian plateau. A total of more than 1,600,000 people lived in the region of the Straits.[48]

It was this small, nationalistic Turkish republic which had surprised the entire world by its ability to recuperate, reorganize and consolidate after more than a decade of conflict ending with the world war and the Greco-Turkish struggle of 1919-1922. The new Turkish republic had defeated the Greeks and brought about a veritable diplomatic revolution in the Near East, had won its political, financial and economic independence at Lausanne, and had set out upon the path of modernization. An ancient polyglot empire had failed to solve its problem and had given way of necessity to a new national republic.

The years following the conference of Lausanne had witnessed diplomatic changes and developments of the first magnitude and importance. Russia and Turkey signed the treaty of December 1925 because both were threatened by Great Britain—Russia in the region of the Straits; Turkey in the cession of Mosul to the British mandate of Iraq. While Russia, despite the treaty of 1925, continued to view her Black sea shores as menaced through the internationalization of the Straits, Turkey offset the 1925 treaty in 1928 by the first political agreement with a western European Power—Italy. Between 1928 and 1930 Great Britain not only appeared to be regaining her position of

influence and trust in the Middle East, lost to Russia during the post-war period, but had renewed contacts with Turkey in the treaty of March 1930.[49] Turkey appeared to be definitely turning away from communist Russia toward western Europe. Finally, the new Turkey seemed to be well on the way toward settling her difficult internal problems, was developing along peaceful lines toward becoming a distinctly stabilizing influence in the Near East, and gave fair prospect of continuing in the path of progress.

3.

## General Conclusion

The treaty of Lausanne was the final step in the long process of the dissolution of the Ottoman Empire, which had begun at Karlowitz in 1699. From 1699 to the twentieth century the Turkish Empire steadily declined, being preserved only through the rivalries of the European states and the principle of the balance of power. The final stages of the partition of Turkey began with the Austrian annexation of Bosnia and Herzegovina in 1908, and continued through the Italo-Turkish war (1911-1912) and the Balkan wars (1912-1913). The conference of Lausanne (1922-1923), following the world war, completed the dissolution of the empire.

After the Balkan wars, it was apparent that the European Powers were discounting in advance their shares of the Ottoman Empire. It was apparent also that the empire could not long endure without serious internal reforms. The German government took advantage of the situation by sending the military mission of Liman von Sanders to Constantinople, which was to reorganize the army and prepare it for future eventualities. With the Bagdad railway, the mission enabled Germany either to preserve the Turkish Empire under German domination, or to obtain a large share of it, if it went to pieces. Agreements were initiated with both Austria-Hungary and Italy in 1913, while France and England concluded agreements with Germany in 1914, leading to a possible political partition of Turkey.

Threatened in the vital region of the Straits, Russia protested against the German mission, and called the two secret conferences of January and February 1914, which decided against war, in view of the unpreparedness of Russia. St. Petersburg might have solved the problem of her relations with the Ottoman Porte by a direct *entente* in 1914, had

347

not German influence at Constantinople entered a checkmate. German action in Turkey led to the Turco-German alliance of August 2, 1914, and brought that country into the war in November, 1914.

Allied attempts to bring Italy and the Balkan states into the war caused considerable difficulties, most of which centered about various phases of the Turkish question. Russia tried to bring Turkey into the war as an ally in 1914, only to be blocked by England and France. Russia refused Greek participation at the Dardanelles, as a British puppet, with Constantinople as the objective. Russia objected to large Anglo-French offers to Italy on the Adriatic (at Serbian expense), and in Asia Minor. Serbia and Greece rejected concessions to Bulgaria in Macedonia, unless guaranteed territory elsewhere. Rumania refused to cede the Dobruja unless Bulgaria were certain to enter the war on the side of the Entente. Having failed to make Greece the pivot of a new Balkan alliance, England then attempted to win supremacy over Russia in Bulgaria. The Balkan alliance was not re-formed, and Allied policy in the pensinsula proved a fiasco.

The Dardanelles campaign, under British leadership, forced Russia to make an outright demand for Constantinople and the Straits on March 4, 1915. France and England reluctantly conceded to the wishes of the Muscovite. This raised the issue of Asiatic Turkey, which was partitioned by a series of secret agreements among England, France, Russia and Italy in 1915-1917. France obtained Syria, Russia Armenia and England Mesopotamia. Palestine was internationalized, while an independent Arab confederation was to be created in the British and French zones of influence. Italy was to retain the Dodecanese, and was promised the Adalia-Smyrna region. Simultaneous British promises to the Arabs conflicted with the secret agreements and caused considerable difficulties at the Paris conference.

While the Powers represented at Paris were agreed that the Ottoman Empire should be partitioned, so conflicting were their aims, that a settlement was impossible. Mr. Wilson favored the mandate principle, and under this system the empire was divided up. England, having obtained her *desiderata* among the Arabs, supported the Greeks (1919-1922), in order to obtain control of the Straits. This policy reached its apogée in the abortive treaty of Sèvres, of August 1920.

In 1921 the hard-pressed Turks renewed friendships with France and Italy, settled accounts with their neighbors, and made an arrangement with Soviet Russia. Neither France nor Italy cared to see Great Britain dominant at Constantinople, and Soviet Russia saw in the

British position a constant menace to her southern shores. Under the guiding genius of Mustapha Kemal Pasha the Turks inflicted a disastrous defeat on the Greeks in 1922, and threatened the British position in the region of the Dardanelles.

The conference of Lausanne (November 1922-July 1923) was called to make peace between Turkey and Greece, to draw the Turks from the Russian moorings, and to make a new régime for the Straits. At Lausanne, the Turks won their economic, financial, judicial and political independence but gave way to an international régime at the Straits, which were demilitarized, but not guaranteed against attack. Such a solution, placing the Straits at the mercy of the greatest sea Power, and endangering both Turkey and Soviet Russia, may not prove to be definitive. France has been placed in Syria, and Great Britain in Iraq and Palestine, with control over the Arabian peninsula and Egypt. Italy has remained in the Dodecanese. Greece, checked in her Asiatic dreams, is consolidating her position at home. All this may prove beneficial to Turkey as a national state, freed from the corrupting influences of an antiquated empire. Out of her defeat in the world war —from her amazing revival after more than ten years of constant struggle—came the new Turkey.

# APPENDIX

## DRAMATIS PERSONAE (OF PRINCIPAL NAMES)

Aehrenthal, Baron A. von, Austrian ambassador in St. Petersburg, 1899-1906; foreign minister, 1906-1912.

Asquith, H. H., (Earl of Oxford and Asquith), prime minister, 1906-1916.

Avarna, Duke of, Italian ambassador in Vienna, 1904-15.

Balfour, A. J. (Earl of), prime minister, 1902-05; in coalition government; 1916-19; lord president of the council, 1919-28.

Basili, N. A., Russian diplomat; vice director of the chancellery of the ministry of foreign affairs, 1912-1916; director of the diplomatic chancellery of general head-quarters, 1916-17.

Benckendorff, Count A. K., Russian diplomat; ambassador in London, 1903-1917.

Berchtold, Count L. von, Austrian ambassador in St. Petersburg, 1906-11; foreign minister, 1912-15.

Bertie, Sir Francis (Lord), British ambassador in Paris, 1905-18.

Bethmann-Hollweg, T. von, German minister for home affairs, 1905-7; chancellor, 1909-17.

Bompard, M., French ambassador in Constantinople, 1909-14.

Bratianu, J., Rumanian statesman; premier, 1914-1917.

Buchanan, Sir George (Lord), British ambassador in St. Petersburg, 1910-1918.

Buxton, Noel, Chairman of the Balkan committee; minister for agriculture, 1929.

Cambon, Paul, French ambassador in Madrid, 1886-91; in Constantinople, 1891-98; in London, 1898-1920.

Carlotti, (Marquis), Italian diplomat; ambassador in St. Petersburg, 1913-1918.

Chamberlain, Sir Austen, English statesman; foreign minister, 1924-29.

Chicherin, George, Soviet commissar for foreign relations.

Churchill, Winston Spencer, first lord of the admiralty, 1911-15; minister of munitions, 1917-18; minister of war, 1918-21; chancellor of the exchequer, 1924-29.

Clemenceau, G., French prime minister, 1906-09; 1917-20.

Curzon, G. N. (Marquess), Viceroy of India, 1899-1905; foreign secretary, 1919-23.

Czernin, Count Ottokar, Austrian diplomat, minister in Rumania, 1913-1916; minister of foreign affairs, 1916.

Delcassé, T. French foreign minister, 1898-1905; ambassador in Russia; minister of foreign affairs, 1914-1915.

Demidov, E. P., Russian minister in Athens, 1912-17.

Djavid Bey, Turkish statesman, Young Turk, finance minister in 1914.

Djemal Pasha, Turkish statesman, Young Turk, minister of marine in 1914.

Elliot, Sir Francis, minister at Athens, 1903-17.

Enver Pasha, Turkish military attaché in Berlin, 1909, 1912-13; minister of war, 1914.

Ferdinand, King of Bulgaria, 1887-1918.

Fisher, Admiral Sir John (Lord), first sea lord, 1904-1910.

Forgách von Ghymes and Gács, Count, Austrian minister at Belgrade, 1907-11.

Ghenadiev, Bulgarian statesman; minister of foreign affairs, 1913.

Geshov, I. E., Bulgarian statesman; premier, 1911-1913.

Giolitti, G., Italian premier, 1903-5, 1906-9, 1911-14.

Goltz, von der (Pasha), German general, Turkish field marshal.

Grey, Sir Edward (Viscount), foreign secretary, 1905-1916.

Gounaris, Greek statesman; premier, 1915.

Halil Bey, Turkish statesman; president of Deputies, 1914.

Helfferich, K., Director of the Anatolian Railway Company, 1906-8; of the Deutsche Bank, 1908-14.

Hötzendorf, Conrad von (Baron), general, chief of Austrian general staff, 1907-11.

Ironside, Sir H. Bax., British minister in Sofia, 1914-15.

Ismet Pasha, Turkish soldier and diplomat; premier of Turkey since 1925.

Isvolsky, A. P., Russian statesman; minister of foreign affairs, 1906-10; ambassador in Paris, 1910-1917.

Krupensky, Russian diplomat; ambassador in Rome, 1914-1916.

Kudashev, Prince N., director of the diplomatic chancellery of general headquarters, 1914-1916.

Leontiev, Russian general; Russian military agent in Constantinople, 1913-14.

Lichnowsky, Prince von, German ambassador in London, 1912-14.

Liman von Sanders, German general; December 1913, chief of the German military mission in Constantinople; January 1914, General inspector of the Turkish army.

Limpus, Admiral, English admiral in the Turkish fleet, 1912-14.

Lloyd George, David, chancellor of the Exchequer, 1908-16; prime minister, 1916-22.

Mahmud Mukhtar Pasha, Turkish soldier and diplomat; ambassador in Berlin, 1913-14.

Mallet, Sir Louis, British ambassador in Turkey, 1913-14.

Marschall von Bieberstein, Baron A., ambassador of Germany in Constantinople, 1897-1912; ambassador in England, 1912.

Miliukov, Professor Paul, Russian foreign minister, 1917.

Mustapha Kemal Pasha (Ghazi), Turkish soldier and statesman; president of Turkey, 1923, 1927.

Neratov, A. A., Russian diplomat; vice-director of department in ministry of foreign affairs, 1906-1910; assistant to minister of foreign affairs, 1911-1917.

Paléologue, M., French diplomat; ambassador in Petrograd, 1914-1917.

Pallavicini, Marquis, Austrian ambassador in Constantinople, 1906-18.

Pashich, N., Serbian statesman; premier, 1913 ff.

Pichon, M., French foreign minister, 1906-11, 1913, 1917-20.

Poklevsky-Koziell, Russian minister in Rumania, 1913-1917.

Radoslavov, V., Bulgarian premier, 1913-17.

Said Halim, Prince, grand vizier of Turkey, 1914.

Savinsky, A. A., Russian minister in Bulgaria, 1913-1915.

Sazonov, S. D., Russian statesman; chargé in London, 1904-6; diplomatic agent to the Vatican, 1906-1910; minister of foreign affairs, 1910-1916.

Talaat Bey, Turkish minister of the interior, 1909-13; minister of interior and of finances, 1913-1917.

Tarnowsky, Count, Austrian minister in Bulgaria, 1914-15.

Tirpitz, Admiral A. von, secretary to the German admiralty, 1897-1916.

Tisza, Count Stephen, Hungarian minister president.

Tschirschky, H. von, German ambassador in Vienna, 1907-16.

Trubetskoi, Prince G., Russian minister to Serbia, 1914-17; director of the diplomatic chancellery of general headquarters, 1917.

Venizelos, E., Greek statesman; premier of the Cretan government, 1909; premier of Greece, 1910-1915; chief of the government of Salonica, 1916; premier of Greece.

Wangenheim, Hans, Baron von, German diplomat; at Constantinople, 1899-1904; minister at Athens, 1909-12; ambassador in Constantinople, 1912-15.

2.

# SIGNIFICANT DATES IN THE PARTITION OF TURKEY

*Origins and development*

1058. Seljuk Turks (Togrul Bey, Alp Arslan, Malek Shah) attain dignity of *Emir al Omra*.

1092. Seljuk empire separated into small sultanates—Iran, Kerman, Aleppo, Damascus, Iconium (Roum).

1326. The Turks capture Brusa.

1354. The Turks take Gallipoli and enter Europe.

1389. The battle of Kossovo, Serbia crushed.

1402. Bayezid I defeated by Timur the Lame at Angora.

1453. May 29. The capture of Constantinople by Mohammed II.

1517. Conquest of Egypt under Selim I.

1520-1566. The reign of Suleiman the Magnificent.

1526. The victory of Mohacs, Hungary crushed.

1529. The first siege of Vienna.

1535. February. France acquires privileged position in Ottoman Empire by capitulations agreement and alliance; consular jurisdiction and protection of Catholic Christians.

1571. Selim II makes war on Venice; capture of Cyprus.

1571. Don Juan of Austria defeats Turks at Lepanto.

1669. Conquest of Crete by Ahmed Kiuprili.

1675. Capitulations and peace, between Great Britain and Turkey.

1676. War on Poland and acquisition of Podolia.

1683. Second siege of Vienna, July-September. Kara Mustapha.

1696. Capture of Azov by Peter the Great.

1699. January 26. *The peace of Karlowitz.* 1. Turkey received the Banat of Temesvar; Austria obtained rest of Hungary and Transylvania. 2. Venice received Morea. 3. Russia acquires Azov.

### The Decline of the Ottoman Empire

1711. July 21. The treaty of the Pruth; Turks force Russia to surrender Azov.

1718. July 21. *The peace of Passarowitz.* 1. Austria received the Banat of Temesvar, part of Serbia, with Belgrade and Little Wallachia. 2. Venice retains Dalmatia; surrenders Morea.

1739. September 18. *The peace of Belgrade.* Austria forced to restore Orsova, Belgrade, Serbia and Little Wallachia to Turkey.

1774. July 10. *The treaty of Kuchuk-Kainardji*, ending Russo-Turkish war of 1768-74. 1. Russia received Kinburn, Yenikale and Kertch in the Crimea. 2. Russia received right of free navigation in Turkish waters for commercial vessels. 3. Tartars in Crimea and on Kuban become "independent." 4. Moldavia and Wallachia placed under Russian "protection." 5. Russia obtained embassy in Constantinople, and certain privileges over Christians in Turkey.

1775. Austria obtains Bukovina from Turkey.

1784. July 24. Austria receives free navigation of commercial vessels in Turkish waters.

1792. January 9. *The peace of Jassy.* Russia received Otchakov, and land between lower Dnieper, Bug and Dniester.

1798. December 23. Russo-Turkish treaty of alliance.

1799. October 30. England received free navigation rights for commercial vessels in Turkish waters. Reaffirmed, 1802.

1802. June 25. France received free navigation rights for commercial vessels in Turkish waters.

1804. Serbian revolt against Turkey, under Karageorge.

1806. July 17. Prussia received free navigation rights for commercial vessels in Turkish waters.

1807. July 7. Treaty of Tilsit. Failure of Alexander I and Napoleon to agree on a partition of Ottoman Empire.

1809. January 5. Alliance between Turkey and England. First formal assertion of principle of closure of Straits in international treaty.

1812. May 28. *The peace of Bucharest.* Pruth river became boundary between Turkey and Russia; Russia retains Bessarabia.

1821-29. The war of Grecian independence.

1826.   October 7. Convention of commerce between Russia and Turkey, signed at Ackermann.

1829.   September 14. *The treaty of Adrianople.* 1. Serbian autonomy recognized, under Russian protection. 2. Russian protectorate over Danubian principalities extended. 3. Greek independence recognized in advance. (Announced by London conference in 1830). 4. Russia secures final control over east coast of Black sea and Caucasus range. 5. Russian trading and commercial rights extended.

1830.   May 7. Treaty of commerce and navigation between United States and Turkey.

1833.   July 8. *Treaty of Unkiar-Eskelessi.* Russia guarantees the territorial integrity of Turkey (Mehemet Ali), and receives rights of passage of Straits for Russian warships. Closure to all other warships.

1840.   July 15. *Treaty of London,* between England, Austria, Prussia and Russia. Alliance to protect Porte against Mehemet Ali. International guarantee of principle of closure of Straits to warships.

1841.   July 13. Convention between Great Britain, Austria, France, Prussia, Russia, and Turkey, respecting the Straits of the Dardanelles. Closure recognized by France.

1844, 1853.   Russian proposal (Nicholas I) with reference to partition of Ottoman Empire, if it crumbled. 1. Serbia, Bosnia, Bulgaria and principalities of Danube to become independent under *Russian* protection. 2. Constantinople to be occupied provisionally and temporarily by Russian troops. 3. England to acquire Crete and Egypt.

1853-54-56.   The Crimean war.

1856.   March 30. *Treaty of Paris.* 1. Russia ceded mouths of Danube and small part of Bessarabia on left bank of lower Danube. 2. Russia renounced protectorate over Christians in Turkey. 3. Russia restored Kars, and was not to establish arsenals or forts on Black sea, nor to maintain warships in Black sea. 4. Restoration of Sebastopol to Russia. 5. Reaffirmation of closure of Straits to warships.

1870.   October 31, November 1. Russia denounces the part of the treaty of 1856, relative to the limitation of naval forces in the Black sea.

1871.   March 13. *The treaty of London* abrogates the restrictive clauses of the treaty of 1856, limiting Russia's forces on the Black sea.

1878.   March 3. *The peace of San Stefano* between Russia and Turkey, ending the war of 1877-78. 1. Montenegro and Serbia gain in territory and are recognized as independent; also Rumania. 2. Bulgaria remains tributary to Porte, but receives Christian prince, under Russian influence. 4. Turkey paid Russia 300,000,000 rubles, and ceded parts of Armenia and the Dobruja to Russia. Russia to give Dobruja to Rumania in return for part of Bessarabia, ceded to Rumania in 1856.

June 4. Turkey concluded treaty with England, wherein England received Cyprus and was to protect Turkey in Asia against Russia.

July 13. *Treaty of Berlin.* 1. Montenegro, Serbia, Rumania became independent. 2. Principality of Bulgaria limited to land between Danube and Balkans, in-

357

cluding Sofia. E. Rumelia (southern Bulgaria) placed under Christian governor, but under Porte. 3. Russian troops to evacuate E. Rumalia and Bulgaria inside nine months, Rumania within year. 5. Turkey ceded to Austria military occupation of sanjak of Novibazar and military occupation and administration of Bosnia and Herzegovina. 6. Porte advised to cede part of Epirus and Thessaly to Greece. 7. Russia received in Asia, Batum as free port, Kars, Ardahan, and border territories.

1879.  September 24. The Austro-German alliance.

1881.  June 18. The Three Emperors' League. *Status quo* in the Balkans; closure of the Straits.

December 20. Ottoman Public Debt Administration founded.

1883.  January 18. The khedive of Egypt abolishes dual (Anglo-French) control and British become masters of Egypt.

1885.  September 18. Revolution in E. Rumelia; union with Bulgaria.

1887.  February 20. Renewal of Triple Alliance; Italy arranged with Austria-Hungary for compensation if *status quo* gives way in Balkans or on Ottoman coasts.

June 18. Reinsurance treaty between Germany and Russia. Recognizes Russia's interests in Balkans; closure of Straits.

1896-97.  Cretan revolt and Greco-Turkish war. December 4, treaty of Constantinople.

1903.  March 5. The Bagdad railway concession is signed at Constantinople.

1907.  August 31. The Anglo-Russian convention.

1908.  July 3. Young Turk revolution begins in Macedonia.

July 24. Sultan of Turkey proclaims restoration of constitution of 1876.

October 5. Prince Ferdinand of Bulgaria proclaims independence of Bulgaria.

October 7. Austria-Hungary asserts sovereignty over Bosnia and Herzegovina.

1911.  September 29. Italy declared war on Turkey. Turco-Italian war, 1911-1912.

1912.  March 13. Treaty of alliance between Bulgaria and Serbia, guaranteeing independence and integrity. Macedonia to be partitioned between them.

April 18. Dardanelles closed; reopened on May 18.

May 29. Treaty of alliance between Bulgaria and Greece.

October 8. The first Balkan war begins.

October 18. *Treaty of Lausanne* between Italy and Turkey. Italian acquisition of Tripolitania and Cyrenaica; "temporary" occupation of the Dodecanese islands.

1913.  May 30. *Treaty of London.* Turkey surrendered Crete and territory in Europe west of Enos-Midia line. Delimitation of Albanian boundaries and disposition of Aegean isles left to decision of Powers. Financial questions to be settled by international financial commission at Paris.

June 1. Alliance of Serbia and Greece against Bulgaria.

June 29-August 10. The second Balkan war.

August 10. *The treaty of Bucharest.* Serbia and Greece (and Bulgaria) divide Macedonia; Greece receives Crete; Rumania obtains Silistria-Balchik.

358

September 29. *Treaty between Turkey and Bulgaria.* Turkey retains Adrianople, Kirk Kilissé and Dimotika.

November 14. Treaty between Turkey and Greece settling differences growing out of Balkan war.

December 14. General Liman von Sanders, head of the German military mission, arrives in Constantinople.

1914. August 2. The Turco-German alliance is signed.

August 10. The *Goeben* and *Breslau* pass the Dardanelles.

September 27. Closure of the Straits of Dardanelles.

October 1. Abolition of capitulations.

October 29. Turco-German warships bombard Russian Black sea ports.

October 30. Russia declares state of war with Turkey.

November 4. Britain formally annexed Cyprus.

November 5. England and France announce state of war with Turkey.

November 16. Turks announce holy war (Jihad).

December 17. British announce protectorate over Egypt.

1915. February 19. Allies begin bombardments of forts of Dardanelles.

March 4. Russia demands that France and Great Britain recognize her right to Constantinople and Straits.

March 12. Great Britain assents to Russian proposal, but Russia is to recognize British and French interests. Britain to have neutral zone in Persia.

April 10. France assents to Russian proposal; receives recognition of rights in Syria.

April 26. Great Britain, France, Russia and Italy sign secret treaty of London. Italy to receive territory at Austrian expense; in Turkey, the Dodecanese islands, and territory in Adalia region.

August 21. Italy declares war on Turkey.

September 6. Bulgaria signs treaty with Germany and Austria to fight Serbia.

September 25. Bulgaro-Turkish treaty signed.

October 21. Britain offers island of Cyprus to Greece; rejected.

1916. April 26. England and France conclude secret agreement with Russia for partition of Asiatic Turkey. 1. England to obtain s. Mesopotamia, with Bagdad, and two ports on Syrian coast. 2. France to have Syria, Adana vilayet, and w. Kurdistan. 3. Russia to obtain Trebizond, Erzerum, Bitlis, Van and part of s. Kurdistan. 4. Arab state or confederation to be formed in French and British spheres of influence. 5. Palestine to be under international régime. May 9-16. The Sykes-Picot agreement signed. Affirming stipulations of above agreement, between France and England.

June 27. Hussein ibn Ali, sherif of Mecca, proclaims new state of Arabia.

August 18. Rumania signs treaty of alliance with Entente. To receive Banat, Transylvania to Tisza. and Bukovina to Pruth.

1917. January 1. Turkey renounces treaties of 1856 and 1878.

April 19-21. St. Jean de Maurienne agreement between Great Britain, France and Italy. Italy assents to Sykes-Picot accord, and receives concessions in Alexandretta, Haifa and Akka.

November 2. Balfour Palestine declaration.

November 8. Bolshevik Russia denounces secret treaties with reference to Asiatic Turkey and begins their publication (November 24).

1918. January 5. Lloyd George announces intention not to molest Turkish "homelands." Straits to be internationalized.

January 8. President Wilson announces "Fourteen Points."

March 3. Treaty of Brest-Litovsk between Bolshevik Russia and Central Powers.

April 13. Armenia and Georgia reject cession of land under Brest-Litovsk treaty; fighting breaks out in Batum, Kars, Ardahan, when Turks begin operations.

July 28. Kars, Batum and Ardahan (plebiscite) to unite with Turkey.

September 29. Bulgaria surrenders to Allies.

October 30. Turkey signs armistice of Mudros. Constantinople and all forts of Dardanelles and Bosphorus to be occupied by Allies; Turkish forces to be demobilized.

1919. April 29. Italian forces land at Adalia.

May 14. Greek forces land at Smyrna. Beginning of Greco-Turkish war, 1919-22.

June 29. Treaty between Allies and Germany.

July 11. Mustapha Kemal Pasha outlawed by Constantinople government.

July 23. Mustapha Kemal presides over the Erzerum nationalist congress.

July 29. Venizelos-Tittoni accord on Rhodes, Dodecanese, and Asiatic Turkey.

September 9. Mustapha Kemal presides over the Sivas congress. The Declaration of the Congress.

November 27. Treaty of Neuilly, between Allies and Bulgaria.

### The Formation of New Turkey

1920. January 28. The Constantinople parliament ratifies the Turkish national pact.

March 16. Allied (British) occupation of Constantinople; arrest and deportation of prominent Turkish nationalists.

April 18-27. Conference of San Remo. Great Britain to be mandatory for Mesopotamia and Palestine; France for Syria. Armenian mandate offered to U. S. Oil agreement.

April 23. Grand National Assembly of Turkey adopts national pact at Angora. Law of fundamental organization.

August 10. *Treaty of Sèvres with Turkey.* Hejaz independent (British control); Armenia independent; British mandate in Palestine, Mesopotamia, Transjordania; French mandate in Syria, sphere in Cilicia. Italian sphere in s. Ana-

tolia. Greece to receive Smyrna, Thrace, Adrianople, Gallipoli, Imbros, Tenedos and Dodecanese islands (except Rhodes and Castellorizzo). Straits" internationalized."

October 30. Turks in possession of Kars.

December 3. Turco-Armenian peace; Armenia reduced to Erivan and Lake Gokcha.

December 23. Anglo-French agreement on Mandates.

1921. March 1. Turco-Afghan treaty of Moscow providing for mutual defence.

March 9. Franco-Turkish agreement regarding evacuation of Cilicia. Not ratified.

March 12. Turco-Italian treaty for economic exploitation of southern Anatolia.

March 16. Turco-Russian treaty of Moscow. Recognition of Turkish territories as in national pact; security pact. Kars and Ardahan to Turkey

October 13. Treaty of Kars between Turkey and the states of Caucasus—Armenia, Georgia, Azerbaijan. Georgia received Batum; free port for Turkey.

October 20. Treaty of Angora (Franklin-Bouillon). France cedes to Turkey about 10,000 square kilometers, including Cilicia, territory e. and w. from gulf of Alexandretta to Tigris opposite Jeziret-ibn-Omar.

1922. January 2. Treaty of friendship with Ukrainian S. S. R.

February 28. British protectorate over Egypt terminated.

March 20. Treaty of friendship (Tiflis) with Georgian S. S. R.

August 5. Lloyd George's speech against the Kemalists in the House of Commons.

September 9. The Turks occupy Smyrna.

September 15. The appeal of the British to the Dominions and Balkan States for aid against Turkey.

October 10. Anglo-Iraq treaty regulating relations.

October 11. The armistice of Mudania brings end to Turco-Greek war; Turks return to Eastern Thrace.

November 1. Abolition of the sultanate.

November 17. Abdul Medjid called to caliphate.

November 20. Opening of the Lausanne conference.

1923. February 4. Breakup of first conference at Lausanne.

July 24. *Treaty of Lausanne.* 1. Turkey surrendered claim to Hejaz, Palestine, Mesopotamia, Syria, Dodecanese, Cyprus, Egypt, Tripoli. 2. Turkey retained Smyrna, Turkish Armenia, Cilicia, Anatolia, Adalia, Constantinople, Gallipoli, Adrianople and eastern Thrace. 3. Exchange of Greek inhabitants in Turkey for Turk inhabitants in Greece; protection of minorities. 4. Abolition of capitulations. 5. Demilitarization of Straits. 6. Renunciation of indemnities.

August 13. Grand National Assembly chooses Mustapha Kemal as president.

August 14. Soviet government signs Straits convention of Lausanne at Rome.

August 6. Turco-American treaty of Lausanne signed.

September 29. Palestine and Syrian mandates into effect.

October 6. Turkish forces occupy Constantinople.

October 14. Angora voted the new Turkish capital.

1924. March 3. G. N. A. abolishes dynasty, the caliphate, and commissariat of sheriat and Evkaff, and attaches all educational institutions to commissariat of public education.

April 20. Basic revised constitution of Turkey adopted.

September 27. League Council approves Iraq mandate.

1925. December 16. Mosul awarded to Iraq (England) by the Council of the League of Nations.

December 17. Turco-Russian treaty of friendship and neutrality.

1926. January 13. Mosul treaty of Bagdad, between Great Britain and Iraq.

February 17. Swiss civil code adopted by G. N. A.

March 1. Italian criminal code adopted by G. N. A.

May 29. German commercial code adopted by G. N. A.

June 5. Mosul treaty of Angora (Great Britain-Turkey-Iraq). Awarded Mosul to Iraq.

1927. November 1. Mustapha Kemal reëlected president of republic.

1928. April 9. Constitutional amendment eliminating Islam as religion of state, passed by G. N. A.

May 30. Political treaty between Turkey and Italy.

November 3. New Latin alphabet is introduced into Turkey.

1929. December 17. Russo-Turkish neutrality pact.

March. Woman suffrage.

1930. March 1. Anglo-Turkish treaty of commerce and navigation.

June 10. Greco-Turkish pact of friendship.

(Based in part on Ploetz' *Manual of Universal History*. Translated and enlarged by W. H. Tillinghast. Revised under H. E. Barnes. (Boston 1925); G. Jäschke and E. Pritsch, *Die Türkei seit dem Weltkriege. Geschichtskalender 1918-1928* (Berlin 1929); E. G. Mears, *Modern Turkey* (N. Y. 1924); Turkey no. 16 (1878). *Treaties and other documents relating to the Black sea, the Dardanelles and the Bosphorus: 1535-1877. Cmd. 1953.*

3.

## SELECTED BIBLIOGRAPHY

### Unpublished Documents

(Many of the documentary materials cited below are now available in *Aussenpolitik*. Originally obtained from the Austrian archives in Vienna).

*Geheim XLIV-15.*

*Frage der Unterstützung der serbischen Oppositionsparteien, Sommer 1913.*

Entwurf "von Serbien zu leistende Garantien für sein künftiges freundliches Verhalten—aus der gleichen Zeit."

*Geheim XLIV-16.*

*Aufzeichnungen des Grafen Forgach über eine Unterredungen mit Staatssekretär von Jagow in Berlin am 25 September 1913.*

*Geheim XLIV-18. 1912-1913.*

*Denkschrift des Gesandten von Szilassy über unsere Politik gegenüber Russland und den Balkanstaaten, 1912-1913.*

*Geheim XLIV-18.*

*Herr von Szilassy, 9 Jänner 1914. Die Beziehungen zwischen O-U und Griechenland, und die internationale Politik O-U in Allegemeinen.*

*Geheim XLIV-20.*

*Tagesbericht vom 30. Jänner 1914, 506. Unterredung des Minister Graf Berchtold mit dem Griechischen Minister-präsidenten Venizelos.*

*Russland Varia: 1912-1913. Geheim XLIV-21.*

*Aufzeichnung dd. Abbazia, 18. April 1914, über die Unterredungen des Ministers Graf Berchtold mit dem italienischen Minister des Aeussern Marchese San Giuliano.*

*Geheim XLV-15.*

*Nr. 3009. Herrn von Merey. Rom. Wien, am 26. Juni 1913. Streng vertraulich.*

*Nr. 3117 prodomo. Privatschreiben S. E. des Herrn Ministers an Grafen Szögyény in Berlin. Wien, 1. Juli 1913.*

*Geheim XLV-16. Notiz Nr. 3733.*

*Der Kabinetts-Direktor. Sr. k.u.k. Apostol. Majestat. Ischl. 27. Juli 1913.*

*Abschrift eines geheimen Erlasses an Gf. Szögyény in Berlin, ddto Wien, 1. August 1913, Nr. 3685.*

*Geheim XLV-16. Notiz Nr. 3733.*

*Nr. 3763. Gf. Szögyény. Berlin. Wien 4. August 1913.*

*Geheim XLV-17.*

*Aeusserungen K. Wilhelms ganz im Sinne der Unterredung mit Gf. Berchtold in Schönbrunn 26-10 1913. Confidentiell München, den 16, Dezember 1913.*

*Abschrift eines streng geheimen Privat-schreibens an Gf. Szögyény, Wien, 24. November 1913.*

*Pallavicini an Berchtold. Konstantinopel, 29. Dezember 1913, Nr. 82. A-o.*

*Aufzeichnung über Unterredungen S. M. des Königs von Bulgarien mit Gf. Berchtold am 6. November 1913.*

*Geheim XLV-23.*

*Aufzeichnung über die Unterredung des Min. Gf. Berchtold mit M. d. A. Také Jonescu. 9. September 1913.*

*Geheim XLV-25.*

This collection contains several reports from January to May 1914 dealing with alliance proposals to bring Bulgaria and Turkey under the Triplice. Berchtold-Tarnowsky-Pallavicini.

*Geheim XLV-26.*

*Eine Kopie dieses Tagesberichtes wurde S. E. dem Herrn Minister behufs Vor-trages bei S. M. am 28-10. unterbreitet. 28 Oktober 1913. Nr. 5097.*

*Geheim XLVII.*

This collection contains several dispatches dealing with alliance projects imme-diately before the outbreak of the world war. The desire to make an alliance with both Turkey and Bulgaria is evident.

*No. 289/2221. Telegramm. Ref. 1. Sekretiert.*

*Von: Graf Tarnowski, ddto. Sofia, 6. September 1915. No. 1024.* Contains text of Austro-Bulgarian alliance, September 6, 1915.

*Fasz. 856. Liasse "Krieg" 6.*

Contains Berchtold-Tisza-Conrad correspondence with reference to Bulgaria, fall of 1914.

*Fasz. 857.*

Contains Conrad-Burian-Falkenhayn correspondence on Turco-Bulgarian al-liance, 1915.

## Published Documents

Adamov, E. A. (ed.)

*Evropeiskie derzhavi i Gretsia v epokhy mirovoi voini.* Moscow 1922. Russian documents dealing with Greece during the world war.

*Konstantinopol i prolivy.* Moscow 1925-26. 2 vols. The authoritative Russian source on cession of Constantinople and Straits problem during the war.

*Razdel Aziatskoi Turtsii.* Moscow 1924. Partition of Asiatic Turkey according to secret documents of former imperial Russian foreign office. Of great importance in understanding ambitions of Powers in Near East.

Austria-Hungary.

*Ministère des affaires étrangères. Documents diplomatiques concernant les rap-ports entre l'Autriche-Hongrie et la Roumanie. 22 juillet 1914-27 août 1916. Vienna 1916.*

*Veröffentlichungen der Kommission für neuere Geschichte Österreichs 23. Öster-reich-Ungarns Aussenpolitik von der bosnischen Krise 1908 bis zum Kriegsaus-bruch 1914. Diplomatische Aktenstücke des Österreichisch-Ungarischen Minis-teriums des Äussern. Ausgewahlt von Ludwig Bittner, Alfred Francis Pribram, Heinrich Srbik und Hans Uebersberger. Bearbeitet von Ludwig Bittner und Hans Uebersberger. Österreichischer Bundesverlag für Unterricht, Wissenschaft und Kunst. Wien und Leipzig, 1930.* The Austrian documents on the causes of the world war, 1908-1914. 9 vols. The writer has used expecially volumes V to VIII. Indispensable for diplomacy in Near East and Turkey.

*Austrian Red Book.* Official files pertaining to pre-war history, June 28 to August 27, 1914. London (Allen and Unwin), n. d. 3 parts. These are the official Austrian documents on the outbreak of the war and are valuable. English translations of documents later published in *Aussenpolitik.*

Baker, R. S., *Woodrow Wilson and World Settlement*. New York, Doubleday Page, 1922. 3 vols. Volume III is especially valuable for documentary materials on the Paris conference.

Baker, R. S., and Dodd, W. E., *The Public Papers of Woodrow Wilson*. New York, Harpers, 1927. 3 vols. Vol III deals with the Paris conference.

Barbusse, Henri (intro.), *The Soviet Union and Peace*. New York, International, 1929. The most important of the documents issued by the government of the U. S. S. R. concerning peace and disarmament from 1917-1929.

Bogichevich, M., *Die auswartige Politik Serbiens 1903-1914*. Geheimakten aus serbischen Archiven. Berlin 1928. 3 volumes. A principal source on Serbian foreign policy.

Brown, Carroll N. (tr.), "Reply of the Hellenic Delegation to the Statements submitted to the Peace Conference by the Bulgarian Delegation with Regard to the Policy of Bulgaria and its Claims to Thrace," *American Hellenic Society Publication No. 10. 1920*. Oxford University Press, New York.

Bulgaria.

"Die Bulgarischen Dokumente zum Kriegsausbruch 1914," *Die Kriegsschuld-frage*, VI, no. 3 (March 1928), pp. 227-59. Translations from the *Bulgarian Orange Book* on the outbreak of the war.

*Doklad na parlamentarnata izpitatelna komisya*, I. Sofia, State Printing office, 1918. Documents dealing with Bulgarian activities in the Balkan wars.

Ministry of Foreign Affairs, *Diplomatic Documents on the Entrance of Bulgaria into the World War*. Tomes I-II. 1913-1918. Sofia, State Printing Office, 1920-21. The Bulgarian Orange Book. Two large volumes of Bulgarian documents.

*The Bulgarian Question and the Balkan States*. Sofia, State Printing Office, 1919. Deals mostly with the Macedonian question. The Bulgarian claims at the Paris conference.

Carnegie Endowment for International Peace. *The Treaties of Peace, 1919-1923*. New York, Carnegie, 1924. 2 vols. Contains treaties of Versailles, Sèvres, St. Germain, Trianon, Neuilly, Lausanne.

Cocks, F. Seymour, *The Secret Treaties*. London, Union of Democratic Control, 1918. The secret understandings on Asiatic Turkey. Should be used with care.

Cummings, C. K., and Pettit, W. W., *Russian-American Relations, March 1917-March 1920. Documents and Papers*. New York, Harcourt, 1920.

Dickinson, G. Lowes, *Documents and Statements Relative to the Peace*. New York, Macmillan, 1919. Peace proposals of the various belligerents. Very valuable.

Earle, E. M., "The Turkish Petroleum Company," *Political Science Quarterly*, XXXIX (June 1924), 265-79. Original documents on the company's concession of 1914.

"The Secret Anglo-German Convention of 1914 Regarding Asiatic Turkey," *Political Science Quarterly*, XXXVIII (March 1923), 24-44. The Anglo-German convention regarding the Bagdad railway, June 15, 1914.

*European Economic and Political Survey*, II, no. 8, p. 7. December 31, 1925. Text of Russo-Turkish agreement of December 17, 1925. Vol. II, no. 12, pp. 46-50, contains text of Franco-Russian treaty of May 1926.

Vol. II, no. 22, pp. 24 ff. Text of Anglo-Persian company's concession from Iraq, June 14, 1926.

l'*Europe nouvelle*, V, nos. 29-40, 1922. Notes and documents on the Mudania armistice, and situation leading to Lausanne conference.

VI, no. 19 (May 12, 1923), 599-604. Documents on the Chester concession.

IX, no. 417 (February 13, 1926). Text of the treaty between Russia and Turkey, December 17, 1925.

France.

*Haut commissariat de la république française en Syrie et au Liban. La Syrie et le Liban en 1922.* Paris 1922.

*Ministère des affaires étrangères. République française. Documents diplomatiques. Les affaires balkaniques, 1912-1914. Tome III.* Paris, Imprimerie nationale, 1922.

*Documents diplomatiques. Conférence de Lausanne sur les affaires du proche-orient. (1922-1923). Recueil des actes de la conférence.* Paris, Imprimerie nationale, 1923. Première série. Tome I contains protocols of first commission; Tome IV documents on negotiations of February 1 to April 22, 1923. *Deuxième série,* Tome I, *procès-verbaux* and documents on second part of conference, April 23-July 24, 1923. Tome II contains final acts of conference.

*Rapport sur la situation de la Syrie et du Liban, année 1924.* Paris, 1925.

*Ministère des affaires étrangères. Rapport sur la situation de la Syrie et du Liban, juillet 1922-juillet 1923.* Paris, Imprimerie nationale, 1923.

*German White Book. Concerning Responsibility of the Authors of the War.* Tr. by Carnegie Endowment for International Peace. Division of International Law. New York, Oxford, 1924.

Gidel, Gilbert, professeur à la faculté de droit de l'université de Paris, et à l'école libre des sciences politiques, *Consultation sur l'artcile 3, paragraphe 2 du traité de Lausanne concernant la Turquie et l'Irak.* Paris, Imprimerie et librairie centrales des chemins de fer, 1925. The opinion for the Turks on Mosul.

Golder, Frank A., *Documents of Russian History, 1914-1917.* New York, Century, 1927. Contains documents on Russian pre-war and war policy. Excellent for early Bolshevik policies.

Great Britain.

Air Ministry. Note on the method of employment of the air arm in Iraq. *Cmd. 2217.*

Arabia. Agreements with the Sultan of Nejd regarding certain questions relating to the Nejd-Trans-Jurdan and Nejd-Iraq frontiers. December 1925. *Cmd. 2566.*

*Collected diplomatic Documents Relating to the Outbreak of the European War.* London, H. M. S. O., 1915.

*Documents on the Origins of the War, 1898-1914.* Edited by G. P. Gooch and Harold Temperley. Vol. I, *The End of British Isolation, 1897-1904,* H. M. S. O., 1927; Vol. IV, *The Anglo-Russian Rapprochement, 1903-1907,* H. M. S. O., 1929. Vol. XI, *The Outbreak of War, June 28-August 4, 1914,* H. M. S. O., 1926. Cited as B. D.

Dardanelles Commission. First Report. *Cmd. 8490.* Supplementary Report. *Cmd. 8502* (1917). Final Report. *Cmd. 371* (1919). An official British investigation of Dardanelles campaign.

Dispatch to H. M. Ambassador at Washington, enclosing a memorandum on the petroleum situation. April 1921. *Cmd. 1351.*

Mesopotamia Commission. Report of the Commission Appointed to Inquire into the Origin, Inception, and Operations of War in Mesopotamia. With separate Report by Com. J. J. Wedgewood. *Cmd. 8610* (1917).

*Miscellaneous no. 13* (1914). Correspondence Respecting Events Leading to the Rupture of Relations with Turkey. *Cmd. 7628.*

*Miscellaneous no. 14* (1914). Dispatch from H. M. Ambassador at Constantinople summarizing Events Leading up to the Rupture of Relations with Turkey and Reply thereto. *Cmd. 7716.*

*Miscellaneous no. 11* (1920). Memorandum of Agreement (San Remo, April 24, 1920) between M. Philippe Berthelot, *Directeur des affaires politiques et commerciales au ministère des affaires étrangères,* and Professor Sir John Cadman, director in charge of H. M. Petroleum Department. *Cmd. 675.*

*Miscellaneous no. 3* (1921). Draft Mandates for Mesopotamia and Palestine as Submitted for the Approval of the League of Nations. *Cmd. 1176.*

*Miscellaneous no. 4* (1921). Franco-British Convention of December 23, 1920, on Certain Points Connected with the Mandates for Syria and the Lebanon, Palestine and Mesopotamia. *Cmd. 1195.*

*Miscellaneous no. 10* (1921). Correspondence between H. M. Government and the United States Respecting Economic Rights in Mandated Territories. *Cmd. 1226.*

*Miscellaneous no. 17* (1925). League of Nations. Decision Relating to the Turco-Iraq Frontier Adopted by the Council of the League of Nations, Geneva, December 16, 1925. *Cmd. 2562.*

Pronouncement by Three Allied Prime Ministers for Foreign Affairs Respecting the Near East Situation. March 27, 1922. *Cmd. 1641.*

Review of the Civil Administration of Mesopotamia. An Account of the Civil Administration during the Military Occupation to the Summer of 1920. *Cmd. 1061* (1920).

*Treaty Series no. 11* (1920). Treaty of Peace with Turkey. Signed at Sèvres, August 10, 1920. *Cmd. 964.*

*No. 13* (1920). Treaty Between the Principal Allied and Associated Powers and Greece. Signed at Sèvres, August 10, 1920. *Cmd. 960.*

*No. 12* (1920). Tripartite Agreement between the British Empire, France, and Italy Respecting Anatolia. Signed at Sèvres, August 10, 1920. *Cmd. 963.*

*No. 13* (1921). Treaty Between the Allied and Associated Powers and Greece Relative to Thrace. Signed at Sèvres, August 10, 1920. *Cmd. 1390.*

*Turkey No. 2* (1921). Dispatch from H. M. Ambassador at Paris Enclosing the Franco-Turkish Agreement Signed at Angora on October 20, 1921. *Cmd. 1556.*

*Turkey no. 1* (1922). Correspondence Between H. M. Government and the French Government Respecting the Angora Agreement of October 20, 1921. *Cmd. 1570.*

*Turkey no. 1 (1923)*. Lausanne Conference on Near Eastern Affairs, 1922-23. *Cmd. 1814*. The records of proceedings and the draft terms of peace. The British records do not go beyond the ending of the first conference, February 1923. Official only for the British Delegates.

*Treaty Series no. 16 (1923)*. Treaty of Peace with Turkey, and Other Instruments Signed at Lausanne on July 24, 1923. *Cmd. 1929*.

*Treaty Series no. 17 (1925)*. Treaty of Alliance Between Great Britan and Iraq signed at Bagdad, October 10, 1922; and Protocol of Treaty of Alliance Between Great Britain and Iraq of October 10, 1922, signed at Bagdad, April 20, 1923; together with Agreements Subsidiary to the Treaty of Alliance Between Great Britain and Iraq of October 10, 1922, signed at Bagdad, March 25, 1924. *Cmd. 2370*.

*Turkey no. 1 (1926)*. Treaty Between the United Kingdom and Iraq and Turkey Regarding the Settlement of the Frontier Between Turkey and Iraq, together with notes exchanged. With map. *Cmd. 2679*.

*War Speeches by British Ministers, 1914-1918*. London, Unwin, 1917. Addresses by Asquith, Grey, Balfour and others.

*Greek White Book*. Supplementary Diplomatic Documents, 1913-1917, issued by the ministry of foreign affairs of the Greek Government. Translated from the French edition by T. P. Ion, and Carroll N. Brown, American Hellenic Society, Publication no. 9. New York, Oxford, 1919. Cited as G. W. B.

*Greek White Book*. Diplomatic documents, 1913-1917, issued by the Greek ministry of foreign affairs concerning the Greco-Serbian treaty of alliance and the Germano-Bulgarian invasion into Macedonia. American Hellenic Society, Publication no. 5. New York, Oxford, 1919. Cited as G. W. B.

*(Die) Grosse Politik der Europäischen Kabinette, 1871-1914*. Deutsche Verlagsgesellschaft für Politik und Geschichte. M. B. H. Berlin, 1922-1927. Vol. 27 deals with the Balkan League. Vols. 34 and 35 with the Balkan wars; vol. 38 with Liman von Sanders. Cited as G. P.

*International Conciliation*, no. 166, September 1921. Constitution of ePrmanent Mandates Commission; terms of "C" mandates; Franco-British Convention of December 23, 1920; correspondence between Great Britain and United States on Economic Rights in Mandated Territories; San Remo oil agreement.

No. 86. January 1915. Documents Regarding the European War, series no. IV. I. Turkish official documents, November 1914.

Ionescu, Také, *The Policy of National Instinct*. A speech delivered by Ionescu in the Rumanian Chamber of Deputies during the sitting of December 16-17, 1915. London, Causton, 1916.

Ismet Pasha, *Speech by the Prime Minister of the Turkish Republic in the Grand National Assembly on the Report of General Laidoner*. London, Oldhams, 1925.

Iraq.

*Report on Iraq Administration, October 1920-March 1922*. London, H. M. S. O., 1922.

*Report on Iraq Administration, April 1922-March 1923. Colonial no. 4*. London, H. M. S. O., 1923.

Report by H. B. M. Government on the Administration of Iraq for the Period
April 1923-December 1924. Colonial no. 13. London, H. M. S. O., 1925.

Report by H. B. M. Government to the Council of the League of Nations on the
Administration of Iraq for the Year 1925. Colonial no. 21. London, H. M. S. O.,
1926. First official report to the League of Nations.

Treaty with King Feisal, Signed at Bagdad, January 13, 1926. With Explanatory
Note. February 1926. Cmd. 2587.

Italy.

Ministero degli affari esteri. (Italian Green Book). Diplomatic Documents, Submitted to the Italian Parliament by the Ministry of Foreign Affairs. Austria-
Hungary. Session of May 20, 1915. London, Hodder and Stoughton, 1915.

Journal officiel. Débats parlementaires. Chambre. Senat. Debates in the French Chamber and Senate are particularly valuable on Turkey, Syria, etc., from 1918-1925.

Kautsky, Karl, Outbreak of the World War. German documents collected by Kautsky
and edited by Max Montegelas and W. Schucking. Tr. by Carnegie Endowment.
Division of International Law. New York, Oxford Press, 1924.

"King-Crane Report on the Near East. A suppressed official document of the United
States Government," Editor and Publishers, LV, no. 27 (December 2, 1922),
pp. i-xxvii. A most important document dealing with the Turkish question at
the Paris conference.

Krasnyi Archiv, Istoricheskii Zhurnal. Moskva, 1923 ff. Vols. 8, 9, 15, deal with
Balkan league.

Laloy, Emile, Les documents secrets des archives du ministère des affaires étrangères
de Russie. Paris, Bossard, 1920. Treaties, conventions and documents published
by the Bolsheviks.

League of Nations.

Assignment of the Mandates. Arab Countries. Letter, dated 8 May 1920, from
the secretary general of the Hedjaz Delegation in Paris. Document du Conseil
KI.20-4-96. H. M. S. O., 1920.

Document C. 500. M. 147. VII. Question of the Frontier Between Turkey and
Iraq. Report submitted to the Council by the Commission instituted by the
Council resolution of September 30, 1924.

Document C. 494. 1924. VII. Frontier Between Turkey and Iraq. Letter and
memorandum from the Turkish government.

Permanent Mandates Commission. Minutes of the First Session, held in Geneva,
October 4-8, 1921. C. 416. M. 296. 1921. VI.

Official Journal. (Authorized edition). The minutes of the Council deal with the
Turkish problem, the mandates, particularly with the Mosul question, from
1920-26, as cited.

Permanent Mandates Commission. Minutes of the Second Session Held in
Geneva, August 1-11, 1922. A. 36. 1922. VI.

Permanent Mandates Commission. Minutes of the Fifth Session (Extraordinary),
held at Geneva, October 23-November 6, 1924.

Treaty Series, XXVIII. Text of the Lausanne treaty of July 24, 1923.

*Mandates.* Final Drafts of the Mandates for Mesopotamia and Palestine for the Approval of the League of Nations. 1921. *Cmd. 1500.*

Marchand, René, *Un livre noir. Diplomatie d'avant guerre et de guerre. D'après les documents des archives russes, 1914-1917.* III. Paris 1926. The correspondence of Isvolsky, Benckendorff and Sazonov.

Massignon, Louis, "*Documents sur les revendications islamiques,*" *Revue du monde musulman,* XL-XLI (September-December 1920), 165-215. (1) Authorized French translation of address presented to the viceroy of India at Delhi, 19 January 1920; (2) Manifesto voted at Session, 15-17 February 1920, Conference All Indian Khalifate, Bombay; (3) Minutes of interview of Indian Khalifate deputation with David Lloyd George, London, 19 March 1920; (4) Protest addressed to D. L. G. at Paris, 10 July 1920, by delegation criticizing peace with Turkey.

Mirkine-Guetsevitch, B. (ed. and tr.), "*Documents: Russie et Turquie en août 1914,*" *Le monde slave,* IV, no. 4 (April 1927), 128-45. Based on Pokrovsky documents.

"*Documents: L'Entrée en guerre de l'Italie,*" *Le monde slave,* II, no. 6 (June 1928), 410-53; III, no. 7 (July 1928), 122-158.

"*Documents: Entrée en guerre de la Roumanie, 1914-1916,*" *Le monde slave,* 5th yr., III, no. 9 (September 1928), 423-71.

"*Documents: l'entrée en guerre de la Bulgarie,*" *Le monde slave,* VI, no. 4 (April 1929), 115-44; no. 5 (May 1929), 275-301; no. 6 (June 1929). French translations of Pokrovsky documents.

"*Documents sur la Conférence interalliée de Petrograd (1917),*" *Le monde slave,* IV, no. 9 (September 1927), 460-71. Pokrovsky to tsar on Greek situation and memorandum of Lord Milner to tsar, February 4-17, 1917.

"*Documents: la diplomatie russe dans les Balkans pendant la grande guerre,*" *Le monde slave,* V, no. 3 (March 1928), 422-51.

Miller, David Hunter, *My Diary at the Conference of Paris, with Documents.* New York, Appeal Printing Company, 1928. 22 vols. The authoritative documentary source for the Paris peace conference, 1918-1919.

Palestine.

*An Interim Report on the Civil Administration of Palestine during the Period 16 July 1920-30 June 1921. Cmd. 1499 (1921).*

*Report of H. B. M. Government on the Palestine Administration, 1923. Colonial no. 9 (1925).*

Colonial Office, Great Britain. *Report on the Administration under Mandate of Palestine and Trans-Jordan for the Year 1924.* London, H. M. S. O., 1925. *Colonial no. 12.*

*Report of the High Commissioner on the Administration of Palestine, 1920-1925. Colonial no. 19.*

*Parliamentary Debates* (authorized edition). Fifth series, House of Commons and House of Lords. For the years 1914 and following, as cited.

Pokrovsky, Professor M., *Drei Konferenzen (zur Vorgeschichte des Krieges). Herausgegeben vom der Redaktion Russische Korrespondenz.* Berlin 1920.

*Das Zaristische Russland im Weltkriege. Neue Documente aus den russischen Staatsarchiven über den Eintritt der Türkei, Bulgariens, Rumaniens, und Italiens*

*in den Weltkrieg. Herausgegeben von der Zentralstelle für Erforschung der Krieg-sursachen.* Deutsche Verlagsgesellschaft für Politik und Geschichte m. b. h. Berlin 1927. German translation of *Tsarskaia Rossia v Mirovoi voine.*

Polonsky, J. (ed. and tr.), *Documents diplomatiques secrets russes, 1914-1917. D'après les archives du ministère des affaires étrangères à Petrograd.* Paris, Payot, 1928. French translations of the Russian documents published in full by Adamov and Pokrovsky. Deals with Turkey, Bulgaria, Rumania, Italy and the question of the Straits.

*Le Pont Euxin devant le congrès de la paix. Mémoire présenté à la conférence de la paix par les délégués du Pont-Euxin.* Paris, February 1919. Greek claims for the Trebizond region.

Price, Crawfurd, "The Austro-Bulgar Treaties," *Balkan Review,* I, no. 3 (April 1919), 200-209.

Prince Lvov, S. D. Sazonov, N. M. Chaikovsky, B. Maklakov, *Mémoire présenté au président de la conférence de la paix.* Paris, 5 juillet 1919. Paris, Fournier, 1919. Presents the Russian claim for a mandate over the Constantinople region.

Publications of the Permanent Court of International Justice. Series B. Collection of Advisory opinions. *No. 12, Article 3, Paragraph 2, of the Treaty of Lausanne. Frontier Between Turkey and Iraq.* Leyden, Sijthoff, 1925.

Series C. Acts and Documents Relating to Judgments and Advisory Opinions Given by the Court. No. 10. Ninth Session. *Documents Relating to Advisory Opinion no. 12. Treaty of Lausanne, Article 3, Paragraph 2.* Leyden, Sijthoff, 1925.

*Rapport de la commission des détroits à la société des nations.* Année 1925. Constanti-nople, Imprimerie française, L. Mourkides, 1926. *Année 1926* (1927). *Année 1927* (1928). Documents on the organization and work of the Commission of the Straits, valuable statistics and account.

Russia.

*Ministerstvo inostrannykh diel. Materialy po istorii franko-russkikh otnoshenii.* Moscow 1922. Valuable for the Russian documents on the alliance between France and Russia.

Imperial Russian Ministry of Foreign Affairs. *Diplomatic Documents.* Negotia-tions covering the period from July 19-August 1 to October 19-November 1, 1914. Preceding the war with Turkey. Translation of the Russian and French texts. Appendix: Speech of Sazonov in the Duma of the Empire, January 27 (February 9), 1915. Petrograd, Impremirie de l'État, 1915. English translation, H. M. S. O.

Rumania.

*Mémoire du gouvernement roumain dans la question du Danube.* Bucharest 1925. *Ministerul afacerilor straine. Documents diplomatiques. Les événements de la péninsule balkanique. L'action de la Roumanie. 20 septembre 1912—1 août 1913.* Bucharest, Imprimeria statului, 1913.

*Ministère des affaires étrangères. Le traité de paix de Bucarest du 28 juillet (10 août) 1913. Précédé des protocoles de la conférence.* Bucharest, Imprimerie de l'État, 1913.

Scott, James Brown (ed.), *The Austrian Red Book* (no. 2). Ministry of Foreign Affairs. *Diplomatic Documents Concerning the Relations of Austria-Hungary with Italy*

*from July 20, 1914 to May 23, 1915.* (Reprinted in *Documents Relating to the Outbreak of the European War.* Carnegie, 1916, I, 127-346.)

Siebert, Baron de, and Schreiner, G., *Entente Diplomacy and the World, 1909-1914.* New York, Knickerbocker, 1922. The correspondence of Isvolsky, Benckendorff and Sazonov.

Siebert, Benno von, *Graf Benckendorffs diplomatischer Schriftwechsel.* 3 vols. Berlin, Walter de Gruyter, 1928. About 100 new documents of the correspondence.

*Statement of the Zionist Organization Concerning Palestine.* February 3, 1919. Paris, Dupont, 1919. Summary of the case before the Paris conference.

Stieve, F., *Das Russische Orangebuch über den Kriegsausbruch mit der Türkei.* Berlin. Verlag für Kulturpolitik, 1926. Supplements the Russian edition of 1915.

*Iswolski im Weltkriege; diplomatische Schriftwechsel Iswolskis, 1914-1917.* Berlin, D. V. P. G., m. b. h., 1925.

Tisza, Graf Stephen, *Briefe,* I (1914-1918). *Nach der von Ungärischen Academie der Wissenschafter veroffentlichten originalausgabe herausgegeben und mit einer Einleitung versehen von Oskar von Wertheimer.* Berlin, Verlag von Reimer, 1928. Indications of Tisza's attitude on the world war, and on Balkan policy during the war.

Turkey.

*Ministère des affaires étrangères. Le livre rouge. La question de Mossoul. De la signature du traité d'armistice de Moudros.* (30 Octobre 1918 au 1 mars 1925). Constantinople, Imprimerie Ahmed Ihsan & Cie., 1925. Very valuable for the Turkish attitude on the Mosul question. Constantinople conference, 1924; Lausanne conference; League of Nations sessions.

*La question de Mossoul à la 35me session du Conseil de la Société des Nations.* September 3, 1925. Lausanne, Imprimerie de la Société suisse de publicité, 1925. *La question de Mossoul à la 35me session du Conseil de la Société des Nations (Genève).* September 19, 1925. Lausanne, Imprimerie de la Société suisse de publicité, 1925.

Turkish Delegation. *Observations générales présentées par la délégation ottomane à la conférence de la paix. 8 juillet 1920.* (n. p., n. d.). A Turkish document of forty seven pages presenting a scathing denunciation of the treaty of Sèvres.

*République turque. Présidence du conseil. Office central de statistique. Population de la Turquie. Par vilayets et cazas. Par villes et villages. D'après le recensement du 28 octobre 1927.* Angora, Imprimerie Turk-odjak, 1928.

*Présidence du conseil. Office central de statistique. Annuaire statistique. Premier volume, 1928.* Angora, Imp. Zellitch Frères, 1928.

United States.

*Congressional Record.* (Authorized edition). For years 1920-24, as cited.
Senate Document no. 266, 66 Congress, 2nd Session. *Conditions in the Near East.* Report of the American military mission to Armenia, by Major General James G. Harbord.

Department of State. *Papers Relating to the Foreign Relations of the United States. 1914 supplement. The World War.* Washington, U. S. Government Printing Office, 1928.

Division of Near Eastern Affairs. *Mandate for Palestine.* Washington, Government Printing Office, 1927. The correspondence between Great Britain and the United States over Palestine and Mesopotamia, with treaty.

Venizelos, E. K., *Greece in Her True Light.* Her position in the world-wide war as expounded by El. K. Venizelos. Translated and published by Socrates A. Xanthaky and Nicholas G. Sakellarios. New York 1916.

*The Vindication of Greek National Policy, 1912-1917.* Introduction by J. Gennadius, Greek minister at London. London, Allen and Unwin, 1918. A report of speeches delivered in the Greek Chamber, August 24-26, 1917.

*Greece Before the Peace Congress of 1919.* A memorandum dealing with the rights of Greece. New York, Oxford Press, American Hellenic Society Publication, no. 7, 1919.

World Peace Foundation. *War Aims of Belligerents as Elicited by Russia's Attempts to Secure a General Peace.* I, no. 3 (February 1918).

## Memoirs and Biographies

Ahmed Djemal Pasha, *Memories of a Turkish Statesman, 1913-1919.* New York, Doran, 1922. Light on Turkey and war.

Arthur, Sir George, *Life of Lord Kitchener.* New York, Macmillan, 1920. 3 vols. Vol. III contains material of value on the war, Dardanelles, etc.

Bertie, Lord Francis, *The Diary of Lord Bertie.* London, Hodder and Staughton, 1924. 2 vols. The diary of the former British ambassador at Paris. Very anti-Russian.

Bethmann-Hollweg, T. von, *Reflections on the World War.* London, Thornton Butterworth, 1920.

Bosdari, Allessandro de, *Delle guerre balcaniche della grande guerra e di alcuni fatti precedenti ad esse.* Milan, Modadori, 1928.

Buchanan, Sir George, *My Mission to Russia and Other Diplomatic Memories.* 2 vols. Boston, Little, Brown & Co., 1922. Memoirs of the former British ambassador in Russia.

Burian, Graf Stephen, *Austria in Dissolution.* New York, Doran, 1925. Memoirs of the former Austrian foreign minister. Excellent for analysis of the Rumanian, Bulgarian and Italian policies during the war.

Caracciolo, Colonel Mario, *L'intervento della Grecia nella guerra mondiale e l'opera della diplomazia alleata.* Rome, Strini, 1925.

Chirol, Sir Valentine, *Fifty Years in a Changing World.* New York, Harcourt, Brace, 1928. An account of a Balkan mission during the war.

Churchill, Winston S., *The World Crisis.* New York, Scribner's, 1928. 4 vols. The brilliant memoirs of the British statesman. Valuable for his relationship to the Dardanelles expedition.

*The Aftermath.* New York, Scribner's, 1929. The analysis of the post war period.

Czernin, Count Ottokar, *In the World War.* New York, Cassell, 1919. Czernin was Austrian minister at Bucharest at the outbreak of the war, and later Austrian foreign minister.

Deville, Gabriel, *L'entente, la Grèce et la Bulgarie*. Paris, E. Figuiere, n. d. Memoirs of the former French minister at Athens.

Edib, Halidé, *Memoirs of Halidé Edib*. New York, Century, n. d.
*The Turkish Ordeal*. New York, Century, 1928. 2 vols. Memoirs.

Einstein, Lewis, *Inside Constantinople*. A diplomat's diary during the Dardanelles expedition, April 8-September 1915. London, Murray, 1917. Mr. Einstein was a special agent of the American Embassy at Constantinople.

Falkenhayn, General von, *German General Staff*. New York, Dodd, Mead, 1920.

Fisher, Admiral Lord (Sir John), *Memories and Records*. 2 vols. New York, Doran, 1920. Important for Dardanelles campaign.

Geshov, I. E., *The Balkan League*. London, Murray, 1915. Very valuable. An author-itative account of formation of Balkan league by the former Bulgarian prime minister. Documentary.

Giolitti, Giovanni, *Memoirs of My Life*. London, Chapman and Dodd, 1923. Very valuable for Italian policy in war.

Grey, Viscount of Fallodon, *Twenty-five Years, 1892-1916*. New York, Stokes, 1925. Valuable for documents, but leaves much to be desired.

Hoetzendorf, Conrad von, *Aus Meiner Dienstzeit*. 5 vols. Rikola Verlag, Vienna and Berlin, 1921. Memoirs of the Austrian chief of staff. Vols. 1 and 2 deal with period of 1909 to 1912.

Ionescu, Také, *Some Personal Impressions*, New York, Stokes, 1920. Memoirs of the late Rumanian statesman. Valuable for Balkan policy.

Izzet Pasha, *Denkwürdigkeiten des Marshalls Izzet Pascha. Ein kritischer Beitrag zur Kriegsschuldfrage aus dem original-manuscript übersetzt, eingeleitet und erstmalig herausgegeben von Karl Klinghardt*. Leipzig, Verlag von K. F. Köehler, 1927.

Jagow, G. von, *Ursachen und Ausbruch des Weltkrieges*. Berlin, Hobbing Verlag, 1919.

Judet, Ernest, *Georges Louis*. Paris, Rieder, 1925.

Kerofilas, Dr. C., *Eleftherios Venizelos; His Life and Work*. New York. Dutton, 1915. Contains Venizelos' memoranda of January 1915 on Cavalla and Asia Minor.

Lawrence, T. E., *Revolt in the Desert*. Garden City, New York, Garden City Publish-ing Co., 1927. The interesting memoirs of the man who aroused and led the Arabs during the war.

Leslie, Shane, *Mark Sykes, His Life and Letters*. London, Cassell, 1923. Much material on the Sykes-Picot accord including an official British version.

Lichnowsky, Prince Karl Mas, *Heading for the Abyss*. New York, Pason and Clarke, 1928. Important for pre-war policy in Turkey.

Louis, Georges, *Les Carnots de Georges Louis*. Paris, Rieder, 1926.

Ludendorff, General Eric von, *Ludendorff's Own Story*. New York, Harper's, 1919. 2 vols.
*The General Staff*. London, Hutchinson, 1920.

Melas, Major George M., *Ex-King Constantine and the War*. London, Hutchinson, n. d.

Mukhtar Pasha, Gen. M., *La Turquie, l'Allemagne et l'Europe depuis le traité de Berlin jusqu'à la guerre mondiale*. Paris, Berger-levrault, 1924. The memoirs of the former Turkish ambassador in Berlin. Very important for Turkish pre-war policy. Favored direct Turco-Russian *entente*.

Nekliudov, Anatolii Vasilevich, *Diplomatic Reminiscences Before and During the World War, 1911-1917*. London, Murray, 1920. Memoirs of the Russian minister at Sofia during the Balkan wars.

Oxford, and Asquith, Earl of, *Memories and Recollections*. Boston, Little, Brown, 1928. 2 vols.

Paléologue, Maurice, *An Ambassador's Memoirs*. London, Hutchinson, 1923. Memoirs of the former French ambassador to Russia. 3 vols.

Poincaré, R., *The Origins of the War*. London, Cassell, 1922.
*The Memoirs of Raymond Poincaré*, II, 1913-1914. Tr. and adapted by Sir G. Arthur. Garden City, N. Y., Doubleday, Doran, 1928.

Pomiankowski, F. M. Lt. Joseph, *Der Zusammenbruch des Ottomanischen Reiches. Erinnerungen an die Turkei der Zeit des Weltkrieges*. Wien, Amalthea-Verlag, 1928. Memoirs of the Austrian military attaché at Constantinople. Valuable for pre-war policy and war activities.

Radoslavov, Dr. Vasil, *Bulgarien und die Weltkrise*. Berlin, Ullstein, 1923. The memoirs of the war-time Bulgarian prime minister. Invaluable for Bulgarian policy. Thoroughly documented.

Rodd, Sir J. Rennell, *Social and Diplomatic Memories*, III, 1902-1919. London Arnold, 1925. The memoirs of the former British Ambassador to Italy.

Ronaldshay, the Earl of, *The Life of Lord Curzon*. Being the authorized biography of George Nathaniel Marquess Curzon of Kedleston, K. G. London, New York, Boni and Liveright, Benn, 1928. 3 vols. The third volume deals with the war and the Near East after the war.

Savinsky, A. A., *Recollections of a Russian Diplomat*. London, Hutchinson, 1927(?). Memoirs of the former Russian minister to Bulgaria. Well documented.

Sazonov, S. D., *Fateful Years*. New York, Stokes, 1928. The memoirs of the Russian foreign minister. Very valuable for statements of Russian policy.

Shelking, Eugene N. de, *Recollections of a Russian Diplomat*. New York, Macmillan, 1918. Important for memorandum on Rumania and the war.

Street, C. J. C., *Lord Reading*. London, Butler and Tanner, 1928. Throws light on the Moslem agitation over Constantinople.

Stuermer, Dr. Harry, *Two War Years in Constantinople*. New York, Doran, 1917. Memoirs of the late correspondent of the *Kölnische Zeitung* in Constantinople, 1915-1916.

Talaat Pasha, "Posthumous Memoirs of Talaat Pasha," *Current History*, XV, no. 2 (November 1921), 298ff.

Taube, Baron M. de, *La politique russe d'avant-guerre et la fin de l'empire des tsars (1904-1917)*. Paris, Leroux, 1928. The memoirs of the former senator and member of the Council of the Empire of Russia. Valuable for pre-war and war policy on Turkey.

Tirpitz, Grand Admiral von, *My Memoirs*. 2 vols. New York, Dodd, Mead and Company, 1919.

Townshend, General C. V. F., *My Campaign*. New York, James McCann Company, 1920. Very important for the Mesopotamian campaign, and the armistice of Mudros.

Vopicka, C. J., *Secrets of the Balkans; Seven Years of a Diplomat's Life in the Storm Center of Europe*. Chicago, Rand, McNally, 1921. Memoirs of the former American minister in the Balkans.

## Works

Abbott, G. F., *Greece and the Allies, 1914-1922*. London, Methuen, 1922. Anti-Venizelos.

Ahmed Emin, *Turkey in the World War*. New Haven, Yale, 1930. Published for the Carnegie Endowment for International Peace in the Economic and Social History of the World War. A valuable contribution to the history of the period in Turkey.

Ahmed Hakki, *Les événements de Turquie depuis l'armistice du 31 octobre 1918*. Lausanne, Bovard-Giddey, 1919.

Ahmed Rustem Bey, *La crise proche-orientale et la question des détroits de Constantinople*. Geneva, Sonor, 1922. A penetrating analysis of the question by the former Turkish ambassador to the United States.

Armstrong, Hamilton Fish, *The New Balkans*. New York, Harpers, 1926.
*Where the East Begins*, New York, Harpers, 1929.

Aspinall-Oglander, Br. Gen. C. F., *Military Operations. Gallipoli*. Based on official documents. By direction of the historical section of the Committee of Imperial Defence. London, Heinemann, 1929. Vol I.

Auerbach, Bertrand, *L'Autriche et la Hongrie pendant la guerre depuis le début des hostilités jusqu'à la chute de la monarchie, août 1914-novembre 1918*. Paris, Felix Alcan, 1925.

'Balkanicus' (Stojan Protich), *The Aspirations of Bulgaria*. London, Simpkin, Marshall, Hamilton, Kent, 1915. Translated from the Serbian of Balkanicus. Good Serbian case on Balkan wars.

Blaisdell, Donald C., *European Financial Control in the Ottoman Empire*. New York, Columbia, 1929. Authoritative English account of the problem.

Bogichevich, Milosh, *Causes of the War*. London, Allen and Unwin, 1920.

Buxton, Noel and C. R., *The War and the Balkans*. London, Allen and Unwin, 1915. Documentary, very valuable.

Buxton, N. and Leese, C. L., *Balkan Problems and European Peace*. London, Allen and Unwin, 1919. Valuable for the Balkans and the war. Documentary.

Corbett, Sir Julian S., *Naval Operations*. 5 vols. London, Longmans, Green, 1920. History of the Great War based on official documents. By direction of the historical section of the Committee of Imperial Defence.

Cosmin, S., *L'Entente et la Grèce pendant la grande guerre, 1914-1917*. 3 vols. Paris, Société Mutuelle d'Édition, 1926. English translation: E. P. P. Cosmetatos, *The Tragedy of Greece*, New York, 1928.

Dascovici, Nicolas, *La question du Bosphore et des Dardanelles*. Geneva, Georg, 1915. The Rumanian thesis on the Straits.

De la Tramerye, P. E., *The World Struggle for Oil*. New York, Knopf, 1924. Translated from the French. Popular, but penetrating.

Delaisi, Francis, *Oil—Its Influence on Politics*. London, Labour Publishing Company, 1922. A penetrating study.

Davenport, E. H. and Cooke, S. R., *The Oil Trusts and Anglo-American Relations*. London, Macmillan, 1923. Important for discussions of oil and diplomacy.

Djuvara, T. L., *Ministre de Roumanie en Belgique et au Luxembourg, ancien chargé à Belgrade, Sofia, et Constantinople. Pref. de L. Renault. Cent projets de partage de la Turquie du XIIIe siècle jusqu'au traité de Bucarest* (1913). Paris. Alçan, n. d.

Djuvara, Mircea, *La guerre roumaine, 1916-1918*. Pref. E. Boutroux. Nancy, Paris, Strasbourg, Berger-Levrault, 1919. Rumanian peace conference propaganda.

Driault, Edouard, *La réprise de Constantinople et l'alliance franco-russe*. Paris, Alçan, 1915.

Driault, Edouard et Lheritier, Michel, *Histoire diplomatique de la Grèce de 1821 à nos jours. Tome V. La Grèce et la grande guerre de la revolution turque au traité de Lausanne (1908-1923)*. Paris, Les presses universitaires de France, 1926. Based on archival material from Athens, but should be used with care.

Earle, E. M., *Turkey, the Great Powers, and the Bagdad Railway*. New York, Macmillan, 1923. Good account of the growth and development of the Bagdad line. Written before publication of *Die Grosse Politik*.

Edib, Halidé, *Turkey Faces West*, New Haven, Yale, 1930. A Turkish view of recent changes and their origin. With an introduction by E. M. Earle.

Fay, Professor S. B., *The Origins of the World War*. New York, Macmillan, 1928. (Revised, 1930). 2 vols. Scholarly and thorough.

Fischer, Louis, *The Soviets in World Affairs*, London, Cape, 1930. 2 vols. A pro-Soviet, scholarly treatise on the foreign policies of Soviet Russia.

Frangulis, A. F., *ancien ministre de Grèce, ancien délégué de la Grèce à la S. d. N., La Grèce et la crise mondiale*. 2 vols. Paris, Alçan, 1926. Best documented source on Greece during the war and after.

Fuad, Ali, *La question des détroits*. Paris, Savouret, 1928. An important work from the Turkish viewpoint.

Gaillard, Gaston, *The Turks and Europe*. London, Murby, 1921. A popular, but valuable account because thoroughly documented. Pro-Turkish.

Gauvain, Auguste, *L'Europe au jour le jour*. Paris, Bossard, 1917. These are the comments which appeared in the *Journal des débats*. Good for war years.

Godovoi otchet za 1923 g. Narodnago kommissariata po inostrannym delam II s'ezdu sovetov SSSR. (Mezhdunarodnaia politika v 1923 g.). Moscow 1924. Deals with the Lausanne conference in pp. 7-32.

Gontaut-Biron, Comte R. de, *Comment la France s'est installée en Syrie, 1918-1919*. Paris, Plon, 1923.

Gontaut-Biron, Comte R. de, et Le Révérend, L., *D'Angora à Lausanne, les étapes d'une échéance*. Paris, Plon, 1924. A French point of view on the rise of the new Turkey and the decline of France in the east.

377

Goos, Roderich, *Das Wiener Kabinett und die Entstehung des Weltkrieges*. Vienna, Siedel, 1919. The outbreak of the war.

Helfferich, Karl Theodor, *Die Deutsche Türkenpolitik*. Berlin, Vossische Buchhandlung, 1921. Contains analysis of German policy.

Hesse, Fritz, *Die Mossulfrage*. Berlin, Vowinckel, 1925. Brief discussion.

Hosono, Gunji, *International Disarmament*. New York, Ph. D., Columbia University, 1926.

House, E. M., and Seymour, C. (ed.), *What Really Happened at Paris*. New York, Scribner's, 1921.

Iorga, N., *Points de vue sur l'histoire du commerce de l'orient, à l'époque moderne, Conférences données en Sorbonne*. Paris, Gamber, 1925.

Jaszi, Oscar, *The Dissolution of the Habsburg Monarchy*. Chicago, Chicago U., 1929. Excellent discussion of South Slav question.

Jung, Eugène, *La révolte arabe*. Paris, Colbert, 1925. 2 vols. Excellent.

Kuhne, Victor. *Les Bulgares peints par eux-mêmes. Documents et commentaires. Recueillis et rédigés par Victor Kuhne. Préface d'Auguste Gauvain*. Paris, Payot, 1917. Lausanne.

Kunke, Max, *Die Kapitulationen der Türkei, deren Aufhebung, und die neuen Deutsche-Türkischen Rechtsvertrage*. München, Schweitzer, 1918.

Larcher, Commandant M., *La guerre turque dans la guerre mondiale. Préface de M. le Maréchal Franchet d'Espérey*. Paris, Berger-Levrault, 1926. Based on the official Turkish documents. Best and most authoritative account of the war from the Turkish side.

*La grande guerre dans les Balkans. Direction de la guerre. Préface du Maréchal Franchet d'Espérey*. Paris, Payot, 1929.

Levermore, C. H., *League of Nations. Second, third, and fourth yearbooks*. New York, Brooklyn Eagle, 1922, 1923, 1924. Excellent materials for consecutive development of questions.

Lodor, J. de V., *The Truth about Mesopotamia, Palestine and Syria*. London, Allen & Unwin, 1923. A good treatment from the British point of view.

Logio, George C., *Bulgarian Problems and Politics*. London, Heinemann, 1919. Brief but important for Bulgaria's entrance into the war.

Lyautey, Pierre, *Le drame oriental et le rôle de la France. Préface de M. Maurice Barrès*. Paris, 1923.

Mach, Richard von, *Aus bewegter Balkanzeit 1879-1918*. Berlin, Mittler, 1928.

Mandelstam, André, *Le sort de l'empire ottoman*. Paris, Librairie Payot et Cie, 1917. Best account from Russian viewpoint.

*La Société des nations et les puissances devant le problème arménien. Édition spéciale de la revue générale de droit international public*. Paris, A. Pedone, 1926. The best single work on the Armenian question for recent years.

Marguerite, Victor (ed.), *Les alliés contre la Russie*. Paris, Delpeuch, 1927. Very important articles by Russian experts on Allied policy toward Russia during the war.

Mears, E. G., *Modern Turkey*. New York, Macmillan, 1924. Contains a valuable documentary appendix.

378

*Mezhdunarodnaia Politika RSFRS v 1922 g. Narodnago komissariata po inostrannym delam. Moscow,* 1923. Russian yearbook on foreign affairs.

Mileff, Milu, *La Bulgarie et les détroits. Essai d'histoire diplomatique.* Paris, Jouve, 1927.

Miliukov, Paul N., *Russlands Zusammenbruch.* Berlin, Obelisk-Verlag, 1925-26. A good analysis of Russian policy at Lausanne.

Milne, Admiral Sir A. Berkeley, *The Flight of the Goeben and Breslau.* London, Nash, 1921. The defence of the commander of the Mediterranean fleet. In reply to Sir Julian Corbett in "Naval Operations," official naval historian of the war.

Mohr, Anton, *The Oil War.* New York, Harcourt, 1926. Valuable discussion of the struggle between the United States and Great Britain for oil.

Paillarès, Michel, *Le Kémalisme devant les alliés.* Constantinople, Paris, Édition du "Bosphore", 1922. A good account of the rise of the new Turkey.

Peace Handbooks, Issued by the Historical Section of the Foreign Office. Vol. X, London, H. M. S. O., 1920. *Turkey in Asia* (general), no. 58; *Syria and Palestine,* no. 60; *Zionism,* no. 162; XI. *Turkey in Asia, Armenia and Kurdistan,* no. 62; *Mesopotamia,* no. 63. *The Eastern Question,* no. 15. Prepared for the British delegates to the Peace Conference. These volumes contain much valuable information.

Phillipson, C., and Buxton, N., *The Question of Bosphorus and Dardanelles.* London, Stevens and Haynes, 1917. A British account of the Straits Question.

Pokrovsky, M. N., *Pages d'histoire.* Paris, Éditions sociales internationales, 1929. The method of historical materialism applied to some concrete historical problems. The question of Constantinople, the Straits, the partition of Turkey are treated in pages 78 to 156.

Pribram, A. F., *Austrian Foreign Policy, 1908-1918.* London, Allen and Unwin, 1923.

Price, Clair, *The Rebirth of Turkey.* New York, Seltzer, 1923. Journalistic production of a journalist in the Near East. Useful.

Price, Crawfurd, *Light on the Balkan Darkness.* London, Simkin, Marshall, Hamilton, Kent & Co., 1915.

Puleston, William D., *The Dardanelles Expedition.* U. S. Naval Institute, 1926. An American naval officer's study.

*Report of the International Commission to Inquire into the Causes and Conduct of the Balkan Wars.* Washington, Carnegie, 1914.

Rizov, D. (Pref.), *The Bulgarians in their Historical, Ethnographical and Political Frontiers.* Berlin, K. Hoflithographie, hof-buch und steindruckerei Wilhelm Greve, 1917. Ethnographical section by Dr. A. Ishirkoff, historical section by Dr. B. Zlatarski. (Tr. for Peace Conference in English, French, and German).

Rohrbach, Paul, *Germany's Isolation; an Exposition of the Economic Causes of the War.* Chicago, McClure, 1915.

Savadjian, Léon, *La Bulgarie en Guerre.* Geneva, Georg, 1917. Represents the Bulgarian opposition to the Radoslavov policy.

Schiclin, Jean, *Angora . . . l'aube de la Turquie nouvelle, 1919-1922.* Paris, Berger-Levrault. A popular French account of the new Turkey.

Seton-Watson, R. W., *Roumania and the Great War*. London, Constable, 1915. An excellent analysis.

*Sarajevo*. London, Hutchinson and Company, 1925. A study of the Southern Slav question. Balkan league.

Sforza, Count Carlo, *Diplomatic Europe Since the Treaty of Versailles*. New Haven, Yale Press, 1928. An interesting chapter on Turkey after the war.

Schmitt, B. E., *The Coming of the War; 1914*. New York, Scribner's 1930. Most detailed and complete study of the immediate origins of the war.

Slivensky, Ivan, *La Bulgarie depuis le traité de Berlin et de la paix dans les Balkans*. Paris, Jouve, 1927.

Steinmetz, Edward Ritter von, *Rings um Sazonov*. Berlin, Verlag für Kultur Politik, 1928. Statements of Berchtold, Hoyos, Machion, Szapary, Jagow, Lucius, Wiesner.

Stieve, F., *Isvolsky and the World War*. New York, Knopf, 1926. Contains English translations of the Russian secret conferences of January-February 1914.

Stieve, Friedrich, und Montegelas, Graf Max, *Russland und der Weltkonflikt*. Berlin, Verlag für Kulture-politik, 1927.

Temperley, H. W. V., *A History of the Peace Conference*, vol. VI. London, Hodder and Staughton, 1924. Deals with the Near Eastern and Turkish problems before the Peace Conference. The British view.

Thompson, Charles T., *The Peace Conference Day by Day. A presidential pilgrimage leading to the discovery of Europe*. New York, Brentano, 1920. Valuable for the Peace Conference.

Toynbee, Arnold J., *The Western Question in Turkey and Greece*. London, Constable, 1922. A valuable work for understanding the Greco-Turkish war, 1919-1922.

*Survey of International Affairs, 1920-1923*. London, Oxford, 1925. An excellent treatment of Near Eastern affairs for the period.

*Survey of International Affairs, 1925*. Vol. I. London, Oxford (Royal Institute of International Affairs), 1927. The Islamic World.

*Survey of International Affairs, 1928*. London, Oxford, 1929.

Toynbee, A. J. and Kirkwood, *Turkey*. New York, Scribner's, 1926.

Tsacalkas, Antoine, *Le Dedécanèse. Étude de droit international*. Alexandria, Egypt (Cassimatis and Jonas), 1928.

Vellay, Charles, *Le problème méditerranéen*. Paris, Berger-Levrault, 1913. Foresees partition of Turkey in 1913.

Viaud, Julien (Pierre Loti), *La mort de notre chère France en orient*. Paris, Calmann-Levy, 1920. Copy of supposed secret Anglo-Turkish treaty, September 1919.

Woolf, Leonard Sidney, *The Future of Constantinople*. London, Unwin, 1917. Favors internationalization.

Young, George, *Nationalism and War in the East*. New York, Clarendon Press, 1915. A well balanced treatment of the Balkan wars and their results. By a diplo-matist.

Only the most important periodical articles have been cited:

Ancel, Jacques, "Les bases géographiques de la question des détroits," *Le monde slave*, 5th year, I, no. 2 (février 1928), 238-53.

Andréadès, André, "The Macedonian Question," *Nineteenth Century*, LXXVII (February 1915), 352-61.

"L'union balkanique: I. La Grèce," (with five maps), *Revue hebdomadaire*, III-IV, no. 11 (March 13, 1915), 128-62.

Barker, J. Ellis, "The Future of Constantinople," *Nineteenth Century*, LXXIX (March 1915), 483-522. Historical—Constantinople a source of weakness to Russia.

"Le Bolchevisme et l'Islam, II. Hors de Russie; les relations russo-turques depuis l'avenement du bolchevisme," *Revue du monde musulman*, LII (1922), 181-206. Valuable for understanding basis on which Turkish treaty with Soviet government was made.

Buell, Raymond L., "Oil Interests in the Fight for Mosul," *Current History*, XVII, no. 6 (March 1923), 931-39.

Danilov, General J., "Les tentatives de constitution d'un 'bloc balkanique' en 1914-1915," *Le monde slave*, II, no. 5 (May 1928), 202-29; II, no. 6 (June 1928), 352-378. An excellent analysis.

Deny, J., "Moustafa Kemal Pacha," I. Sa biographie d'après le nouvel annuaire officiel de Turquie. *Revue du monde musulman*, LXIII (1926), 146-67.

Diamandy, C. J., "La grande guerre vue du versant oriental," I. (1912-1914). *Revue des deux mondes*, XLIII (December 15, 1927), 781-804. II. "L'entrevue de Constantza," *ibid.*, XLIII (January 1, 1928), 129-43. III. "Ma mission en Russie," *ibid.*, IXL (15 February 1929). Formerly Rumanian minister in Petrograd in the war.

Florinsky, Michael T., "A Page of Diplomatic History. Russian Military Leaders and the Problem of Constantinople During the War," *Political Science Quarterly*, XLIV, no. 1 (March 1929), 108-15.

"Russia and Constantinople: Count Kokovtzov's Evidence," *Foreign Affairs* (N. Y.), VIII (October 1929), 138-39. A letter of Kokovtzov to the author, April 23, 1929.

Frantz, Gunther, "Die Meerengenfrage in der Vorkriegspolitik Russlands," *Deutsche Rundschau*, vol. 210 (February 1927), 142-60.

Hoschiller, Max, "La Russie sur le chemin de Byzance," *Revue de Paris*, XXII, no. 15 (August 1, 1915), 590-616; XXII, no. 16 (August 15, 1915), 766-96. A valuable study based on Russian sources.

Iorga, N., "The Attitude of Roumania," *Quarterly Review*, v. 223, no. 443 (April 1915), 439-50.

Jasich, Gregoire, "La Bulgarie et les alliés," *Revue hebdomadaire*, I-II, no. 8 (19 February 1916), 407-24; XI-XII, no. 50 (11 December 1915), 277-300. Radoslavov letter of July 6, 1913, reprints from articles, etc.

Jonquière, A. de la, "Angora et Moscou," l'Asie française, XXIV, no. 225 (September-October 1924), 333-340.

Kerner, Robert J., "Austro-Hungarian War Aims in the Winter of 1915-1916, as Revealed by Secret Documents," Journal of International Relations, X (1919-20), 444-70.

"Austrian Plans for a Balkan Settlement," New Europe, XVI, no. 206 (23 September 1920), 280-4.

"The Mission of Liman von Sanders. I. Its Origin," Slavonic Review, VI, no. 16 (June 1927), 12-27. II. "The Crisis," ibid., VI, no. 17 (December 1927), 344-63; (III), ibid., VI, no. 18 (March 1928), 543-60. (IV). "The Aftermath," ibid., VIII, no. 19 (June 1928), 90-112. This is the most thoroughgoing and soundest analysis of the origin, development, and results of the mission of Liman von Sanders.

"Russia, the Straits, and Constantinople, 1914-1915," Journal of Modern History, I, no. 3 (September 1929), 400-15. Excellent account based on the Russian documents.

"Russia and the Straits, 1915-1917," Slavonic Review, VIII, no. 24 (March 1930), 589-93. A fundamental analysis based on Russian sources.

Krajewski, Leon, "Le Nedjd et les Wahabites," Revue politique et parlementaire, CXXVII (April 1926), 105-22.

"La creation du royaume du Hedjaz," ibid., CXXVII (June 1926) 441-59.

"Le triomphe du wahabisme," ibid., CXXIX (November 1926), 260-79.

"La politique anglaise en Arabie (1915-1927)," Revue de Paris, no. 6 (March 15, 1928), 378-419.

Langer, William L., "Russia, the Straits Question and the Origins of the Balkan League, 1908-1912," Political Science Quarterly, XLIII, no. 3 (September 1928), 329-37.

"Levant," Asie française, XIV, 157 (April 1924). Italy and Austria in Asia Minor, p. 162. Adalia-Kos-Cilicia. Also San Giuliano statement on May 26, 1914, no. 158 (May 1914), 209-10.

London Times. The files of the London Times for the period 1922-26 have been particularly useful.

Ludwig, Emil, "Les croisières du 'Goeben' et du 'Breslau'," Les archives de la grande guerre, V, no. 13 (March 1920), 68-87; no. 14. (April 1920), 243-56.

Lybyer, Albert Howe, "Turkey under the Armistice," Journal of International Relations, XII, no. 4 (April 1922), 447-73.

Martel, René, "L'orient et la guerre après les archives diplomatiques russes," Le monde slave, III, no. 10 (October 1926), 118-155.

"Un discours de Moustafa Kemal," Asie française, XXI, no. 193 (June 1921), 250-52. Discourse of March 1, 1921.

New York Times. The New York Times has been very useful both on the Straits and on the Mosul question for the period 1922-1926.

Outis, "Problems of Diplomacy in the Near East," Fortnightly Review, CIII (April 1915), 583-91. Discounts value or necessity of Constantinople to Russia. Source of Weakness, but France and England ought to grant.

Pernot, Maurice, "Costantinople sous le controle interallié," *Revue des deux mondes*, VII (January 15, 1922), 276-314.

Pingaud, Albert, "L'entente et les balkaniques aux premiers mois de la guerre. (Août-décembre 1914)." *Revue des deux mondes*, LIV, (November 1, 1929), 48-83.

Politicus, "The Future of Turkey," *Fortnightly Review*, CIII (April 1915), 604-16. Russian opinion on Constantinople. Favors Russian possession; a source of weakness to Russia.

Poidébard, A., "Mossoul et la route des Indes," no. 8. Supplement to *Asie française*, XXIII, no. 211 (May 1923), 23-30. Economic, political and scientific documents.

A. Rustem Bey, "Les victoires d'Angora," *Revue de Genève*, V, no. 30. (December 1922), 771-86.

Seton-Watson, R. W., "Italy's Balkan Policy in 1914," *Slavonic Review*, V, no. 13 (June 1926), 48-65.

"Italian Intervention and the Secret Treaty of London," *ibid.*, V, no. 14 (December 1926), 271-297.

"William II's Balkan Policy," *Slavonic Review*, VII, no. 19. (June 1928), 1-29. Contains memorandum of Berchtold, Vienna, October 28, 1913, from Geheim XLV-26, and Report of Austro-Hungarian Chargé d'affaires at Munich, to Berchtold, December 16, 1913.

"Unprinted Documents. Austro German Plans for the Future of Serbia (1915)," *ibid.*, VII (March 1929), 705-24.

Shatzky, B. E., "La question de Constantinople et des détroits," *Revue d'histoire de la guerre mondiale*, IV, no. 4 (October 1926), 289-311; V, no. 1 (January 1927), 19-43. One of the best analyses of the question.

Sokolovich, P. P. de, "Le mirage bulgare et la guerre européenne," *Revue d'histoire diplomatique*, XXXI-XXXII (1917-18), 7-36, 309-70. The first article deals with the immediate pre-war situation in Bulgaria; the second has much of historical value.

Tardieu, André, "Mossoul et le pétrole," *L'Illustration*, v. 155, no. 1033 (June 19, 1920), 380-82.

V. F. M., "The Mosul Question," *Reference Service on International Affairs*, Bulletin nos. 9-10, American Library, Paris (April 1926).

Viner, Jacob, "International Finance and Balance of Power Diplomacy," *Southwestern Political and Social Science Quarterly*, IX, no. 4 (March 1929), 407-51.

Visscher, Fernand de, "Le régime nouveau des détroits," *Revue de droit international et législation comparée*, IV, no. 6 (1923), 537-72; V, nos. 1-2 (1924), 13-57.

# CHAPTER NOTES

# CHAPTER I

*Note 1.* For an indication of the various projects for the partition of Turkey, see T. G. Djuvara, *Cent projets de partage de la Turquie, 1281-1914* (Paris 1914).

*Note 2.* The various agreements between Russia, Germany and Austria on the Balkans and Turkey, from 1876-1897; may be found in A. F. Pribram, *The Secret Treaties of Austria-Hungary* (Cambridge 1921), 2 vols.

*Note 3.* For Isvolsky's memorandum on the Buchlau conversations, see Bertie to Grey, October 4, 1908, in *British Documents on the Origins of the War, 1898-1914*, V, *The Near East*, no. 292, pp. 383-84. For Grey's memorandum on the Straits, October 14, 1908, see *ibid.*, V, no. 377, p. 441 and E. A. Adamov, *Konstantinopel i Prolivy* (Moscow 1925-26), II, 5. See also Viscount Grey, *Twenty-Five Years* (N. Y., 1925), ch. 11. The Austrian angle of the Bosnian crisis may now be followed in *Osterreich-Ungarns Aussenpolitik von der bosnischen Krise 1908 bis zum Kriegsausbruch 1914. Diplomatische Aktenstücke des Osterreichisch-Ungarischen Ministeriums des Aussern.* (Vienna and Leipzig, 1930), I, 92-895; II, 2-285. (Hereafter cited as *Aussenpolitik*). The reader should also consult such works as S. B. Fay, *The Origins of the World War* (N. Y. 1928), I, 368-413, and B. E. Schmitt, *The Coming of the War: 1914* (N. Y. 1930), I, 13-18, 121-43.

*Note 4.* For Italo-Russian relations, see Siebert and Schreiner, *Entente Diplomacy and the World* (N. Y. 1921), chs. 11-12; R. Marchand, *Un livre noir*, II, 143 ff, 356-58.

*Note 5.* The treaty of Lausanne, October 18, 1912, may be found in Djuvara, *op. cit.*, 528-31. Tripolitania consisted of about 350,000 square miles; Cyrenaica of about 230,000 square miles. The combined population is now about 800,000.

*Note 6.* M. Hartwig, Russian minister at Belgrade, a pan-Slavist, was especially opposed, since his project called for a Balkan league against Turkey. See *Die Belgischen Dokumente zur Vorgeschichte des Weltkrieges*, IV, no. 134, 136, pp. 375-77, 379-81. Ahmed Emin, *Turkey in the World War* (New Haven 1930), 65-66.

*Note 7.* R. J. Kerner, "The Mission of Liman von Sanders," *Slavonic Review*, VI, no. 16 (June 1927), 1-16; William L. Langer, "Russia, the Straits Question and the Origins of the Balkan League, 1908-1912," *Political Science Quarterly*, XLIII, no. 3 (September 1928); Fay, I, 413-29; Schmitt, I, 82-87. See also Siebert, *op. cit.*, ch. 5, for Russian documents on the exchange.

*Note 8.* See *Die Grosse Politik* (hereafter G. P.), XXX, nos. 10987, 10988, 10989, 10991, 10993, 10998, for exchanges between Baron Marshall von Bieberstein, German ambassador to the Porte, and the Foreign Office (December 4-11, 1911).

*Note 9.* G. P., XXX (i), nos. 11000, 11002, 11003 (December 16-19, 1911).

*Note 10.* For discussion of these negotiations, see the following: I. E. Geshov, *The Balkan Alliance* (London 1915); Balkanicus (Stojan Protich), *The Balkan Aspirations of Bulgaria;* A. V. Nekliudov, *Diplomatic Reminiscences before and during the World War* (London 1920), chs. 5-6; Siebert, *op. cit.*, ch. 6; G. P., XXXIII, 1-47; *Ministère des affaires étrangères, Les affaires balkaniques*, I, 3ff; L. N., II, contains much valuable material. See also *Krasnyi Arkhiv*, VIII (1925), 3-31.

*Note 11.* The text of this treaty may be found in Djuvara, *op. cit.*, 560-61; Ministry of Foreign Affairs (Sofia), *Doklad na Parlamentarnata Ispitatelna Komisiya* (State Printing Office, 1918), I, 159-60. (Hereafter cited as D. P. I. K.) Geshov, *op. cit.*, 112-17; British *Peace Hand Book*, no. 15, pp. 115-26.

*Note 12.* Djuvara, *op. cit.*, 561-3; D. P. I. K., I, 161-63.

*Note 13.* *Les affaires balkaniques*, I, no. 57, p. 38; S. D. Sazonov, *Fateful Years* (N. Y. 1928), 52-55.

*Note 14.* Siebert, *op. cit.*, no. 396, p. 339. This is a note of Sazonov to Benckendorff, March 30, 1912. The Sofia government was in sad need of money at this time and negotiations were already in progress in Paris in April 1912.

*Note 15.* Geshov, 117-27; D. P. I. K., I, 163-65, 167-68.

*Note 16.* See Geshov, 128-33, and *Peace Hand Book*, no. 15, pp. 127-32, for text. A military convention was signed on September 22-October 5, 1912. Greece was to furnish 120,000 men, Bulgaria 300,000. The Greek fleet was to be used to secure naval supremacy over Turkey in the Aegean, interrupting communications between Asia Minor and European Turkey. See also J. D. Bourchier's articles in the London *Times*, June 4, 5, 11, 1913.

*Note 17.* Nekliudov to Sazonov, June 20, 1912; Siebert, *op. cit.*, no. 400, pp. 340-41. Also *ibid.*, nos. 406, 407, pp. 346-48.

*Note 18.* Hartwig to Sazonov, May 11, 1912; Siebert, no. 401, p. 341. Also *ibid.*, nos. 402, 403, pp. 341-42.

*Note 19.* For the various notes exchanged in this crisis, see Geshov, 52-60. See also A. F. Pribram, *Austrian Foreign Policy, 1908-1918*, pp. 36ff.

*Note 20.* Grey, *Twenty-Five Years*, I, ch. 14; R. Poincaré, *The Memoirs of Raymond Poincaré, 1913-1914* (London 1928), ch. 5.

*Note 21.* Sazonov to Benckendorff, October 31, 1912; Siebert, no. 443, pp. 382-83. This note was sent to Sofia also.

*Note 22.* Same to same, November 2, 1912; *ibid.*, no. 447, pp. 383-84.

*Note 23.* Benckendorff to Sazonov, November 2, 1912; *ibid.*, no. 448, pp. 384-85.

*Note 24.* Sazonov to Isvolsky, November 4, 1912; *ibid.*, no. 449, pp. 385-86.

*Note 25.* Same to same, November 6, 1912; *ibid.*, no. 452, p. 387.

*Note 26.* Benckendorff to Sazonov, November 7, 1912; *ibid.*, no. 454, pp. 388-89.

*Note 27.* Isvolsky to Sazonov, November 26, 1912; *ibid.*, no. 489, p. 414.

*Note 28.* Sazonov to Isvolsky, November 28, 1912; *ibid.*, no. 491, pp. 415-17.

*Note 29.* See George Young (A diplomatist), *Nationalism and War in the East* (N. Y. 1915), 400-01, and D. P. I. K., I, 350-51, for text. Note Sazonov's statement on Bulgarian request for arbitration; L. N., II, 92-93.

*Note 30.* See *Peace Hand Book* no. 15, *Eastern Question*, 40-41; Crawford Price, *Light on the Balkan Darkness*, 34ff. The delimitation of the Albanian frontiers and the formation of the régime in that country were reserved to the European Powers.

*Note 31.* Sazonov to Benckendorff, May 1, 1913; Siebert, no. 493, pp. 418-21. The question had been raised in connection with the financial commission in Paris.

*Note 32.* Giers to Sazonov, May 10, 1913; *ibid.*, no. 494, p. 421.

*Note 33.* The treaty was for a ten-year period. A military convention was signed the same day. For text, see the *Greek White Book, Diplomatic Documents, 1913-1917* (American Hellenic Society, no. 5), 20-34. (Hereafter G. W. B.)

*Note 34.* See especially Berchtold to Tarnowsky, December 19, 1912; Tarnowsky to Berchtold, December 20, 1912; Mensdorff to Berchtold, December 27, 1912; *Aussenpolitik*, V, nos. 4983, 4999, 5080, pp. 175-6, 187-90, 249-50.

About the same time Germany began to fear for the future of Turkey, hoped for the localizing of any trouble which might develop, and wished to avoid any "danger in Asia-Minor (Armenia)". Pallavicini reported a conversation with Wangenheim on January 18, 1913, in which the latter expressed his fears for Turkey, and stated that "in the future this land would find a mighty protection in Germany." See Berchtold's memoranda of conversations with the German and Italian ambassadors, January 17, 1913; Pallavicini to Berchtold, January 18, 1913; *ibid.*, V, nos. 5415, 5434, 5585, pp. 469-70, 480, 575-76.

*Note 35.* Berchtold to Tarnowsky, December 19, 1912; *ibid.*, V, no. 4983, pp. 175-76.

*Note 36.* See Tarnowsky to Berchtold, March 4, 1913; *ibid.*, V, no. 6021, p. 873. Also same to same, February 21, 1913; *ibid.*, V, no. 5895, p. 788-93.

*Note 37.* Same to same, March 10, 1913; *ibid.*, V, no, 6094, p. 918. Already the Germans were showing considerable distrust of the Bulgarian government. See Szögyény to Berchtold, March 8, 1913; Berchtold to Jagow, March 13, 1913; Szögyény to Berchtold, March 13, 1913; *ibid.*, V, nos. 6065, 6126, 6127, pp. 899-901, 937-42.

*Note 38.* Tarnowsky to Berchtold, March 18, 1913; *ibid.*, V, no. 6211, pp. 1002-3. They explained that "orienting of Bulgarian policy in the sense of a connection to Austria-Hungary would be impossible", if Austria supported Rumania. See also same to same, March 26, 1913; *ibid.*, no. 6318, pp. 1070-1. Already Bulgaria had met Austrian wishes in the matter of Salonica, when she promised that Salonica (if in Bulgarian hands) would be made a free port, and that Austria should be given an influence in the administration and exploitation of the port. Tarnowsky to Berchtold, March 14, 1913; *ibid.*, V, no. 6156, pp. 970-1.

*Note 39.* Tarnowsky to Berchtold, May 29, 1913; *ibid.*, VI, nos. 7201-02, pp. 554-57. On May 2, an Austrian ministerial council had reached certain definite conclusions with reference to the Balkan situation. These were: (1) Creation of an independent Albania; (2) keeping Serbia from the Adriatic; (3) keeping the Serbian elements in their natural frontiers; (4) compensations for Rumania. On the Adriatic, it was held that Scutari was the key of the program, because without it Albania would be an impossibility. San Giovanni di Medua was the natural port for Montenegro. See Protocol of the meeting of May 2, 1913, council for general affairs; *ibid.*, VI, no. 6870, pp. 324-36.

*Note 40.* Berchtold to Tarnowsky, May 30, 1913; Tarnowsky to Berchtold, May 30, 1913; *ibid.*, VI, nos. 7214, 7215, pp. 561-3.

*Note 41.* On June 1, 1913, Tarnowsky reported a conversation with M. Ghika, the Rumanian minister at Sofia, who told him: "We have decided to be paid and I shall leave no doubt to M. Geshov that our friendship is to be purchased and that we have only to choose. If M. Geshov hesitates we shall ask him not to reflect too long and will make him understand that the longer the bargaining lasts the dearer it will be." See Same to same, June 1, 1913; *ibid.*, VI, no. 7248, p. 579. See also Szápáry to Tarnowsky, June 3, 1913; *ibid.*, V, no. 7265, pp. 589-90.

*Note 42.* Tarnowsky to Berchtold, June 18, 1913; Berchtold to Tarnowsky, June 20, 1913; *ibid.*, V, nos. 7408, 7433, pp. 670-1, 688-89. In a telegram of June 13

Szögyény reported that Jagow had told him a "warlike outbreak between Bulgaria and Serbia, which would hasten the breakup of the Balkan alliance, from the stand, point of the *Dreibund,* would be very desirable." Szögyény to Berchtold, June 13, 1913; *ibid.,* V, no. 7355, pp. 640-1.

*Note 43.* Berchtold to Tarnowsky, June 24, 1913, *ibid.,* no. 7486, pp. 721-2. See also Schmitt, I, 136-137, note. See especially Balkanicus, 1-76; Geshov, 99ff; R. W. Seton-Watson, *Sarajevo* (London 1925), ch. 2; Bogichevich, *Causes of the War,* 49ff. P. P. Sokolovich, "Le mirage bulgare et la guerre européenne." *Revue d'histoire diplomatique,* XXX-XXXI, no. 1. (1917-1918), 27-28, contains excerpts of Tisza's speech of June 13, 1913, in which he urged the right of each state to settle disputes as it saw fit. Berchtold authorized Tarnowsky to make his declaration in writing to the Bulgarian government on June 28. See Berchtold to Tarnowsky, June 28, 1913; *ibid.,* VI, 761.

*Note 44.* Geshov, 99-100; Young, *War and Nationalism in the Near East,* 261-71; S. Panaretoff, *Near Eastern Affairs and Conditions* (New Haven 1922), 184-92; Sokolovich, *loc.-cit.,* 7-20. There was much severe fighting, claims and counter claims of atrocities committed were made. See the Carnegie Endowment for International Peace, *Report of the International Commission to Inquire into the Causes and Conduct of the Balkan Wars* (Washington, 1914), 49-69; W. H. C. Price, *The Balkan Cockpit,* 231-74.

*Note 45.* See *Les affaires balkaniques,* II, nos. 413, 416, 426, pp. 263ff. Also Note verbale of the Turkish Embassy, July 21, 1913; *Aussenpolitik,* VI, no. 7894, pp. 975-6.

*Note 46.* *Ministerul Afacerilor Straine, Documents diplomatiques. Les événements de la péninsule balkanique. L'action de la Roumainie. 20 septembre 1912—1 août 1913.* (Bucharest, Imprimeria Statului, 1913). Hereafter cited as R. D. Report by T. Maiorescu, Sinaia, 3 October, 1912; R. D., no. 1, p. 1.

*Note 47.* Misu (London) to M. F. A., January 2, 1913; R. D., no. 23, pp. 18-19. See also *Les affaires balkaniques,* II, no. 22.

*Note 48.* The Rumanian attitude on the dispute may be followed in R. D., nos. 61-90, pp. 43-66. See also Berchtold to Tarnowsky, April 3, 1913; Tarnowsky to Berchtold, April 4, 1913; Tarnowsky to Berchtold, April 12, 13, 1913; *Aussenpolitik,* VI, nos. 6441, 6455, 6599, 6607, pp. 27-8, 34-5, 136, 141. Berchtold (April 3) advised Bulgaria to cede something in Silistria to Rumania in order to guarantee her neutrality "in case of a future complication in the Balkans." Geshov (April 12), after hearing of a possible decision at St. Petersburg, giving Silistria to Rumania, said: "If we do not have Salonica and if they do not give us satisfaction on the subject of our western frontier, the cession of Silistria would become a calamity for the government."

*Note 49.* Protocol of St. Petersburg, May 9, 1913; R. D., no. 131, pp. 99-100.

*Note 50.* Rumania's insistence on her claims may be followed in R. D., nos. 155-63, June 23-June 30, 1913, when the commission failed to agree.

*Note 51.* Maiorescu to King Carol, May 2, 28, June 22, 1913; Geshov 83-86. See also Tarnowsky to Berchtold, June 29, 30, July 2, 1913; *Aussenpolitik,* VI, nos. 7553, 7564, 7592, pp. 769-70, 775-6, 789.

*Note 52.* See R. D., nos. 166, 172, 177, pp. 141 ff. The circular telegram from the minister of foreign affairs, July 3, 1913; R. D., no. 181, p. 149.

*Note 53.* Minister of foreign affairs to Ghika, July 10, 1913; R. D., no. 193, p. 154; Ghika to Danev, July 13 (June 27), 1913; D. P. I. K., I, 796-97.

*Note 54.* Maiorescu to legations abroad, July 16, 1913; R. D., no. 206, pp. 160-61.

*Note 55.* Telegram from M. F. A. of Bulgaria to Rumanian government, through the Italian legation at Bucharest, July 19, 1913; R. D., no. 222, p. 169.

*Note 56.* M. F. A. of Bulgaria to Rumanian government, July 20, 1913; R. D., no. 228, pp. 171-72.

*Note 57.* See especially Berchtold to Tarnowsky, July 15, 1913; Tarnowsky to Berchtold, July 20, 1913; *Aussenpolitik*, VI, nos, 7780, 7878, 7881, pp. 902-3, 966-68. On July 26, 1913, Francis Joseph expressed his satisfaction to Tsar Ferdinand that he was desirous of closing the war, and stated: "My government cannot admit that the future of Bulgaria depends solely on the fate of arms and it does not cease to exercise in this sense its influence with the belligerents." Telegram to Sofia, July 26, 1913; *ibid.*, no. 8057, p. 1057.

*Note 58.* The protocols of the conference of Bucharest may be found in *Ministère des affaires étrangères. Le traité de paix de Bucarest du 28 juillet* (10 août) *1913. Précédé des protocoles de la conférence.* (Bucarest, Imprimerie de l'État, 1913). For text see *ibid.*, 67-72; Young, 402-05; *Peace Hand Book*, no. 15, pp. 134-38.

*Note 59.* Notice of the Russian ministry of foreign affairs; August 2, 1913; *Aussenpolitik*, VII, pp. 45-6.

*Note 60.* Note especially G. P., XXXVI, nos. 13696, 13698, 13699; and *Les affaires balkaniques*, II, nos. 442, 452, 453, 457, 467.

*Note 61.* Ministère des affaires étrangères, *Le traité de paix de Bucarest*, 48. Statement of Maiorescu, August 8, before the conference.

*Note 62.* *Ibid.*, 60. See also Tarnowsky to Berchtold, August 9, 1913; *Aussenpolitik*, VII, no. 8315, pp. 98-99.

*Note 63.* Mavrocordato to M. F. A., August 18, 1913; R. D., no. 272, p. 193. Zimmermann to von Treutler, August 3, 1913; G. P., XXXV, no. 13707, pp. 334-35.

*Note 64.* Nano to M. F. A., August 14, 1913; R. D., no. 282, p. 199. For discussion concerning revision, see G. P., XXXV, nos. 13744-13753, pp. 368-83. On August 15 the Russian government informed Vienna that "Russia would have wished another peace which would have guaranteed more the economic and political interests of Bulgaria. Among the points which answer the least to this idea, the attribution of Cavalla to Greece is, in the opinion of the imperial government, the most important point, that for which the imperial minister at Bucharest was charged to reserve for Russia the liberty of revision conjointly with the other Powers." *Aussenpolitik*, VII, no. 8406, pp. 153-54. Count Tisza considered the treaty of Bucharest a great danger for Austria-Hungary and worked for its revision. See *ibid.*, VII, no. 8343, pp. 112-114.

Greece and Turkey reached an agreement on November 14, 1913, by the terms of which Greece was awarded the islands in dispute, except Tenedos and Imbros, which guarded the Dardanelles. But that the question was not settled, and that it would again flare up to disturb Greco-Turkish relations was beyond doubt. On December 29, 1913, the Turks again protested to the Powers against their policy on the islands, and announced their intention to use every means "to retake from the Greeks those islands indispensable to the Ottoman Empire for the security of its Asiatic possessions." The Porte notified the Powers of its "unbreakable decision . . . to remain in possession of the islands neighboring the shores of the Empire." See *Aussenpolitik*, VII, no. 9137, p. 689. For further discussion see *ibid.*, VII, nos. 8229, 8291, 8428, 8572. For text of the agreement of November 14, 1913, see Young, 406-26.

*Note* 65.   See *Peace Hand Book*, *No.* 15, *Eastern Question*, 41-42, for text. The fact that Bulgaria renounced all claims to Thasos shows the extent of her ambitions in the Aegean.

*Note* 66.   Young, 298-99. Turkey in Europe before the wars consisted of 169,300 square kilometers. It lost 143,000 square kilometers, leaving only 26,300 in European Turkey. In population, Greece advanced from 2,750,000 to 4,750,000; Serbia from 3,000,000 to 4,175,000; Montenegro from 280,000 to 400,000; Bulgaria from 4,500,000 to 4,750,000; Rumania from 7,250,000 to 7,600,000. Turkey in Europe, now with an area of only 10,882 square miles, had a population in Europe of about 2,000,000, most of whom were in Constantinople and its environs. See also *Statesman's Year-Book* (1919), 1306-7. Taken as a whole the Ottoman Empire before the Balkan wars had a total of more than 1,000,000 square miles, and a population of between 35-39,000,000 people.

The reorganization in the Balkan peninsula brought about the creation of an independent Albania, on the Adriatic coast, under an international commission of control. Prince William of Wied, however, finally was chosen as ruler of the country, and began his short and troublesome reign in March 1914. The writer has made no attempt to detail the history of these developments, which can be traced in Miss Edith P. Stickney's *Southern Albania or Northern Epirus in European International Affairs, 1912-1923* (Stanford University Press, 1926), and in C. A. Chekrezi, *Albania Past and Present* (N. Y., 1919).

*Note* 67.   Bogichevich, *Causes of the War*, 53; Seton-Watson, *Sarajevo*, 56ff. This did not necessarily mean that Pashich was ready to plot a world war in order to achieve a greater Serbia.

*Note* 68.   See Von Tschirschky to F. O., June 4, 1913; G. P., XXXV, no. 13361, p. 8.

*Note* 69.   See Same to same, July 3, 1913; Zimmermann to Tchirschky, July 6, 1913; G. P., XXXV, 122-24, 129-30. For comment, see Fay, I, 447-55; Schmitt, I, 135-38. See also *Collected Diplomatic Documents Relating to the Outbreak of the European War* (London 1915), Speech of M. Giolitti to Italian Chamber, December 5, 1914, pp. 400-01; Giovanni Giolitti, *Memoirs of My Life* (London 1923), 372-73; Sir Rennell Rodd, *Social and Diplomatic Memories, 1902-1919*, III, 175-76; Balkanicus, 135; Seton-Watson, 50. Count Max Montegelas, *Case for the Central Powers*, 81-84, states the German case. Ionescu states that in May 1913, Vienna notified him in Bucharest that "Austria will defend Bulgaria by force of arms." See Také Ionescu, *Some Personal Impressions* (N. Y. 1920), 120-21.

*Note* 70.   Von Tschirschky to Bethmann-Hollweg, August 5, 1913; G. P., XXXV, no. 13724, pp. 346-49. See also *Geheim XLIV-15* (August 21-28, 1913) for memoranda on guarantees from Serbia for future good conduct toward Austria-Hungary, and outlining projects for buying off the opposition parties in Serbia with Austrian gold, during the late summer of 1913. Contained in part in *Aussenpolitik*, VII, no. 8437, pp. 171-3.

*Note* 71.   Balkanicus, 143, and ch. 2, for details. See also G. C. Logio, *Bulgarian Problems and Politics* (London 1919), 96-98. Radoslavov came into power on July 27, 1913.

*Note* 72.   Grey, *Twenty-Five Years*, I, 254. See also Sir George Buchanan, *My Mission to Russia and Other Diplomatic Memories*, (Boston 1922), I, 137-38; Maurice Paléologue, *An Ambassador's Memoirs* (London 1923), II, 22-23. Paléologue quotes

Tsar Ferdinand as saying, "Ma vengeance sera terrible." Note also Nekliudov, *Diplomatic Reminiscences*, 203-219. Professor Miliukov's analysis may be found in the *Report* of the International Commission to Inquire into the causes and conduct of the Balkan wars (Carnegie Endowment, Washington, 1914), 157-58. George Young, *op. cit.*, 340 ff., has a balanced estimate of the results of the wars.

## CHAPTER II

*Note 1.* Talaat Pasha, "Posthumous Memoirs of Talaat Pasha," *Current History*, XV, no. 2 (November 1921), p. 288; Djemal Pasha, *Memoirs of a Turkish Statesman*, 1913-1919 (N. Y. 1922), 65-66.

*Note 2.* The most exhaustive treatment of the mission of Liman von Sanders is Professor R. J. Kerner's "The Mission of Liman von Sanders," *Slavonic Review*, VI (June, December, 1927; March, 1928); 12-27, 244-63, 543-69; VII (June, 1928), 90-112. The Turks already had M. Laurent as a financial advisor, Count Léon Ostrorog as a judicial advisor, and General Baumann—all Frenchmen—to assist in training the gendarmerie. Admiral Limpus was in charge of the navy, while Sir Richard Crawford was in the customs service and Sir William Willcocks was engaged in irrigation projects in Mesopotamia. General von der Goltz Pasha had been in the Turkish military service since the 1880's.

*Note 3.* Baron von Wangenheim to Bethmann-Hollweg, April 26, 1914; G. P., XXXVIII, no. 15439, pp. 196-200.

*Note 4.* Wangenheim to Bethman-Hollweg, May 21, 1913; G. P., XXXVIII, no. 15312, pp. 41-48. See also Pallavicini to Berchtold, January 28, May 13, 1913; *Aussenpolitik* V, no. 5574, p. 560-4, and VI, no. 7009, p. 427-8.

*Note 5.* Kerner, "The Mission of Liman von Sanders," *Slavonic Review*, VI (June 1927), 7; Fay, I, 499 ff; Schmitt, I, 92-3.

*Note 6.* Jagow to the kaiser, September 20, 1913; G. P., XXXVIII, no. 15444, pp. 204-05. For the contract see Carl Mühlmann, *Deutschland und die Turkei*, 1913-1914 (Berlin 1929), 88-92.

*Note 7.* Sazonov's report to the tsar, October 24, 1913; L. N., II, 362-63. See also Berchtold's memorandum of a visit of the German chargé, October 24, 1913; *Aussenpolitik*, VII, no. 8906, pp. 491-2.

*Note 8.* For a record of these conversations see L. N., II, 385-417, Kokovtsev's report to the tsar, December 2, 1913; Bethmann's memorandum, November 18, 1913; G. P., XXXVIII, no. 15450, pp. 212-17.

*Note 9.* Sazonov to the Russian chargé at London, November 25, 1913; E. D., no. 782, p. 678.

*Note 10.* Isvolsky to Sazonov, November 26, 1913; *ibid.*, no. 784, pp. 678-79.

*Note 11.* Pichon to Bompard, December 3, 1913; *Les affaires balkaniques*, III, no. 157, p. 96. See also Russian chargé at London to Sazonov, December 2, 1913; E. D., nos. 786, 787, pp. 680-81.

*Note 12.* Sazonov to chargé at London, December 7, 1913; E. D., no. 788, p. 681. See also Pallavicini to Berchtold, December 8, 1913, and Pomiankowski to Conrad (enclosure); *Aussenpolitik*, VII, no. 9069, pp. 632-7.

*Note 13.* Benckendorff to Sazonov, December 12, 1913; E. D., no. 800, p. 688. Wangenheim to German F. O., December 5-6, 1913; G. P., XXXVIII, no. 15468, pp. 237-38, for terms of the Limpus contract in the Turkish navy.

*Note 14.* Benckendorff to Sazonov, December 9, 1913; E. D., no. 792. pp. 683-84. See also Benckendorff to Sazonov, December 9, 1913; E. D., nos. 789, 790, pp. 682-83.

*Note 15.* Sazonov to Benckendroff, December 10, 1913; *ibid.*, no. 793, pp. 684-5. See also Kerner, *loc. cit.*, VI, 543 ff.

*Note 16.* Sazonov to Benckendorff, December 11, 1913; Benckendorff to Sazonov, December 12, 1913; Benno von Siebert, *Graf Benckendorffs diplomatischer Schriftwechsel* (Berlin 1928), III, nos. 990, 994, 995, pp. 216, 219, 220-21. Hereafter cited as B. D. S. Giers to Sazonov, December 10, 1913; Sazonov to Benckendorff, December 11, 1913; E. D., nos. 796, 797, pp. 686-87.

*Note 17.* Sazonov to Benckendorff, December 12, 1913; *ibid.*, nos. 798, 799, pp. 687-88.

*Note 18.* Benckendorff to Sazonov, December 14, 1913; Giers to Sazonov, December 15, 1913; *ibid.*, nos. 803, 805, pp. 689, 690. Also Giers to Sazonov, December 13, 1913; B. D. S., III, no. 998, p. 222.

*Note 19.* Giers to Sazonov, December 16, 1913; E. D., no. 807, p. 691.

*Note 20.* See Isvolsky to Sazonov, December 18, 1913; *ibid.*, no. 812, p. 693. Grey also told Lichnowsky that the Anglo-Russian understanding was based on the idea that "Constantinople should remain Turkish and that no other Power should be given a predominant influence there." See Lichnowsky to the F. O., December 15, 1913; Prince Lichnowsky, *Heading for the Abyss* (London 1928), 325-26.

*Note 21.* Liman von Sanders, *Five Years in Turkey* (Annapolis 1927), 3. See also Pallavicini to Berchtold, December 17, 1913; *Aussenpolitik*, VII, no. 9100, pp. 661-3.

*Note 22.* Kerner, *loc. cit.*, VI, 556 ff. See also Mühlmann, 10-25.

*Note 23.* Russian chargé at London to Sazonov, December 29, 31, 1913; E. D., nos. 818, 822, 823, pp. 696, 699.

*Note 24.* Isvolsky to Sazonov, December 30, 1913; *ibid.*, no. 819, pp. 697-98; L. N., II, 218-19; *Materially po istorii franko-ruskikh otnoshenii za 1910-1914* (Moscow 1922), 674-75.

*Note 25.* Sazonov's memorandum to the tsar, December 6, 1913; L. N., II, 363-72. For an analysis of the background of this memorandum see Kerner, *loc. cit.*, VII, 90 ff. See also the views of Fay (I, 524-29) and Schmitt (I, 87-88).

*Note 26.* Sazonov's memorandum to the tsar, December 6, 1913; L. N., II, 363-72.

*Note 27.* *Ibid.*, 363, 372. See also Kerner, *loc. cit.*

*Note 28.* For text of the minutes of this conference see F. Stieve, *Isvolsky and the War* (London 1926), 219-29; M. N. Pokrovsky, *Drei Konferenzen* (Berlin 1920), 32 ff; for a German view of the mission see M. Montegelas, *Case for the Central Powers*, 92-6; Gunther Frantz, "Die Meerengenfrage in der vorkriegs Politik Russlands," *Deutsche Rundschau*, v. 210 (February 1927), 142-60; Bethmann-Hollweg, *Reflections on the War*, 105-116. See also Kerner, *loc. cit.*, VII, 556 ff; Fay, I, 526-41; G. Michon, *L'alliance franco-russe*, 229-31.

*Note 29.* Stieve, 229. Grey used a "moderating" influence on St. Petersburg. Lichnowsky saw him on January 7, and was told that "Constantinople was after all Russia's most sensitive spot and he did not think that people in St. Petersburg would be pacified unless we could find some way out." Grey feared that "Russia's attitude might place him in an awkward position and that under the circumstances

he would not venture to leave the Russians in the lurch in this matter." Lichnowsky to Bethmann-Hollweg, January 7, 1914; Lichnowsky, 327-28.

*Note 30.* *German White Book, concerning the Responsibility of the Authors of the War* (Carnegie, N. Y., 1924), 131. Pourtales to Jagow, January 15, 1914. Sazonov did not receive confirmation at this time however, (Hereafter cited as G. W. B.)

*Note 31.* Sverbeiev to Sazonov, January 16, 1914; E. D., no. 836, pp. 706-08. See also Otto Czernin to Berchtold, January 17, 1914; Pomiankowski to Conrad, January 19, 1914; *Aussenpolitik*, VII, nos. 9202, 9211, pp. 738-9, 745-47.

*Note 32.* Evidently Professor Fay considers the problem as settled at this time. He seems to make little connection between the military mission and the secret conferences of January and February 1914, which grew directly out of the mission. See Fay, I, 522-24. See also R. J. Kerner, *loc. cit.*, VII, 90-106, and Schmitt, I, 96-99.

*Note 33.* For text of the minutes of the conference of February 21, see Stieve, 230-46; Pokrovsky, 46ff; Laloy, *Documents secrets*, 74-100; G. W. B., 136-43.

*Note 34.* Vice-Director of the chancellery of the ministry of foreign affairs, Basili, had drawn up a memorandum for the conference, urging preparations for operations against the Straits. Russian sovereignty over the Straits was the *desideratum*. "The operations for the occupation of the Straits must be based solely upon our own forces, and must not assume the presence of assistance from without." It was probable "that we have before us the prospect of solving the question of the Straits during a European war." The fleets of France and England could check that of Germany, but Greece could not be depended on as she had dreams of Constantinople which "will probably henceforth form an obstacle to a further *rapprochement* between Greece and ourselves." For text of Basili memorandum, see G. W. B., 133-36.

*Note 35.* See Buchanan, I, 137-38. Also Kerner, *loc. cit.*, VII, 106-08; Schmitt, I, 99.

*Note 36.* Isvolsky to Sazonov, April 9, 1914; E. D., no. 843, pp. 715-16. See Paléologue to Doumergue, February 15, 1914; Cambon to Doumergue, February 16, 1914; same to same, February 19, 1914; Doumergue to Paléologue, February 28, 1914; *Les affaires balkaniques*, III, nos. 191, 194, 197, 202, pp. 113-14, 115, 117, 120.

*Note 37.* Benckendorff to Sazonov, May 12, 1914; same to same, May 16, 1914, and May 18, 1914; E. D., nos. 844-46, pp. 716-21. See also Sazonov, 127-32. See also Kerner, *loc. cit.*

*Note 38.* See the interesting estimate of George Young (a diplomatist), *op. cit.*, 365-66. For German views see Stieve and Montegelas, *Russland und der Weltkonflikt* (Berlin 1927), 87 ff; Ritter von Steinitz, *Rings um Sazonov* (Berlin 1928), 143-46. For conservative Russian views of the mission, see the statements of Durnovo, February 1914, and Markov, May 1914, reprinted in F. A. Golder, *Documents of Russian History* (N. Y. 1928), 3ff, 24-28. Baron Taube, a member of the council of state, criticizes Sazonov's policy rather severely during this period, but carefully notes that Sazonov neither "plotted" a war for the Straits, nor was aggressive, but stood for the existing *status quo* in Turkey. See Baron Taube, *La politique russe d'avant-guerre et fin de l'empire des tsars* (1904-1917) (Paris 1928), 314-23.

In a letter to M. T. Florinsky, April 23, 1929, Count Kokovtsev states that there was no difference between himself and Sazonov at this time. "During the whole of our collaboration in the government, at first under the presidency of Stolypin and then later when I succeeded him, until the very day of my resignation, Sazonov was never in favor of an aggressive policy against Turkey. His fundamental view, that

a weak Turkey is advantageous to Russia, and that Russia should not hasten her collapse, is clearly stated in his report and recurs over and over again in his declarations . . . .

"He was perfectly aware of our military unpreparedness and on this particular question we were in complete agreement . . .. Sazonov was not at that time, in January, 1914, under the influence of our Ministry of War and of the Admiralty . . ..

"My own part consisted not so much in trying to prove that the measures suggested by the minister of foreign affairs were inacceptable in principle and at the same time impracticable, as in arguing the two following propositions: (1) the complete improbability that the point of view of the report would be accepted by France and especially by England; and (2) the close connection of this problem with the general problem of European peace and the danger of even raising it." See M. T. Florinsky, "Russia and Constantinople: Count Kokovtzov's Evidence," *Foreign Affairs* (N. Y.), VIII (October 1929), 138-139.

*Note 39.* Mühlmann, *op. cit.*, 7.

*Note 40.* See Donald C. Blaisdell, *European Financial Control in the Ottoman Empire* (N. Y. 1929), chs. 1-4; E. G. Mears, *Modern Turkey* (N. Y. 1924), 440; Sir Vincent Caillard, "Turkey—Finance," *Encyclopedia Britannica*, 11th ed., XXXII, 430-42.

*Note 41.* One member each for syndicates in Germany, Austria-Hungary, England, France, Italy, Turkey and the Ottoman Bank. See Blaisdell, ch. 5 and *passim*.

*Note 42.* The history of the Bagdad railway may be traced in full in E. M. Earle, *Turkey, the Great Powers and the Bagdad Railway* (N. Y. 1923), which, however, was written before the publication of *Die Grosse Politik*. See Earle, 58-84; Blaisdell, 128; Caillard, *loc. cit.* Also G. B. Ravndal, *Turkey—A Commercial and Industrial Handbook*. Trade Promotion Series, no. 28. Department of Commerce. (Washington 1926). Discussion of railways, pp. 46-57.

*Note 43.* Earle, 77-80; Ravndal, 52-3.

*Note 44.* The Bagdad concession stipulated, among other things, that Turkey was to (1) issue in imperial Ottoman bonds, 275,000 francs for each kilometer of the line; (2) grant a gross receipt guarantee of 4500 francs for each kilometer open to traffic; (3) grant land for the right of way, with wood and timber free, and give the right of operation of mines twenty kilometers on each side; (4) give large tax exemptions, etc.; (5) grant the right of construction at Bagdad, Basra and a terminus on the Persian gulf all the necessary facilities, with rights of navigation on the Tigris, Euphrates and the Shatt-el-Arab. The Ottoman public debt administration was allowed to collect the revenues pledged for construction, and to supervise payments. See Earle, *loc. cit.*, and Blaisdell, 127-29.

*Note 45.* See Caillard, *loc. cit.*; Mears, 367; *Statesman's Year Book* (1919), 1317-18. The *Statesman's* Year Book gives the figures for 1914 as follows: Turkish government—1,116 miles, or 31 per cent; German nationals—1,327 miles, or 36.8 per cent; French nationals—760 miles, or 21 per cent; British nationals—378 miles, or 10.5 per cent; Belgian nationals—25 miles, or 0.7 per cent.

*Note 46.* E. A. Adamov, *Razdel Aziatskoi Turtsii* (Moscow 1924), 15. For a very good analysis of the economic position of the European Powers in Turkey, see *ibid.*, 5-28.

*Note 47.* Mears, 357. By 1914 the P. D. A. was responsible for a total of 1,628,966,000 francs in loans, of which 401,000,000 francs were under the *Deutsche*

*Bank* (German) and 416,966,000 under the Ottoman Bank (French). Total French loans under the P. D. A. were 1,191,966,000. In round figures the investments in the public debt of Turkey were: France—2,500,000,000 francs (60.31 per cent); Germany —867,000,000 (21.31 per cent); England—580,000,000 (14.36 per cent); Italy— 120,000,000 (3 per cent). Of investments in private enterprises, France controlled 53.55 per cent, Germany 32.77 per cent, and England 13.66 per cent. See Blaisdell, 147; Ravndal, 214; Adamov, 9.

*Note 48.* Earle, 105; *Statesman's Year Book* (1919), 1316-17.

*Note 49.* Sir N. O'Connor to Sir T. Sanderson, Précis of despatches, April 29, 1903; B. D., II, no. 202, pp. 174-76. For financial background, see also Mr. (Later Sir) Adam Block's memorandum on Franco-German penetration in Turkey, June 18, 1906; B. D., V, Enclosure 1 in no. 147, pp. 174-80.

*Note 50.* Bethmann to Pourtalès, November 8, 1910; G. P., XXVII, no. 10155, pp. 840-42. Sazonov's report to the tsar, November 17, 1910; L. N., II, 331-34. Bethmann to Pourtalès, November 15, 1910; G. P., XXVII, no. 10159, pp. 846-49.

*Note 51.* For the correspondence with reference to the final signature see L. N., II; E. D., 501-76; Bethmann to Pourtalès, July 16, 1911; Kiderlen to Pourtalès, July 27, 1911; Pourtalès to F. O., July 31—August 25, 1911; G. P., XXVII, nos. 10218-10220, pp. 950-62. See also Earle, ch. 10.

*Note 52.* L. N., II, 363.

*Note 53.* *Peace Handbook*, no. 63, Mesopotamia, 96-97; Earle, 255-56; L. N., 93-94. See also Mr. J. A. C. Tilley's memorandum of January 5, 1914; B. D., I, 333-34.

*Note 54.* Pallavicini to Berchtold, May 22, 31, 1913; Mensdorff to Berchtold, May 23, 1913; *Aussenpolitik*, VI, nos. 7108, 7277, 7129, pp. 495-6, 569-70, 502-03.

*Note 55.* See Pallavicini to Berchtold, February 6, 1913 and April 24, 1913; *ibid.*, V, no. 6592, p. 646-8; VI, no. 6743, p. 229-31.

*Note 56.* Oscar Jaszi, *The Dissolution of the Habsburg Monarchy* (Chicago 1929), 411-412.

*Note 57.* Tschirschky to Jagow, May 18, 1913; G. P., XXXVII (ii), no. 15045, pp. 643-45. See also Berchtold's memorandum of the conversation with the German ambassador, May 17, 1913; *Aussenpolitik*, VI, no. 7034, p. 443-44.

*Note 58.* Jagow to Flotow, May 22, 1913; G. P., XXXVII (ii), no. 15046, pp. 645-46. See also *ibid.*, nos. 15407-51, May 24-July 4, 1913, pp. 646-54, and nos. 15052-54, no. 15097, pp. 655-8, 690-93.

*Note 59.* Jagow to Tschirschky, July 6, 1913; G. P., XXXVII (ii), no. 15052, pp. 655-56. See also Wangenheim to Jagow, May 21, 1913; G. P., XXXVIII, no. 15312, pp. 41-48. The map is not in G. P.

*Note 60.* Jagow to Bollati, July 16, 1913; G. P., XXXVII (ii), no. 15056, p. 600; XXXVIII, no. 15360, p. 106. Austria was opposed to Italy in the Adalia vilayet on the ground of prior interest.

*Note 61.* See Report of conversations with the German and Italian ambassadors (Berchtold), July 7, 1913; Mérey to Berchtold, July 7, 1913; Berchtold's memorandum of conversation with the German ambassador, July 11, 1913; Mérey to Berchtold, July 17, 1913; *Aussenpolitik*, VI, nos. 7671, 7676, 7722, 7812, pp. 836-7, 839-41, 868-9, 920-22. See also Giovanni Giolitti, *Memoirs of My Life* (London 1923), 374-75.

*Note 62.* Memorandum of Count Forgach on an interview with Jagow in Berlin, September 25, 1913; *Aussenpolitik*, VII, no. 8708, pp. 353-8.

*Note 63.* Pallavicini to Berchtold, December 29, 1913; *ibid.*, VII, no. 9133, pp. 685-8. See also Pallavicini's report of December 8, 1913; *ibid.*, VII, no. 9068, pp. 629-30. The conversation with Zimmermann does not appear in *Aussenpolitik.* Footnote c to no. 9068 states: "He (Zimmermann) does not doubt that it will come to a breakup of Asiatic Turkey. A map lay before him, where all Asiatic Turkey (also Syria) appeared partitioned among the Powers in colored zones. Only the district Adalia appeared without a master."

It is interesting to note that Delcassé advised his government on November 30, 1913: "The falling to pieces of Turkey has already begun, or is beginning, and Germany, with her assistance to the Ottoman government, will occupy a position assuring to her all the advantages of a partition." See E. A. Adamov, *Konstantinopol i Prolivy* (Moscow 1925), I, 59.

*Note 64.* Bollati to Jagow, January 28, 1914; G. P., XXXVIII, no. 15101, p. 697.

*Note 65.* Szögyény to Berchtold, January 31, 1914; *Aussenpolitik*, VII, no. 9285, pp. 820-2.

*Note 66.* Pallavicini to Berchtold, March 23, 1914; *ibid.*, no. 9503, pp. 994-6. Wangenheim drew the conclusion that Germany and Russia could work together in this new orientation of Russian policy, according to Pallavicini!

*Note 67.* Interview of Count Berchtold with San Giuliano, April 18, 1914; *Aussenpolitik*, VII, no. 9592, pp. 1063-69.

*Note 68.* See *Asie française*, XIV, no. 157 (April 1914), 162.

*Note 69.* Giolitti, *Memoirs*, 374-5. Writer's italics.

*Note 70.* For part text of the address of San Giuliano, see *Asie française*, XIV, no. 158 (May 1914), 209-11. See also the letter of Lichnowsky to Bethmann-Hollweg, February 21, 1914; Lichnowsky, 323-24.

*Note 71.* Mukhtar Pasha, *La Turquie, l'Allemagne et l'Europe depuis le traité de Berlin jusqu'à la guerre mondiale* (Paris 1924), 191 ff.

*Note 72.* Graf von Jagow, *Ursachen und Ausbruch des Weltkrieges* (Berlin 1919), 60-62; Bethmann-Hollweg, *Reflections on the World War*, 60-61, 114-16.

*Note 73.* Lichnowsky to Jagow, June 2, 1913; Lichnowsky, 318-19.

*Note 74.* Same to same, June 26, 1913; *ibid.*, 322.

*Note 75.* The negotiations had been going on since May 1913. See G. P., XXXVII (ii), 479-639, for these negotiations. For the text of the agreement see G. P., XXXVII (ii), no. 14996, pp. 583-88.

*Note 76.* *Peace Handbook*, no. 60, Syria and Palestine, pp. 65-87. Various projects and counter projects may be found in G. P., XXXVII (ii), nos. 14936, 14963, 14969, etc. Also Earle, 244-52.

*Note 77.* Salisbury's policy dates from about 1895. On January 25, 1898, Salisbury suggested to O'Conor in St. Petersburg, that Russia and England might coöperate in Turkey and China, but stated that "we aim at no partition of territory, but only a partition of preponderance." Salisbury to O'Conor, January 25, 1898; B. D., I, no. 9, p. 8.

*Note 78.* Earle, ch. 8, gives a consideration of the British interests involved.

*Note 79.* Lichnowsky to Bethmann-Hollweg, June 22, 1914; G. P., XXXVII (i), no. 14907, pp. 453-65. For various projects of agreement, see *ibid.*, pp. 196-205, 237-39, 240-51, 263-6, 266-71, 274-76, 278-83, 291-314, 339-43, 362-6, 367-9, 382-6, 400-03, 408-14, 415-19, 440-42. The agreement was initialed in London on June 14,

1914, signed by the Germans on July 27, and on July 30, was forwarded back to Lichnowsky. Text also in Earle, *Political Science Quarterly*, XXXVIII (March 1923), 22-44. See also M. E. Townsend, *The Rise and Fall of the German Colonial Empire* (N. Y. 1930), 341-3.

*Note 80.* Lichnowsky to Bethmann-Hollweg, May 7, 1914; Lichnowsky, 320-1. See also Blaisdell, chs. 7, 8.

*Note 81.* Sazonov to Isvolsky, November 7, 1913; L. N., II, 178. See also Isvolsky to Sazonov, July 3, 1913; Sazonov to Isvolsky, July 14, 1913; Sazonov to Isvolsky, July 26, 1913; L. N., II, 104-09, 114-15, 117. Also Siebert, ch. 9, pp. 656-65.

*Note 82.* Pallavicini to Berchtold, March 23, 1914; *Aussenpolitik*, VII, no. 9503, pp. 994-96. Sazonov's memorandum, December 6, 1913, (L. N., II, 363-72) is a confirmation of this statement.

*Note 83.* Lichnowsky, 62-63. There is no indication, however, that direct negotiations with Russia were undertaken with reference to a sphere in Armenia.

*Note 84.* See Lt. F. M. Pomiankowski, *Der Zusammenbruch des Ottomanischen Reiches. Erinnerungen an die Türkei der Zeit des Kreiges.* (Vienna 1928), 35-41, 51-52. Also Paul Rohrbach, *Germany's Isolation and German World Policies* (Chicago 1915); Karl Hellferich, *Die deutsche Türkenpolitik* (Berlin 1921); M. Jastrow, *The War and the Bagdad Railroad* (Philadelphia 1917); Charles Vellay, *Le problème mediterranean* (Paris 1913).

*Note 85.* See Berchtold's memorandum of a conversation with the Serbian minister-president, Nikola Pashich (on October 4, 1913), 10-11 October, 1913; *Aussenpolitik*, VII, no. 8813, pp. 425-27. Note the comments of Schmitt, I, 138-41, and see Bogichevich, 65, 68-73.

*Note 86.* The ultimatum was presented to Belgrade on October 18, and demanded that Serbia respect the decisions of the conference of ambassadors at London, and abstain from all military measures in Albania. "The Imperial and Royal Government is pleased to hope that the Serbian Government will not delay to proceed to the evacuation (integral) of Albanian territory in a period of eight days. Otherwise, the Imperial and Royal Government would see itself, to its great regret, in the necessity of having recourse to the means proper to assure the realization of its demands." Within two days the Serbian government made the necessary promise. See Berchtold to Storck, October 17, 1913; Memorandum on a visit of the Serbian minister, October 20, 1913; Circular, October 18, 1913; *Aussenpolitik*, VII, nos. 8850, 8879, 8854, pp. 453, 474, 455-7. See also Clément-Simon (French chargé at Belgrade) to Pichon, October 27, 1913; *Les affaires balkaniques*, III, no. 112, pp. 71-72. Conrad, III, 464-66, 729-31. Note also the comments of Fay, I, 463-75.

*Note 87.* This is explained in part by the distrust of Tsar Ferdinand and the German interests in Rumania as a route to the Black sea and Constantinople. See N. Iorga, *Points de vue sur l'histoire du commerce de l'orient à l'époque moderne* (Paris 1925), 119-20.

*Note 88.* Memorandum of the Hungarian minister-president, August 25, 1913; *Aussenpolitik*, VII, no. 8474, pp. 198-201. See also Berchtold to Szögyény, July 1, August 1, 1913; *ibid.*, VI, no. 7566, pp. 776-8; VII, no. 8157, pp. 1-7.

*Note 89.* Jagow to Wangenheim, September 13, 1913; G. P., XXXVI, no. 13823, p. 60.

*Note 90.* Pallavicini to Berchtold, September 8, 1913; Tarnowsky to Berchtold, September 16, 18, 1913; Flotow to Berchtold, September 23, 1913; *Aussenpolitik,* VII, nos. 8561, 8647, 8665, 8682, 8683, pp. 260, 310-11, 321-22, 333-36.

*Note 91.* Memorandum of Count Berchtold, Vienna, October 28, 1913; *Secret XLV-26.* The translation is from R. W. Seton-Watson, "William II's Balkan Policy," *Slavonic Review,* VII, no. 19 (June 1928), pp. 24-27, 28-29. See also *Aussenpolitik,* VII, no. 8934, pp. 512-5.

*Note 92.* Memorandum of an interview with H. M. the king of Bulgaria with Count Berchtold, November 6, 1913; *Aussenpolitik,* VII, no. 8969, pp. 542-5.

*Note 93.* Berchtold sent this telegram to London, Paris, Berlin, St. Petersburg, Constantinople, Bucharest, Sofia, Athens, Belgrade and Cetinje. See *Aussenpolitik,* VII, no. 8981, pp. 551-2.

*Note 94.* Ribot to Paris, November 19, 1913; Dard to Paris, November 23, 1913; *Les affaires balkaniques,* III, nos. 134, 138, pp. 82, 84. Dard viewed this as a move toward Austria, and noted Austrian support in Sofia to hold both Serbia and Rumania in line.

*Note 95.* See Dard to Paris, December 2, 1913; *ibid.,* III, no. 156, p. 945. Berchtold to Szögyény, November 24, 1913; *Aussenpolitik,* VII, no. 9025, pp. 657-9.

*Note 96.* See Isvolsky's two notes of November 6, 1913, to Sazonov; L. N., II, 167-72. Ghenadiev denied that an Austrian loan, then being negotiated, had any political strings.

*Note 97.* Sazonov to Isvolsky, November 7, 1913; *ibid.,* 198-99.

*Note 98.* Pallavicini to Berchtold, November 17, 1913; *Aussenpolitik,* VII, no. 9008, pp. 571-3. See also Haymerle to Berchtold, November 1, 1913; Szögyény to Berchtold; November 13, 1913; Fürstenberg, November 15, 1913; *ibid.,* nos. 8945, 8991, 8999-9000, pp. 522-5, 556-7, 562-4.

*Note 99.* See Czernin to Berchtold, December 5, 1913; *ibid.,* no. 9051, 9052, pp. 608-14. Also Berchtold to Czernin, December 18, 1913; *ibid.,* no. 9103, pp. 664-5. More details as to the situation may be seen in Czernin-Berchtold exchange, November 26, December 8, November 30, 1913; *ibid.;* nos. 9032, 9039, pp. 588-94, 587-60; Conrad, III, 634.

*Note 100.* Tarnowsky to Berchtold, December 11, 29, 1913; *Aussenpolitik,* VII, nos. 9080, 9136, pp. 643-5, 689-91.

*Note 101.* Pallavicini to Berchtold, December 29, 1913; *Aussenpolitik,* VII, no. 9131, pp. 682-4. The pro-Austro-German and pro-Turkish position of the Rado-slavov government is not difficult to understand. Only a loan could consolidate the financial position. His cabinet itself depended on the fourteen Moslem deputies from western Thrace (Talaat Pasha's district) who controlled the narrow balance in the Sobranje See Logio, 101ff; *Turkey in Europe, Peace Handbook,* no. 16, pp. 55-56; Jaksich, "La Bulgarie et les alliés," *Revue hebdomadaire,* I, no. 8 (February 19, 1915), 419-20.

On December 15, 1913, the Emperor William told Velics, the Austrian chargé at Munich that "the Serbs must be harnessed before the car of the Monarchy—in one way or another: they must also remain conscious that they are held in respect by a firm will, which indeed offers them a powerful friendship, but is also instantly ready to give its troops marching orders at the first hostile provocation. The final decision in the south-east of Europe may involve sooner or later a serious armed conflict,

and we Germans then stand with you and behind you, but it can in no case be indifferent, whether twenty divisions of your army are earmarked for operations against the Southern Slavs, or not." But William II was not prepared yet to support Austria's project in Bulgaria. "Emperor William closed by saying that it seemed to him that a more important and more successful task beckoned to us in Serbia than among the Bulgars, whose king was untrustworthy and always inclined towards intrigue, and had proved himself such in the last crisis." See Velics to Berchtold, December 16, 1913; Seton-Watson, *Slavonic Review*, VII (1928), 28-29; *Aussenpolitik*, VII, 657-59

*Note 102.*    Tarnowsky to Berchtold, January 28, 1914; *ibid*, VII, no. 9625, pp 802-03

*Note 103.*    See no 13828, pp. 67-9 in G. P., XXXVI, for July 18, 1913.

*Note 104.*    See Cambon to M. F. A., October 2, 1913; Pichon to Cambon, October 16, 1913; Pichon to Berlin, etc., October 21, 1913; Delcassé to Pichon, November 8, 1913; Note of Russian embassy, December 14, 1913; *Les affaires balkaniques*, III, nos. 94, 104, 107, 122, 158, pp. 61-62, 67, 68-9, 77, 80-81, 96-97. See also Note of the Turkish embassy, December 29, 1913; Trauttmansdorff (note to no. 9193), January 14, 1914; *Aussenpolitik*, VII, no. 9137, p. 689 and p. 733. For a full discussion of the issue of northern Epirus and the Aegean islands from a Greek position, see E. Driault, *Histoire diplomatique de la Grèce* (Paris 1926), V, 136-58. See also Giolitti, 368ff.

*Note 105.*    Wangenheim to F. O., August 29, 1913; G. P., XXXVI (i), no. 13935, p. 72.

*Note 106.*    These memoranda of Szilassy may be found in Secret XLIV-18. They do not appear to be in *Aussenpolitik*. According to Szilassy, Albania would become a client state of Austria-Hungary.

*Note 107.*    Memorandum of January 30, 1914, of an interview of Minister Count Berchtold with Minister-President Venizelos; *Aussenpolitik*, VII, no. 9272, pp. 806-11.

*Note 108.*    Bethmann-Hollweg to F. O., April 17, 1914; G. P., XXXVI (ii), no. 14564, pp. 758-59. Von Mutius was in Athens in March 1914, and on March 8, sounded Major George Melas, secretary to King Constantine on conceding Mitylene, Chios, Samos, etc., to Turkish sovereignty. Constantine, apparently, favored the idea of a Greco-Turkish *entente* under German tutelage, in a Balkan *bloc*. George Melas, *Ex-King Constantine and the War*, 217-19.

*Note 109.*    Bassewitz to F. O., Athens, April 27, 1914; Von Mutius to F. O., Pera, April 29, 1914; G. P., XXXVI (ii), nos. 14575, 14578, pp. 767-68, 770-71.

*Note 110.*    Wangenheim to F. O., May 7, 1914; *ibid.*, no. 14587, pp. 779-84. See also enclosure, pp. 784-88.

*Note 111.*    See Pallavicini to Berchtold, May 4, 8, 9, 1914; *Aussenpolitik*, VIII, nos. 9636, 9637, 9652, 9658, pp. 10-11, 11-12, 20-21, 27.

*Note 112.*    Wangenheim to F. O., May 25, 1914; von Quadt to F. O., Athens, May 28, 1914; Wangenheim to Bethmann-Hollweg, June 17, 1914; G. P., XXXVI (ii), nos. 14596, 14598, 14626, pp. 799, 799-80, 823-24.

Pallavicini explained the Grecophil tendencies of the German government not so much on the basis of the German kaiser's desire to see his sister, the queen of Greece "as empress of Byzantium," as on the basis of desiring to have "the Greeks in Constantinople in place of the Turks," if Turkish rule came to an end. See Pallavicini to Berchtold, October 2, 1913; *Aussenpolitik*, VII, no. 8772, pp. 392-94.

*Note 113.* See Tarnowsky to Berchtold, January 27, 1914; Pallavicini to Berchtold, January 28, 1914; Tarnowsky to Berchtold, February 18, 1914; Pallavicini to Berchtold, February 23, 1914; Pallavicini to Berchtold, May 25, 1914 (containing a project for military convention between Turkey and Bulgaria); *Aussenpolitik,* VII, nos. 9252, 9258, 9393, 9415, pp. 786-8, 794-5, 893-4, 911-12. See also *Secret XLV-25.*

*Note 114.* For text of this document see H. Marczali, "Papers of Count Tisza, 1914-1918," *American Historical Review,* XXIX (January 1924), 303-310; *Aussenpolitik,* VII, no. 9482, pp. 974-79. This memorandum became the basis of a later one drawn up in the Ballplatz in May 1914, which outlined definitely the policy to be followed in the Balkans. *Vide infra,* note 140.

*Note 115.* See Report of Pashich on his conversation with the tsar, February 2, 1914; G. W. B. (1919), 99-105; Bogichevich, 126-34; Bogichevich, *Die auswartige Politik, Serbiens,* I, 414-21. Both Pashich and Venizelos made good impressions on the government at St. Petersburg.

*Note 116.* See especially Poklevsky-Koziel to Sazonov, January 24, 1914; chargé at Bucharest to Sazonov, February 17, 1914; Poklevsky-Koziel to Sazonov, February 24, 1914; E. D., nos. 520, 521, 522, pp. 436-41.

*Note 117.* Paléologue to M. F. A., April 18, 1914; L. N., II, 258. For the Venizelos-Ionescu statements on Greco-Rumanian friendship, and the treaty of Bucharest, see Djuvara, *Cent projets,* 579-80. Also Také Ionescu, 191-93.

*Note 118.* Report of Sazonov to the tsar on his trip to Rumania in June 1914; L. N., II, 377-84. See also Grand Duke Nikolai Mikhailovich to the tsar, September 2, 1916; Golder, 70-72. Also Bompard to M. F. A., June 19, 1914; *Les affaires balkaniques,* III, no. 233, p. 138.

*Note 119.* L. N., II, 380. See also Viviani to ministers (in Europe), June 21, 1914; *Les affaires balkaniques,* III, no. 233, p. 138. Akers-Douglas (Bucharest) to Grey, June 22, 1914; Buchanan to Nicolson, June 25, 1914; B D., XI, nos. 2, 3, pp. 2-4. Note Sazonov's post-war account. Sazonov, 114; and C. J. Diamandy, "La grande guerre vue du versant oriental: l'entrevue de Constantza," *Revue des deux mondes,* XLIII (January 1, 1928), 132-37.

*Note 120.* Sazonov to Savinsky, March 2, 1914; E. D., no. 523, pp. 441-42. Russian ambassador at Vienna to Sazonov, April 3, 1914; *ibid.,* no. 524, pp. 442-43.

*Note 121.* Savinsky to Sazonov, April 22, 26, 1914; *ibid.,* nos. 534, 535, pp. 449-51. The German government had considerable difficulty in getting German banks to foster the Bulgarian loan, and the banks, in turn, insisted on very onerous terms. See Berchtold to Szögyény, February 27, 1914; Szögyény to Berchtold, March 1, 1914; Berchtold to Szögyény and Tarnowsky, June 8, 1914; Tarnowsky to Berchtold, June 8, 1914; *Aussenpolitik,* VII, nos. 9422, 9428, pp. 890-91, 918-20; VIII, nos. 9832, 9837, pp. 124-25, 126.

*Note 122.* Isvolsky to Sazonov, April 29, 1914; Savinsky to Sazonov, May 13, 1914; Isvolsky to Sazonov, May 18, 1914; Savinsky to Sazonov, June 6, 29, 30, 1914; E. D., nos. 536, 537, 538, 544, 545-57. pp. 450-51, 455-56.

*Note 123.* See John Buchan, *Bulgaria and Romania* (London 1924), 92-93, Logio quoting document no. 735 of the *Bulgarian Orange Book.* Tschirschky, German ambassador at Vienna is reported as telling the Bulgarian minister at Vienna that "even when the loan was advanced to you, it was understood that your policy would assume an unhesitating course." The loan was for 500,000,000 francs. A German syndicate secured control of state coal mines, the railway to be constructed from central

Bulgaria to the Aegean, Porto Logos, and a monopoly of the tobacco export. See also Vasil Radoslavov, *Bulgarien und die Weltkrise* (Berlin 1923), 132. A good brief account is in Jacob Viner, "International finance and Balance of Power Diplomacy," *Southwestern Political and Social Science Quarterly*, IX, no. 4 (March 1929), 438-443.

*Note 124.* A. A. Savinsky, *Recollections of a Russian Diplomat* (London 1927), 218-19.

*Note 125.* Ali Fuad, *La question des détroits* (Paris 1928), 66. The entire volume is a good Turkish demonstration of this principle. Interesting in this connection, is Count Herbert Bismarck's acceptance of this general principle. In a memorandum of November 4, 1887, he wrote that Russian policy was directed toward avoiding war with Turkey, and reaching a friendly solution of the question of the Straits. Russia desired control of the Straits, but this could be secured more cheaply and conveniently by a protective alliance with the Porte. If Russia obtained control of the Straits, through such an agreement with the Sultan, she would achieve her purposes without war. Moreover, in view of certain schemes for partition at the time, Count Bismarck thought the sultan might see his way clear to make that kind of arrangement. See Count Herbert Bismarck to Count Monts, chargé in Vienna, November 4, 1887; G. P., VI, 358.

*Note 126.* See Mukhtar Pasha, 197; Ahmed Emin, *Turkey in the World War* (New Haven 1930), 66. Writer's italics. Also Halidé Edib, *Turkey Faces West* (New Haven 1930), 133-134.

*Note 127.* Russia had proposed a project for reforms in 1913, which was reported to the conference of six ambassadors. To this project the Austrian and German ambassadors raised serious objections. In September 1913, however. Russia and Germany had reached agreement, which, in turn, was opposed by the Porte. On February 8, 1914, a final agreement between Russia and Turkey was signed at last. See G. P., XXXVIII, 3-189; A. Mandelstam, *Le sort de l'empire ottoman* (Paris 1917), 236-38, for text of agreement; A. Mandelstam, *La société des nations et les puissances devant le problème arménien* (Paris 1926), 39-42; Djemal Pasha, 262-76.

*Note 128.* Pallavicini to Berchtold, March 23, 1914; *Aussenpolitik*, VII, no. 9503. pp. 994-46.

*Note 129.* Same to same, April 4, 1914; *ibid.*, VII, no. 9550, pp. 1028-31.

*Note 130.* Same to same, April 13, 1914; *ibid.*, VII, no. 9577, pp. 1051-53.

*Note 131.* Sazonov; 133-38; Mukhtar Pasha, 196-97; Talaat Pasha, "Posthumous Memoirs of Talaat Pasha," *Current History*, XV, no. 2 (November 1922), 288ff. See also Pallavicini to Berchtold, May 4, 5, 8, 1914; *Aussenpolitik*, VIII, nos. 9637, 9641, 9650, pp. 11-12, 15, 20. See also G. P., XXXVI, 797, note. Izzet Pasha, *Denkwürdigkeiten des Marshalls Izzet Pasha* (Leipzig 1927), 236-37, gives a Turkish point of view.

*Note 132.* Pallavicini to Berchtold, May 13, 1914; *Aussenpolitik*, VIII, nos. 9664, 9665, pp. 32-34, 35.

*Note 133.* "La politique asiatique de la Russie," *L'Asie française*, XIV, no. 158 (May 1914), 181.

*Note 134.* See especially Pallavicini to Berchtold, May 19, 1914; Berchtold to Sofia, Constantinople, Bucharest, Budapest, May 14, 1914; Mittag to Berchtold, June 13, 1914; Pallavicini to Berchtold, June 24, 1914; *Aussenpolitik*, VIII, nos. 9692, 9669, 9855, 9911, pp. 53, 37-38, 139-41, 180-82. For a German view, see Jagow to Tschirschky, May 27, 1914; G. P. XXXVI, 795, note.

*Note 135.* Mukhtar Pasha, 198-99. Writer's italics.

*Note 136.* See Viner, "International Finance and Balance of Power Diplomacy," *Southwestern Political and Social Science Quarterly,* IX, no. 4 (March 1929), 428-36; Earle, 249-50. This included the famous Angora Sivas-Samsun railway project. See Ravndal, 54.

*Note 137.* Djemal Pasha, 105-107; Mukhtar Pasha, 202 ff. Djemal states that the proposal was blocked by Russian policy. The question of the Aegean islands and Armenia raised the other difficulties involved. England would not consent to a cession of the islands, Imbros and Tenedos, commanding the Straits, to Turkey. Russia did not desire to see Armenia placed under English administrators.

*Note 138.* Mukhtar Pasha, 236, 238.

*Note 139.* Sazonov, *Fateful Years,* 138.

*Note 140.* For text of this memorandum, see Karl Kautsky, *German Documents on the Outbreak of the World War* (Carnegie 1924), no. 14, pp. 70-77. (Hereafter cited as K. D.). The Austrian original, dated July 1, 1914, is in *Aussenpolitik,* VIII, no. 9984 (memorandum), pp. 253-61. Aside from Tisza's memorandum of March 16, 1914, for the bases of this document, see the memorandum of Flotow, May 1914, and that of Matscheko (n. d); *Aussenpolitik,* VIII, nos. 9627, 9918, pp. 1-3, 186-95. A history of the memorandum may be found in R. Goos, *Das Wiener Kabinett und die Entstehung des Weltkrieges* (Vienna 1919), 3-25; Pribram, 54, 72-73; Fay, II, 193-98; Schmitt, I, 161-68. Drawn up in May by Baron Flotow, the memorandum was modified by Matscheko, and fundamentally altered by Count Berthtold, who changed any idea of *rapprochement* of Austria to Serbia. Berchtold received the memorandum on June 24, and approved it, with his changes, on June 28. Since the memorandum was drawn up before the murder of the archduke, the conclusions are essentially independent of any connection with that event.

Interesting in this connection is the fact that Pallavicini had advised Ionescu in Bucharest as early as December 1913, that Rumania should improve her relations with Bulgaria at Serbian expense, and in the spring of 1914, inquiring of the Rumanian alliance, hinted at a Bulgarian connection as a substitute. Ionescu, *Some Personal Impressions,* 35-38, 39.

*Note 141.* The emperor of Austria to the emperor (delivered July 5, 1914); K. D., no. 13, pp. 68-69; *Aussenpolitik,* VIII, no. 9984, pp. 250-52. In the emperor's letter it is stated that "the efforts of my government must in the future be directed toward the isolation and diminution of Serbia." The plan for a new Balkan alliance with Bulgaria as the pivot is then elaborated. For the German *carte blanche* to Austria-Hungary, see Szögyény to Berchtold, July 5, 1914; *Austrian Red Book* (London, n. d.), I, no. 6, pp. 18-19. (Hereafter cited as A. R. B.). Also in Austrian original, *Aussenpolitik,* VIII, no. 10058, pp. 306-07.

*Note 142.* Relation of the Hungarian Premier Count Tisza to Franz Josef, July 1, 1914. Tisza's position was: (1) that Austria could not count on Rumania, and Bulgaria was exhausted; (2) a diplomatic constellation must be created to change the situation in Austria-Hungary's favor; (3) an alliance with Bulgaria and Greece was necessary, and Rumania must (with German aid) be made to join the Triple Alliance openly. See A. R. B., I, no. 2, pp. 14-15; Graf Stefan Tisza, *Briefe* (Berlin 1928), I, 37-38; *Aussenpolitik,* VIII, no. 9978, pp. 248-9.

*Note 143.* Council of ministers for common concerns, July 7, 1914; A.. R, B. I, no. 8, pp. 21-32; *Aussenpolitik,* VIII, no. 10118, pp. 343-51. This was also printed in *Current History,* XI, no. 3 (December 1919), 455-460. On July 6, Szögyény had

wired Berchtold that "both the imperial chancellor and the under-secretary of state were of opinion that it would be best to negotiate a treaty with Bulgaria only at present and to leave it to the future whether Turkey and eventually Greece would bind themselves to Bulgaria. Chancellor remarked that in view of the great interests which Germany has in Turkey, this country's accession would be most desirable." Szögyény to Berchtold, July 6, 1914; A. R. B., I, no. 7, pp. 20-21; *Aussenpolitik*, VIII, no. 10076, pp. 319-20.

*Note 144.*   Tisza to the emperor, July 8, 1914; A. R. B., I, no. 12, pp. 37-39.

*Note 145.*   Tschirschky to the imperial chancellor, July 14, 1914; K. D., no. 49, pp. 112-13.

*Note 146.*   Council of ministers for common affairs, July 19, 1914; A. R. B., I, no. 26, pp. 53-58; *Aussenpolitik*, VIII, no. 10393, pp. 511-14. It was pointed out that "the strategically necessary corrections of the frontier lines, or the reduction of Serbia's territory to the advantage of other states or the unavoidable temporary occupation of Serbian territory is not precluded by this resolution. See also Goos, 101 ff.

*Note 147.*   See also Schmitt, I, 173-74.


## CHAPTER III

*Note 1.*   Djemal Pasha, *op. cit.*, 107-09.

*Note 2.*   For Francis Joseph's statement, see Emperor of Austria to the Emperor of Germany, received July 5, 1914; K. D., no. 13, pp. 68-69. For Jagow's statement, see Jagow to Tschirschky and Wangenheim, July 14, 1914; K. D., no. 45, p. 109. Pallavicini's position in Pallavicini to Berchtold, July 16, 1914; *Aussenpolitik*, VIII, no. 10303, pp. 460-1. See also Szögyény to Berchtold, July 11, 1914; *ibid.*, no. 10196, p. 399.

*Note 3.*   Wangenheim to F. O., July 18, 1914; K. D., no. 71, p. 130. See also H. Morgenthau, *Ambassador Morgenthau's Story*, 96-104. Wangenheim notes that Pallavicini's idea was for "the arrangement of new alliances, and would like therefore to attach Turkey to Austria through Bulgaria. I oppose this idea most actively. Turkey is today without any question worthless as an ally." See also Maurice Bompard (former ambassador of France at Constantinople), "L'entrée en guerre de la Turquie," *Revue de Paris*, XXVIII (July 1, 1921), 60-85. Also Pallavicini to Berchtold, July 20, 1914; *Aussenpolitik*, VIII, no. 10410, pp. 530-32.

*Note 4.*   Wangenheim to F. O., July 22, 1914; K. D., no. 117, pp. 156-58.

*Note 5.*   *Ibid.* Also Pallavicini to Berchtold, July 21, 1914; *Aussenpolitik*, VIII, nos. 10453-5, pp. 562-63.

*Note 6.*   Jagow to Wangenheim, July 24, 1914; K. D., no. 144, p. 175.

*Note 7.*   Wangenheim to F. O., July 23, 1914; K. D., no. 149, p. 178. Writer's italics.

*Note 8.*   Same to same, July 27, 1914; K. D., no. 256, pp. 242-4. Writer's italics. It is to be noted that German command of the navy gave Germany command of the two great branches of the Turkish armed forces. Szögyény, Austro-Hungarian ambassador in Berlin, telegraphed the substance of the kaiser's orders to Berchtold on July 25, and on July 27, it was relayed to Constantinople and Sofia. Berchtold to Pallavicini, Tarnowsky and Szögyény; *Aussenpolitik*, VIII, no. 10657 (Szögyény to Berchtold), pp. 705, 776, 791, 808.

*Note 9.* Wangenheim to F. O., July 28, 1914; K. D., no. 285, p. 265.

*Note 10.* Bethmann-Hollweg to Wangenheim, July 28, 1914; K. D., no. 320, pp. 286-7. See also Djemal Pasha, *op. cit.*, 108-9; Talaat Pasha, *loc. cit.*, Mukhtar Pasha, *op. cit.*, 250-4.

*Note 11.* Wangenheim to F. O., July 30, 1914; K. D., no. 411, p. 355.

*Note 12.* Szögyény to Berchtold, July 31, 1914; A. R. B., III, no. 58, pp. 50-2. See also Wangenheim to F. O., July 29, 1914; K. D., no. 398, p. 346. Urging alliance, Berchtold advised that Russia was about to force the Straits. Berchtold to Pallavicini, July 31, 1914; *Aussenpolitik*, VIII, no. 11149, p. 955.

*Note 13.* Wangenheim to F. O., August 3, 1914; K. D., no. 733, p. 529. In a note attached, Wangenheim explained that "General Liman . . . had officially informed me in advance that he had arranged a detailed agreement with the minister of war Enver which provided the military mission with the actual chief command— as required by your telegram 275." See also Liman von Sanders, *op. cit.*, 22-3, and Mühlmann, *Deutschland und die Türkei, 1913-1914*, pp. 28-43. Article 4 of the treaty of alliance appears in Ahmed Emin, *Turkey in the World War*, 67 (translated from the Turkish) and in Johannes Hohlfeld, *Deutsche Reichsgeschichte in Dokumenten, 1849-1926* (Berlin 1927), II, 520-1.

*Note 14.* See M. Bompard, "L'entrée en guerre de la Turquie," *Revue de Paris*, XVIII (July 15, 1921), 261-4. Von Moltke desired immediate publication of the treaty and a Turkish declaration of war on Russia "as soon as possible." Moltke to F. O., August 2, 1914; K. D., no. 662, p. 493. The coming of the *Goeben* and *Breslau* into the eastern Mediterranean and the desire of Germany for their entrance into the Dardanelles, which would be a breach of Turkish neutrality, led to further demands. The grand vizier demanded more definite guarantees of Turkish integrity, and the return of the Aegean islands in case Greece joined the Entente. The territories desired in the Caucasus region included Kars, Ardahan and Batum. See Mühlmann, *op. cit.*, 44-45, and Wangenheim to F. O., August 6, 1914; *ibid.*, 96-7. A brief summary of the Germany negotiations with Turkey may be found in Schmitt, II, 431-40.

*Note 15.* Bethmann-Hollweg to chargé at Bucharest, July 6, 1914; K. D., no. 16, pp. 79-80. Szögyény to Berchtold, July 5, 1914; A. R. B., I, no. 6, pp. 18-9. Direct report of Berchtold, July 7, 1914; Berchtold to von Mérey, July 12, 1914; A. R. B., I, nos. 9, 16, pp. 33-4, 43-4. See also Savinsky, *op. cit.*, 226, 239. Kaiser to Emperor of Austria, July 14, 1914; K. D., no. 26, pp. 89-90.

The Austrian draft for a Bulgaro-Austrian alliance provided: (1) Mutual friendship, with an obligation not to enter any agreement directed again either; (2) if Bulgaria, without provocation, is attacked by two states one of which borders on Austria-Hungary, the latter is bound to come to Bulgaria's assistance, and vice versa; (3) both parties desire to preserve friendly relations with Rumania, Bulgaria recognizing the treaty of Bucharest, which can only be altered by aggression of Rumania; Austria takes note of Bulgarian claims in Macedonia; (4) war and peace in common, matters to be regulated by military convention; (5) duration of the treaty, which was to be secret. See Tarnowsky to F. O., July 19, 1914; *Aussenpolitik* VIII, no. 10389, pp. 506-7.

*Note 16.* See Tarnowsky to Berchtold, July 23, 28, 30, 31, 1914; *Aussenpolitik* VIII, nos. 10555, 10556, 10926, 11105, 11188.

*Note 17.* Toshev to M. F. A., July 17, 1914; *Kriegsschuldfrage*, VI, no. 3 (March 1928), no. 192, pp. 230-5. These are German translations from the *Bulgarian Orange Book* on Bulgaria's entrance into the world war.

*Note 18.* Toshev to M. F. A., July 21, 1914, and Rizov (Rome) to M. F. A., July 24, 1914; *ibid.*, 195, 202, 211, pp. 236-7, 238-9, 241-3. See also Sir Rennell Rodd (Rome) to Grey, July 23, 1914; B. D., XI, no. 163, pp. 116-7.

*Note 19.* See Berchtold to Tarnowsky, July 23, 28, 1914; *Aussenpolitik VIII*, nos. 10550, 10874. See Schmitt, II, 441-2.

*Note 20.* Michahelles to Jagow, July 25, 1914; K. D., no. 162, p. 190. The kaiser urged: "Hurry it up!" Sir H. Bax-Ironside, British minister at Sofia, thought an agreement had been arrived at as early as July 24. See Bax-Ironside to Grey, July 24, 1914; B. D., XI, no. 95, p. 76.

*Note 21.* Michahelles to Jagow, July 28, 1914; K. D., no. 381, pp. 285-6.

*Note 22.* See nos. 251, 316, 512, 548; K. D., pp. 305, 414, 436-7. Also Jagow to Tschirschky, August 1, 1914, and Tschirschky to Jagow, August 1, 1914; K. D., nos. 544, 597, pp. 435, 462.

*Note 23.* Michahelles to Jagow, August 2, 1914; K. D., no. 673, p. 500.

*Note 24.* Bethmann-Hollweg to Michahelles, August 2, 1914, and same to Tschirschky, August 2, 1914; K. D., 697-8, pp. 512-3.

*Note 25.* Jagow to Wangenheim, August 3, 1914, and Bethmann-Hollweg to chargé at Bucharest, August 3, 1914; K. D., nos. 711, 729, pp. 519, 527.

*Note 26.* Bethmann-Hollweg to Michahelles, August 3, 1914; K. D., no. 728, p. 527.

*Note 27.* Tschirschky to F. O., August 4, 1914; K. D., no. 798, p. 564.

*Note 28.* Jagow to Michahelles, August 4, 1914; K. D., no. 816, p. 573.

*Note 29.* Michahelles to F. O., August 4, 1914; K. D., no. 857, pp. 590-1.

*Note 30.* Jagow to Michahelles, August 4, 1914; Jagow to Tschirschky, August 5, 1914; Jagow to Michahelles, August 5, 1914; K. D., nos. 866, 872, 873, pp. 594, 597, 598.

*Note 31.* Pribram, op. cit., 72-33. Czernin, *In the World War* (London 1921), 82. Crawford Price, in the *Balkan Review*, no. 3 (April 1919), 204-5, reproduces the text of the treaty, which he dates from September, 1914. It is, however, the treaty which was signed in 1915. Undoubtedly the basis was laid down at the time of these negotiations. See also *Greek White Book, 1913-1917* (American Hellenic Society no. 5) Theotoky to Streit, July 25, 1914, no. 13, pp. 44-45; same to Constantine, August 4, 1914, no. 19, pp. 49-50; same to same, August 4, 1914, no. 20, pp. 50-1. Also Bax-Ironside to Grey, July 24, 1914 and Sir R. Rodd to Grey, July 30, 1914; B. D., XI, nos. 95, 649, pp. 76, 334.

*Note 32.* Czernin, *op. cit.*, 90-1.

*Note 33.* Emperor to king of Rumania, July 31, 1914; K. D., no. 472, p. 391. Szögyény to Berchtold, July 31, 1914; A. R. B., III, no. 57, pp. 49-50.

*Note 34.* Waldburg to F. O., August 1, 1914; K. D., no. 582, pp. 454-5.

*Note 35.* Ibid.

*Note 36.* Waldthausen to F. O., August 2, 1914 and August 3, 1914; K. D., nos. 699, 786, pp. 513, 558-9, 562.

*Note 37.* Same to same, August 4, 1914; K. D., no. 811, pp. 570-1, U. S. *Foreign Relations* (1914 War Supplement), Vopicka to Bryan, August 11, 1914, p. 64. Radev to M. F. A., July 31, 1914; *Kriegsschuldfrage VI*, no. 3 (March 1928), no. 244, p. 252. See also Ionescu, *Some Personal Impressions*, 51-58, 91-101, 125-38; Negulescu, *Rumania's Sacrifice*, 26-32; Czernin, *op. cit.*, 79-82.

*Note 38.* For the terms and negotiations of this alliance of June 21, 1913, see G. W. B. (1913-17), American Hellenic Society, no. 9, pp. 20-42.

*Note 39.* Venizelos to Streit, July 25, 1914; *ibid.*, no. 14, p. 45. See also Streit to Alexandropoulos, August 2, 1914; *ibid.*, nos. 17-8, p. 47-8.

*Note 40.* Alexandropoulos to Venizelos, July 25, 1914; *ibid.*, no. 12, p. 43.

*Note 41.* Frangulis, A. F., *La Grèce et la crise mondiale* (Paris 1926), I, 142 King of Greece to the Emperor, July 27, 1914; K. D., no. 243.

*Note 42.* William II to Constantine, July 31, 1914, Constantine to William II, August 2, 1914; K. D., nos. 504, 702, pp. 388, 411, 515.

*Note 43.* Theotoky to Constantine, August 4, 1914; G. W. B., (1913-1917), nos. 19, 20, pp. 49-50. Streit to Theotoky, August 7, 1914; *ibid.*, no. 21, p. 50. See also Cosmin, *L'entente et la Grèce pendant la grande guerre* (Paris 1926): English translation—S. P. P. Cosmetatos, *The Tragedy of Greece* (N. Y. 1928); A. F. Frangulis, *La Grèce et la crise mondiale* (Paris 1926); Paxton Hibben, *Constantine I and the Greek People* (N. Y. 1922), 3-16; Bosdari, *Delle guerre balcaniche della grande guerra*, 103ff; M. Carracciolo, *L'intervento della Grecia nella guerra mondiale e l'opera della diplomazia alleata* (Rome 1925), 28-30; Venizelos, *Vindication of Greek National Policy* (1912-1917), 70ff.

It should be remembered that when on June 12, 1914, Athens appealed to Belgrade for support in a possible Greco-Turkish war (in which Bulgaria would hardly have remained neutral), Serbia, though hard pressed, made a timely *démarche* with the Porte (June 16, 1914) which served to pass over the crisis. See *Greek White Book* (supplement), nos. 1-6, pp. 1-7.

*Note 44.* See Morgenthau to Bryan, August 17, 1914; *U. S. Foreign Relations* (1914 supplement), 66. Giers to Sazonov, August 15, 1914; J. Polonsky, *Documents diplomatiques secrets russes, 1914-1917* (Paris 1928), 79-80; M. N. Pokrovsky, *Zaristische Russland im Weltkrieg* (Berlin 1927), no. 38, p. 23. See also Giers to Sazonov, August 15, 1915; Polonsky, 80-1; Pokrovsky, nos. 39, 40, 41, pp. 23-24. Poklevsky to Sazonov, August 25 and September 12, 1914; Pokrovsky, nos. 21, 31, pp. 172, 177. Savinsky to Sazonov, August 18, 1914; Polonsky, 15-6; Pokrovsky, no. 13, pp. 74-5. Take Ionescu, *Some Personal Impressions*, 189-200, throws light on the incident in Bucharest. While Radoslavov told Savinsky on August 18 that no compact had "yet" been signed, Logio (Buchan, *Bulgaria and Rumania*, ch. 13), states that on August 19 a formal treaty was signed between Turkey and Bulgaria, guaranteeing Bulgarian neutrality in case of a Turkish war against the Entente, and promising mutual support in case of attack by another Balkan state. Radoslavov admits that a treaty of alliance and friendship was signed on August 6, 1914, but this does not appear to have given the Turks much confidence. See Radoslavov, 117. See also "A travers les journaux," in *Revue du monde musulman*, XXX, 1915, pp. 292ff, which gives summaries of *Tanin* and *Ikdam*, two Constantinople newspapers, during this period.

*Note 45.* Excellent discussions of the geographical phases of the Turkish (Constantinople) position are to be found in Vaughn Cornish, *The Great Capitals*, 89-103; Cornish, *Strategic Geography of the Great Powers*, 26-33; Cornish, *Strategic Geography of the British Empire*, 111-13; J. Ancel, "Les bases géographiques de la question des détroits," *Le monde slave*, 5th yr., II, no. 2 (February 1928), 238-53.

*Note 46.* Prince Sabaheddine, nephew of the sultan, living at Paris at the outbreak of the war, opposed Turkey's fighting the Entente. On August 1, 1914, he

warned Talaat of disasters to follow such a step. German triumph, he argued, would mean German seizure of Asia Minor. It was, therefore, to Turkey's interest to ally with the Balkan states under the Entente. He followed this two weeks later with a second plea. When at last the sultan had drawn the sword, he wrote, "Your government condemns our country to death." See Sabaheddine to Talaat Bey, August 1, 15, 1914; same to sultan, November 6, 1914; in "La Turquie et les alliés," *La revue*, (February 1915)—, CX, 206-09.

*Note 47.*   Evidently Giers, Russian ambassador at the Porte, heard of it on August 8, 1914. See F. Stieve, *Das Russische Orangebuch über den Kriegsausbruch mit der Türkei* (Berlin 1926), no. 15, p. 54, containing the note of Giers to Sazonov, August 8, 1914.

*Note 48.*   See Grey, *op. cit.*, II, 171; Winston Churchill, *World Crisis*, I, 536-7; Buchanan, *op. cit.*, I, 223-4; Corbett, *Naval Operations*, I, 92ff; Mandelstam, *op. cit.*, 76-7.

*Note 49.*   Grey to Bertie, August 15, 1914; Grey, *op. cit.*, II, 172-3.

*Note 50.*   Jagow to Wangenheim, August 3, 1914; K. D., no. 751, p. 541.

*Note 51.*   Ottoman embassy to the secretary of state, August 8, 1914; *U. S. Foreign Relations* (1914 Supplement), 50-1. M. de Bunsen (Vienna) to Grey, July 24, 1914, and Beaumont to Grey, July 26, 1914; B. D., XI, nos. 97, 151, pp. 76-7, 106. Giers to Sazonov, August 1-3, 1914; Stieve, *op. cit.*, nos. 1-5. The grand vizier told Giers that Austria was urging Turkey to take action against Russia.

*Note 52.*   Grey to Beaumont, August 4, 1914; B. D., XI, no. 589 p. 313.

*Note 53.*   Tewfik Pasha to Grey, August 4, 1914; *ibid.*, no. 598, p. 316. Beaumont to Grey, August 3, 1914; *ibid.*, no. 605, pp. 317-8. For an interesting view of the Turkish position written August 29, 1914, see A. Rustem Bey, former Turkish ambassador to the United States, on "The Position of Turkey," *World's Work*, XXVIII, (September 1914), 518-23, and "Enver Pasha," *ibid.*, XXIX (November 1914), 300-1.

*Note 54.*   Russia also complained of the ships. See the Benckendorff-Sazonov exchange, June 1914; Siebert, *op. cit.*, nos. 853, 854, 855.

*Note 55.*   Giers to Sazonov, August 8, 1914; Stieve, *op. cit.*, no. 10, p. 46. See also the exchanges between Beaumont and Grey, and Mallet and Grey, particularly August 9, 1914 (no. 6), and August 18, 1914; *Misc. 13 (1914)*. Correspondence respecting the Outbreak of the War with Turkey. *Cmd. 7628*, nos. 1-6, pp. 1-3; no. 20, pp. 41-2. See also Ahmed Emin, *op. cit.*, 69.

*Note 56.*   Grey to Mallet, August 25, 1914; *Cmd. 7628*, no. 34, p. 11. See also Giers to Sazonov, October 5, 1914: Imperial Russian Ministry of Foreign Affairs, *Diplomatic Documents. Negotiations Preceding the War with Turkey.* (London 1915). Hereafter cited as R. O. B., II.

*Note 57.*   See Djemal Pasha, *op. cit.*, 83-4, 93-5, 97; Talaat Pasha, *op. cit.*, 291., Mukhtar Pasha, *op. cit.*, 269-76; Churchill, *op. cit.*, I, 522; Corbett, *op. cit.*, I, 58; Baron Schilling, *How the War Began*, 98.

*Note 58.*   There is an interesting account in Ludwig, Emil, "Les croisières du *Goeben* et du *Breslau*," *Les archives de la grande guerre*, V, no. 13 (March 1920), pp. 68-87, no. 14, (April 1920) pp. 243-56; Larcher, Commandant M., *La guerre turque dans la guerre mondiale* (Paris 1926), 30-1. Larcher is based on the official Turkish sources. The *Breslau* had been in the Mediterranean since 1913.

*Note 59.* Corbett, *op. cit.*, I, 35·7. For the Russian view see the article by A. Stahl, "La *Goeben* dans la mer noire," in Margueritte, V., *Les alliés contre la Russie*, 105·18, Sazonov to London and Paris, August 6, 1914; Polonsky, *op. cit.*, 71·2.

*Note 60.* Sinclair to Grey, August 2, 1914, Bertie to Grey, August 3, 1914, Bertie to Grey, August 4, 1914; B. D., XI, nos. 480, 559, 616, pp. 272, 301, 321. Wangenheim to F. O., August 1, 1914, von Mutius to F. O., August 2, 1914, Jagow to Wangenheim, August 3, 1914, Tirpitz to Jagow, August 4, 1914; K. D., nos. 652, 683, 712, 870, pp. 488, 505, 520, 597.

*Note 61.* Corbett, *op. cit.*, I, 70·1; Morgenthau, *op. cit.*, 70·1; Ludwig, *op. cit.*, (ii), 247ff. See also Corbett, I, 349·50; Tirpitz to Jagow, August 4, 1914; K. D., no. 870, p. 597; Tirpitz, *My Memoirs*, II, 81·3.

*Note 62.* Tirpitz to Jagow, August 3, 1914; K. D., no. 775, p. 552. On August 4 Theotoky, Greek minister in Berlin, reported to Constantine that the kaiser told him "the German ships which are in the Mediterranean will be joined with the Turkish fleet in order to act together." Theotoky to Constantine, August 4, 1914; G. W. B., (1913·1914), no. 19, p. 50. See also Melas, *op. cit.*, 210·15; Cosmin, 21·3.

*Note 63.* Jagow to Wangenheim, August 3, 1914; K. D., no. 751, p. 541.

*Note 64.* There were thirteen French, three British cruisers and five Anglo-French naval bases in the western Mediterranean. See Margueritte, *op. cit.*, 113ff; Ludwig (ii), 247ff.

*Note 65.* *Loc. cit.* See also Tirpitz, II, 81·3. Many Constantinople officials remained in the dark about the incident. See Djemal Pasha, 122·7. Wangenheim to F. O., August 4, 1914; K. D., no. 852, p. 588.

*Note 66.* Sazonov to Giers, August 8, 1914; Stieve, no. 11, p. 47. See also Giers to Sazonov, August 8, 1914 and Sazonov to Giers, August 8, 9, 1914; *ibid.*, nos. 12, 14, 18, pp. 48, 50, 54. Grey-Beaumont exchange, August 11, 1914; *Cmd. 7628*, nos. 7, 8, pp. 2·3. See also Ahmed Emin, *op. cit.*, 72·3.

*Note 67.* Djemal Pasha, *loc. cit.* See also Halidé Edib, *op. cit.*, 139.

*Note 68.* Grey to Bertie, August 15, 1914; Grey, II, 172ff.

*Note 69.* Grey to Mallet, August 2, 1914; *loc. cit.*

*Note 70.* Beaumont to Grey, August 11, 1914; *Cmd. 7628*, no. 9, p. 3. Morgenthau reported on August 11 that Turkey had (purchased?) the vessels. Wangenheim told him that the admiral and men would enter the Turkish service. "German military mission to be duplicated by naval mission. This completely changes situation here." See Morgenthau to Bryan, August 11, 1914; *Foreign Relations* (1914 Supplement), 62·3.

*Note 71.* Sazonov to Giers, August 11, 1914; Stieve, no. 26, p. 64. Djemal Pasha, 121·22; Mukhtar Pasha, 277·280; Talaat Pasha, 293ff. Demidov to Sazonov, August 10, 1914; Stieve, no. 46, p. 88; R. O. B., II, no. 27, pp. 14·5. See also Liman von Sanders, 32·3.

*Note 72.* Beaumont to Grey, August 15, 1914; *Cmd. 7628*, no. 16, p. 5. Giers to Sazonov, August 13, 1914; R. O. B., II, no. 22, p. 12. Larcher, *La guerre turque*, 54·5.

*Note 73.* Djemal Pasha, *loc. cit.*, Talaat Pasha, *loc. cit.*, Pokrovsky, no. 31, p. 19.

*Note 74.* Corbett, II, 181ff.

*Note 75.* Grey, I, 89-90; Morgenthau, 70-1; Mandelstam, 77-80. See Mallet to Grey, September 7, 1914; *Cmd. 7628*, no. 64, pp. 21-2.

*Note 76.* Mallet to Grey, August 19, 1914; *Cmd. 7628*, no. 22, p. 7.

*Note 77.* Morgenthau, 80. Morgenthau quotes Wangenheim: "We've got our foot on Russia's tow and we propose to keep it there." After the advent of the vessels, on the fall of Brussells, when Djavid Bey tried to comfort a distinguished Belgian jurist, saying, "I have terrible news for you . . . The Germans have captured Brussels," he replied, "I have even more terrible news for you . . . The Germans have captured Turkey." *Ibid.*, 80-1. Tirpitz says, "The whole Turkish question received its favorable ending through the success of this break-through . . . . The support which the German navy was able to give to Turkey . . . is an episode of itself and it can only be mentioned here that our navy took a leading part in the glorious defence of the Dardanelles, thus assisting in the saving of Constantinople. On this depended victory or defeat on the Balkan front, which was so important for the Central Powers. The approach from the Mediterranean to Russia thus remained closed, while the maintenance of communications with Asia Minor rendered possible our serious threats against the English in Egypt and Mesopotamia." Tirpitz, II, 82-3.

See also Rafael de Nogales, *Four Years Beneath the Crescent*, 12-30; Pomiankowski, 73-5; David Robert, *Le drame ignoré de l'armée d'orient*, 14-6. Admiral Milne, commander of the British Mediterranean fleet which gave chase to the vessels, has written of the episode in his *The Flight of the Goeben and Breslau*.

*Note 78.* The documents on these negotiations may be found in Pokrovsky, 3-60; Polonsky, 61-102; B. Mirkine-Guetsevitch, "Russie et Turquie en août, 1914," *Le monde slave*, IV, no. 4 (April 1927).

*Note 79.* Giers to Sazonov, August 5, 1914; Polonsky, 67-8, Pokrovsky, no. 9, pp. 7-8. The grand vizier had explained to Giers and Bompard that Liman von Sanders had been ordered to remain in Turkey, even though he had indicated a willingness to release him. Giers to Sazonov, August 3, 1914; R. O. B., II, no. 6, p. 5. See also Liman von Sanders, 22-3.

*Note 80.* Giers to Sazonov, August 5, 1914; Polonsky, 68-9; Pokrovsky, no. 11, p. 9.

*Note 81.* Giers to Sazonov, August 5, 1914; Polonsky, 69-70; Pokrovsky, no. 12, pp. 9-10. As a matter of fact negotiations had been going on for some time.

*Note 82.* *Ibid.* See also Giers to Sazonov, August 5, 6, 1914; Polonsky, 70-1; Pokrovsky, nos. 13, 14, p. 10.

*Note 83.* Giers to Sazonov, August 9, 1914; Polonsky, 74-5, Pokrovsky, no. 20, pp. 13-14. Giers had heard a rumor of the German-Turkish alliance on the previous day.

*Note 84.* Sazonov to Giers, August 9, 1914; Pokrovsky, no. 21, p. 14.

*Note 85.* Giers to Sazonov, August 9, 1914; *ibid.*, no. 23, p. 15, Polonsky, 75-6.

*Note 86.* Sazonov to Giers, August 10, 1914; Pokrovsky, no. 24, p. 15; Polonsky, 76; Stieve, no. 21, p. 57. The telegram was dispatched to Paris and London.

*Note 87.* Isvolsky to Sazonov, August 10, 1914; L. N., III, 2-3; Stieve, no. 69, p. 38.

*Note 88.* Isvolsky to Sazonov, August 11, 1914; L. N., III, 3-4; Stieve, no. 28, p. 66.

*Note 89.* Giers to Sazonov, August 10, 1914; Pokrovsky, no. 25, p. 16.

*Note 90.* Giers to Sazonov, August 11, 1914; *ibid.*, no. 26, pp. 16-7.

*Note 91.* Giers to Sazonov, August 12, 1914; Polonsky, 76-7; Pokrovsky, no. 30, pp. 30-1.

*Note 92.* Giers to Sazonov, August 13, 1914; Pokrovsky, no. 32, pp. 19-20.

*Note 93.* Sazonov to Benckendorff, August 15, 1914; Pokrovsky, no. 37, p. 76.

*Note 94.* As has been indicated, Talaat Pasha and Halil Pasha had gone to Bucharest and Sofia, ostensibly to settle the question of the Aegean islands—actually in the interest of drawing both Rumania and Bulgaria in the German alliance. On August 9 the war cabinet (composed of the grand vizier and the ministers of interior, war-marine and finance) had decided to do the following: (1) have the German alliance examined from the legal standpoint; (2) seek alliances with Bulgaria and Rumania; (3) convince the Entente of Turkish neutrality; (4) not to allow either the German ambassador or Liman von Sanders to interfere with politics or military affairs; (5) not to enter the war until the negotiations with Rumania, Bulgaria and Greece had turned out favorably; (6) to open negotiations with both France and Russia. See Ahmed Emin, *op. cit.,* 72.

*Note 95.* Sazonov to Benckendorff, August 16, 1914; Polonsky, 81-2; Pokrovsky, no. 42, p. 25.

*Note 96.* Giers to Sazonov, August 16, 1914; *ibid.,* 83, Pokrovsky; no. 44, p. 26.

*Note 97.* Sazonov to Isvolsky and Benckendorff, August 16, 1914; Polonsky, 83-4; Pokrovsky, no. 45, p. 26; Stieve, no. 41, p. 81. Mukhtar Pasha, the Turkish ambassador in Berlin, supported a Russian *rapprochement* until Turkey's entrance into the war. He writes, "Knowing . . . the perils which threatened Turkey while she counted on Germany, I had recommended with insistence an orientation toward Russia which alone could have consolidated with us . . . . That was my conviction to the world war . . . . We had no reason to lean by sentiment more to one side than to the other . . . ." He adds, "What Turkey could the least desire, during the world war, was the triumph of panslavism and a Russian supremacy in the Orient. This could be realized if she (Turkey) facilitated the provisioning of the Russians by the Straits and favored thus a Balkan coalition against the Central (Powers) . . . . But the Entente was scarcely disposed to it. Alone M. Giers, ambassador of the tsar, seemed inclined . . . ." Mukhtar Pasha, 256-7.

*Note 98.* Isvolsky to Sazonov, August 17, 1914; L. N., III, 4; Stieve, no. 42, p. 82. See also Isvolsky to Sazonov, August 17, 1914, Stieve, no. 43, p. 84.

*Note 99.* Benckendorff to Sazonov, August 17, 1914; Stieve, no. 44, p. 85-6; *Iswolski im Weltkriege,* no. 117, p. 61. Cambon agreed with Grey. See also Michon, *L'alliance franco-russe,* 266-8, for a French comment on these negotiations.

*Note 100.* Giers to Sazonov, August 17, 1914; Pokrovsky, no. 46, p. 27.

*Note 101.* Giers to Sazonov, August 18, 1914; Polonsky, 84-5; Pokrovsky, no. 48, p. 28.

*Note 102.* Same to same, August 19, 1914; Pokrovsky, no. 49, pp. 29-30.

*Note 103.* It was about this time, as has been indicated, that Talaat and Halil were in Bucharest with a Balkan *bloc* under Austria and Germany in mind. Zaïmis and Politis had come from Athens for the meeting, in reference to the question of the islands. Talaat tried to inveigle the Greeks into war, it is said. Ionescu calmed him. He explained then that Rumania would not at all support the Central Powers. See Ionescu, *Some Personal Impressions,* 194-200.

*Note 104.* Giers to Sazonov, August 20, 1914; Pokrovsky, no. 51, p. 31,

*Note 105.* Same to same, August 20, 1914; *ibid.*, no. 52, pp. 31-2. Polonsky, 96-7; R. O. B., II, no. 31, pp. 16-7.

*Note 106.* Sazonov to Isvolsky, August 20, 1914; Polonsky, 87; Pokrovsky, no. 53, p. 32.

*Note 107.* Sazonov to Isvolsky and Benckendorff, August 20, 1914; Pokrovsky, no. 54, p. 32.

*Note 108.* See Ahmed Emin, *op. cit.*, 69-73; Halidé Edib, *op. cit.*, 133ff. For a Communist point of view see M. N. Pokrovsky's *Pages d'histoire* (Paris 1929). Pokrovsky (pp. 122-33) admits that Giers was sincere in his negotiations with the Turks, but insists that Sazonov was not, and that the *Goeben* and *Breslau* really "saved Russia from the *danger* of the Turkish alliance." In the face both of the evidence involved and of the consequences of the incident, such an assertion is ridiculous.

*Note 109.* Mallet to Grey, August 20, 1914; *Cmd.* 7628, no. 24, p. 8. See also Giers to Sazonov, August 19, 20, 1914; Stieve, nos. 48-50, pp. 90-3. For the capitulations in general see Philip Marshall Brown, *Foreigners in Turkey* (Princeton 1914). Halidé Edib, *op. cit.*, 137, states that the Turks "saw that an independent Turkey was an impossibility as long as capitulations continued . . . . These were the two important facts—Russia and capitulations—which the new *régime* was facing when the great war broke out."

*Note 110.* Mallet to Grey, August 20, 1914; *Cmd.* 7628, no. 24, p. 8.

*Note 111.* Sazonov to Giers, August 23, 1914; Stieve, no. 54, pp. 97-8. See also Giers to Sazonov, August 23, 1914, Isvolsky to Sazonov, August 24, 1914, Giers to Sazonov, August 26, 1914; *ibid.*, nos. 55, 56, 57, pp. 99-101. Same correspondence in R. O. B., II, nos. 34-6, pp. 18-19. See also Pokrovsky, no. 55, p. 33, and Polonsky, 87-8.

*Note 112.* Giers to Sazonov, August 27, 1914; Polonsky, 88-9; Pokrovsky, no. 56, pp. 34-5.

*Note 113.* Isvolsky to Sazonov, August 27, 1914; L. N., III, p. 8; Stieve, no. 58, pp. 102-3.

*Note 114.* Giers to Sazonov, August 30, 1914; Pokrovsky, no. 61, pp. 36-7; Polonsky, 89-90. See also Isvolsky to Sazonov, August 29, 1914; Stieve, no. 65, p. 112.

*Note 115.* Giers to Sazonov, September 8, 1914; Stieve, no. 72, p. 120.

*Note 116.* Mallet to Grey, September 9, 1914; *Cmd.* 6628, no. 69, p. 22. Same to same, September 9, 1914; *ibid.*, no. 70, pp. 22-3.

*Note 117.* Giers to Sazonov, September 9, 1914; Stieve, no. 73, p. 121, R. O. B., II, no. 42, p. 23.

*Note 118.* Mallet to Grey, September 9, 1914; *Cmd.* 7628, no. 70, pp. 22-3. See also Bompard, "L'entrée en guerre de la Turquie," *Revue de Paris*, XXVIII (July 15, 1914), 272ff; Letter of Bompard to the director of the *Revue d'histoire de la guerre mondiale*, November 30, 1926 in *ibid.*, V, no. 1, January 1927, pp. 94-6.

*Note 119.* Mallet to Grey, September 9, 1914; *Cmd.* 7628, no. 71, p. 23. Text of Turkish note of September 9, 1914, in R. O. B., II, 26-7; Jean A. Mazard, *Le régime des capitulations en Turquie pendant la guerre de 1914* (Paris 1923), 207-10; *Cmd.* 7628, no. 142, p. 53.

*Note 120.* Sazonov to Giers, September 10, 1914; Stieve, no. 79, p. 127.

*Note 121.* Grey to Mallet, September 15, 16, 1914; *Cmd.* 7628, nos. 76-7, pp. 24-5.

*Note 122.*   Giers to Sazonov, September 15, 1914; R. O. B., II, no. 54, pp. 32-3; Stieve, no. 85, p. 133.

*Note 123.*   Sazonov to Giers, September 19, 1914; *ibid.*, no. 56, p. 34, Stieve, no. 87, p. 135. See also Giers to Sazonov, September 17, 1914; *ibid.*, no. 55, p. 33, Stieve, no. 86, p. 134.

*Note 124.*   Giers to Sazonov, September 25, 1914; R. O. B., II, no. 63, p. 37. See also Giers to Sazonov, September 22, 1914, Sazonov to Giers, September 24, 1914, Giers to Sazonov, September 25, 1914; R. O. B., II, nos. 60, 61, 62, p. 36; Stieve, nos. 91-4, pp. 139-42. The increase in customs was from 11 per cent to 15 per cent *ad valorem* and 8 per cent to 11 per cent.

*Note 125.* Grey to Mallet, September 25, 1914; *Cmd.* 7628, no. 93, p. 21. Giers to Sazonov, September 26, 1914; Stieve, no. 96, p. 143.

*Note 126.*   Sazonov to Giers, September 26, 1914; R. O. B., II, no. 65, p. 38.

*Note 127.*   Note verbale communicated to the Sublime Porte, October 1, 1914; *Cmd.* 7628, no. 142, p. 143. For Delcassé see Isvolsky to Sazonov, September 23, 24, 1914; L. N., III, 16-7.

*Note 128.*   Giers to Sazonov, September 30, 1914; R. O. B., II, nos. 42-3. The Italian, Austro-Hungarian and German offices were closed. See also Giers to Sazonov, October 1, 1914; *ibid.*, no. 73, p. 42. Also Giers to Sazonov, September 30, 1914, October 1, 1914; Stieve, nos. 103-4, pp. 152-3.

*Note 129.*   Giers to Sazonov, October 1, 1914; R. O. B., II, no. 74, pp. 42-3; Stieve, no. 105, pp. 154-5.

*Note 130.*   Giers to Sazonov, October 3, 1914, Sazonov to Giers, October 4, 1914, Giers to Sazonov, October 5, 1914; R. O. B., II, nos. 78, 79, 81.

*Note 131.*   Giers to Sazonov, October 5, 1914; *ibid.*, no. 80, pp. 46-7.

*Note 132.*   On January 11, 1917, a Turco-German treaty was ratified which provided for (1) the abolition of the capitulations and (2) the abolition of the treaties of Paris (1856) and the treaty of Berlin (1878) as well as the privileges of the Lebanon. For the Turks this meant a recognition of her right to throw off foreign tutelage and assume her place in the public law of Europe. The final settlement came, however, only in the treaty of Lausanne in 1923, when the capitulations régime was abolished. See Mandelstam, *Le sort de l'empire ottoman;* Gabriel Bie Ravndal, "The Origins of the Capitulations and the Consular Institution," *Senate Document no. 34, 67th Congress;* J. A. Mazard, *Le régime des capitulations en Turquie pendant la guerre de 1914;* Habib Abi-Chahla, *L'extinction des capitulations en Turquie et dans les régions arabes;* Max Kunke, *Die Kapitulationen der Türkei, deren Aufhebung und die neuen deutsch-türkischen Rechtsvertrage.*

*Note 133.*   Giers to Sazonov, September 13, 1914; R. O. B., II, no. 51, p. 31. See also B. Shatzky, "La question de Constantinople et des détroits," *Revue d'histoire de la guerre mondiale*, IV, no. 4 (October 1916), p. 296; V, no. 1 (January 1927), 94-7.

*Note 134.*   Halidé Edib, *Turkey Faces West*, 138. See also Djemal Pasha, 115ff; Shatzky, 289-309; Mazard, ch. 4; Ahmed Emin, 69-73.

*Note 135.*   Djemal Pasha, 127-8; Talaat Pasha, 289-90; Morgenthau, 123ff; Mandelstam, 90-92; Ahmed Emin, 72-3.

*Note 136.*   See the Sazonov-Giers notes (August 1914); R. O. B., II, nos. 26, 28, 36, 37, 39, pp. 14, 15, 19-20, 21. Mallet to Grey, August 26, 28, 1914; *Cmd.* 7628,

nos. 39, 46, pp. 12-3, 15. It was reported on August 14 that 150 men had arrived, and on August 15, 800 men with officers had arrived. See in general Mühlmann, *op. cit.*, 49-76.

*Note 137.* Giers to Sazonov, September 3, 1914; Stieve, no. 70, pp. 117-8.

*Note 138.* Mallet to Grey, September 20, 1914; Cmd. 7628, no. 84, pp. 27-8.

*Note 139.* Sazonov to Giers, August 14, 1914; R. O. B., II, no. 25, pp. 13-4; Stieve, no. 36, p. 75. See also Beaumont to Grey, August 17, 1914, Mallet to Grey, August 30, 1914, same to same, September 1, 6, 19, 1914; Cmd. 7628, nos. 18, 48, 50, 64, 82, pp. 5-6, 16, 20-1, 27.

*Note 140.* Ahmed Emin, *op. cit.*, 74.

*Note 141.* Mallet to Grey, September 23, 1914; Cmd. 7628, no. 88, p. 29.

*Note 142.* Same to same, August 26, 28 and September 5, 1914; *ibid.*, nos. 39, 46, 60, pp. 12, 15, 18.

*Note 143.* Mallet to Grey, September 27, 1914; Cmd. 7628, no. 97, pp. 32-3. Giers to Sazonov, September 27, 30, 1914; R. O. B., II, nos. 67, 68, 70, pp. 39-40, 41. Morgenthau to Bryan, September 27, 1914; *U. S. Foreign Relations* (1914 Supplement), 113-4. For Turkish regulations of warships in territorial waters see note verbale communicated by Sublime Porte, and reply in Cmd. 7628, no. 145 (with enclosures), pp. 58-62.

*Note 144.* Mallet to Grey, September 27, 1914; Cmd. 7628, no. 98, p. 33. Giers to Sazonov, September 28, 1914; R. O. B., II, no. 69, p. 40; Pokrovsky, no. 79, pp. 45-6; Polonsky, 95-6.

*Note 145.* Grey to Mallet, September 30, 1914; Cmd. 7628, no. 102, p. 34. Isvolsky to Sazonov, October 1, 1914; R. O. B., II, no. 71, p. 41; *Livre noir*, III, p. 19.

*Note 146.* Grey to Mallet, October 3, 1914; Cmd. 7628, no. 105, p. 35. See Liman von Sanders, 33. Admiral von Usedom had arrived in the fall and was later given command of the Dardanelles and Bosphorus.

*Note 147.* Grey to Mallet, October 4, 1914; Cmd. 7628, no. 107, p. 36.

*Note 148.* Ahmed Emin, *op. cit.*, 74.

*Note 149.* Giers to Sazonov, August 20, r914; R. O. B., II, no. 29, p. 15. Same to same, August 29, 1914, Benckendorff to Sazonov, August 28, 1914; R. O. B., II, nos. 38-9, pp. 20-1. See also Liman von Sanders, 32-3. Morgenthau telegraphed on August 27, 1914, that Wangenheim told him Germany desired Turkish neutrality "but intends to prevent Russia from taking Constantinople . . . . Dardanelles are . . . as well fortified as Cuxhaven and impregnable against both British and French fleets . . . ." Morgenthau to Bryan, August 27, 1914; *U. S. Foreign Relations*, 79-80.

*Note 150.* Liman von Sanders, 23. Italics mine. Liman had been refused once before in August 1914. General Hans Kannengiesser Pasha states in his *The Campaign in Gallipoli* (London 1917), 24-25, that the kaiser sent the following telegram: "Whilst fully recognizing the services rendered by you in the past, I appeal to your sense of duty and to that of my officers who are serving under you, to persevere undisturbed by politics in the work I have allotted to you until you receive further orders from me. I consider your duties there at the present critical period to be equivalent to any services you could render me here, if you successfully carry out your difficult task in Turkey, which may perhaps often demand self-sacrifice, but which is of such importance to us here."

*Note 151.* Giers to Sazonov, September 10, 1914; R. O. B., II, nos. 46, 47, pp. 28-9. See also Sanders, 25. General Liman states that in the latter part of August

a military conference took place in which he, Souchon, Wangenheim, military and naval attachés, Enver and others took part. An attack on the Suez was discussed, as well as one on Odessa, which seemed more practicable.

*Note 152.* Grey to Mallet, September 8, 1914, Mallet to Grey, September 8, 1914, communication read to sultan by Mallet, September 21, 1914 (with enclosures); *Cmd.* 7628, nos. 67, 68, 112, pp. 21-2, 38-40. Giers to Sazonov, September 13, 1914; R. O. B., II, no. 52, p. 31; Stieve, no. 83, p. 131.

*Note 153.* Giers to Sazonov, September 14, 1914; R. O. B., II, no. 53, p. 32.

*Note 154.* Giers to Sazonov, September 22, 1914; R. O. B., II, no. 58, p. 35. See Morgenthau to Bryan, September 20, 1914; *U. S. Foreign Relations,* 111. Also Liman von Sanders, 32.

*Note 155.* Giers to Sazonov, September 22, 1914; R. O. B., II, no. 59, p.35, same to same, September 27, 1914; *ibid.,* no. 66, p. 39. See also Pallavicini's note of September 2, 1914; Polonsky, 90-1; Pokrovsky, no. 64, p. 38.

*Note 156.* Giers to Sazonov, October 2, 1914; R. O. B., II, no. 75, p. 43.

*Note 157.* Giers to Sazonov, October 2, 1914; R. O. B., II, no. 76, pp. 44-5. Mallet was reporting similar news about frontier incidents and war preparations in Syria, Mesopotamia, along the Egyptian frontier and in Persia. See especially Mallet to Grey (September-October 1914); *Cmd.* 7628, nos. 100, 104, 108, 109, 113, 125 (with enclosures), 129, 143 (with enclosures).

*Note 158.* Giers to Sazonov, October 6, 1914; R. O. B., II, no. 83, p. 48. Enver did not share the grand vizier's views. He desired to force Bulgaria's hand. Giers to Sazonov, September 24, 1914; Polonsky, 94; Pokrovsky, nos. 76, 77, pp. 44-5. See also Mallet to Grey, October 5, 1914; *Cmd.* 7628, no. 108, p. 36.

*Note 159.* Giers to Sazonov, October 16, 18, 1914; R. O. B., II, nos. 87, 88, pp. 49-50. See also Giers to Sazonov, October 19, 1914; Polonsky, 100. Bompard had wired Delcassé on September 30 that when the Porte had received the desired money it would act immediately. See Isvolsky to Sazonov, September 30, 1914; Polonsky, 98-9.

*Note 160.* Mallet to Grey, October 6, 1914; *Cmd.* 7628, no. 147, enclosures 1 and 2, pp. 63-4.

*Note 161.* Same to same, October 22, 1914; *ibid.,* no. 157, p. 66. Giers had the same information. See Giers to Sazonov, October 18, 20, 1914; R. O. B., II, nos. 88, 89, p. 50.

*Note 162.* Giers to Sazonov, October 25, 1914; Polonsky, 101-2. This includes a Pallavicini dispatch of October 19, 1914. See also Morgenthau to Bryan, October 19, 1914; *Foreign Relations,* 119-21.

*Note 163.* Mühlmann, *op. cit.,* nos. 9-10, pp. 101-2.

*Note 164.* Mallet to Grey, October 27, 1914; *Cmd.* 7628, no. 169, p. 170. See also the Giers dispatches, October 15-29, 1914; R. O. B., II, nos. 86-91, pp. 49-51, and *Livre noir,* III, 24-27.

*Note 165.* Giers to Sazonov, October 29, 1914; R. O. B., II, no. 90, pp. 50-1. Liman von Sanders states that the news of the attack was a surprise to him. He says that Djemal Pasha, minister of marine, must have known. Both Talaat and Djemal, however, denied all prior knowledge of the attack. See Talaat Pasha, 292-93; Djemal Pasha, 132-3; Mukhtar Pasha, 281-5; Liman von Sanders, 31-2. Ahmed Emin (*op. cit.,* 75), states that "the actual aggression took place without the knowledge of any member of the Turkish government." See also Morgenthau to Bryan, October 29, 1914;

*Foreign Relations*, 281-82, and Bompard, "L'entrée en guerre de la Turquie," *Revue de Paris*, XXVIII, (July 15, 1921), 283-8. In the Turkish official history it is stated that on October 20, Souchon was prevented from entering the Black sea by the Turks. On October 23, he was forbidden again. On October 27, he was authorized by the vice-commander of the Bosphorus forts to go for instruction purposes. Then came the attack. See Larcher, *La guerre turque*, 51-2. See also Mühlmann, *op. cit.*, 71-7.

*Note 166.* Sazonov to Giers, October 29, 1914; R. O. B., no. 91, p. 51. Morgenthau to Bryan, October 29, 1914; *Foreign Relations*, 127. Grey to Mallet, October 30, 1914; *Cmd.* 7628, no. 179, p. 72.

*Note 167.* Giers to Sazonov, October 30, 1914; R. O. B., II, no. 94, p. 52. Morgenthau to Bryan, October 29, 1914; *Foreign Relations*, 127.

*Note 168.* Benckendorff to Sazonov, October 31, 1914; R. O. B., II, no. 96, p. 53. Morgenthau to Bryan, October 30, 1914; *Foreign Relations*, 127-8.

*Note 169.* Sazonov to Isvolsky and Benckendorff, November 1, 1914; R. O. B., II, no. 97, pp. 53-4.

*Note 170.* Ahmed Emin, *op. cit.*, 75-6.

*Note 171.* Liman von Sanders, 33. Liman could not vouch for the correctness of the information, but the Russian documents prove this to have been the case. See also Halidé Edib, *op. cit.*, 132-40, and Ahmed Emin, *op. cit.*, 76.

*Note 172.* See Corbett, I, 374; Djemal Pasha, 392-3; Grey, II, 176; Buchanan, I, 223-4; Paléologue, I, 181ff; Morgenthau, 123-9. See also Hans Kannengiesser, *op. cit.*, chs. 1-3, and Ahmed Emin, *op. cit.*, 75-7.

*Note 173.* See Victor Margueritte, *Les alliés contre la Russie* (Paris 1927), 118.

*Note 174.* Morgenthau, 109-10; Buchanan, I, 223-4; Paléologue, I, 151; Falkenhayn, *German General Staff*, 20-21; Pomiankowski, 17-18. See also the Lloyd George statements in the House of Commons, August 4, 1923 (*Parliamentary Debates*, v. 157, col. 1998), and in the New York *Times*, September 23, 1922.

*Note 175.* Paléologue, I, 178; Buchanan, *loc. cit.*

*Note 176.* Morgenthau, 157-180; Corbett, I, 375-6; Mandelstam, 81-4; Falkenhayn, 53-4; Liman von Sanders, ch. 5; Larcher, *La guerre turque*, 38-44. For a review of incidents leading to the war see *Dispatch from H. M. Ambassador at Constantinople Summarizing Events Leading to the Rupture of Relations with Turkey and Reply Thereto. Cmd. 7716. Miscellaneous no. 14 (1914);* Giers to Sazonov, November 13, 1914; R. O. B., II, no. 98, p. 58; Sir Edward Cook, *Britain and Turkey, Causes of the Rupture* (London 1915); A. Thomazi, *La guerre navale aux Dardanelles*, 21-31; Pomiankowski, 75-88.

*Note 177.* For text see Mears, *Modern Turkey*, 608-9; *International Conciliation*, no. 68 (January 1915); Larcher, *op. cit.*, 44-9. Text of "Fetva" in Horne and Austin, *The Great Events of the Great War*, II, 398-400. See also Ahmed Emin, *op. cit.*, 174-80; Halidé Edib, *op. cit.*, 141. Turkey declared war on France, England and Russia on November 12, 1914.

*Note 178.* The Turco-German alliance of January 11, 1915, provided in the main that: (1) both the parties would offer mutual aid with all their forces in case one of them were the object of an attack on the part of Russia, France or England, or of a coalition of at least two Balkan states; (2) in case of an attack by England, the engagement assumed by Germany was to apply only in case Turkey were engaged

simultaneously with a second European state. Another treaty signed September 28, 1916, stipulated that (1) neither of the two parties would sign a peace treaty as long as the territory of one of them was occupied by the enemy, and (2) that neither would conclude a separate peace. See Mühlmann, *op. cit.*, 98-101, for texts.

*Note 179.* War Speeches by British Ministers, 1914-1916 (London 1917), 55-6.

*Note 180.* Ahmed Emin, *op. cit.*, 75.

## CHAPTER IV

*Note 1.* The documentary publications of the Soviet government are: E. A. Adamov (ed.), *Konstantinopol i prolivy* (2 vols. Moscow 1925-26); M. N. Pokrovsky (ed.), *Tsarskaia Rossiia v mirovoi voine*, (Leningrad 1926). German edition: *Zaristiche Russland im Weltkriege* (Berlin 1927); E. A. Adamov (ed.), *Razdel Aziatskoi Turtsii* (Moscow 1924); F. Stieve, *Iswolski im Weltkriege* (Berlin 1925); J. Polonsky, *Documents diplomatiques secrets russes, 1914-1917* (Paris 1928), consisting of translations from the Adamov and Pokrovsky publications. F. Stieve, *Das Russische Orangebuch über den Kriegsausbruch mit der Türkei* (Berlin 1926); V. Margueritte, *Livre noir*, III (Paris 1927). See also Professor R. J. Kerner, "Russia, the Straits and Constantinople, 1914-1915," *Journal of Modern History*, I, no. 3 (September 1929), 400-15, and Professor B. Shatzky, "La question de Constantinople et des détroits," *Revue d'histoire de la guerre mondiale*, IV, no. 4 (October 1926, 289-309; V, no. 1 (January 1927) 19-43.

*Note 2.* For a Communist point of view on the fulfilment of Russia's "historic task," see M. N. Pokrovsky, *Pages d'histoire* (Paris 1929), 122-56. In his chapter entitled "La Russia tsariste et la guerre pendant l'hiver 1914-1915," he argues against the attempt to solve the problem of the "free sea," in the Mediterranean, on the ground that it is not in reality "free" since the British, through Cyprus, the Suez canal, Egypt, Malta, Gibraltar and general naval supremacy, control that sea. On similar grounds, however, it could be argued that there is no free sea in any fundamental sense as long as one Power has such a large naval force. Pokrovsky's argument could not vitiate the principle of the fundamental necessity of Russia to get an outlet to the sea.

*Note 3.* Paléologue, I, 178. Paléologue to Delcassé, September 26, 1914; L. N., III, 17-19. M. Krivochine had expressed a similar view, stating, however, that Constantinople might become a neutral city like Tangier. Sazonov was undecided. The naval coaling station was to be at Bujukdere.

*Note 4.* Isvolsky to Sazonov, October 13, 1914; *ibid.*, 20-21; Stieve, *Iswolski im Weltkriege*, nos. 224, 225, pp. 118-20; *Isvolsky and the World War*, 247-48.

*Note 5.* Paléologue, I, 178. Sazonov, with many others, looked on the possession of Constantinople with some misgiving, as a source of political weakness for Russia. See Sazonov, *op. cit.*, 245-46; Alexinsky, *Russia and the Great War*, 302-5; Philipson and Buxton, *The Question of the Bosphorus and the Dardanelles*, 194ff; Hoschiller, M., "La Russie sur le chemin de Byzance," *Revue de Paris*, XXII, no. 16 (August 15, 1915), 779-84. Apparently Isvolsky himself shared the same view, as indicated in his letter to the *Journal des Débats*, (October 3, 1918), written September 30, 1918.

*Note 6.* Isvolsky to Sazonov, November 7, 1914; L. N., III, 28.

*Note 7.* Benckendorff to Sazonov, November 9, 1914; Adamov, *Konstantinopol i prolivy*, I, 228. See also R. Martel, "L'Orient et la guerre d'après les archives diplo-

matiques russes," *Le monde slave*, III, no. 10 (October 1926), 135. It should be remembered that on September 5, 1914, France, England and Russia agreed to make war and peace in common. See *Livre noir*, III, 116, for text. See also Grey, II, 159; Mowat, *Select Treaties and Documents* (Oxford pamphlets, 1914-15), XVIII, no. 81, p. 19.

*Note 8.*   Benckendorff to Sazonov, November 13, 1914; Polonsky, 249.

*Note 9.*   Churchill, II, 198; Corbett, II, 204; Buchanan, I, 224-5; Paléologue, I, 186-7. The memorandum is to be found in Adamov, I, 233-4. British memorandum to Sazonov, November 14, 1914.

*Note 10.*   Paléologue, I, 188. On November 5, 1914, the British government proclaimed martial law in Egypt, and on the same day annexed Cyprus. The work of partition of the Turkish Empire, for Britain, was a matter of acting, not of asking. Egypt formally became a protectorate on December 18, 1914, and Hussein became sultan of Egypt on December 19, 1914. See Knabenshue to Bryan, August 7, 1914; Arnold to Bryan, November 5, 1914, December 20, 1914; Spring-Rice to Bryan, December 18, 1914, in *U. S. Foreign Relations. War Supplement*, (1914), 49, 144, 152-3. Isvolsky to Sazonov, December 18, 1914; L. N., III, 41-3, and proclamation in *ibid.*, 119. See also George Young, *Egypt*, 200-5; *Cyprus, Peace Handbook*, no. 65, pp. 68-71: text of notes in *l'Europe nouvelle*, V, no. 12 (March 25, 1922), 373, and Mowat, *op. cit.*, 95-8.

*Note 11.*   Paléologue, I, 192-3.

*Note 12.*   *Loc. cit.*

*Note 13.*   Isvolsky to Sazonov, November 20, 1914; L. N., III, 31-2.

*Note 14.*   Motono, Japanese ambassador at Petrograd, to Kato, November 23, 1914; *ibid.*, 35.

*Note 15.*   Corbett, II, 67. See also Commandant M. Larcher, *La grande guerre dans les balkans*, ch. 2.

*Note 16.*   Corbett, *loc. cit.*

*Note 17.*   Churchill, II, 485-95.

*Note 18.*   Fisher, *Records and Memories*, I, 76, 82; Corbett, I, 154; Grey, II, 78-80; Churchill, II, 185-6; Morgenthau, 184. See also *Cmd. 8490* (1917). *Dardanelles Commission. First Report*, 19.

*Note 19.*   Fisher, I, 94.

*Note 20.*   *Cmd. 8490*, p. 14.

*Note 21.*   J. H. Williams, *The Emperor Nicholas as I Knew Him* (London 1922), 23-25.

*Note 22.*   Churchill, II, 85-6. See also *Cmd. 8490*, p. 15; Arthur, Life of Lord Kitchener, III, 100-101. Kudashev to Sazonov, December 31, 1914; Adamov, II, 128-29. According to Prince Kudashev, the grand duke pointed out that Russia would follow the French plan of attack on Germany and Austria, and if it were best to advance against Turkey, it might be desirable to attack her at one of several sensitive points. See also R. J. Kerner, "Russia, Constantinople, and the Straits," J. M. H., I, no. 3, (September 1929).

*Note 23.*   Churchill, *loc. cit.*, Arthur,   *loc. cit.*

*Note 24.*   Churchill, II, 87; *Cmd. 8490*, 15ff.

*Note 25.*   *Cmd. 8490*, p. 21. Arguments were heard from Kitchener, Churchill, Fisher and Sir A. Wilson. See also Callwell, *The Dardanelles*, 7-13.

*Note 26.*   *Cmd. 8490*, p. 21.

*Note 27.*   Churchill, II, 113-4.

*Note 28.* See Kerner, *loc. cit.;* M. T. Florinsky, "Russian Military Leaders and the Problem of Constantinople during the War," *Political Science Quarterly,* XLIV, no. 1 (March 1929), 111-2. Prince Kudashev had drawn up a memorandum at Grand Duke Nicholas' suggestion on December 18, 1914, stating that "seizure of the Straits by our troops alone was entirely out of the question." See also Isvolsky to Sazonov, February 20, 1915; L. N., III, 66-7. Delcassé urged aid of the Russian fleet in the attack and simultaneous arrival at Constantinople. See also Sazonov, 255-6.

*Note 29.* Churchill, II, 161-2. An official British account of the initiation of the Dardanelles campaign is Brig. General Aspinall-Oglander, *Military Operations. Gallipoli* (London 1929), I, 39-106.

*Note 30.* As early as August 1914, Venizelos had favored the Allies, and was the active partisan of the Entente. The peculiarly Greek phase of the question will be considered in Chapter V. See Venizelos' speech of August 26, 1917, before the Greek chamber of deputies, in *The Vindication of Greek National Policy,* 73ff.

*Note 31.* See the speech of Venizelos of August 26, 1917; *ibid.,* 84-7. Also Frangulis, *La Grèce et la crise mondiale,* I, 186-7; Cosmin, *L'Entente et la Grèce,* I, 33-8; Melas, 150ff; Demidov to Sazonov, March 6, 1914, in Polonsky, 268-9.

*Note 32.* Venizelos to London, Paris, Petrograd, March 5, 1915; Frangulis, I, 195-6. This telegram was also communicated to Clemenceau. See also H. R. H. Prince Nicholas of Greece, *My Fifty Years* (London 1928), 265-66.

*Note 33.* Genadius to Athens, March 6, 1915; Cosmin, I, 38-9. See also Asquith, *Memories and Reflections,* II, 77-8.

*Note 34.* Sicilanos to Athens, March 7, 1915; Cosmin, I, 39, and Frangulis, I, 200.

*Note 35.* Demidov to Sazonov, February 27, 1915; Polonsky, 265.

*Note 36.* Sazonov to Demidov, March 7, 1915; *ibid.,* 287.

*Note 37.* Same to same, March 2, 1915; *ibid.,* 266.

*Note 38.* This was on March 3, 1915. The Quai d'Orsay was informed that "the Russian government would not *at any price* accept the coöperation of Greece in Constantinople." See Churchill, II, 203. See also *Parliamentary Debates,* (H. C.), January 5, 1916, vol. 77, cols. 934-5; February 24, 1916, vol. 80, cols. 782-4. See also Ivolsky to Sazonov, March 4, 6, 1915; L. N., III, 74-6. Same to same, March 6 (?), 1915; Polonsky, 254-5. Delcassé felt that the Russian government should not refuse the Greeks, as England desired their entrance into the war.

*Note 39.* Benckendorff to Sazonov, March 4, 1915; Polonsky, 266-7.

*Note 40.* Churchill, II, 205. This note was not sent. See Churchill's note to Grey, March 6, 1915; *ibid,* 205.

*Note 41.* Dragoumis to Athens, March 7, 1915; Cosmin, I, 39; Frangulis, I, 199-200. See also Martel, in *Le monde slave,* III, no. 10, October 1926, 120-24. Sazonov told Dragoumis that England would cede Smyrna and large part of Asia Minor to Greece. He realized Greece had no "aims" on Constantinople, but public opinion had to be reassured. The British official version of the Dardanelles campaign asserts that Demidov asked Constantine point blank whether Greece would participate in the Dardanelles operations (in certain eventualities), as early as August 1914. Neither the Russian evidence nor the Russian attitude are consonant with this view. See Aspinall-Oglander, 39-40.

*Note 42.* Stavridi to Venizelos, London, March 5, 1915; Frangulis, I, 191-2, footnote citation of the complete text.

*Note 43.* Baron M. de Taube, *La politique russe d'avant-guerre* (Paris 1928), 394-9. Taube had criticized Sazonov for being too aggressive in the Liman von Sanders crisis and too mild in his November 1914 demands on Constantinople and the Straits,

*Note 44.* Paléologue, 273-5. Also Max Hoschiller, "La Russie sur le chemin de Byzance," *Revue de Paris*, XXVII, no. 16 (August 15, 1915), 784-90. Prince Trubetskoy, eminent liberal leader, wrote at this time in March 1915, in the *Russkaia Viedomosti*, "Constantinople and the Straits must become Russian." Excerpts from Russian speeches and articles may be found in *Politicus*, "The Future of Turkey," *Fortnightly Review*, v. 103 (April 1, 1915), 605-16. See also J. W. Bienstock, "Dostoievsky et la guerre," *Revue hebdomadaire*, V, no. 21 (May 22, 1915), 501-22. The full text of Sazonov's speech to the Duma, February 9, 1915, is in R. O. B., II, 59-68. For Communist point of view, see Pokrovsky, *Pages d'histoire*, 146-50.

*Note 45.* Sazonov to Isvolsky and Benckendorff, January 20, 1915; Memorandum of Buchanan to Sazonov, February 11, 1915; Polonsky, 250-1. Grey stated that "he had no intention at all of changing what he (Grey) had said on the subject of the Straits."

*Note 46.* Isvolsky to Sazonov, February 23, 1915; L. N., III, 67-8. Prince Kudashev at this same time had given up any hope of solving the problem of the Straits for the reason that Russia could not afford the troops. However, on the next day, Danilov had agreed to the sending of an army corps. See M. T. Florinsky, *op. cit.*, 112-3. See Kerner, *op. cit.*, 409-10.

*Note 47.* Isvolsky to Sazonov, February 25, 1915; L. N., III, 69; Polonsky, 298-9.

*Note 48.* Sazonov to Benckendorff and Isvolsky, February 28, 1915; Polonsky, 299-300. See also Isvolsky to Sazonov, March 4, 1915; *ibid.*, 300.

*Note 49.* *Parliamentary Debates*, (H. C.), v. 70, February 25, 1915, co. 364. Mr. Outhwaite asked if Grey had seen Sazonov's statement "that Russia intended permanently to occupy Constantinople," and whether the statement was made with the knowledge and approval of the British government.

*Note 50.* Expressions of public opinion may be found in Hoschiller, "La Russie sur le chemin de Byzance," *Revue de Paris*, XXII, no. 16 (August 15, 1915), 784-94. See also Sazonov, *op. cit.*, 250-2.

*Note 51.* Paléologue, I. 295. Buchanan, I, 223-4.

*Note 52.* Buchanan to Grey, March 1, 1915; Grey, II, 199-200.

*Note 53.* Grey to Buchanan, March 2, 1915; Grey, II, 199-200. See also Mears, *op. cit.*, 609ff.; Corbett, II, 204; Benckendorff to Sazonov, March 7, 1915 in Stieve, *Iswolski im Weltkriege*, no. 263, p. 173.

*Note 54.* Paléologue, I, 299; Buchanan, I, 225-6.

*Note 55.* Isvolsky to Sazonov, March 1, 1915; L. N., III, 69-70.

*Note 56.* Same to same, March 4, 1915; *ibid.*, 73-4.

*Note 57.* Same to same, March 2, 4, 1915; *ibid.*, III, 71-3.

*Note 58.* Memorandum of Sazonov to Paléologue and Buchanan, March 4, 1915; Polonsky, 252; L. N., III, 122-3; Cocks, *Secret Treaties*, 19-24; Mears, 610-11; Laloy, 107-110. Originally published in *Pravda*, November 23, 1917. See also Sazonov, 256-7, and Kerner, *loc. cit.*

*Note 59.* Isvolsky to Sazonov, March 6, 1915, March 10, 1915; L. N., III, 76-8.

*Note 60.* Memorandum of the French ambassador at Petrograd to Sazonov, March 8, 1915; Polonsky, 255-6.

*Note* 61. Isvolsky to Sazonov, March 9, 1915; L. N., III, 77.

*Note* 62. Same to same, March 10, 1915; *ibid.*, 79. At the same time Delcassé wanted precise information as to fortifications; whether Russia admitted an international organ like that on the Danube, and whether Constantinople would be a free port. Sazonov on the same day asked that the press be censored on the subject, and Isvolsky undertook measures in that direction. See Sazonov to Isvolsky, March 10, 1915; Polonsky, 257.

*Note* 63. Isvolsky to Sazonov (two telegrams), March 10, 1915; L. N., III, 79-81. Information from Raffalovitch, a Russian agent in the Russo-Asiatic Bank in Paris. He suggested Raffalovitch, already designated on the council of the debt, as the one to draw up the plans.

*Note* 64. Memorandum of the British embassy at Petrograd to Sazonov, March 6, 1915; Polonsky, 253-4.

*Note* 65. Memorandum of the British embassy at Petrograd, March 12, 1915; Golder, 60-2. See also Pokrovsky, *op. cit.*, 150-6, for comment.

*Note* 66. Sazonov to Benckendorff, March 20, 1915; L. N., III, 124-5. He asked also that Ispahan and Yezd, the zone forming the corner of the Russo-Afghan frontier, be attributed to Russia. See also Sazonov to Benckendorff, March 20, 1915; Polonsky, 292-3.

*Note* 67. Memorandum of the British embassy, March 12, 1915; Polonsky, 257.

*Note* 68. Sazonov to Isvolsky, March 18, 1915; L. N., III, 123.

*Note* 69. Basili to Kudashev, March 14, 1915 (two telegrams); same to same, March 15, 1915; Sazonov to Neratov, March 15, 1915; Polonsky, 288-9; L. N., III, 83-4.

*Note* 70. Neratov to Sazonov, March 15, 1915; Polonsky, 290.

*Note* 71. Sazonov to Isvolsky, March 16, 1915; Polonsky, 290. See the formula for the subject of the holy places proposed by Paléologue, March 16, 1915; *ibid.*, 290-21, and L. N., III, 85-6.

*Note* 72. Isvolsky to Sazonov, March 17, 1915; *ibid.*, 291, and L. N., III, 82.

*Note* 73. Paléologue, I, 299.

*Note* 74. Isvolsky to Sazonov, March 26, 1915; L. N., III, 93-4.

*Note* 75. Isvolsky to Sazonov, March 28, 1915; L. N., III, 96-7. As early as March 19, 1915, *Le Temps* pronounced in favor of Russia having the Straits. See reprint in L. N., III, 126-8. The historian, Edouard Driault, writing in *Revue des études napoléoniennes*, VII, (May-June, 1915), 360-411 (reprinted as *La réprise de Constantinople et l'alliance franco-russe* (Paris 1915), declared: "Constantinople is necessary to the total independence and grandeur of Russia." See also J. Aulneau, "*La Turquie et la guerre* (Paris 1916)", 332-3, who expresses a similar opinion. See also Isvolsky to Sazonov, March 18, 19, 1915; L. N., III, 86. On April 12 Sazonov appointed Prince Trubetskoi as one of the Allied high commissioners in Constantinople. Sazonov to Trubetskoi; April 12, 1915; Polonsky, 271.

*Note* 76. Isvolsky to Sazonov, April 1, 5, 1915; L. N., III, 99, 101.

*Note* 77. Verbal note of the French embassy, April 10, 1915; Adamov, I, 295. For Sazonov's attitude on the French negotiations, see Sazonov, 253-5.

*Note* 78. Memorandum of British embassy at Petrograd, April 22, 1915; Sazonov's memorandum to Buchanan, April 22, 1915; Pokrovsky, nos. 93-4, pp. 310-20; *Le monde slave*, III, no. 7, (July 1928), nos. 93, 94, pp. 145-6. See also Poincaré to Nicholas II, April 23, 1915; Pokrovsky, no. 95, p. 321; *Le monde slave*, III, no. 7,

no. 96, p. 147. Also British memorandum, April 23, 1915; French memorandum, April 24, 1915; Adamov, I, 332. For later developments on the partition of Turkey, see below, ch. 9.

*Note 79.* See the decision of the committee on imperial defence regarding the Straits, February 11, 1903. Memorandum by Sir Charles Hardinge. Memorandum respecting the passage of Russian warships through the Dardanelles. Foreign office, November 15, 1906; *British Documents*, IV, 59-60. Also Corbett, 204.

*Note 80.* See Georges Louis, *Les carnots de Georges Louis* (Paris 1926), 136; Ernest Judet, *Georges Louis* (Paris 1925), 143.

*Note 81.* Grey, II, 186-9. See also Charles Seymour, *Intimate Papers of Colonel House*, I, 354-5, 363, 393; II, 181. See also *Politicus*, "The Future of Turkey," *Fortnightly Review*, v. 103 (April 1, 1915), 604-16; Outis, "Problems of diplomacy in the Near East," *ibid.*, 583-91; J. B. Firth, "England, Russia, and Constantinople," *ibid.*, 645-54; J. Ellis Barker, "The Future of Constantinople," *Nineteenth Century*, LXXXVII (March 1915), 493-522. All these writers tend to justify Russian claims, but minimize the importance of Constantinople.

*Note 82.* Lord Bertie, *Diary of Lord Bertie*, I, 121. Note of February 25, 1915. M. Odahari, military attaché of Japan in Russia, noted on March 3, 1915, that in Petrograd "they say that the operations against the Dardanelles have been undertaken by England and France to prevent the Straits from falling under the power of Russia." Odahari to Kazehava, March 3, 1915; Polonsky, 251-2. See also Kerner, "Russia, the Staits and Constantinople, 1914-1915," *Journal of Modern History*, I, no. 3 (September 1929), 410, and B. Shatzky, "La question de Constantinople et des détroits," *Revue d'histoire de la guerre mondiale*, V, no. 1, 19-43.

*Note 83.* Bacheracht to Sazonov, Berne, April 9, 1915; Sazonov to Isvolsky, May 21, 1915; Polonsky, 300-1. Djavid denied any such intentions.

*Note 84.* Isvolsky to Sazonov, May 23, 1915; *ibid.*, 301-2.

*Note 85.* Isvolsky to Sazonov, May 28, 1915; *Polonsky*, 301-2.

*Note 86.* Sazonov to Isvolsky, May 30, 1915; *ibid.*, 302-3.

*Note 87.* Janushkevich to Sazonov, April 3, 1915; Polonsky, 259-61. Kudashev, apparently had given up hope and was later inclined toward a separate peace with Turkey. An army corps being unavailable, it was suggested in the spring of 1915, that 4,500 men be sent. On the objections of the British to this, Danilov complained, "they simply don't want us to take part in the operation, they don't want us to enter Constantinople together with them." See Florinsky, "Russian Military Leaders and the Problem of Constantinople," *Political Science Quarterly*, XLIV, no. 1 (March 1929), 113-14.

*Note 88.* Private letters of Princess Vasilchikova to Emperor Nicholas II, March 10, 30 and May 27, 1915; Golder, 41-7, and Polonsky, 318-26.

*Note 89.* Nekliudov to Sazonov, July 20, 1915, July 28, 1915; Kaklamanos to Gounaris, August 2, 1915; Polonsky, 326-9.

*Note 90.* Paléologue, II, 150. Good studies of the Dardanelles campaign may be found in Captain W. D. Puleston, *The Dardanelles Expedition* (Annapolis 1926); Liman von Sanders, *op. cit.*, chs. 7-9; General Hans Kannengiesser Pasha, *The Campaign in Gallipoli* (London 1927); Larcher, *La guerre turque*, 191-242; Larcher, *La grande guerre dans les Balkans*, ch. 2; Churchill, II, 190-1, 324-46, 47-105; Lt. Gen. Ellison, *Perils of Amateur Strategy* (London 1926); Callwell, *The Dardanelles* (New York 1916); Ellis Ashmead-Bartlett, *The Uncensored Dardanelles* (London 1928?); Corbett,

III, 230-58; Morgenthau, 171-252. The official British reports on the campaign are: Dardanelles Commission. *First Report. Cmd. 8490* (1917) Dardanelles Commission. *Supplement to First Report. Cmd. 8502* (1917). *The Final Report of the Dardanelles Commission. Cmd. 371.* British official history of the Dardanelles campaign, Aspinall-Oglander, *op. cit.*, (entire). See also A. Kolenkovsky, *Dardanellskaia operatsia* (Moscow 1930).

*Note 91.* Kudashev to Sazonov, February 18, 1916; Laloy, 127-31. See also Rosen, *Forty Years of Diplomacy*, II, 212-13; Florinsky, 114-15; Martel, 151-2. For the tsar's statement, see Polonsky, 305.

*Note 92.* Seymour, *Intimate Papers of Colonel House*, II, 181.

*Note 93.* See Memorandum of Sir Edward Grey, February 22, 1916; Seymour, *op. cit.*, II, 201-2. Also interview of February 10, 1916 in *ibid*, 170.

*Note 94.* This statement is from a letter of Colonel House to the writer, dated August 18, 1930. Colonel House seems to be perfectly consistent in this attitude, which he had always taken. However, the *Intimate Papers* (II, 170 fn) seem to indicate a more definite statement. Professor Seymour, in a letter to the writer, October 1, 1930, state that while there is no evidence to show that House ever went beyond offering free access to the open sea to Russia through internationalization and neutralization of the Straits, he never vigorously opposed the Allied policy because of a possible threat to breaking the "understanding" with Grey and the danger of driving Russia out of the alliance.

*Note 95.* Cox, 17. The negotiations with reference to publication of the agreement may be found in Adamov, *Konstantinopol i prolivy*, I, 412-48. Britain and France finally consented in principle, but were glad Russia was contented with the Duma announcement. The best discussion of this entire matter is in R. J. Kerner, "Russia and the Straits, 1915-1917," *Slavonic Review*, VIII, no. 24 (March 1930), 589-93.

*Note 96.* F. J. C. Hearnshaw, in A. W. Ward and G. P. Gooch, *Cambridge History of British Foreign Policy* (Cambridge 1923), II, 357-58.

*Note 97.* See below, ch. 9. Some phases of the Constantinople cession have a direct bearing on the secret treaties with reference to Asiatic Turkey and will be treated in that connection. These phases deal with Italy's final assent to the Constantinople agreement, the attitude of the provisional government in Russia, the agreement fixing the western boundary of France and the eastern boundary along the Russo-German frontier, and the final denunciation of the secret agreements by the Bolshevik government in the winter of 1917.


## CHAPTER V

*Note 1.* The Italian declaration may be found in P. Fauchille, *La guerre de 1914* (Paris, n. d.), I, 284. See also Rodd, 204.

*Note 2.* Italy had complained that during the war with Tripoli, Austrian action had prevented her from carrying out operations which would have shortened the war. See M. F. A. to Avarna, December 9, 1914; *Italian Green Book* (London 1915), no. 1, pp. 11-12. (Hereafter I. G. B.). Article VII of the 1912 treaty of the Triple Alliance provided for reciprocal compensations in case either party moved in Balkans, the Adriatic or Aegean Sea. See A. F. Pribram, *Secret Treaties*, I, 249-50; Berchtold report, July 25, 1914; A. R. B., II, no. 46, pp. 39-40.

*Note 3.* Avarna to M. F. A., December 20, 1914; I. G. B., no. 7, pp. 17-18; Berchtold to Macchio, December 21, 1914; A. R. B., no. 2 (J. B. Scott, Carnegie Endowment, 1916), I, no. 78, pp. 194-97.

*Note 4.* Sonnino to Italian ambassadors in Berlin and Vienna, December 20, 1914; I. G. B., no. 8, pp. 18-19.

*Note 5.* Same to same, January 15, 1915; I G. B., no. 11, pp. 22-24.

*Note 6.* Avarna to Sonnino, January 18, 1915; I. G. B., no. 12, pp. 25-27; Burian to Macchio, January 20, 1915; A. R. B., no. 2, no. 98, pp. 211-214.

*Note 7.* Avarna to Sonnino, March 27, 1915; I. G. B., no. 56, pp. 75-6; Same to same, March 28, 1915; A. R. B., no. 2, no. 131, pp. 252-53.

*Note 8.* Sonnino to Avarna, March 31, 1915; I. G. B., no. 58, pp. 77-9; Burian to Macchio, March 31, 1915; A. R. B., no. 2, no. 132, pp. 253-54. See also Krupensky to Sazonov, March 19, 1915; Pokrovsky, no. 62, p. 294.

*Note 9.* Sonnino to Avarna, April 8, 1915; I. G. B., no. 64, pp. 82-4; Burian to Macchio, April 11, 1915; A. R. B., no. 2, no. 141, pp. 263-6.

*Note 10.* Avarna to Sonnino, April 16, 1915; I. G. B., no. 71, pp. 86-9; Hohenlohe to Macchio, April 12, 1915; A. R. B., no. 2, no. 142, pp. 266-7.

*Note 11.* For additional light on these negotiations see Rodd, III, 227-50; Giolitti, 393ff; Salandra, *La neutralita italiana* (Milan 1928), 82-114; T. H. Page, *Italy and the World War* (N. Y. 1920), 191-207; Pribram, *Austrian Foreign Policy*, 77-87; Burian, *Austria in Dissolution* (N. Y. n. d.), 19-63; B. Auerbach, *L'Autriche et la Hongrie pendant la guerre*, 57-92; R. W. Seton-Watson, "Italy's Balkan Policy in 1914," *Slavonic Review*, V, no. 13 (June 1926), 48-65.

*Note 12.* Isvolsky to Sazonov, August 2, 1914; Sazonov to Isvolsky, August 4, 1914; Polonsky, 168, 215. The Italian negotiations may be traced from the Russian angle in the Pokrovsky documents and the Polonsky translations. See also *Le Monde slave*, II, no. 6, (June 1928), 410 ff, and III, no. 7 (July 1928), 125-28. See also Churchill, *World Crisis*, (1915), 16. An excellent summary is in Prof. R. W. Seton-Watson's "Italian Intervention and the Secret Treaty of London", *Slavonic Review*, V, no. 14 (December 1926), 271-97.

*Note 13.* Sazonov to Isvolsky, August 4, 1914; Polonsky, 216; Pokrovsky, no. 2, pp. 263-4.

*Note 14.* Isvolsky to Sazonov, August 5, 1914; L. N., III, 1. Doumergue reserved the subject of the national aspirations of France.

*Note 15.* Same to same, August 7, 1914; *ibid.*, 1-2.

*Note 16.* Sazonov to Krupensky, August 7, 1914; Polonsky, 216-7. See also Sazonov to Paris, London, Rome, August 7-10, 1914; Pokrovsky, 266-9.

*Note 17.* Sazonov to London, Paris, Rome, August 10, 1914; Polonsky, 217-18; Pokrovsky, no. 14, p. 269.

*Note 18.* Benckendorff to Sazonov, August 11, 1914; Sazonov to Benckendorff, August 17, 1914; Polonsky, 218; Pokrovsky, nos. 15, 18, pp. 270-1. On August 15, the Italian government informed Krupensky it could take no action at the time. See Krupensky to Sazonov, August 15, 1914; Pokrovsky, no. 17, pp. 270-1.

*Note 19.* Sazonov to Benckendorff, August 17, 1914; Sazonov to Krupensky, August 18, 1914; Pokrovsky, nos. 19, 20, pp. 271-2.

*Note 20.* Krupensky to Sazonov, no. 95, August 22, 1914; Polonsky, 220; Pokrovsky, no. 25, p. 274. See also Sazonov to Krupensky, August 26, 1914; Polonsky, 221, Pokrovsky, no. 29, p. 276.

*Note 21.* Krupensky to Sazonov, August 27, 1914; Sazonov to Isvolsky and Benckendorff, August 29, 1914; Polonsky, 223-4; Pokrovsky, no. 29, p. 276.

*Note 22.* Sazonov to Paris, London and Rome, September 19, 1914; Polonsky, 224; Pokrovsky, no. 35, p. 279.

*Note 23.* Grey to Buchanan, October 4, 1914; Sazonov to Krupensky, October 4, 1914; Polonsky, 225-6.

*Note 24.* Krupensky to Sazonov, December 4, 1914, December 8, 1914; Pokrovsky, nos. 44, 45, pp. 283-4.

*Note 25.* Sazonov to Isvolsky and Benckendorff, December 10, 1914; Trubetz-koy to Sazonov, December 28, 1914; Sazonov to Isvolsky and Benckendorff, January 7, 1915; Demidov to Sazonov, January 8, 1914; Pokrovsky, nos. 45-49, pp. 284-7. Carlotti promised not to land at Durazzo.

*Note 26.* Demidov to Sazonov, January 21, 1915; Rizov to Radoslavov, January 30, 1915; Krupensky to Sazonov, February 26, 1915. Pokrovsky, nos. 50-3, pp. 287-88. See also Churchill, *op. cit.*, (1915) 200-1.

*Note 27.* Sazonov to Buchanan and Paléologue, March 7, 1915; Sazonov to Isvolsky and Benckendorff, March 8, 1915; Pokrovsky, nos. 54-5, pp. 289-90; Polonsky, 228. Also Asquith, II, 77.

*Note 28.* Isvolsky to Sazonov, March 10, 1915; Pokrovsky, no. 56, p. 290. See also Isvolsky to Sazonov, March 4, 1915; L. N., III, 73-5. Delcassé, learning of Sazonov's opposition to Italian participation in the Dardanelles, feared repelling Italy.

*Note 29.* Benckendorff to Sazonov, March 10, 1915; Neratov to Sazonov, March 15, 1915; Pokrovsky, nos. 57, 59, pp. 290-1, 292.

*Note 30.* Sazonov to Rome, Paris and London, March 15, 1915; Pokrovsky, no. 60, pp. 292-4.

*Note 31.* Sazonov to Benckendorff, March 24, 1915; Pokrovsky, no. 60, p. 295.

*Note 32.* Same to same, March 25, 1915; *ibid.*, no. 65, pp. 295-6.

*Note 33.* British memorandum, March 26, 1915; *ibid.*, no. 66, pp. 296-7; Isvolsky to Sazonov, March 26, 1915; L. N., III, 91-3.

*Note 34.* Sazonov to London, March 28, 1915, March 30, 115; Polonsky, 229-30; Pokrovsky, nos. 67-8, pp. 297-8. Also Isvolsky to Sazonov March 27, 28, 1915; L. N., III, 95, 97. The Serbs had heard of the concessions and now were alarmed definitely.

*Note 35.* Benckendorff to Sazonov, March 30, 1915; Sazonov to Benckendorff, March 31, 1915; Sazonov to Buchanan and Paléologue, March 31, 1915; Polonsky, 231-2; Pokrovsky, nos. 70-1, pp. 299-301. Also Isvolsky to Sazonov, March 30, 1915; L. N., III, 97-8. Again slight concessions were made, but Sazonov warned that if Italy did not enter the war immediately, Russia would withdraw her consent.

*Note 36.* Sazonov to Benckendorff, March 31, 115; Benckendorff, to Sazonov, April 2, 1915; Polonsky, 233-5; Pokrovsky, nos. 73-4, pp. 302-4; Isvolsky to Sazonov, April 1, 1915; L. N., III, 99-100.

*Note 37.* Sazonov to chief of staff of commander in chief, Grand Duke Nicholas, April 4, 1915; Sazonov to G. D. Nicholas, April 6, 1915; Same to Benckendorff, April 6, 1915; Pokrovsky, nos. 75-7, pp. 304-5; Isvolsky to Sazonov, April 5-6, 1915; L. N., III, 100-2.

*Note 38.* British memorandum, April 10, 15, 1915; Sazonov to Grand Duke Nicholas, April 15, 1915; Sazonov to Benckendorff, April 15, 1915; Pokrovsky, nos. 79-82, pp. 307-10; Polonsky, 237-8.

*Note* 39. Sazonov to Benckendorff, April 16, 1915; British memorandum, April 16, 1915; Sazonov to Benckendorff and Isvolsky, April 17, 1915; Pokrovsky, nos. 83-5, pp. 310-13; Polonsky, 238-9. Also Isvolsky to Sazonov, April 16, 17, 1915; L. N., III, 104-5, 105-6.

*Note* 40. Benckendorff to Sazonov, April 18, 1915; Pokrovsky, no. 87, p. 314. The best treatment of this aspect of the Italian question is Kerner, *loc. cit.*, I, 414-5.

*Note* 41. Poincaré to Nicholas II, April 19, 1915; Pokrovsky, no. 88, p. 315; Polonsky, 239-40.

*Note* 42. Buchanan to Sazonov (from Grey), April 20, 1915; Polonsky, 241-2; Pokrovsky, no. 90, 316-17.

*Note* 43. Grey to Buchanan, April 21, 1915; Sazonov to Benckendorff, April 21, 1915; Pokrovsky, no. 91, 92, pp. 317-9; Polonsky, 242-3. Also Isvolsky to Sazonov, April 20, 21, 1915; L. N., III, 106-9.

*Note* 44. British memorandum, April 22, 1915; Pokrovsky, no. 93, p. 319.

*Note* 45. Poincaré to Nicholas II, April 20, 24, 1915; Nicholas II to Poincaré, April 21, 25, 26, 1915; L. N., III, 129-31; Pokrovsky, no. 96, p. 137. See also Kerner, *loc. cit.*

*Note* 46. Sazonov to Isvolsky, April 25, 1915; Pokrovsky, no. 97, pp. 321-2. Also, Sazonov, *Fateful Years*, 262-4.

*Note* 47. For detailed discussion of the Asia Minor concession, see chapter VI below.

*Note* 48. Sonnino to Avarna, May 3, 1915; Avarna, May 3, 1915; Avarna to Sonnino, May 4, 1915; I. G. B., nos. 76-7, pp. 85-6. For vigorous protest of Serbs, see Alexander of Serbia to Grand Duke Nicholas; Nicholas to Alexander, May 4, 5, 1915; *Le monde slave*, V, no. 3, March 1928, 424-6. See also Gordon Gordon-Smith, "The Genesis of the Secret Treaty of London," *Current History* XI, no. 2, November 1919, 249-57.

*Note* 49. Alexandroupolos (Belgrade) to Venizelos, July 25, 1914; Venizelos to Streit, July 25, 1914; Venizelos to Alexandroupolos, July 26, 1914; Streit to Alexandroupolos, August 2, 1914; *Greek White Book. Diplomatic Documents*, 1913-1917 (American Hellenic Society, Publication no. 5, N. Y., n. d. Hereafter G. W. B., I.), nos. 12, 14, 15, 18, pp. 43, 45-6, 48-9. Venizelos reserved his opinion on the question of the alliance of May 5, 1913, but stated that Greece could not tolerate an attack upsetting the Bucharest treaty. At any rate the treaty bound Greece to mobilize 40,000 men. Whether Greece was obligated to go to war is much disputed. It was a defensive alliance aimed at Bulgaria in a Balkan war. However, the military convention of June 1, 1913 (art. 1) stated that "in case of war between one of the allied states and a third Power, arising in the circumstances provided for by the treaty of alliance between Serbia and Greece", the two states promised mutual military support. For text see *ibid.*, 20-34. For criticism see Abbott, *Greece and the Allies, 1914-1922* (London 1922), 114-20, 158-62; Léon Maccas, "L'alliance greco-serbe," *Correspondant*, v. 262, no. 4 (February 25, 1916), 717-48.

*Note* 50. See above, ch. 2. Theotoky to Constantine, August 4, 1914; Constantine to Theotoky, August 7, 1914; G. W. B., I, nos. 19, 21, pp. 49-50, 51. Theotoky, Greek minister at Berlin, continually urged action in concert with Germany. See his August 1914 telegrams in G. W. B., I, nos. 20-4, pp. 50-3.

*Note* 51. See British note to Athens, French note, August 18, 1914; Dragoumis to Streit, August 22, 1914. Frangulis, *La Grèce et la crise mondiale*, I, (Paris 1926),

153, 159. E. Venizelos, *The Vindication of Greek National Policy* (1912-1917), address of August 26, 1917, pp. 73-7. See also Abbott, 12-14. Deville, *L'Entente, la Grèce et la Bulgarie* (Paris 1919), 119-20; Driault, V, 165-7. M. Streit resigned as minister of foreign affairs following Venizelos' démarche. See also Churchill (1911-1914), 485-6; Grey, II, 172-6.

*Note 52.* Venizelos to Constantine, September 7, 1914; *Greek White Book. Supplement, 1913-1917.* (American Hellenic Society, Publication no. 9. N. Y., 1919. Hereafter G. W. B., II), no. 6, pp. 7-10. Constantine to Venizelos, September 7, 1914; G. M. Melas, *Ex-King Constantine and the War* (London, n. d.), 244-5. See also Churchill, *World Crisis*, I, 529-30, 532-37.

*Note 53.* See ch. 3 above. The Turks were, on the other hand, trying to induce Bulgaria and Rumania to ally under the Triplice.

*Note 54.* See below for discussion of Bulgaria.

*Note 55.* Laloy, *Documents secrets* (Paris 1919), 134-35. *New York Evening Post:* full texts of secret treaties as revealed at Petrograd, reprinted February 1918, p. 7; Deville, 131; Cosmin, I, 27-8.

*Note 56.* Grey to Elliot, January 23, 1915; Frangulis, I, 172-3; Cosmin, I, 28. See also Laloy, 135. Text in Venizelos, *Greece in Her True Light* (N. Y. 1916), 12-14.

*Note 57.* Text of first memorandum to Constantine, January 23, 1915 in Venizelos, *op. cit.*, 25-32; Paxton Hibben, *Constantine I and the Greek People* (N. Y. 1920), 551-5; C. Kerofilas, *E. Venizelos* (London 1915), 175-84.

*Note 58.* Text of second memorandum, January 30, 1915; Venizelos, *op. cit.*, 33-40; Hibben, 556-60. See also, Chester, *Life of Venizelos* (N. Y. 1921), 221-3; H. A. Gibbons, *Venizelos*, 209-15. For contemporary comment see André Andreadès, "The Macedonian Question," *Nineteenth Century*, LXII (February 1915), 352-61; Andreadès, "L'union balkanique: I. La Grèce", *Revue hebdomadaire*, III-LV, no. 11 (March 13, 1915), 128-62. Andreadès viewed a Balkan league as the best possibility for a settlement of the Straits question. See also Alfred Sharpe, "A Postscript," *Nineteenth Century*, LXXIX (November 1915), 1041-43. How Delcassé felt on giving Smyrna to Greece is apparent. On January 23, 1915, he told Isvolsky that France had interests there and that "the fate of Smyrna is strictly bound to the general question of Asiatic Turkey," and before attributing this locality to Greece, Russia, France and England must in general be in accord on the partition. His attitude depended on what France obtained. Isvolsky to Sazonov, January 23, 1915; L. N., III, 47-8.

*Note 59.* See chapter 4 above. The minutes of the crown councils are in the *Balkan Review*, IV, no. 5 (December 1920), 384-5. See also Venizelos, *Vindication*, 81-7; Crawfurd Price, *Light on the Balkan Darkness* (London 1915), 49, 60-7; Driault, V, 174-85; Deville, 157-8; Robert David, *Le Drame ignoré de l'armée d'orient* (Paris 1917), 157-8; S. P. P. Cosmetatos, *The Tragedy of Greece* (N. Y. 1928), 14-16. Also Romanos to M. F. A., March 11, 1915; G. W. B., II, no. 1, p. 16. Delcassé had won Russian consent to Greek aid "in principle." See also Nicholas of Greece, "La Grèce pendant la grande guerre," *Revue de Paris*, XXXIV, (July 15, 1917), no. 14, pp. 241-66.

*Note 60.* R. J. Kerner, *loc. cit.*, I (1929), 408-415.

*Note 61.* Allied note to Greek government, April 12, 1915. Frangulis, I, 210; Cosmin, I, 69-70. See also Melas, 150-2.

*Note 62.* This conversation, April 12, 1915, is in Frangulis, I, 210-11. For Gounaris ministry see, Driault, V, 185-98; Caracciolo, 42-53.

*Note 63.* Zographos to London, Paris, Petrograd, April 14, 1915; Frangulis, I, 215-16; Cosmetatos, 23-24. Also, Laloy, 135.

*Note 64.* Same to same, May 1, 1915; Cosmetatos, 27. See also Zographos to Paris, Petrograd, April 20, 1915; Romanos to M. F. A., April 21, 1915; same to same, April 25, 30, 1915; Prince George's conversations with the Quai d'Orsay and Poincaré; Frangulis, I, 220-22, 222-3, 227-8, 228-9. Also Melas, 167-9, especially Constantine to Romanos, April 19, 1915.

Under no conditions were the Greeks to enter Constantinople with that as their objective. The offer of Cyprus was undesirable because it gave Greece supremacy near the Straits. See Sazonov to Isvolsky and Benckendorff, April 21, 1915; Polonsky, 272.

*Note 65.* Constantine to Greek legation, Paris, May 9, 1915; Romanos to M. G. A., May 10, 1915; Cosmin, I, 85-6; Cosmetatos, 30. See also Guillemin interview with Zographos, May 13, 1915 (in which he affirmed France had not promised Cavalla to Bulgaria); Zographos on Elliot interview, May 4, 1915; Romanos to M. F. A., May 4, 1915; Frangulis, I, 229-31, 232, 233. For other details see M. Larcher, *La grande guerre dans les balkans,* ch. 2.

*Note 66.* Romanos to M. F. A., May 7, 1915, and May 11, 1915; Frangulis, I, 234-36, 236-7.

*Note 67.* Romanos to M. F. A. (two letters), May 11, 1915; Frangulis, I, 239, 241-43.

*Note 68.* Cosmin, I, 102-5.

*Note 69.* Note of Greece to Allied governments, August 12, 1915; Elliot to Venizelos, August 17, 1915; Grey to Elliot, August 20, 1915; Frangulis, I, 253-5, 255-6, 256-7.

*Note 70.* Cosmin, I, 127-35. See also Elliot to Grey, September 22, 1915; Grey, II, 223-24.

The origin of the Salonica expedition goes back, in reality, to November 1914. It was a conception of Colonel de Lardemelle, chief of staff of General d'Espérey's Fifth Army, who urged an attack on Germany from the rear through the Balkans, *via* Salonica. It materialized when Venizelos made his request of September 23, 1915. By December 1915, a total of 150,000 men were landed, of whom 85,000 were English. For details see Larcher, *op. cit.,* 58-61, 74-85, 99-109 and *passim:* annex no. 3, pp. 268-9. Also Gordon Gordon-Smith, *From Serbia to Jugo-Slavia* (London 1920).

*Note 71.* For the English attitude see Grey to Elliot, October 1, 1915; Frangulis, I, 273. Elliot to Grey, October 2, 1915; Grey, II, 225-26. See also Cosmin, I, 136-39, and Alexandre Ribot, *Lettres à un ami* (Paris 1924), 329-30.

*Note 72.* Venizelos, *Greece in Her True Light,* 43-105; address of October 4, 1915; Cosmin, I, 139-40; Venizelos, *Vindication,* 66 ff, address of August 26, 1917. Grey to Bertie, October 6, 1915; Grey to Elliot, October 6, 1915; Grey, II, 226-7. See also Venizelos to Constantine, September 12, 1915; Melas, 254-7. Leon Maccas, "La crise hellenique," *Revue de Paris,* XXIII, February 1916, 646-72. Not until 1917 did Venizelos discover the *universal* application of the Serbo-Greek treaty.

*Note 73.* Cosmin, I, 154-56. Zaïmis to all royal legations, October 8, 1915; G. W. B., I, no. 33, p. 60.

*Note 74.* Zaïmis to Alexandroupolos, October 12, 1915; G. W. B., I, no. 34, pp. 60-1; Cosmin, I, 165-7; Cosmetatos, 63-5; Frangulis, I, 284.

*Note 75.* Grey to Elliot, October 16, 1915; Frangulis, I, 288. Sazonov had learned of an offer to Greece of Bulgarian Thrace and was willing to offer it if she would come to the aid of Serbia. See Sazonov to London, Paris and Rome, October 17, 1915; Demidov to Sazonov, October 17, 1915; E. A. Adamov, *Evropeiskie Dershavi i Gretsiia* (Moscow 1922), 20; Frangulis, I, 290. See also Cosmetatos, 69, 70-1.

*Note 76.* For Venizelos' criticism of Zaïmis see address of October 11, 1915, and two addresses of November 4, 1915; Venizelos, *Greece in Her True Light*, 106-92.

*Note 77.* See treaty arrangements defining the international relations of Greece, May 7, 1832; G. W. B., I, pp. 1-19. The Entente acted as guaranteeing Powers. See Skouloudis to all royal legations; same to Panourias, November 8, 1915; Skouloudis to Paris, Rome, London and Petrograd, November 8, 1915; G. W. B., I, nos. 35-37, pp. 63-4.

*Note 78.* See Demidov to Sazonov, December 28, 1915; Adamov, 55; Frangulis, I, 421. See also Abbott, 85-86. The revolt in Castellorizo had been prepared by the French.

*Note 79.* Demidov's report of the audience given by the king to the British minister Sir F. Elliot, December 28, 1915; Cosmetatos, 126-27.

*Note 80.* Romanos to Skouloudis, April 10, 1916; Skouloudis to Romanos, April 11, 1916; note verbal of the Serbian government, April 20, 1916; Skouloudis to Paris and London, April 27, 1916; G. W. B., I, nos. 39-42, pp. 67-73. France was playing the important rôle in these negotiations, under M. Guilleman. Because of Skouloudis' attitude, France refused a loan of 150,000,000 francs, which the Greeks then borrowed in Berlin (March 7, 1916), of which 40,000,000 were paid.

*Note 81.* For the Rupel affair see G. W. B., II, 22-49, and G. W. B., I, 74-109. Brief summaries in Abbott, 98 ff; Driault, V, 232-48. See also Venizelos, *Greece in Her True Light*, 195-200. An address to King Constantine, Athens, September 10, 1916. Prince Nicholas of Greece to Sturmer, August 11, 25, 28, 1916; *Le monde slave*, V, no. 3 (March 1928), 426-30.

As a consequence of the Rupel affair, the French, British and Russian ministers addressed a joint note to the Athens government on June 21, 1916, demanding: (1) immediate demobilization; (2) replacement of existing ministry by cabinet of "no political complexion;" (3) dissolution of chamber of deputies followed by general election; (4) removal of all officials objectionable to Allies. The Zaïmis cabinet, in a note of June 23 promised to carry out the demands. See Cmd. 8298. *Collective note addressed to the Greek government.* Miscellaneous no. 27 (1916). Also Cosmetatos, 182-6.

*Note 82.* A proclamation to the Greek people issued by Venizelos and Condourates at Canea, Crete, September 27, 1916; Venizelos, *Greece in Her True Light*, 201-8; Gibbons, *op. cit.*, 274-300.

*Note 83.* Giers to M. F. A., June 1, 1917; Demidov to M. F. A., June 4, 1917; same to same, June 5, 7, 1917; Adamov, 191, 192, 194. Cosmin, I, 437-447; Cosmetatos, 260-92; Frangulis, I, 530-1, 556. For the Italian attitude see Bosdari, *Delle guerre balcaniche della grande guerra* (Milan 1928), 193-99. See also Ribot, *op. cit.*, 327-9; Abbott, 186-99, Driault, V, 295-305; Larcher, *op. cit.*, ch. 5.

*Note 84.* Abbott, 200-16; Driault, V, 305-19; Bosdari, 200-14. See also Venizelos, *Vindication*, address of August 26, 1917, pp. 90-162. A strongly pro-Venizelist account of the Greek question is Auguste Gauvain, *The Greek Question* (American Hellenic Society, Publication no. 1, N. Y. 1918). Also T. P. Ion, "The Hellenic Crisis

from the Standpoint of International Law," *American Journal of International Law*, XI (January 1917), 46-73, (April 1917), 327-57.

*Note 85.* See Morgenthau, 262, 265; V. Radoslavov, *Bulgarien und die Weltkrise* (Berlin 1923), 132-33; Larcher, 13-37. Serbia's strategic position is well portrayed in Dr. Niko Zupovich, "The Strategical Significance of Serbia," *Nineteenth Century*, XXXIX, 1011-20. In September 1915 Wangenheim told Morgenthau: "We cannot hold the Dardanelles without the military support of Bulgaria."

*Note 86.* See ch. 2 above. Something of Bulgarian opinion after the Balkan wars and preceding the worl war may be gathered from G. Jasich, "La Bulgarie et les alliés," (1) *Revue hebdomadaire*, I-II, no. 8 (February 19, 1916), 407-24, and XI-XII, no. 50 (December 11, 1915), 277-85, 293-300, including extracts from Bulgarian periodicals and journals. See also Savinsky to Sazonov, July 29, 1914; Polonsky, 105-6. Also Alexander Savinsky, *Recollections*, 239, and André Cheradame, "La Bulgarie au seuil de la guerre européenne," *Correspondant*, v. 256, no. 4 (August 25, 1914), 621-52.

*Note 87.* Sazonov to Strandtmann, August 5, 1914; Sazonov to Savinsky, August 3, 1914; Polonsky, 106-7, 107-8. See also Laloy, 101-06 and Radoslavov, 136-7.

*Note 88.* Strandtmann to Sazonov, August 6, 1914; Laloy, 103-5, Pashich thought Russia might say that Serbia would concede "territory whose exact limits cannot be determined at present."

*Note 89.* Savinsky to Sazonov, August 9, 1914; Polonsky, 108-10. Also Albert Pingaud, "L'Entente et les balkaniques aux premiers mois de la guerre (Août-Décembre 1914)". *Revue des deux mondes*, LIV (November 1929), 48-83.

*Note 90.* Sazonov to Savinsky, August 9, 1914; same to same, August 9, 1914; Savinsky to Sazonov, August 11, 12, 1914; Pokrovsky, nos. 7-10, pp. 68-70; Polonsky, 110-11. Text of August 8 note in Radoslavov, 137-8. On August 5, Savinsky had a conversation with Tsar Ferdinand in which he warned him against adopting a hostile attitude, and allowing Bulgarian *comitadji* to menace the Serbs in Macedonia. See Savinsky to Sazonov, August 15, 1914; Polonsky, 111-15, and Savinsky, 240-42.

*Note 91.* Savinsky to Sazonov, August 18, 1914; Polonsky, 115-16. Loggio (in Buchanan, *Bulgaria and Rumania*, 105-6) states that an an agreement was signed on August 19, 1914. See Isvolsky to Sazonov, September 14, 1914; L. N., III, 13; and Radoslavov, 117.

*Note 92.* Sazonov to Athens, Nish, Bucharest, Sofia, Paris, London, Constantinople, August 23, 1914; Pokrovsky, no. 15, pp. 76-7. Isvolsky to Sazonov, August 17, 1914; L. N., III, 4. Giers to Sazonov, September 6, 1914; Stieve, *Orangebuch*, no. 71, p. 119. Sazonov was in the midst of the Turkish negotiations, which neither France nor England approved.

*Note 93.* Sazonov to Savinsky, August 24, 25, 1914; Polonsky, 116-17.

*Note 94.* Sazonov to Savinsky, August 30, 1914; Polonsky, 117. See also Savinsky to Sazonov, August 25, 28, 1914; Sazonov to Benckendorff, August 29, 1914; Pokrovsky, nos. 18-20, pp. 77-80. Also Isvolsky to Sazonov, August 29, 1914; Stieve, *op. cit.*, no. 65, p. 112, and Deville, *op. cit.*, 120.

*Note 95.* Memorandum submitted to Sir Edward Grey by Mr. Noel Buxton, August 1914; Buxton and Lease, *Balkan Problems and European Peace* (London 1919), 68-69. Conditions for securing Bulgarian neutrality were (1) guarantee against Turkey; (2) England, France and Russia to act together in guarantee; (3) definite approach

from England; (4) revision of Bucharest treaty; (5) a loan. Buxton was taken to Salonica on the H. M. S. *Hussar*.

*Note 96.* Churchill to Buxton, August 31, 1914; *ibid.*, 70-2; Churchill, *op. cit.* (1911-14), 486-7. On October 15 an attempt was made to assassinate Buxton at Bucharest. His accomplishments will be detailed later.

*Note 97.* Radoslavov to Savinsky, October 1, (September 18), 1914; *Diplomatic Documents Relative to the Intervention of Bulgaria in the Great War, 1913-1918,* I, (Sofia 1920), 232-33. In Bulgarian. (Hereafter *Bulgarian Orange Book*, B. O. B.)

*Note 98.* See ch. 4 above.

*Note 99.* Savinsky to Sazonov, October 4, 1914; Polonsky, 118.

*Note 100.* Same to same, October 4, 1914; *ibid.*, 118-19. Savinsky told Radoslavov that Serbia and Greece would take no action against the *comitadii* in Macedonia, and advised him to take energetic measures.

*Note 101.* Giers to Sazonov, October 29, 1914; Savinsky to Sazonov, October 29 and November 1, 1914; Pokrovsky, nos. 27, 28, 30, pp. 83-4, 84-6. Delcassé declared to Isvolsky that the Entente should secure Bulgaria's aid against Turkey by inducing Greece and Serbia to make concessions, and offering a part of Thrace with Adrianople. See Isvolsky to Sazonov, October 30, 1914; L. N., III, 24.

*Note 102.* Savinsky to Sazonov, November 2, 1914; Sazonov to Savinsky, November 4, 1914; Polonsky, 120-22. Demidov reported from Athens that Passarov had outlined Bulgarian difficulties as follows: (1) fear for littoral, without defence; (2) uncertainty of Moslem population; (3) difficulties with the Macedonian party. The Serb minister at Athens told Demidov that Serbia would withdraw all troops from the Austrian front if Bulgaria attempted a seizure. Demidov to Sazonov, November 4, 1914; Polonsky, 122-3.

*Note 103.* Sazonov to Savinsky, November 5, 1914; British memorandum, November 5, 1914; Polonsky, 123-4. See also Isvolsky to Sazonov, November 7, 1914; L. N., III, 28-9, and Auguste Gauvain on negotiations with Bulgaria, November 7, 1914, in *L'Europe au jour le jour* (Paris 1920), VII, 304-6.

*Note 104.* Savinsky to Sazonov, November 8, 1914; Polonsky, 124-6.

*Note 105.* Sazonov to Isvolsky and Benckendorff, transmitted to Savinsky, November 9, 1914; Polonsky, 126.

*Note 106.* Savinsky to Sazonov, November 10, 1914; Polonsky, 125-8. Radoslavov, 143-6.

*Note 107.* Savinsky to Sazonov, November 16, 1914; same to same, November 17, 1914; Polonsky, 129-30. See also Sazonov to Savinsky, November 15, 1914; Pokrovsky, no. 44, p. 96. The text is also in B. O. B., I, November 3-16, 1914, p. 327.

*Note 108.* Savinsky to Sazonov, November 13, 1914; Polonsky, 128. See also Grey to Bax-Ironside, November 13, 1914; Grey, II, 191-92. Isvolsky to Sazonov, November 14, 1914; L. N., III, 29-30. The best single article on the Balkan union is General Danilov, "Les tentatives de constitution d'un bloc balkanique en 1914-1915," (1) *Le monde slave*, 5th year, (II), no. 5 (May 1928), 201-08.

*Note 109.* Savinsky to Sazonov, November 17, 1914; Polonsky, 130-32. Savinsky noted that "for the historic prestige of Russia her own representative should play the first rôle." See also B. O. B., I, 328-29 for text of November 24 note.

*Note 110.* Sazonov to Savinsky, November 18, 1914; Sazonov to Isvolsky and Benckendorff, November 20, 1914; Savinsky to Sazonov, November 21, 22, 1914;

Sazonov to Savinsky, November 22, 1914; Savinsky to Sazonov, November 24, 1914; Sazonov to Savinsky, November 29, 1914; Savinsky to Sazonov, November 30, 1914; Polonsky, 133-37; Pokrovsky, nos. 49-56, pp. 100-03. See also Isvolsky to Sazonov. November 20, 23, 1914; L. N., III, 32-33. On November 21 Savinsky declared it as the opinion of all three ministers that immediate possession of Macedonia to the Vardar, and the Goline-Okhrida-Struga line at the end of the war was necessary. Text of the Bulgarian reply of November 26, 1914; B. O. B., I, 329. See also Savinsky, 253.

*Note 111.*    French memorandum, November 21, 1914; M. F. A. to Panafeu, December 20, 1914; M. F. A. to Allied Powers, December 24, 1914, and December 28, 1914; B. O. B., I., nos. 557, 604, 608, pp. 286-87, 309-10, 311-12, 315-16. See also Gauvain, VII, 344-45.

*Note 112.*    Sazonov to Savinsky, December 1, 1914; Polonsky, 137-38.

*Note 113.*    Savinsky to Sazonov, December 9, 1914; *ibid.*, 139-40. Also Deville, 128-30. The Bulgarian reply stated that "while safeguarding the interests of the country which must have an importance predominant over all other considerations," it would remain neutral.

*Note 114.*    See Delcassé's proposal to divide Albania between Greece and Serbia in the hope of getting a Bulgaro-Serb accord. Isvolsky to Sazonov, November 28, 1914; L. N., III, 37, and Isvolsky to Sazonov, December 20, 1914; *ibid.*, 43. For Sazonov's warning to Madjarov, see Sazonov to Savinsky, December 10, 11, 1914; Pokrovsky, nos. 61-62, pp. 105-06.

*Note 115.*    Vopicka to Bryan, November 30 (received December 22), 1914; *U. S. Foreign Relations, 1914 Supplement. The World War*, 155-6. Radoslavov declared to Sir Alfred Sharpe in December 1914, that Bulgaria demanded Drama, Seres and Cavalla from Greece and Macedonia on the 1912 basis from Serbia. See Sharpe, "A Definite Policy in the Balkans," *Nineteenth Century*, LXVIII (September 1915), 542 note.

*Note 116.*    Tarnowsky to Berchtold, December 2, 1914; same to same, December 13, 1914; Polonsky, 138-9, 140-41; Pokrovsky, no. 58, 63, pp. 138-39, 140-42. As early as October the Germans were willing to have Bulgaria occupy Macedonia and were urging Turkey to cede part of Thrace. Savinsky to Sazonov, October 18, 1914; Polonsky, 132-33; Pokrovsky, no. 48, pp. 99-100. See also Richard von Mach, *Aus bewegten Balkan Zeit, 1879-1918* (Berlin 1928), 199-200.

*Note 117.*    Jasich, "La Bulgarie et les alliés," *Revue hebdomadaire*, XI-XII, no. 50, (December 11, 1915), quoted pp. 285-7. Ghenadiev, leader of the Stambulovist party, was in Italy, where on January 30, 1915, he gave assurance of his pro-German sympathies. See Tarnowsky to Burian, January 16, 1915; Pokrovsky, no. 65, p. 109. For Ghenadiev's statement see Jasich, *loc. cit.*, 288, from *Le Temps*, January 30, 1915. See also Gauvain, VII, 451-56.

*Note 118.*    See Savinsky to Sazonov, July 31, 1914; same to same, September 22, 1914; Sazonov to Savinsky, November 4, 1914; Bakametev to Sazonov, December 14, 1914; Demidov to Sazonov, March 3, 1915; Savinsky to Sazonov, March 17, 1915; Adamov, *Konstantinopol i prolivy*, II, 236-7, 239-40, 243-4, 245-6, 257, 263.

*Note 119.*    Tarnowsky to Burian, January 23, 1915; Polonsky, 143; Pokrovsky, no. 66, pp. 109-110.

*Note 120.* See *Near East*, VIII, no. 194, (January 22, 1915), p. 317, and VIII no. 197 (February 12, 1915). An official statement declared that the *Disconto Gessellschaft had* placed at the disposal of Bulgaria 75,000,000 francs of the loan concluded in Berlin, in July 1914. 120,000,000 francs had been paid, and another 75,000,-000 would be paid in ten weeks. The rest was to follow every two weeks. The proceeds were to be used on debt and supplies. See also *ibid.*, VIII, no. 200, (March 5 1915), p. 508, and E. J. Dillon, "Bulgaria and Entente Diplomacy," *Fortnightly Review*, CIII (May 1, 1915), 755-66. For the loan see Radoslavov, 132; Savinsky, 218; Pribram, 87-88; Gauvain, VIII, 13-16. For the dispatches: Savinsky to Sazonov, January 28, 1915, February 4, 7, 1915; Pokrovsky, nos. 69-73, pp. 111-12, 113-14, 116-17. Isvolsky to Sazonov, January 7, 1915; L. N., III, 43-44. Grey to Bax-Ironside, February, 6, 13, 1915; Grey, II, 195-96, 196-97.

*Note 121.* Isvolsky to Sazonov, December 20, 1914; L. N., III, 43. For the military situation in Serbia see Larcher, *op. cit.*, 30-7. See also Pingaud, *loc. cit.*, LIV (1929), 73-83.

*Note 122.* Text of memorandum in Buxton and Lease, *op. cit.*, 77-89. See also Noel and C. R. Buxton, *The War and the Balkans*, (London 1915), 102-12.

*Note 123.* Isvolsky to Sazonov, January 10, 1915 (two telegrams), and same to same, January 23, 25, 1915; L. N., III, 45-6, 47-8.

*Note 124.* Isvolsky to Sazonov, January 28, 1915; L. N., III, 49-50. Though Delcassé did not believe Venizelos willing to cede Cavalla in return for the Asiatic concessions, his two memoranda of January 24, 30, 1915, indicate the contrary. See ch. 5 above.

*Note 125.* Mr. des Graz to Grey, February 1, 1915 (two telegrams); Grey, 192-94. Isvolsky to Sazonov, February 6, 1915; L. N., III, 58.

*Note 126.* Savinsky to Sazonov, February 8, 1915, February 9, 1915; Sazonov to Savinsky, February 9, 1915; Polonsky, 145-6; Pokrovsky, nos. 75-77, pp. 145-6. His concession was the Egri-Palanka, Koprülü-Okhrida line in Macedonia. Savinsky had instructions to act when his colleagues had similar instructions.

*Note 127.* Isvolsky to Sazonov, February 2, 1915; L. N., III, 51.

*Note 128.* Savinsky to Sazonov, January 28, February 7, 8, 10, 1915; Polonsky, 143-44, 144-45, 147-48; Pokrovsky, nos. 68, 74, 75, 78, pp. 110-11, 114-15, 116-17. Isvolsky to Sazonov, February 15, 1915; L. N., III, 59-60.

*Note 129.* Isvolsky to Sazonov, February 2, 3, 4, 11, 15, 1915; L. N., 58-60. Larcher, *op. cit.*, 54-60.

*Note 130.* Churchill, *op. cit.*, I, 202.

*Note 131.* Grey to Buchanan, February 15, 1915; Grey, II, 198; Isvolsky to Sazonov, February 24, 1915; L. N., III, 68-69. See also Savinsky, 257-58.

*Note 132.* Savinsky to Sazonov, February 26, 1915; Polonsky, 148.

*Note 133.* Radoslavov to Kadjimishev, March 1, 1915; Polonsky, 119. At the same time he warned the minister at Petrograd against premature conclusions with reference to Rumania. See Radoslavov to Madjarov, March 6, 1915; Polonsky, 150. See also Radoslavov, 153-54.

*Note 134.* Isvolsky to Sazonov, March 22, 1915; L. N., III, 90-91.

*Note 135.* Madjarov to Radoslavov, March 25, 1915; Pokrovsky, no. 86, p. 120-21.

*Note 136.* Isvolsky to Sazonov, April 10, 1915; *L. N.*, III, 102; Savinsky, 260-61. See also Grey to Bax-Ironside, March 25, 1915; Grey to Buchanan, March 22, 1915; Grey, II, 200, 205. Savinsky to Sazonov, April 5, 1915, Sazonov to Savinsky, April 5, 15, 1915; Pokrovsky, nos. 89-90, 92, pp. 123, 124-5. For Macedonian invasions, Serbian protest and Radoslavov answer, see Gauvain, VIII, 118-21, 125-28; Stantsiov (Paris) to M. F. A., April 12, 1915; B. O. B., I, 441-42, and Demidov to Sazonov, February 27, 1915; Polonsky, 265.

*Note 137.* For the Rumanian negotiations see below.

*Note 138.* Sazonov to Savinsky, April 25, 1915, Savinsky to Sazonov, April 27, 1915; Pokrovsky, nos. 95-6, pp. 127-28. On March 29, Radoslavov declared in the *Sobranje:* "The government will cede to no pressure; it will not allow itself to be entrained by any vain promise. It has no engagement with any one. It cannot be engaged prematurely, for it would be sure to lose. When our interests permit we shall take into consideration the necessary decisions . . . . The Balkan federation is impossible because it is difficult to conciliate our interests with those of the Balkan peoples who hold their eyes on Bulgaria to snatch her last morsel." Gauvain, VIII, 112-14. See "The Balkan States and the War," *Quarterly Review*, no. 443 (April 1915), 424-38. Larcher, *loc. cit.*

*Note 139.* Sazonov to Savinsky, May 4, 1915; Kadjimishev to Radoslavov, May 12, 1915; Sazonov to Savinsky, May 19, 1915; Savinsky to Sazonov, May 21, 1915; Sazonov to Savinsky, May 23, 24, 1915; Pokrovsky, nos. 99-105, pp. 129-33. See also conversations of Bulgarian minister with Grey, April 28, 1915; B. O. B., I, no. 801, pp. 461-62.

*Note 140.* Savinsky to Sazonov, May 25, 1915; Polonsky, 151-52; Pokrovsky, no. 106, pp. 133-34.

*Note 141.* Sazonov to Nish, May 26, 1915; Polonsky, 152-53; Pokrovsky, no. 108, pp. 134-35.

*Note 142.* Grey to Rodd, May 26, 1915; Grey, II, 205-06.

*Note 143.* Sazonov to Rome, May 28, 1915, Savinsky to Sazonov, May 29, 1915. Pokrovsky, nos. 109-10, p. 135. See also Radoslavov, 154-55; Richard von Mach, *op. cit.*, 208-09. For text of the joint Allied note, May 29, 1915; see B. O. B., I, no. 879, pp. 503-04.

*Note 144.* Text of Austrian note of May 23-June 5, 1915; B. O. B., I, no. 894, pp. 514-15; Radoslavov, 156-57. See also Tisza to Czernin and Tarnowsky, May 21, 1915; Tisza to Burian, May 23, 1915; June 5, 1915; Tisza, *Briefe*, I, 221-22, 223-25, 228-31.

*Note 145.* Savinsky to Sazonov, June 4, 16, 1915; Sazonov to Savinsky, June 5, 1915; Pokrovsky, nos. 112-14, pp. 137-39; Grey to Bertie, July 7, 1915; Grey, II, 206-07. Text of the Bulgarian note of June 14, in B. O. B., I, pp. 680-81; Radoslavov, 158-60. See also Savinsky, 262 ff; Loggio, 121-25.

*Note 146.* Savinsky to Sazonov, July 20, 1915; Gounaris to Caclamanos, July 27, 1915; Savinsky to Sazonov, July 28, 1915; Pokrovsky, nos. 115-117, pp. 139-41. See also Radoslavov, 165. The Germans were working through the embassy at Constantinople through the intermediary of Colonel von Leipzig, military attaché and Prince Hohenlohe.

*Note 147.* Sir Valentine Chirol, *Fifty Years in a Changing World* (N. Y. 1928), 311-17.

*Note 148.* Grey to O'Beirne, July 28, 1915; Grey, II, 208-09. See also Savinsky, 268-71. See also Einstein, L., *Inside Constantinople* (London, 1917), 209-10. Einstein was a special agent in the American diplomatic service at Constantinople, and believed this would be a master stroke, as it would force the hand of Greece, hold Bulgaria, facilitate Serbian concessions, render the German position in Turkey difficult, and facilitate a Serbian offensive.

*Note 149.* Grey to de Graz, July 20, 1915, and July 26, 1915; Grey, II, 207-08, 209-10. Chirol, *loc. cit.*

*Note 150.* Text of the identical declaration of the four ministers in Serbia to Pasich, August 5, 1915; Savinsky to Sazonov, August 18, 1915; Pokrovsky, nos. 118-19, pp. 141-43. See also Danilov, "Les tentatives de constitution d'un bloc balkanique en 1914-15" (ii), *Le monde slave*, 5th yr., II, no. 6, (June 1928) 352-54. See also Passarov to Radoslavov, August 9, 1915. Frangulis, I, 252-55. Chirol, *loc. cit.* Ghenadiev was in Italy in July, and was claiming satisfaction of four irredenta: Thrace, Macedonia (Greek and Serb), and the Dobruja. In a statement to the Naples *Mattino* he said: "We wish to be paid." See Gauvain, VIII, 308-312, and Rodd, III, 262-65.

*Note 151.* Text of Allied note of August 3, 1915; B. O. B. I. 682-84; Radoslavov, 162-64. See also Savinsky, 271-72..

*Note 152.* O'Beirne to Grey, August 20, 1915; Grey, II, 211-12. See also Savinsky, 273 ff. However, on August 15, Dobrovitch, secretary to Ferdinand, expressed his gratification at Allied victories. See Joseph Reinach, *Les commentaires de Polybe* (Paris 1915), 381-90.

*Note 153.* Falkenhayn, *The German General Staff and its Decisions* (N. Y. 1920), 179-82. There is an excellent summary in Larcher, *La grande guerre dans les Balkans*, 62-74.

*Note 154.* Savinsky to Sazonov, August 31, 1915; Polonsky, 155; Pokrovsky, no. 123, p. 144. See also Savinsky, 276-77.

*Note 155.* See R. W. Seton-Watson, "Unprinted Documents. Austro-German Plans for the Future of Serbia (1915)," *Slavonic Review*, VII, no. 21 (March 1929), 705-24. Especially note Count Tarnowsky to Vienna, May 22, 1915; Count Czernin to Vienna, August 13, 1915; Prince Gotfried Hohenlohe to Vienna, September 27, 1915; Ballplatz to Hohenlohe, n. d.; Count Tarnowsky to Vienna, September 30, 1915; *ibid.*, 708-11.

*Note 156.* Sazonov to Savinsky, August 21, 1915; Polonsky, 154. See also Danilov, *loc. cit.*, (ii), 257-8.

*Note 157.* Danilov, *loc. cit.*, 361-63, and Léon Savadjian, *La Bulgarie en guerre* (Geneva 1917), 16-21.

*Note 158.* See Radoslavov, 165ff; Einstein, 222-23, 242, 268-9; Harry Stuermer, *Two War Years in Constantinople* (N. Y. 1917), 84-6. Also Conrad to Burian and Falkenhayn, Op. Nr. 129-31 v. 17. VII. 15: *Operationen gegen Serbien und Verhältnis Türkei-Bulgarien*. July 17, 1915. P. A. *Fasz. 857, Liasse "Krieg" 6a.*

*Note 159.* Radoslavov, 165ff, 171-2. Colonel von Leipzig, German military attaché in Constantinople was murdered by the Turks for his part in the alliance negotiations. See Stuermer, *loc. cit.*

*Note 160.* The texts of these agreements may be found in the Austrian documents, Ref. I. No. 289-2221 and No. 6101-2226. The Bulgarian-German treaty of September 6, 1915, and military conventions, B. O. B., I, 687, 689-90; Radoslavov, 186-92. Military convention between Germany, Austria and Bulgaria in 1915; *Miller*

*Diary*, XVIII, 11-14. See also Savinsky to Sazonov, September 11, 1915; Polonsky, 156-58; Falkenhayn, 179-82; Burian, 133-35 and Marcel Dunan, *L'été bulgare, juillet-octobre* (Paris 1917), 268-69.

*Note 161.* Allied note of September 13, 1915; B. O. B., I, 691-92. See also Savinsky to Sazonov, September 14, 1915; Pokrovsky, nos. 126-7, pp. 148-9.

*Note 162.* Radoslavov to Tarnowsky, September 17, 1915; B. O. B., I, 635. Also Savinsky to Sazonov, September 21, 1915; Polonsky, 160. Gauvain, VIII, 353-56.

*Note 163.* The complete acquisition of the territory was fixed for the day the Bulgarians attacked Serbia. See Einstein, 242 note.

*Note 164.* Sazonov to Savinsky, September 21, 1915; Polonsky, 160-1. Also Paléologue, II, 81-2. Sazonov would not allow a preventive Serb attack on Bulgaria which Delcassé was urging. See Radoslavov, 178-9.

*Note 165.* See Sazonov to Savinsky, September 22, 24, 1915 and Savinsky to Sazonov, September 22, 23, 25, 1915; Pokrovsky, nos. 132-37, pp. 151-55; Polonsky, 16. See also *Parliamentary Debates* (H. C.), September 28, 1915, v. 74, cols. 731-2. See also Gauvain, VIII, 357-66. The speech disquieted both the Serbs and the Greeks.

*Note 166.* Sazonov to Savinsky, October 2, 1915; Polonsky, 162. Panafeu to Radoslavov, October 5, 1915; O'Beirne to Radoslavov, October 4, 1915; B. O. B., I, 692-3, 696-7. See also Savinsky, 298-9; Radoslavov, *loc. cit.;* Paléologue, II, 84-5, 86-8; Danilov, *loc. cit.* (ii), 375-8. For the Bulgarian note of October 4, 1915, see Bulgarian note, B. O. B., I, 6968-9; Savinsky, 299-300; Radoslavov, 179-84. For French and British notes, October 4, 5, 1915, see B. O. B., I, 696-7, 699-700; Radoslavov to Savinsky, October 5, 1915; *ibid.,* 698-9. See also Crawfurd Price, "Bulgaria and Peace," *Fortnightly Review*, CXII (September 1, 1917), 418-31, and "Why Bulgaria Made War," *Balkan Review*, I, no. 1 (February 1919), 14-31; Noel Buxton, "New Departure in Balkan Diplomacy," *Nineteenth Century*, LXXXI (June 1917), 1215-24; A. E. White, "Balkan Unity and the 'New Departure,' " *Nineteenth Century*, LXXXII (July 1917), 211-20.

*Note 167.* Wilhelm to Ferdinand, September 20, 1915; extracts from code telegrams, October 10, 12, 1915; *Miller Diary*, XVIII, 17-19.

*Note 168.* Summary of Note Drawn from German Embassy in Vienna, November 4, 1915; *Slavonic Review*, VII, no. 21 (March 1929), 713.

*Note 169.* Marquis Pallavicini to Baron Burian, December 1, 1915; *ibid*, 714-16.

*Note 170.* Count Tisza to Francis Joseph, December 4, 1915 and Count Tisza to Baron Burián, December 30, 1915; *ibid.,* 717-23. Prince Danilo of Montenegro had offered himself already to the Central Powers. See *ibid.,* 723-4.

*Note 171.* See Buchanan, *op. cit.,* 108-13; Loggio, 143-6; Gentizon, *Le drame bulgare* (Paris 1924), 11-15; Savadjan, 22-5; Savinsky, 287ff. Text of Radoslavov's address, October 11, 1915; Horne and Austin, *Great Events of the Great War*, III, 336-40. See also Victor Kuhne, *Les Bulgares peints par eux-mêmes* (Lausanne 1917), 34-46, 163-83. I. Slivensky, *La Bulgarie depuis le traité de Berlin et la paix dans les Balkans* (Paris 1927), 134ff; Sazonov, 228-9, 233-4. For the tsar's proclamation of October 19, 1915, see Paléologue, II, 95-6. See also M. Mileff, *La Bulgarie et les détroits* (Paris 1927) 124-39.

*Note 172.* For the Macedonian issue see D. Michev, "La Bulgarie et les alliés," *La Revue*, CXII, no. 12 (June 1915), 131-38; Un Bulgare, "Les raisons de la Bulgarie," *Revue de Paris*, XXII, (July-August 1915), 666-76; A. Shopov, "La Bulgarie

437

et la question macédonienne: II. Cavalla. La population en Macédoine," *Revue hebdomadaire*, VII-VIII, no. 35 (August 28, 1915), 450-71; Shopov, "Les états balkaniques et le principe confederatif," *Revue hebdomadaire*, VII-VIII, no. 34 (August 21, 1915), 305-24; Yves Guyot, "La question bulgare," *Journal des économistes*, ser. 6, XLVIII, no. 3 (December 1915), 353-78. See also (Anon.) *Ferdinand of Bulgaria* (London 1916); "Ferdinand, Tsar des bulgares," *Revue hebdomadaire*, III-IV, no. 10 (March 10, 1917), 245-60; E. Daudet, "Le suicide bulgare. Autour d'une couronne. Notes et souvenirs, 1875-1915. I I. Le tsar des bulgares. La rupture avec l'Entente." *Revue des deux mondes*, XXXVI (December 1916), 565-600.

*Note 173.* Sazonov, *op. cit.*, 626-67.

*Note 174.* See ch. 3 above. Poklevsky to Sazonov, July 25, 27, 28, 1914; Pokrovsky, nos. 1-3, pp. 161-63. Same to same, August 1-3, 1914; *ibid.*, nos. 6, 9, 14, pp. 164-66, 167-70; Polonsky, 168-71. Czernin to Berchtold, August 4, 6, 1914; Ministère des affaires étrangères. *Documents diplomatiques concernant les rapports entre l'Autriche-Hongrie et la Roumanie. 22 juillet 1914-27 août 1916* (Vienna 1916). Hereafter cited as A. R. B. (Rumania), nos. 4, 7, pp. 3-4, 5-6. See also Auerbach, *op. cit.*, 118-23; Ionescu, *op. cit.*, 125-38; Baron Jehan de Witte, "Carol 1er, roi de Roumanie," *Revue des deux mondes*, XXIV (November 1, 1914), 81-93; H. de Gallier, "La décision de la Roumanie. Les partis et les hommes," *Correspondant*, v. 264, no. 5 (September 10, 1916), 850-77. See also C. Diamandy, "Ma mission en Russie," (i), *Revue des deux mondes*, IXL, (February 15, 1929), 817.

*Note 175.* Mircea Djuvara, *La guerre roumaine, 1916-1918* (Paris 1919), 73-75. For the irredentist problem, see Seton-Watson, *Rumania and the Great War* (London 1915); N. Iorga, *A History of Roumania* (London 1925), ch. 12 and "The Attitude of Roumania," *Fortnightly Review*, XCVIII (December 1915), 1067-78; Politicus, "Roumania and the Eastern Question," *Fortnightly Review*, v. 100 (October 1916), 549-62; Henri Nevill, "La Roumanie, les balkaniques et la guerre," *La revue*, v. 111, no. 6 (March 1915), 35-50; Seton-Watson, "The Roumanians of Hungary," *New Europe*, I (October 19, 1916), 20-27.

*Note 176.* Sazonov to Poklevsky, July 30, 1914; Isvolsky to Sazonov, August 1, 1914; Polonsky, 167-68. Also Sazonov to Isvolsky, August 2, 1914; *ibid.*, 169-70.

*Note 177.* Poklevsky to Sazonov, August 3, 1914, *ibid.*, 170-71.

*Note 178.* Sazonov to Isvolsky and Benckendorff, August 9, 1914; Isvolsky to Sazonov, August 11, 1914; Poklevsky to Sazonov, August 28, 1914; Polonsky, 171-73; Pokrovsky, nos. 16, 18, 23, pp. 170, 171, 172-3.

*Note 179.* Poklevsky to Sazonov, September 12, 1914; Sazonov to Poklevsky, September 3, 1914; Poklevsky to Sazonov, September 8, 1914; Pokrovsky, nos. 24-26, pp. 173-75; Polonsky, 173-74.

*Note 180.* Giers to Sazonov, September 6, 1914; Isvolsky to Sazonov, September 8, 1914; Poklevsky to Sazonov, September 11, 1914; Polonsky, 173, 174-75; Pokrovsky, nos. 27, 29, 30, pp. 175, 176-77.

*Note 181.* Isvolsky to Sazonov, September 16, 1914; Poklevsky to Sazonov, September 22, 1914; Pokrovsky, nos. 33, 39, pp. 178, 182. See also Czernin to Berchtold, September 7, 1914; Tisza to Czernin, September 7, 1914, September 28, 1914; Tisza, *Briefe*, I. 74-75, 82. Also Auerbach, 120-23.

*Note 182.* Sazonov to Poklevsky, September 16, 17; Polonsky, 176.

*Note 183.* Poklevsky to Sazonov, September 21, 1914; Sazonov to Poklevsky, September 22, 1914; Pokrovsky, nos. 37-38, pp. 180-92; Polonsky, 177.

*Note 184.* Poklevsky to Sazonov, September 26, 1914; Sazonov to Poklevsky, September 26, 1914; Pokrovsky, nos. 40-41, pp. 182-84; Polonsky, 178-79.

*Note 185.* The agreement stipulated: (1) a Russian engagement to oppose any injury to Rumanian integrity; (2) Rumania's right to Austro-Hungarian territories "peopled with Rumanians"; the frontier to be delimited on a nationality basis; (3) Rumania to occupy these territories when opportune; (4) Russia to obtain French and English consent to the agreement; (5) Rumania to observe a benevolent neutrality toward Russia: (6) the agreement to remain secret. See Note to the Rumanian minister in Russia, October 1, 1914; Laloy, 106-07; Poklevsky to Sazonov, September 28, 1914; Sazonov to Poklevsky, October 3, 1914; Pokrovsky, nos. 42, 44, pp. 184, 185-86. For a characterization of Poklevsky's policy, see Arseniev (2nd secretary at Bucharest) to Sazonov, February 8, 1915; *Le Monde slave,* 5th yr. no. 3 (March 1928), 437-51.

*Note 186.* Poklevsky to Sazonov, October 6, 1914; Polonsky, 180-82; Pokrovsky, no. 45, pp. 186-87. Neither England nor France were explicitly informed of this agreement, though the general lines were revealed. See also Danilov, in *Le monde slave,* II, no. 5 (May 1928), 209.

*Note 187.* Same to same, October 30, 1914; Pokrovsky, no. 46, pp. 188-89. See also Burian, 64-66; Czernin, 107 ff; Negulescu, 29-32; Djuvara, 83.

*Note 188.* Czernin to Berchtold, November 14, 1914; same to same, December 2, 1914; A. R. B. (Rumania), nos. 24, 25, pp. 14-16.

*Note 189.* Kudashev (Belgium) to Sazonov, November 20, 1914; Poklevsky to Sazonov, December 2, 1914; Pokrovsky, nos. 51-52, pp. 190-191; Polonsky, 183-84.

*Note 190.* Isvolsky to Sazonov, December 2, 1914; L. N., III, 38. Sazonov to Poklevsky, December 2, 1914; Pokrovsky, no. 53, pp. 191-92. See also Larcher, *Les balkans,* ch. 4.

*Note 191.* Sazonov to Poklevsky, December 2, 1914; Poklevsky to Sazonov, December 12, 1914; Pokrovsky, nos. 54-5, pp. 192-3.

*Note 192.* Trubetzkoy to Sazonov, December 14, 1914; Sazonov to Poklevsky, December 16, 1914 (communicated to Nish, Paris, and London); Pokrovsky, nos. 57, 58, pp. 194-95; Polonsky, 184-85.

*Note 193.* Isvolsky to Sazonov, December 20, 1914; L. N., III, 43.

*Note 194.* Czernin, 110, 120-22. See also Tisza to Czernin telegraphic to M. F. A., through Burian, October 10, 1914; same to same, October 20, 1914; Tisza to Berchtold, telephonic communication through Burian, November 1, 1914; Tisza to Tschirschky, November 5, 1914; Tisza, I, 91-92, 95, 101-02, 104 06, 109. Tisza seems to have been convinced that concessions would not win Rumania.

*Note 195.* See Buchanan memorandum, January 9, 1915; Adamov, *Konstantinopol i prolivy,* I, 365-66. Also Sazonov to Poklevsky, January 10, 1915; Poklevsky to Sazonov, January 15, 1915; Kudashev to Sazonov, January 22, 1915; Pokrovsky, nos. 60-62, pp. 196-97.

*Note 196.* Sonnino to Carlotti, February 19, 1915; Buchanan memorandum, March 26, 1915; Adamov, I, 371, 376-77.

*Note 197.* Madjarov to Radoslavov, March 3, 1915; Pokrovsky, no. 64, pp. 198-99.

*Note 198.* Poklevsky to Sazonov, April 21, 1915; Pokrovsky, no. 66, p. 200. See also Isvolsky to Sazonov, April 17, 21, 1915; L. N., III, 105-06, 106-08.

*Note 199.*   Neratov to Isvolsky, April 30, 1915; Polonsky, 188; Pokrovsky, no. 68, p. 201. See also Blondel to Delcassé, April 23, 1915; Polonsky, 187; Pokrovsky, no. 67, pp. 200-01.

*Note 200.*   Poklevsky to Sazonov, May 1, 1915; Isvolsky to Sazonov, May 1, 1915; Pokrovsky, nos. 69, 70, pp. 202-03.

*Note 201.*   Sazonov to Isvolsky and Benckendorff, May 2, 1915; same to Isvolsky, Benckendorff and Poklevsky, May 3, 1915; Polonsky, 188-89; Pokrovsky, 71-72, pp. 203-04. How the Serbs felt about the Banat may be seen in G. Jasich, "Le Banat," *Revue hebbdomadaire*, VII-VIII (August 7, 1915), no. 32-100-23.

*Note 202.*   Grand Duke Nicholas to Neratov, May 3, 1915; Polonsky, 189-90.

*Note 203.*   Poklevsky to Sazonov, May 4, 1915; Pokrovsky, no. 74, pp. 204-05.

*Note 204.*   Sazonov to Poklevsky, May 14, 1915; Sazonov to Poklevsky, May 19, 1915; Sazonov to Isvolsky, May 19, 1915; Pokrovsky, nos. 80-84, pp. 207-12; Polonsky, 191-93. See also Danilov, *Le monde slave*, (May 1928), 223-24.

*Note 205.*   Czernin to Tisza, May 21, 1915; Tisza to Czernin, May 25, 1915 (telephone). Tisza, 222-23, 225-26, 227. See also Burian, 66-67; Czernin, 121-24.

*Note 206.*   See Tisza to Burian, December 20, 1915; Conrad to Francis Joseph, October 27, 1915; R. J. Kerner, "Austro-Hungarian War Aims in the Winter of 1915-1916 as Revealed by Secret Documents," *Journal of International Relations*, X, no. 3 (January 1920), 444-470. See also R. J. Kerner, "Austrian Plans for a Balkan Settlement," *New Europe*, XVI, no. 206 (September 23, 1920), 280-84.

*Note 207.*   Burian to Czernin, May 23, 1915; A. R. B. (Rumania), no. 31, p. 19. He advised Czernin on June 10. "Let no one imagine at Bucharest that in the long run Russia will tolerate that ten million of Rumanians bar the road to Constantinople." *Ibid.*, no. 34, p. 21.

*Note 208.*   Burian, 68-69. See Tisza to Burian, June 5, 1915; Tisza to Erzberger, June 12, 1915; Erzberger to Tisza, June 15; Tisza-Czernin exchange, June 8, 12, 1915; Tisza memorandum of June 17, 1915; Tisza, 228-231, 233-34, 236, 244, 247-48, 251-53.

*Note 209.*   Burian 69-71. Tisza to Czernin, June 30, 1915; Tisza, I, 254-57.

*Note 210.*   Poklevsky to Sazonov, June 18, 1915; Polonsky, 194; Pokrovsky, no. 89, p. 216.

*Note 211.*   Janushkevitch to G. H. Q., June 20, 1915; Polonsky, 194-96; Pokrovsky, no. 90, pp. 216-17.

*Note 212.*   Poklevsky to Sazonov, June 23, 1915; Isvolsky to Sazonov, June 27, 1915; Pokrovsky, nos. 91-92, pp. 217-18; Polonsky, 196.

*Note 213.*   Isvolsky to Sazonov, June 29, 1915; Polonsky, 197-98; Pokrovsky, no. 93, p. 219.

*Note 214.*   Sazonov to Paris and Rome, June 30, 1915; Polonsky, 198; Pokrovsky, no. 94, p. 219.

*Note 215.*   Isvolsky to Sazonov, July 8, 1915; Sazonov to Benckendorff, July 10, 1915; Pokrovsky, nos. 96-97, pp. 220-21; Polonsky, 198.

*Note 216.*   Sazonov to Poklevsky, July 10, 1915; Sazonov to Paris, London, Rome, Bucharest, July 14, 1915; Pokrovsky, nos. 98-99, pp. 221-22.

*Note 217.*   Sazonov to Poklevsky, August 2, 1915; Polonsky, 199; Pokrovsky, no. 100, p. 222.

*Note 218.*   Poklevsky to Sazonov, August 14, September 18, 1915; Pokrovsky, nos. 101-02, p. 223. Bratianu indicated his favorable attitude toward the Balkan *bloc*

project in August, but insisted on Rumania's interests in the Straits. See Poklevsky to Sazonov, nos. 471, 472, August 21, 1915; Adamov, I, 378-79.

*Note 219.* Isvolsky to Sazonov, October 12, 1915; Polonsky, 199-200; Pokrovsky, no. 103, pp. 224-25.

*Note 220.* Poklevsky to Sazonov, November 1, 1915; Polonsky, 200-01.

*Note 221.* Paléologue, II, 97-98. See also Poklevsky to Sazonov, October 14, 17, 1915, letter of Poklevsky to Sazonov, November 15, 1915; Pokrovsky, nos. 104-05, 107, pp. 225-26, 226-31. Larcher, *op. cit.*, 122-28.

*Note 222.* Sazonov to Paris, London and Rome, November 24, 1915; Laloy, no. 28, pp. 122-23.

*Note 223.* Paléologue, II, 316. See also A. Gauvain, "La question des détroits et la Roumanie," February 24, 1915, VIII; N. Dascovici, *La question du Bosphore et des Dardanelles* (Geneva 1915), 272-300; Jean Finot, "Une crise diplomatique. Autour de Constantinople." *La Revue*, CXIII, (November 1915). pp. 381-3.

*Note 224.* Také Ionescu, *The Policy of National Instinct* (London 1916).

*Note 225.* That Russian policy was much influenced by the Straits question is indicated by General Polivanov's memorandum of November 20, 1916: "In the future this state (Rumania) could hardly have been friendly disposed toward Russia and would scarcely have abandoned the design of realizing its national dreams in Bessarabia and the Balkans." See Cocks, 56-67.

*Note 226.* Paléologue, II, 154-56. See also Poklevsky to Sazonov, January 22, 1916, Sazonov to Poklevsky, January 24, 1916; Poklevsky to Sazonov, January 25, 1916, Sazonov to Poklevsky, January 26, 1916; Pokrovsky, nos. 108-11, pp. 231-35; Polonsky, 201-02.

*Note 227.* Paléologue, II, 159-60, 164-65, 166-67. General Alexeiev's plan provided: (1) ten divisions to support Rumania; (2) concentration in northern Moldavia to menace the right flank of the Austro-Germans; (3) Rumania to repel the Bulgarians and cover Transylvania; (4) military convention.

*Note 228.* Paléologue, II, 197-98, 200-03. Filipescu was in Petrograd at the time taking stock of the situation. See Isvolsky to Sazonov, March 2, 1916 and Sazonov to Poklevsky, March 4, 1916; Pokrovsky, nos. 114-15, p. 237.

*Note 229.* Auerbach, 124-31. Sazonov to Poklevsky, April 19, 1916; Polonsky, 202; Pokrovsky, no. 119, p. 239. Also Burian, 72, and Larcher, *loc. cit.*

*Note 230.* Memorandum of N. A. Basili, April 1916; Polonsky, 306-09. Particularly dangerous would be Russia's position in the Dobruja. See also Paléologue, II, 235-36, 244; Larcher, 128-134.

*Note 231.* Basili to Sazonov, May 27, 1916; Polonsky, 203.

*Note 232.* Burian, 73-74; Paléologue, II, 284, 286, 290; Laloy, no. 36, pp. 143-47; Larcher, *loc. cit.* See also General Brusilov, "L'Offensive russe de 1916," *Revue des deux mondes*, LI, (i) May 15, 1929, pp. 365-70; (ii) June 15, 1929, pp. 903-29.

*Note 233.* The conditions were: (1) Guarantee of war supplies; (2) general offensive of the Allies; (3) situation of the Russian army in Galicia and Bukovina to be held; (4) guarantee from a Bulgarian attack. See Poklevsky to Sazonov, June 29, July 4, 1916; Polonsky, 204-05; Pokrovsky, nos. 123-24, pp. 242-43. Czernin knew of these conditions, see Czernin to Burian, June 19, 28, 1916 and Burian to Hohenlohe (Berlin), July 18, 1916; A. R. B. (Rumania), nos. 61, 66, 74, pp. 39-40, 43-44, 51-53. See also Larcher, 134-142.

*Note 234.* Poklevsky to Sazonov, July 5, 1916, Sazonov to Basili, July 7, 1916; Pokrovsky, nos. 125-26, pp. 243-45; Polonsky, 205-06.

*Note 235.* Paléologue, II, 295-96. Text of Briand to Blondel, July 9, 1916.

*Note 236.* Basili to M. F. A., July 27, 1916; same to same, July 28, 1916; Polonsky, 206-07. Czernin reports an audience with King Ferdinand on this date. Ferdinand did not think that Bratianu was over-obligating himself, and at any rate the king himself was not bound. However, he felt that Bratianu wanted to be "in on it," if it were "a question of dismembering the Monarchy, but that he does not intend to coöperate to lead to this dismemberment." Czernin to Burian, July 27, 1916; A. R. B. (Rumania), no. 80, pp. 56-57.

*Note 237.* See Sturmer to London, Paris and Rome, nos. 1-2, August 8, 1916, Sturmer to Paris and London, August 8, 1916; Pokrovsky, nos. 133-34, pp. 249-51; Polonsky, 208-09.

*Note 238.* Poklevsky to Sturmer, August 9, 1916, Sturmer to Poklevsky, August 13, 1916, and Poklevsky to Sturmer, August 18, 1916; Pokrovsky, nos. 135-36, 139, pp. 251-52, 257; Polonsky, 209-10.

*Note 239.* For text of military convention, August 13, 1916 see Pokrovsky, No. 137, pp. 252-57; Laloy, 149-54. See also Negulescu, 52-63, Paléologue, II, 306-07, 309-10, 311-15, 319-20. Larcher, *loc. cit.*

*Note 240.* See Burian to Czernin, August 10, 1916 and Czernin to Burian, August 26, 1916; A. R. B. (Rumania), nos. 93, 108, 109, pp. 66, 72-74. The text of the war declaration may be found in A. R. B., no. 110, pp. 74-77; Negulescu, 34-39, 39-51. See also Poklevsky to Sturmer, August 28, 1916; Valeiev to Sturmer, August 28, 1916; Pokrovsky, nos. 139-140, pp. 258-59; Polonsky, 211. For comment see Burian, 74-75; Czernin, 112-20; Auerbach, 135-38.

*Note 241.* Auerbach, 138-46; Burian, 75-77. See also General Polivanov's memorandum, November 20, 1916; Cocks, 56-57. De Schelking, *Recollections of a Russian Diplomat* (N. Y. 1918), Report of September 15, 1916, pp. 315-27. For military operations see Djuvara, *op. cit.*, (entire); Negulescu, 64-136; Churchill, III, 197-212; Larcher, 142-176. See also Gourko to Joffre; Paléologue, III, 126-27, December 26, 1916. For Bulgaria and the war with Rumania see Radoslavov, *op. cit.*, 203ff.


## CHAPTER VI


*Note 1.* See above, chs. IV, V. See also René Martel, "L'Orient et la guerre d'après les archives diplomatiques russes." *Le monde slave*, III, no. 10 (October 1926), 124-27.

*Note 2.* Mesopotamia, *Peace Handbook*, no. 63, 43-44.

*Note 3.* See R. S. Baker, *Woodrow Wilson and World Settlement*, I, 64ff.

*Note 4.* See above, ch. IV.

*Note 5.* *Miscellaneous No. 7* (1920). Agreement between France, Russia, Great Britain, and Italy, signed at London, April 26, 1915; *Cmd. 671*. See also Asquith, II, 70-71, 78.

*Note 6.* Memorandum of the ambassador of Great Britain to Sazonov, March 20, 1917; Polonsky, 291.

*Note 7.* Shane Leslie, *Mark Sykes, His Life and Letters* (London 1923), 249, 256-57. See also *The Arrangement Between Great Britain, France and Russia, regarding Syria, Mesopotamia, and Eastern Asia Minor, commonly known as the Sykes-Picot Agreement of May 1916* (an official foreign office version of the agreements), in *ibid.*, 250-8.

*Note 8.* These negotiations of March-April, 1916, may be followed in E. A. Adamov (ed.), *Razdel Aziatskoi Turtsii* (Moscow, 1924), 154-88. See especially the Franco-British memorandum of March 9, 1916, pp. 154-57; Mark Sykes' memorandum of March 12, 1916, pp. 158-59; Sazonov memorandum of March 13, 1916, pp. 160-61; General Beliaev memorandum, April 6, 1916, pp, 178-82. See also the letters of Grand Duke Nikolai Mikhailovich, May to October 1915; Golder *op. cit.*, 63-77.

*Note 9.* The French territory was bounded on the south by the Aintab-Mardin line to the future Russian frontier; on the north by the Ala-Dagh-Zara-Egin Kharput line.

*Note 10.* See Sazonov-Paléologue agreement, April 26, 1916; Sazonov memorandum, March 13, 1916; Adamov, 160-61, 185-86. See also Sazonov, 200-61. For translations and summaries of this agreement see Mears, 617-18. See also Baker, I, 66-67.

*Note 11.* The territory in southern Kurdistan ran along the line Mush-Sert-Ibn Omar-Amadia-Persian frontier.

*Note 12.* The Sykes-Picot agreement may be found in various sources: *Le livre rouge (Turkish Red Book* on the Mosul question, 1925), no. 170, pp. 316-17; Mears, 615-16; *Asie française*, XVII, no. 176, (August-November 1919), 243 ff; *Current History*, XI, no. 3 (March 1920), 499 ff; Loder, *The Truth About Mesopotamia, Syria, and Palestine* (London 1923), 161-64.

*Note 13.* This is clear from Paléologue's conversations with the tsar in November 1914, on the Constantinople accord. See also Cressaty, "La France et la question des lieux saints," *Revue politique et parlementaire*, LXXXIV (September 1915), 334 ff; Etienne Flandin, "Nos droits en Syrie et en Palestine," *Revue hebdomadaire*, V-VI, no. 23 (June 5, 1915), 17-32; Driault, *La reprise de Constantinople*, 39; Gontaut-Biron et Reverend, *D'Angora à Lausanne* (Paris 1924), 1 ff; Gontaut-Biron, *Comment la France s'est installée en Syrie* (Paris 1922), 1-35.

*Note 14.* Shane Leslie, 249-50.

*Note 15.* For text of the Saint Jean de Maurienne agreement see Mears, 619-20; Adamov, 348-49; *Current History*, XI, no. 3 (March 1920), 499 ff. See also David Hunter Miller, *My Diary at the Conference of Paris*, XX, 335-38, for an anonymous, undated document, explaining the circumstances of the agreement. (Hereafter cited as M. D.) Also Martel, "L'Orient et la guerre d'après les archives diplomatiques russes," *Le monde slave*, III, no. 10 (October 1926), pp. 129-30.

*Note 16.* Baker, I, 69-70. An interesting Russian view of the partition of Turkey may be found in Vladimir Zabotinsky, *Turkey and the War* (London 1917), 149-264.

*Note 17.* The best single work on the British campaigns in Mesopotamia is Edmund Dane, *The Campaigns in the Nearer East, 1914-1918* (2v., London 1919). See also Townshend, *My campaign in Mesopotamia; Mesopotamia commission. Report of the commission appointed by act of parliament to enquire into the operation*

of war in Mesopotamia, etc. Cmd. 8610 (1917); Review of the civil administration of Mesopotamia, Cmd. 1061. (1917); Liman von Sanders, 109, 132-141; Larcher, La La guerre turque, 318-41.

Note 18. For the Armenians during the war see Mandelstam, Le sort de l'empire ottoman, 245-331; La société des nations et les puissances devant le problème arménien, 43-51; Lepsius, Deutschland und Armenien; Morgenthau, 300-96; Djemal Pasha, ch. 9; Stuermer, Two War Years in Constantinople, ch. 7; A. J. Toynbee, The Treatment of the Armenians in the Ottoman Empire (1915-16). Misc. No. 31 (1916). Lewis Einstein, Inside Constantinople. A diplomatist's diary during the Dard-anelles expedition, April-September, 1915 (London 1917), 155-208. For the campaigns in the Caucasus and Armenia see Larcher, 367-412. See also, Ahmed Emin, 212-23.

Note 19. Djemal Pasha, 145-161; Douin, L'attaque de canal de Suez (3 février 1915) (Paris 1922).

Note 20. See Liman von Sanders, 144-45; Djemal Pasha, 197-237; Larcher, 245-62. There can be no question, of course, as to the British intrigue, or as to the separatist tendencies of the Arabs, but as Liman indicates, Djemal's policy proved "a complete fiasco," and the British were able to operate in a friendly country, while the Turks "in defense of their own country had to fight against a population directly hostile."

Note 21. L. Gaillard, The Turks and Europe (London 1921), 310-12; Loder, 16-20; Krajevski, L., "La politique anglaise en Arabie, 1915-1927," Revue de Paris, XXV, no. 6 (March 15, 1928), 378-79; Temperley, A History of the Peace Conference, VI, 120-21; Coke, The Heart of the Middle East, 143 ff.

Note 22. See Loder, 20-21; Krajevski, 380; Jung, E., La révolte arabe (Paris 1924), I, 131-2; Current History, XI, no. 2 (November 1919), pp. 339-41, contains the revelations of Col. Lawrence in a communication to the Manchester Guardian, September 12, 1919. See also the letter of Lawrence in the London Times, September 6, 1919, which is reprinted in Mears, 613-14. Also Gaillard, 312-13.

Note 23. Loder, 21-22; Gaillard, 313; Krajevski, 380-81.

Note 24. Jung, I, 132.

Note 25. Krajevski, 381; Loder, 22-23; Gaillard, 313. Of course, the Turks were informed of the Arab events, but Djemal's policy, as indicated, had already failed in dealing with the Arabs. See also, C. A. Hooper, L'Iraq et la société des nations (Paris 1928), 8-13. Stoyanovsky, The Mandate for Palestine (London 1928), 5-8.

Note 26. See Winston Churchill's statement in the House of Commons, July 11, 1922; Parliamentary Debates, vol. 156, col. 1033.

Note 27. Krajevski, 391-93; Toynbee, Survey of International Affairs, 1925, I. Islamic World, 282-83. This treaty was first published in 1924 and 1925 in the Egyptian press and was not denied by either party. See also Peace Handbook, no. 61, Arabia, 28, 30, 32, 34; Coke, 151; Temperley, VI, 120.

Note 28. Hussein received £120,000 gold a month, while Feisal, his son, received £105,000. By 1924, Ibn Saud had received only about £300,000.

Note 29. See Baker, I, 75, and below, ch. VII. For Toynbee's views on the engagements, see Toynbee, 284-88. The best that can be said is that the engagements were so general in nature as to be misleading to all other parties—except the British.

Note 30. Temperley, VI, 124-25.

Note 31. Temperley, VI. 126-28. See also Toynbee, 272-73.

*Note 32.*   Texts of this proclamation may be found in *The King of the Hedjaz and Arab Independence* (London 1917), 6-11; Hurgronje, *The Revolt in Arabia* (N. Y. 1917), 43-50; "Textes historiques sur le réveil arabe au Hedjaz," *Revue du monde musulman*, XLVII (October 1921), 1-27; Mandelstam, 358-64. See also "La révolte du grand cherif de la Mecque," *Asie française*, XVI, no. 166 (July-September 1916), 119-22; and "La révolte du cherif de la Mecque," *Asie française*, no. 165 (April-June 1916), 81-84.

*Note 33.*   See Maude's proclamation to the Arabs, March 19, 1917, in *The King of the Hedjaz and Arab Independence*, 12-15.

*Note 34.*   *Cmd.* 1061, ch. 6; Coke, *op. cit.*, 151ff, 158-9; Baker, III, 1-5. For Colonel Lawrence's exploits see his *Revolt in the Desert;* Robert Graves, *Lawrence and the Adventure;* Lowell Thomas, *With Lawrence in Arabia.* Edmund Dane is good for the British campaigns; Also General F. J. Moberly, *The Campaign in Mesopotamia,* 1914-1918 (London 1923). For the Turco-German angle, see Liman von Sanders, 140-320; Larcher, *La guerre turque,* 341-64, 254-317. An excellent treatment of the Arab question may be found in Richard Coke, *The Arab's Place in the Sun* (London 1929), especially ch. 12.

*Note 35.*   Sonnino-Giers exchange of notes, December 2, 1916; Adamov, *Konstantinopol i Prolivy,* I, 354-55. Kerner, "Russia and the Straits, 1915-1917," *Slavonic Review,* VIII (March 1930), 591.

*Note 36.*   Sazonov to Isvolsky, March 8, 1916. Other conditions were that Sweden be turned from a war against Russia; failing, Norway was to be won over; useless efforts in Rumania were to cease; the question of excluding the Germans from the Chinese markets was reserved.

*Note 37.*   Isvolsky to Pokrovsky, February 13, 1917; Polonsky, 263-64. Pokrovsky to Paléologue, February 14, 1917; Isvolsky to Pokrovsky, March 11, 1917; Laloy, 156-57. See also Paléologue, III, 183-84, 192-93. Also Kerner, *Slavonic Review,* VIII, 591-3.

*Note 38.*   Basili to Pokrovsky, March 11, 1917; Polonsky, 277-80.

*Note 39.*   Basili to Miliukov, April 5, 1917; Basili to Neratov, April 24, 1917; Polonsky, 280-86.

*Note 40.*   Miliukov's note on Policy of Provisional Government, March 18, 1917; Golder, 323-24; Adamov, I, 466-67. The first declaration of the Provisional Government of March 20, 1917, stated: "The Government will sacredly observe the alliances which bind us to other Powers, and will unswervingly carry out the agreements entered into by the Allies." Golder, 311-3.

*Note 41.*   Call by the Petrograd Soviet to the Peoples of the World, March 27, 1917; *ibid.,* 325-6. See also Miliukov to Nabakov, March 29, 1917; Adamov, I, 415.

*Note 42.*   Giers to Miliukov, March 23, 1917; Nabakov to Miliukov, March 23, 1917; Isvolsky to Miliukov, March 23, 1917; Adamov, I, 470-71.

*Note 42a.*   Golder, 329-31 and G. Lowes Dickinson, *Documents and Statements Relative to the Peace* (N. Y. 1919), 43-44. In an interview in *Temps,* April 9, 1917, Miliukov declared: ". . . The Straits to Russia, is, in my opinion, the only way to liquidate the problem (of peace). Neutralization of the Straits would always signify a series of great dangers for peace, and Russia would be obliged to have in the Black Sea a powerful fleet of war ready to defend her coasts. Neutralization of the Straits would give to the warships of all countries the means of penetrating freely in the internal Russian sea, which the Black sea is, and that could entrain great misfortunes

impossible to foresee . . . . We Russians, we need the Straits to assure our exportation and importation without interference and menace of any sort . . . ." B. Nikitine, "Le problème musulman selon le schefs de l'émigration russe," *Revue du monde musulman*, LII, (December 1922), 36.

*Note 42b.* Resolution of the All-Russian Conference of the Soviet of Workers' and Soldiers' Deputies, April 25, 1917; Miliukov's note on war aims, May 1, 1917; Soviet on Miliukov's note, May 3, 1917; Explanation of the Provisional Government, May 5, 1917; Golder, 331-3, 333-4, 334-6.

*Note 43.* Reprinted from the *Riech*, no. 109, May 24, 1917, in Golder, 334. See also the resolution passed by the All-Russian Conference of Bolsheviks at Petrograd, May 7-12, 1917; Appeal by the Petrograd Soviet of Workers' and Soldiers' Deputies to the Socialists of All Countries, May 15, 1917; *ibid.*, 337-343.

*Note 43a.* See Declaration of the New Provisional Government, May 18, 1917; Note of the Provisional Government, June 15, 1917; *ibid.*, 353-6. M. I. Tereschenko became minister of foreign affairs on the resignation of Miliukov. See also Kerner, *Slavonic Review*, VIII, 596-600.

*Note 44.* Seymour, III, 38-9, 43-5. These are conversations of April 22, 28, 1917. See also Mary R. Frear, "Did President Wilson Contradict Himself on the Secret Treaties," *Current History*, June, 1929.

*Note 45.* There was much talk of internationalization of the Straits at this time. Ramsey MacDonald stated in the House of Commons on February 12, 1917: "There are two points on the continent of Europe which I venture to say this empire ought not willingly to surrender to the possession of a Great Power. One is Belgium. And the other is Constantinople. You simply have to look at the map to see that, if this empire is going to rest in security, you must not allow a large European Power to take possession of Belgium, and you ought not to allow it to take possession of Constantinople. I rather like to avoid prophesying, but I venture to say that if a Great Power has taken possession of Constantinople and has fortified it and the Dardanelles, this country will be busy with an attempt to solve the problem of imperial communication in a form which it has never had to face before. Your only reply is to make Egypt a fortified station. You could not afford to do other . . . ." *Parliamentary Debates*, v. 90, col. 348. For House's statement, see Seymour, *loc. cit.*

*Note 46.* Seymour, III, *loc. cit.*

*Note 47.* *Parliamentary Debates* (H.C.), v. 99, col. 838, November 2, 1917; *Zionism, Peace Handbook*, no. 162, p. 44. For the identical announcement of Balfour to Lord Rothschild, see the facsimile in Leonard Stein, *Zionism* (N. Y. 1926). There is a good history of the Balfour declaration in *ibid.*, ch. 4. On August 31, 1918, President Wilson expressed his "satisfaction" to Rabbi Stephen S. Wise concerning the progress of the Zionist movement since the Balfour declaration. See Baker and Dodd, *Public Papers of Woodrow Wilson*, III (i), 243. The statement from Asquith is from his *Memories and Reflections*, II, 78.

*Note 48.* Golder, *op. cit.*, 646-8. See also W. P. F. *War Aims of Belligerents as Russia's Attempts to Secure a General Peace. A League of Nations.* I. n. 3, February 1918, 107-08. Dickinson, 79-80. This was followed by similar declarations for a peace of no annexations and no indemnities in December 1917. See also the general statement of principles at Brest-Litovsk, December 12, 1917, and Trotzky's invitation to the Allied Powers, December 29, 1917, and his statement of November 22, 1917; Dickinson, 100-04, 80-1.

*Note 49.*    Decree of Peace, November 8, 1917; *The Soviet Union and Peace* (N. Y. 1929), 22-25. See also Golder, 620-3 and Cumming and Petit, *Russian-American Relations*, March 1917-March 1920. *Documents and Papers*. (N. Y. 1920), no. 25, p. 43.

*Note 49a.*    Note from R. S. F. S. R. People's Commissariat for Foreign Affairs to Allied Ambassadors, November 22, 1917; Appeal by Council of People's Commissars for the R. S. F. S. R. to the People of the Belligerent Countries with a proposal to join in the negotiations for an armistice, November 28, 1917; *Soviet Union and Peace*, 26-28. Writer's italics.

*Note 49b.*    Appeal of People's Commissars of R.S.F.S.R. to all Mohammedan workers in Russia and the East, December 7, 1917; *ibid.*, 28-30.

*Note 50.*    Shane Leslie, *op. cit.*, 253-54; Temperley, VI. 137-8.

*Note 50a.*    Declaration made by the R. S. F. S. R. Delegation at the First Plenary Session of the Peace Conference in Brest-Litovsk, December 22, 1917; Declaration of February 10, 1918; *Soviet Union and Peace*, 33-41.

*Note 51.*    For text of the Brest-Litovsk treaty, see *Text of the Russian Treaty* (Washington, Government printing office, 1918); *Current History*, XIV, 11. See also Czernin, 214ff; Hoffmann, *War of Lost Opportunities*, 202-32. The Russian position in the Trans-Caucasus is discussed in Larcher, 412-26.

*Note 52.*    For the Bulgarian position at Brest-Litovsk, see Radoslavov, *Bulgarien und die Weltkrise*, 292-313. See also Karl F. Nowak, *The Collapse of Central Europe* (London 1924), ch. 1, and the brilliant memoirs of Leon Trotsky, *My Life* (N. Y. 1930), chs. 21-22.

*Note 53.*    *Parliamentary Debates*, House of Commons, v. 100, col. 2220.

*Note 54.*    W. P. F., I, no. 3 (February 1918), 121. See also L. S. Woolf, *The Future of Constantinople* (London 1917).

*Note 55.*    Lloyd George's speech of January 5, 1918 may be found in Dickinson, *Documents and Statements*, 108-115, especially, 109, 113.

*Note 56.*    For the views of Lord Curzon, see Ronaldshay, *Life of Lord Curzon*, III, 151-61.

*Note 57.*    Baker and Dodd, III, 160-61. Seymour, III, 332. See also *Report* made in January 1918 by the American Inquiry to President Wilson regarding "War aims and peace terms," Baker, III, 23-41.

*Note 58.*    Dickinson, 130-31.

*Note 59.*    W. P. F., I, no. 2 (February 1918), 145 note.

*Note 60.*    Dickinson, 157.

*Note 61.*    See Mr. Balfour's speech in the House of Commons, February 27, 1918; *Parliamentary Debates*, v. 103, cols, 1468-74.

*Note 62.*    The broad lines of a Balkan settlement, P.I.D-F.O., August 2, 1918. Bulgaria—002; M. D., XX, 272-280. The document is anonymous.

*Note 63.*    The Bessarabian question and the act of union with Rumania. P.I.D.-F.O. Rumania-001. August 12, 1918; M.D., XX, 294-312.

*Note 64.*    Robert Lansing, *The Peace Negotiations* (Boston 1921), 192-97.

*Note 65.*    Seymour, IV, 199-200. See also Miller's draft memorandum of July 31, 1918, a portion of which deals with Turkey. Point XII, he argues, excludes complete sovereignty over certain portions of the empire but not necessarily requires its abandonment over Armenia, Syria, Palestine and Arabia. "Possibly one or more

states may be created from what has been Turkish territory." International control over the waters and shores of the Straits is recommended; M.D., II, Document 85, pp. 428-37.

*Note 65a.* Note from Chicherin, People's Commissar for Foreign Affairs, to Woodrow Wilson, President of the United States of America, October 24, 1918; *Soviet Union and Peace*, 48-57.

*Note 66.* Larcher, *La guerre turque*, 416-26 See also Sir Percy Sykes, "The British Flag on the Caspian: a Side-show of the Great War," *Foreign Affairs*, II, no. 2 (December 15, 1923), 282-94; A. Rawlinson, *Adventures in the Near East, 1918-1922* (London 1923).

In this connection it is interesting to note that on December 23, 1917, Lord Milner and Clemenceau signed a convention in Paris with reference to French and English activity in southern Russia. French activity was to be developed north of the Black sea; English activity was to be directed southeast of the Black sea, against the Turks. The French zone of influence was to be: Bessarabia, the Ukraine, the Crimea; the English was in the Cossack territories, the Caucasus, Armenia, Georgia, Kurdistan. For text, see Louis Fischer, *The Soviets in World Affairs* (N. Y., 1930), II, 836. See also W. S. Churchill, *The Aftermath* (N. Y. 1929), 167-168.

*Note 67.* Larcher, 542, estimates the total British forces operating against Turkey at 2,551,000, with losses of 262,000. 900,000 operated in Mesopotamia, Palestine and Syria.

*Note 67a.* Plan of action of General d'Espérey, October 5, 1918; Larcher, *Les Balkans*, Annex no. 21, pp. 286-87. See also *ibid.*, 239-242.

*Note 67b.* Plan of action of the Entente in the East, October 7, 1918; *ibid.*, Annex no. 22, pp. 287-9. Also *ibid.*, 243ff.

*Note 68.* Telegram no. 1930 of E. M. A., October 7, 1918 to C. A. A.; *ibid.*, 289 and 244ff. See also Larcher, *La guerre turque*, 542-43; Gaillard, 155-6; Gontaut et le Réverend, 6-7; Townshend, *My Campaign in Mesopotamia*, II, ch. 20, especially 281-2, 290-7. Also Nowak, *op. cit.*, ch. 5.

*Note 69.* Larcher, *La guerre turque*, 544.

*Note 70.* *Loc. cit.*

*Note 71.* The French had asked to participate in the negotiations on October 27, but were already virtually presented with a *fait accompli*. See Larcher, 544; Sforza, *Diplomatic Europe Since the Treaty of Versailles* (New Haven 1925), 51-53.

*Note 72.* *Livre rouge (Turkish Red Book*, 1925), no. 1; Mears, 624-6.

*Note 73.* Gaillard, 155.

*Note 74.* Ali Ihsan, commander of the Sixth Turkish Army, on October 31, 1918, asked the British commander Marshall to declare the zone between the two armies neutral, but Marshall advanced his troops "in the interest of order and of law," and instructed the Turks to withdraw five miles to the rear. See the Ali Ihsan-Marshall exchange in *Livre rouge*, nos. 4-8, pp. 9-15.

*Note 75.* See the Ali Ihsan-Marshall exchanges of November 1918; *ibid.*, nos. 9, 13-22, pp. 16ff. See also *Cmd. 1061*, ch. 5; Toynbee and Kirkwood, 274ff.

*Note 76.* Text in *Current History*, XIII, no. 2 (February 1921), 243; Temperley, VI, 140-1; Loder, 32-3; Jung, II, 102-3. See also the French instructions to M. Georges Picot, who was sent out to Syria and Palestine as commissioner, with a small contingent of troops in April 1917; *Current History*, XI, no. 3 (March 1920), 502-3.

*Note 77.* Temperley, VI, 140-5; Gaillard, 318-9.

Note 78. See the Secret Minutes of the Conference, March 20, 1919; Baker, III, 1-19.

Note 79. Ibid. The French memorandum has never been published.

Note 80. Journal officiel. Senat (1920), 1525. See also Briand's address to the chamber, June 25, 1920; Journal officiel. Débats parlementaires (1920:2), 2434-35.

Note 81. André Tardieu, "Mossoul et le pétrole," L'Illustration, v. 155, no. 4033 (June 19, 1920), 380-2.

Note 82. Journal officiel. Chambre. (1918:2), 3716.

## CHAPTER VII

Note 1. Leonard Woolf, The Future of Constantinople (London 1917), 1.

Note 2. See especially Report of American Inquiry to President Wilson, January 1918; Baker, III, 23-41. The American Program and International Law, Draft Memorandum, July 31, 1918; Miller Diary, II, Document 85, pp. 428-37. David Hunter Miller, Preliminary outline association of nations (ca) November 29, 1918; ibid., II, Doc. 22, pp. 133.

Note 3. Baker, I, 64ff; Thompson, C. T., The Peace Conference Day by Day (N. Y. 1920), 76-85.

Note 4. The Smuts Plan—a practical suggestion by Lieut. Gen. the Rt. Hon. J. C. Smuts, P. C., December 16, 1918; David Hunter Miller, The Drafting of the Covenant (N. Y. Putnam), Doc. 5, 26-32.

Note 5. Wilson's Second Draft or First Paris Draft, January 10, 1919 with Comments and Suggestions by D. H. M; ibid., II, 65-93 (entire), and ibid., I, 40ff. See also Wilson's Third Paris Draft, February 2, 1919; ibid., II, 145-54.

Note 6. The minutes of this conference are in Secretary's Notes of a Conversation Held at M. Pichon's Room at the Quai d'Orsay, Paris, on Thursday, January 20, 1919, at 11 A. M.; ibid., II, 194-201.

Note 7. Secretary's Notes of a Conversation Held at M. Pichon's Room at the Quai d'Orsay, Paris, on Thursday, January 30, 1919, at 3:30 P. M.; ibid., II, 220-227.

Note 8. Resolutions in reference to mandatories, January 30, 1919; M. D., XIV, 130-31. See also Doc. 252, pp. 302-4 for resolution in regard to mandatories of tenth meeting of League of Nations Commission; Miller, Drafting of the Covenant, II, Doc. 19, p. 333, art. 19.

Note 9. Minutes of the Supreme Council, February 3, 1919; M. D., XIV, 19091. "To Sum up, Greece claimed all the islands of the eastern Mediterranean, including the Dodecanese, Imbros, Tenedos, Kastelorizo, Rhodes and Cyprus."

Note 10. Ibid., XIV, 192-95, 195-97. The frontiers proposed were: from the summit of Koula, northeast of the Greco-Bulgarian frontier, line following the course of the Arda to the Maritza junction to the Turco-Bulgarian frontier of 1913, to Cape India on the Black sea. The Maritza cuts Thrace into eastern and western Thrace.

Note 11. M. D., XIV, 199-209. The committee was composed of Professors Westermann and Day for the United States, Sir Robert Borden and Sir Eyre Crowe for the British Empire, MM. Jules Cambon and Gout for France, and M. de Martino and Colonel Coltoldi for Italy. Greek claims are also to be found in a memorandum of Venizelos, December 30, 1918, Greece before the Conference (Paris 1918); American

Hellenic Society, Publication no. 7 (N. Y. 1919). See also Polybius, *Greece Before the Conference* (London, n.d). For Greece and the Dodecanese see *White Book. The Dodecanese, Resolutions and Documents Concerning the Dodecanese, 1912-1919. Second edition with a map of the Dodecanese* (London 1919); *The Dodecanese and the British Press* (London 1919).

*Note 12.* M. D., XVII, 11 Bulletin no. 57, March 5, 1919. See also Report of Committee on Greek Territorial Claims, March 6, 1919; M. D., X, 286-92, Annex 2. Italian reservations in regard to northern Epirus; M. D., X, 296-8. Neither Greece nor Albania was represented on the commission. For Thrace see Bulletin no. 57, March 5, 1919., XVII, 112; Report of March 6, 1919, M. D., X, 286-92, Annex 3. Italian reservations regarding Bulgarian Thrace, Annex 4; Italian reservations regarding eastern Thrace, Annex 5; M. D., X, 298-300.

*Note 13.* Report of March 6, 1919, Annex 5, Italian reservations in regard to Asia Minor; M. D., X, 286-92; M. D., XVII, 105-6. In a memorandum of November 2, 1918, Venizelos informed Lloyd George that the principal obstacle to Greek Asiatic claims would be Italy, due to the promises of 1915. He stated that after separating Syria, Palestine and Asia Minor, maintenance of the Ottoman Empire would be impossible, and that Greece must have western Asia Minor. Constantinople, with Turkish Thrace, should be international. Frangulis, II, 21-27.

*Note 14.* Bulletin no. 53, March 3, 1919; M. D., XVII, 105-6. Report of March 6, 1919; M. D., X, 286-92. Summary report of the meeting of the Central Committee on Territorial Questions, of March 17, 1919; M. D., XVII, 228-29.

*Note 15.* Memorandum from Westermann to Mezes, March 25, 1919; M. D. VII, no. 605, p. 107. The Report of the Commission, March 6, 1919, should be compared with the Recommendations of Plenipotentiaries, January 21, 1919, no. 246, M. D., IX, 249: (1) that the frontiers of Greece in the north and northeast remain as in 1914, and as established after the second Balkan war, and (2) that Rhodes and the Dodecanese be assigned to Greece.

*Note 16.* Venizelos to Dutasta, March 13, 1919, submitting a memorandum on Greek claims, March 8, 1919; M. D., XVII, Bulletin no. 118, March 29, 1919, pp. 335-40.

*Note 17.* Gaillard, 318-19; Lansing, Robert, *The Big Four* (N. Y. 1921), 161-77.

*Note 18.* Memorandum of the Emir Feisal, January 31, 1918; M. D. IV, no. 250, pp. 297-99, no. 251, p. 300. Territorial claims of the government of the Hejaz.

*Note 19.* Supreme Council, February 6, 1919. Statement of Emir Feisal; M. D., XIV, 227-28. Feisal's expenses were paid by the British government. See also Arabia. *Aperçu sur l'illégitimité du sultan turc en tant que Khalife. Quelques remarques relatives aux prétendues visées turques sur Constantinople. D'après les sources arabes et l'opinion des islamistes les plus célèbres* (Paris 1919). Shows separatist tendencies in religion among Arabs and Turks.

*Note 20.* M. D., XIV, 229-32. The Intelligence Section Report (American), January 21, 1919, recommended for Arabia: (1) that the desert section of Arabia be separated from Syria and the Tigris and Euphrates valleys and be treated as a block; (2) that no definite action be taken concerning the tribal states; (3) this region including territory south of the Euphrates below the town of Hit, thence stretching out to the west to the Red sea, the eastern boundary of Palestine, to the agricultural parts of Syria; (4) the policing of the Red sea, Indian ocean and Persian gulf coasts of Arabia be left to the British Empire; (5) that Hejaz not be allowed to stretch its

dominion over unwilling tribes. However if Syria desired union with the Arab confederation, no obstacle was to be placed in its way. A Mesopotamian state under mandate was recommended, and it was to be allowed union with the Arabian confederation if it desired. M. D., IX, no. 246, pp. 259-64.

Note 21. M. D., XIV, 392-99. February 13, 1919. Supreme Council.

Note 22. M. D., XIV, 399-416, February 13, 1919. See also M. D., XIV, February 15, 1919, pp. 429-33. The statements of Damad Bey Mamon, President of the Great Administrative Council of Mount Lebanon, Negile Bey Malek, Druse delegate and Abdel Halim Haffar, Musulman delegate. The expenses of these delegates were paid by the French government.

Note 23. M. D., XIV, 503.

Note 24. Supreme Council, February 26, 1919. M. D., XV, 86-92. See also *The Armenian Question before the Peace Conference. A memorandum presented officially by the representatives of Armenia to the Peace Conference at Versailles, on February 26, 1919.* See also *Le Pont-Euxin devant le Congrès de la Paix. Mémoire présenté à la Conference de la Paix par les délégués du Pont-Euxin* (Paris 1919). Claims conflict with those of Armenians. The American Intelligence Report recommended on January 21, that (1) Armenians of Transcaucasian state unite with Armenia; (2) provisional independence for Azerbaijan Tartars; (3) provisional independence for Georgia. For Armenia proper a separate state was recommended under League mandatory. The Adana region of Cilicia is included, as well as Kars and Erivan, while Trebizond was assigned as a harbor on the Black sea. See Doc. 246, M. D., IV, 229-259. See also House and Seymour, *What Really Happened at Paris*, ch. 8.

Note 25. M. D., XV, 104-08. Dr. Weizmann made a similar statement, ibid., 110-17. See also the memorandum of the Zionist organization regarding Palestine; M. D., V, Doc. 315, pp. 15-29, dated February 27, 1919, and *Statement of the Zionist Organization Concerning Palestine* (Paris 1919). The boundaries desired were outlined in the memorandum. The American Intelligence Report recommended: (1) a separate state of Palestine be established; (2) that the state be under a British mandate; (3) that the Jews be invited to return, and that when Palestine becomes a Jewish state in fact, it be so recognized; (4) that the holy places and the rights of all creeds be put under League protection. M. D., IV, Doc. 246, p. 264.

Note 26. Agreement between the King of the Hejaz and the Zionists, London, January 3, 1919; M. D., III, Doc. 141, pp. 188-89.

Note 27. *Responsabilité des Jeunes Turcs; Mémoire sur les révendications des Kurdes; Memorandum no. 339, February 6, 1919; M. D., V., Docs. 337, 339, pp. 134-42.

Note 28. The Secret Minutes of the Conference of the Four Heads of States, March 20, 1919; Baker, III, 1-19.

Note 29. Baker, III, 3-6. See also Briand's statement in the French Chamber, June 25, 1920; *Journal officiel. Débats parlementaires* (1920:2), 2434-35.

Note 30. Baker, III, 6.

Note 31. Ibid., 7.

Note 32. Ibid., 8.

Note 33. Ibid., 8-9.

Note 34. Baker, III, 9-10.

Note 35. Loc. cit.

Note 36. Ibid., 10-11.

Note 37.   Ibid., 14-16.

Note 38.   Ibid., 16-19.

Note 39.   Baker, I, 77-87. See also A. H. Lybyer, "Turkey under the Armistice," *Journal of International Relations*, XII, no. 4 (April 1922), 455-59.

Note 40.   The results of the commission's report will be detailed later.

Note 41.   Gaillard, 319-21; Coke, *The Arab's Place in the Sun*, ch. 13.

Note 42.   Memorandum on Syria, March 26, 1919; M. D., VII, 169-70. Probably British.

Note 43.   M. D., I, 27-28.

Note 44.   M. D.. I, 74.

Note 45.   Miller, *Drafting of the Covenant*, I, 47, 103. See also Thompson, 10-11, note of April 16, 1919. House favored the idea of the Constantinople mandate. See Lansing, *The Peace Negotiations* (Boston 1921), 158-60. Whatever the motive, the United States, on account of its geographical situation, and consequent dis-interestedness (more or less), was best suited to this task.

Note 46.   The Constantinople Region and Greek Claims, March 9 (?), 1919, (Mezes?); M. D., VI, Doc. 471, pp. 284-86. The Italians had insisted on this proposi-tion on March 1, 1919.

Note 47.   Memorandum re Turkey and Constantinople State (written by some of the American experts, date uncertain); M. D., VI, Doc. 492, p. 320. The population of the Asiatic side of the Constantinople state would total about 900,000 (520,000 Turks, 255,000 Greeks, 125,000 various) which added to 1,500,000 on the European shore, would total about 2,400,000. About half rural.

Note 48.   Italian policy in Asia Minor, January-October, 1919; M. D., XIX, 557-9.

Note 49.   *Loc. cit.* The Italians had sent two cruisers and some destroyers. Lloyd George said they were stirring up trouble between the Turks and Greeks. According to Clemenceau there were seven battleships.

Note 50.   M. D., XIX, 559.

Note 51.   Ibid., 559-60.

Note 52.   The Dodecanese, January-October, 1919; M. D., XIX, 570.

Note 53.   M. D., XIX, 559-60, 570. Wilson excluded the Meander valley and country south of it, but proposed a Greek mandate over "the larger area claimed by M. Venizelos."

Note 54.   Ibid., 560-61.

Note 55.   Ibid., 562. This was a tentative program as a part of an offer to Italy. Wilson approved the assignment of the Meander valley to Greece. Lloyd George thought that Italy would insist on the ports of Scala Nuova and Mersina.

Note 56.   M. D., XIX, 562-3.

Note 57.   Venizelos to Clemenceau, April 12, 1919. Bulletin no. 197, April 23, 1919; M. D., XVIII, 7-9. Frangulis, II, 623, Venizelos to High Commissioner at Constantinople, May 6, 1919. See also Ahmed Hakki, *Les événements de Turquie depuis l'armistice du 31 octobre, 1918* (Lausanne 1919).

Note 58.   Thompson, 373-74. Venizelos' reasons for landing were later found to be almost entirely false. The Greeks did their share of massacring at this time. See the conclusions of the committee of inquest, Frangulis, II, 64-67.

Note 59.   M. D., XIX, 563. The Balfour memorandum of May 17, 1919, may be found in Baker, III, 303-07.

Note 60.　Ibid., 564. On May 18, Orlando had asked Lloyd George for a mandate for all Anatolia. "At last M. Orlando had let out that he really did not care a scrap about Asia Minor if he could get Fiume." See also Thompson, 374-75; Seymour, op. cit., IV, 467. Note of May 16, 1919.

Note 61.　M. D., XIX, 564. Lloyd George suggested it worth while to concede Fiume to get Italy out of Asia Minor. The Moslems were also opposed to Italy in the Caucasus.

Note 62.　M. D., XIX, 565

Note 63.　Ibid., 566. See also Thompson, 377-78.

Note 64.　M. D., XIX, 566.

Note 65.　Loc. cit. See Venizelos' letter to Wilson, May 19, 1919, and Wilson's acceptance; Frangulis, II, 50-51.

Note 66.　Ibid., 566-67. Renewed Italian landings brought Lloyd George's declaration on May 26, that if Italy did not withdraw he would entirely disinterest himself in Italian claims in Asia Minor.

Note 67.　Supreme Council, June 17, 1919; M. D., XVI, 419-21. See also Damad Ferid to Clemenceau, June 23, 1919; ibid., 479-84.

Note 68.　Clemenceau to Damad Ferid Pasha, June 25, 1919. Approved by Council of Allied and Associated Powers, June 23, 1919; M. D., XVI, 475-79.

Note 69.　Minutes of the Supreme Council, June 25, 1919; M. D., XVI, 459-61.

Note 70.　Loc. cit.

Note 71.　M. D., XIX, 567-68. See also Lansing, The Peace Negotiations, 158-60.

Note 72.　Ibid., 568. For Lord Curzon's attitude on these problems, see Ronald-shay, Life of Lord Curzon (London, N. Y., 1928), III, 262-68. He favored eliminating the Turk from Constantinople. Naturally, he favored, also, British rule over the new Arab kingdom in Mesopotamia and Arabia.

Note 73.　M. D., XVI, 459-61.

Note 74.　See "The King-Crane Report on the Near East. A suppressed official document of the United States government." Editor and Publisher, LV, no. 27 (December 2, 1922), i-xvii.

The mission found considerable anti-French sentiment in Syria, and great popular support for Feisal. It recommended that a mandate in Syria should be of limited term, the unity of Syria be preserved, and Cilicia be united with Asia Minor. The Lebanon should be under a decentralized régime. Syria, it felt, should be under one mandatory, with Feisal as head of a new constitutional monarchy in a united Syrian state.

Serious modifications of the Zionist program were recommended. The United States appeared to be first choice as the mandatory, but if not accepted, the mandatory should be England. For Mesopotamia, including Basra, Bagdad and Mosul, the commission proposed a limited British mandate. A constitutional monarchy, with popular election appeared best as a form of government. British evidence indicated a son of Hussein as the choice.

The Ottoman Empire, subject to historic abuses by the Turks (and for geographical reasons) was to be broken up, but on a just and fair basis. A separate Armenian state was recommended, though Professor Lybyer, the general advisor, was not in favor of an extended territory. Professor Lybyer recommended a state including Russian Armenia, the area crossed by commercial routes through Erzingan and Erzerum between Anatolia and Persia and Transcaucasia, through Trebizond toward the Persian gulf. This would guarantee Kars, Erivan, Erzerum, Mush and

Van. The problem of the Turkish state involved Anatolia, about 10,000,000 people, with ample outlets to the sea. An American mandate was desired. The mandates for Anatolia, Armenia and Constantinople were to be held by one Power. The commission did not favor Greek claims in Smyrna.

A separate Constantinopolitan state, with internationalization and neutralization of the Straits, under an American mandate, was another important recommendation. Such a mandate, it was felt, would take this world problem "out of politics" and give a genuine solution to it. Professor Lybyer desired to include in this state, both shores of the Straits (Bosphorus and Dardanelles) and the Marmora littoral. In European Turkey, the existing frontiers, with the 1915 Bulgaro-Turkish modifications were recommended. Turkish Thrace would be retained. On the Asiatic shore, a frontier beginning on the Black sea coast, just east of the Sakaria river, running east of the river to Ak Sofu Dagh, to Geuk Dagh, south between Irmik and Yeni Shehir and westward along the heights south of Mudania and Panderma, to the boundary of Biga, following to the sea south of Mt. Ida. The total population of the area would be about sixty per cent Turkish, twenty-five per cent Greek, and ten per cent Armenian, a total of 2,000,000.

For French criticism of the report see R. de Gontaut-Biron, *Comment la France s'est installée en Syrie*, 262-82; Michel Paillarès, *Le Kémalisme devant les alliés* (Constantinople-Paris, 1922), 1-31.

*Note 75.* Supreme Council, February 1, 1919; M. D., XIV, 162-82. Bulletin no. 23, February 18, 1919. Proceedings of the commission for the study of Rumanian territorial questions; M. D., XVII, 13, also M. D., XVII, Bulletin no. 57. The American recommendation is in document 246, M. D., IV, 233. The Rumanians had then been in occupation for more than a year, following the Russian revolution.

*Note 76.* See Russian Political Conference (Lvov, Sazonov, Chaikovsky, Maklakov) to the president of the Peace Conference, March 22, 1919; M. D., XVIII, 435-40.

*Note 77.* Russian Political Conference (Lvov, Sazonov, Chaikovsky, Maklakov), *Memorandum Presented to the President of the Conference of Peace*, Paris, July 5, 1919 (Paris 1919). The committee stated that 40% of the total Russian export, 54% of maritime export, 74% of cereals, 88% of napthha, 93% of manganese, 61% of iron were exported by the Black and Azov seas. They urged a Russian mandate in a "better" day.

*Note 78.* For text of the Venizelos-Tittoni accord, see Frangulis, II, 100-01; C. D., and I. B., Booth, *Italy's Aegean Possessions* (London 1928), 297-303; Antoine Tsacalkis, *Le Dodécanèse. Étude de droit international* (Alexandria 1928), 66-72.

*Note 79.* Treaty of Versailles, June 28, 1919; *The Treaties of Peace, 1919-1923* (Carnegie, N. Y., 1924), 91.

*Note 80.* *Ibid.*, 92-93.

*Note 81.* The treaty of St. Germain, September 10, 1919, articles 86, 102; treaty of Trianon (with Hungary), articles 70, 86; *ibid.*, 296, 302, 486-7, 492.

*Note 82.* See League of Nations *Covenant*, article XXIII and President Wilson's address of February 14, 1919; Baker and Dodd, III,(i) 421.

*Note 83.* Many of the proposals may be found in the *Miller Diary*: Venizelos to Clemenceau, May 16, 1919, with memorandum on the Bulgarian frontier, Bulletin 281, M. D., XVIII, 281-3; treaty with Bulgaria, political clauses, July 28, 1919; *ibid.*, XIII, 317-20; frontiers of Bulgaria in Thrace; *ibid.*, X 303-5, 307-10. Bulgaria,

like the other enemy states, was not allowed to deliberate with the victors at the Conference. Many pamphlets and memoranda were presented however. Some of these are: J. Ivanov, *La région de Cavalla* (Berne 1918); Ministry of Foreign Affairs, *The Bulgarian Question and the Balkan States* (Sofia 1919); D. Rizov, *The Bulgarians in Their Historical, Ethnological and Political Frontiers*, with 40 maps (Berlin 1917). See also the *Reply of the Hellenic Delegation to the Statements Submitted to the Peace Conference by the Bulgarian Delegation with regard to the Policy of Bulgaria and its Claims to Thrace* (American Hellenic Society, Publication no. 10 (N. Y. 1920)

*Note 84.* Treaty of Neuilly, November 27, 1919, article 27; *The Treaties of Peace* (Carnegie), II, 658-61. Article 48 put Thrace at the disposal of the Allied Powers.

*Note 85.* Agreement between H. B. M. Government and the Persian Government, signed at Teheran, August 9, 1919; Persia no. 1 (1919). See also *International Conciliation*, no. 145 (December 1919), 18-25. For Lord Curzon's position, see Ronaldshay, III, 208-23. The French position is detailed in Gontaut-Biron et Le Réverend, *D'Angora à Lausanne*, 8-10. There is a very brief but good survey of British policy in A. H. Lybyer, "British Policy in the Near East," *Current History*, XXVI, no. 3 (June 1927), 498-502.

*Note 86.* Telegram from Polk, Paris, received September 16, 1919, for President and Secretary of State, September 16, 1919; M. D., XX, 416-19. Lloyd George memorandum, September 13, 1919; M. D., XVI, 509-13.

*Note 87.* See Gontaut-Biron, *Comment La France s'est installée en Syrie, 1918-1919* (Paris 1923), 309-22.

*Note 88.* The text of this supposed treaty is in Pierre Loti, *La Mort de notre chère France en Orient* (Paris 1920), 153-55. The treaty is denied by both governments, but fits exactly into English policy at this time. Mr. Winston Churchill and MM. Fraster and Nolan (English) and Damad Ferid Pasha (Turkish) were the supposed negotiators.

*Note 89.* Memorandum of Agreement, San Remo, April 24, 1920. *Cmd. 675.* See also Lloyd George's statement in the House of Commons; *Parliamentary Debates*, v. 131, cols. 35-36.

*Note 90.* *Misc. 11. (1921).* Correspondence between H. M. Government and the United States ambassador respecting economic rights in mandated territories. *Cmd. 1226.* Text also in *International Conciliation*, no. 166 (September 1921). For further details of the controversy see below, chs. 8, 9.

*Note 91.* *Parliamentary Debates*, v. 128 (H.C.) col. 1470. See also Millerand's statement in the French Senate, April 29, 1920; *Journal officiel*. Senate (1920), 545-46. See also Frangulis, II, 158-59. The official documents and statements relative to San Remo are in *L'Europe Nouvelle*, 3rd yr., no. 15 (May 8, 1920), 602-08.

*Note 92.* See *Congressional Record*, LIX, 7533-34 for Wilson's message of May 24, 1920, and *ibid.*, June 1, 1920, v. LIX, pt. 8, pp. 8051-73 for the rejection by the Senate. The State Department had recognized Armenia on April 23, 1920. This was confirmed by the Senate on May 13, 1920. See *ibid.*, LIX, pt. 7, pp. 6978-9. Armenia had declared her own independence on May 28, 1918 and was recognized by Great Britain and France on January 19, 1920.

*Note 93.* The first protest came on January 11, 1920 to the viceroy at Delhi from the Delegation for the Defence of the Caliphate. See Gaillard, 122-37; Street, *Life of Lord Reading.* (London 1928), 200-27. See also *Parliamentary Debates* (H.C.),

v. 125, pp. 1278-9, February 23, 1920. The full text of the interview of the Indian delegation with Lloyd George, March 19, 1920 may be found in *La revue du monde Musulman*, XL-XLI (1920), 178-200. Just a month before the treaty of Sèvres was signed, on July 10, 1920, the Moslem delegation filed a written protest with Lloyd George; *ibid.*, 200-15. The address to Baron Chelmsford; *ibid.*, 166-73. Manifesto in name of Congress of All India for Defence of Caliphate; *ibid.*, 174-77.

*Note 94.* See *Observations générales présentées par la délégation ottomane à la conférence de la paix*, July 8, 1920 (n. p., n. d.). This is a strongly worded, carefully prepared proptest of some forty-seven pages against the treaty. Hussein bitterly objected to the San Remo agreement and refused to sign the Sèvres treaty, which in turn, deprived the Hejaz of representation at Lausanne. See League of Nations. *Assignment of the Mandates over Arab Countries.* Letter dated May 8, 1920, from the Secretary-General of the Hejaz Delegation in Paris. Document du Conseil KI, 20-4-96. H. M. S. O., London, 1920. San Remo, the Hejaz protested, put an end to the hope of Arab independence.

*Note 95.* For treaty of Sèvres, see *Treaty Series no. 11* (1920). Treaty of peace with Turkey, signed at Sèvres, August 10, 1920. Cmd. 964. Turkey recognized the mandate system, the terms of which were to be submitted to the League Council for approval after being drawn up by the Allied Powers. See especially articles 94-6, 98-100, 132.

*Note 96.* *Ibid.*, arts. 65-83, 84-87.

*Note 97.* *Ibid.*, arts. 88-93. Mr. Wilson agreed to this in answer to a letter from M. Paul Hymans, President of the League Council November 30, 1920; Baker and Dodd, III, 511-12. The Wilson boundary for Armenia ran from the Black sea east of Kerasun, southeast crossing the Kara Su, including Mush, Bitlis, Van, Baye-zid, etc. Wilson was to have sent Mr. Morgenthau to Armenia, but when Soviet Russia absorbed Armenia, and the Powers did not back him up, he had nothing more to do with it. See L. N., *Official Journal*, February 1921, p. 81. See also the *Harbord Report*, Senate Document no. 266, 66th Congress, 2nd Session. For the Aegean islands, see treaty of Sèvres, arts. 101-17, 121-22. The islands included Stampalia, Rhodes, Calki, Scarpanto, Casos, Pscopis, Misiras, Calymnas, Leros, Patmos, Lipsos, Simi and Cos, and Castellorizo.

*Note 98.* *Ibid.*, arts. 37-57. Among the duties over which the commission had charge were: (1) improvements of channels; (2) lighting and buoying of channels; (3) control of pilotage; (4) control of anchorage; (5) control of wrecks and salvage, and lighterage.

*Note 99.* *Ibid.*, Annex. There are six articles in the Annex. With Russia and the United States the Great Powers had 12 votes against 4 for the minor states. Great Britain, France, Italy and Japan alone had 8 votes.

*Note 100.* Blaisdell, *European Financial Control in the Ottoman Empire*, 196-7. For entire discussion of Sèvres see *ibid.*, 193-7.

*Note 101.* *Treaty Series no. 12* (1920). Tripartite Agreement between the British Empire, France, and Italy respecting Anatolia. Signed at Sèvres, August 10, 1920. Cmd. 963.

*Note 102.* With reference to railroads: The Mersina-Tarsus, Adana line, and the part of the Bagdad railroad in Anatolia were under French-British-Italian capital. France reserved the right to work her own lines including the above in her own sphere. See also treaty of Sèvres, Part XI, on waterways and railways.

Note 103. These included Stampalia, Calymnos, Léros, Patmos, Lipsos, Simi and Cos, as well as the islets dependent on them.

Note 104. For the text of this accord see Cmd. 963 (1920); Booth, 303-06; Tsakalkis, 74-77. The American Senate adopted the Lodge resolution on May 17, 1920 stating "northern Epirus . . . the twelve islands of the Aegean and the western coast of Asia Minor, where a strong Greek population predominates, should be awarded by the Peace Conference to Greece and become incorporated in the kingdom of Greece." Congressional Record, LIX, pt. 7. (May 17, 1920), 7160.

Note 105. Treaty Series no. 13 (1921). Treaty between the Principal Allied and Associated Powers and Greece. Signed at Sèvres , August 10, 1921. Cmd. 960.

Note 106. See B. Nikitine, "Le problème musulman selon les chefs de l'émigration russe," Revue du monde musulman, LII (December 1922), 38-40. Also Ali Fuad, La question des détroits (Paris 1928), 130-33; Ahmed Rustem Bey, La Crise proche orientale et la question des détroits de Constantinople (Geneva 1922), 1 ff. For a French view see Gontaut-Biron et le Révérend, 10-16; L'Islam et la politique contemporaine (Paris 1927), René Pinon on "L'islam et le proche orient," pp. 73-91.

Note 107. Miscellaneous no. 4 (1921). Franco-British Convention of December 23, 1920 on certain points connected with the Mandates for Syria and the Lebanon, Palestine and Mesopotamia. Cmd. 1195. French concessions were granted expressly for "the maintenance for the benefit of France of the provisions of the Franco-British agreement of San Remo regarding oil."

Note 108. Ibid., arts. 5-7. Also W. R. Batsell, "The United States and the Mandates System," International Conciliation, no. 213 (October 1925), 276-77.


CHAPTER VIII


Note 1. Observations générales présentées par la délégation ottomane à la conférence de la paix, July 8, 1920.

Note 2. Bonar Law declared in the House of Commons on July 5, 1920, that "the Greek government were permitted to land troops at Smyrna in May 1919, for the protection of their nationals;" Parliamentary Debates, v. 131, col. 1001. For Winston Churchill's reactions to the new Turkey, see The Aftermath (N. Y. 1929), 373-401.

Note 3. See A. J. Toynbee, The Western Question in Greece and Turkey (London 1922), 84ff, 178ff.

Note 4. Mustapha Kemal Pasha, "Creating a Nation," Living Age, v. 333, no. 4319 (December 1, 1927), 974. This is only a fragment of the Ghazi's famous six-day speech before the Grand National Assembly at Angora.

Note 5. J. Deny (tr.) "Moustafa Kemal Pacha: Sa biographie d'après le nouvel annuaire officiel de Turquie," Revue du monde musulman, LXIII (1926), 146-7; Gaillard, 179-83. For text of Sivas declaration of September 9, 1919, see Mears, 627-8. For more biography of Mustafa Kemal, see Abdul Adam, Book of Mustafa Kemal, (Constantinople, 1926); J. W. Hall, Eminent Asians (N. Y. 1929), 249-337.

Note 6. Mustapha Kemal Pasha, op. cit., 974-77. See also Toynbee and Kirkwood, Turkey (N. Y. 1926), 84-5, and Report of the Military Mission to Armenia (Harbord Report), Senate Document no. 266, 66th Congress, 2nd Session.

Note 7. Toynbee, op. cit., 209-10, for English translation.

*Note 8.* Mears, *op. cit.*, no. 19, p. 631. On February 29 British marines paraded in Pera, on March 1 in Stambul, and on March 3 in Scutari. See Sforza, 55-9; Toynbee and Kirkwood, 88; Claire Price, *Rebirth of Turkey*, ch. 18; Jean Schicklin, *Angora . . . . L'Aube de la Turquie nouvelle*, ch. 1; Paillarès, *Le Kémalisme devant les alliés* (Paris 1922), 136-9; Maurice Pernot, "Constantinople sous le controle interallié," *Revue des deux mondes*, VII, (January 15, 1922), 276-314, and "Angora—les Turcs entre l'occident et l'orient," *ibid.*, 549-79.

*Note 9.* *Parliamentary Debates*, v 125, February 26, 1920. See especially the statements of Sir Douglas Maclean, cols. 1951-4, Sir Edward Carson, cols. 1957, Lloyd George, cols. 1959-70. While the British were gaining control at Constantinople, the French were courting the Angora government. In September 1919, M. Picot went to Sivas where Kemal and his lieutenants proposed recognition of a French economic "mandate" over Turkey in return for a special régime in Cilicia admitting control of "consuls à compétence plus étendue." See Gontaut et le Réverend, 12.

*Note 10.* J. Deny, *op. cit.*, 162-4; Sforza, 60; Gaillard, 183-6. Shortly after the occupation of Constantinople, Kemal addressed a letter of protest to Millerand. See Gaillard, 186-7.

*Note 11.* See Miss G. E. Knox's chapter on "Government" (ch. 18) in Mears, *Modern Turkey*.

*Note 12.* Stavridi to Venizelos, London, March 5, 1915; Frangulis, I, 191-2; Venizelos to M. F. A., London, March 19, 1920 and Romanos to Venizelos, March 24, 1920; Frangulis, II, 121-2, 137-8, 138-9. See also Churchill to the Prime Minister, March 29, 1920; Churchill, *The Aftermath*, 418-19.

*Note 13.* See Sforza, 60-61; Frangulis, II, 160-61, Romanos to Venizelos, June 21, 1920.

*Note 14.* Frangulis, II, 162-63; Sforza, 61-62.

*Note 15.* *Parliamentary Debates* (H. C.), v. 132, July 21, 1920, cols. 477-78. Italics mine.

*Note 16.* See the Allied note of December 3, 1920; Frangulis, II, 173. The Greek reply, Rhally to the Allied Powers, December 29, 1920; *ibid.*, 177-78.

*Note 17.* It was decided at Paris, January 25, 1921, to call a meeting of the Greek, Turkish and Allied delegates at London to settle the question. See "Résultats de la conférence de Paris," *l'Europe nouvelle*, 4th yr., no. 6 (February 5, 1921), p. 187.

*Note 18.* See notes of the English secretary on the Allied Conference held in the St. James Palace, London, February 21, 1921; Frangulis, II, 183-94.

*Note 19.* "Les résultats de la conférence de Londres, 21 février (March 19, 1921), 380-82; Official communiqués of the Conference. From this time on Lord Curzon, who no longer believed in the possibility of Greek victory, diverged from the policy of Lloyd George. See Ronaldshay, III, 277-78.

*Note 20.* Calogeroupoulos to Athens, February 25, 1921; M. F. A. to same, March 4, 1921; Turkish memorandum, March 4, 1921; Frangulis, II, 198, 200-04, 207.

*Note 21.* Calogeroupoulos to M. F. A, March 9, 1921; Notes on a conversation at 10 Downing Street, London, March 10, 1921; Gounaris, March 10, 1921; notes on a meeting at 10 Downing Street, March 18, 1921; *ibid.*, II, 207, 209-12, 219-20, 224-8.

On June 11 Winston Churchill voiced his disapproval of the policy of Sèvres, and was willing to support the Greeks under certain conditions. But on June 21 Churchill wrote the prime minister that if Greece refused the offer of mediation

(which they did), England should make its policy effective, "as we shall have an absolutely unreasonable Kemal to deal with." He was particularly afraid that if the Greeks started an offensive in a disheartened manner "it may produce irretrievable disaster if it fails." See Churchill, *op. cit.*, 419-21.

*Note 22.* Italo-Turkish agreement for Italian economic development in Anatolia, March 13, 1921; Sforza, 104-5. A definitive agreement was to be laid down later. For the whole of Sforza's policy toward Turkey see: Sforza, *Makers of Modern Europe*, Indianapolis, Bobbs Merrill Co. Ch. XXXIV.

*Note 23.* Toynbee, *op. cit.*, 228-9. Chamberlain was informed of a later agreement (April 24, 1922). The British government had assurances that there were no counter concessions. See *Parliamentary Debates* (H. C.), v. 153 (May 3, 1922), cols. 1344-45.

*Note 24.* The armistice gave France large concessions in Cilicia and other parts of Turkey. Though never ratified, it did stop the war and paved the way for the accord of October, 1921. See *l'Europe nouvelle*, 4th yr., no. 13 (March 26, 1921), 407-8, for text. See also Mohr, *The Oil War* (N. Y. 1926), 174-5; Driault, V, 402-5. France had from 80,000 to 100,000 men in Syria.

*Note 25.* See *Turkey no. 1* (1922). Correspondence between H. M. Government and the French Government respecting the Angora Agreement of October 20, 1921. *Cmd. 1570.* Especially nos. 1 and 2 of the Curzon-Saint Aulaire correspondence.

*Note 26.* *Turkey no. 2* (1921). Dispatch from H. M. Ambassador at Paris enclosing the Franco-Turkish Agreement signed at Angora on October 20, 1921. *Cmd. 1556.*

*Note 27.* *Ibid.*, art. 10.

*Note 28.* *Ibid.* Especially Yussuf Kemal Bey to M. Franklin-Bouillon, October 20, 1921, and the rest of this interesting correspondence.

*Note 29.* Proclamation of Franklin-Bouillon, of Muhedin Pasha and Damad Bey, Adana, December 1, 1921; Proclamation of Mustapha Kemal Pasha, December 5, 1921; Proclamation of General Gouraud; Gontaut-Biron et le Réverend, *op. cit.*, 216-21.

*Note 30.* See *Cmd. 1570* for this correspondence. Considerable discussion took place in the Council and Assembly of the League of Nations over the fate of Armenia, but very little was or could be done about it. See *Official Journal* (February 1922), 175-77.

*Note 31.* B. Nikitine, *Revue du monde musulman*, LII, (December 1922) 38-40. An excellent review of Russo-Turkish relations from 1918-1923, (London 1925), 362-76.

*Note 32.* For texts of these various treaties, see Malbone W. Graham, "The Soviet Security System," *International Conciliation*, (September 1929), no. 252, 277ff, 381-5, 388-91, and *Soviet Union and Peace*, 271-3. See also Georges Ducrocq, "La politique du gouvernement des soviets en Perse," *Revue du monde musulman*, LII, 109-15 and in general. pp. 84-180.

*Note 33.* *Soviet Union and Peace*, 273-4.

*Note 34.* W. "Les relations russo-turques depuis l'avenement du Bolchevisme," *Revue du monde musulman*, LII, 197-200. At the end of the Turkish operations in Georgia and Armenia, Kars and Ardahan were in Kemal's hands, while Russia obtained Batum. Russia had ceded about 10,000 square miles of territory near Kars by the Alexandropol agreement of 1920.

459

*Note 35.* Kemal had sent an official letter to Chicherin in 1920, which the latter answered on June 4, 1920. For text see W., *op. cit.*, 194-6. See also Kemal's address before the Grand National Assembly, March 1, 1921; *Asie française*, XXI, no. 193 (June 1921), 250-2. For treaty of Moscow, March 16, 1921, see *Current History*, XVII, no. 2 (November 1922), 277,79, and *Soviet Union and Peace*, 274.

*Note 36.* *Current History*, XVII, no. 2, pp. 277-79. See also Charles Levermore, *Third Yearbook of the League of Nations*, 326.

*Note 37.* See Temperley, VI, 86ff. The Turks made a treaty with the Erivan republic ceding the western and southwestern part of this territory to Turkey, when the Turks almost clashed with the Red army in the winter of 1920. This was confirmed in the treaty of March 1921 and also in the treaty with the Transcaucasian republics in October 1921. Questions concerning the Turco-Russian negotiations were raised in the House of Commons, but on December 9, 1920, the government denied any knowledge of them. See *Parliamentary Debates* (H. C.), v. 134, cols. 2258 (December 9, 1920) and v. 143, col. 25 (June 13, 1921).

*Note 38.* See W., *op. cit.*, LII, 201-3, 205-6, and appendix I, "Moustafa Bey Sabhi et le Yeni Dunya," 207-08. Note especially Kemal's statement at the end of 1921.

*Note 39.* Treaty of Kars, October 13, 1921; *Current History*, XVII, no. 5 (February 1923), 769-70. A treaty of mutual alliance was signed by Turkey and Afghanistan on March 1, 1921, and on June 3, 1921 Persia and Afghanistan signed a similar treaty—all under the influence of Russia. A Turco-Ukraine treaty, January 2, 1922 contained provisions on the Straits identical with those of Kars and Moscow, and internationalized the rivers flowing into the Black sea, only with their participation. The only missing link in the entire chain of treaties was one between Persia and Turkey. For text of Turco-Ukraine treaty see *Current History* XVII, 770. See also A. J. Toynbee, *Survey of International Affairs*, 1928 (London 1929), 361-2; A. L. P. Dennis, *The Foreign Policy of Soviet Russia* (N. Y. 1924), chs. 9, 10, and *passim;* Louis Fischer, *The Soviets and World Affairs* (London 1930), I, 382-99.

*Note 40.* Ronaldshay, III, 278. See also the March proposals, Frangulis, II, 212-14, 217-18.

*Note 41.* Allied Note to Greece, June 22, 1921; Greek Reply, June 28, 1921; Frangulis, II, 282, 283-85. See also Churchill, *The Aftermath*, 419-21.

*Note 42.* Official communiqué, Supreme Council, August 10, 1921; Frangulis, II, 292.

*Note 43.* Gounaris to M. F. A., October 25, 1921; Frangulis, II, 310-11.

*Note 44.* Exposé of Curzon to Gounaris and Baltazzi, October 26, 1921; Gounaris-Baltazzi Memorandum, November 1921; Frangulis, II, 312ff. See also Ronaldshay, III, 279.

*Note 45.* Gounaris to M. F. A., November 1921; Frangulis, II, 319-20.

*Note 46.* Ronaldshay, III, 280-83; Gounaris to M. F. A., Cannes, January 13, 1922; Gounaris to M. F. A., January 28, 1922; Frangulis, II, 325-26.

*Note 47.* Gounaris to Curzon, February 15, 1922; Frangulis, II, 350-52.

*Note 48.* Curzon to Gounaris, March 6, 1922; Frangulis, II, 352-53. See also Chargé of Greece at London, March 14, 1922; *ibid.*, 353, and Ronaldshay, III, 283-84.

*Note 49.* Ronaldshay, III, 284-86. For circumstances of the communication see Street, *Life of Lord Reading*, 211-34.

*Note 50.* *Misc. no. 3* (1922). Pronouncement by Three Allied Ministers for Foreign Affairs Respecting the Near Eastern Situation. Paris, March 27, 1922. Cmd.

*1641*. See also Lord Curzon's statement in the House of Lords, on March 30, 1922. *Parliamentary Debates* (H. L.), v. 49, cols. 985-1003. The Frangulis Memorandum of March 1922(?); Frangulis, II, 366-71. See also the proposition of March 22, 1922; *l'Europe nouvelle*, V, no. 27 (July 8, 1922), 851.

*Note 51.* Curzon-Schanzer-Poincaré note of March 28, 1922: *l'Europe nouvelle*, V, no. 27 (July 8, 1922), 851-53.

*Note 52.* Response of the Sublime Porte, April 8, 1922, *ibid.*, 853-54.

*Note 53.* Response of the Angora government April 5, 1922; *ibid.*, 854-5.

From April 10 to May 19, 1922, the Genoa conference was in session. Soviet Russia desired the presence of Turkey at the conference, but the Allies rejected the idea, and the Turks announced their refusal to abide by any decisions in their regard. See Reply of the Russian delegation to the memorandum sent on May 3, 1922, May 11, 1922. Papers relating to the International Economic Conference, Genoa, April-May 1922. *Cmd. 1667*, p. 42, and *Soviet Union and Peace*, 96-104. See also London *Times*, February 16, 1922, and Mr. Churchill to Lord Curzon, April 26, 1922; Churchill, 440-1.

*Note 54.* The Hellenic note stated that "the Hellenic government has arrived at the conclusion that only the occupation of Constantinople, capital of the Empire by the Hellenic army, will impose the conclusion of peace." Greek note to Allied Powers, July 29, 1922; Allied verbal note, Athens, July 31, 1922; Frangulis, II, 392-3. See also British memorandum, Athens, August 2 1922 and Baltazzi aide-mémoire, August 4, 1922, to London; *ibid.*, 394, 396-7. Also Ronaldshay, III, 298.

*Note 55.* *Parliamentary Debates* (H. C.), August 4, 1922, v. 157, cols. 2004-5. Writers' italics.

*Note 56.* See Ronaldshay, III, 298-9; Driault, V, 400-14; Churchill, 442-4. A fire broke out in Smyrna on September 13, 1922, destroying the Greek, Armenian and free quarter. The Turkish center was not destroyed. Churchill was not unaware of the fundamental nature of British support to the Greeks. His memorandum to Curzon, April 26, 1922, complains: "At the same time the policy which has been imposed upon us in regard to Turkey has been a policy contrary not only to the interests of France, but to those of Great Britain. Our continued bolstering up of the Greeks and hostility towards the Turks has been incomprehensible to the French, who have been unable in their minds to discern any British interest behind it, and consequently have continually suspected all sorts of extraordinary motives . . . ." Churchill, 440-41.

*Note 57.* London *Times*, September 12, 1922, and September 13, 1922. Also Churchill, 447ff.

*Note 58.* N. Y. *Times*, September 13, 1922. Bonar Law justified Britain's appeal in a letter to the London *Times*, October 7, 1922: "We are at the Straits and Constantinople not by our action alone, but by the will of the Allied Powers which won the war, and America is one of these Powers."

*Note 59.* Toynbee, *Survey* (1920-23), 374.

*Note 60.* RSFSR. *Godovoi Otchet k IX S'ezdu Sovetov 1920 g.* (*1921*), 45.

*Note 61.* *Ibid.*, 113-4.

*Note 62.* *Mezhdunarodnaia Politika RSFSR v 1922* (Moscow 1923), 56-7. Russia protested to France, England and Italy on July 19, 1922, against Greek entry into the Dardanelles. Balfour maintained that the Greek fleet, which bombarded Samsun July 7, had not violated the régime of the Straits.

*Note 63.* *Ibid.*, 57. The text was published in the London *Times*, as of September 14, 1922; *Times*, September 23, 1922. Also in *l'Europe nouvelle*, V, no. 39 (September 30, 1922), 1240-1.

*Note 64.* London *Times*, September 14, 1922. Texts of notes.

*Note 65.* Churchill, 450-54; N. Y. *Times*, September 17, 1922; London *Times*, September 18, 1922; *l'Europe nouvelle*, V, no. 39, 1239-40; *Asie française*, XXII, no. 205, 351-2. See also Ronaldshay, III, 300-02.

*Note 66.* See Poincaré's address to the French Chamber, November 10, 1922, giving texts of notes to London, *Journal officiel. Chambre.* (1922:3), 3056-60.

*Note 67.* London *Times*, September 19, 1922; *ibid.*, September 20, 1922. See also *Asie française*, XXII, no. 205 (September-October 1922), 352.

*Note 68.* For text, see London *Times*, September 21, 1922. See also Churchill, 454-6.

*Note 69.* Official communiqué of the conference of Paris, September 20, 1922; *l'Europe nouvelle*, V, no. 39 (September 30, 1922), 1241. Invitation to Angora, September 23, 1922, *ibid.*, 1231. See also Ronaldshay, III, 303-4, and Churchill, *loc. cit.*, The official communiqués are also in *Asie française* (1922), 351-4.

Count Sforza says in his *Makers of Modern Europe*, Ch. VIII, that Lord Curzon ended by admitting with him that the mistake (of a policy of force against Turkey) had been his, and that it was he, who for all his apparent excess of conciliatory spirit had best tried to safeguard the interests of the West.

*Note 70.* Official communiqué of the conference of Paris, September 25, 1922; *l'Europe nouvelle*, V, no. 39, p. 1241. Text of September 23 invitation to Turkey in London *Times*, September 25, 1922.

*Note 71.* Text of Lloyd George announcement in N. Y. *Times*, September 24, 1922.

*Note 72.* *Mezhdunarodnaia Politika RSFSR v 1922* (Moscow 1923), 57.

*Note 73.* Yussuf Kemal Bey to Poincaré, September 29, 1922; *l'Europe nouvelle*, V, no. 40 (October 7, 1922), 1271. Franklin-Bouillon was sent to Smyrna, arriving September 28, conversed with Kemal and persuaded him in favor of peace. See *Asie française*, XXII, 354-5.

*Note 74.* Mustapha Kemal to Harrington, September 25, 1922; Harrington to Kemal, September 27, 1922; *l'Europe nouvelle*, V, no. 40, 1270-1. The Harrington-Kemal exchange is also in the London *Times*, September 29, 1922. See also Churchill, 456-64.

*Note 75.* Statement of Secretary Hughes, September 26, 1922; London *Times*, September 27, 1922.

*Note 76.* Soviet note to Curzon, Moscow, September 27, 1922; *l'Europe nouvelle*, V, no. 40, 1271.

*Note 77.* Soviet note to London, September 30, 1922; *ibid.*, 1271-2. See also *Mezhdunarodnaia Politika RSFSR v 1922*, p. 57. For general position of Soviet Russia, see Fischer, I, 399-403.

*Note 78.* The text of the Mudania armistice is in Mears, 658-59, and *l'Europe nouvelle*, V, 1366-67. M. Franklin-Bouillon negotiated for the French government. The Greeks signed on October 14, 1922.

*Note 79.* Text of Constantine's abdication in London *Times*, September 29, 1922. Resignation of September 27, 1922. Many Greeks attribute the defeat to a

fatalist policy of Venizelos, which is not likely. See Frangulis, II, 409ff. The royalist ministers were overthrown and later executed. See *ibid.*, II, 435-40, 461-544.

*Note 80.* For Lloyd George's fall, see Ronaldshay, III, 309-31; Paxton Hibben, "Betrayal of Greece by Lloyd George," *Current History,* XVII, no. 4 (January 1923), 544-51. See also Lloyd George's statement of September 24, 1922, in the N. Y. *Times,* September 24, 1922, and his address before the Manchester Reform Club, on October 14, 1922, in the London *Times,* October 16, 1922. Britain's desire, he explains, was to assure freedom of the Straits, though this was not a task for England alone. It should be regulated as an international concern under the League of Nations. For the Turkish side, see Dr. Reshad Bey, Angora diplomatic agent in London, reply in London *Times,* October 16, 1922. See also Halidé Edib, *The Turkish Ordeal* (N. Y., 1928): *Memoirs of Halidé Edib* (N. Y., n. d.). *Turkey Faces West* (New Haven 1930), 149-201; and Ahmed Emin, *Turkey in the World War* (New Haven 1930), 271-279.

## CHAPTER IX

*Note 1.* See Curzon's statement in the House of Lords, February 13, 1923; *Parliamentary Debates* (H. L.), v. 53, cols. 31-42.

*Note 2.* Mezhdunarodnaia Politika RSFSR v 1922, 57.

*Note 3.* Ibid., 57-8. Also Godovoi otchet za 1923 g. narodnago komissariata po inostrannym Delam II sezdu sovetov SSSR. Mezhdunarodnaia Politika v 1922 g. (Moscow 1924), 7. A Russian protest of September 25 warned the Allies that Moscow would abide by no decision on the Straits taken without her. See also Charles Levermore, *Third Yearbook of the League of Nations,* 343; N. Y. *Times,* September 27, 1922.

*Note 4.* See Toynbee, I, 50-1; A. P. Newman. *The Mediterranean and its Problems* (London 1927), 149-50; Levermore, 357. A few days later the sultan embarked on H. M. S. *Malaya* for Malta.

*Note 5.* Official communiqué, November 18, 1922; N. Y. *Times,* November 19, 1922.

*Note 6.* See N. Y. *Times,* November 1, 1922.

*Note 7.* A. Rustem Bey, "Les victoires d'Angora," *Revue de Genève,* V, no. 30 (December 1922), 771-86.

*Note 8.* *Turkey no. 1* (1923). Lausanne Conference on Near Eastern Affairs, 1922-1923. Cmd. *1814.* Also Ministère des affaires étrangères. Documents diplomatiques. Conférence de Lausanne sur les affaires du proche-orient (1922-1923). Recueil des Actes de la Conférence. Première série, tomes I-IV; Deuxième série, tomes I-II. These contain the procès-verbaux and acts of the Conference. The minutes of the session of November 20 are in Cmd. *1814,* pp. 1-5.

*Note 9.* The work of the Conference was divided into three commissions. Lord Curzon presided over the first, dealing with territorial questions, the problem of minorities and the régime of the Straits. Marquis Garroni, of Italy, presided over the second commission which dealt with the régime of foreigners, including judicial and economic questions. M. Barrère, of France, was president of the third commission, dealing with financial and economic questions, ports, railways and sanitary problems.

*Note 10.* Cmd., *1814,* p. 11.

*Note 11.* Ibid., 28.

*Note 12.* Ismet Pasha to the Presidents of the British, French and Italian Delegations, Lausanne, February 4, 1923; Cmd. *1814,* 837-41. See also A. J. Toynbee,

"The Breakdown at Lausanne," *New Republic*, XXXIV, no. 431 (March 7, 1923), 39-40.

Note 13.   *Current History*, XVII, no. 6 (March 1923), 930.

Note 14.   Ibid., XVIII, no. 1 (April 1923), 176.

Note 15.   London *Times*, March 8, 1923.

Note 16.   Ismet Pasha to the Ministers of Foreign Affairs of the inviting Powers, March 8, 1923; *Documents diplomatiques. Conférence de Lausanne*. 1er série, IV, 26-33. (Hereafter cited as *Recueil*).

Note 17.   Ibid., 70-2. See also London *Times*, April 2, 1923.

Note 18.   *Recueil*, IV, 73-4.

Note 19.   Levermore, *Fourth Yearbook of the League of Nations*, 123.

Note 20.   The work of the second conference was divided among three commissions. Sir Horace Rumbold presided over the first commission on territorial and military questions; General Pellé with the second commission dealt with the financial problems; and Mr. Montagna presided over the third commission which was to solve the economic issues. Mr. Grew, now American ambassador to Turkey, was the American observer. Since the question of the Straits was not considered settled, Russia was not invited. The Soviet delegation, headed by M. Vorovsky, representative at Rome, came to discuss the question, but M. Vorovsky, was assassinated.

Note 21.   *Treaty of peace between the Allied and Associated Powers and Bulgaria, signed at Neuilly-sur-Seine, November 27, 1919*. Cmd. 522 (1920), art. 47.

Note 22.   *Treaty Series no. 13* (1921). Treaty between the Allied and Associated Powers and Greece Relative to Thrace. Signed at Sèvres, August 10, 1920, Cmd. 1390.

Note 23.   For the treaty of Sèvres, see Cmd. 564 (1920), arts. 27,84.

Note 24.   For Mudania armistice, see Mears, *op. cit.*, 658, art. 2.

Note 25.   Cmd. 1814, pp. 21-22. Ismet based his argument on the Mudania armistice, wherein the Allies accepted the retrocession of eastern Thrace, with Adrianople, to Turkey. He demanded, also, the return of Karagatch, and the territory including the Kuleli-Burgas-Mustapha-Pashà railway between Adrianople and Constantinople, and claimed that the majority of the people west of the Maritza was Turkish.

Note 26.   Cmd. 1814, pp. 22-8.

Note 27.   Ibid., 30-33.

Note 28.   Ibid., 34-8.

Note 29.   Ibid., 47.

Note 30.   Ibid., 47-8. Ismet reaffirmed the fairness of a plebiscite for western Thrace.

Note 31.   Annex (A) to no. 7; ibid., 77-79.

Note 32.   Note by the Bulgarian delegation, statement of M. Morphof; *ibid.*, 68-73, 80.

Note 33.   Cmd. 1814, pp. 64-65, 67. Venizelos agreed that demilitarization without a guarantee was useless. Ismet was willing to grant supervision of the railway from Dedeagatch to the Bulgarian frontier, but did not want supervision to intervene in the management.

Note 34.   Ibid., 65-66.

Note 35.   Ibid., 67. Both agreed on "deferring" the question. Ismet took the position that since Turkey was to renounce her means of defence, "it was perfectly

just that she should claim in return corresponding guarantees— that is to say, military and political."

Note 36.   Ibid., 87-94. This territory included the railway station at Karagatch, and the center of the railway connecting the Maritza bridge with Karagatch.

Note 37.   See Lord Curzon's statement; Cmd. 1814, p. 431.

Note 38.   Ibid., 687. Art. 2.

Note 39.   Draft convention respecting the frontiers of Thrace; ibid., 785-90. The restriction of 20,000 men was dropped on February 3-4, as a concession to Turkey.

Note 40.   Draft convention, art. 5; ibid., 789.

Note 41.   Turkish note, February 4, 1923; ibid., 838.

Note 42.   Recueil, 1er ser., IV, 230-31.

Note 43.   Ibid., 228.

Note 44.   Ibid., 2e ser., I, 137-38.

Note 45.   Draft convention regarding Dedeagatch; Cmd. 1814, pp. 461-64. The negotiations with Bulgaria henceforth lapsed, though a Bulgarian note protested the Karagatch arrangements on May 27. Sir Horace Rumbold assured Bulgaria of her rights under both the treaty of Neuilly and under the Thracian agreement with Greece, of 1920. See Recueil, 2e ser., I, 229, 230, ff, 240. See also Cmd. 1814, pp. 458-61.

Note 46.   Cmd. 1814, 98. Riza Nur Bey stated they were to be put under a neutral and independent political existence.

Note 47.   Ibid., 98-99.

Note 48.   Cmd. 1814, p. 100. The commission was to meet when the Straits question was being considered.

Note 49.   Loc. cit.

Note 50.   Ibid., 108-09. The Turkish delegation reserved on the question of aviation and military contingents. For the report of the sub-commission, see ibid., 109-11.

Note 51.   Ibid., 691. This gave Greece Lemnos, Samothrace, Mitylene, Chios, Samos and Nikaria. By article 15, Turkey renounced in favor of Italy Stampalia (Astropalia), Rhodes (Rhodos), Calki (Kharki), Scarpanto, Casos (Casso), Piscopis (Tilos), Misiros (Nisyros), Calimnos (Kalymnos), Leros, Patmos, Lipsos (Lipso), Simi (Symi), and Cos (Kos), then occupied by Italy, the dependent islets, and also Castellorizzo. Article 12 stipulated that (save where the treaty declares the con-trary) the islands within three miles of the Asiatic coast remained Turkish.

Note 52.   Cmd. 1814, p. 838.

Note 53.   Recueil, 2e ser., I, 8, 10, 125, 126.

Note 54.   Ibid., 12, 147.

Note 55.   Ibid., 13, 15, 126.

Note 56.   Cmd. 1814, p. 127.

Note 57.   Ibid., 128-31. Fischer, I, 403-04.

Note 58.   Loc. cit.

Note 59.   See Ali Fuad, La question des détroits (Paris 1928), 138-40. Fischer, I, 404.

Note 60.   Cmd. 1814., pp. 131-2. See also Mémoire du gouvernement roumain dans la question du Danube (Bucharest 1925). See also Hamilton Fish Armstrong, The New Balkans (N. Y. 1926); A. Babel, La Bessarabie (Paris 1926), 354-55.

Note 61.   Cmd. 1814, pp. 131-2. See also Aurel Cosma, La petite entente,

(Paris 1926), 108-10; Robert Machray, *The Little Entente* (London 1929), 207-09; A. L. P. Dennis, *The Foreign Policies of Soviet Russia* (N. Y. 1924), 222-28.

*Note 62.*   Cmd. *1814*, pp. 138-41. Fischer, I, 404-06.

*Note 63.*   Cmd. *1814*, pp. 141-2. Fischer, I, 406-08.

*Note 64.*   See Annex (A) to no. 13. Document communicated to the Territorial and Military Commission on December 6, 1922, by the British, French and Italian Delegations; Cmd. *1814*, pp. 151-2.

*Note 65.*   Cmd. *1814*, pp. 142-45. Barrère and Carroni supported Lord Curzon. See the Allied drafts, *ibid.*, 151-4, and Toynbee *Survey*, 1920-1923, p. 375.

*Note 66.*   Cmd. *1814*, 145-46. Had Mr. Child represented another Power he could have applied identically the same argument to the American position at Panama, and the British position at Suez—as M. Chicherin was to do later at the Conference.

*Note 67.*   *Ibid.*, 156-59. According to the Turkish thesis, particularly harmful were: (1) the inclusion of the Marmora in the demilitarized zones; (2) demilitarization of the Bosphorus; (3) prohibition of troop movements in the Bosphorus; (4) prohibition of arsenals and naval establishments at Constantinople and the Straits; (5) extended demilitarized zones.

*Note 68.*   *Ibid.*, 159-63. See also M. Duca's reply to Chicherin, on behalf of Rumania.

*Note 69.*   Cmd. *1814*, 167-69. The Allied experts were uncertain as to Turkey's intention on a minimum means of defence at Gallipoli.

*Note 70.*   *Ibid.*, 172-73.

*Note 71.*   *Current History*, XVII, no. 5 (February 1923), p. 743.

*Note 72.*   Third draft, December 14, 1922; Cmd. *1814*, 243-50.

*Note 73.*   *Ibid.*, 250. The vote of the Power alleged to have imperiled the Straits would not count. See also the speeches of Curzon, Barrère and Garroni; *ibid.*, 230-36.

*Note 74.*   Cmd. *1814*, 236-38.

*Note 75.*   The Russian draft, December 18, 1922; *ibid.*, 250-53.

*Note 76.*   *Ibid.*, 250. Article 4. The Straits were to include: the Dardanelles, Marmora, Bosphorus, islands of the Aegean (Samothrace, Imbros, Tenedos, Lemnos, and the Rabbit islands). Likewise, military aircraft were to be forbidden from the zones.

*Note 77.*   Cmd. *1814*, 263, 275-76. See also Ali Fuad, 138-40. An additional declaration of the Russian, Ukrainian, Georgian delegation noted, in event of acceptance, their intention to call a conference of the riverain states in the interest of the mutual security of their coasts.

*Note 78.*   *Ibid.*, 253-61. The Turks proposed to limit the *entire force* entering the Black sea to the strength of the largest Black sea fleet. See Ismet Pasha's speech; *ibid.*, 235-36, and Ali Fuad, 140-42.

*Note 79.*   Cmd. *1814*, pp. 262-68. The Turks demanded a 5,000 garrison at Gallipoli, but the Allies refused.

*Note 80.*   *Ibid.*, 268-71.

*Note 81.*   Cmd. *1814*, 274.

*Note 82.*   *Ibid.*, 280-83. The American delegation opposed the institution of an international commission of the Straits. See *Current History*, XXVIII, no. 5 (February 1923), 744.

*Note 83.*   Cmd. *1814*, 449,50. London *Times*, January 9, 1923.

*Note 84.*   Cmd. *1814*, 454-56. See also Lord Curzon's replies; *ibid.*, 451-54, 456-57. See also Toynbee, *Survey* (1920-23), 376; Professor Paul Miliukov, *Russlands Zusammenbruch* (Berlin 1925), I, 197-206.

*Note 85.*   London *Times*, March 8, 1923. See also *Godovoi otchet za 1923 g.*, 7-32, for the Lausanne Conference.

*Note 86.*   See London *Times*, July 23, 1923, and *Recueil*, 2e ser., I, 161, 531. See also *Soviet Union and Peace*, 130-32. Fischer, I, 409-412.

*Note 87.*   The Straits convention may be found in *Treaty series no. 16* (1923). *Treaty of peace with Turkey and other instruments signed at Lausanne on July 24, 1923.* Cmd. *1929.*

*Note 88.*   The demilitarized zones in the Gallipoli peninsula begin southeast of a point on the gulf of Xeros four kilometers northeast of Bakla-Burmu, reaching the Marmora at Kumbaghi, but excluding Kavak. On the southeast the area is between the coast and a line drawn twenty kilometers from the coast, beginning at Stambul and running to Karabiga on the Marmora. On the west the area to a line fifteen kilometers from the eastern shore of the Bosphorus is demilitarized.

*Note 89.*   See the analysis of Ali Fuad, *op. cit.*, 145-67. A juridical study of the régime of the Straits may be found in Fernand de Visscher, "Le régime nouveau des détroits. (Convention de Lausanne concernant le régime des détroits, signée le 24 juillet 1923)" *Revue de droit international et de législation comparée*, 3e ser., IV (1923), 537-72; V (1924), 13-57. Also Fischer, I, 412-14.

*Note 90.*   See A. Poidébard, "Mossoul et la route des Indes," *Asie française*, XXIII, no. 211 (May 1923, supplement no. 8), 23-30.

*Note 91.*   Apparently conversations had taken place the latter part of November, lasting until December 14, 1922. Then began a futile exchange of memoranda in which each presented his claims. For this correspondence see Cmd. *1814*, p. 363-393.

*Note 92.*   Curzon to Ismet Pasha, December 31, 1922; Cmd. *1814*, p. 393.

*Note 93.*   *Ibid.*, 351-52.

*Note 94.*   Cmd. *1814*, p. 352-60.

*Note 95.*   *Ibid.*, 360.

*Note 96.*   *Ibid.*, 360-61.

*Note 97.*   Statement presented by the United States delegation, January 23, 1923, Cmd. *1814*, p. 405, annex.

*Note 98.*   *Ibid.*, 361-62. Bompard and Garroni agreed.

*Note 99.*   *Ibid.*, 395-98. This statement was made in the evening.

*Note 100.*   *Ibid.*, 400-01. Lord Curzon should have known (or did?) that parties to a dispute before the League do not vote in determining this unanimity, so that neither Turkey nor Great Britain (theoretically) would have a voice.

*Note 101.*   *Ibid.*, 402.

*Note 102.*   *Ibid.*, 404.

*Note 103.*   *Official Journal* (March 1923), 249. Curzon's note, January 25, 1923, in document C. 88. *1923*. VII, annex 440 to no. 2. See also Cmd. *1814*, pp. 426-7.

*Note 104.*   Ismet Pasha to the Presidents of the British, French and Italian Delegations, February 4, 1923; Cmd. *1814*, pp. 837-8.

*Note 105.*   *Ibid.*, 842.

*Note 106.*   *Ibid.*, 846, 851.

*Note 107.*   *Recueil*, 1e ser., II, 129. Bompard so informed Poincaré.

*Note 108.*   *Journal officiel. Chambre* (1922:3), 4201.

*Note 109.*   *Recueil,* 2e ser., I, 7.

*Note 110.*   *Ibid.,* 110.

*Note 111.*   *Ibid.,* 124-5.

*Note 112.*   *Ibid.,* 147. For the projects and counter projects on this article (art. 2, par. 3), see *ibid.,* 1er ser., I, 348; *Cmd. 1814,* pp. 687-8; counter project, *Recueil,* 1er ser., IV, 333-4.

*Note 113.*   *Recueil,* 2e ser., II, 410. The full text of the treaty of Lausanne may be found in *Cmd. 1929* (1923).

*Note 114.* See below, ch. 10, for the League decision on the subject.

*Note 115.*   *Cmd. 1814,* pp. 113-17.

*Note 116.*   *Ibid.,* 117-18.

*Note 117.*   *Cmd. 1814,* pp. 175-80. Both Garroni and Barrère supported Curzon.

*Note 118.*   *Ibid.,* 190-204, for text of Ismet's address.

*Note 119.*   *Ibid.,* 182-85.

*Note 120.*   *Cmd. 1814,* pp. 185-87.

*Note 121.*   *Ibid.,* 181-82, 185-90.

*Note 122.*   *Ibid.,* 206-07.

*Note 123.*   *Ibid.,* 207-10. Ismet granted freedom of movement for minorities, but rejected exemption from military duties.

*Note 124.*   *Ibid.,* 210-15.

*Note 125.*   *Cmd. 1814,* pp. 217-21.

*Note 126.*   *Ibid.,* 221-23.

*Note 127.*   *Ibid.,* 223-26. Rumbold stated that Dr. Nansen, invited by the high commissioners at Constantinople to attend a meeting held there, had suggested compulsory exchange. Nansen approached Hamid Bey, Angora representative, who said it could be considered only on a compulsory basis; *ibid.,* 227.

*Note 128.*   *Ibid.,* 303-13, for text of report of January 7, 1923.

*Note 129.*   *Ibid.,* 295-300.

*Note 130.*   *Cmd. 1814,* pp. 317-19.

*Note 131.*   *Ibid.,* 319-25.

*Note 132.*   *Ibid.,* 325-27.

*Note 133.*   Report of the sub-commission; *ibid.,* 328-37.

*Note 134.*   Convention concerning the exchange of Greek and Turkish populations, signed at Lausanne, January 30, 1923; *ibid.,* 817-27.

*Note 135.*   Articles 37 and 46 dealt with the minorities. See *Cmd. 1929,* for text. The convention stipulated general amnesty. Dr. Nansen declares that it would have been better had the diplomats never uttered the name of Armenia: "And after all, it was only a massacred, but gifted little nation, with no oil fields or gold mines." Fridtjof Nansen, *Armenia and the Near East* (London 1928), 324.

*Note 136.*   For text, see Toynbee, *Western Question in Greece and Turkey.* 207-10.

*Note 137.*   *Cmd. 1814,* pp. 466-68.

*Note 138.*   *Cmd. 1814,* p. 468.

*Note 139.*   *Ibid.,* 468-69.

*Note 140.*   *Ibid.,* 470.

*Note 141.*   Turkish memorandum, December 2, 1922; *ibid.,* 471-80.

*Note 142.*   *Cmd. 1814*, pp. 481-84.

*Note 143.*   *Ibid.*, 484-88. Rumbold was British commissioner in Constantinople. For his report of December 23, 1922, see *ibid.*, 500-04; Turkish counter proposals, *ibid.*, 504-05; draft respecting jurisdiction in matters other than personal status, *ibid.*, 506-08.

*Note 144.*   *Ibid.*, 488-92.

*Note 145.*   *Ibid.*, 492-93.

*Note 146.*   *Ibid.*, 493-94.

*Note 147.*   *Ibid.*, 495-98.

*Note 148.*   *Ibid.*, 509-15.

*Note 149.*   *Cmd. 1814*, pp. 515-20. Especially the speeches of Garroni, Curzon and Barrère.

*Note 150.*   *Ibid.*, 522-24.

*Note 151.*   *Ibid.*, 524-25. Guarantees for religious, educational and benevolent institutions were asked. The third sub-commission on nationality and antiquities had reached complete agreement under M. Montagna. See *ibid.*, annex B, 532-35.

*Note 152.*   *Ibid.*, 695. Article 26 of the draft.

*Note 153.*   *Cmd. 1814*, pp. 790-803.

*Note 154.*   *Ibid.*, 834-36.

*Note 155.*   *Ibid.*, 852-53. The jurists were to come from countries not taking part in the world war.

*Note 156.*   *Recueil*, 2e ser., I, 40-41, 50-51.

*Note 157.*   *Ibid.*, 96-97, 107-09.

*Note 158.*   For the text of the convention see *Cmd. 1929* (1923).

*Note 159.*   *Cmd. 1814*, pp. 537-8. These problems included the Ottoman public debt, concessions and protection of foreign interests. Sub-commissions were appointed to consider the questions.

*Note 160.*   *Ibid.*, 538-9.

*Note 161.*   See Mears, *op. cit.*, 364, 403; Blaisdell, *European Financial Control in the Ottoman Empire*, 197ff. By August 31, 1921, the total public debt was £T148,-000,000 ($651,200,000), separate from the war debt. By all odds the most interested financial power in Turkey after the war (1922) was France, holding 66.34% of the unified debt of Turkey, while Great Britain held 11%, Germany and Belgium held almost 8%, with Holland and Italy holding each 1.75%.

*Note 162.*   *Cmd. 1814*, pp. 543-49. This was rather a strange position for Venizelos, in view of his actual intentions in Asia Minor, and the circumstances surrounding the Greek venture of May 1919.

*Note 163.*   *Ibid.*, 549-50.

*Note 164.*   *Ibid.*, 550-2.

*Note 165.*   *Ibid.*, 552-54. Albania participated in these negotiations as one of the succession states.

*Note 166.*   Report of sub-commission on Finance. Ottoman public debt; *ibid.*, 575-87. The sub-commission on communications and transport completed its work and reported on December 8, the report being accepted with little change. *Ibid.*, 557-59. See also annex with draft articles, *ibid.*, 559-62.

*Note 167.*   *Cmd. 1814*, pp. 565-66.

*Note 168.*   *Ibid.*, 566-67. Garroni supported his colleagues. Venizelos resumed his previous arguments. *Ibid.*, 568-69.

Note 169.   Ibid., 570-71.

Note 170.   Ibid., 573-74.

Note 171.   Ibid., 594-98. For report of the sub-commission see ibid., 628-35.

Note 172.   Cmd. 1814, pp. 611-12.

Note 173.   Ibid., 624-25.

Note 174.   Levermore, Fourth Yearbook, 72; N. Y. Times, January 28, 1923.

Note 175.   Cmd. 1814, pp. 438-41. The debt of £T140,000,000 in 1914 was reduced to £T102,000,000.

Note 176.   Ibid., 832-33. Summary and explanation of concessions offered to Ismet Pasha on February 3-4, 1923.

Note 177.   Cmd. 1814, pp. 839-40.

Note 178.   Ibid., 845-46, 851-52.

Note 179.   Ibid., 846.

Note 180.   Ibid., 847-51.

Note 181.   Recueil, 2e ser., I, 207-08.

Note 182.   Levermore, Fourth Yearbook, 170.

Notr 183.   Recueil, 2e ser., I, 215-17, 219-21.

Note 184.   Ibid., 230-33. Jugoslavia withdrew objections, and the Bulgarian protest that it endangered her outlet to the Aegean was ignored. Ibid., 233-34, 240.

Note 185.   Ibid., 243-48.

Note 186.   Levermore, 161; Current History, XVIII, no. 5 (August 1923), 895-96.

Note 187.   Current History XVIII, no. 5 (August 1923), 896.

Note 188.   Levermore, 176. The Americans insisted they were merely urging the "open door." On July 3, 1923, Mr. Leland Harrison, assistant secretary of state, in a letter to Judson King, denied any diplomatic support to the Chester concession. Ibid., 212-13, for text.

Note 189.   For further details see below, ch. 10.

Note 190.   Recueil, 2e ser., I, 379-80.

Note 191.   Ibid., 379.

Note 192.   Recueil, 2e ser., II, 121ff; Cmd. 1929, 203-11. Protocol relating to certain concessions granted in the Ottoman Empire.

Note 193.   Ibid., articles 2, 9. See also Davenport and Cooke, 154ff; Mohr, 195.

Note 194.   Mohr, loc. cit.

Note 195.   In mid-June a compromise for payment in gold on a three-fourths paper valuation was accepted, but Poincaré objected on principle. Current History, XVIII, no. 5 (August 1923), 856.

Note 196.   Cmd. 1929, arts. 46-57, and annex.

Note 197.   See Mears, op. cit., ch. 17 Ahmed Emin, 302-05.

Note 198.   Blaisdell, op. cit., 204-7, 208-38.

Note 199.   See the statement of Secretary Hughes before the Council on Foreign Relations, January 23, 1924 in Foreign Affairs, II, no. 2, p. xiv.

Note 200.   "The Turco-American Treaty," Current History, XIX, no. 1 (October 1923), 160-61.

Note 201.   Current History, XX, no. 5 (August 1924), 739 contains the platform of the Democratic party of 1924, which condemned the treaty. See also the Congressional Record, LXVIII, no. 29, pp. 1962, 1966, and Senator King's resolution

of December 22, 1926; Senate resolution no. 306, 69th Congress, 2nd Session. Oil and Armenia were the issues involved—as well as the American interest in the capitulations.

*Note 202.* See the exchange of notes, February 17, 1927 in *Current History,* XXVII, no. 2 (May 1927), 328-29. Also *ibid.,* XXVII, no. 3 (December 1927), 448. Formal announcement of Grew's appointment was made May 20, 1927; *ibid.,* XXVI, no. 5 (July 1927), 665. For background of the Turco-American treaty see E. W. Turlington, "The American Treaty of Lausanne," *World Peace Foundation,* XII (1924), no. 10, pp. 565-602.

*Note 203.* For an excellent summary of the situation after Lausanne see A. J. Toynbee, "The East after Lausanne," *Foreign Affairs,* II, no. 1 (September 1923), 84-99.


## CHAPTER X


*Note 1.* See especially Leonard Stein, *Syria* (N. Y. 1926), 26ff; Haut commissariat de la république française en Syrie et au Liban, *La Syrie et le Liban en 1922* (Paris 1922), 41-43; Freda White, *Mandates* (London 1926), 64-65; Loder, *op. cit.,* 68-73.

*Note 2.* George Samné, *La Syrie* (Paris 1921), 536-81, 582-98.

*Note 3.* *Journal Officiel. Chambre* (1920:2), 2434-5.

*Note 4.* *Parliamentary Debates* (H. C.), v. 132, col. 148.

*Note 5.* For the text see *Current History,* XIII, no. 2 (February 1921), 251-4; *l'Europe nouvelle,* December 12, 1920. For discussion see Loder, 76-8; E. P. MacCallum, *The Nationalist Crusade in Syria* (N. Y. 1928), 30-1; Leonard Stein, *Syria, passim;* Lyautey, *Le drame oriental,* 164-8.

*Note 6.* Haut commissariat de la république française en Syrie et au Liban, *op. cit.,* 45-6; Ministère des affaires étrangères, *Rapport sur la situation de la Syrie et du Liban, juillet 1922-juillet 1923* (Paris 1923), Annex I sur la situation de la Syrie et du Liban au 1er juillet 1922, pp. 37ff. See also statement of Robert de Caix before the Permanent Mandates Commission in League of Nations. P. M. C. *Minutes of the Fifth (Extraordinary) Session, October 23-November 6, 1924,* pp. 99-103. Feisal's own account is in *Current History,* XIII, no. 2 (February 1921), 254-5.

*Note 7.* Haut commissariat, 77-82; Lyautey, 182-6; Toynbee, *Survey* (1925). I, *Islamic World,* 356-60; Loder, 80-6. For the French troubles in Syria during the period 1924-25, see MacCallum (entire) and Leonard Stein, *Syria.*

*Note 8.* *Palestine, Report of the High Commissioner on the Administration of Palestine, 1920-1925. Colonial no. 15, p. 48.* See also *An Interim Report on the Civil Administration of Palestine during the Period, July 1, 1920-June 30, 1921. Cmd. 1449* (1921). For brief general account, see Leonard Stein, *Zionism* (N. Y. 1926), ch. 4.

*Note 9.* For the Arab complaints on Palestine, see *Correspondence with the Palestine Delegation and the Zionist Organization. Cmd. 1700* (June 1922); *Papers Relating to the Elections for the Palestine Legislative Council, 1923. Cmd. 1889.* See also *Colonial no. 15,* pp. 24-47; Toynbee, *Survey* (1925), I, 386-406, and Sir Herbert Samuel's statement before the Permanent Mandates Commission, October 28, 1924 in *Minutes of the Fifth Session,* (1924), 54-7.

*Note 10.* *Interim Report, Cmd. 1499* (1921), 20-22; *Colonial no. 15,* pp. 53-5; *Colonial no. 12,* pp. 65-70; statement of Sir Herbert Samuel, October 28, 1924 before Permanent Mandates Commission, *Fifth Session,* 59-61; Toynbee, 362-3.

*Note 11.* *Review of the Civil Administration of Mesopotamia. Cmd. 1061* (1920), 126-47; Sir Aylmer Haldane, *The Insurrection in Mesopotamia* (London 1922); Loder, *op. cit.,* 87-98. For a personal view of the events see Lady Bell, *The Letters of Gertrude Bell,* 439-503. Miss Bell was in the British colonial service.

*Note 12.* Institution of the Council of State, November 11, 1920; *Report on Iraq Administration, October 1920-March 1922,* II, 123-4.

*Note 13.* *Ibid.,* 10-11. See appendix 6, withdrawal of Sayid Talib Pasha from the government and Bagdad, April 18, 1921, pp. 125-6.

*Note 14.* For Churchill's statement see *Parliamentary Debates* (H. C.), (June 14, 1921), cols. 265-78. See also Bell, II, 597-609.

*Note 15.* *Iraq Report* (1920-1922), 12, 14, 15, 19.

*Note 16.* In May 1921 the high commissioner tried to institute a system of local autonomy for the Kurdish districts, directly under the British, subject to Iraq in general. It was then that Suleimania rejected inclusion with Iraq and remained "at its express wish under direct British control, exercised through a political officer." See appendix VII on Kurdistan, *ibid.,* 126. In Bagdad the condition was laid down that there should be no foreign domination. The Kurdish element asked for a Kurdish government, but were against inclusion in Suleimania. Some Turcomans favored a Turkish ruler. *Ibid.,* 1415 and Bell, II, 616-21.

*Note 17.* Suleimania and Kirkuk were not represented at the coronation because of general opposition to the system. See *ibid.,* 15 and the review of events by Sir Percy Cox and that of Sir Henry Dobbs in Bell, II, 504-41, 542-60.

*Note 18.* The Philadelphia *Public Ledger* had obtained and published a copy of the terms. See *Parliamentary Debates* (H. C.), v. 139, col. 923. From the date of its announcement there was much criticism of the British position in the House of Commons.

*Note 19.* *Miller Diary,* IX, 459.

*Note 20.* For the oil controversy over concessions, see R. L. Buell, "Oil Interests in the Fight for Mosul," *Current History,* (March 1923); Henry Woodhouse, "Americans Oil Claims in Turkey," *Current History* (March 1922); John Carter, "The Bitter Conflict over Turkish Oil Fields," *Current History,* (January 1926). The best general treatments of the oil struggle are: W. H. Davenport and S. R. Cooke, *The Oil Trusts and Anglo-American Relations* (London, 1923); Francis Delaisi, *Oil—Its Influence on Politics* (London 1922); Pierre l'Espagnol de la Tramerye, *The World Struggle for Oil* (N. Y. 1924); Louis Fischer, *Oil Imperialism* (N. Y. 1926); Anton Mohr, *The Oil War* (N. Y. 1926). For the Turkish Petroleum Company's history, see Peace Handbook, XI, *Mesopotamia,* no. 63; E. M. Earle, *Turkey, the Great Powers and the Bagdad Railway, passim;* Earle, "The Turkish Petroleum Company," *Political Science Quarterly,* XXXIX, (June 1924), 265-79, contains text of 1914 agreement. The Anglo-Persian Company was newly founded in 1909, and by 1919 the British government owned two-thirds of the ordinary shares besides debentures.

*Note 21.* Peace Handbook, *Mesopotamia,* no. 63, p. 34. See also Earle, in *Political Science Quarterly,* XXXIX.

*Note 22.* *Correspondence between H. M. Government and the U. S. Ambassa-dor Respecting Economic Rights in Mandated Territories. Cmd. 1226 (1921).* Also U. S. Department of State. Division of Near Eastern Affairs. *Mandate for Palestine* (Washington 1928). Davis to Curzon, May 12, 1920, no. 1, *Cmd. 1226,* See also E. H. Davenport and S. R. Cooke, *Oil Trusts and Anglo-American Relations,* ch. 11. Lloyd George stated in the House of Commons on March 23, 1923, that the British intended not only to conquer Mesopotamia and found an Arab state, but to have the predominant rights of exploitation. See *Parliamentary Debates,* v. 161, col. 2433.

*Note 23.* Davis to Curzon, July 28, 1920 and Curzon to Davis, August 9, 1920; *Cmd. 1226,* nos. 2-3. See also W. R. Batsell, "The United States and the System of Mandates," *International Conciliation,* no. 213 (October 1925). 214, and Anton Mohr, *The Oil War,* 46ff. Davenport and Cooke, *op. cit.,* 211-14 and the *Federal Trade Commission Report* (1923), 132 are useful.

*Note 24.* The American position is brought out clearly not only in the diplo-matic exchange but in the joint resolution of Congress, July 2, 1921, preliminary to the treaty with Germany; *42 U. S. Statutes at Large,* pt. 2, p. 1940; statement of Bonar Law in House of Commons, March 8, 1921; *Parliamentary Debates.* v. 139, col. 238.

*Note 25.* Colby to Curzon, November 20, 1920; *Cmd. 1226,* no. 4. See also Levermore, *Second Yearbook of the League of Nations,* 408-18.

*Note 26.* Colby to Curzon, November 20, 1920. See also Curzon to Davis, February 28, 1921, upholding the Turkish Petroleum Company; *Cmd. 1226* no. 5. For discussion, see F. Delaisi, *op. cit.,* 85-6; Mohr, *op. cit.,* ch. 9; de la Tramerye, *op. cit.,* ch. 8.

*Note 27.* Batsell, *op. cit.,* 13. See also Ormsby-Gore's statement in the House of Commons, March 20, 1923; *Parliamentary Debates,* v. 161, col. 2450.

*Note 28.* L. N. *Minutes of the 12th Session of the Council,* XII,. 10-11.

*Note 29.* Wallace to da Cunha, February 21, 1921; da Cunha to Wallace, February 22, 1921; Colby to da Cunha, February 21, 1921, enclosing Colby to Curzon (November 20, 1921); *ibid.,* annexes 154, 154a, 154b, pp. 68-74.

*Note 30.* Da Cunha to Colby, March 1, 1921; *ibid.,* annex 154c, pp. 75-6.

*Note 31.* Batsell, *loc. cit.,* Levermore, *Second Yearbook,* 136-7.

*Note 32.* *O. J.,* July-August, 1921, pp. 441-2.

*Note 33.* *Minutes of the 13th Session of the Council,* 49.

*Note 34.* *Minutes of the 14th Session of the Council,* 16-17. See also P. M. C. *Minutes of the 1st Session of the Permanent Mandates Commission, October 4-8, 1921* (C.416.M.296.1921.VI), 5-6.

*Note 35.* For texts see *Draft Mandates for Mesopotamia and Palestine. Cmd.* 1500 (1921).

*Note 36.* *O. J.,* June-August, 1922, 546-9. For the Anglo-American corre-spondence on Palestine, see U. S. Department of State, *Palestine,* 49-103.

*Note 37.* *O. J.,* June-August 1922, 798-802.

*Note 38.* *Ibid.,* 818-23.

*Note 39.* *Ibid.,* 825.

*Note 40.* *O. J.,* November 1922, pp. 1390-1. See also *Mandate for Palestine, together with a note by the Secretary General Relating to its Application to the Terri-tory known as Trans-Jordan under the Provisions of Article 25. Cmd. 1785 (1922).*

*Note 41.* U. S. Treaty Series. *Convention Between the United States and France. Rights in Syria and the Lebanon, April 4, 1924.* (Washington 1924).

*Note 42. Palestine,* 107-14; *Cmd. 2559* (1925). Ratification took place on December 3, 1925.

*Note 43. Cmd. 1785,* art. 1.

*Note 44 O. J.,* August 1922, no. 8, II, 1013-17.

*Note 45.* Many difficulties confronted the negotiation of this treaty. The extremist press had caused considerable trouble. Many were opposed to the British mandate, and some leaders were deported. See *Colonial no. 4,* pp. 14ff. Announcement of British government policy, appendix 4, *ibid.,* 186-7.

*Note 46. Treaty Series no. 17* (1925). *Cmd. 2370.* The subsidiary agreements dealt with the appointment of officials, a military accord, judicial and financial agreement.

*Note 47. Ibid.,* enclosure no. 2.

*Note 48. Colonial no. 4,* pp. 22-3. Only 69 out of 100 members were present, the vote being 37 to 24, with 8 not voting. Mr. Thomas, the Labor colonial secretary, did not regard the rider as affecting the validity of the treaty or imposing any new responsibilities on England. See *Parliamentary Debates* (H. C.), July 21, 1924, v. 176, col. 869.

*Note 49.* Fisher so informed the Council as early as November 1921. See Fisher *Report; O. J.,* November 1921, pp. 1215-17.

*Note 50. O. J.,* July 1924, p. 923. See also *ibid.,* 1013-15, annex 651 for May 1924, communications to the Council, in which note was taken of this change, and the new conditions laid down for the mandate.

*Note 51. O. J.,* October 1924, 1314-15.

*Note 52. O. J.,* October 1924, pp. 1346-7. For the draft instrument of British government, see annex 678, *ibid.,* 1563-4.

*Note 53. Colonial no. 21,* pp. 23-4. Also Toynbee, *Survey of International Affairs,* 1928, (London 1929), 336, 338. In June 1929, the Syro-Turkish boundary was fixed running from Jeziret-ibn-Omar on the Tigris to a point on the Alexandretta south of Payas.

*Note 54. Treaty Series no. 13* (*1923*). Agreement Between H. M. Government and the French Government Respecting the Boundary line between Syria and Palestine from the Mediterranean to El Hamné. *Cmd. 1910.*

*Note 55.* In general see Richard Coke, *The Arab's Place in the Sun* (London 1929), chs. 13-14. Excellent accounts of the rise of Ibn Saud are: Toynbee, *Survey* (1925), I, 271-324; Léon Krajevski, "Le Nejd et les wahabites," *Revue politique et parlementaire,* CXXVII (April 1926), 105-22; "La création du royaume du Hedjaz," *ibid.* (June 1926), 441-59; "La politique anglaise en Arabie (1915-1927)," *Revue de Paris,* XXXV, no. 6 (March 15, 1928), 378-419.

*Note 56.* Hussein appears to have received from £1,200,000 to £6,000,000 while Ibn Saud received only some £232,908 by 1922. In the year ending March 1924, he had received £50,000. See Ormsby-Gore's statement in the Commons, November 28, 1922; Parliamentary Debates, v. 159 (1922), col. 490. Mr. Thomas announced that the payments would be discontinued during the financial year. *Parliamentary Debates,* v. 171 (March 24, 1924), col. 938. See also Toynbee, *Survey* (1925), I, 272-74; L. "Downing Street and Arab Potentates," *Foreign Affairs,* V, no. 2 (January 1927) 233-40.

*Note 57.* For the negotiations of this treaty see *Asie française*, XXIII, no. 212 (June 1923), 197-98; no. 214 (August-September 1923), 305. The text of the treaty is in *Asie française*, XXIV, no. 225 (September-October 1924), 362.

*Note 58.* *Parliamentary Debates*, (H. C.), v. 177, cols. 141-2. October 1, 1924.

*Note 59.* For the Nejd-Hejaz war, see Toynbee, I, 272-4, 280-96, 296-24.

*Note 60.* *Asie française*, XXIV, no. 226 (November 1924), 407.

*Note 61.* For the Bahra agreement see *Cmd. 1566 (1925). Arabia. Agreements with the Sultan of Nejd relating to the Nejd-Trans-Jordan and Nejd-Iraq frontiers.* Also *Colonial no. 4*, appendix II, 183-6, for treaty of Muhammarah, December 2, 1922; *Colonial no. 13*, pp. 42-51; *Colonial no. 21*, p. 27. See Toynbee, I, 324-46 for summary. For the treaty of February 24, 1930, see A. H. Lybyer, "The Near and Middle East," *Current History*, XXXII, no. 1 (April 1930), 171-2.

*Note 62.* *Cmd. 1592 (1922)*, 29-30 and the dispatch of March 15, 1922; *Cmd. 1617 (1922)*.

*Note 63.* Pierre Crabites, "The Problem of the Nile," *Current History*, XXXII, no. 4 (July 1930), 737-42. See also Toynbee, *Survey* (1928), 234-283, and *Current History*, XXX, no. 6 (September 1929).

*Note 64.* See MacCallum, *op. cit., passim;* Stein, *op. cit.* Latest development in *Current History*, XXXII, no. 4 (July 1930), 811-2. Also Toynbee, *Survey* (1928), 328-32, 336-8.

*Note 65.* A. H. Lybyer, "The Conflict Between Jews and Arabs in Palestine," *Current History*, XXXI, no. 1 (October 1929), 190-5; Ameen Rihani, "Palestine Arabs Claim to be Fighting for National Existence," and Meyer W. Weisgae, "Zionism as a Spiritual Ideal and a Blessing to Palestine," *Current History*, XXXI, no. 2 (November 1929), 272-85. For background of the struggle, see Leonard Stein, *Zionism* and John Haynes Holmes, *Palestine—Today and Tomorrow* (N. Y. 1929). See Lybyer, "Near and Middle East," *Current History*, XXXII, no. 2 (May 1930), 395-8 for summary of official report, also *Current History*, XXXII, no. 4 (July 1930), 807-09.

*Note 66.* Toynbee, *Survey* (1928), 284-307, 321-8.

*Note 67.* *Cmd. 2587. Iraq. Treaty with King Feisal signed at Bagdad, January 13, 1926. With explanatory Note. February, 1926.*

*Note 68.* For the preliminaries of this treaty, see Toynbee, *Survey* (1928), 339-42. For text, see *ibid.*, 442-43.

*Note 69.* See Lybyer, "British Plan for Independence of Iraq," *Current History*, XXXI, no. 2 (November 1929), 404-5.

*Note 70.* See S. H. Slater, "Iraq," *Nineteenth Century*, v. 99 (April 1926), 479ff. and F. W. Chardin, "The Land of the Two Rivers," *Living Age.* v. 328, (January 1926), 148-53.


## CHAPTER XI

*Note 1.* See Toynbee, *Survey* (1925), I, 50-51.

*Note 2.* There is an excellent discussion of all these reforms in Turkey in Toynbee, *Survey* (1928), 192-7, 200-13, 216-34.

*Note 3.* *Ibid.*, 200-206. See also Lybyer's summary in *Current History*, XXXII, no. 2 (May 1930), 398. For the position of the minorities, see Toynbee, *op. cit.*, 197-200.

*Note 3a.* See Halidé Edib, *Turkey Faces West*, 260-61, 200-61. See also Ahmed Emin, *Turkey in the World War*, 280-96; and Léon Ostrorog, *The Angora Reform* (London 1927).

*Note 4.* The treaty of Lausanne, article 3, paragraph 2, stipulated that the two parties were to settle the dispute within nine months, or failing that, to refer it to the Council of the League of Nations.

*Note 5.* For the procès-verbaux of the Constantinople Conference, see Turkey. Ministère des affaires étrangères. *Le livre rouge. La question de Mossoul.* (30 octobre 1918-1 mars 1925), 180-200.

*Note 6.* *Ibid.*, 195.

*Note 7.* *O. J.*, October 1924, pp. 1463-4.

*Note 8.* The British contended that the question was one of a frontier settlement—which frontier could be moved either north or south of Mosul. *Ibid.*, 1566.

*Note 9.* *O. J.*, October 1924, p. 1570. The Turkish memorandum.

*Note 10.* *Ibid.*, 1337-39; *O. J.*, November 1924, pp. 1659-62.

*Note 11.* Count Paul Teleki (Hungary), M. de Wirsen (Sweden), Colonel Paulis (Belgium), were the members of the commission. *Ibid.*, 1662ff. See also *Colonial no. 21* (1925), 8-10.

*Note 12.* See League of Nations document C.494,1924.VII. *Frontier between Turkey and Iraq. Report submitted to the Council by the Commission Instituted by the Council Resolution of September 30, 1924.* The Kurds were the local problem in Mosul, being about 500,000 in number. At Sèvres, the British talked of an autonomous Kurdistan under British influence. For details see *Iraq Report*, 1920-22, 114ff; *Colonial no. 4*, pp. 33-41; *Colonial no. 13*, pp. 29-33; *Colonial no. 21*, pp.20ff, 101ff. For the troubles in 1922-23, see *La question de Mossoul (Livre rouge)*, 55-73; *Cmd. 2217. Air Ministry. Note on the Employment of Air Arm in* Iraq. For the Turkish troubles with the Kurds, see Toynbee and Kirkwood, 266ff. The Assyro-Chaldean problem in Iraq may be found in *Iraq Report*, 1920-22, pp. 102-110 and in H. C. Luke, *Mosul and Its Minorities* (London 1925).

*Note 13.* *O. J.*, October 1925, pp. 1307-10.

*Note 14.* *O. J.*, October 1925, pp. 1310ff.

*Note 15.* *Ibid.*, 1327.

*Note 16.* *Ibid.*, 1379. See also Rushdi Bey's letter to the Secretary General, September 24, 1925 in *Le livre rouge. La question de Mossoul à la 35me session du conseil de la société des nations*, September 19, 1925, pp. 35ff.

*Note 17.* See *Publications de la cour permanente de justice internationale. Série C. no. 10.*

*Note 18.* *Publications of the Permanent Court of International Justice. Series B. no. 12.* Article 3, paragraph 2 of the treaty of Lausanne. Frontier between Turkey and Iraq. The Turks employed Professor Gilbert Gidel to give them a legal opinion. See *Consultation sur l'article 3, paragraphe 2 du traité de Lausanne concernant la frontière entre la Turquie et l'Irak.* See also Gidel, "L'avis consultatif de la cour permanente de justice," *l'Europe nouvelle*, XXVIII, 608-10.

*Note 19.* *O. J.*, February 1926, pp. 121-7.

*Note 20.* See Rushdi Bey's letter in *La question de Mossoul à la 37me session du conseil de la société de nations*, 22-30.

*Note 21.* *O. J.*, February 1926, pp. 192ff. Rushdi informed the Council that "our sovereign rights over the whole of the vilayet of Mosul remain intact." *Ibid.*,

187. See also *Speech by the Prime Minister of the Turkish Republic in the Grand National Assembly on the Report of General Laidoner, December 12, 1925* (London 1925).

Note 22.    *Parliamentary Debates* (H. C.), v. 189, cols. 2076-2151; *ibid.*, (H. L.), v. 62, cols. 1680ff.

Note 23.    *European Economic and Political Survey*, no. 8, p. 7 (December 31, 1925); *l'Europe nouvelle*, 9e année, no. 417 (13 février 1926), 221; Graham, "Soviet Security System," *International Conciliation*, no. 252 (September 1929), 400-1.

Note 24.    N. Y. *Times*, December 19, 1925; *Current History*, February 1926, p. 765.

Note 25.    See Lybyer, "Turkish Relations to Mosul Decision," *Current History* (February 1926), 765; Earle, "Mosul—Settled or Unsettled," *New Republic*, v. 45 (February 10, 1926), 314-6. See also the statement of the Turkish ambassador (?) in London *Times*, January 1, 1926, and *Current History* (March 1926), 922.

Note 26.    *Cmd. 2587* (1926).

Note 27.    For text, see *European Economic and Political Survey*, II, no. 21, pp. 46-50; *l'Europe nouvelle*, VIII, no. 419 (February 27, 1926), 258ff.

Note 28.    *Turkey no. 1* (1926). Treaty between the United Kingdom and Turkey Regarding the Settlement of the Frontier between Turkey and Iraq with Notes Exchanged. With map of Boundary. *Cmd. 2679*. Iraq accepted the treaty on June 14, 1926, and the Council took note of it on June 7, 1926. See *European Economic and Political Survey*, no. 20, p. 30 and *O. J.*, July 1926, pp. 859, 1040-41. For criticism of the boundary decision, see Major H. I. Lloyd, "The Geography of the Mosul Boundary," *Geographical Journal*, LXVII, no. 2 (August 1926), 106ff.

Note 29.    N. Y. *Times*, June 17, 1926, and *Economist* (London, June 1926), CII, 1245-46.

Note 30.    *Current History*, March 1923, pp. 484-9, and *l'Europe nouvelle*, (May 12, 1923), VI, no. 19, pp. 599-604 contain texts.

Note 31.    See Levermore, *Fourth Yearbook of the League of Nations*, 176, 212-3; Anton Mohr, *Oil War*, 194ff; Davenport and Cooke, *op. cit.*, 151-3. It will be seen readily that this far-reaching concession contravened the claims of both the *Régie générale* and the Turkish Petroleum Company.

Note 32.    See League of Nations Document C.400.M.147.1925.VII. *Report Submitted to the Council by the Commission Instituted by the Council Resolution of September 30, 1924.*

Note 33.    The American group held 25 %, Anglo-Persian 25 %, Royal Dutch 25 %, *Compagnie française des pétroles* 25 %. The American companies were Standard of N. Y., Standard of New Jersey, Pan-American Petroleum and Transport Company. See N. Y. *Times*, June 15, 1926 and July 24, 1926; V. F. M., "The Mosul Question," *Reference Service on International Affairs* (American Library, Paris, April 1926, Bulletins nos. 9-10.) For details see *Colonial no. 21*, p. 109; N. Y. *Times*, March 16, 1925; Fritz Hesse, *Die Mossulfrage*, 38-9.

Note 34.    *Soviet Union and Peace*, 115-118. Writer's italics.

Note 35.    *Ibid.*, 126-8. For attitude on exclusion at Washington Conference, see *ibid.*, 78-81. Writer's italics.

Note 36.    The conference met as a naval sub-commission of the Temporary Mixed Commission of the League of Nations to extend the principles of the Washing-

ton Conference to non-signatories. See *Annex 622a*, *C.76.1924.IX.*, *O. J.*, V, no. 4 (April 1924), 707-09. Note by the Naval Delegate of the U. S. S. R., February 21, 1924. For Russian fleet tonnage of 1917, 1921, 1924, see *ibid.*, 709-10. See also Gunji Hosono, *International Disarmament* (N. Y. 1926), 286-7; John C. Shillock, "The Post-War Developments to Reduce Naval Armaments," *International Conciliation*, no. 245 (December 1928), 595-607.

*Note 37.* Professor Malbone W. Graham, *op. cit.*, 363-4, states that "in a very real sense, the amount of security afforded Russia by the Straits Convention plus the Treaty of Paris is substantial. Little did the Lausanne Conference realize when it drafted the Straits Convention that it was forging a definite link in the Soviet security system." It is difficult to accept such a conclusion if one considers the fundamental nature of the Straits convention and the circumstances which brought about the treaty with Turkey, of 1925. Certainly Russia was still endangered in the Straits and was at this very time beginning to lose hold in both the Near and Middle East. See also Dennis, *op. cit.*, 222-8; and Fischer, II, 726-34.

*Note 38.* See A. de Jonquière, "Angora et Moscou," *l'Asie française*, XXIV, no. 225 (September-October 1924), 333-40. Trotzky later denied the remarks.

*Note 39.* See Denys P. Myers, "Origin and Conclusion of the Paris Pact," *W. P. F. Pamphlets*, XII, no. 2, 1929, pp. 71-4. For documents see *ibid.*, 375-7 (text of Paris Pact) and *ibid.*, 387-92. Russian note of August 31, 1928. See also *Soviet Union and Peace*, 245ff for documents relative to Paris pact. At the conference of Moscow on February 9, 1929, called to put the pact into operation in eastern Europe, M. Litvinov referred to Rumania and the Bessarabian question when he spoke of a state not then in normal diplomatic relations with Russia and "with which serious unsolved dissensions, not solved by this protocol have long existed . . . ." The Rumanian foreign minister shortly after declared that the pact of Paris pledged the Powers "not to resort to war and to settle their differences by peaceful methods." See Meyers, *op. cit.*, 294, and *Soviet Union and Peace*, 267-9. There is a summary in H. F. Armstrong, *Where the East Begins* (N. Y. 1929), 116-7.

*Note 40.* *Commission des détroits. Rapport* (1925), 16. The specific rules are laid down and elaborated by the commission in the *Rapports* for 1925, 1926 and 1927. See especially *Rapport* (1926), 11-14 and *Rapport* (1927), 13-14.

*Note 41.* Toynbee, *Survey* (1928), 362-74. The treaties of significance are the Russo-Turkish, December 17, 1925; Turco-Persian, April 22, 1926 (with protocol of June 15, 1928); Russo-Afghan, August 31, 1926; Russo-Persian, October 1, 1927; Perso-Alghan, November 28, 1927 (with protocol of June 15, 1928); Turco-Afghan, May 25, 1928. Only one of the eight treaties was signed at Moscow. See also *Soviet Union and Peace*, 276-80; Graham, *op. cit.*, 408-12, 416-23; Fischer, II, 726-34.

*Note 42.* See *Commission des détroits, Rapport* (1925), 49-50; *Rapport* (1926), 78; and *Rapport* (1927), 63. Russian tonnage passing through the Straits had advanced from 172,402 tons in 1924 to 295,004 in 1927. The Black sea and sea of Azov continued to be the principal center of export trade by water with 4,936 thousand metric tons in 1926-27, while imports by water in the same region stood at 226,000 tons. The bulk of the trade in the Black sea region consisted in exports in oil products, grain, ores and coal.

*Note 43.* Toynbee, *op. cit.*, 158-61; Armstrong, *Where the East Begins*.

*Note 44.* See Lybyer's summary in *Current History*, XXXI, no. 3 (December 1929), 613 and in *Current History*, XXXII, no. 2 (May 1930), 398.

Note 45.   *Current History*, XXXI, no. 6 (March 1930), 1233.

Note 46.   See MacDonald's address in the House of Commons, February 25, 1924 in *Parliamentary Debates*, v. 170, cols. 28-9. For the American position, see the Lodge resolution, May 17, 1920 in *Congressional Record*, LIX, pt. 7, p. 7160. See also H. F. Armstrong, *The New Balkans* (N. Y. 1926), 85-113, and his *Where the East Begins;* Jacques Ancel, *Les balkans face à l'Italie* (Paris 1928).

Note 47.   These figures are based largely on the *Statesman's Year Book* (1929). The territories under British influence included the Hejaz, Imamate of Yemen, Sultanate of Koweit, Sultanate of Oman, Protectorate of Oman. This does not include, of course, a large part of Arabia. Nor does it include Egypt or Cyprus.

Note 48.   The figures for Turkish population are based on *République turque. Présidence du conseil. Office central de statistique. Population de la Turquie par vilayets et cazas par villes et villages. D'après le recensement du 28 octobre 1927.* (Angora 1927); *Annuaire statistique*, I (Angora 1928). In Europe the boundaries of the new Turkish republic include Constantinople and Eastern Thrace, and run east and west from the mouth of the Resvaya river (Black sea) to the Maritza river, fifteen miles northwest of Adrianople. The boundary with Greece follows the Maritza to Enos, on the Aegean, excepting Karagatch. In Asia Minor, the Caucasian frontier (with Russia) is defined by the treaty of Kars, leaving Kars and Ardahan to Turkey, and running south of Batum to the northwest corner of Persia. The Turco-Persian frontier continues from near Mt. Ararat to the Iraq frontier, as delimited by the Anglo-Turkish agreement of 1926, giving Mosul to Iraq. The Syrian boundary with Turkey runs from Jeziret-ibn-Omar on the Tigris, to a point on the gulf of Alexandretta below Payas, as defined in t he treaty of June 1929, between France and Turkey. Imbros, Tenedos and the Rabbit islands are included in the new republic. Seventy-two vilayets make up the state.

Note 49.   Toynbee, *op. cit.*, 366, states that this change in the relations between western Europe in general, and Great Britain in particular, and the Near and Middle East, was due to the recession of imperialistic designs. "Noting this tendency, the Middle Eastern peoples gradually became less afraid of the Western Powers, and in proportion as their recent fear of these diminished, their old suspicion of Russia showed signs of revival."

# INDEX

## M

Macedonia, 21, 32, 75, 142, 152f, 172, 176.
MacMahon, Sir H., 188f.
Mallet, Sir I.., 103, 107f.
Mandates, 317-28.
Marmora (See Straits), 120.
Mesopotamia, 48, 51, 58, 184f, 206, 241, 317, 320f.
Miliukov, P., 125, 194.
Miller, D. H., 226, 231.
Milne, General, 208.
Montenegro, 20, 23, 32.
Moslems (of India), 235, 243.
Mosul, 48, 184f, 210-12, 229, 297-301, 320f, 336-40.
Mudania, armistice of, 272-3.
Mudros, armistice of, 208, 209.
Mukhta Pasha, 73, 74.
Mustapha Kemal Pasha, 134, 242, 253f, 277.

## N

Nekliudov, 21, 23, 133.
Neuilly, treaty of, 240-1.
Nicholas II, of Russia, 40, 113, 119, 133, 147.
Nicholas, Grand Duke N. N., 123, 134.
Nogara concern, 55.

## O

Ottoman Bank, 58, 313.
Ottoman Empire, 19, 20, 21, 35, 47, 72, 103 (See also Turkey, etc.).
Ottoman Public debt, 47, 48, 308-13.

## P

Paléologue, 121, 126, 127, 130.
Pallavicini, Margrave, 52, 55, 62, 64, 66, 73, 83, 104, 109.
Palestine, 130, 184f, 229f, 241, 319-20.
Panama canal, 198, 231, 289, 296.
Pashich, Nikola K., 21, 61, 68, 152f.
Persia, 241.

Petrograd Soviet, 195f.
Picot, Georges, 185.
Pichon, M., 212, 227f. 193f.
Poincaré, R., 22, 147.
Poklevsky-Koziel, 166f.
Pokrovsky, M. N., 193f.
Potsdam accord, of 1911, 50-51.
Provisional government, of Russia, 194f.

## R

Radoslavov, V., 35, 63, 69, 152f.
Railways, in Turkey, 48, 49.
Rome naval conference, 341.
Rumania, 61, 69f, 89-90, 142, 166-76.
Rupel, fort, 151.
Russia, 19, 21f, 32, 49, 59, 68f, 77-79, 96f, 111-115, 119, 124, 131-32, 136-37, 141f, 173, 182-3, 248, 266, 272.
Russo-Turkish accord (1921), 263-4; (1925), 338-9; (1929), 344.

## S

Salonica, 26.
Salonica expedition, 134, 151, 175.
Savinsky, 70, 153f.
Samuel, Sir Herbert,197, 319.
San Remo oil agreement, 242-3, 323.
San Remo conference, 243.
San Giuliano, 56.
Sazonov, S. D., 23, 24, 25, 41-44, 45-46, 59, 69, 72, 91-96, 98-99, 101, 103, 105, 111, 119, 124, 125, 126, 127, 128, 129, 130, 147, 154f, 166f, 193-194, 239.
Serbia, 20f, 35f, 148, 149, 151.
Sonnino, 144.
Sèvres, treaty of, 242-49.
Sforza, 260.
Smuts, J. C., 219f.
Souchon, 110.
Soviet Russia, 198f, 262f, 277f.
Stahl, 112-13.
Standard Oil Company, 299, 312, 313, 340.
St. Jean de Maurienne agreement, 186-7.

Straits (see also Constantinople, Turkey, etc.), 21, 25, 26, 43-45, 49, 91f, 107, 108, 113, 115, 119, 173, 193f, 208f, 244-46, 256-57, 263, 269, 271, 272, 281, 285-97, 340-43.
Suez Canal, 198, 289, 296.
Sykes, Sir Mark, 184f.
Sykes-Picot accord (1916), 184-86.
Syria, 48, 130, 184f, 206, 211, 225, 241, 217-18.
Szögyény, 55, 61.

## T

Talaat Bey, 104, 109.
Tarnowsky, 28, 29, 62, 67, 87f, 161, 163, 183.
Tisza, Count Stephen, 61, 67, 171.
Thrace, 103, 152, 201, 222, 247, 281-4.
Transylvania, 166f.
Trepov, 136.
Triple Alliance, 64, 65, 79.
Tripolitania, 20.
Trotzky, Leon, 200, 342.
Turco-German alliance (1914), 75, 77, 79, 83f, 417.
Turco-Russian alliance negotiations, 96f.
Turkey (see also Ottoman Empire, Constantinople, Straits, etc.), 19, 20, 21, 33, 34, 52, 55, 56, 57, 59, 65, 68, 83f, 100, 101, 106-115, 137, 206f, 233, 237f, 305f, 314.
Turkish Petroleum Company, 299, 312, 323, 340.
Turkish republic, 335-49.
Tschirschky, 52.

## U

United States, 102, 135-36, 231, 232, 233, 235, 239, 246, 279, 288, 289, 299, 321f.

## V

Valona, 103, 145.
Vasilchikova, Princess Maria, 133.
Venizelos, E., 32, 68, 100, 123, 148f, 222f, 234, 259, 308-9.
Versailles, treaty of, 240.

## W

Wangenheim, Baron von, 40, 59, 65, 66, 83f, 104, 108, 109.
William II, of Germany, 39, 66, 90-91, 108, 163.
Williams, General Sir J. H., 122.
Wilson, Woodrow, 135, 196, 202, 213, 218, 219f, 231f, 243.

Composed at Norman by the University of Oklahoma Press on the Monotype in Kennerley, designed by Frederic W. Goudy, who also designed the initial letters in Forum. The Kennerley italic is based on the handwriting of Petrarch. Forum is a modern adaptation of the lapidary characters of Roman days.
First printed September, 1931